Software Engineering   Seventh Edition

International Computer Science Series

Selected titles in the series

Operating Systems
J Bacon and T Harris

Programming Language Essentials
H E Bal and D Grune

Programming in Ada 95, 2nd ed
J G P Barnes

Java Gently, 3rd ed
J Bishop

Software Design, 2nd ed
D Budgen

Concurrent Programming
A Burns and G Davies

Real-Time Systems and Programming Languages
A Burns and A Wellings

Database Systems, 4th ed
T Connolly and C Begg

Distributed Systems, 3rd ed
G Coulouris, J Dollimore and T Kindberg

Principles of Object-Oriented Software Development, 2nd ed
A Eliëns

Fortran 90 Programming, 2nd ed
T M R Ellis, I R Phillips and T M Lahey

Program Verification
N Francez

Introduction to Programming using SML
M Hansen and H Rischel

Functional C
P Hartel and H Muller

Algorithms and Data Structures, 2nd ed
J Kingston

Introductory Logic and Sets for Computer Scientists
N Nissanke

Human-Computer Interaction
J Preece et al

Algorithms
F Rabhi and G Lapalme

Ada 95 From the Beginning, 3rd ed
J Skansholm

C++ From the Beginning
J Skansholm

Java From the Beginning, 2nd ed
J Skansholm

Software Engineering, 6th ed
I Sommerville

Object-Oriented Programming in Eiffel, 2nd ed
P Thomas and R Weedon

Miranda
S Thompson

Haskell, 2nd ed
S Thompson

Discrete Mathematics for Computer Scientists, 2nd ed
J K Truss

Compiler Design
R Wilhem and D Maurer

Discover Delphi
S Williams and S Walmsley

Comparative Programming Languages, 3rd ed
L B Wilson and R G Clark

Software Engineering with B *J B
Wordsworth*

Software Engineering

Seventh Edition

Ian Sommerville

PEARSON

Addison
Wesley

Boston San Francisco New York
London Toronto Sydney Tokyo Singapore Madrid
Mexico City Munich Paris Cape Town Hong Kong Montreal

Pearson Education Limited
Edinburgh Gate
Harlow
Essex CM20 2JE
England

and Associated Companies around the World.

Visit us on the World Wide Web at:
www.pearsoneduc.com

First published 1982
Second Edition 1984
Third Edition 1989
Fourth Edition 1992
Fifth Edition 1995
Sixth Edition 2001
Seventh Edition 2004

ISBN 0-321-21026-3

British Library Cataloguing-in-Publication Data
A catalogue record for this book can be obtained from the British Library

Library of Congress Cataloging-in-Publication Data
Sommerville, Ian
    Software engineering / Ian Sommerville. — 7th ed.
       p. cm.
    ISBN 0-321-21026-3
       1. Software engineering.   I. Title.
    QA76.758S657   2004
    005.1—dc22   2004007038

10 9 8 7 6 5 4 3 2
08 07 06 05 04

Typeset by 35 in 10/12.5pt Times
Printed and bound in the United States of America

Preface

The first edition of this textbook on software engineering was published more than twenty years ago. That edition was written using a dumb terminal attached to an early minicomputer (a PDP-11) that probably cost about $50,000. I wrote this edition on a wireless laptop that cost less than $2,000 and is many times more powerful than that PDP-11. Software then was mostly mainframe software, but personal computers were just becoming available. None of us then realised how pervasive these would become and how much they would change the world.

Changes in hardware over the past twenty or so years have been absolutely remarkable, and it may appear that changes in software have been equally significant. Certainly, our ability to build large and complex systems has improved dramatically. Our national utilities and infrastructure—energy, communications and transport—rely on very complex and, largely, very reliable computer systems. For building business systems, there is an alphabet soup of technologies—J2EE, .NET, EJB, SAP, BPEL4WS, SOAP, CBSE—that allow large web-based applications to be deployed much more quickly than was possible in the past.

However, although much appears to have changed in the last two decades, when we look beyond the specific technologies to the fundamental processes of software engineering, much has stayed the same. We recognised twenty years ago that the waterfall model of the software process had serious problems, yet a survey published in December 2003 in *IEEE Software* showed that more than 40% of companies are still using this approach. Testing is still the dominant program validation technique, although other techniques such as inspections have been used more effectively since the mid 1970s. CASE tools, although now based around the UML, are still essentially diagram editors with some checking and code-generation functionality.

Our current software engineering methods and techniques have made us much better at building large and complex systems than we were. However, there are still too many projects that are late, are over budget and do not deliver the software that meets the customer's needs. While I was writing this book, a government enquiry in the UK reported on the project to provide a national system to be used in courts that try relatively minor offenders. The cost of this system was estimated at £156 million and it was scheduled for delivery in 2001. In 2004, costs have escalated to £390 million and it is still not fully operational. There is, therefore, still a pressing need for software engineering education.

Over the past few years, the most significant developments in software engineering have been the emergence of the UML as a standard for object-oriented system description and the development of agile methods such as extreme programming. Agile methods are geared to rapid system development, explicitly involve the user in the development team, and reduce paperwork and bureaucracy in the software process. In spite of what some critics claim, I think these approaches embody good software engineering practice. They have a well-defined process, pay attention to system specification and user requirements, and have high quality standards.

However, this revision has not become a text on agile methods. Rather, I focus on the basic software engineering processes—specification, design, development, verification, and validation and management. You need to understand these processes and associated techniques to decide whether agile methods are the most appropriate development strategy for you and how to adapt and change methods to suit your particular situation. A pervasive theme of the book is critical systems—systems whose failure has severe consequences and where system dependability is critical. In each part of the book, I discuss specific software engineering techniques that are relevant to critical systems engineering.

Books inevitably reflect the opinions and prejudices of their authors. Some readers will disagree with my opinions and with my choice of material. Such disagreement is a healthy reflection of the diversity of the discipline and is essential for its evolution. Nevertheless, I hope that all software engineers and software engineering students can find something of interest here.

The structure of the book

The structure of the book is based around the fundamental software engineering processes. It is organised into six parts with several chapters in each part:

Part 1: Introduces software engineering, places it in a broader systems context and presents the notions of software engineering processes and management.

Part 2: Covers the processes, techniques and deliverables that are associated with requirements engineering. It includes a discussion of software requirements, system modelling, formal specification and techniques for specifying dependability.

Part 3: This part is devoted to software design and design processes. Three out of the six chapters focus on the important topic of software architectures. Other topics include object-oriented design, real-time systems design and user interface design.

Part 4: Describes a number of approaches to development, including agile methods, software reuse, CBSE and critical systems development. Because change is now such a large part of development, I have integrated material on software evolution and maintenance into this part.

Part 5: Focuses on techniques for software verification and validation. It includes chapters on static V & V, testing and critical systems validation.

Part 6: The final part covers a range of management topics: managing people, cost estimation, quality management, process improvement and configuration management.

In the introduction to each part, I discuss the structure and organisation in more detail.

Changes from the 6th edition

There are significant changes to the organisation and content from the previous edition. I have included four new chapters and made major revisions of 11 other chapters. All other chapters have been updated and, where appropriate, new material has been added. More and more systems have high availability and reliability requirements, and I believe that we have to consider dependability as a basic driver for software engineering, so the chapters on critical systems have now been integrated into other sections. To avoid content creep, I have reduced the amount of material on software maintenance and have integrated material on maintenance and evolution with other chapters in the book. There are two running case studies—one on a document management system used in a library and the other on a medical system—that I draw on in several chapters.

The case study material is indicated by margin icons. Table 1 summarises the changes, with the number in parentheses indicating the corresponding chapter in the 6th edition. Further information on the changes is available on the book's web site.

Table 1 Chapter revisons

New chapters
Chap. 13: Application architectures
Chap. 17: Rapid software development
Chap. 19: Component-based software engineering
Chap. 21: Software evolution

Chapters with significant new material and/or major structural revisions

Chap. 2: Socio-technical systems (2)
Chap. 4: Software processes (3)
Chap. 7: Requirements engineering processes (6)
Chap. 9: Critical systems specification (17)
Chap. 12: Distributed systems architectures (11)
Chap. 16: User interface design (15)
Chap. 18: Software reuse (14)
Chap. 23: Software testing (20)
Chap. 25: Managing people (22)
Chap. 24: Critical systems validation (21)
Chap. 28: Process improvement (25)

Updated chapters

Chap. 1: Introduction (1)
Chap. 3: Critical systems (16)
Chap. 5: Project management (4)
Chap. 6: Software requirements (5)
Chap. 8: System models (7)
Chap. 10: Formal specification (9)
Chap. 11: Architectural design (10)
Chap. 14: Object-oriented design (12)
Chap. 15: Real-time systems design (13)
Chap. 20: Critical systems development (18)
Chap. 22: Verification and validation (19)
Chap. 26: Software cost estimation (23)
Chap 27: Quality management (24)
Chap. 29: Configuration management (29)

Deleted chapters

Software prototyping (8)
Legacy systems (26)
Software change (27)
Software re-engineering (28)

Readership

The book is aimed at students taking undergraduate and graduate courses and at software engineers in commerce and industry. It may be used in general software engineering courses or in courses such as advanced programming, software specification, and software design or management. Software engineers in industry may find the book useful as general reading and as a means of updating their knowledge on particular topics such as requirements engineering, architectural design, dependable systems development and process improvement. Wherever practicable, the examples in the text have been given a practical bias to reflect the type of applications that software engineers must develop.

Using the book for teaching

I have designed the book so that it can be used in three types of software engineering course:

1. *General introductory courses in software engineering* For students who have no previous software engineering experience, you can start with the introductory section then pick and choose chapters from the other sections of the book. This will give students a general overview of the subject with the opportunity of more detailed study for those students who are interested. If the course's approach is project-based, the early chapters provide enough material to allow students to get started on projects, consulting later chapters for reference and further information as their work progresses.

2. *Introductory or intermediate courses on specific software engineering topics* The book supports courses in software requirements specification, software design, software engineering management, dependable systems development and software evolution. Each part can serve as a text in its own right for an introductory or intermediate course on that topic. As well as further reading associated with each chapter, I have also included information on other relevant papers and books on the web site.

3. *More advanced courses in specific software engineering topics* The chapters can form a foundation for a specific software course, but they must be supplemented with further reading that explores the topic in greater detail. For example, I teach an MSc module in systems engineering that relies on material here. I have included details of this course and a course on critical systems engineering on the web site.

The benefit of a general text like this is that it can be used in several related courses. At Lancaster, we use the text in an introductory software engineering course and in courses on specification, design and critical systems. Courses on component-based software engineering and systems engineering use the book along with additional papers that are distributed to students. Having a single text presents students with a consistent view of the subject—and they don't have to buy several books.

To reinforce the student's learning experience, I have included a glossary of key terms, with additional definitions on the web site. Furthermore, each chapter has:

- A clearly defined set of objectives set out on the first page

- A list of key points covered in the chapter

- Suggested further reading—either books that are currently in print or easily available papers (lists of other suggested readings and links can be found on my web site)

- Exercises, including design exercises.

The Software Engineering Body of Knowledge project (http://www.swebok.org) was established to define the key technical knowledge areas that are relevant to professional software engineers. These are organised under 10 headings: requirements, design, construction, testing, maintenance, configuration management, management, process, tools and methods, and quality. While it would be impossible to cover all of the knowledge areas proposed by the SWEBOK project in a single textbook, all of the top-level areas are discussed in this book.

Web pages

The web site that is associated with the book is:

http://www.software-engin.com

This offers a wide range of supplementary material on software engineering. From there, you can access web pages dedicated to supporting both this and previous editions of *Software Engineering*.

It has been my policy, both in the previous edition and in this edition, to keep the number of web links in the book to an absolute minimum. The reason for this is that these links are subject to change and, once printed, it is impossible to update them. Consequently, the book's web page includes a large number of links to resources and related material on software engineering. If you use these and find problems, please let me know and I will update the links.

To support the use of this book in software engineering courses, I have included a wide range of supplementary material on the web site. If you follow the Material for Instructors links, you can find:

- Lecture presentations (PowerPoint and PDF) for all chapters in the book
- Class quiz questions for each chapter
- Case studies
- Project suggestions
- Course structure descriptions
- Suggestions for further reading and links to web resources for each chapter
- Solutions for a selection of the exercises associated with each chapter and for the quiz questions (instructor's only).

I welcome your constructive comments and suggestions about the book and the web site. You can contact me at ian@software-engin.com. I recommend that you include [SE7] in the subject of the e-mail message to ensure that my spam filters do not accidentally reject your mail. I regret that I do not have time to help students with their homework, so please do not ask me how to solve any of the problems in the book.

Acknowledgements

A large number of people have contributed over the years to the evolution of this book and I'd like to thank everyone (reviewers, students and book users who have e-mailed me) who has commented on previous editions and made constructive suggestions for change. The editorial and production staff at Pearson Education in England and the US were supportive and helpful, and produced the book in record time. So thanks to Keith Mansfield, Patty Mahtani, Daniel Rausch, Carol Noble, and Sharon Burkhardt for their help and support.

Finally, I'd like to thank my family, who tolerated my absence when the book was being written and my frustration when the words were not flowing. A big thank-you to my wife, Anne, and daughters, Ali and Jane, for their help and support.

Ian Sommerville,
February 2004

Contents at a glance

Contents

Trademark Notice

The following are trademarks or registered trademarks of their respective companies:

Java, JavaBeans and Modula-2 are trademarks of Sun Microsystems, Inc.; Lotus Notes is a trademark of Lotus Development Corporation; Mac OS is a trademark of Apple Computer, Inc.; Microsoft, PowerPoint, Windows, Visual Basic and Visual C++ are trademarks of Microsoft Corporation; Unix is a trademark licensed through X/Open Company Ltd.

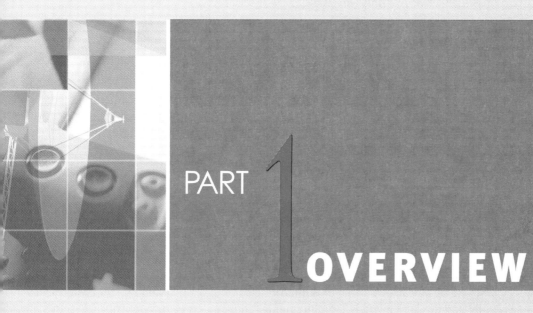

PART 1 OVERVIEW

The basic structure of this book follows the essential software processes of specification, design, development, verification and validation, and management. However, rather than plunge immediately into these topics, I have included this overview section so that you can get a broad picture of the discipline. The chapters in this part are:

Chapter 1 is a general introduction to software engineering. To make this accessible and easy to understand, I have organised it using a question/answer structure where I pose and answer questions such as 'what is software engineering'. I also introduce professionalism and ethics in this chapter.

Chapter 2 introduces socio-technical systems, a topic that I believe is absolutely essential for software engineers. Software is never used on its own but always as part of some broader system including hardware, people and, often, organisations. These profoundly affect the software requirements and operation. In this chapter I cover the emergent system properties, systems engineering processes and some of the ways in which organisational and human concerns affect software systems.

Chapter 3 discusses 'critical systems'. Critical systems are systems where failure has severe technical, economic or human consequences, and where system safety, security and availability are key requirements. Chapters on aspects of critical systems are included in each part of the book. In this chapter, I also introduce the first of the running case studies in the book—the software for an insulin pump used in the treatment of diabetic patients.

The first three chapters set the scene for software engineering and Chapter 4 continues this by introducing software process and software process models. I introduce basic software engineering processes, the subject of the book, in this chapter. I also briefly discuss the Rational Unified Process, which is geared to object-oriented system development. The final section of the chapter discusses how software processes can be supported with automated software tools.

Chapter 5 introduces project management. Project management is part of all professional development projects and I describe basic project planning, scheduling and risk estimation here. Students in a software engineering course involved in a student project should find the information they need here to draw up bar charts for a project schedule and resource allocation.

1

Introduction

Objectives

The objectives of this chapter are to introduce software engineering and to provide a framework for understanding the rest of the book. When you have read this chapter, you will:

■ understand what software engineering is and why it is important;

■ know the answers to key questions that provide an introduction to software engineering;

■ understand some ethical and professional issues that are important for software engineers.

Contents

Virtually all countries now depend on complex computer-based systems. National infrastructures and utilities rely on computer-based systems and most electrical products include a computer and controlling software. Industrial manufacturing and distribution is completely computerised, as is the financial system. Therefore, producing and maintaining software cost-effectively is essential for the functioning of national and international economies.

Software engineering is an engineering discipline whose focus is the cost-effective development of high-quality software systems. Software is abstract and intangible. It is not constrained by materials, or governed by physical laws or by manufacturing processes. In some ways, this simplifies software engineering as there are no physical limitations on the potential of software. However, this lack of natural constraints means that software can easily become extremely complex and hence very difficult to understand.

The notion of *software engineering* was first proposed in 1968 at a conference held to discuss what was then called the 'software crisis'. This software crisis resulted directly from the introduction of new computer hardware based on integrated circuits. Their power made hitherto unrealisable computer applications a feasible proposition. The resulting software was orders of magnitude larger and more complex than previous software systems.

Early experience in building these systems showed that informal software development was not good enough. Major projects were sometimes years late. The software cost much more than predicted, was unreliable, was difficult to maintain and performed poorly. Software development was in crisis. Hardware costs were tumbling whilst software costs were rising rapidly. New techniques and methods were needed to control the complexity inherent in large software systems.

These techniques have become part of software engineering and are now widely used. However, as our ability to produce software has increased, so too has the complexity of the software systems that we need. New technologies resulting from the convergence of computers and communication systems and complex graphical user interfaces place new demands on software engineers. As many companies still do not apply software engineering techniques effectively, too many projects still produce software that is unreliable, delivered late and over budget.

I think that we have made tremendous progress since 1968 and that the development of software engineering has markedly improved our software. We have a much better understanding of the activities involved in software development. We have developed effective methods of software specification, design and implementation. New notations and tools reduce the effort required to produce large and complex systems.

We know now that there is no single 'ideal' approach to software engineering. The wide diversity of different types of systems and organisations that use these systems means that we need a diversity of approaches to software development. However, fundamental notions of process and system organisation underlie all of these techniques, and these are the essence of software engineering.

Software engineers can be rightly proud of their achievements. Without complex software we would not have explored space, would not have the Internet and modern telecommunications, and all forms of travel would be more dangerous and expensive. Software engineering has contributed a great deal, and I am convinced that, as the discipline matures, its contributions in the 21st century will be even greater.

1.1 FAQs about software engineering

This section is designed to answer some fundamental questions about software engineering and to give you some impression of my views of the discipline. The format that I have used here is the 'FAQ (Frequently Asked Questions) list'. This approach is commonly used in Internet newsgroups to provide newcomers with answers to frequently asked questions. I think that it is a very effective way to give a succinct introduction to the subject of software engineering.

Figure 1.1 summarises the answers to the questions in this section.

1.1.1 What is software?

Many people equate the term *software* with computer programs. However, I prefer a broader definition where software is not just the programs but also all associated documentation and configuration data that is needed to make these programs operate correctly. A software system usually consists of a number of separate programs, configuration files, which are used to set up these programs, system documentation, which describes the structure of the system, and user documentation, which explains how to use the system and web sites for users to download recent product information.

Software engineers are concerned with developing software products, i.e., software which can be sold to a customer. There are two fundamental types of software product:

1. *Generic products* These are stand-alone systems that are produced by a development organisation and sold on the open market to any customer who is able to buy them. Examples of this type of product include software for PCs such as databases, word processors, drawing packages and project management tools.

2. *Customised (or bespoke) products* These are systems which are commissioned by a particular customer. A software contractor develops the software especially for that customer. Examples of this type of software include control systems for electronic devices, systems written to support a particular business process and air traffic control systems.

Question	Answer
What is software?	Computer programs and associated documentation. Software products may be developed for a particular customer or may be developed for a general market.
What is software engineering?	Software engineering is an engineering discipline which is concerned with all aspects of software production.
What is the difference between software engineering and computer science?	Computer science is concerned with theory and fundamentals; software engineering is concerned with the practicalities of developing and delivering useful software.
What is the difference between software engineering and system engineering?	System engineering is concerned with all aspects of computer-based systems development, including hardware, software and process engineering. Software engineering is part of this process.
What is a software process?	A set of activities whose goal is the development or evolution of software.
What is a software process model?	A simplified representation of a software process, presented from a specific perspective.
What are the costs of software engineering?	Roughly 60% of costs are development costs, 40% are testing costs. For custom software, evolution costs often exceed development costs.
What are software engineering methods?	Structured approaches to software development which include system models, notations, rules, design advice and process guidance.
What is CASE (Computer-Aided Software Engineering)?	Software systems which are intended to provide automated support for software process activities. CASE systems are often used for method support.
What are the attributes of good software?	The software should deliver the required functionality and performance to the user and should be maintainable, dependable and usable.
What are the key challenges facing software engineering?	Coping with increasing diversity, demands for reduced delivery times and developing trustworthy software.

Figure 1.1 Frequently asked questions about software engineering

An important difference between these types of software is that, in generic products, the organisation that develops the software controls the software specification. For custom products, the specification is usually developed and controlled by the organisation that is buying the software. The software developers must work to that specification.

However, the line between these types of products is becoming increasingly blurred. More and more software companies are starting with a generic system and customising it to the needs of a particular customer. Enterprise Resource Planning (ERP) systems, such as the SAP system, are the best examples of this approach. Here, a large and complex system is adapted for a company by incorporating information about business rules and processes, reports required, and so on.

1.1.2 What is software engineering?

Software engineering is an engineering discipline that is concerned with all aspects of software production from the early stages of system specification to maintaining the system after it has gone into use. In this definition, there are two key phrases:

1. *Engineering discipline* Engineers make things work. They apply theories, methods and tools where these are appropriate, but they use them selectively and always try to discover solutions to problems even when there are no applicable theories and methods. Engineers also recognise that they must work to organisational and financial constraints, so they look for solutions within these constraints.

2. *All aspects of software production* Software engineering is not just concerned with the technical processes of software development but also with activities such as software project management and with the development of tools, methods and theories to support software production.

In general, software engineers adopt a systematic and organised approach to their work, as this is often the most effective way to produce high-quality software. However, engineering is all about selecting the most appropriate method for a set of circumstances and a more creative, less formal approach to development may be effective in some circumstances. Less formal development is particularly appropriate for the development of web-based systems, which requires a blend of software and graphical design skills.

1.1.3 What's the difference between software engineering and computer science?

Essentially, computer science is concerned with the theories and methods that underlie computers and software systems, whereas software engineering is concerned with the practical problems of producing software. Some knowledge of computer science is essential for software engineers in the same way that some knowledge of physics is essential for electrical engineers.

Ideally, all of software engineering should be underpinned by theories of computer science, but in reality this is not the case. Software engineers must often use *ad hoc* approaches to developing the software. Elegant theories of computer science cannot always be applied to real, complex problems that require a software solution.

1.1.4 What is the difference between software engineering and system engineering?

System engineering is concerned with all aspects of the development and evolution of complex systems where software plays a major role. System engineering is therefore concerned with hardware development, policy and process design and system deployment as well as software engineering. System engineers are involved in spec-ifying the system, defining its overall architecture and then integrating the different parts to create the finished system. They are less concerned with the engineering of the system components (hardware, software, etc.).

System engineering is an older discipline than software engineering. People have been specifying and assembling complex industrial systems such as aircraft and chem-ical plants for more than a hundred years. However, as the percentage of software in systems has increased, software engineering techniques such as use-case mod-elling and configuration management are being used in the systems engineering pro-cess. I discuss system engineering in Chapter 2.

1.1.5   What is a software process?

A software process is the set of activities and associated results that produce a soft-ware product. There are four fundamental process activities (covered later in the book) that are common to all software processes. These are:

1. *Software specification* where customers and engineers define the software to be produced and the constraints on its operation.

2. *Software development* where the software is designed and programmed.

3. *Software validation* where the software is checked to ensure that it is what the customer requires.

4. *Software evolution* where the software is modified to adapt it to changing cus-tomer and market requirements.

Different types of systems need different development processes. For example, real-time software in an aircraft has to be completely specified before development begins whereas, in e-commerce systems, the specification and the program are usu-ally developed together. Consequently, these generic activities may be organised in different ways and described at different levels of detail for different types of soft-ware. However, use of an inappropriate software process may reduce the quality or the usefulness of the software product to be developed and/or increase the develop-ment costs.

Software processes are discussed in more detail in Chapter 4, and the important topic of software process improvement is covered in Chapter 28.

1.1.6   What is a software process model?

A software process model is a simplified description of a software process that pre-sents one view of that process. Process models may include activities that are part of the software process, software products and the roles of people involved in software engineering. Some examples of the types of software process model that may be produced are:

1. *A workflow model* This shows the sequence of activities in the process along with their inputs, outputs and dependencies. The activities in this model represent human actions.

2. *A dataflow or activity model* This represents the process as a set of activities, each of which carries out some data transformation. It shows how the input to the process, such as a specification, is transformed to an output, such as a design. The activities here may represent transformations carried out by people or by computers.

3. *A role/action model* This represents the roles of the people involved in the software process and the activities for which they are responsible.

Most software process models are based on one of three general models or paradigms of software development:

1. *The waterfall approach* This takes the above activities and represents them as separate process phases such as requirements specification, software design, implementation, testing and so on. After each stage is defined it is 'signed-off', and development goes on to the following stage.

2. *Iterative development* This approach interleaves the activities of specification, development and validation. An initial system is rapidly developed from very abstract specifications. This is then refined with customer input to produce a system that satisfies the customer's needs. The system may then be delivered. Alternatively, it may be reimplemented using a more structured approach to produce a more robust and maintainable system.

3. *Component-based software engineering (CBSE)* This technique assumes that parts of the system already exist. The system development process focuses on integrating these parts rather than developing them from scratch. I discuss CBSE in Chapter 19.

I return to these generic process models in Chapter 4 and Chapter 17.

1.1.7   What are the costs of software engineering?

There is no simple answer to this question as the distribution of costs across the different activities in the software process depends on the process used and the type of software that is being developed. For example, real-time software usually requires more extensive validation and testing than web-based systems. However,

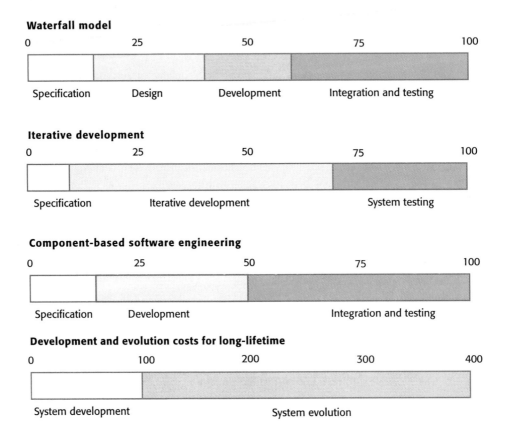

Waterfall model

| 0 | 25 | 50 | 75 | 100 |

| Specification | Design | Development | Integration and testing |

Iterative development

| 0 | 25 | 50 | 75 | 100 |

| Specification | Iterative development | System testing |

Component-based software engineering

| 0 | 25 | 50 | 75 | 100 |

| Specification | Development | Integration and testing |

Development and evolution costs for long-lifetime

| 0 | 100 | 200 | 300 | 400 |

| System development | System evolution |

Figure 1.2 Software engineering activity cost distribution

each of the different generic approaches to software development has a different profile of cost distribution across the software process activities. If you assume that the total cost of developing a complex software system is 100 cost units then Figure 1.2 illustrates how these are spent on different process activities.

In the waterfall approach, the costs of specification, design, implementation and integration are measured separately. Notice that system integration and testing is the most expensive development activity. Normally, this is about 40% of the total development costs but for some critical systems it is likely to be at least 50% of the system development costs.

If the software is developed using an iterative approach, there is no hard line between specification, design and development. Specification costs are reduced because only a high-level specification is produced before development in this approach. Specification, design, implementation, integration and testing are carried out in parallel within a development activity. However, you still need an independent system testing activity once the initial implementation is complete.

Component-based software engineering has only been widely used for a short time. We don't have accurate figures for the costs of different software development activities in this approach. However, we know that development costs are reduced relative to integration and testing costs. Integration and testing costs are increased because you have to ensure that the components that you use actually meet their specification and work as expected with other components.

On top of development costs, costs are also incurred in changing the software after it has gone into use. The costs of evolution vary dramatically depending on the type of system. For long-lifetime software systems, such as command and control systems that may be used for 10 years or more, these costs are likely to exceed the development costs by a factor of 3 or 4, as illustrated in the bottom bar in Figure 1.3. However, smaller business systems have a much shorter lifetime and correspondingly reduced evolution costs.

These cost distributions hold for customised software that is specified by a customer and developed by a contractor. For software products that are (mostly) sold for PCs, the cost profile is likely to be different. These products are usually developed from an outline specification using an evolutionary development approach. Specification costs are relatively low. However, because they are intended for use on a range of different configurations, they must be extensively tested. Figure 1.3 shows the type of cost profile that might be expected for these products.

The evolution costs for generic software products are particularly hard to estimate. In many cases, there is little formal evolution of a product. Once a version of the product has been released, work starts on the next release and, for marketing reasons, this is likely to be presented as a new (but compatible) product rather than as a modified version of a product that the user has already bought. Therefore, the evolution costs are not assessed separately as they are in customised software but are simply the development costs for the next version of the system.

1.1.8 What are software engineering methods?

A software engineering method is a structured approach to software development whose aim is to facilitate the production of high-quality software in a cost-effective way. Methods such as Structured Analysis (DeMarco, 1978) and JSD (Jackson, 1983) were first developed in the 1970s. These methods attempted to identify the basic functional components of a system; function-oriented methods are still used. In the 1980s and 1990s, these function-oriented methods were supplemented by object-oriented (OO) methods such as those proposed by Booch (Booch, 1994) and Rumbaugh (Rumbaugh, et al., 1991). These different approaches have now been integrated into a single unified approach built around the Unified Modeling Language (UML) (Booch, et al., 1999; Rumbaugh, et al., 1999a; Rumbaugh, et al., 1999b).

Figure 1.3 Product development costs

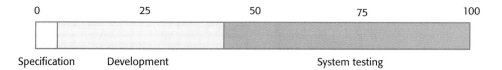

0	25	50	75	100

Specification   Development   System testing

Component	Description	Example
System model descriptions	Descriptions of the system models which should be developed and the notation used to define these models.	Object models, data-flow models, state machine models, etc.
Rules	Constraints which always apply to system models.	Every entity in a system model must have a unique name.
Recommendations	Heuristics which characterise good design practice in this method. Following these recommendations should lead to a well-organised system model.	No object should have more than seven sub-objects associated with it.
Process guidance	Descriptions of the activities which may be followed to develop the system models and the organisation of these activities.	Object attributes should be documented before defining the operations associated with an object.

Figure 1.4 Method components

There is no ideal method, and different methods have different areas where they are applicable. For example, object-oriented methods are often appropriate for interactive systems but not for systems with stringent real-time requirements.

All methods are based on the idea of developing models of a system that may be represented graphically and using these models as a system specification or design. Methods include a number of different components (Figure 1.4).

1.1.9 What is CASE?

The acronym CASE stands for Computer-Aided Software Engineering. It covers a wide range of different types of programs that are used to support software process activities such as requirements analysis, system modelling, debugging and testing. All methods now come with associated CASE technology such as editors for the notations used in the method, analysis modules which check the system model according to the method rules and report generators to help create system documentation. The CASE tools may also include a code generator that automatically generates source code from the system model and some process guidance for software engineers.

1.1.10 What are the attributes of good software?

As well as the services that it provides, software products have a number of other associated attributes that reflect the quality of that software. These attributes are not directly concerned with what the software does. Rather, they reflect its behaviour while it is executing and the structure and organisation of the source program and associated documentation. Examples of these attributes (sometimes called non-functional attributes) are the software's response time to a user query and the understandability of the program code.

The specific set of attributes that you might expect from a software system obviously depends on its application. Therefore, a banking system must be secure, an

Figure 1.5 Essential attributes of good software

Product characteristic	Description
Maintainability	Software should be written in such a way that it may evolve to meet the changing needs of customers. This is a critical attribute because software change is an inevitable consequence of a changing business environment.
Dependability	Software dependability has a range of characteristics, including reliability, security and safety. Dependable software should not cause physical or economic damage in the event of system failure.
Efficiency	Software should not make wasteful use of system resources such as memory and processor cycles. Efficiency therefore includes responsiveness, processing time, memory utilisation, etc.
Usability	Software must be usable, without undue effort, by the type of user for whom it is designed. This means that it should have an appropriate user interface and adequate documentation.

interactive game must be responsive, a telephone switching system must be reliable, and so on. These can be generalised into the set of attributes shown in Figure 1.5, which, I believe, are the essential characteristics of a well-designed software system.

1.1.11 What are the key challenges facing software engineering?

Software engineering in the 21st century faces three key challenges:

1. *The heterogeneity challenge* Increasingly, systems are required to operate as distributed systems across networks that include different types of computers and with different kinds of support systems. It is often necessary to integrate new software with older legacy systems written in different programming languages. The heterogeneity challenge is the challenge of developing techniques for building dependable software that is flexible enough to cope with this heterogeneity.

2. *The delivery challenge* Many traditional software engineering techniques are time-consuming. The time they take is required to achieve software quality. However, businesses today must be responsive and change very rapidly. Their supporting software must change equally rapidly. The delivery challenge is the challenge of shortening delivery times for large and complex systems without compromising system quality.

3. *The trust challenge* As software is intertwined with all aspects of our lives, it is essential that we can trust that software. This is especially true for remote software systems accessed through a web page or web service interface. The trust challenge is to develop techniques that demonstrate that software can be trusted by its users.

Of course, these are not independent. For example, it may be necessary to make rapid changes to a legacy system to provide it with a web service interface. To address these challenges, we will need new tools and techniques as well as innovative ways of combining and using existing software engineering methods.

1.2 Professional and ethical responsibility

Like other engineering disciplines, software engineering is carried out within a legal and social framework that limits the freedom of engineers. Software engineers must accept that their job involves wider responsibilities than simply the application of technical skills. They must also behave in an ethical and morally responsible way if they are to be respected as professionals.

It goes without saying that you should always uphold normal standards of honesty and integrity. You should not use your skills and abilities to behave in a dishonest way or in a way that will bring disrepute to the software engineering profession. However, there are areas where standards of acceptable behaviour are not bounded by laws but by the more tenuous notion of professional responsibility. Some of these are:

1. *Confidentiality* You should normally respect the confidentiality of your employers or clients irrespective of whether a formal confidentiality agreement has been signed.

2. *Competence* You should not misrepresent your level of competence. You should not knowingly accept work that is outside your competence.

3. *Intellectual property rights* You should be aware of local laws governing the use of intellectual property such as patents and copyright. You should be careful to ensure that the intellectual property of employers and clients is protected.

4. *Computer misuse* You should not use your technical skills to misuse other people's computers. Computer misuse ranges from relatively trivial (game playing on an employer's machine, say) to extremely serious (dissemination of viruses).

Professional societies and institutions have an important role to play in setting ethical standards. Organisations such as the ACM, the IEEE (Institute of Electrical and Electronic Engineers) and the British Computer Society publish a code of professional conduct or code of ethics. Members of these organisations undertake to follow that code when they sign up for membership. These codes of conduct are generally concerned with fundamental ethical behaviour.

The ACM and the IEEE have cooperated to produce a joint code of ethics and professional practice. This code exists in both a short form, shown in Figure 1.6, and a longer form (Gotterbarn, et al., 1999) that adds detail and substance to the

Software Engineering Code of Ethics and Professional Practice

ACM/IEEE-CS Joint Task Force on Software Engineering Ethics and Professional Practices

PREAMBLE
The short version of the code summarizes aspirations at a high level of the abstraction; the clauses that are included in the full version give examples and details of how these aspirations change the way we act as software engineering professionals. Without the aspirations, the details can become legalistic and tedious; without the details, the aspirations can become high sounding but empty; together, the aspirations and the details form a cohesive code.

Software engineers shall commit themselves to making the analysis, specification, design, development, testing and maintenance of software a beneficial and respected profession. In accordance with their commitment to the health, safety and welfare of the public, software engineers shall adhere to the following Eight Principles:

1. PUBLIC – Software engineers shall act consistently with the public interest.
2. CLIENT AND EMPLOYER – Software engineers shall act in a manner that is in the best interests of their client and employer consistent with the public interest.
3. PRODUCT – Software engineers shall ensure that their products and related modifications meet the highest professional standards possible.
4. JUDGMENT – Software engineers shall maintain integrity and independence in their professional judgment.
5. MANAGEMENT – Software engineering managers and leaders shall subscribe to and promote an ethical approach to the management of software development and maintenance.
6. PROFESSION – Software engineers shall advance the integrity and reputation of the profession consistent with the public interest.
7. COLLEAGUES – Software engineers shall be fair to and supportive of their colleagues.
8. SELF – Software engineers shall participate in lifelong learning regarding the practice of their profession and shall promote an ethical approach to the practice of the profession.

Figure 1.6 ACM/IEEE
Code of Ethics
(©IEEE/ACM 1999)

shorter version. The rationale behind this code is summarised in the first two paragraphs of the longer form:

> *Computers have a central and growing role in commerce, industry, government, medicine, education, entertainment and society at large. Software engineers are those who contribute by direct participation or by teaching, to the analysis, specification, design, development, certification, maintenance and testing of software systems. Because of their roles in developing software systems, software engineers have significant opportunities to do good or cause harm, to enable others to do good or cause harm, or to influence others to do good or cause harm. To ensure, as much as possible, that their efforts will be used for good, software engineers must commit themselves to making software engineering a beneficial and respected profession. In accordance with that commitment, software engineers shall adhere to the following Code of Ethics and Professional Practice.*

> *The Code contains eight Principles related to the behaviour of and decisions made by professional software engineers, including practitioners, educators, managers, supervisors and policy makers, as well as trainees and students of*

the profession. The Principles identify the ethically responsible relationships in which individuals, groups, and organizations participate and the primary obligations within these relationships. The Clauses of each Principle are illustrations of some of the obligations included in these relationships. These obligations are founded in the software engineer's humanity, in special care owed to people affected by the work of software engineers, and the unique elements of the practice of software engineering. The Code prescribes these as obligations of anyone claiming to be or aspiring to be a software engineer.

In any situation where different people have different views and objectives, you are likely to be faced with ethical dilemmas. For example, if you disagree, in principle, with the policies of more senior management in the company, how should you react? Clearly, this depends on the particular individuals and the nature of the disagreement. Is it best to argue a case for your position from within the organisation or to resign in principle? If you feel that there are problems with a software project, when do you reveal these to management? If you discuss these while they are just a suspicion, you may be overreacting to a situation; if you leave it too late, it may be impossible to resolve the difficulties.

Such ethical dilemmas face all of us in our professional lives and, fortunately, in most cases they are either relatively minor or can be resolved without too much difficulty. Where they cannot be resolved, the engineer is faced with, perhaps, another problem. The principled action may be to resign from their job, but this may well affect others such as their partner or their children.

A particularly difficult situation for professional engineers arises when their employer acts in an unethical way. Say a company is responsible for developing a safety-critical system and because of time-pressure, falsifies the safety validation records. Is the engineer's responsibility to maintain confidentiality or to alert the customer or publicise, in some way, that the delivered system may be unsafe?

The problem here is that there are no absolutes when it comes to safety. Although the system may not have been validated according to predefined criteria, these criteria may be too strict. The system may actually operate safely throughout its lifetime. It is also the case that, even when properly validated, a system may fail and cause an accident. Early disclosure of problems may result in damage to the employer and other employees; failure to disclose problems may result in damage to others.

You must make up your own mind in these matters. The appropriate ethical position here depends entirely on the views of the individuals who are involved. In this case, the potential for damage, the extent of the damage and the people affected by the damage should influence the decision. If the situation is very dangerous, it may be justified to publicise it using the national press (say). However, you should always try to resolve the situation while respecting the rights of your employer.

Another ethical issue is participation in the development of military and nuclear systems. Some people feel strongly about these issues and do not wish to participate in any systems development associated with military systems. Others will work on military systems but not on weapons systems. Yet others feel that national security is an overriding principle and have no ethical objections to working on weapons systems.

In this situation it is important that both employers and employees should make their views known to each other in advance. Where an organisation is involved in military or nuclear work, it should be able to specify that employees must be willing to accept any work assignment. Equally, if an employee is taken on and makes clear that he does not wish to work on such systems, employers should not put pressure on him to do so at some later date.

The general area of ethics and professional responsibility is one that has received increasing attention over the past few years. It can be considered from a philosophical standpoint where the basic principles of ethics are considered, and software engineering ethics are discussed with reference to these basic principles. This is the approach taken by Laudon (Laudon, 1995) and to a lesser extent by Huff and Martin (Huff and Martin, 1995).

However, I find their approach is too abstract and difficult to relate to everyday experience. I prefer the more concrete approach embodied in codes of conduct and practice. I think that ethics are best discussed in a software engineering context and not as a subject in their own right. In this book, therefore, I do not include abstract ethical discussions but, where appropriate, include examples in the exercises that can be the starting point for a group discussion on ethical issues.

KEY POINTS

■ Software engineering is an engineering discipline that is concerned with all aspects of software production.

■ Software products consist of developed programs and associated documentation. Essential product attributes are maintainability, dependability, efficiency and acceptability.

■ The software process includes all of the activities involved in software development. The high-level activities of software specification, development, validation and evolution are part of all software processes.

■ Methods are organised ways of producing software. They include suggestions for the process to be followed, the notations to be used, system models to be developed and rules governing these models and design guidelines.

■ CASE tools are software systems that are designed to support routine activities in the software process such as editing design diagrams, checking diagram consistency and keeping track of program tests that have been run.

■ Software engineers have responsibilities to the engineering profession and society. They should not simply be concerned with technical issues.

■ Professional societies publish codes of conduct that set out the standards of behaviour expected of their members.

FURTHER READING

Fundamentals of Software Engineering. A general software engineering text that takes a rather different perspective on the subject than this book. (C. Ghezi, et. al., Prentice Hall, 2003.)

'Software engineering: The state of the practice'. A special issue of *IEEE Software* that includes several articles discussing current practice in software engineering, how this has changed and the extent to which new software technologies are used. (*IEEE Software*, 20 (6), November 2003.)

Software Engineering: An Engineering Approach. A general text that takes a rather different approach to my book but which includes a number of useful case studies. (J. F. Peters and W. Pedrycz, 2000, John Wiley & Sons.)

Professional Issues in Software Engineering. This is an excellent book discussing legal and professional issues as well as ethics. I prefer its practical approach to more theoretical texts on ethics. (F. Bott, et al., 3rd edition, 2000, Taylor & Francis.)

'Software engineering code of ethics is approved'. An article that discusses the background to the development of the ACM/IEEE Code of Ethics and includes both the short and long form of the code. (*Comm. ACM*, D. Gotterbarn, et al., October 1999.)

'No silver bullet: Essence and accidents of software engineering'. In spite of its age, this paper is a good general introduction to the problems of software engineering. The essential message of the paper, that there is no simple answer to the problems of software engineering, hasn't changed. (F. P. Brooks, *IEEE Computer,* 20 (4), April 1987.)

EXERCISES

1.1   By making reference to the distribution of software costs discussed in Section 1.1.6, explain why it is appropriate to consider software to be more than the programs that can be executed by end-users of a system.

1.2   What are the differences between generic software product development and custom software development?

1.3   What are the four important attributes which all software products should have? Suggest four other attributes that may sometimes be significant.

1.4   What is the difference between a software process model and a software process? Suggest two ways in which a software process model might be helpful in identifying possible process improvements.

1.5   Explain why system testing costs are particularly high for generic software products that are sold to a very wide market.

1.6   Software engineering methods became widely used only when CASE technology became available to support them. Suggest five types of method support that can be provided by CASE tools.

1.7   Apart from the challenges of heterogeneity, rapid delivery and trust, identify other problems and challenges that software engineering is likely to face in the 21st century.

1.8   Discuss whether professional engineers should be certified in the same way as doctors or lawyers.

1.9   For each of the clauses in the ACM/IEEE Code of Ethics shown in Figure 1.6, suggest an appropriate example that illustrates that clause.

1.10   To help counter terrorism, many countries are planning the development of computer systems that track large numbers of their citizens and their actions. Clearly this has privacy implications. Discuss the ethics of developing this type of system.

2

Socio-technical systems

Objectives

The objectives of this chapter are to introduce the concept of a socio-technical system—a system that includes people, software and hardware—and to discuss the systems engineering process. When you have read this chapter, you will:

■ know what is meant by a socio-technical system and understand the difference between a technical computer-based system and a socio-technical system;

■ have been introduced to the concept of emergent system properties such as reliability, performance, safety and security;

■ understand the activities that are involved in the systems engineering process;

■ understand why the organisational context of a system affects its design and use;

■ know what is meant by a 'legacy system', and why these systems are often critical to the operation of many businesses.

Contents

The term *system* is one that is universally used. We talk about computer systems, operating systems, payment systems, the educational system, the system of government, and so on. These are all obviously quite different uses of the word *system* although they share the characteristic that, somehow, the system is more than simply the sum of its parts.

Very abstract systems such as the system of government are well outside the scope of this book. Consequently, I focus here on systems that include computers and that have some specific purpose such as to enable communication, support navigation, and compute salaries. Therefore, a useful working definition of these types of systems is:

> *A system is a purposeful collection of interrelated components that work together to achieve some objective.*

This general definition embraces a vast range of systems. For example, a very simple system such as a pen may only include three or four hardware components. By contrast, an air traffic control system includes thousands of hardware and software components plus human users who make decisions based on information from the computer system.

Systems that include software fall into two categories:

- *Technical computer-based systems* are systems that include hardware and software components but not procedures and processes. Examples of technical systems include televisions, mobile phones and most personal computer software. Individuals and organisations use technical systems for some purpose but knowledge of this purpose is not part of the system. For example, the word processor I am using is not aware that is it being used to write a book.

- *Socio-technical systems* include one or more technical systems but, crucially, also include knowledge of how the system should be used to achieve some broader objective. This means that these systems have defined operational processes, include people (the operators) as inherent parts of the system, are governed by organisational policies and rules and may be affected by external constraints such as national laws and regulatory policies. For example, this book was created through a socio-technical publishing system that includes various processes and technical systems.

Essential characteristics of socio-technical systems are as follows.

1. They have emergent properties that are properties of the system *as a whole* rather than associated with individual parts of the system. Emergent properties depend on both the system components and the relationships between them. As this is so complex, the emergent properties can only be evaluated once the system has been assembled.

2. They are often nondeterministic. This means that, when presented with a specific input, they may not always produce the same output. The system's behaviour depends on the human operators, and people do not always react in the same way. Furthermore, use of the system may create new relationships between the system components and hence change its emergent behaviour.

3. The extent to which the system supports organisational objectives does not just depend on the system itself. It also depends on the stability of these objectives, the relationships and conflicts between organisational objectives and how people in the organisation interpret these objectives. New management may re-interpret the organisational objective that a system is designed to support, and a 'successful' system may then become a 'failure'.

In this book, I am concerned with socio-technical systems that include hardware and software, which have defined operational processes and which offer an interface, implemented in software, to human users. Software engineers should have some knowledge of socio-technical systems and systems engineering (White, et al., 1993; Thayer, 2002) because of the importance of software in these systems. For example, there were fewer than 10 megabytes of software in the US Apollo space program that put a man on the moon in 1969, but there are about 100 megabytes of software in the control systems of the Columbus space station.

A characteristic of all systems is that the properties and the behaviour of the system components are inextricably intermingled. The successful functioning of each system component depends on the functioning of some other components. Thus, software can only operate if the processor is operational. The processor can only carry out computations if the software system defining these computations has been successfully installed.

Systems are usually hierarchical and so include other systems. For example, a police command and control system may include a geographical information system to provide details of the location of incidents. These other systems are called *sub-systems*. A characteristic of sub-systems is that they can operate as independent systems in their own right. Therefore, the same geographical information system may be used in different systems.

Because software is inherently flexible, unexpected systems problems are often left to software engineers to solve. Say a radar installation has been sited so that ghosting of the radar image occurs. It is impractical to move the radar to a site with less interference, so the systems engineers have to find another way of removing this ghosting. Their solution may be to enhance the image-processing capabilities of the software to remove the ghost images. This may slow down the software so that its performance becomes unacceptable. The problem may then be characterised as a 'software failure' whereas, in fact, it was a failure in the design process for the system as a whole.

This situation, where software engineers are left with the problem of enhancing software capabilities without increasing hardware cost, is very common. Many so-called software failures were not a consequence of inherent software problems; they were the result of trying to change the software to accommodate modified system engineering requirements. A good example of this was the failure of the Denver airport baggage system (Swartz, 1996), where the controlling software was expected to deal with several limitations in the equipment used.

Software engineering is therefore critical for the successful development of complex, computer-based socio-technical systems. As a software engineer, you should not simply be concerned with the software itself but you should also have a broader awareness of how that software interacts with other hardware and software systems and how it is supposed to be used. This knowledge helps you understand the limits of software, to design better software and to participate as equal members of a systems engineering group.

2.1 Emergent system properties

The complex relationships between the components in a system mean that the system is more than simply the sum of its parts. It has properties that are properties of the system as a whole. These *emergent properties* (Checkland, 1981) cannot be attributed to any specific part of the system. Rather, they emerge only once the system components have been integrated. Some of these properties can be derived directly from the comparable properties of sub-systems. However, more often, they result from complex sub-system interrelationships that cannot, in practice, be derived from the properties of the individual system components. Examples of some emergent properties are shown in Figure 2.1.

There are two types of emergent properties:

1. *Functional emergent properties* appear when all the parts of a system work together to achieve some objective. For example, a bicycle has the functional property of being a transportation device once it has been assembled from its components.

2. *Non-functional emergent properties* relate to the behaviour of the system in its operational environment. Examples of non-functional properties are reliability, performance, safety and security. These are often critical for computer-based systems, as failure to achieve some minimal defined level in these properties may make the system unusable. Some users may not need some system functions so the system may be acceptable without them. However, a system that is unreliable or too slow is likely to be rejected by all its users.

To illustrate the complexity of emergent properties, consider the property of system reliability. Reliability is a complex concept that must always be considered at the system level rather than at the individual component level. The components in

Figure 2.1 Examples of emergent properties

Property	Description
Volume	The volume of a system (the total space occupied) varies depending on how the component assemblies are arranged and connected.
Reliability	System reliability depends on component reliability but unexpected interactions can cause new types of failure and therefore affect the reliability of the system.
Security	The security of the system (its ability to resist attack) is a complex property that cannot be easily measured. Attacks may be devised that were not anticipated by the system designers and so may defeat built-in safeguards.
Repairability	This property reflects how easy it is to fix a problem with the system once it has been discovered. It depends on being able to diagnose the problem, access the components that are faulty and modify or replace these components.
Usability	This property reflects how easy it is to use the system. It depends on the technical system components, its operators and its operating environment.

a system are interdependent, so failures in one component can be propagated through the system and affect the operation of other components. It is often difficult to anticipate how the consequences of component failures propagate through the system. Consequently, you cannot make good estimates of overall system reliability from data about the reliability of system components.

There are three related influences on the overall reliability of a system:

1. *Hardware reliability* What is the probability of a hardware component failing and how long does it take to repair that component?

2. *Software reliability* How likely is it that a software component will produce an incorrect output? Software failure is usually distinct from hardware failure in that software does not wear out. Failures are usually transient so the system carries on working after an incorrect result has been produced.

3. *Operator reliability* How likely is it that the operator of a system will make an error?

All of these are closely linked. Hardware failure can generate spurious signals that are outside the range of inputs expected by software. The software can then behave unpredictably. Operator error is most likely in conditions of stress, such as when system failures are occurring. These operator errors may further stress the hardware, causing more failures, and so on. Thus, the initial, recoverable failure can rapidly develop into a serious problem requiring a complete system shutdown.

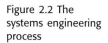

Figure 2.2 The
systems engineering
process

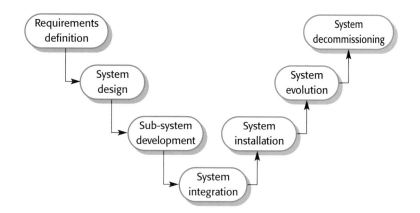

Like reliability, other emergent properties such as performance or usability are
hard to assess but can be measured after the system is operational. Properties such
as safety and security, however, pose different problems. Here, you are not simply
concerned with an attribute that is related to the overall behaviour of the system
but are concerned with behaviour that the system should *not* exhibit. A secure system is one that does not allow unauthorised access to its data but it is clearly impossible to predict all possible modes of access and explicitly forbid them. Therefore,
it may only be possible to assess these properties by default. That is, you only know
that a system is insecure when someone breaks into it.

2.2 Systems engineering

Systems engineering is the activity of specifying, designing, implementing, validating,
deploying and maintaining socio-technical systems. Systems engineers are not just concerned with software but also with hardware and the system's interactions with users
and its environment. They must think about the services that the system provides, the
constraints under which the system must be built and operated and the ways in which
the system is used to fulfil its purpose. As I have discussed, software engineers need
an understanding of system engineering because problems of software engineering are
often a result of system engineering decisions (Thayer, 1997; Thayer, 2002).

The phases of the systems engineering process are shown in Figure 2.2. This
process was an important influence on the 'waterfall' model of the software process that I describe in Chapter 4.

There are important distinctions between the system engineering process and the
software development process:

Figure 2.3 Disciplines
involved in systems
engineering

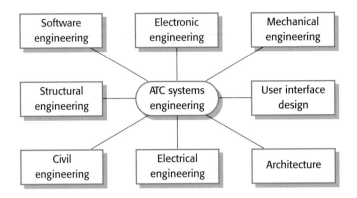

1. *Limited scope for rework during system development* Once some system engineering decisions, such as the siting of base stations in a mobile phone system, have been made, they are very expensive to change. Reworking the system design to solve these problems is rarely possible. One reason software has become so important in systems is that it allows changes to be made during system development, in response to new requirements.

2. *Interdisciplinary involvement* Many engineering disciplines may be involved in system engineering. There is a lot of scope for misunderstanding because different engineers use different terminology and conventions.

   Systems engineering is an interdisciplinary activity involving teams drawn from various backgrounds. System engineering teams are needed because of the wide knowledge required to consider all the implications of system design decisions. As an illustration of this, Figure 2.3 shows some of the disciplines that may be involved in the system engineering team for an air traffic control (ATC) system that uses radars and other sensors to determine aircraft position.

   For many systems, there are almost infinite possibilities for trade-offs between different types of sub-systems. Different disciplines negotiate to decide how functionality should be provided. Often there is no 'correct' decision on how a system should be decomposed. Rather, you may have several possible alternatives, but you may not be able to choose the best technical solution. Say one alternative in an air traffic control system is to build new radars rather than refit existing installations. If the civil engineers involved in this process do not have much other work, they may favour this alternative because it allows them to keep their jobs. They may then rationalise this choice with technical arguments.

2.2.1 System requirements definition

System requirements definitions specify what the system should do (its functions) and its essential and desirable system properties. As with software requirements analysis (discussed in Part 2), creating system requirements definitions involves consultations with system customers and end-users. This requirements definition phase usually concentrates on deriving three types of requirement:

1. *Abstract functional requirements* The basic functions that the system must provide are defined at an abstract level. More detailed functional requirements specification takes place at the sub-system level. For example, in an air traffic control system, an abstract functional requirement would specify that a flight-plan database should be used to store the flight plans of all aircraft entering the controlled airspace. However, you would not normally specify the details of the database unless they affected the requirements of other sub-systems.

2. *System properties* These are non-functional emergent system properties such as availability, performance and safety, as I have discussed above. These non-functional system properties affect the requirements for all sub-systems.

3. *Characteristics that the system must not exhibit* It is sometimes as important to specify what the system must *not* do as it is to specify what the system should do. For example, if you are specifying an air traffic control system, you might specify that the system should not present the controller with too much information.

An important part of the requirements definition phase is to establish a set of overall objectives that the system should meet. These should not necessarily be expressed in terms of the system's functionality but should define why the system is being procured for a particular environment.

To illustrate what this means, say you are specifying a system for an office building to provide for fire protection and for intruder detection. A statement of objectives based on the system functionality might be:

> *To provide a fire and intruder alarm system for the building that will provide internal and external warning of fire or unauthorised intrusion.*

This objective states explicitly that there needs to be an alarm system that provides warnings of undesired events. Such a statement might be appropriate if you were replacing an existing alarm system. By contrast, a broader statement of objectives might be:

> *To ensure that the normal functioning of the work carried out in the building is not seriously disrupted by events such as fire and unauthorised intrusion.*

If you set out the objective like this, you both broaden and limit the design choices. For example, this objective allows for intruder protection using sophisticated locking technology—without any internal alarms. It may also exclude the use of sprinklers for fire protection because they can affect the building's electrical systems and so seriously disrupt work.

Figure 2.4 The
system design
process

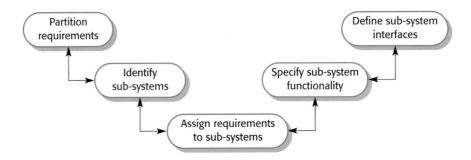

A fundamental difficulty in establishing system requirements is that the problems that complex systems are usually built to help tackle are usually 'wicked problems' (Rittel and Webber, 1973). A 'wicked problem' is a problem that is so complex and where there are so many related entities that there is no definitive problem specification. The true nature of the problem emerges only as a solution is developed. An extreme example of a 'wicked problem' is earthquake planning. No one can accurately predict where the epicentre of an earthquake will be, what time it will occur or what effect it will have on the local environment. We cannot therefore completely specify how to deal with a major earthquake. The problem can only be tackled after it has happened.

2.2.2 System design

System design (Figure 2.4) is concerned with how the system functionality is to be provided by the components of the system. The activities involved in this process are:

1. *Partition requirements* You analyse the requirements and organise them into related groups. There are usually several possible partitioning options, and you may suggest a number of alternatives at this stage of the process.

2. *Identify sub-systems* You should identify sub-systems that can individually or collectively meet the requirements. Groups of requirements are usually related to sub-systems, so this activity and requirements partitioning may be amalgamated. However, sub-system identification may also be influenced by other organisational or environmental factors.

3. *Assign requirements to sub-systems* You assign the requirements to sub-systems. In principle, this should be straightforward if the requirements partitioning is used to drive the sub-system identification. In practice, there is never a clean match between requirements partitions and identified sub-systems. Limitations of externally purchased sub-systems may mean that you have to change the requirements to accommodate these constraints.

4. *Specify sub-system functionality* You should specify the specific functions provided by each sub-system. This may be seen as part of the system design phase

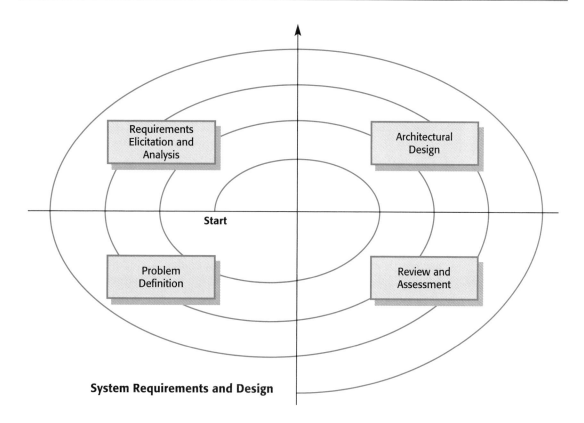

Figure 2.5 A spiral
model of
requirements and
design

or, if the sub-system is a software system, part of the requirements specification activity for that system. You should also try to identify relationships between sub-systems at this stage.

5. *Define sub-system interfaces* You define the interfaces that are provided and required by each sub-system. Once these interfaces have been agreed upon, it becomes possible to develop these sub-systems in parallel.

As the double-ended arrows in Figure 2.4 imply, there is a lot of feedback and iteration from one stage to another in this design process. As problems and questions arise, you often have to redo work done in earlier stages.

Although I have separated the processes of requirements engineering and design in this discussion, in practice they are inextricably linked. Constraints posed by existing systems may limit design choices, and these choices may be specified in the requirements. You may have to do some initial design to structure and organise the requirements engineering process. As the design process continues, you may discover problems with existing requirements and new requirements may emerge. Consequently, one way to think of these linked processes is as a spiral, as shown in Figure 2.5.

The spiral process reflects the reality that requirements affect design decisions and vice versa, and so it makes sense to interleave these processes. Starting in the

Figure 2.6 A simple
burglar alarm system

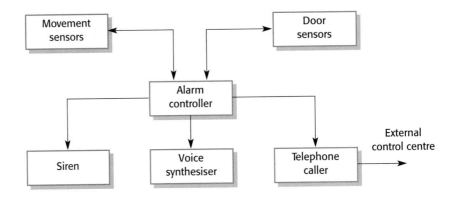

centre, each round of the spiral may add detail to the requirements and the design.
Some rounds may focus on requirements, some on design. Sometimes, new knowledge collected during the requirements and design process means that the problem
statement itself has to be changed.

For almost all systems, there are many possible designs that meet the requirements. These cover a range of solutions that combine hardware, software and human
operations. The solution that you chose for further development may be the most
appropriate technical solution that meets the requirements. However, wider organisational and political considerations may influence the choice of solution. For example, a government client may prefer to use national rather than foreign suppliers for
its system, even if the national product is technically inferior. These influences usually take effect in the review and assessment phase in the spiral model where designs
and requirements may be accepted or rejected. The process ends when the review
and evaluation shows that the requirements and high-level design are sufficiently
detailed to allow the next phase of the process to begin.

2.2.3 System modelling

During the system requirements and design activity, systems may be modelled as
a set of components and relationships between these components. These are normally illustrated graphically in a system architecture model that gives the reader an
overview of the system organisation.

The system architecture may be presented as a block diagram showing the major
sub-systems and the interconnections between these sub-systems. When drawing a
block diagram, you should represent each sub-system using a rectangle, and you
should show relationships between the sub-systems using arrows that link these rectangles. The relationships indicated may include data flow, a 'uses'/'used by' relationship or some other type of dependency relationship.

For example, Figure 2.6 shows the decomposition of an intruder alarm system
into its principal components. The block diagram should be supplemented by brief
descriptions of each sub-system, as shown in Figure 2.7.

Sub-system	Description
Movement sensors	Detects movement in the rooms monitored by the system
Door sensors	Detects door opening in the external doors of the building
Alarm controller	Controls the operation of the system
Siren	Emits an audible warning when an intruder is suspected
Voice synthesiser	Synthesises a voice message giving the location of the suspected intruder
Telephone caller	Makes external calls to notify security, the police, etc.

At this level of detail, the system is decomposed into a set of interacting sub-systems. Each sub-system should be represented in a similar way until the system is decomposed into functional components. Functional components are components that, when viewed from the perspective of the sub-system, provide a single function. By contrast, a sub-system usually is multifunctional. Of course, when viewed from another perspective (say that of the component manufacturer), a functional component may itself be a system in its own right.

Historically, the system architecture model was used to identify hardware and software components that could be developed in parallel. However, this hardware/software distinction is becoming increasingly irrelevant. Almost all components now include some embedded computing capabilities. For example, a network linking machines will consist of physical cables plus repeaters and network gateways. The repeaters and the gateways include processors and software to drive these processors as well as specialised electronic components.

At the architectural level, it is now more appropriate to classify sub-systems according to their function before making decisions about hardware/software trade-offs. The decision to provide a function in hardware or software may be governed by non-technical factors such as the availability of off-the-shelf components or the time available to develop the component.

Block diagrams may be used for all sizes of system. Figure 2.8 shows the architecture of a much larger system for air traffic control. Several major sub-systems shown are themselves large systems. The arrowed lines that link these systems show information flow between these sub-systems.

2.2.4 Sub-system development

During sub-system development, the sub-systems identified during system design are implemented. This may involve starting another system engineering process for

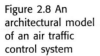

Figure 2.8 An architectural model of an air traffic control system

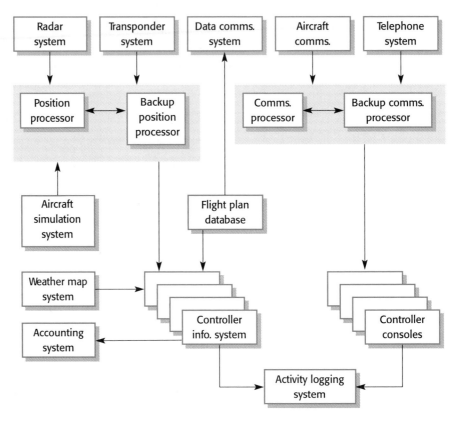

individual sub-systems or, if the sub-system is software, a software process involving requirements, design, implementation and testing.

Occasionally, all sub-systems are developed from scratch during the development process. Normally, however, some of the sub-systems are commercial, off-the-shelf (COTS) systems that are bought for integration into the system. It is usually much cheaper to buy existing products than to develop special-purpose components. At this stage, you may have to reenter the design activity to accommodate a bought-in component. COTS systems may not meet the requirements exactly but, if off-the-shelf products are available, it is usually worth the expense of rethinking the design.

Sub-systems are usually developed in parallel. When problems are encountered that cut across sub-system boundaries, a system modification request must be made. Where systems involve extensive hardware engineering, making modifications after manufacturing has started is usually very expensive. Often 'work-arounds' that compensate for the problem must be found. These 'work-arounds' usually involve software changes because of the software's inherent flexibility. This leads to changes in the software requirements so, as I have discussed in Chapter 1, it is important to design software for change so that the new requirements can be implemented without excessive additional costs.

2.2.5 Systems integration

During the systems integration process, you take the independently developed sub-systems and put them together to make up a complete system. Integration can be done using a 'big bang' approach, where all the sub-systems are integrated at the same time. However, for technical and managerial purposes, an incremental integration process where sub-systems are integrated one at a time is the best approach, for two reasons:

1. It is usually impossible to schedule the development of all the sub-systems so that they are all finished at the same time.

2. Incremental integration reduces the cost of error location. If many sub-systems are simultaneously integrated, an error that arises during testing may be in any of these sub-systems. When a single sub-system is integrated with an already working system, errors that occur are probably in the newly integrated sub-system or in the interactions between the existing subsystems and the new sub-system.

Once the components have been integrated, an extensive programme of system testing takes place. This testing should be aimed at testing the interfaces between components and the behaviour of the system as a whole.

Sub-system faults that are a consequence of invalid assumptions about other sub-systems are often revealed during system integration. This may lead to disputes between the various contractors responsible for the different sub-systems. When problems are discovered in sub-system interaction, the contractors may argue about which sub-system is faulty. Negotiations on how to solve the problems can take weeks or months.

As more and more systems are built by integrating COTS hardware and software components, system integration is becoming increasingly important. In some cases, there is no separate sub-system development and the integration is, essentially, the implementation phase of the system.

2.2.6 System evolution

Large, complex systems have a very long lifetime. During their life, they are changed to correct errors in the original system requirements and to implement new requirements that have emerged. The system's computers are likely to be replaced with new, faster machines. The organisation that uses the system may reorganise itself and hence use the system in a different way. The external environment of the system may change, forcing changes to the system.

System evolution, like software evolution (discussed in Chapter 21), is inherently costly for several reasons:

1. Proposed changes have to be analysed very carefully from a business and a technical perspective. Changes have to contribute to the goals of the system and should not simply be technically motivated.

2. Because sub-systems are never completely independent, changes to one sub-system may adversely affect the performance or behaviour of other sub-systems. Consequent changes to these sub-systems may therefore be needed.

3. The reasons for original design decisions are often unrecorded. Those responsible for the system evolution have to work out why particular design decisions were made.

4. As systems age, their structure typically becomes corrupted by change so the costs of making further changes increases.

Systems that have evolved over time are often reliant on obsolete hardware and software technology. If they have a critical role in an organisation, they are known as *legacy systems*—systems that the organisation would like to replace but where the risks of introducing a new system are high. I discuss some issues with legacy systems in Section 2.4.

2.2.7 System decommissioning

System decommissioning means taking the system out of service after the end of its useful operational lifetime. For hardware systems this may involve disassembling and recycling materials or dealing with toxic substances. Software has no physical decommissioning problems, but some software may be incorporated in a system to assist with the decommissioning process. For example, software may be used to monitor the state of hardware components. When the system is decommissioned, components that are not worn can therefore be identified and reused in other systems.

If the data in the system that is being decommissioned is still valuable to your organisation, you may have to convert it for use by some other system. This can often involve significant costs as the data structures may be implicitly defined in the software itself. You have to analyse the software to discover how the data is structured and then write a program to reorganise the data into the required structures for the new system.

2.3 Organisations, people and computer systems

Socio-technical systems are enterprise systems that are intended to help deliver some organisational or business goal. This might be to increase sales, reduce material used in manufacturing, collect taxes, maintain a safe airspace, etc. Because they are embedded in an organisational environment, the procurement, development and use of these system is influenced by the organisation's policies and procedures and by its working culture. The users of the system are people who are influenced by the way the organisation is managed and by their interactions with other people inside and outside of the organisation.

Therefore, when you are trying to understand the requirements for a socio-technical system you need to understand its organisational environment. If you don't, the systems may not meet business needs, and users and their managers may reject the system.

Human and organisational factors from the system's environment that affect the system design include:

1. *Process changes* Does the system require changes to the work processes in the environment? If so, training will certainly be required. If changes are significant, or if they involve people losing their jobs, there is a danger that the users will resist the introduction of the system.

2. *Job changes* Does the system de-skill the users in an environment or cause them to change the way they work? If so, they may actively resist the introduction of the system into the organisation. Designs that involve managers having to change their way of working to fit the computer system are often resented. The managers may feel that their status in the organisation is being reduced by the system.

3. *Organisational changes* Does the system change the political power structure in an organisation? For example, if an organisation is dependent on a complex system, those who know how to operate the system have a great deal of political power.

These human, social and organisational factors are often critical in determining whether or not a system successfully meets its objectives. Unfortunately, predicting their effects on systems is very difficult for engineers who have little experience of social or cultural studies. To help understand the effects of systems on organisations, various methodologies have developed such as Mumford's socio-technics (Mumford, 1989) and Checkland's Soft Systems Methodology (Checkland and Scholes, 1990; Checkland, 1981). There have also been extensive sociological studies of the effects of computer-based systems on work (Ackroyd, et al., 1992).

Ideally, all relevant organisational knowledge should be included in the system specification so that the system designers may take it into account. In reality, this is impossible. System designers have to make assumptions based on other comparable systems and on common sense. If they get these wrong, the system may malfunction in unpredictable ways. For example, if the designers of a system do not understand that different parts of an organisation may actually have conflicting objectives, then any organisation-wide system that is developed will inevitably have some dissatisfied users.

2.3.1 Organisational processes

In Section 2.2, I introduced a system engineering process model that showed the sub-processes involved in system development. However, the development process is not the only process involved in systems engineering. It interacts with the

Figure 2.9
Procurement,
development and
operational
processes

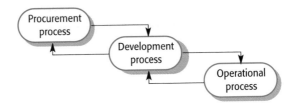

system procurement process and with the process of using and operating the system. This is illustrated in Figure 2.9.

The procurement process is normally embedded within the organisation that will buy and use the system (the client organisation). The process of system procurement is concerned with making decisions about the best way for an organisation to acquire a system and deciding on the best suppliers of that system.

Large complex systems usually consist of a mixture of off-the-shelf and specially built components. One reason why more and more software is included in systems is that it allows more use of existing hardware components, with the software acting as a 'glue' to make these hardware components work together effectively. The need to develop this 'glueware' is one reason why the savings from using off-the-shelf components are sometimes not as great as anticipated. I discuss COTS systems in more detail in Chapter 18.

Figure 2.10 shows the procurement process for both existing systems and systems that have to be specially designed. Some important points about the process shown in this diagram are:

1. Off-the-shelf components do not usually match requirements exactly, unless the requirements have been written with these components in mind. Therefore, choosing a system means that you have to find the closest match between the system requirements and the facilities offered by off-the-shelf systems. You may then have to modify the requirements and this can have knock-on effects on other sub-systems.

2. When a system is to be built specially, the specification of requirements acts as the basis of a contract for the system procurement. It is therefore a legal, as well as a technical, document.

3. After a contractor to build a system has been selected, there is a contract negotiation period where you may have to negotiate further changes to the requirements and discuss issues such as the cost of changes to the system.

I have already outlined the main phases of the system development process. Complex systems are usually developed by a different organization (the supplier) from the organization that is procuring the system. The reason for this is that the procurer's business is rarely system development so its employees do not have the

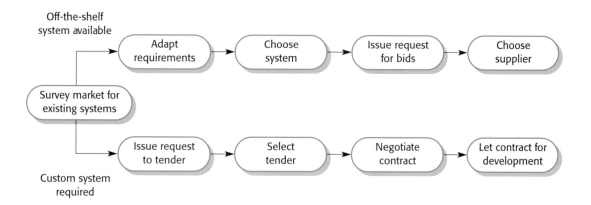

Off-the-shelf
system available

Survey market for
existing systems

Custom system
required

Figure 2.10 The
system procurement
process

skills needed to develop complex systems themselves. In fact, very few single organisations have the capabilities to design, manufacture and test all the components of a large, complex system.

This supplier, who is usually called the *principal contractor*, may contract out the development of different sub-systems to a number of sub-contractors. For large systems, such as air traffic control systems, a group of suppliers may form a consortium to bid for the contract. The consortium should include all of the capabilities required for this type of system, such as computer hardware suppliers, software developers, peripheral suppliers and suppliers of specialist equipment such as radars.

The procurer deals with the contractor rather than the sub-contractors so that there is a single procurer/supplier interface. The sub-contractors design and build parts of the system to a specification that is produced by the principal contractor. Once completed, the principal contractor integrates these different components and delivers them to the customer buying the system. Depending on the contract, the procurer may allow the principal contractor a free choice of sub-contractors or may require the principal contractor to choose sub-contractors from an approved list.

Operational processes are the processes that are involved in using the system for its defined purpose. For example, operators of an air traffic control system follow specific processes when aircraft enter and leave airspace, when they have to change height or speed, when an emergency occurs and so on. For new systems, these operational processes have to be defined and documented during the system development process. Operators may have to be trained and other work processes adapted to make effective use of the new system. Undetected problems may arise at this stage because the system specification may contain errors or omissions. While the system may perform to specification, its functions may not meet the real operational needs. Consequently, the operators may not use the system as its designers intended.

The key benefit of having people in a system is that people have a unique capability of being able to respond effectively to unexpected situations even when they have never had direct experience of these situations. Therefore, when things go wrong, the operators can often recover the situation, although this may sometimes mean that the defined process is violated. Operators also use their local knowledge to adapt and improve processes. Normally, the actual operational process is different from that anticipated by the system designers.

This means that designers should design operational processes to be flexible and adaptable. The operational processes should not be too constraining, they should not require operations to be done in a particular order, and the system software should not rely on a specific process being followed. Operators usually improve the process because they know what does and does not work in a real situation.

An issue that may only emerge after the system goes into operation is the problem of operating the new system alongside existing systems. There may be physical problems of incompatibility, or it may be difficult to transfer data from one system to another. More subtle problems might arise because different systems have different user interfaces. Introducing the new system may increase the operator error rate for existing systems as the operators mix up user interface commands.

2.4 Legacy systems

Because of the time and effort required to develop a complex system, large computer-based systems usually have a long lifetime. For example, military systems are often designed for a 20-year lifetime, and much of the world's air traffic control still relies on software and operational processes that were originally developed in the 1960s and 1970s. It is sometimes too expensive and too risky to discard such business-critical systems after a few years of use. Their development continues throughout their life with changes to accommodate new requirements, new operating platforms, and so forth.

Legacy systems are socio-technical computer-based systems that have been developed in the past, often using older or obsolete technology. These systems include not only hardware and software but also legacy processes and procedures—old ways of doing things that are difficult to change because they rely on legacy software. Changes to one part of the system inevitably involve changes to other components,

Legacy systems are often business-critical systems. They are maintained because it is too risky to replace them. For example, for most banks the customer accounting system was one of their earliest systems. Organisational policies and procedures may rely on this system. If the bank were to scrap and replace the customer accounting software (which may run on expensive mainframe hardware) then there would be a serious business risk if the replacement system didn't work properly. Furthermore, existing procedures would have to change, and this may upset the people in the organisation and cause difficulties with the bank's auditors.

Figure 2.11 illustrates the logical parts of a legacy system and their relationships:

Figure 2.11 Legacy
system components

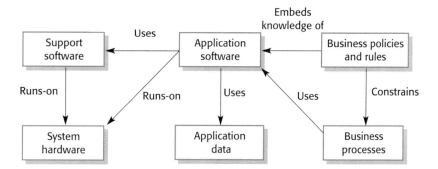

1. *System hardware* In many cases, legacy systems have been written for main-frame hardware that is no longer available, that is expensive to maintain and that may not be compatible with current organisational IT purchasing policies.

2. *Support software* The legacy system may rely on a range of support software from the operating system and utilities provided by the hardware manufacturer through to the compilers used for system development. Again, these may be obsolete and no longer supported by their original providers.

3. *Application software* The application system that provides the business services is usually composed of a number of separate programs that have been developed at different times. Sometimes the term *legacy system* means this application software system rather than the entire system.

4. *Application data* These are the data that are processed by the application system. In many legacy systems, an immense volume of data has accumulated over the lifetime of the system. This data may be inconsistent and may be duplicated in several files.

5. *Business processes* These are processes that are used in the business to achieve some business objective. An example of a business process in an insurance company would be issuing an insurance policy; in a manufacturing company, a business process would be accepting an order for products and setting up the associated manufacturing process. Business processes may be designed around a legacy system and constrained by the functionality that it provides.

6. *Business policies and rules* These are definitions of how the business should be carried out and constraints on the business. Use of the legacy application system may be embedded in these policies and rules.

An alternative way of looking at these components of a legacy system is as a series of layers, as shown in Figure 2.12. Each layer depends on the layer immediately below it and interfaces with that layer. If interfaces are maintained, then you should be able to make changes within a layer without affecting either of the adjacent layers.

Figure 2.12 Layered model of a legacy system

Socio-technical system

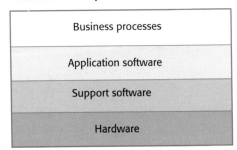

| Business processes |
| Application software |
| Support software |
| Hardware |

In practice, this simple encapsulation rarely works, and changes to one layer of the system may require consequent changes to layers that are both above and below the changed level. The reasons for this are:

1. Changing one layer in the system may introduce new facilities, and higher layers in the system may then be changed to take advantage of these facilities. For example, a new database introduced at the support software layer may include

KEY POINTS

■ Socio-technical systems include computer hardware, software and people, and are situated within an organisation. They are designed to help the organisation meet some broad goal.

■ The emergent properties of a system are characteristic of the system as a whole rather than of its component parts. They include properties such as performance, reliability, usability, safety and security. The success or failure of a system is often dependent on these emergent properties.

■ The systems engineering process includes specification, design, development, integration and testing. System integration, where sub-systems from more than one supplier must be made to work together, is particularly critical.

■ Human and organisational factors such as organisational structure and politics have a significant effect on the operation of socio-technical systems.

■ Within an organisation, there are complex interactions between the processes of system procurement, development and operation.

■ A legacy system is an old system that still provides essential business services.

■ Legacy systems are not just application software systems. They are socio-technical systems so include business processes, application software, support software and system hardware.

facilities to access the data through a web browser, and business processes may be modified to take advantage of this facility.

2. Changing the software may slow the system down so that new hardware is needed to improve the system performance. The increase in performance from the new hardware may then mean that further software changes which were previously impractical become possible.

3. It is often impossible to maintain hardware interfaces, especially if a radical change to a new type of hardware is proposed. For example, if a company moves from mainframe hardware to client-server systems (discussed in Chapter 11) these usually have different operating systems. Major changes to the application software may therefore be required.

FURTHER READING

'Software system engineering: A tutorial'. A good general overview of systems engineering, although Thayer focuses exclusively on computer-based systems and does not discuss socio-technical issues. (R. H. Thayer, *IEEE Computer*, April 2002.)

'Legacy information systems: Issues and directions'. An overview of the problems of legacy systems with a particular focus on the problems of legacy data. (J. Bisbal, et al., *IEEE Software*, September/October 1999.)

Systems Engineering: Coping with Complexity. At the time of this writing, this is still the best available systems engineering book. It focuses on systems engineering processes with good chapters on requirements, architecture and project management. (R. Stevens, et al., 1998, Prentice Hall.)

'Airport 95: Automated baggage system'. An excellent, readable case study of what can go wrong with a systems engineering project and how software tends to get the blame for wider systems failures. (*ACM Software Engineering Notes*, 21, March 1996.)

EXERCISES

2.1 Explain why other systems within a system's environment can have unanticipated effects on the functioning of a system.

2.2 Explain why specifying a system to be used by emergency services for disaster management is an inherently wicked problem.

2.3 Suggest how the software systems used in a car can help with the decommissioning (scrapping) of the overall system.

2.4 Explain why it is important to produce an overall description of a system architecture at an early stage in the system specification process.

2.5 Consider a security system that is an extended version of the system shown in Figure 2.6, which is intended to protect against intrusion and to detect fire. It incorporates smoke sensors, movement sensors, door sensors, video cameras under computer control, located at various places in the building, an operator console where the system status is reported, and external communication facilities to call the appropriate services such as the police and fire departments. Draw a block diagram of a possible design for such a system.

2.6 A flood warning system is to be procured which will give early warning of possible flood dangers to sites that are threatened by floods. The system will include a set of sensors to monitor the rate of change of river levels, links to a meteorological system giving weather forecasts, links to the communication systems of emergency services (police, coastguard, etc.), video monitors installed at selected locations, and a control room equipped with operator consoles and video monitors.

Controllers can access database information and switch video displays. The system database includes information about the sensors, the location of sites at risk and the threat conditions for these sites (e.g., high tide, southwesterly winds), tide tables for coastal sites, the inventory and location of flood control equipment, contact details for emergency services, local radio stations, and so on.

Draw a block diagram of a possible architecture for such a system. You should identify the principal sub-systems and the links between them.

2.7 A multimedia virtual museum system offering virtual experiences of ancient Greece is to be developed for a consortium of European museums. The system should provide users with the facility to view 3-D models of ancient Greece through a standard web browser and should also support an immersive virtual reality experience. What political and organisational difficulties might arise when the system is installed in the museums that make up the consortium?

2.8 Explain why legacy systems may be critical to the operation of a business.

2.9 Explain why legacy systems can cause difficulties for companies that wish to reorganise their business processes.

2.10 What are the arguments for and against considering system engineering as a profession in its own right such as electrical engineering or software engineering?

2.11 You are an engineer involved in the development of a financial system. During installation, you discover that this system will make a significant number of people redundant. The people in the environment deny you access to essential information to complete the system installation. To what extent should you, as a systems engineer, become involved in this? Is it your professional responsibility to complete the installation as contracted? Should you simply abandon the work until the procuring organisation has sorted out the problem?

3

Critical systems

Objectives

The objective of this chapter is to introduce the idea of a critical system—a system in which dependability is its most important property. When you have read this chapter, you will:

■ understand that in a critical system, system failure can have severe human or economic consequences;

■ understand four dimensions of system dependability: availability, reliability, safety and security;

■ understand that to achieve dependability you need to avoid mistakes during the development of a system, to detect and remove errors when the system is in use and to limit the damage caused by operational failures.

Contents

Software failures are relatively common. In most cases, these failures cause inconvenience but no serious, long-term damage. However, in some systems failure can result in significant economic losses, physical damage or threats to human life. These systems are called *critical systems*. Critical systems are technical or socio-technical systems that people or businesses depend on. If these systems fail to deliver their services as expected then serious problems and significant losses may result.

There are three main types of critical systems:

1. *Safety-critical systems* A system whose failure may result in injury, loss of life or serious environmental damage. An example of a safety-critical system is a control system for a chemical manufacturing plant.

2. *Mission-critical systems* A system whose failure may result in the failure of some goal-directed activity. An example of a mission-critical system is a navigational system for a spacecraft.

3. *Business-critical systems* A system whose failure may result in very high costs for the business using that system. An example of a business-critical system is the customer accounting system in a bank.

The most important emergent property of a critical system is its dependability. The term *dependability* was proposed by Laprie (Laprie 1995) to cover the related systems attributes of availability, reliability, safety and security. As I discuss in Section 3.2, these properties are inextricably linked, so having a single term to cover them all makes sense.

There are several reasons why dependability is the most important emergent property for critical systems:

1. *Systems that are unreliable, unsafe or insecure are often rejected by their users.* If users don't trust a system, they will refuse to use it. Furthermore, they may also refuse to buy or use products from the same company as the untrustworthy system, believing that these products perhaps cannot be trusted.

2. *System failure costs may be enormous.* For some applications, such as a reactor control system or an aircraft navigation system, the cost of system failure is orders of magnitude greater than the cost of the control system.

3. *Untrustworthy systems may cause information loss.* Data is very expensive to collect and maintain; it may sometimes be worth more than the computer system on which it is processed. A great deal of effort and money may have to be spent duplicating valuable data to guard against data corruption.

The high cost of critical systems failure means that trusted methods and techniques must be used for development. Consequently, critical systems are usually developed using well-tried techniques rather than newer techniques that have not been subject to extensive practical experience. Rather than embrace new techniques and methods, critical systems developers are naturally conservative. They prefer to use older techniques whose strengths and weaknesses are understood rather than new techniques which may appear to be better but whose long-term problems are unknown.

Expensive software engineering techniques that are not cost-effective for non-critical systems may sometimes be used for critical systems development. For example, formal mathematical methods of software development (discussed in Chapter 10) have been successfully used for safety and security critical systems (Hall, 1996; Hall and Chapman, 2002). One reason why these formal methods are used is that it helps reduce the amount of testing required. For critical systems, the costs of verification and validation are usually very high—more than 50% of the total system development costs.

Although a small number of control systems may be completely automatic, most critical systems are socio-technical systems where people monitor and control the operation of computer-based systems. The costs of critical systems failure are usually so high that we need people in the system who can cope with unexpected situations, and who can often recover from difficulties when things go wrong.

Of course, while system operators can help recover from problems, they can also cause problems if they make mistakes. There are three 'system components' where critical systems failures may occur:

1. System hardware may fail because of mistakes in its design, because components fail as a result of manufacturing errors, or because the components have reached the end of their natural life.

2. System software may fail because of mistakes in its specification, design or implementation.

3. Human operators of the system may fail to operate the system correctly. As hardware and software have become more reliable, failures in operation are now probably the largest single cause of system failures.

These failures can be interrelated. A failed hardware component may mean system operators have to cope with an unexpected situation and additional workload. This puts them under stress—and people under stress often make mistakes. This can cause the software to fail, which means more work for the operators, even more stress, and so on.

As a result, it is particularly important that designers of critical systems take a holistic, systems perspective rather than focus on a single aspect of the system. If the hardware, software and operational processes are designed separately without taking the potential weaknesses of other parts of the system into account, then it is more likely that errors will occur at interfaces between the various parts of the system.

Figure 3.1 Insulin
pump structure

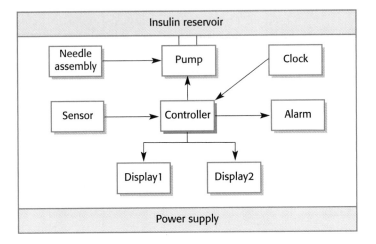

3.1 A simple safety-critical system

There are many types of critical computer-based systems, ranging from control systems for devices and machinery to information and e-commerce systems. They could be excellent case studies for a software engineering book, as advanced software engineering techniques are often used in their development. However, understanding these systems can be very difficult, as you need to understand the features and constraints of the application domain where they operate.

Consequently, the critical systems case study that I use in several chapters in this book is a medical system that simulates the operation of the pancreas (an internal organ). I have chosen this because we all have some understanding of medical problems and it is clear why safety and reliability are so important for this type of system. The system chosen is intended to help people who suffer from diabetes.

Diabetes is a relatively common condition where the human pancreas is unable to produce sufficient quantities of a hormone called *insulin*. Insulin metabolises glucose in the blood. The conventional treatment of diabetes involves regular injections of genetically engineered insulin. Diabetics measure their blood sugar levels using an external meter and then calculate the dose of insulin that they should inject.

The problem with this treatment is that the level of insulin in the blood does not just depend on the blood glucose level but is a function of the time when the insulin injection was taken. This can lead to very low levels of blood glucose (if there is too much insulin) or very high levels of blood sugar (if there is too little insulin). Low blood sugar is, in the short term, a more serious condition, as it can result in temporary brain malfunctioning and, ultimately, unconsciousness and death. In the long term, continual high levels of blood sugar can lead to eye damage, kidney damage, and heart problems.

Current advances in developing miniaturised sensors have meant that it is now possible to develop automated insulin delivery systems. These systems monitor blood sugar levels and deliver an appropriate dose of insulin when required. Insulin delivery systems

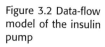

Figure 3.2 Data-flow model of the insulin pump

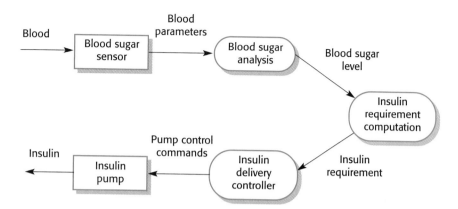

like this already exist for the treatment of hospital patients. In the future, it may be possible for many diabetics to have such systems permanently attached to their bodies.

A software-controlled insulin delivery system might work by using a micro-sensor embedded in the patient to measure some blood parameter that is proportional to the sugar level. This is then sent to the pump controller. This controller computes the sugar level and the amount of insulin that is needed. It then sends signals to a miniaturised pump to deliver the insulin via a permanently attached needle.

Figure 3.1 shows the components and organisation of the insulin pump. Figure 3.2 is a data-flow model that illustrates how an input blood sugar level is transformed to a sequence of pump control commands.

There are two high-level dependability requirements for this insulin pump system:

1. The system shall be available to deliver insulin when required.

2. The system shall perform reliably and deliver the correct amount of insulin to counteract the current level of blood sugar.

Failure of the system could, in principle, cause excessive doses of insulin to be delivered and this could threaten the life of the user. It is particularly important that overdoses of insulin should not occur.

3.2 System dependability

All of us are familiar with the problem of computer system failure. For no obvious reason, computer systems sometimes crash and fail to deliver the services that have been requested. Programs running on these computers may not operate as expected and, occasionally, may corrupt the data that is managed by the system. We have

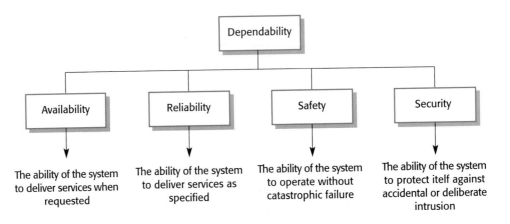

Figure 3.3
Dimensions of
dependability

learned to live with these failures, and few of us completely trust the personal computers that we normally use.

The dependability of a computer system is a property of the system that equates to its trustworthiness. Trustworthiness essentially means the degree of user confidence that the system will operate as they expect and that the system will not 'fail' in normal use. This property cannot be expressed numerically, but we use relative terms such as 'not dependable', 'very dependable' and 'ultra-dependable' to reflect the degrees of trust that we might have in a system.

Trustworthiness and usefulness are not, of course, the same thing. I don't think that the word processor that I used to write this book is a very dependable system, but it is very useful. However, to reflect my lack of trust in the system I frequently save my work and keep multiple backup copies of it. I compensate for the lack of system dependability by actions that limit the damage that could be caused if the system failed.

There are four principal dimensions to dependability, as shown in Figure 3.3:

1. *Availability* Informally, the availability of a system is the probability that it will be up and running and able to deliver useful services at any given time.

2. *Reliability* Informally, the reliability of a system is the probability, over a given period of time, that the system will correctly deliver services as expected by the user.

3. *Safety* Informally, the safety of a system is a judgement of how likely it is that the system will cause damage to people or its environment.

4. *Security* Informally, the security of a system is a judgement of how likely it is that the system can resist accidental or deliberate intrusions.

These are complex properties that can be decomposed into a number of other, simpler properties. For example, *security* includes *integrity* (ensuring that the systems program and data are not damaged) and *confidentiality* (ensuring that information can only be accessed by people who are authorised). *Reliability* includes *correctness* (ensuring the system services are as specified), *precision* (ensuring information is delivered at an appropriate level of detail) and *timeliness* (ensuring that information is delivered when it is required).

The dependability properties of availability, security, reliability and safety are all interrelated. Safe system operation usually depends on the system being available and operating reliability. A system may become unreliable because its data has been corrupted by an intruder. Denial-of-service attacks on a system are intended to compromise its availability. If a system that has been proved to be safe is infected with a virus, safe operation can no longer be assumed. It is because of these close links that the notion of system dependability as an encompassing property was introduced.

As well as these four main dimensions, other system properties can also be considered under the heading of dependability:

1. *Repairability* System failures are inevitable, but the disruption caused by failure can be minimised if the system can be repaired quickly. In order for that to happen, it must be possible to diagnose the problem, access the component that has failed and make changes to fix that component. Repairability in software is enhanced when the organisation using the system has access to the source code and has the skills to make changes to it. Unfortunately, this is becoming increasingly uncommon as we move towards system development using third-party, black-box components (see Chapter 19).

2. *Maintainability* As systems are used, new requirements emerge. It is important to maintain the usefulness of a system by changing it to accommodate these new requirements. Maintainable software is software that can be adapted economically to cope with new requirements and where there is a low probability that making changes will introduce new errors into the system.

3. *Survivability* A very important attribute for Internet-based systems is survivability, which is closely related to security and availability (Ellison, et al., 1999). Survivability is the ability of a system to continue to deliver service whilst it is under attack and, potentially, while part of the system is disabled. Work on survivability focuses on identifying key system components and ensuring that they can deliver a minimal service. Three strategies are used to enhance survivability—namely, resistance to attack, attack recognition and recovery from the damage caused by an attack (Ellison, et al., 1999; Ellison, et al., 2002).

4. *Error tolerance* This property can be considered as part of usability (discussed in Chapter 16) and reflects the extent to which the system has been designed so that user input error are avoided and tolerated. When user errors occur, the system should, as far as possible, detect these errors and either fix them automatically or request the user to re-input their data

Figure 3.4
Cost/dependability
curve

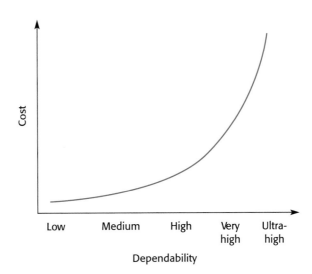

Because availability, reliability, safety and security are the fundamental dependability properties, I concentrate on them in this chapter and in later chapters that cover critical systems specification (Chapter 9), critical systems development (Chapter 20) and critical systems validation (Chapter 24).

Of course, these dependability properties are not all applicable to all systems. For the insulin pump system, introduced in Section 3.1, the most important properties are availability (it must work when required), reliability (it must deliver the correct dose of insulin) and safety (it must never deliver a dangerous dose of insulin). Security, in this case, is less likely to be an issue, as the pump will not maintain confidential information and is not networked so cannot be maliciously attacked.

Designers must usually make a trade-off between system performance and system dependability. Generally, high levels of dependability can only be achieved at the expense of system performance. Dependable software includes extra, often redundant, code to perform the necessary checking for exceptional system states and to recover from system faults. This reduces system performance and increases the amount of store required by the software. It also adds significantly to the costs of system development.

Because of additional design, implementation and validation costs, increasing the dependability of a system can significantly increase development costs. In particular, validation costs are high for critical systems. As well as validating that the system meets its requirements, the validation process may have to prove to an external regulator such as the Federal Aviation Authority that the system is dependable.

Figure 3.4 shows the relationship between costs and incremental improvements in dependability. The higher the dependability that you need, the more that you have to spend on testing to check that you have reached that level. Because of the exponential nature of this cost/dependability curve, it is not possible to demonstrate that a system is 100% dependable, as the costs of dependability assurance would then be infinite.

3.3 Availability and reliability

System availability and reliability are closely related properties that can both be expressed as numerical probabilities. The reliability of a system is the probability that the system's services will be correctly delivered as specified. The availability of a system is the probability that the system will be up and running to deliver these services to users when they request them.

Although they are closely related, you cannot assume that reliable systems will always be available and vice versa. For example, some systems can have a high availability requirement but a much lower reliability requirement. If users expect continuous service then the availability requirements are high. However, if the consequences of a failure are minimal and the system can recover quickly from these failures then the same system can have low reliability requirements.

An example of a system where availability is more critical than reliability is a telephone exchange switch. Users expect a dial tone when they pick up a phone so the system has high availability requirements. However, if a system fault causes a connection to fail, this is often recoverable. Exchange switches usually include repair facilities that can reset the system and retry the connection attempt. This can be done very quickly, and the phone user may not even notice that a failure has occurred. Therefore, availability rather than reliability is the key dependability requirement for these systems.

A further distinction between these characteristics is that availability does not simply depend on the system itself but also on the time needed to repair the faults that make the system unavailable. Therefore, if system A fails once per year, and system B fails once per month, then A is clearly more reliable then B. However, assume that system A takes three days to restart after a failure, whereas system B takes 10 minutes to restart. The availability of system B over the year (120 minutes of down time) is much better than that of system A (4,320 minutes of down time).

System reliability and availability may be defined more precisely as follows:

1. *Reliability* The probability of failure-free operation over a specified time in a given environment for a specific purpose.

2. *Availability* The probability that a system, at a point in time, will be operational and able to deliver the requested services.

One of the practical problems in developing reliable systems is that our intuitive notions of reliability and availability are sometimes broader than these limited definitions. The definition of *reliability* states that the environment in which the system is used and the purpose that it is used for must be taken into account. If you measure system reliability in one environment, you can't assume that the reliability will be the same in another environment where the system is used in a different way.

For example, let's say that you measure the reliability of a word processor in an office environment where most users are uninterested in the operation of the software. They follow the instructions for its use and do not try to experiment with the system. If you measure the reliability of the same system in a university environment, then the reliability may be quite different. Here, students may explore the boundaries of the system and use the system in unexpected ways. These may result in system failures that did not occur in the more constrained office environment.

Human perceptions and patterns of use are also significant. For example, say a car has a fault in its windscreen wiper system that results in intermittent failures of the wipers to operate correctly in heavy rain. The reliability of that system as perceived by a driver depends on where they live and use the car. A driver in Seattle (wet climate) will probably be more affected by this failure than a driver in Las Vegas (dry climate). The Seattle driver's perception will be that the system is unreliable, whereas the driver in Las Vegas may never notice the problem.

A further difficulty with these definitions is that they do not take into account the severity of failure or the consequences of unavailability. People, naturally, are more concerned about system failures that have serious consequences, and their perception of system reliability is influenced by these consequences. For example, say a failure of initialisation in the engine management software causes a car engine to cut out immediately after starting, but it operates correctly after a restart that corrects the initialisation problem. This does not affect the normal operation of the car, and many drivers would not think that a repair was needed. By contrast, most drivers will think that an engine that cuts out while they are driving at high speed once per month (say) is both unreliable and unsafe and must be repaired.

A strict definition of reliability relates the system implementation to its specification. That is, the system is behaving reliably if its behaviour is consistent with that defined in the specification. However, a common cause of perceived unreliability is that the system specification does not match the expectations of the system users. Unfortunately, many specifications are incomplete or incorrect and it is left to software engineers to interpret how the system should behave. As they are not domain experts, they may not, therefore, implement the behaviour that users expect.

Reliability and availability are compromised by system failures. These may be a failure to provide a service, a failure to deliver a service as specified, or the delivery of a service in such a way that is unsafe or insecure. Some of these failures are a consequence of specification errors or failures in associated systems such as a telecommunications system. However, many failures are a consequence of erroneous system behaviour that derives from faults in the system. When discussing reliability, it is helpful to distinguish between the terms *fault, error* and *failure*. I have defined these terms in Figure 3.5.

Human errors do not inevitably lead to system failures. The faults introduced may be in parts of the system that are never used. Faults do not necessarily result in system errors, as the faulty state may be transient and may be corrected before erroneous behaviour occurs. System errors may not result in system failures, as the behaviour may also be transient and have no observable effects or the system may

Figure 3.5 Reliability
terminology

Term	Description
System failure	An event that occurs at some point in time when the system does not deliver a service as expected by its users
System error	An erroneous system state that can lead to system behaviour that is unexpected by system users.
System fault	A characteristic of a software system that can lead to a system error. For example, failure to initialise a variable could lead to that variable having the wrong value when it is used.
Human error or mistake	Human behaviour that results in the introduction of faults into a system.

include protection that ensures that the erroneous behaviour is discovered and corrected before the system services are affected.

This distinction between the terms shown in Figure 3.5 helps us identify three complementary approaches that are used to improve the reliability of a system:

1. *Fault avoidance* Development techniques are used that either minimise the possibility of mistakes and/or that trap mistakes before they result in the introduction of system faults. Examples of such techniques include avoiding error-prone programming language constructs such as pointers and the use of static analysis to detect program anomalies.

2. *Fault detection and removal* The use of verification and validation techniques that increase the chances that faults will be detected and removed before the system is used. Systematic system testing and debugging is an example of a fault-detection technique.

3. *Fault tolerance* Techniques that ensure that faults in a system do not result in system errors or that ensure that system errors do not result in system failures. The incorporation of self-checking facilities in a system and the use of redundant system modules are examples of fault tolerance techniques.

I cover the development of fault tolerant systems in Chapter 20, where I also discuss some techniques for fault avoidance. I discuss process-based approaches to fault avoidance in Chapter 27 and fault detection in Chapters 22 and 23.

Software faults cause software failures when the faulty code is executed with a set of inputs that expose the software fault. The code works properly for most inputs. Figure 3.6, derived from Littlewood (Littlewood, 1990), shows a software system as a mapping of an input to an output set. Given an input or input sequence, the program responds by producing a corresponding output. For example, given an input of a URL, a web browser produces an output that is the display of the requested web page.

Figure 3.6 A system
as an input/output
mapping

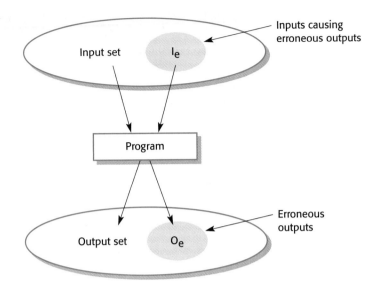

Some of these inputs or input combinations, shown in the shaded ellipse in Figure 3.6, cause erroneous outputs to be generated. The software reliability is related to the probability that, in a particular execution of the program, the system input will be a member of the set of inputs, which cause an erroneous output to occur. If an input causing an erroneous output is associated with a frequently used part of the program, then failures will be frequent. However, if it is associated with rarely used code, then users will hardly ever see failures.

Each user of a system uses it in different ways. Faults that affect the reliability of the system for one user may never be revealed under someone else's mode of working (Figure 3.7). In Figure 3.7, the set of erroneous inputs correspond to the shaded ellipse in Figure 3.6. The set of inputs produced by User 2 intersects with this erroneous input set. User 2 will therefore experience some system failures. User 1 and User 3, however, never use inputs from the erroneous set. For them, the software will always be reliable.

Figure 3.7 Software
usage patterns

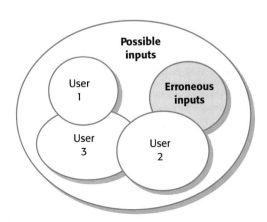

The overall reliability of a program, therefore, mostly depends on the number of inputs causing erroneous outputs during normal use of the system by most users. Software faults that occur only in exceptional situations have little effect on the system's reliability. Removing software faults from parts of the system that are rarely used makes little real difference to the reliability as seen by system users. Mills et al. (Mills, et al., 1987) found that, in their software, removing 60% of known errors in their software led to only a 3% reliability improvement. Adams (Adams, 1984), in a study of IBM software products, noted that many defects in the products were only likely to cause failures after hundreds or thousands of months of product usage.

Users in a socio-technical system may adapt to software with known faults, and may share information about how to get around these problems. They may avoid using inputs that are known to cause problems so program failures never arise. Furthermore, experienced users often 'work around' software faults that are known to cause failures. They deliberately avoid using system features that they know can cause problems for them. For example, I avoid certain features, such as automatic numbering in the word processing system that I used to write this book. Repairing the faults in these features may make no practical difference to the reliability as seen by these users.

3.4 Safety

Safety-critical systems are systems where it is essential that system operation is always safe. That is, the system should *never* damage people or the system's environment even if the system fails. Examples of safety-critical systems are control and monitoring systems in aircraft, process control systems in chemical and pharmaceutical plants and automobile control systems.

Hardware control of safety-critical systems is simpler to implement and analyse than software control. However, we now build systems of such complexity that they cannot be controlled by hardware alone. Some software control is essential because of the need to manage large numbers of sensors and actuators with complex control laws. An example of such complexity is found in advanced, aerodynamically unstable military aircraft. They require continual software-controlled adjustment of their flight surfaces to ensure that they do not crash.

Safety-critical software falls into two classes:

1. *Primary, safety-critical software* This is software that is embedded as a controller in a system. Malfunctioning of such software can cause a hardware malfunction, which results in human injury or environmental damage. I focus on this type of software.

2. *Secondary safety-critical software* This is software that can indirectly result in injury. Examples of such systems are computer-aided engineering design systems whose malfunctioning might result in a design fault in the object being

designed. This fault may cause injury to people if the designed system malfunctions. Another example of a secondary safety-critical system is a medical database holding details of drugs administered to patients. Errors in this system might result in an incorrect drug dosage being administered.

System reliability and system safety are related but separate dependability attributes. Of course, a safety-critical system should be reliable in that it should conform to its specification and operate without failures. It may incorporate fault-tolerant features so that it can provide continuous service even if faults occur. However, fault-tolerant systems are not necessarily safe. The software may still malfunction and cause system behaviour, which results in an accident.

Apart from the fact that we can never be 100% certain that a software system is fault-free and fault-tolerant, there are several other reasons why software systems that are reliable are not necessarily safe:

1. The specification may be incomplete in that it does not describe the required behaviour of the system in some critical situations. A high percentage of system malfunctions (Nakajo and Kume, 1991; Lutz, 1993) are the result of specification rather than design errors. In a study of errors in embedded systems, Lutz concludes:

    ...difficulties with requirements are the key root cause of the safety-related software errors which have persisted until integration and system testing.

2. Hardware malfunctions may cause the system to behave in an unpredictable way and may present the software with an unanticipated environment. When components are close to failure they may behave erratically and generate signals that are outside the ranges that can be handled by the software.

3. The system operators may generate inputs that are not individually incorrect but which, in some situations, can lead to a system malfunction. An anecdotal example of this is when a mechanic instructed the utility management software on an aircraft to raise the undercarriage. The software carried out the mechanic's instruction perfectly. Unfortunately, the plane was on the ground at the time—clearly, the system should have disallowed the command unless the plane was in the air.

A specialised vocabulary has evolved to discuss safety-critical systems, and it is important to understand the specific terms used. In Figure 3.8, I show some definitions that I have adapted from terms initially defined by Leveson (Leveson, 1985).

The key to assuring safety is to ensure either that accidents do not occur or that the consequences of an accident are minimal. This can be achieved in three complementary ways:

1. *Hazard avoidance* The system is designed so that hazards are avoided. For example, a cutting system that requires the operator to press two separate buttons at the same time to operate the machine avoids the hazard of the operator's hands being in the blade pathway.

Figure 3.8 Safety
terminology

Term	Description
Accident (or mishap)	An unplanned event or sequence of events which results in human death or injury, damage to property or to the environment. A computer-controlled machine injuring its operator is an example of an accident.
Hazard	A condition with the potential for causing or contributing to an accident. A failure of the sensor that detects an obstacle in front of a machine is an example of a hazard.
Damage	A measure of the loss resulting from a mishap. Damage can range from many people killed as a result of an accident to minor injury or property damage.
Hazard severity	An assessment of the worst possible damage that could result from a particular hazard. Hazard severity can range from catastrophic where many people are killed to minor where only minor damage results.
Hazard probability	The probability of the events occurring which create a hazard. Probability values tend to be arbitrary but range from *probable* (say 1/100 chance of a hazard occurring) to implausible (no conceivable situations are likely where the hazard could occur).
Risk	This is a measure of the probability that the system will cause an accident. The risk is assessed by considering the hazard probability, the hazard severity and the probability that a hazard will result in an accident.

2. *Hazard detection and removal* The system is designed so that hazards are detected and removed before they result in an accident. For example, a chemical plant system may detect excessive pressure and open a relief valve to reduce the pressure before an explosion occurs.

3. *Damage limitation* The system may include protection features that minimise the damage that may result from an accident. For example, an aircraft engine normally includes automatic fire extinguishers. If a fire occurs, it can often be controlled before it poses a threat to the aircraft.

Accidents generally occur when several things go wrong at the same time. An analysis of serious accidents (Perrow, 1984) suggests that they were almost all due to a combination of malfunctions rather than single failures. The unanticipated combination led to interactions that resulted in system failure. Perrow also suggests that it is impossible to anticipate all possible combinations of system malfunction, and that accidents are an inevitable part of using complex systems. Software tends to increase system complexity, so using software control *may* increase the probability of system accidents.

However, software control and monitoring can also improve the safety of systems. Software-controlled systems can monitor a wider range of conditions than electro-mechanical systems. They can be adapted relatively easily. They involve the use of computer hardware, which has very high inherent reliability and which is physically small and lightweight. Software-controlled systems can provide sophisticated safety interlocks. They can support control strategies that reduce the amount of time people need to spend in hazardous environments. Therefore, although software control may introduce more ways in which a system can go wrong, it also allows better monitoring and protection and hence may improve the safety of the system.

In all cases, it is important to maintain a sense of proportion about system safety. It is impossible to make a system 100% safe, and society has to decide whether or not the consequences of an occasional accident are worth the benefits that come from the use of advanced technologies. It is also a social and political decision about how to deploy limited national resources to reduce risk to the population as a whole.

3.5 Security

Security is a system attribute that reflects the ability of the system to protect itself from external attacks that may be accidental or deliberate. Security has become increasingly important as more and more systems are connected to the Internet. Internet connections provide additional system functionality (e.g., customers may be able to access their bank accounts directly), but Internet connection also means that the system can be attacked by people with hostile intentions. The Internet connection also means that details of specific system vulnerabilities may be easily disseminated so that more people may be able to attack the system. Equally, however, the connection can speed up the distribution of system patches to repair these vulnerabilities.

Examples of attacks might be viruses, unauthorised use of system services and unauthorised modification of the system or its data. Security is important for all critical systems. Without a reasonable level of security, the availability, reliability and safety of the system may be compromised if external attacks cause some damage to the system.

The reason for this is that all methods for assuring availability, reliability and safety rely on the fact that the operational system is the same as the system that was originally installed. If this installed system has been compromised in some way (for example, if the software has been modified to include a virus), then the arguments for reliability and safety that were originally made can no longer hold. The system software may be corrupted and may behave in an unpredictable way.

Conversely, errors in the development of a system can lead to security loopholes. If a system does not respond to unexpected inputs or if array bounds are not checked, then attackers can exploit these weaknesses to gain access to the system. Major security incidents such as the original Internet worm (Spafford, 1989) and the Code Red worm more than 10 years later (Berghel, 2001) took advantage of the fact that programs in C do not include array bound checking. They overwrote part of memory with code that allowed unauthorised access to the system.

Figure 3.9 Security
terminology

Term	Description
Exposure	Possible loss or harm in a computing system. This can be loss or damage to data or can be a loss of time and effort if recovery is necessary after a security breach.
Vulnerability	A weakness in a computer-based system that may be exploited to cause loss or harm.
Attack	An exploitation of a system's vulnerability. Generally, this is from outside the system and is a deliberate attempt to cause some damage.
Threats	Circumstances that have potential to cause loss or harm. You can think of these as a system vulnerability that is subjected to an attack.
Control	A protective measure that reduces a system's vulnerability. Encryption would be an example of a control that reduced a vulnerability of a weak access control system.

Of course, in some critical systems, security is the most important dimension of system dependability. Military systems, systems for electronic commerce and systems that involve the processing and interchange of confidential information must be designed so that they achieve a high level of security. If an airline reservation system (say) is unavailable, this causes inconvenience and some delays in issuing tickets. However, if the system is insecure and can accept fake bookings then the airline that owns the system can lose a great deal of money.

There are three types of damage that may be caused through external attack:

1. *Denial of service* The system may be forced into a state where its normal services become unavailable. This, obviously, then affects the availability of the system.

2. *Corruption of programs or data* The software components of the system may be altered in an unauthorised way. This may affect the system's behaviour and hence its reliability and safety. If damage is severe, the availability of the system may be affected.

3. *Disclosure of confidential information* The information managed by the system may be confidential, and the external attack may expose this to unauthorised people. Depending on the type of data, this could affect the safety of the system and may allow later attacks that affect the system availability or reliability.

As with other aspects of dependability, there is a specialised terminology associated with security. Some important terms, as discussed by Pfleeger (Pfleeger, 1997), are defined in Figure 3.9.

There is a clear analogy here with some of the terminology of safety so that an exposure is analogous to an accident and a vulnerability is analogous to a hazard.

Therefore, there are comparable approaches that may be used to assure the security of a system:

1. *Vulnerability avoidance* The system is designed so that vulnerabilities do not occur. For example, if a system is not connected to an external public network then there is no possibility of an attack from members of the public.

2. *Attack detection and neutralisation* The system is designed to detect vulnerabilities and remove them before they result in an exposure. An example of vulnerability detection and removal is the use of a virus checker that analyses incoming files for viruses and modifies these files to remove the virus.

KEY POINTS

■ In a critical system, failure can lead to significant economic losses, physical damage or threats to human life. Three important classes of critical systems are safety-critical systems, mission-critical systems and business-critical systems.

■ The dependability of a computer system is a property of the system that reflects the user's degree of trust in the system. The most important dimensions of dependability are availability, reliability, safety and security.

■ The availability of a system is the probability that it will be able to deliver services to its users when requested to do so. Reliability is the probability that system services will be delivered as specified.

■ Reliability and availability are usually considered to be the most important dimensions of dependability. If a system is unreliable, it is difficult to ensure system safety or security, as they may be compromised by system failures.

■ Reliability is related to the probability of an error occurring in operational use. A program may contain known faults but may still be seen as reliable by its users. They may never use features of the system that are affected by these faults.

■ The safety of a system is a system attribute that reflects the system's ability to operate, normally or abnormally, without threatening people or the environment.

■ Security is important for all critical systems. Without a reasonable level of security, the availability, reliability and safety of the system may be compromised if external attacks cause some damage to the system.

■ To improve dependability, you need to take a socio-technical approach to system design, taking into account the humans in the system as well as the hardware and software.

3. *Exposure limitation* The consequences of a successful attack are minimised. Examples of exposure limitation are regular system backups and a configuration management policy that allows damaged software to be recreated.

The vast majority of vulnerabilities in computer-based systems result from human failings rather than technical problems. People chose easy-to-guess passwords or write down their passwords in places where they can be found. System administrators make errors in setting up access control or configuration files and users forget to install or use protection software. To improve security, therefore, we need to take a socio-technical perspective and to think about how systems are actually used and not just about their technical characteristics.

FURTHER READING

'The evolution of information assurance'. An excellent article discussing the need to protect critical information in an organisation from accidents and attacks. (R. Cummings, *IEEE Computer*, 35 (12), December 2002.)

Practical Design of Safety-critical Computer Systems. A general overview of safety-critical systems design that discusses safety issues and which takes a systems and not merely a software perspective. (W. R. Dunn, Reliability Press, 2002.)

Secrets and Lies: Digital Security in a Networked World. An excellent, very readable book on computer security which approaches it from a socio-technical perspective. (B. Schneier, 2000, John Wiley & Sons.)

'Survivability: Protecting your critical systems'. An accessible introduction to the topic of survivability and why it is important. (R. Ellison et al., *IEEE Internet Computing*, Nov./Dec. 1999.)

Computer-related Risks. A collection drawn from the Internet Risks Forum of incidents that have occurred in automated systems. It shows how much can actually go wrong in safety-related systems. (P. G. Neumann, 1995, Addison-Wesley.)

EXERCISES

3.1   What are the three principal types of critical system? Explain the differences between these.

3.2   Suggest six reasons why dependability is important in critical systems.

3.3   What are the most important dimensions of system dependability?

3.4   Why is the cost of assuring dependability exponential?

3.5 Giving reasons for your answer, suggest which dependability attributes are likely to be most critical for the following systems:

  ▪ An Internet server provided by an ISP with thousands of customers

  ▪ A computer-controlled scalpel used in keyhole surgery

  ▪ A directional control system used in a satellite launch vehicle

  ▪ An Internet-based personal finance management system.

3.6 Identify six consumer products that contain, or that may contain in the future, safety-critical software systems.

3.7 Reliability and safety are related but distinct dependability attributes. Describe the most important distinction between these attributes and explain why it is possible for a reliable system to be unsafe and vice versa.

3.8 In a medical system that is designed to deliver radiation to treat tumours, suggest one hazard that may arise and propose one software feature that may be used to ensure that the identified hazard does not result in an accident.

3.9 Explain why there is a close relationship between system availability and system security.

3.10 In computer security terms, explain the differences between an attack and a threat.

3.11 Is it ethical for an engineer to agree to deliver a software system with known faults to a customer? Does it make any difference if the customer is told of the existence of these faults in advance? Would it be reasonable to make claims about the reliability of the software in such circumstances?

3.12 As an expert in computer security, you have been approached by an organisation that campaigns for the rights of torture victims and have been asked to help the organisation gain unauthorised access to the computer systems of an American company. This will help them confirm or deny that this company is selling equipment that is used directly in the torture of political prisoners. Discuss the ethical dilemmas that this request raises and how you would react to this request.

4

Software processes

Objectives

The objective of this chapter is to introduce you to the idea of a software process—a coherent set of activities for software production. When you have read this chapter, you will:

■ understand the concept of software processes and software process models;

■ understand three generic software process models and when they might be used;

■ understand, in outline, the activities involved in software requirements engineering, software development, testing and evolution;

■ understand how the Rational Unified Process integrates good software process practice to create a modern, generic process model;

■ have been introduced to CASE technology that is used to support software process activities.

Contents

A software process is a set of activities that leads to the production of a software product. These activities may involve the development of software from scratch in a standard programming language like Java or C. Increasingly, however, new software is developed by extending and modifying existing systems and by configuring and integrating off-the-shelf software or system components.

Software processes are complex and, like all intellectual and creative processes, rely on people making decisions and judgements. Because of the need for judgement and creativity, attempts to automate software processes have met with limited success. Computer-aided software engineering (CASE) tools (discussed in Section 4.5) can support some process activities. However, there is no possibility, at least in the next few years, of more extensive automation where software takes over creative design from the engineers involved in the software process.

One reason the effectiveness of CASE tools is limited is because of the immense diversity of software processes. There is no ideal process, and many organisations have developed their own approach to software development. Processes have evolved to exploit the capabilities of the people in an organisation and the specific characteristics of the systems that are being developed. For some systems, such as critical systems, a very structured development process is required. For business systems, with rapidly changing requirements, a flexible, agile process is likely to be more effective.

Although there are many software processes, some fundamental activities are common to all software processes:

1. *Software specification* The functionality of the software and constraints on its operation must be defined.

2. *Software design and implementation* The software to meet the specification must be produced.

3. *Software validation* The software must be validated to ensure that it does what the customer wants.

4. *Software evolution* The software must evolve to meet changing customer needs.

I discuss these activities briefly in this chapter and discuss them in much more detail in later parts of the book.

Although there is no 'ideal' software process, there is scope for improving the software process in many organisations. Processes may include outdated techniques or may not take advantage of the best practice in industrial software engineering. Indeed, many organisations still do not take advantage of software engineering methods in their software development.

Software processes can be improved by process standardisation where the diversity in software processes across an organisation is reduced. This leads to improved communication and a reduction in training time, and makes automated process support more economical. Standardisation is also an important first step in introducing new software engineering methods and techniques and good software engineering practice. I discuss software process improvement in more detail in Chapter 28.

4.1 Software process models

As I explained in Chapter 1, a software process model is an abstract representation of a software process. Each process model represents a process from a particular perspective, and thus provides only partial information about that process. In this section, I introduce a number of very general process models (sometimes called *process paradigms*) and present these from an architectural perspective. That is, we see the framework of the process but not the details of specific activities.

These generic models are not definitive descriptions of software processes. Rather, they are abstractions of the process that can be used to explain different approaches to software development. You can think of them as process frameworks that may be extended and adapted to create more specific software engineering processes.

The process models that I cover here are:

1. *The waterfall model* This takes the fundamental process activities of specification, development, validation and evolution and represents them as separate process phases such as requirements specification, software design, implementation, testing and so on.

2. *Evolutionary development* This approach interleaves the activities of specification, development and validation. An initial system is rapidly developed from abstract specifications. This is then refined with customer input to produce a system that satisfies the customer's needs.

3. *Component-based software engineering* This approach is based on the existence of a significant number of reusable components. The system development process focuses on integrating these components into a system rather than developing them from scratch.

These three generic process models are widely used in current software engineering practice. They are not mutually exclusive and are often used together, especially for large systems development. Indeed, the Rational Unified Process that I cover in Section 4.4 combines elements of all of these models. Sub-systems within a larger system may be developed using different approaches. Therefore, although it is convenient to discuss these models separately, you should understand that, in practice, they are often combined.

All sorts of variants of these generic processes have been proposed and may be used in some organisations. The most important variant is probably formal system development, where a formal mathematical model of a system is created. This model

Figure 4.1 The
software life cycle

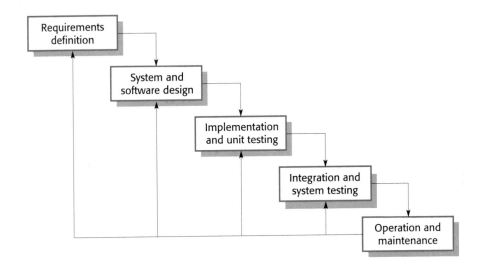

is then transformed, using mathematical transformations that preserve its consistency, into executable code.

The best-known example of a formal development process is the Cleanroom process, which was originally developed by IBM (Mills, et al., 1987; Selby, et al., 1987; Linger, 1994; Prowell, et al., 1999). In the Cleanroom process each software increment is formally specified and this specification is transformed into an implementation. Software correctness is demonstrated using a formal approach. There is no testing for defects in the process, and the system testing is focused on assessing the system's reliability.

Both the Cleanroom approach and another approach to formal development based on the B method (Wordsworth, 1996) are particularly suited to the development of systems that have stringent safety, reliability or security requirements. The formal approach simplifies the production of a safety or security case that demonstrates to customers or certification bodies that the system does actually meet the safety or security requirements.

Outside of these specialised domains, processes based on formal transformations are not widely used. They require specialised expertise and, in reality, for the majority of systems this process does not offer significant cost or quality advantages over other approaches to system development.

4.1.1 The waterfall model

The first published model of the software development process was derived from more general system engineering processes (Royce, 1970). This is illustrated in Figure 4.1. Because of the cascade from one phase to another, this model is known as the waterfall model or software life cycle. The principal stages of the model map onto fundamental development activities:

1. *Requirements analysis and definition* The system's services, constraints and goals are established by consultation with system users. They are then defined in detail and serve as a system specification.

2. *System and software design* The systems design process partitions the requirements to either hardware or software systems. It establishes an overall system architecture. Software design involves identifying and describing the fundamental software system abstractions and their relationships.

3. *Implementation and unit testing* During this stage, the software design is realised as a set of programs or program units. Unit testing involves verifying that each unit meets its specification.

4. *Integration and system testing* The individual program units or programs are integrated and tested as a complete system to ensure that the software requirements have been met. After testing, the software system is delivered to the customer.

5. *Operation and maintenance* Normally (although not necessarily) this is the longest life-cycle phase. The system is installed and put into practical use. Maintenance involves correcting errors which were not discovered in earlier stages of the life cycle, improving the implementation of system units and enhancing the system's services as new requirements are discovered.

In principle, the result of each phase is one or more documents that are approved ('signed off'). The following phase should not start until the previous phase has finished. In practice, these stages overlap and feed information to each other. During design, problems with requirements are identified; during coding design problems are found and so on. The software process is not a simple linear model but involves a sequence of iterations of the development activities.

Because of the costs of producing and approving documents, iterations are costly and involve significant rework. Therefore, after a small number of iterations, it is normal to freeze parts of the development, such as the specification, and to continue with the later development stages. Problems are left for later resolution, ignored or programmed around. This premature freezing of requirements may mean that the system won't do what the user wants. It may also lead to badly structured systems as design problems are circumvented by implementation tricks.

During the final life-cycle phase (operation and maintenance), the software is put into use. Errors and omissions in the original software requirements are discovered. Program and design errors emerge and the need for new functionality is identified. The system must therefore evolve to remain useful. Making these changes (software maintenance) may involve repeating previous process stages.

The advantages of the waterfall model are that documentation is produced at each phase and that it fits with other engineering process models. Its major problem is its inflexible partitioning of the project into distinct stages. Commitments must be made at an early stage in the process, which makes it difficult to respond to changing customer requirements.

Figure 4.2
Evolutionary
development

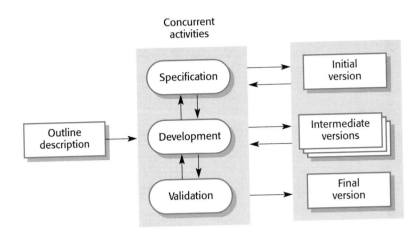

Therefore, the waterfall model should only be used when the requirements are well understood and unlikely to change radically during system development. However, the waterfall model reflects the type of process model used in other engineering projects. Consequently, software processes based on this approach are still used for software development, particularly when the software project is part of a larger systems engineering project.

4.1.2 Evolutionary development

Evolutionary development is based on the idea of developing an initial implementation, exposing this to user comment and refining it through many versions until an adequate system has been developed (Figure 4.2). Specification, development and validation activities are interleaved rather than separate, with rapid feedback across activities.

There are two fundamental types of evolutionary development:

1. *Exploratory development* where the objective of the process is to work with the customer to explore their requirements and deliver a final system. The development starts with the parts of the system that are understood. The system evolves by adding new features proposed by the customer.

2. *Throwaway prototyping* where the objective of the evolutionary development process is to understand the customer's requirements and hence develop a better requirements definition for the system. The prototype concentrates on experimenting with the customer requirements that are poorly understood.

An evolutionary approach to software development is often more effective than the waterfall approach in producing systems that meet the immediate needs of customers. The advantage of a software process that is based on an evolutionary approach is that the specification can be developed incrementally. As users develop a better understanding of their problem, this can be reflected in the software system. However, from an engineering and management perspective, the evolutionary approach has two problems:

1. *The process is not visible* Managers need regular deliverables to measure progress. If systems are developed quickly, it is not cost-effective to produce documents that reflect every version of the system.

2. *Systems are often poorly structured* Continual change tends to corrupt the software structure. Incorporating software changes becomes increasingly difficult and costly.

For small and medium-sized systems (up to 500,000 lines of code), I think that the evolutionary approach is the best approach to development. The problems of evolutionary development become particularly acute for large, complex, long-life-time systems, where different teams develop different parts of the system. It is difficult to establish a stable system architecture using this approach, which makes it hard to integrate contributions from the teams.

For large systems, I recommend a mixed process that incorporates the best features of the waterfall and the evolutionary development models. This may involve developing a throwaway prototype using an evolutionary approach to resolve uncertainties in the system specification. You can then reimplement the system using a more structured approach. Parts of the system that are well understood can be specified and developed using a waterfall-based process. Other parts of the system, such as the user interface, which are difficult to specify in advance, should always be developed using an exploratory programming approach.

Evolutionary development processes and process support are covered in more detail in Chapter 17, along with system prototyping and agile software development. Evolutionary development is also incorporated in the Rational Unified Process that I discuss later in this chapter.

4.1.3 Component-based software engineering

In the majority of software projects, there is some software reuse. This usually happens informally when people working on the project know of designs or code which is similar to that required. They look for these, modify them as needed and incorporate them into their system. In the evolutionary approach, described in Section 4.1.2, reuse is often essential for rapid system development.

This informal reuse takes place irrespective of the development process that is used. However, in the last few years, an approach to software development called component-based software engineering (CBSE), which relies on reuse, has emerged and is becoming increasingly used. I briefly introduce this approach here but cover it in more detail in Chapter 19.

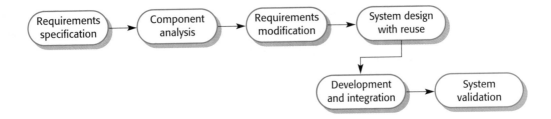

Figure 4.3
Component-based
software engineering

This reuse-oriented approach relies on a large base of reusable software components and some integrating framework for these components. Sometimes, these components are systems in their own right (COTS or commercial off-the-shelf systems) that may provide specific functionality such as text formatting or numeric calculation. The generic process model for CBSE is shown in Figure 4.3.

While the initial requirements specification stage and the validation stage are comparable with other processes, the intermediate stages in a reuse-oriented process are different. These stages are:

1. *Component analysis* Given the requirements specification, a search is made for components to implement that specification. Usually, there is no exact match, and the components that may be used only provide some of the functionality required.

2. *Requirements modification* During this stage, the requirements are analysed using information about the components that have been discovered. They are then modified to reflect the available components. Where modifications are impossible, the component analysis activity may be re-entered to search for alternative solutions.

3. *System design with reuse* During this phase, the framework of the system is designed or an existing framework is reused. The designers take into account the components that are reused and organise the framework to cater to this. Some new software may have to be designed if reusable components are not available.

4. *Development and integration* Software that cannot be externally procured is developed, and the components and COTS systems are integrated to create the new system. System integration, in this model, may be part of the development process rather than a separate activity.

Component-based software engineering has the obvious advantage of reducing the amount of software to be developed and so reducing cost and risks. It usually also leads to faster delivery of the software. However, requirements compromises are inevitable and this may lead to a system that does not meet the real needs of users. Furthermore, some control over the system evolution is lost as new versions of the reusable components are not under the control of the organisation using them.

CBSE has much in common with an emerging approach to system development that is based on integrating web services from a range of suppliers. I cover this service-centric development approach in Chapter 12.

4.2 Process iteration

Change is inevitable in all large software projects. The system requirements change as the business procuring the system responds to external pressures. Management priorities change. As new technologies become available, designs and implementation change. This means that the software process is not a one-off process; rather, the process activities are regularly repeated as the system is reworked in response to change requests.

Iterative development is so fundamental to software that I devote a complete chapter to it later in the book (Chapter 17). In this section, I introduce the topic by describing two process models that have been explicitly designed to support process iteration:

1. *Incremental delivery* The software specification, design and implementation are broken down into a series of increments that are each developed in turn.

2. *Spiral development* The development of the system spirals outwards from an initial outline through to the final developed system.

The essence of iterative processes is that the specification is developed in conjunction with the software. However, this conflicts with the procurement model of many organisations where the complete system specification is part of the system development contract. In the incremental approach, there is no complete system specification until the final increment is specified. This requires a new form of contract, which large customers such as government agencies may find difficult to accommodate.

4.2.1 Incremental delivery

The waterfall model of development requires customers for a system to commit to a set of requirements before design begins and the designer to commit to particular design strategies before implementation. Changes to the requirements require rework of the requirements, design and implementation. However, the separation of design and implementation should lead to well-documented systems that are amenable to change. By contrast, an evolutionary approach to development allows requirements and design decisions to be delayed but also leads to software that may be poorly structured and difficult to understand and maintain.

Incremental delivery (Figure 4.4) is an in-between approach that combines the advantages of these models. In an incremental development process, customers identify, in

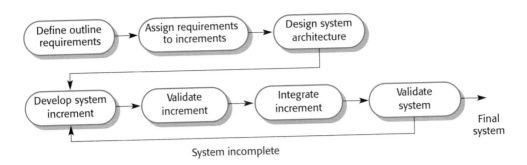

Figure 4.4
Incremental delivery

outline, the services to be provided by the system. They identify which of the services are most important and which are least important to them. A number of delivery increments are then defined, with each increment providing a sub-set of the system functionality. The allocation of services to increments depends on the service priority with the highest priority services delivered first.

Once the system increments have been identified, the requirements for the services to be delivered in the first increment are defined in detail, and that increment is developed. During development, further requirements analysis for later increments can take place, but requirements changes for the current increment are not accepted.

Once an increment is completed and delivered, customers can put it into service. This means that they take early delivery of part of the system functionality. They can experiment with the system that helps them clarify their requirements for later increments and for later versions of the current increment. As new increments are completed, they are integrated with existing increments so that the system functionality improves with each delivered increment. The common services may be implemented early in the process or may be implemented incrementally as functionality is required by an increment.

This incremental development process has a number of advantages:

1. Customers do not have to wait until the entire system is delivered before they can gain value from it. The first increment satisfies their most critical requirements so they can use the software immediately.

2. Customers can use the early increments as prototypes and gain experience that informs their requirements for later system increments.

3. There is a lower risk of overall project failure. Although problems may be encountered in some increments, it is likely that some will be successfully delivered to the customer.

4. As the highest priority services are delivered first, and later increments are integrated with them, it is inevitable that the most important system services receive the most testing. This means that customers are less likely to encounter software failures in the most important parts of the system.

However, there are problems with incremental delivery. Increments should be relatively small (no more than 20,000 lines of code), and each increment should deliver some system functionality. It can be difficult to map the customer's requirements onto increments of the right size. Furthermore, most systems require a set of basic facilities that are used by different parts of the system. As requirements are not defined in detail until an increment is to be implemented, it can be hard to identify common facilities that are needed by all increments.

A variant of this incremental approach called *extreme programming* has been developed (Beck, 2000). This is based around the development and delivery of very small increments of functionality, customer involvement in the process, constant code improvement and pair programming. I discuss extreme programming and other so-called agile methods in Chapter 17.

4.2.2 Spiral development

The spiral model of the software process (Figure 4.5) was originally proposed by Boehm (Boehm, 1988). Rather than represent the software process as a sequence of activities with some backtracking from one activity to another, the process is represented as a spiral. Each loop in the spiral represents a phase of the software process. Thus, the innermost loop might be concerned with system feasibility, the next loop with requirements definition, the next loop with system designand so on. Each loop in the spiral is split into four sectors:

1. *Objective setting* Specific objectives for that phase of the project are defined. Constraints on the process and the product are identified and a detailed management plan is drawn up. Project risks are identified. Alternative strategies, depending on these risks, may be planned.

2. *Risk assessment and reduction* For each of the identified project risks, a detailed analysis is carried out. Steps are taken to reduce the risk. For example, if there is a risk that the requirements are inappropriate, a prototype system may be developed.

3. *Development and validation* After risk evaluation, a development model for the system is chosen. For example, if user interface risks are dominant, an appropriate development model might be evolutionary prototyping. If safety risks are the main consideration, development based on formal transformations may be the most appropriate and so on. The waterfall model may be the most appropriate development model if the main identified risk is sub-system integration.

4. *Planning* The project is reviewed and a decision made whether to continue with a further loop of the spiral. If it is decided to continue, plans are drawn up for the next phase of the project.

The main difference between the spiral model and other software process models is the explicit recognition of risk in the spiral model. Informally, risk simply means

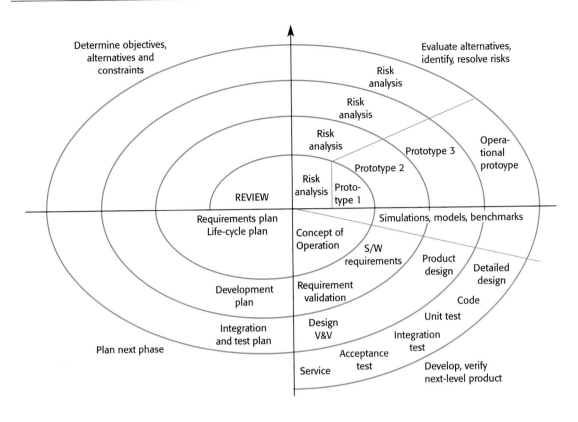

Determine objectives,
alternatives and
constraints

Evaluate alternatives,
identify, resolve risks

Risk
analysis

Risk
analysis

Risk
analysis

Opera-
tional
protoype

Prototype 3

Prototype 2

Risk
analysis

Proto-
type 1

REVIEW

Simulations, models, benchmarks

Requirements plan
Life-cycle plan

Concept of
Operation

S/W
requirements

Product
design

Detailed
design

Development
plan

Requirement
validation

Code

Unit test

Integration
and test plan

Design
V&V

Integration
test

Plan next phase

Acceptance
test

Develop, verify
next-level product

Service

Figure 4.5 Boehm's
spiral model of the
software process
(©IEEE, 1988)

something that can go wrong. For example, if the intention is to use a new programming language, a risk is that the available compilers are unreliable or do not produce sufficiently efficient object code. Risks result in project problems such as schedule and cost overrun so risk minimisation is a very important project management activity. Risk management, an essential part of project management, is covered in Chapter 5.

A cycle of the spiral begins by elaborating objectives such as performance and functionality. Alternative ways of achieving these objectives and the constraints imposed on each of them are then enumerated. Each alternative is assessed against each objective and sources of project risk are identified. The next step is to resolve these risks by information-gathering activities such as more detailed analysis, prototyping and simulation. Once risks have been assessed, some development is carried out, followed by a planning activity for the next phase of the process.

4.3 Process activities

The four basic process activities of specification, development, validation and evolution are organised differently in different development processes. In the waterfall model, they are organised in sequence, whereas in evolutionary development they are interleaved. How these activities are carried out depends on the type of software, people and organisational structures involved. There is no right or wrong way to organise these activities and my goal in this section is simply to provide you with an introduction to how they can be organised.

4.3.1 Software specification

Software specification or requirements engineering is the process of understanding and defining what services are required from the system and identifying the constraints on the system's operation and development. Requirements engineering is a particularly critical stage of the software process as errors at this stage inevitably lead to later problems in the system design and implementation.

The requirements engineering process is shown in Figure 4.6. This process leads to the production of a requirements document that is the specification for the system. Requirements are usually presented at two levels of detail in this document. End-users and customers need a high-level statement of the requirements; system developers need a more detailed system specification.

There are four main phases in the requirements engineering process:

1. *Feasibility study* An estimate is made of whether the identified user needs may be satisfied using current software and hardware technologies. The study considers whether the proposed system will be cost-effective from a business point of view and whether it can be developed within existing budgetary constraints. A feasibility study should be relatively cheap and quick. The result should inform the decision of whether to go ahead with a more detailed analysis.

2. *Requirements elicitation and analysis* This is the process of deriving the system requirements through observation of existing systems, discussions with

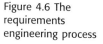

Figure 4.6 The requirements engineering process

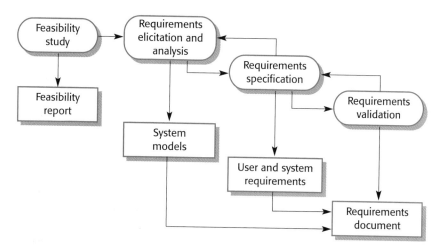

potential users and procurers, task analysis and so on. This may involve the development of one or more system models and prototypes. These help the analyst understand the system to be specified.

3. *Requirements specification* The activity of translating the information gathered during the analysis activity into a document that defines a set of requirements. Two types of requirements may be included in this document. *User requirements* are abstract statements of the system requirements for the customer and end-user of the system; *system requirements* are a more detailed description of the functionality to be provided.

4. *Requirements validation* This activity checks the requirements for realism, consistency and completeness. During this process, errors in the requirements document are inevitably discovered. It must then be modified to correct these problems.

Of course, the activities in the requirements process are not simply carried out in a strict sequence. Requirements analysis continues during definition and specification, and new requirements come to light throughout the process. Therefore, the activities of analysis, definition and specification are interleaved. In agile methods such as extreme programming, requirements are developed incrementally according to user priorities, and the elicitation of requirements comes from users who are part of the development team.

4.3.2 Software design and implementation

The implementation stage of software development is the process of converting a system specification into an executable system. It always involves processes of software design and programming but, if an evolutionary approach to development is used, may also involve refinement of the software specification.

A software design is a description of the structure of the software to be implemented, the data which is part of the system, the interfaces between system components and, sometimes, the algorithms used. Designers do not arrive at a finished design immediately but develop the design iteratively through a number of versions. The design process involves adding formality and detail as the design is developed with constant backtracking to correct earlier designs.

The design process may involve developing several models of the system at different levels of abstraction. As a design is decomposed, errors and omissions in earlier stages are discovered. These feed back to allow earlier design models to be improved. Figure 4.7 is a model of this process showing the design descriptions that may be produced at various stages of design. This diagram suggests that the stages of the design process are sequential. In fact, design process activities are interleaved. Feedback from one stage to another and consequent design rework is inevitable in all design processes.

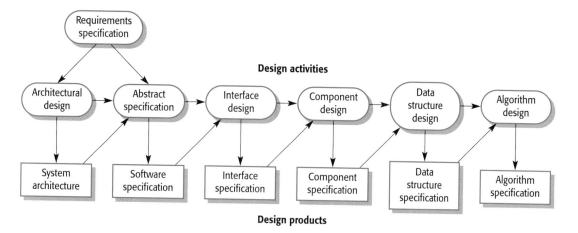

Figure 4.7 A general model of the design process

A specification for the next stage is the output of each design activity. This specification may be an abstract, formal specification that is produced to clarify the requirements, or it may be a specification of how part of the system is to be realised. As the design process continues, these specifications become more detailed. The final results of the process are precise specifications of the algorithms and data structures to be implemented.

The specific design process activities are:

1. *Architectural design* The sub-systems making up the system and their relationships are identified and documented. This important topic is covered in Chapters 11, 12 and 13.

2. *Abstract specification* For each sub-system, an abstract specification of its services and the constraints under which it must operate is produced.

3. *Interface design* For each sub-system, its interface with other sub-systems is designed and documented. This interface specification must be unambiguous as it allows the sub-system to be used without knowledge of the sub-system operation. Formal specification methods, as discussed in Chapter 10, may be used at this stage.

4. *Component design* Services are allocated to components and the interfaces of these components are designed.

5. *Data structure design* The data structures used in the system implementation are designed in detail and specified.

6. *Algorithm design* The algorithms used to provide services are designed in detail and specified.

This is a general model of the design process and real, practical processes may adapt it in different ways. Possible adaptations are:

1. The last two stages of design—data structure and algorithm design—may be delayed until the implementation process.

2. If an exploratory approach to design is used, the system interfaces may be designed after the data structures have been specified.

3. The abstract specification stage may be skipped, although it is usually an essential part of critical systems design.

Increasingly, where agile methods of development are used (see Chapter 17), the outputs of the design process will not be separate specification documents but will be represented in the code of the program. After the system architecture has been designed, later stages of the design are incremental. Each increment is represented as program code rather than as a design model.

A contrasting approach is taken by *structured methods* for design that rely on producing graphical models of the system (see Chapter 8) and, in many cases, automatically generating code from these models. Structured methods were invented in the 1970s to support function-oriented design (Constantine and Yourdon, 1979; Gane and Sarson, 1979). Various competing methods to support object-oriented design were proposed (Robinson, 1992; Booch, 1994) and these were unified in the 1990s to create the Unified Modeling Language (UML) and the associated unified design process (Rumbaugh, et al., 1991; Booch, et al., 1999; Rumbaugh, et al., 1999a; Rumbaugh, et al., 1999b). At the time of this writing, a major revision to UML (UML 2.0) is underway.

A structured method includes a design process model, notations to represent the design, report formats, rules and design guidelines. Structured methods may support some or all of the following models of a system:

1. An object model that shows the object classes used in the system and their dependencies.

2. A sequence model that shows how objects in the system interact when the system is executing.

3. A state transition model that shows system states and the triggers for the transitions from one state to another.

4. A structural model where the system components and their aggregations are documented.

5. A data flow model where the system is modelled using the data transformations that take place as it is processed. This is not normally used in object-oriented methods but is still frequently used in real-time and business system design.

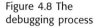

Figure 4.8 The
debugging process

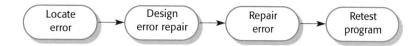

In practice, structured 'methods' are really standard notations and embodiments of good practice. Following these methods and applying the guidelines can result in a reasonable design. Designer creativity is still required to decide on the system decomposition and to ensure that the design adequately captures the system specification. Empirical studies of designers (Bansler and Bødker, 1993) have shown that they rarely follow methods slavishly. They pick and choose from the guidelines according to local circumstances.

The development of a program to implement the system follows naturally from the system design processes. Although some classes of programs, such as safety-critical systems, are usually designed in detail before any implementation begins, it is more common for the later stages of design and program development to be interleaved. CASE tools may be used to generate a skeleton program from a design. This includes code to define and implement interfaces, and in many cases the developer need only add details of the operation of each program component.

Programming is a personal activity and there is no general process that is usually followed. Some programmers start with components that they understand, develop them, and then move on to less well-understood components. Others take the opposite approach, leaving familiar components till last because they know how to develop them. Some developers like to define data early in the process then use this to drive the program development; others leave data unspecified for as long as possible.

Normally, programmers carry out some testing of the code they have developed. This often reveals program defects that must be removed from the program. This is called *debugging*. Defect testing and debugging are different processes. Testing establishes the existence of defects. Debugging is concerned with locating and correcting these defects.

Figure 4.8 illustrates the stages of debugging. Defects in the code must be located and the program modified to meet its requirements. Testing must then be repeated to ensure that the change has been made correctly. Thus the debugging process is part of both software development and software testing.

When debugging, you generate hypotheses about the observable behaviour of the program then test these hypotheses in the hope of finding the fault which caused the output anomaly. Testing the hypotheses may involve tracing the program code manually. You may write new test cases to localise the problem. Interactive debugging tools that show the intermediate values of program variables and a trace of the statements executed may be used to help the debugging process.

Figure 4.9 The
testing process

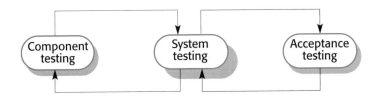

4.3.3 Software validation

Software validation or, more generally, verification and validation (V & V) is intended
to show that a system conforms to its specification and that the system meets the
expectations of the customer buying the system. It involves checking processes, such
as inspections and reviews (see Chapter 22), at each stage of the software process
from user requirements definition to program development. The majority of validation costs, however, are incurred after implementation when the operational system is tested (Chapter 23).

Except for small programs, systems should not be tested as a single, monolithic
unit. Figure 4.9 shows a three-stage testing process where system components are
tested, the integrated system is tested and, finally, the system is tested with the customer's data. Ideally, component defects are discovered early in the process and
interface problems when the system is integrated. However, as defects are discovered the program must be debugged and this may require other stages in the testing process to be repeated. Errors in program components, say, may come to light
during system testing. The process is therefore an iterative one with information
being fed back from later stages to earlier parts of the process.

The stages in the testing process are:

1. *Component (or unit) testing* Individual components are tested to ensure that they
    operate correctly. Each component is tested independently, without other sys-
    tem components. Components may be simple entities such as functions or object
    classes, or may be coherent groupings of these entities.

2. *System testing* The components are integrated to make up the system. This pro-
    cess is concerned with finding errors that result from unanticipated interactions
    between components and component interface problems. It is also concerned with
    validating that the system meets its functional and non-functional requirements
    and testing the emergent system properties. For large systems, this may be a multi-
    stage process where components are integrated to form sub-systems that are indi-
    vidually tested before they are themselves integrated to form the final system.

3. *Acceptance testing* This is the final stage in the testing process before the sys-
    tem is accepted for operational use. The system is tested with data supplied by
    the system customer rather than with simulated test data. Acceptance testing may
    reveal errors and omissions in the system requirements definition because the
    real data exercise the system in different ways from the test data. Acceptance
    testing may also reveal requirements problems where the system's facilities do
    not really meet the user's needs or the system performance is unacceptable.

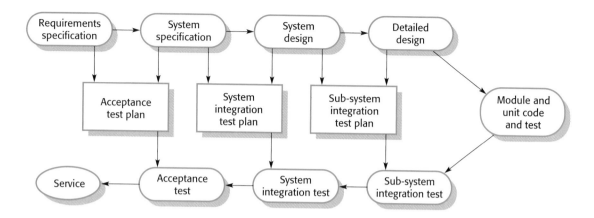

Figure 4.10 Testing phases in the software process

Normally, component development and testing are interleaved. Programmers make up their own test data and incrementally test the code as it is developed. This is an economically sensible approach, as the programmer knows the component best and is therefore the best person to generate test cases.

If an incremental approach to development is used, each increment should be tested as it is developed, with these tests based on the requirements for that increment. In extreme programming, tests are developed along with the requirements before development starts. This helps the testers and developers to understand the requirements and ensures that there are no delays as test cases are created.

Later stages of testing involve integrating work from a number of programmers and must be planned in advance. An independent team of testers should work from preformulated test plans that are developed from the system specification and design. Figure 4.10 illustrates how test plans are the link between testing and development activities.

Acceptance testing is sometimes called alpha testing. Custom systems are developed for a single client. The alpha testing process continues until the system developer and the client agree that the delivered system is an acceptable implementation of the system requirements.

When a system is to be marketed as a software product, a testing process called beta testing is often used. Beta testing involves delivering a system to a number of potential customers who agree to use that system. They report problems to the system developers. This exposes the product to real use and detects errors that may not have been anticipated by the system builders. After this feedback, the system is modified and released either for further beta testing or for general sale.

4.3.4 Software evolution

The flexibility of software systems is one of the main reasons why more and more software is being incorporated in large, complex systems. Once a decision has been made to procure hardware, it is very expensive to make changes to the hardware

Figure 4.11 System
evolution

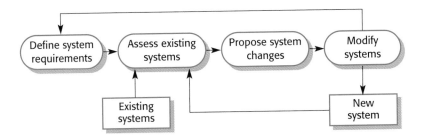

design. However, changes can be made to software at any time during or after the system development. Even extensive changes are still much cheaper than corresponding changes to system hardware.

Historically, there has always been a split between the process of software development and the process of software evolution (software maintenance). People think of software development as a creative activity where a software system was developed from an initial concept through to a working system. However, they sometimes think of software maintenance as dull and uninteresting. Although the costs of 'maintenance' are often several times the initial development costs, maintenance processes are sometimes considered to be less challenging than original software development.

This distinction between development and maintenance is becoming increasingly irrelevant. Few software systems are now completely new systems, and it makes much more sense to see development and maintenance as a continuum. Rather than two separate processes, it is more realistic to think of software engineering as an evolutionary process (Figure 4.11) where software is continually changed over its lifetime in response to changing requirements and customer needs.

4.4 The Rational Unified Process

The Rational Unified Process (RUP) is an example of a modern process model that has been derived from work on the UML and the associated Unified Software Development Process (Rumbaugh, et al., 1999b). I have included a description here as it is a good example of a hybrid process model. It brings together elements from all of the generic process models (Section 4.1), supports iteration (Section 4.2) and illustrates good practice in specification and design (Section 4.3).

The RUP recognises that conventional process models present a single view of the process. In contrast, the RUP is normally described from three perspectives:

1.   A dynamic perspective that shows the phases of the model over time.

2.   A static perspective that shows the process activities that are enacted.

3.   A practice perspective that suggests good practices to be used during the process.

Figure 4.12 Phases
in the Rational
Unified Process

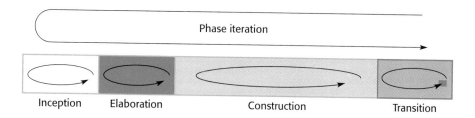

Most descriptions of the RUP attempt to combine the static and dynamic perspectives in a single diagram (Krutchen, 2000). I think that makes the process harder to understand, so I use separate descriptions of each of these perspectives.

The RUP is a phased model that identifies four discrete phases in the software process. However, unlike the waterfall model where phases are equated with process activities, the phases in the RUP are more closely related to business rather than technical concerns. Figure 4.12 shows the phases in the RUP. These are:

1. *Inception* The goal of the inception phase is to establish a business case for the system. You should identify all external entities (people and systems) that will interact with the system and define these interactions. You then use this information to assess the contribution that the system makes to the business. If this contribution is minor, then the project may be cancelled after this phase.

2. *Elaboration* The goals of the elaboration phase are to develop an understanding of the problem domain, establish an architectural framework for the system, develop the project plan and identify key project risks. On completion of this phase, you should have a requirements model for the system (UML use cases are specified), an architectural description and a development plan for the software.

3. *Construction* The construction phase is essentially concerned with system design, programming and testing. Parts of the system are developed in parallel and integrated during this phase. On completion of this phase, you should have a working software system and associated documentation that is ready for delivery to users.

4. *Transition* The final phase of the RUP is concerned with moving the system from the development community to the user community and making it work in a real environment. This is something that is ignored in most software process models but is, in fact, an expensive and sometimes problematic activity. On completion of this phase, you should have a documented software system that is working correctly in its operational environment.

Iteration within the RUP is supported in two ways, as shown in Figure 4.12. Each phase may be enacted in an iterative way with the results developed incrementally. In addition, the whole set of phases may also be enacted incrementally, as shown by the looping arrow from Transition to Inception in Figure 4.12.

Workflow	Description
Business modelling	The business processes are modelled using business use cases.
Requirements	Actors who interact with the system are identified and use cases are developed to model the system requirements.
Analysis and design	A design model is created and documented using architectural models, component models, object models and sequence models.
Implementation	The components in the system are implemented and structured into implementation sub-systems. Automatic code generation from design models helps accelerate this process.
Testing	Testing is an iterative process that is carried out in conjunction with implementation. System testing follows the completion of the implementation.
Deployment	A product release is created, distributed to users and installed in their workplace.
Configuration and change management	This supporting workflow manages changes to the system (see Chapter 29).
Project management	This supporting workflow manages the system development (see Chapter 5).
Environment	This workflow is concerned with making appropriate software tools available to the software development team.

Figure 4.13 Static
workflows in
Rational Unified
Process

The static view of the RUP focuses on the activities that take place during the development process. These are called *workflows* in the RUP description. There are six core process workflows identified in the process and three core supporting workflows. The RUP has been designed in conjunction with the UML—an object-oriented modelling language—so the workflow description is oriented around associated UML models. The core engineering and support workflows are described in Figure 4.13.

The advantage in presenting dynamic and static views is that phases of the development process are not associated with specific workflows. In principle at least, all of the RUP workflows may be active at all stages of the process. Of course, most effort will probably be spent on workflows such as business modelling and requirements at the early phases of the process and in testing and deployment in the later phases.

The practice perspective on the RUP describes good software engineering practices that are recommended for use in systems development. Six fundamental best practices are recommended:

1. *Develop software iteratively*. Plan increments of the system based on customer priorities and develop and deliver the highest priority system features early in the development process.

2. *Manage requirements*. Explicitly document the customer's requirements and keep track of changes to these requirements. Analyse the impact of changes on the system before accepting them.

3. *Use component-based architectures.* Structure the system architecture into components as discussed earlier in this chapter.

4. *Visually model software.* Use graphical UML models to present static and dynamic views of the software.

5. *Verify software quality.* Ensure that the software meets the organisational quality standards.

6. *Control changes to software.* Manage changes to the software using a change management system and configuration management procedures and tools (see Chapter 29).

The RUP is not a suitable process for all types of development but it does represent a new generation of generic processes. The most important innovations are the separation of phases and workflows, and the recognition that deploying software in a user's environment is part of the process. Phases are dynamic and have goals. Workflows are static and are technical activities that are not associated with a single phase but may be used throughout the development to achieve the goals of each phase.

4.5 Computer-Aided Software Engineering

Computer-Aided Software Engineering (CASE) is the name given to software used to support software process activities such as requirements engineering, design, program development and testing. CASE tools therefore include design editors, data dictionaries, compilers, debuggers, system building tools and so on.

CASE technology provides software process support by automating some process activities and by providing information about the software that is being developed. Examples of activities that can be automated using CASE include:

1. The development of graphical system models as part of the requirements specification or the software design.

2. Understanding a design using a data dictionary that holds information about the entities and relations in a design.

3. The generation of user interfaces from a graphical interface description that is created interactively by the user.

4. Program debugging through the provision of information about an executing program.

5. The automated translation of programs from an old version of a programming language such as COBOL to a more recent version.

CASE technology is now available for most routine activities in the software process. This has led to some improvements in software quality and productivity, although these have been less than predicted by early advocates of CASE. Early advocates suggested that orders of magnitude improvement were likely if integrated CASE environments were used. In fact, the improvements that have been achieved are of the order of 40% (Huff, 1992). Although this is significant, the predictions when CASE tools were first introduced in the 1980s and 1990s were that the use of CASE technology would generate huge savings in software process costs.

The improvements from the use of CASE are limited by two factors:

1. Software engineering is, essentially, a design activity based on creative thought. Existing CASE systems automate routine activities but attempts to harness artificial intelligence technology to provide support for design have not been successful.

2. In most organisations, software engineering is a team activity, and software engineers spend quite a lot of time interacting with other team members. CASE technology does not provide much support for this.

CASE technology is now mature, and CASE tools and workbenches are available from a wide range of suppliers. However, rather than focus on any specific tools, I simply present an overview of tools here with some discussion of specific support in other chapters. In my web pages, I include links to other material on CASE and links to CASE tool suppliers.

4.5.1 CASE classification

CASE classifications help us understand the types of CASE tools and their role in supporting software process activities. There are several ways to classify CASE tools, each of which gives us a different perspective on these tools. In this section, I discuss CASE tools from three of these perspectives:

1. *A functional perspective* where CASE tools are classified according to their specific function.

2. *A process perspective* where tools are classified according to the process activities that they support.

3. *An integration perspective* where CASE tools are classified according to how they are organised into integrated units that provide support for one or more process activities.

Figure 4.14 is a classification of CASE tools according to function. This table lists a number of different types of CASE tools and gives specific examples of each

Figure 4.14
Functional
classification of
CASE tools

Tool type	Examples
Planning tools	PERT tools, estimation tools, spreadsheets
Editing tools	Text editors, diagram editors, word processors
Change management tools	Requirements traceability tools, change control systems
Configuration management tools	Version management systems, system building tools
Prototyping tools	Very high-level languages, user interface generators
Method-support tools	Design editors, data dictionaries, code generators
Language-processing tools	Compilers, interpreters
Program analysis tools	Cross reference generators, static analysers, dynamic analysers
Testing tools	Test data generators, file comparators
Debugging tools	Interactive debugging systems
Documentation tools	Page layout programs, image editors
Reengineering tools	Cross-reference systems, program restructuring systems

one. This is not a complete list of CASE tools. Specialised tools, such as tools to support reuse, have not been included.

Figure 4.15 presents an alternative classification of CASE tools. It shows the process phases supported by a number of types of CASE tools. Tools for planning and estimating, text editing, document preparation and configuration management may be used throughout the software process.

The breadth of support for the software process offered by CASE technology is another possible classification dimension. Fuggetta (Fuggetta, 1993) proposes that CASE systems should be classified in three categories:

1. *Tools* support individual process tasks such as checking the consistency of a design, compiling a program and comparing test results. Tools may be general-purpose, standalone tools (e.g., a word processor) or grouped into workbenches.

2. *Workbenches* support process phases or activities such as specification, design, etc. They normally consist of a set of tools with some greater or lesser degree of integration.

3. *Environments* support all or at least a substantial part of the software process. They normally include several integrated workbenches.

Figure 4.15 Activity-based classification of CASE tools

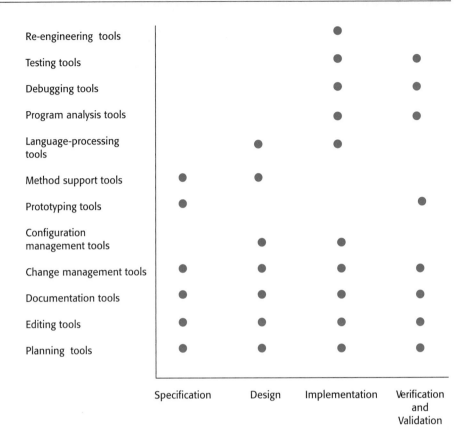

Figure 4.16 illustrates this classification and shows some examples of these classes of CASE support. Of course, this is an illustrative example; many types of tools and workbenches have been left out of this diagram.

General-purpose tools are used at the discretion of the software engineer who makes decisions about when to apply them for process support. Workbenches, however, usually support some method that includes a process model and a set of rules/guidelines, which apply to the software being developed. I have classified environments as integrated or process-centred. Integrated environments provide infrastructure support for data, control and presentation integration. Process-centred environments are more general. They include software process knowledge and a process engine which uses this process model to advise engineers on what tools or workbenches to apply and when they should be used.

In practice, the boundaries between these classes are blurred. Tools may be sold as a single product but may embed support for different activities. For example, most word processors now provide a built-in diagram editor. CASE workbenches for design usually support programming and testing, so they are more akin to environments than specialised workbenches. It may therefore not always be easy to position a product using a classification. Nevertheless, classification provides a useful first step to help understand the extent of process support that a tool provides.

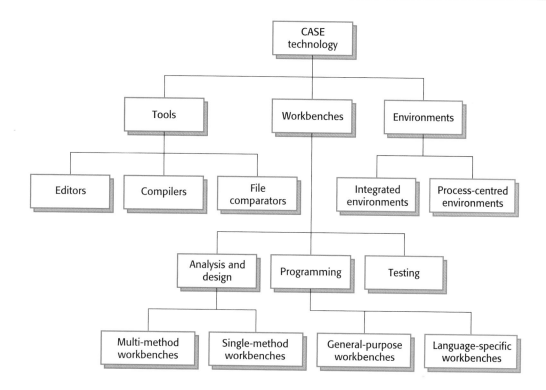

Figure 4.16 Tools, workbenches and environments

KEY POINTS

■ Software processes are the activities involved in producing a software system. Software process models are abstract representations of these processes.

■ All software processes include software specification, software design and implementation, software validation and software evolution.

■ Generic process models describe the organisation of software processes. Examples of generic models include the waterfall model, evolutionary development and component-based software engineering.

■ Iterative process models present the software process as a cycle of activities. The advantage of this approach is that it avoids premature commitments to a specification or design.

Examples of iterative models include incremental development and the spiral model.

■ Requirements engineering is the process of developing a software specification. Specifications are intended to communicate the system needs of the customer to the system developers.

■ Design and implementation processes are concerned with transforming a requirements specification into an executable software system. Systematic design methods may be used as part of this transformation.

■ Software validation is the process of checking that the system conforms to its specification and that it meets the real needs of the users of the system.

■ Software evolution is concerned with modifying existing software systems to meet new requirements. This is becoming the normal approach to software development for small and medium-sized systems.

■ The Rational Unified Process is a modern generic process model that is organised into phases (inception, elaboration, construction and transition) but that separates activities (requirements, analysis and design, etc.) from these phases.

■ CASE technology provides automated support for software processes. CASE tools support individual process activities; workbenches support a set of related activities; environments support all or most software process activities.

FURTHER READING

Extreme Programming Explained: Embrace Change. An evangelical book that describes the extreme programming process and extreme programming experiences. The author was the inventor of extreme programming and communicates his enthusiasm very well. (Kent Beck, 2000, Addison-Wesley.)

The Rational Unified Process—An Introduction. This is the most readable book available on the RUP at the time of this writing. Krutchen describes the process well, but I would like to have seen more on the practical difficulties of using the process. (P. Krutchen, 2000, Addison-Wesley.)

Managing Software Quality and Business Risk. This is primarily a book about software management but it includes an excellent chapter (Chapter 4) on process models. (M. Ould, 1999, John Wiley & Sons)

'A classification of CASE technology'. The classification scheme proposed in this article is used in this chapter, but Fuggetta goes into more detail and illustrates how a number of commercial products fit into this scheme. (A. Fuggetta, *IEEE Computer*, 26 (12), December 1993.)

EXERCISES

4.1   Giving reasons for your answer based on the type of system being developed, suggest the most appropriate generic software process model that might be used as a basis for managing the development of the following systems:

■ A system to control anti-lock braking in a car

■ A virtual reality system to support software maintenance

■ A university accounting system that replaces an existing system

■ An interactive system that allows railway passengers to find train times from terminals installed in stations.

4.2   Explain why programs that are developed using evolutionary development are likely to be difficult to maintain.

4.3   Explain how both the waterfall model of the software process and the prototyping model can be accommodated in the spiral process model.

4.4   What are the advantages of providing static and dynamic views of the software process as in the Rational Unified Process?

4.5   Suggest why it is important to make a distinction between developing the user requirements and developing system requirements in the requirements engineering process.

4.6   Describe the main activities in the software design process and the outputs of these activities. Using a diagram, show possible relationships between the outputs of these activities.

4.7   What are the five components of a design method? Take any method you know and describe its components. Assess the completeness of the method that you have chosen.

4.8   Design a process model for running system tests and recording their results.

4.9   Explain why a software system that is used in a real-world environment must change or become progressively less useful.

4.10   Suggest how a CASE technology classification scheme may be helpful to managers responsible for CASE system procurement.

4.11   Survey the tool availability in your local development environment and classify the tools according to the parameters (function, activity, breadth of support) suggested here.

4.12   Historically, the introduction of technology has caused profound changes in the labour market and, temporarily at least, displaced people from jobs. Discuss whether the introduction of advanced CASE technology is likely to have the same consequences for software engineers. If you don't think it will, explain why not. If you think that it will reduce job opportunities, is it ethical for the engineers affected to passively or actively resist the introduction of this technology?

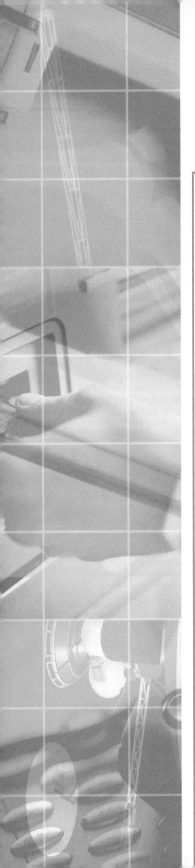

5

Project management

Objectives

The objective of this chapter is to give you an overview of software project management. When you have read this chapter, you will:

■ know the principal tasks of software project managers;

■ understand why the nature of software makes software project management more difficult than other engineering project management;

■ understand the need for project planning in all software projects;

■ know how graphical representations (bar charts and activity charts) can be used by project managers to represent project schedules;

■ have been introduced to the notion of risk management and some of the risks that can arise in software projects.

Contents

Software project management is an essential part of software engineering. Good management cannot guarantee project success. However, bad management usually results in project failure: The software is delivered late, costs more than originally estimated and fails to meet its requirements.

Software managers are responsible for planning and scheduling project development. They supervise the work to ensure that it is carried out to the required standards and monitor progress to check that the development is on time and within budget. We need software project management because professional software engineering is always subject to organisational budget and schedule constraints. The software project manager's job is to ensure that the software project meets these constraints and delivers software that contributes to the goals of the company developing the software.

Software managers do the same kind of job as other engineering project managers. However, software engineering is different from other types of engineering in a number of ways. These distinctions make software management particularly difficult. Some of the differences are:

1. *The product is intangible* The manager of a shipbuilding project or of a civil engineering project can see the product being developed. If a schedule slips, the effect on the product is visible—parts of the structure are obviously unfinished. Software is intangible. It cannot be seen or touched. Software project managers cannot see progress. They rely on others to produce the documentation needed to review progress.

2. *There are no standard software processes* In engineering disciplines with a long history, the process is tried and tested. The engineering process for some types of system, such as bridges and buildings is well understood. However, software processes vary dramatically from one organisation to another. Although our understanding of these processes has developed significantly in the past few years, we still cannot reliably predict when a particular software process is likely to cause development problems. This is especially true when the software project is part of a wider systems engineering project.

3. *Large software projects are often 'one-off' projects* Large software projects are usually different in some ways from previous projects. Therefore, even managers who have a large body of previous experience may find it difficult to anticipate problems. Furthermore, rapid technological changes in computers and communications can make a manager's experience obsolete. Lessons learned from previous projects may not be transferable to new projects.

Because of these problems, it is not surprising that some software projects are late, over budget and behind schedule. Software systems are often new and technically innovative. Engineering projects (such as new transport systems) that are innovative often also have schedule problems. Given the difficulties involved, it is perhaps remarkable that so many software projects are delivered on time and to budget!

Software project management is a huge topic and cannot be covered in a single chapter. Therefore, I simply introduce the subject here and describe three important management activities: project planning, project scheduling and risk management. Later chapters (in Part 6) cover other aspects of software management, including managing people, software cost estimation and quality management.

5.1 Management activities

It is impossible to write a standard job description for a software manager. The job varies tremendously depending on the organisation and the software product being developed. However, most managers take responsibility at some stage for some or all of the following activities:

- Proposal writing

- Project planning and scheduling

- Project cost

- Project monitoring and reviews

- Personnel selection and evaluation

- Report writing and presentations

The first stage in a software project may involve writing a proposal to win a contract to carry out the work. The proposal describes the objectives of the project and how it will be carried out. It usually includes cost and schedule estimates, and justifies why the project contract should be awarded to a particular organisation or team. Proposal writing is a critical task as the existence of many software organisations depends on having enough proposals accepted and contracts awarded. There can be no set guidelines for this task; proposal writing is a skill that you acquire through practice and experience.

Project planning is concerned with identifying the activities, milestones and deliverables produced by a project. A plan is drawn up to guide the development towards the project goals. Cost estimation is a related activity that is concerned with estimating the resources required to accomplish the project plan. I cover these in more detail later in this chapter and in Chapter 26.

Project monitoring is a continuing project activity. The manager must keep track of the progress of the project and compare actual and planned progress and costs. Although most organisations have formal mechanisms for monitoring, a skilled manager can often form a clear picture of what is going on through informal discussions with project staff.

Informal monitoring can often predict potential project problems by revealing difficulties as they occur. For example, daily discussions with project staff might reveal a particular problem in finding some software fault. Rather than waiting for a schedule slippage to be reported, the software manager might assign some expert to the problem or might decide that it should be programmed around.

During a project, it is normal to have a number of formal project management reviews. They are concerned with reviewing overall progress and technical development of the project and checking whether the project and the goals of the organisation paying for the software are still aligned.

The outcome of a review may be a decision to cancel a project. The development time for a large software project may be several years. During that time, organisational objectives are almost certain to change. These changes may mean that the software is no longer required or that the original project requirements are inappropriate. Management may decide to stop software development or to change the project to accommodate the changes to the organisational objectives.

Project managers usually have to select people to work on their project. Ideally, skilled staff with appropriate experience will be available to work on the project. However, in most cases, managers have to settle for a less-than-ideal project team. The reasons for this are:

1. The project budget may not cover the use of highly paid staff. Less experienced, less well-paid staff may have to be used.

2. Staff with the appropriate experience may not be available either within an organisation or externally. It may be impossible to recruit new staff to the project. Within the organisation, the best people may already be allocated to other projects.

3. The organisation may wish to develop the skills of its employees. Inexperienced staff may be assigned to a project to learn and to gain experience.

The software manager has to work within these constraints when selecting project staff. However, problems are likely unless at least one project member has some experience with the type of system being developed. Without this experience, many simple mistakes are likely to be made. I discuss team building and staff selection in Chapter 25.

Project managers are usually responsible for reporting on the project to both the client and contractor organisations. They have to write concise, coherent documents that abstract critical information from detailed project reports. They must be able to present this information during progress reviews. Consequently, if you are a project manager, you have to be able to communicate effectively both orally and in writing.

Plan	Description
Quality plan	Describes the quality procedures and standards that will be used in a project. See Chapter 24.
Validation plan	Describes the approach, resources and schedule used for system validation. See Chapter 19.
Configuration management plan	Describes the configuration management procedures and structures to be used. See Chapter 29.
Maintenance plan	Predicts the maintenance requirements of the system, maintenance costs and effort required. See Chapter 27.
Staff development plan	Describes how the skills and experience of the project team members will be developed. See Chapter 22.

5.2 Project planning

Effective management of a software project depends on thoroughly planning the progress of the project. Managers must anticipate problems that might arise and prepare tentative solutions to those problems. A plan, drawn up at the start of a project, should be used as the driver for the project. This initial plan should be the best possible plan given the available information. It evolves as the project progresses and better information becomes available.

A structure for a software development plan is described in Section 5.2.1. As well as a project plan, managers may also have to draw up other types of plans. These are briefly described in Figure 5.1 and covered in more detail in the relevant chapter elsewhere in the book.

The pseudo-code shown in Figure 5.2 sets out a project planning process for software development. It shows that planning is an iterative process, which is only complete when the project itself is complete. As project information becomes available during the project, the plan should be regularly revised. The goals of the business are an important factor that must be considered when formulating the project plan. As these change, the project's goals also change so changes to the project plan are necessary.

At the beginning of a planning process, you should assess the constraints (required delivery date, staff available, overall budget, etc.) affecting the project. In conjunction with this, you should estimate project parameters such as its structure, size, and distribution of functions. You next define the progress milestones and deliverables. The process then enters a loop. You draw up an estimated schedule for the project and the activities defined in the schedule are started or given permission to continue. After some time (usually about two to three weeks), you should review

Figure 5.2 Project
planning

Establish the project constraints
Make initial assessments of the project parameters
Define project milestones and deliverables
while project has not been completed or cancelled **loop**
    Draw up project schedule
    Initiate activities according to schedule
    Wait (for a while)
    Review project progress
    Revise estimates of project parameters
    Update the project schedule
    Renegotiate project constraints and deliverables
    if (problems arise) **then**
        Initiate technical review and possible revision
    end if
end loop

progress and note discrepancies from the planned schedule. Because initial estimates
of project parameters are tentative, you will always have to modify the original plan.

As more information becomes available, you revise your original assumptions
about the project and the project schedule. If the project is delayed, you may have
to renegotiate the project constraints and deliverables with the customer. If this renegotiation is unsuccessful and the schedule cannot be met, a project technical review
may be held. The objective of this review is to find an alternative approach that
falls within the project constraints and meets the schedule.

Of course, you should never assume that everything will always go well.
Problems of some description nearly always arise during a project. Your initial assumptions and scheduling should be pessimistic rather than optimistic. There should be
sufficient contingency built into your plan so that the project constraints and milestones need not be renegotiated every time round the planning loop.

5.2.1 The project plan

The project plan sets out the resources available to the project, the work breakdown
and a schedule for carrying out the work. In some organisations, the project plan
is a single document that includes the different types of plan (Figure 5.1). In other
cases, the project plan is solely concerned with the development process.
References to other plans are included but the plans themselves are separate.

The plan structure that I describe here is for this latter type of plan. The details
of the project plan vary depending on the type of project and organisation.
However, most plans should include the following sections:

1. *Introduction* This briefly describes the objectives of the project and sets out
    the constraints (e.g., budget, time, etc.) that affect the project management.

2. *Project organisation* This describes the way in which the development team is organised, the people involved and their roles in the team.

3. *Risk analysis* This describes possible project risks, the likelihood of these risks arising and the risk reduction strategies that are proposed. I explain the principles of risk management in Section 5.4.

4. *Hardware and software resource requirements* This specifies the hardware and the support software required to carry out the development. If hardware has to be bought, estimates of the prices and the delivery schedule may be included.

5. *Work breakdown* This sets out the breakdown of the project into activities and identifies the milestones and deliverables associated with each activity. Milestones and deliverables are discussed in Section 5.2.2.

6. *Project schedule* This shows the dependencies between activities, the estimated time required to reach each milestone and the allocation of people to activities.

7. *Monitoring and reporting mechanisms* This defines the management reports that should be produced, when these should be produced and the project monitoring mechanisms used.

You should regularly revise the project plan during the project. Some parts, such as the project schedule, will change frequently; other parts will be more stable. To simplify revisions, you should organise the document into separate sections that can be individually replaced as the plan evolves.

5.2.2 Milestones and deliverables

Managers need information to do their job. Because software is intangible, this information can only be provided as reports and documents that describe the state of the software being developed. Without this information, it is impossible to assess how well the work is progressing, and cost estimates and schedules cannot be updated.

When planning a project, you should establish a series of *milestones,* where a milestone is a recognisable end-point of a software process activity. At each milestone, there should be a formal output, such as a report, that can be presented to management. Milestone reports need not be large documents. They may simply be a short report of what has been completed. Milestones should represent the end of a distinct, logical stage in the project. Indefinite milestones such as 'Coding 80% complete' that can't be checked are useless for project management. You can't check whether this state has been achieved because the amount of code that still has to be developed is uncertain.

A deliverable is a project result that is delivered to the customer. It is usually delivered at the end of some major project phase such as specification or design. Deliverables are usually milestones, but milestones need not be deliverables.

ACTIVITIES

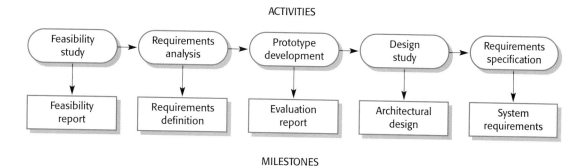

MILESTONES

Figure 5.3 Milestones in the requirements process

Milestones may be internal project results that are used by the project manager to check project progress but which are not delivered to the customer.

To establish milestones, the software process must be broken down into basic activities with associated outputs. For example, Figure 5.3 shows possible activities involved in requirements specification when prototyping is used to help validate requirements. The milestones in this case are the completion of the outputs for each activity. The project deliverables, which are delivered to the customer, are the requirements definition and the requirements specification.

5.3 Project scheduling

Project scheduling is one of the most difficult jobs for a project manager. Managers estimate the time and resources required to complete activities and organise them into a coherent sequence. Unless the project being scheduled is similar to a previous project, previous estimates are an uncertain basis for new project scheduling. Schedule estimation is further complicated by the fact that different projects may use different design methods and implementation languages.

If the project is technically advanced, initial estimates will almost certainly be optimistic even when you try to consider all eventualities. In this respect, software scheduling is no different from scheduling any other type of large advanced project. New aircraft, bridges and even new models of cars are frequently late because of unanticipated problems. Schedules, therefore, must be continually updated as better progress information becomes available.

Project scheduling (Figure 5.4) involves separating the total work involved in a project into separate activities and judging the time required to complete these activities. Usually, some of these activities are carried out in parallel. You have to coordinate these parallel activities and organise the work so that the workforce is used optimally. It's important to avoid a situation where the whole project is delayed because a critical task is unfinished.

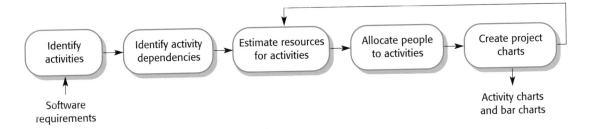

Activity charts
and bar charts

Figure 5.4 The
project scheduling
process

Project activities should normally last at least a week. Finer subdivision means that a disproportionate amount of time must be spent on estimating and chart revision. It is also useful to set a maximum amount of time for any activity of about 8 to 10 weeks. If it takes longer than this, it should be subdivided for project planning and scheduling.

As I have already suggested, when you are estimating schedules, you should not assume that every stage of the project will be problem free. People working on a project may fall ill or may leave, hardware may break down, and essential support software or hardware may be delivered late. If the project is new and technically advanced, certain parts of it may turn out to be more difficult and take longer than originally anticipated.

As well as calendar time, you also have to estimate the resources needed to complete each task. The principal resource is the human effort required. Other resources may be the disk space required on a server, the time required on specialised hardware such as a simulator, and the travel budget required for project staff. I discuss estimation in more detail in Chapter 26.

A good rule of thumb is to estimate as if nothing will go wrong, then increase your estimate to cover anticipated problems. A further contingency factor to cover unanticipated problems may also be added to the estimate. This extra contingency factor depends on the type of project, the process parameters (deadline, standards, etc.) and the quality and experience of the software engineers working on the project. I always add 30% to my original estimate for anticipated problems then another 20% to cover things I hadn't thought of.

Project schedules are usually represented as a set of charts showing the work breakdown, activities dependencies and staff allocations. I describe these in the following section. Software management tools, such as Microsoft Project, are usually used to automate chart production.

5.3.1   Bar charts and activity networks

Bar charts and activity networks are graphical notations that are used to illustrate the project schedule. Bar charts show who is responsible for each activity and when the activity is scheduled to begin and end. Activity networks show the dependencies between the different activities making up a project. Bar charts and activity charts can be generated automatically from a database of project information using a project management tool.

Figure 5.5 Task
durations and
dependencies

Task	Duration (days)	Dependencies
T1	8	
T2	15	
T3	15	T1 (M1)
T4	10	
T5	10	T2, T4 (M2)
T6	5	T1, T2 (M3)
T7	20	T1 (M1)
T8	25	T4 (M5)
T9	15	T3, T6 (M4)
T10	15	T5, T7 (M7)
T11	7	T9 (M6)
T12	10	T11 (M8)

To illustrate how these charts are used, I have created a hypothetical set of activities as shown in Figure 5.5. This table shows activities, their duration, and activity interdependencies. From Figure 5.5, you can see that Activity T3 is dependent on Activity T1. This means that T1 must be completed before T3 starts. For example, T1 might be the preparation of a component design and T3, the implementation of that design. Before implementation starts, the design should be complete.

Given the dependencies and estimated duration of activities, an activity chart that shows activity sequences may be generated (Figure 5.6). This shows which activities can be carried out in parallel and which must be executed in sequence because of a dependency on an earlier activity. Activities are represented as rectangles; milestones and project deliverables are shown with rounded corners. Dates in this diagram show the start date of the activity and are written in British style, where the day precedes the month. You should read the chart from left to right and from top to bottom

In the project management tool used to produce this chart, all activities must end in milestones. An activity may start when its preceding milestone (which may depend on several activities) has been reached. Therefore, the third column in Figure 5.5 shows the corresponding milestone (e.g., M5) that is reached when the tasks finish (see Figure 5.6).

Before progress can be made from one milestone to another, all paths leading to it must be complete. For example, when activities T3 and T6 are finished, then activity T9, shown in Figure 5.6, can start.

Figure 5.6 An activity
network

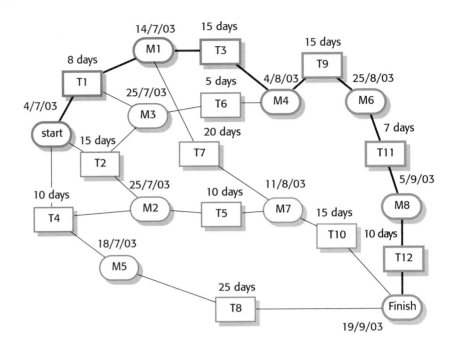

The minimum time required to finish the project can be estimated by considering the longest path in the activity graph (the critical path). In this case, it is 11 weeks of elapsed time or 55 working days. In Figure 5.6, the critical path is shown as a sequence of emboldened boxes. The critical path is the sequence of dependent activities that defines the time required to complete the project. The overall schedule of the project depends on the critical path. Any slippage in the completion in any critical activity causes project delays because the following activities cannot start until the delayed activity has been completed.

However, delays in activities that do not lie on the critical path do not necessarily cause an overall schedule slippage. So long as these delays do not extend these activities so much that the total time for that activity plus future dependent activities does not exceed the critical path, the project schedule will not be affected. For example, if T8 is delayed by two weeks, it will not affect the final completion date of the project because it does not lie on the critical path. Most project management tools compute the allowed delays, as shown in the project bar chart.

Managers also use activity charts when allocating project work. They can provide insights into activity dependencies that are not intuitively obvious. It may be possible to modify the system design so that the critical path is shortened. The project schedule may be shortened because of the reduced amount of time spent waiting for activities to finish.

Inevitably, initial project schedules will be incorrect. As a project develops, estimates should be compared with actual elapsed time. This comparison can be used as a basis for revising the schedule for later parts of the project. When actual figures

Figure 5.7 Activity
bar chart

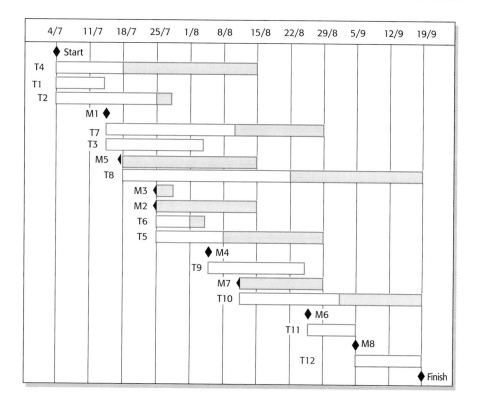

are known, the activity chart should be reviewed. Later project activities may then be reorganised to reduce the length of the critical path.

Figure 5.7 is a complementary way of representing project schedule information. It is a bar chart showing a project calendar and the start and finish dates of activities. Sometimes these are called *Gantt charts*, after their inventor. Reading from left to right, the bar chart clearly shows when activities start and end.

Some of the activities shown in the bar chart in Figure 5.7 are followed by a shaded bar whose length is computed by the scheduling tool. This highlights the flexibility in the completion date of these activities. If an activity does not complete on time, the critical path will not be affected until the end of the period marked by the shaded bar. Activities that lie on the critical path have no margin of error and can be identified because they have no associated shaded bar.

In addition to considering schedules, as a project manager you must also consider resource allocation and, in particular, the allocation of staff to project activities. This allocation can also be input to project management tools and a bar chart generated that shows when staff are employed on the project (Figure 5.8). People don't have to be assigned to a project at all times. During intervening periods they may be on holiday, working on other projects, attending training courses or engaging in some other activity.

Large organisations usually employ a number of specialists who work on a project when needed. In Figure 5.8, you can see that Mary and Jim are specialists who

Figure 5.8 Staff allocation vs. time chart

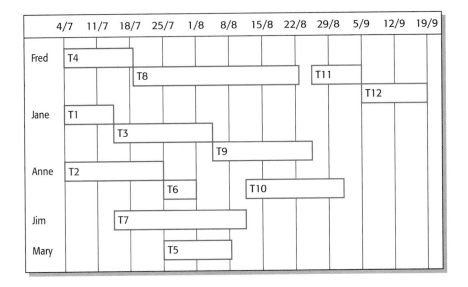

work on only a single task in the project. This can cause scheduling problems. If one project is delayed while a specialist is working on it, this may have a knock-on effect on other projects. They may also be delayed because the specialist is not available.

5.4 Risk management

Risk management is increasingly seen as one of the main jobs of project managers. It involves anticipating risks that might affect the project schedule or the quality of the software being developed and taking action to avoid these risks (Hall, 1998) (Ould, 1999). The results of the risk analysis should be documented in the project plan along with an analysis of the consequences of a risk occurring. Effective risk management makes it easier to cope with problems and to ensure that these do not lead to unacceptable budget or schedule slippage.

Simplistically, you can think of a risk as something that you'd prefer not to have happen. Risks may threaten the project, the software that is being developed or the organisation. There are, therefore, three related categories of risk:

1. *Project risks* are risks that affect the project schedule or resources. An example might be the loss of an experienced designer.

2. *Product risks* are risks that affect the quality or performance of the software being developed. An example might be the failure of a purchased component to perform as expected.

3. *Business risks* are risks that affect the organisation developing or procuring the software. For example, a competitor introducing a new product is a business risk.

Of course, these risk types overlap. If an experienced programmer leaves a project, this can be a project risk because the delivery of the system may be delayed. It can also be a product risk because a replacement may not be as experienced and so may make programming errors. Finally, it can be a business risk because the programmer's experience is not available for bidding for future business.

The risks that may affect a project depend on the project and the organisational environment where the software is being developed. However, many risks are universal—some of the most common risks are shown in Figure 5.9.

Risk management is particularly important for software projects because of the inherent uncertainties that most projects face. These stem from loosely defined requirements, difficulties in estimating the time and resources required for

Figure 5.9 Possible software risks

Risk	Risk type	Description
Staff turnover	Project	Experienced staff will leave the project before it is finished.
Management change	Project	There will be a change of organisational management with different priorities.
Hardware unavailability	Project	Hardware which is essential for the project will not be delivered on schedule.
Requirements change	Project and product	There will be a larger number of changes to the requirements than anticipated.
Specification delays	Project and product	Specifications of essential interfaces are not available on schedule.
Size underestimate	Project and product	The size of the system has been underestimated.
CASE tool under-performance	Product	CASE tools which support the project do not perform as anticipated.
Technology change	Business	The underlying technology on which the system is built is superseded by new technology.
Product competition	Business	A competitive product is marketed before the system is completed.

Figure 5.10 The risk
management process

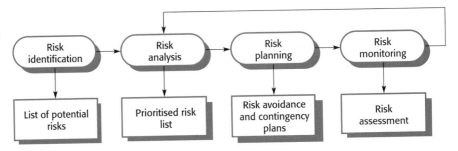

software development, dependence on individual skills and requirements changes due to changes in customer needs. You have to anticipate risks, understand the impact of these risks on the project, the product and the business, and take steps to avoid these risks. You may need to draw up contingency plans so that, if the risks do occur, you can take immediate recovery action.

The process of risk management is illustrated in Figure 5.10. It involves several stages:

1. *Risk identification* Possible project, product and business risks are identified.

2. *Risk analysis* The likelihood and consequences of these risks are assessed.

3. *Risk planning* Plans to address the risk either by avoiding it or minimising its effects on the project are drawn up.

4. *Risk monitoring* The risk is constantly assessed and plans for risk mitigation are revised as more information about the risk becomes available.

The risk management process, like all other project planning, is an iterative process which continues throughout the project. Once an initial set of plans are drawn up, the situation is monitored. As more information about the risks becomes available, the risks have to be reanalysed and new priorities established. The risk avoidance and contingency plans may be modified as new risk information emerges.

You should document the outcomes of the risk management process in a risk management plan. This should include a discussion of the risks faced by the project, an analysis of these risks and the plans that are required to manage these risks. Where appropriate, you should also include in the plan results of the risk management process such as specific contingency plans to be activated if the risk occurs.

5.4.1 Risk identification

Risk identification is the first stage of risk management. It is concerned with discovering possible risks to the project. In principle, these should not be assessed or prioritised at this stage, although, in practice, risks with very minor consequences or very low probability risks are not usually considered.

Risk identification may be carried out as a team process using a brainstorming approach or may simply be based on experience. To help the process, a checklist of different types of risk may be used. There are at least six types of risk that can arise:

1. *Technology risks* Risks that derive from the software or hardware technologies that are used to develop the system.

2. *People risks* Risks that are associated with the people in the development team.

3. *Organisational risks* Risks that derive from the organisational environment where the software is being developed.

4. *Tools risks* Risks that derive from the CASE tools and other support software used to develop the system.

5. *Requirements risks* Risks that derive from changes to the customer requirements and the process of managing the requirements change.

6. *Estimation risks* Risks that derive from the management estimates of the system characteristics and the resources required to build the system.

Figure 5.11 gives some examples of possible risks in each of these categories. When you have finished the risk identification process, you should have a long list of risks that could occur and which could affect the product, the process and the business.

5.4.2 Risk analysis

During the risk analysis process, you have to consider each identified risk and make a judgement about the probability and the seriousness of it. There is no easy way to do this—you must rely on your own judgement and experience, which is why experienced project managers are generally the best people to help with risk management. These risk estimates should not generally be precise numeric assessments but should be based around a number of bands:

- The probability of the risk might be assessed as very low (<10%), low (10–25%), moderate (25-50%), high (50–75%) or very high (>75%).

- The effects of the risk might be assessed as catastrophic, serious, tolerable or insignificant.

You should then tabulate the results of this analysis process using a table ordered according to the seriousness of the risk. Figure 5.12 illustrates this for the risks identified in Figure 5.11. Obviously, the assessment of probability and seriousness is arbitrary here. In practice, to make this assessment you need detailed information about the project, the process, the development team and the organisation.

Figure 5.11 Risks and risk types

Risk type	Possible risks
Technology	The database used in the system cannot process as many transactions per second as expected. Software components which should be reused contain defects which limit their functionality.
People	It is impossible to recruit staff with the skills required. Key staff are ill and unavailable at critical times. Required training for staff is not available.
Organisational	The organisation is restructured so that different management are responsible for the project. Organisational financial problems force reductions in the project budget.
Tools	The code generated by CASE tools is inefficient. CASE tools cannot be integrated.
Requirements	Changes to requirements which require major design rework are proposed. Customers fail to understand the impact of requirements changes.
Estimation	The time required to develop the software is underestimated. The rate of defect repair is underestimated. The size of the software is underestimated.

Of course, both the probability and the assessment of the effects of a risk may change as more information about the risk becomes available and as risk management plans are implemented. Therefore, you should update this table during each iteration of the risk process.

Once the risks have been analysed and ranked, you should assess which are most significant. Your judgement must depend on a combination of the probability of the risk arising and the effects of that risk. In general, catastrophic risks should always be considered, as should all serious risks that have more than a moderate probability of occurrence.

Boehm (Boehm, 1988) recommends identify and monitoring the 'top 10' risks, but I think that this figure is rather arbitrary. The right number of risks to monitor must depend on the project. It might be 5 or it might be 15. However, the number of risks chosen for monitoring should be manageable. A very large number of risks would simply require too much information to be collected. From the risks identified in Figure 5.12, it is appropriate to consider all 8 risks that have catastrophic or serious consequences.

5.4.3 Risk planning

The risk planning process considers each of the key risks that have been identified and identifies strategies to manage the risk. Again, there is no simple process that

Figure 5.12 Risk
analysis

Risk	Probability	Effects
Organisational financial problems force reductions in the project budget.	Low	Catastrophic
It is impossible to recruit staff with the skills required for the project.	High	Catastrophic
Key staff are ill at critical times in the project.	Moderate	Serious
Software components which should be reused contain defects which limit their functionality.	Moderate	Serious
Changes to requirements which require major design rework are proposed.	Moderate	Serious
The organisation is restructured so that different management are responsible for the project.	High	Serious
The database used in the system cannot process as many transactions per second as expected.	Moderate	Serious
The time required to develop the software is underestimated.	High	Serious
CASE tools cannot be integrated.	High	Tolerable
Customers fail to understand the impact of requirements changes.	Moderate	Tolerable
Required training for staff is not available.	Moderate	Tolerable
The rate of defect repair is underestimated.	Moderate	Tolerable
The size of the software is underestimated.	High	Tolerable
The code generated by CASE tools is inefficient.	Moderate	Insignificant

can be followed to establish risk management plans. It relies on the judgement and experience of the project manager. Figure 5.13 shows possible strategies that have been identified for the key risks from Figure 5.12.

These strategies fall into three categories:

1. *Avoidance strategies* Following these strategies means that the probability that the risk will arise will be reduced. An example of a risk avoidance strategy is the strategy for dealing with defective components shown in Figure 5.13.

2. *Minimisation strategies* Following these strategies means that the impact of the risk will be reduced. An example of a risk minimisation strategy is that for staff illness shown in Figure 5.13

Figure 5.13 Risk
management
strategies

Risk	Strategy
Organisational financial problems	Prepare a briefing document for senior management showing how the project is making a very important contribution to the goals of the business.
Recruitment problems	Alert customer of potential difficulties and the possibility of delays, investigate buying-in components.
Staff illness	Reorganise team so that there is more overlap of work and people therefore understand each other's jobs.
Defective components	Replace potentially defective components with bought-in components of known reliability.
Requirements changes	Derive traceability information to assess requirements change impact, maximise information hiding in the design.
Organisational restructuring	Prepare a briefing document for senior management showing how the project is making a very important contribution to the goals of the business.
Database performance	Investigate the possibility of buying a higher-performance database.
Underestimated development time	Investigate buying-in components, investigate the use of a program generator.

3. *Contingency plans* Following these strategies means that you are prepared for the worst and have a strategy in place to deal with it. An example of a contingency strategy is the strategy for organisational financial problems in Figure 5.13.

You can see here the analogy with the strategies used in critical systems to ensure reliability, security and safety. Essentially, it is best to use a strategy that avoids the risk. If this is not possible, use one that reduces the chances that the risk will have serious effects. Finally, have strategies in place that reduce the overall impact of a risk on the project or product.

5.4.4 Risk monitoring

Risk monitoring involves regularly assessing each of the identified risks to decide whether or not that risk is becoming more or less probable and whether the effects of the risk have changed. Of course, this cannot usually be observed directly, so you have to look at other factors that give you clues about the risk probability and its effects. These factors are obviously dependent on the types of risk. Figure 5.14 gives some examples of factors that may be helpful in assessing these risk types.

Risk monitoring should be a continuous process, and, at every management progress review, you should consider and discuss each of the key risks separately.

Figure 5.14 Risk
factors

Risk type	Potential indicators
Technology	Late delivery of hardware or support software, many reported technology problems
People	Poor staff morale, poor relationships amongst team members, job availability
Organisational	Organisational gossip, lack of action by senior management
Tools	Reluctance by team members to use tools, complaints about CASE tools, demands for higher-powered workstations
Requirements	Many requirements change requests, customer complaints
Estimation	Failure to meet agreed schedule, failure to clear reported defects

KEY POINTS

■ Good software project management is essential if software engineering projects are to be developed on schedule and within budget.

■ Software management is distinct from other engineering management. Software is intangible. Projects may be novel or innovative so there is no body of experience to guide their management. Software processes are not well understood.

■ Software managers have diverse roles. Their most significant activities are project planning, estimating and scheduling. Planning and estimating are iterative processes. They continue throughout a project. As more information becomes available, plans and schedules must be revised.

■ A project milestone is a predictable outcome of an activity where some formal report of progress should be presented to management. Milestones should occur regularly throughout a software project. A deliverable is a milestone that is delivered to the project customer.

■ Project scheduling involves the creation of various graphical plan representations of part of the project plan. These include activity charts showing the interrelationships of project activities and bar charts showing activity durations.

■ Major project risks should be identified and assessed to establish their probability and the consequences for the project. You should make plans to avoid, manage or deal with likely risks if or when they arise. Risks should be explicitly discussed at each project progress meeting.

FURTHER READING

Waltzing with Bears: Managing Risk on Software Projects. A very practical and easy-to-read introduction to risks and risk management. (T. DeMarco and T. Lister, 2003, Dorset House.)

Managing Software Quality and Business Risk. Chapter 3 of this book is simply the best discussion of risk that I have seen anywhere. The book is oriented around risk and I think it is probably the best book on this topic currently available. (M. Ould, 1999, John Wiley & Sons.)

The Mythical Man Month (Anniversary Edition). The problems of software management have been unchanged since the 1960s and this is one of the best books on the topic. An interesting and readable account of the management of one of the first very large software projects, the IBM OS/360 operating system. The anniversary edition (published 20 years after the original edition in 1975) includes other classic papers by Brooks. (F. P. Brooks, 1995, Addison-Wesley.)

Software Project Survival Guide. This is a very pragmatic account of software management, but it contains good practical advice. It is easy to read and understand. (S. McConnell, 1998, Microsoft Press.)

See Part 6 for other readings on management.

EXERCISES

5.1   Explain why the intangibility of software systems poses special problems for software project management.

5.2   Explain why the best programmers do not always make the best software managers. You may find it helpful to base your answer on the list of management activities in Section 5.1.

5.3   Explain why the process of project planning is iterative and why a plan must be continually reviewed during a software project.

5.4   Briefly explain the purpose of each of the sections in a software project plan.

5.5   What is the critical distinction between a milestone and a deliverable?

5.6   Figure 5.15 sets out a number of activities, durations and dependencies. Draw an activity chart and a bar chart showing the project schedule.

5.7   Figure 5.5 gives task durations for software project activities. Assume that a serious, unanticipated setback occurs and instead of taking 10 days, task T5 takes 40 days. Revise the activity chart accordingly, highlighting the new critical path. Draw up new bar charts showing how the project might be reorganised.

5.8   Using reported instances of project problems in the literature, list management difficulties that occurred in these failed programming projects. (I suggest that you start with Brooks's book, as suggested in Further Reading.)

Figure 5.15 Task durations and dependencies

Task	Duration (days)	Dependencies
T1	10	
T2	15	T1
T3	10	T1, T2
T4	20	
T5	10	
T6	15	T3, T4
T7	20	T3
T8	35	T7
T9	15	T6
T10	5	T5, T9
T11	10	T9
T12	20	T10
T13	35	T3, T4
T14	10	T8, T9
T15	20	T12, T14
T16	10	T15

5.9 In addition to the risks shown in Figure 5.11, identify six other possible risks that could arise in software projects.

5.10 Fixed-price contracts, where the contractor bids a fixed price to complete a system development, may be used to move project risk from client to contractor. If anything goes wrong, the contractor has to pay. Suggest how the use of such contracts may increase the likelihood that product risks will arise.

5.11 You are asked by your manager to deliver software to a schedule that you know can only be met by asking your project team to work unpaid overtime. All team members have young children. Discuss whether you should accept this demand from your manager or whether you should persuade your team to give their time to the organisation rather than to their families. What factors might be significant in your decision?

5.12 As a programmer, you are offered a promotion to project management but you feel that you can make a more effective contribution in a technical rather than a managerial role. Discuss whether you should accept the promotion.

PART 2

REQUIREMENTS

Perhaps the major problem that we face in developing large and complex software systems is that of requirements engineering. Requirements engineering is concerned with establishing what the system should do, its desired and essential emergent properties, and the constraints on system operation and the software development processes. You can therefore think of requirements engineering as the communications process between the software customers and users and the software developers.

Requirements engineering is not simply a technical process. The system requirements are influenced by users' likes, dislikes and prejudices, and by political and organisational issues. These are fundamental human characteristics, and new technologies, such as use-cases, scenarios and formal methods, don't help us much in resolving these thorny problems.

The chapters in this section fall into two classes—in Chapters 6 and 7 I introduce the basics of requirements engineering, and in Chapters 8 to 10 I describe models and techniques that are used in the requirements engineering process. More specifically:

1. The topic of Chapter 6 is software requirements and requirements documents. I discuss what is meant by a requirement, different types of requirements and how these requirements are organised into a requirements specification document. I introduce the second running case study—a library system—in this chapter.

2. In Chapter 7, I focus on the activities in the requirements engineering process. I discuss how feasibility studies should always be part of requirements engineering, techniques for requirements elicitation and analysis, and requirements validation. Because requirements inevitably change, I also cover the important topic of requirements management.

3. Chapter 8 describes types of system models that may be developed in the requirements engineering process. These provide a more detailed description for system developers. The emphasis here is on object-oriented modelling but I also include a description of data-flow diagrams. I find these are intuitive and helpful, especially for giving you an end-to-end picture of how information is processed by a system.

4. The emphasis in Chapters 9 and 10 is on critical systems specification. In Chapter 9, I discuss the specification of emergent dependability properties. I describe risk-driven approaches and specific issues of safety, reliability and security specification. In Chapter 10, I introduce formal specification techniques. Formal methods have had less impact than was once predicted but they are being increasingly used in the specification of safety and mission-critical systems. I cover both algebraic and model-based approaches in this chapter.

6

Software requirements

Objectives

The objectives of this chapter are to introduce software system requirements and to explain different ways of expressing software requirements. When you have read the chapter, you will:

■ understand the concepts of user requirements and system requirements and why these requirements should be written in different ways;

■ understand the differences between functional and non-functional software requirements;

■ understand how requirements may be organised in a software requirements document.

Contents

The requirements for a system are the descriptions of the services provided by the system and its operational constraints. These requirements reflect the needs of customers for a system that helps solve some problem such as controlling a device, placing an order or finding information. The process of finding out, analysing, documenting and checking these services and constraints is called *requirements engineering* (RE). In this chapter, I concentrate on the requirements themselves and how to describe them. I introduced the requirements engineering process in Chapter 4 and I discuss the RE process in more detail in Chapter 7.

The term *requirement* is not used in the software industry in a consistent way. In some cases, a requirement is simply a high-level, abstract statement of a service that the system should provide or a constraint on the system. At the other extreme, it is a detailed, formal definition of a system function. Davis (Davis, 1993) explains why these differences exist:

> If a company wishes to let a contract for a large software development project, it must define its needs in a sufficiently abstract way that a solution is not predefined. The requirements must be written so that several contractors can bid for the contract, offering, perhaps, different ways of meeting the client organisation's needs. Once a contract has been awarded, the contractor must write a system definition for the client in more detail so that the client understands and can validate what the software will do. Both of these documents may be called the requirements document for the system.

Some of the problems that arise during the requirements engineering process are a result of failing to make a clear separation between these different levels of description. I distinguish between them by using the term *user requirements* to mean the high-level abstract requirements and *system requirements* to mean the detailed description of what the system should do. User requirements and system requirements may be defined as follows:

1. *User requirements* are statements, in a natural language plus diagrams, of what services the system is expected to provide and the constraints under which it must operate.

2. *System requirements* set out the system's functions, services and operational constraints in detail. The system requirements document (sometimes called a functional specification) should be precise. It should define exactly what is to be implemented. It may be part of the contract between the system buyer and the software developers.

Different levels of system specification are useful because they communicate information about the system to different types of readers. Figure 6.1 illustrates the distinction between user and system requirements. This example from a library system shows how a user requirement may be expanded into several system requirements. You can see from Figure 6.1 that the user requirement is more abstract, and the system requirements add detail, explaining the services and functions that should be provided by the system to be developed.

Figure 6.1 User and
system requirements

User requirement definition

> 1. LIBSYS shall keep track of all data required by copyright licensing agencies in the UK and elsewhere.

System requirements specification

> 1.1 On making a request for a document from LIBSYS, the requestor shall be presented with a form that records details of the user and the request made.
> 1.2 LIBSYS request forms shall be stored on the system for five years from the date of the request.
> 1.3 All LIBSYS request forms must be indexed by user, by the name of the material requested and by the supplier of the request.
> 1.4 LIBSYS shall maintain a log of all requests that have been made to the system.
> 1.5 For material where authors' lending rights apply, loan details shall be sent monthly to copyright licensing agencies that have registered with LIBSYS.

You need to write requirements at different levels of detail because different types of readers use them in different ways. Figure 6.2 shows the types of readers for the user and system requirements. The readers of the user requirements are not usually concerned with how the system will be implemented and may be managers who are not interested in the detailed facilities of the system. The readers of the system requirements need to know more precisely what the system will do because they are concerned with how it will support the business processes or because they are involved in the system implementation.

6.1 Functional and non-functional requirements

Software system requirements are often classified as functional requirements, non-functional requirements or domain requirements:

1. *Functional requirements* These are statements of services the system should provide, how the system should react to particular inputs and how the system should behave in particular situations. In some cases, the functional requirements may also explicitly state what the system should not do.

2. *Non-functional requirements* These are constraints on the services or functions offered by the system. They include timing constraints, constraints on the development process and standards. Non-functional requirements often apply to the system as a whole. They do not usually just apply to individual system features or services.

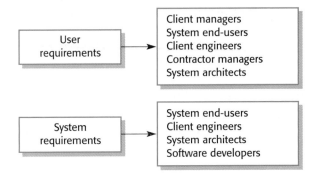

Figure 6.2 Readers of
different types of
specification

3. *Domain requirements* These are requirements that come from the application
    domain of the system and that reflect characteristics and constraints of that domain.
    They may be functional or non-functional requirements

In reality, the distinction between different types of requirements is not as clear-cut
as these simple definitions suggest. A user requirement concerned with security, say,
may appear to be a non-functional requirement. However, when developed in more
detail, this requirement may generate other requirements that are clearly functional,
such as the need to include user authentication facilities in the system.

6.1.1 Functional requirements

The functional requirements for a system describe what the system should do. These
requirements depend on the type of software being developed, the expected users
of the software and the general approach taken by the organisation when writing
requirements. When expressed as user requirements, the requirements are usually
described in a fairly abstract way. However, functional system requirements
describe the system function in detail, its inputs and outputs, exceptions, and so on.

 Functional requirements for a software system may be expressed in a number of
ways. For example, here are examples of functional requirements for a university
library system called LIBSYS, used by students and faculty to order books and documents from other libraries.

1. The user shall be able to search either all of the initial set of databases or select
    a subset from it.

2. The system shall provide appropriate viewers for the user to read documents
    in the document store.

3. Every order shall be allocated a unique identifier (ORDER_ID), which the user
    shall be able to copy to the account's permanent storage area.

These functional user requirements define specific facilities to be provided by
the system. These have been taken from the user requirements document, and they

illustrate that functional requirements may be written at different levels of detail (contrast requirements 1 and 3).

The LIBSYS system is a single interface to a range of article databases. It allows users to download copies of published articles in magazines, newspapers and scientific journals. I give a more detailed description of the requirements for the system on which LIBSYS is based in my book with Gerald Kotonya on requirements engineering (Kotonya and Sommerville, 1998).

Imprecision in the requirements specification is the cause of many software engineering problems. It is natural for a system developer to interpret an ambiguous requirement to simplify its implementation. Often, however, this is not what the customer wants. New requirements have to be established and changes made to the system. Of course, this delays system delivery and increases costs.

Consider the second example requirement for the library system that refers to 'appropriate viewers' provided by the system. The library system can deliver documents in a range of formats; the intention of this requirement is that viewers for all of these formats should be available. However, the requirement is worded ambiguously; it does not make clear that viewers for each document format should be provided. A developer under schedule pressure might simply provide a text viewer and claim that the requirement had been met.

In principle, the functional requirements specification of a system should be both complete and consistent. *Completeness* means that all services required by the user should be defined. *Consistency* means that requirements should not have contradictory definitions. In practice, for large, complex systems, it is practically impossible to achieve requirements consistency and completeness.

One reason for this is that it is easy to make mistakes and omissions when writing specifications for large, complex systems. Another reason is that different system stakeholders (see Chapter 7) have different—and often inconsistent—needs. These inconsistencies may not be obvious when the requirements are first specified, so inconsistent requirements are included in the specification. The problems may only emerge after deeper analysis or, sometimes, after development is complete and the system is delivered to the customer.

6.1.2 Non-functional requirements

Non-functional requirements, as the name suggests, are requirements that are not directly concerned with the specific functions delivered by the system. They may relate to emergent system properties such as reliability, response time and store occupancy. Alternatively, they may define constraints on the system such as the capabilities of I/O devices and the data representations used in system interfaces.

Non-functional requirements are rarely associated with individual system features. Rather, these requirements specify or constrain the emergent properties of the system, as discussed in Chapter 2. Therefore, they may specify system performance, security, availability, and other emergent properties. This means that they are often

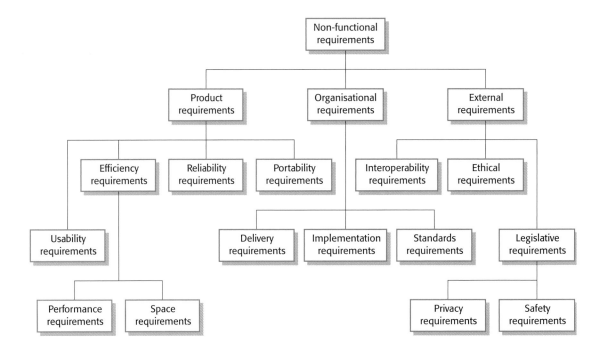

Figure 6.3 Types of
non-functional
requirements

more critical than individual functional requirements. System users can usually find ways to work around a system function that doesn't really meet their needs. However, failing to meet a non-functional requirement can mean that the whole system is unusable. For example, if an aircraft system does not meet its reliability requirements, it will not be certified as safe for operation; if a real-time control system fails to meet its performance requirements, the control functions will not operate correctly.

Non-functional requirements are not just concerned with the software system to be developed. Some non-functional requirements may constrain the process that should be used to develop the system. Examples of process requirements include a specification of the quality standards that should be used in the process, a specification that the design must be produced with a particular CASE toolset and a description of the process that should be followed.

Non-functional requirements arise through user needs, because of budget constraints, because of organisational policies, because of the need for interoperability with other software or hardware systems, or because of external factors such as safety regulations or privacy legislation. Figure 6.3 is a classification of non-functional requirements. You can see from this diagram that the non-functional requirements may come from required characteristics of the software (product requirements), the organization developing the software (organizational requirements) or from external sources.

Figure 6.4 Examples
of non-functional
requirements

Product requirement
8.1 The user interface for LIBSYS shall be implemented as simple HTML without
frames or Java applets.

Organisational requirement
9.3.2 The system development process and deliverable documents shall conform to
the process and deliverables defined in XYZCo-SP-STAN-95.

External requirement
10.6 The system shall not disclose any personal information about system users
apart from their name and library reference number to the library staff who use the
system.

The types of non-functional requirements are:

1. *Product requirements* These requirements specify product behaviour. Examples include performance requirements on how fast the system must execute and how much memory it requires; reliability requirements that set out the acceptable failure rate; portability requirements; and usability requirements.

2. *Organisational requirements* These requirements are derived from policies and procedures in the customer's and developer's organisation. Examples include process standards that must be used; implementation requirements such as the programming language or design method used; and delivery requirements that specify when the product and its documentation are to be delivered.

3. *External requirements* This broad heading covers all requirements that are derived from factors external to the system and its development process. These may include interoperability requirements that define how the system interacts with systems in other organisations; legislative requirements that must be followed to ensure that the system operates within the law; and ethical requirements. Ethical requirements are requirements placed on a system to ensure that it will be acceptable to its users and the general public.

Figure 6.4 shows examples of product, organisational and external requirements taken from the library system LIBSYS whose user requirements were discussed in Section 6.1.1. The product requirement restricts the freedom of the LIBSYS designers in the implementation of the system user interface. It says nothing about the functionality of LIBSYS and clearly identifies a system constraint rather than a function. This requirement has been included because it simplifies the problem of ensuring the system works with different browsers.

The organisational requirement specifies that the system must be developed according to a company standard process defined as XYZCo-SP-STAN-95. The external requirement is derived from the need for the system to conform to privacy legislation. It specifies that library staff should not be allowed access to data, such as the addresses of system users, which they do not need to do their job.

Figure 6.5 System
goals and verifiable
requirements

A system goal
The system should be easy to use by experienced controllers and should be
organised in such a way that user errors are minimised.

A verifiable non-functional requirement
Experienced controllers shall be able to use all the system functions after a total of
two hours' training. After this training, the average number of errors made by
experienced users shall not exceed two per day.

A common problem with non-functional requirements is that they can be difficult to verify. Users or customers often state these requirements as general goals
such as ease of use, the ability of the system to recover from failure or rapid user
response. These vague goals cause problems for system developers as they leave
scope for interpretation and subsequent dispute once the system is delivered. As an
illustration of this problem, consider Figure 6.5. This shows a system goal relating
to the usability of a traffic control system and is typical of how a user might express
usability requirements. I have rewritten it to show how the goal can be expressed
as a 'testable' non-functional requirement. While it is impossible to objectively verify the system goal, you can design system tests to count the errors made by controllers using a system simulator.

Whenever possible, you should write non-functional requirements quantitatively
so that they can be objectively tested. Figure 6.6 shows a number of possible metrics that you can use to specify non-functional system properties. You can measure
these characteristics when the system is being tested to check whether or not the
system has met its non-functional requirements.

In practice, however, customers for a system may find it practically impossible
to translate their goals into quantitative requirements. For some goals, such as maintainability, there are no metrics that can be used. In other cases, even when quantitative specification is possible, customers may not be able to relate their needs to
these specifications. They don't understand what some number defining the
required reliability (say) means in terms of their everyday experience with computer systems. Furthermore, the cost of objectively verifying quantitative non-
functional requirements may be very high, and the customers paying for the system
may not think these costs are justified.

Therefore, requirements documents often include statements of goals mixed with
requirements. These goals may be useful to developers because they give indications of customer priorities. However, you should always tell customers that they
are open to misinterpretation and cannot be objectively verified.

Non-functional requirements often conflict and interact with other functional or
non-functional requirements. For example, it may be a requirement that the
maximum memory used by a system should be no more than 4 Mbytes. Memory
constraints are common for embedded systems where space or weight is limited
and the number of ROM chips storing the system software must be minimised. Another
requirement might be that the system should be written using Ada, a programming

Figure 6.6 Metrics for specifying non-functional requirements

Property	Measure
Speed	Processed transactions/second User/Event response time Screen refresh time
Size	K bytes Number of RAM chips
Ease of use	Training time Number of help frames
Reliability	Mean time to failure Probability of unavailability Rate of failure occurrence Availability
Robustness	Time to restart after failure Percentage of events causing failure Probability of data corruption on failure
Portability	Percentage of target-dependent statements Number of target systems

language for critical, real-time software development. However, it may not be possible to compile an Ada program with the required functionality into less that 4 Mbytes. There therefore has to be a trade-off between these requirements: an alternative development language or increased memory added to the system.

It is helpful if you can differentiate functional and non-functional requirements in the requirements document. In practice, this is difficult to do. If the non-functional requirements are stated separately from the functional requirements, it is sometimes difficult to see the relationships between them. If they are stated with the functional requirements, you may find it difficult to separate functional and non-functional considerations and to identify requirements that relate to the system as a whole. However, you should explicitly highlight requirements that are clearly related to emergent system properties, such as performance or reliability. You can do this by putting them in a separate section of the requirements document or by distinguishing them, in some way, from other system requirements.

Non-functional requirements such as safety and security requirements are particularly important for critical systems. I therefore discuss dependability requirements in more detail in Chapter 9, which covers critical systems specification.

6.1.3 Domain requirements

Domain requirements are derived from the application domain of the system rather than from the specific needs of system users. They usually include specialised domain terminology or reference to domain concepts. They may be new functional require-

Figure 6.7 A domain requirement from a train protection system

The deceleration of the train shall be computed as:

$$D_{train} = D_{control} + D_{gradient}$$

where $D_{gradient}$ is 9.81 ms^2 * compensated gradient/alpha and where the values of 9.81 ms^2/alpha are known for different types of train.

ments in their own right, constrain existing functional requirements or set out how particular computations must be carried out. Because these requirements are specialised, software engineers often find it difficult to understand how they are related to other system requirements.

Domain requirements are important because they often reflect fundamentals of the application domain. If these requirements are not satisfied, it may be impossible to make the system work satisfactorily. The LIBSYS system includes a number of domain requirements:

1. There shall be a standard user interface to all databases that shall be based on the Z39.50 standard.

2. Because of copyright restrictions, some documents must be deleted immediately on arrival. Depending on the user's requirements, these documents will either be printed locally on the system server for manual forwarding to the user or routed to a network printer.

The first requirement is a design constraint. It specifies that the user interface to the database must be implemented according to a specific library standard. The developers therefore have to find out about that standard before starting the interface design. The second requirement has been introduced because of copyright laws that apply to material used in libraries. It specifies that the system must include an automatic delete-on-print facility for some classes of document. This means that users of the library system cannot have their own electronic copy of the document.

To illustrate domain requirements that specify how a computation is carried out, consider Figure 6.7, taken from the requirements specification for an automated train protection system. This system automatically stops a train if it goes through a red signal. This requirement states how the train deceleration is computed by the system. It uses domain-specific terminology. To understand it, you need some understanding of the operation of railway systems and train characteristics.

The requirement for the train system illustrates a major problem with domain requirements. They are written in the language of the application domain (mathematical equations in this case), and it is often difficult for software engineers to understand them. Domain experts may leave information out of a requirement simply because it is so obvious to them. However, it may not be obvious to the developers of the system, and they may therefore implement the requirement in the wrong way.

Figure 6.8 A user
requirement for an
accounting system
in LIBSYS

> **4.5** LIBSYS shall provide a financial accounting system that maintains records of all
> payments made by users of the system. System managers may configure this system
> so that regular users may receive discounted rates.

6.2 User requirements

The user requirements for a system should describe the functional and non-functional requirements so that they are understandable by system users without detailed technical knowledge. They should only specify the external behaviour of the system and should avoid, as far as possible, system design characteristics. Consequently, if you are writing user requirements, you should not use software jargon, structured notations or formal notations, or describe the requirement by describing the system implementation. You should write user requirements in simple language, with simple tables and forms and intuitive diagrams.

However, various problems can arise when requirements are written in natural language sentences in a text document:

1. *Lack of clarity* It is sometimes difficult to use language in a precise and unambiguous way without making the document wordy and difficult to read.

2. *Requirements confusion* Functional requirements, non-functional requirements, system goals and design information may not be clearly distinguished.

3. *Requirements amalgamation* Several different requirements may be expressed together as a single requirement.

As an illustration of some of these problems, consider one of the requirements for the library shown in Figure 6.8.

This requirement includes both conceptual and detailed information. It expresses the concept that there should be an accounting system as an inherent part of LIBSYS. However, it also includes the detail that the accounting system should support discounts for regular LIBSYS users. This detail would have been better left to the system requirements specification.

It is good practice to separate user requirements from more detailed system requirements in a requirements document. Otherwise, non-technical readers of the user requirements may be overwhelmed by details that are really only relevant for technicians. Figure 6.9 illustrates this confusion. This example is taken from an actual requirements document for a CASE tool for editing software design models. The user may specify that a grid should be displayed so that entities may be accurately positioned in a diagram.

Figure 6.9 A user
requirement for an
editor grid

2.6 Grid facilities To assist in the positioning of entities on a diagram, the user
may turn on a grid in either centimetres or inches, via an option on the control
panel. Initially, the grid is off. The grid may be turned on and off at any time during
an editing session and can be toggled between inches and centimetres at any time.
A grid option will be provided on the reduce-to-fit view but the number of grid lines
shown will be reduced to avoid filling the smaller diagram with grid lines.

The first sentence mixes up three kinds of requirements.

1. A conceptual, functional requirement states that the editing system should provide a grid. It presents a rationale for this.

2. A non-functional requirement giving detailed information about the grid units (centimetres or inches).

3. A non-functional user interface requirement that defines how the grid is switched on and off by the user.

The requirement in Figure 6.9 also gives some but not all initialisation information. It defines that the grid is initially off. However, it does not define its units when turned on. It provides some detailed information—namely, that the user may toggle between units—but not the spacing between grid lines.

User requirements that include too much information constrain the freedom of the system developer to provide innovative solutions to user problems and are difficult to understand. The user requirement should simply focus on the key facilities to be provided. I have rewritten the editor grid requirement (Figure 6.10) to focus only on the essential system features.

Whenever possible, you should try to associate a rationale with each user requirement. The rationale should explain why the requirement has been included and is particularly useful when requirements are changed. For example, the rationale in Figure 6.10 recognises that an active grid where positioned objects automatically 'snap' to a grid line can be useful. However, this has been deliberately rejected in favour of manual positioning. If a change to this is proposed at some later stage, it will be clear that the use of a passive grid was deliberate rather than an implementation decision.

To minimise misunderstandings when writing user requirements, I recommend that you follow some simple guidelines:

1. Invent a standard format and ensure that all requirement definitions adhere to that format. Standardising the format makes omissions less likely and requirements easier to check. The format I use shows the initial requirement in boldface, including a statement of rationale with each user requirement and a reference to the more detailed system requirement specification. You may also

Figure 6.10
A definition of an
editor grid facility

2.6.1 Grid facilities

The editor shall provide a grid facility where a matrix of horizontal and vertical lines provide a background to the editor window. This grid shall be a passive grid where the alignment of entities is the user's responsibility.

> *Rationale*: A grid helps the user to create a tidy diagram with well-spaced entities. Although an active grid, where entities 'snap-to' grid lines can be useful, the positioning is imprecise. The user is the best person to decide where entities should be positioned.

Specification: ECLIPSE/WS/Tools/DE/FS Section 5.6

Source: Ray Wilson, Glasgow Office

include information on who proposed the requirement (the requirement source) so that you know whom to consult if the requirement has to be changed.

2. Use language consistently. You should always distinguish between mandatory and desirable requirements. *Mandatory requirements* are requirements that the system must support and are usually written using 'shall'. *Desirable requirements* are not essential and are written using 'should'.

3. Use text highlighting (bold, italic or colour) to pick out key parts of the requirement.

4. Avoid, as far as possible, the use of computer jargon. Inevitably, however, detailed technical terms will creep into the user requirements.

The Robertsons (Robertson and Robertson, 1999), in their book that covers the VOLERE requirements engineering method, recommend that user requirements be initially written on cards, one requirement per card. They suggest a number of fields on each card, such as the requirements rationale, the dependencies on other requirements, the source of the requirements, supporting materials, and so on. This extends the format that I have used in Figure 6.10, and it can be used for both user and system requirements.

6.3 System requirements

System requirements are expanded versions of the user requirements that are used by software engineers as the starting point for the system design. They add detail and explain how the user requirements should be provided by the system. They may be used as part of the contract for the implementation of the system and should therefore be a complete and consistent specification of the whole system.

Ideally, the system requirements should simply describe the external behaviour of the system and its operational constraints. They should not be concerned with how the system should be designed or implemented. However, at the level of detail required to completely specify a complex software system, it is impossible, in practice, to exclude all design information. There are several reasons for this:

1. You may have to design an initial architecture of the system to help structure the requirements specification. The system requirements are organised according to the different sub-systems that make up the system. As I discuss in Chapter 7 and Chapter 18, this architectural definition is essential if you want to reuse software components when implementing the system.

2. In most cases, systems must interoperate with other existing systems. These constrain the design, and these constraints impose requirements on the new system.

3. The use of a specific architecture to satisfy non-functional requirements (such as N-version programming to achieve reliability, discussed in Chapter 20) may be necessary. An external regulator who needs to certify that the system is safe may specify that an architectural design that has already been certified be used.

Natural language is often used to write system requirements specifications as well as user requirements. However, because system requirements are more detailed than user requirements, natural language specifications can be confusing and hard to understand:

1. Natural language understanding relies on the specification readers and writers using the same words for the same concept. This leads to misunderstandings because of the ambiguity of natural language. Jackson (Jackson, 1995) gives an excellent example of this when he discusses signs displayed by an escalator. These said 'Shoes must be worn' and 'Dogs must be carried'. I leave it to you to work out the conflicting interpretations of these phrases.

2. A natural language requirements specification is overflexible. You can say the same thing in completely different ways. It is up to the reader to find out when requirements are the same and when they are distinct.

3. There is no easy way to modularise natural language requirements. It may be difficult to find all related requirements. To discover the consequence of a change, you may have to look at every requirement rather than at just a group of related requirements.

Because of these problems, requirements specifications written in natural language are prone to misunderstandings. These are often not discovered until later phases of the software process and may then be very expensive to resolve.

Notation	Description
Structured natural language	This approach depends on defining standard forms or templates to express the requirements specification.
Design description languages	This approach uses a language like a programming language but with more abstract features to specify the requirements by defining an operational model of the system. This approach is not now widely used although it can be useful for interface specifications.
Graphical notations	A graphical language, supplemented by text annotations is used to define the functional requirements for the system. An early example of such a graphical language was SADT (Ross, 1977) (Schoman and Ross, 1977). Now, use-case descriptions (Jacobsen, et al., 1993) and sequence diagrams are commonly used (Stevens and Pooley, 1999).
Mathematical specifications	These are notations based on mathematical concepts such as finite-state machines or sets. These unambiguous specifications reduce the arguments between customer and contractor about system functionality. However, most customers don't understand formal specifications and are reluctant to accept it as a system contract.

It is essential to write user requirements in a language that non-specialists can understand. However, you can write system requirements in more specialised notations (Figure 6.11). These include stylised, structured natural language, graphical models of the requirements such as use-cases to formal mathematical specifications. In this chapter, I discuss how structured natural language supplemented by simple graphical models may be used to write system requirements. I discuss graphical system modelling in Chapter 8 and formal system specification in Chapter 10.

6.3.1 Structured language specifications

Structured natural language is a way of writing system requirements where the freedom of the requirements writer is limited and all requirements are written in a standard way. The advantage of this approach is that it maintains most of the expressiveness and understandability of natural language but ensures that some degree of uniformity is imposed on the specification. Structured language notations limit the terminology that can be used and use templates to specify system requirements. They may incorporate control constructs derived from programming languages and graphical highlighting to partition the specification.

An early project that used structured natural language for specifying system requirements is described by Heninger (Heninger, 1980). Special-purpose forms were designed to describe the input, output and functions of an aircraft software system. The system requirements were specified using these forms.

Figure 6.12 System
requirements
specification using a
standard form

Insulin Pump/Control Software/SRS/3.3.2

Function	Compute insulin dose: Safe sugar level
Description	Computes the dose of insulin to be delivered when the current measured sugar level is in the safe zone between 3 and 7 units
Inputs	Current sugar reading (r2), the previous two readings (r0 and r1)
Source	Current sugar reading from sensor. Other readings from memory.
Outputs	CompDose—the dose in insulin to be delivered
Destination	Main control loop

Action: CompDose is zero if the sugar level is stable or falling or if the level is increasing but the rate of increase is decreasing. If the level is increasing and the rate of increase is increasing, then CompDose is computed by dividing the difference between the current sugar level and the previous level by 4 and rounding the result. If the result, is rounded to zero then CompDose is set to the minimum dose that can be delivered.

Requires	Two previous readings so that the rate of change of sugar level can be computed.
Pre-condition	The insulin reservoir contains at least the maximum allowed single dose of insulin.
Post-condition	r0 is replaced by r1 then r1 is replaced by r2
Side effects	None

To use a form-based approach to specifying system requirements, you must define one or more standard forms or templates to express the requirements. The specification may be structured around the objects manipulated by the system, the functions performed by the system or the events processed by the system. An example of such a form-based specification is shown in Figure 6.12. I have taken this example from the insulin pump system that was introduced in Chapter 3.

The insulin pump bases its computations of the user's insulin requirement on the rate of change of blood sugar levels. These rates of change computed using the current and previous readings. You can download a complete version of the specification for the insulin pump from the book's web pages.

When a standard form is used for specifying functional requirements, the following information should be included:

1. Description of the function or entity being specified

2. Description of its inputs and where these come from

3. Description of its outputs and where these go to

4. Indication of what other entities are used (the *requires* part)

5. Description of the action to be taken

6. If a functional approach is used, a pre-condition setting out what must be true before the function is called and a post-condition specifying what is true after the function is called

7. Description of the side effects (if any) of the operation.

Using formatted specifications removes some of the problems of natural language specification. Variability in the specification is reduced and requirements are organised more effectively. However, it is difficult to write requirements in an unambiguous way, particularly when complex computations are required. You can see this in the description shown in Figure 6.12, where it isn't made clear what happens if the pre-condition is not satisfied.

To address this problem, you can add extra information to natural language requirements using tables or graphical models of the system. These can show how computations proceed, how the system state changes, how users interact with the system and how sequences of actions are performed.

Tables are particularly useful when there are a number of possible alternative situations and you need to describe the actions to be taken for each of these. Figure 6.13 is a revised description of the computation of the insulin dose.

Graphical models are most useful when you need to show how state changes (see Chapter 8) or where you need to describe a sequence of actions. Figure 6.14 illustrates the sequence of actions when a user wishes to withdraw cash from an automated teller machine (ATM).

You should read a sequence diagram from top to bottom to see the order of the actions that take place. In Figure 6.14, there are three basic sub-sequences:

1. *Validate card* The user's card is validated by checking the card number and user's PIN.

2. *Handle request* The user's request is handled by the system. For a withdrawal, the database must be queried to check the user's balance and to debit the amount withdrawn. Notice the exception here if the requestor does not have enough money in their account.

3. *Complete transaction* The user's card is returned and, when it is removed, the cash and receipt are delivered.

You will see sequence diagrams again in Chapter 8, which covers system models, and in Chapter 14, which covers object-oriented design.

Figure 6.13 Tabular
specification of
computation

Condition	Action
Sugar level falling (r2 < r1)	CompDose = 0
Sugar level stable (r2 = r1)	CompDose = 0
Sugar level increasing and rate of increase decreasing ((r2 − r1) < (r1 − r0))	CompDose = 0
Sugar level increasing and rate of increase stable or increasing. ((r2 − r1) > (r1 − r0))	CompDose = round ((r2 − r1)/4) If rounded result = 0 then CompDose = MinimumDose

Figure 6.14
Sequence diagram of
ATM withdrawal

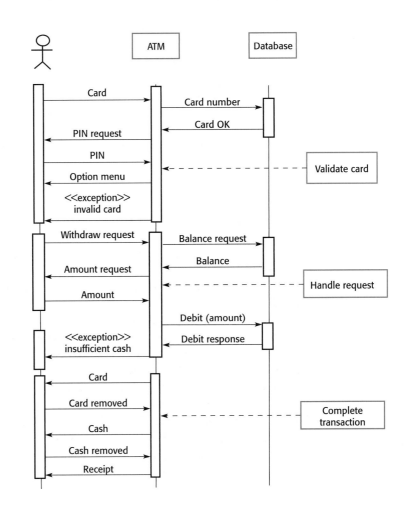

6.4 Interface specification

Almost all software systems must operate with existing systems that have already been implemented and installed in an environment. If the new system and the existing systems must work together, the interfaces of existing systems have to be precisely specified. These specifications should be defined early in the process and included (perhaps as an appendix) in the requirements document.

There are three types of interface that may have to be defined:

1. *Procedural interfaces* where existing programs or sub-systems offer a range of services that are accessed by calling interface procedures. These interfaces are sometimes called Application Programming Interfaces (APIs).

2. *Data structures* that are passed from one sub-system to another. Graphical data models (described in Chapter 8) are the best notations for this type of description. If necessary, program descriptions in Java or C++ can be generated automatically from these descriptions.

3. *Representations of data* (such as the ordering of bits) that have been established for an existing sub-system. These interfaces are most common in embedded, real-time system. Some programming languages such as Ada (although not Java) support this level of specification. However, the best way to describe these is probably to use a diagram of the structure with annotations explaining the function of each group of bits.

Formal notations, discussed in Chapter 10, allow interfaces to be defined in an unambiguous way, but their specialised nature means that they are not understandable without special training. They are rarely used in practice for interface specification although, in my view, they are ideally suited for this purpose. A programming language such as Java can be used to describe the syntax of the interface. However, this has to be supplemented by further description explaining the semantics of each of the defined operations.

Figure 6.15 is an example of a procedural interface definition defined in Java. In this case, the interface is the procedural interface offered by a print server. This manages a queue of requests to print files on different printers. Users may examine the queue associated with a printer and may remove their print jobs from that queue. They may also switch jobs from one printer to another. The specification in Figure 6.15 is an abstract model of the print server that does not reveal any interface details. The functionality of the interface operations can be defined using structured natural language or tabular description.

Figure 6.15 The Java
PDL description of a
print server interface

```
interface PrintServer {

// defines an abstract printer server
// requires: interface Printer, interface PrintDoc
// provides: initialize, print, displayPrintQueue, cancelPrintJob, switchPrinter

    void initialize ( Printer p ) ;
    void print ( Printer p, PrintDoc d ) ;
    void displayPrintQueue ( Printer p ) ;
    void cancelPrintJob (Printer p, PrintDoc d) ;
    void switchPrinter (Printer p1, Printer p2, PrintDoc d) ;
} //PrintServer
```

6.5 The software requirements document

The software requirements document (sometimes called the software requirements specification or SRS) is the official statement of what the system developers should implement. It should include both the user requirements for a system and a detailed specification of the system requirements. In some cases, the user and system requirements may be integrated into a single description. In other cases, the user requirements are defined in an introduction to the system requirements specification. If there are a large number of requirements, the detailed system requirements may be presented in a separate document.

The requirements document has a diverse set of users, ranging from the senior management of the organisation that is paying for the system to the engineers responsible for developing the software. Figure 6.16, taken from my book with Gerald Kotonya on requirements engineering (Kotonya and Sommerville, 1998) illustrates possible users of the document and how they use it.

The diversity of possible users means that the requirements document has to be a compromise between communicating the requirements to customers, defining the requirements in precise detail for developers and testers, and including information about possible system evolution. Information on anticipated changes can help system designers avoid restrictive design decisions and help system maintenance engineers who have to adapt the system to new requirements.

The level of detail that you should include in a requirements document depends on the type of system that is being developed and the development process used. When the system will be developed by an external contractor, critical system specifications need to be precise and very detailed. When there is more flexibility in the requirements and where an in-house, iterative development process is used, the requirements document can be much less detailed and any ambiguities resolved during development of the system.

A number of large organisations, such as the US Department of Defense and the IEEE, have defined standards for requirements documents. Davis (Davis, 1993) discusses some of these standards and compares their contents. The most widely known

Figure 6.16 Users of
a requirements
document

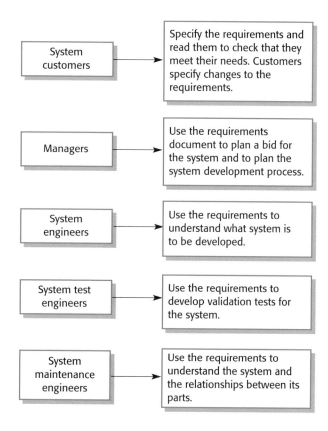

standard is IEEE/ANSI 830-1998 (IEEE, 1998). This IEEE standard suggests the
following structure for requirements documents:

1. **Introduction**
   1.1   Purpose of the requirements document
   1.2   Scope of the product
   1.3   Definitions, acronyms and abbreviations
   1.4   References
   1.5   Overview of the remainder of the document

2. **General description**
   2.1   Product perspective
   2.2   Product functions
   2.3   User characteristics
   2.4   General constraints
   2.5   Assumptions and dependencies

3. **Specific requirements** cover functional, non-functional and interface requirements. This is obviously the most substantial part of the document but because

of the wide variability in organisational practice, it is not appropriate to define a standard structure for this section. The requirements may document external interfaces, describe system functionality and performance, specify logical database requirements, design constraints, emergent system properties and quality characteristics.

4. **Appendices**

5. **Index**

Although the IEEE standard is not ideal, it contains a great deal of good advice on how to write requirements and how to avoid problems. It is too general to be an organisational standard in its own right. It is a general framework that can be tailored and adapted to define a standard geared to the needs of a particular organisation. Figure 6.17 illustrates a possible organisation for a requirements document that is based on the IEEE standard. However, I have extended this to include information about predicted system evolution. This was first proposed by Heninger (Heninger, 1980) and, as I have discussed, helps the maintainers of the system and may allow designers to include support for future system features.

Of course, the information that is included in a requirements document must depend on the type of software being developed and the approach to development that is used. If an evolutionary approach is adopted for a software product (say), the requirements document will leave out many of detailed chapters suggested above. The focus will be on defining the user requirements and high-level, non-functional system requirements. In this case, the designers and programmers use their judgement to decide how to meet the outline user requirements for the system.

By contrast, when the software is part of a large system engineering project that includes interacting hardware and software systems, it is often essential to define the requirements to a fine level of detail. This means that the requirements documents are likely to be very long and should include most if not all of the chapters shown in Figure 6.17. For long documents, it is particularly important to include a comprehensive table of contents and document index so that readers can find the information that they need.

Requirements documents are essential when an outside contractor is developing the software system. However, agile development methods argue that requirements change so rapidly that a requirements document is out of date as soon as it is written, so the effort that is largely wasted. Rather than a formal document, approaches such as extreme programming (Beck, 1999) propose that user requirements should be collected incrementally and written on cards. The user then prioritises requirements for implementation in the next increment of the system.

For business systems where requirements are unstable, I think that this approach is a good one. However, I would argue that it is still useful to write a short supporting document that defines the business and dependability requirements for the system. It is easy to forget the requirements that apply to the system as a whole when focusing on the functional requirements for the next system release.

Figure 6.17
The structure
of a requirements
document

Chapter	Description
Preface	This should define the expected readership of the document and describe its version history, including a rationale for the creation of a new version and a summary of the changes made in each version.
Introduction	This should describe the need for the system. It should briefly describe its functions and explain how it will work with other systems. It should describe how the system fits into the overall business or strategic objectives of the organisation commissioning the software.
Glossary	This should define the technical terms used in the document. You should not make assumptions about the experience or expertise of the reader.
User requirements definition	The services provided for the user and the non-functional system requirements should be described in this section. This description may use natural language, diagrams or other notations that are understandable by customers. Product and process standards which must be followed should be specified.
System architecture	This chapter should present a high-level overview of the anticipated system architecture showing the distribution of functions across system modules. Architectural components that are reused should be highlighted.
System requirements specification	This should describe the functional and non-functional requirements in more detail. If necessary, further detail may also be added to the non-functional requirements, e.g. interfaces to other systems may be defined.
System models	This should set out one or more system models showing the relationships between the system components and the system and its environment. These might be object models, data-flow models and semantic data models.
System evolution	This should describe the fundamental assumptions on which the system is based and anticipated changes due to hardware evolution, changing user needs, etc.
Appendices	These should provide detailed, specific information which is related to the application which is being developed. Examples of appendices that may be included are hardware and database descriptions. Hardware requirements define the minimal and optimal configurations for the system. Database requirements define the logical organisation of the data used by the system and the relationships between data.
Index	Several indexes to the document may be included. As well as a normal alphabetic index, there may be an index of diagrams, an index of functions, etc.

KEY POINTS

■ Requirements for a software system set out what the system should do and define constraints on its operation and implementation.

■ Functional requirements are statements of the services that the system must provide or are descriptions of how some computations must be carried out. Domain requirements are functional requirements that are derived from characteristics of the application domain.

■ Non-functional requirements constrain the system being developed and the development process that should be used. They may be product requirements, organisational requirements or external requirements. They often relate to the emergent properties of the system and therefore apply to the system as a whole.

■ User requirements are intended for use by people involved in using and procuring the system. They should be written using in natural language, with tables and diagrams that are easily understood.

■ System requirements are intended to communicate, in a precise way, the functions that the system must provide. To reduce ambiguity, they may be written in a structured form of natural language supplemented by tables and system models.

■ The software requirements document is the agreed statement of the system requirements. It should be organised so that both system customers and software developers can use it.

■ The IEEE standard for requirements documents is a useful starting point for more specific requirements specification standards.

FURTHER READING

Software Requirements, 2nd ed. This book, designed for writers and users of requirements, discusses good requirements engineering practice. (K. M. Weigers, 2003, Microsoft Press.)

Mastering the Requirements Process. A well-written, easy-to-read book that is based on a particular method (VOLERE) but which also includes lots of good general advice about requirements engineering. (S. Robertson and J. Robertson, 1999, Addison-Wesley.)

Requirements Engineering: Processes and Techniques. This book covers all aspects of the requirements engineering process and discusses specific requirements specification techniques. (G. Kotonya and I. Sommerville, 1999, John Wiley & Sons.)

Software Requirements Engineering. This collection of papers on requirements engineering includes several relevant articles such as 'Recommended Practice for Software Requirements Specification', a discussion of the IEEE standard for requirements documents. (R. H. Thayer and M. Dorfman (eds.), 1997, IEEE Computer Society Press.)

EXERCISES

6.1 Identify and briefly describe four types of requirements that may be defined for a computer-based system

6.2 Discuss the problems of using natural language for defining user and system requirements, and show, using small examples, how structuring natural language into forms can help avoid some of these difficulties.

6.3 Discover ambiguities or omissions in the following statement of requirements for part of a ticket-issuing system.

An automated ticket-issuing system sells rail tickets. Users select their destination and input a credit card and a personal identification number. The rail ticket is issued and their credit card account charged. When the user presses the start button, a menu display of potential destinations is activated, along with a message to the user to select a destination. Once a destination has been selected, users are requested to input their credit card. Its validity is checked and the user is then requested to input a personal identifier. When the credit transaction has been validated, the ticket is issued.

6.4 Rewrite the above description using the structured approach described in this chapter. Resolve the identified ambiguities in some appropriate way.

6.5 Draw a sequence diagram showing the actions performed in the ticket-issuing system. You may make any reasonable assumptions about the system. Pay particular attention to specifying user errors.

6.6 Using the technique suggested here, where natural language is presented in a standard way, write plausible user requirements for the following functions:

- The cash-dispensing function in a bank ATM

- The spelling-check and correcting function in a word processor

- An unattended petrol (gas) pump system that includes a credit card reader. The customer swipes the card through the reader and then specifies the amount of fuel required. The fuel is delivered and the customer's account debited.

6.7 Describe four types of non-functional requirements that may be placed on a system. Give examples of each of these types of requirement.

6.8 Write a set of non-functional requirements for the ticket-issuing system, setting out its expected reliability and its response time.

6.9 Suggest how an engineer responsible for drawing up a system requirements specification might keep track of the relationships between functional and non-functional requirements.

6.10 You have taken a job with a software user who has contracted your previous employer to develop a system for them. You discover that your company's interpretation of the requirements is different from the interpretation taken by your previous employer. Discuss what you should do in such a situation. You know that the costs to your current employer will increase if the ambiguities are not resolved. You have also a responsibility of confidentiality to your previous employer.

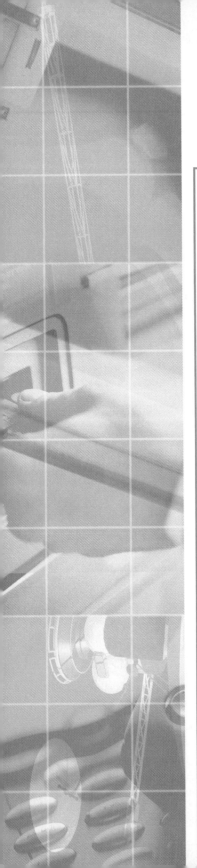

7

Requirements
engineering processes

Objectives

The objective of this chapter is to discuss the activities involved in the requirements engineering process. When you have read this chapter, you will:

- understand the principal requirements of engineering activities and their relationships;

- have been introduced to several techniques of requirements elicitation and analysis;

- understand the importance of requirements validation and how requirements reviews are used in this process;

- understand why requirements management is necessary and how it supports other requirements engineering activities.

Contents

The goal of the requirements engineering process is to create and maintain a system requirements document. The overall process includes four high-level requirements engineering sub-processes. These are concerned with assessing whether the system is useful to the business (feasibility study); discovering requirements (elicitation and analysis); converting these requirements into some standard form (specification); and checking that the requirements actually define the system that the customer wants (validation). Figure 7.1 illustrates the relationship between these activities. It also shows the documents produced at each stage of the requirements engineering process. Specification and documentation are covered in Chapter 6; this chapter concentrates on the other requirements engineering activities.

The activities shown in Figure 7.1 are concerned with the discovery, documentation and checking of requirements. In virtually all systems, however, requirements change. The people involved develop a better understanding of what they want the software to do; the organisation buying the system changes; modifications are made to the system's hardware, software and organisational environment. The process of managing these changing requirements is called requirements management, which is covered in the final section of this chapter.

I present an alternative perspective on the requirements engineering process in Figure 7.2. This presents the process as a three-stage activity where the activities are organised as an iterative process around a spiral. The amount of time and effort devoted to each activity in an iteration depends on the stage of the overall process and the type of system being developed. Early in the process, most effort will be spent on understanding high-level business and non-functional requirements and the user requirements. Later in the process, in the outer rings of the spiral, more effort will be devoted to system requirements engineering and system modelling.

This spiral model accommodates approaches to development in which the requirements are developed to different levels of detail. The number of iterations around the spiral can vary, so the spiral can be exited after some or all of the user requirements have been elicited. If the prototyping activity shown under requirements validation

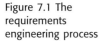

Figure 7.1 The requirements engineering process

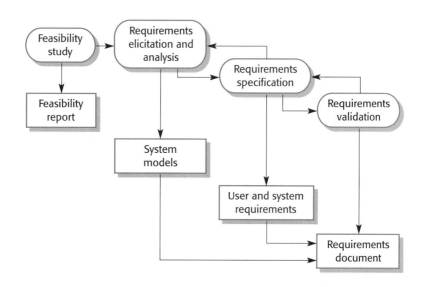

Figure 7.2 Spiral
model of
requirements
engineering
processes

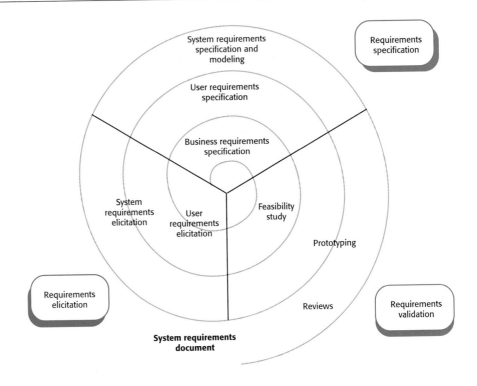

is extended to include iterative development, as discussed in Chapter 17, this model
allows the requirements and the system implementation to be developed together.

Some people consider requirements engineering to be the process of applying a
structured analysis method such as object-oriented analysis (Larman, 2002). This
involves analysing the system and developing a set of graphical system models, such
as use-case models, that then serve as a system specification. The set of models
describes the behaviour of the system and are annotated with additional information describing, for example, its required performance or reliability.

Although structured methods have a role to play in the requirements engineering process, there is much more to requirements engineering than is covered by these methods. Requirements elicitation, in particular, is a human-centred activity and people dislike
the constraints imposed by rigid system models. I focus on general approaches to requirements engineering here and cover structured methods and system models in Chapter 8.

7.1 Feasibility studies

For all new systems, the requirements engineering process should start with a feasibility study. The input to the feasibility study is a set of preliminary business requirements, an outline description of the system and how the system is intended to support

business processes. The results of the feasibility study should be a report that recommends whether or not it is worth carrying on with the requirements engineering and system development process.

A feasibility study is a short, focused study that aims to answer a number of questions:

1. Does the system contribute to the overall objectives of the organisation?

2. Can the system be implemented using current technology and within given cost and schedule constraints?

3. Can the system be integrated with other systems which are already in place?

The issue of whether or not the system contributes to business objectives is critical. If a system does not support these objectives, it has no real value to the business. While this may seem obvious, many organisations develop systems which do not contribute to their objectives because they don't have a clear statement of these objectives, because they fail to define the business requirements for the system or because other political or organisation factors influence the system procurement. Although this is not discussed explicitly, a feasibility study should be part of the Inception phase in the Rational Unified Process, as discussed in Chapter 4.

Carrying out a feasibility study involves information assessment, information collection and report writing. The information assessment phase identifies the information that is required to answer the three questions set out above. Once the information has been identified, you should talk with information sources to discover the answers to these questions. Some examples of possible questions that may be put are:

1. How would the organisation cope if this system were not implemented?

2. What are the problems with current processes and how would a new system help alleviate these problems?

3. What direct contribution will the system make to the business objectives and requirements?

4. Can information be transferred to and from other organisational systems?

5. Does the system require technology that has not previously been used in the organisation?

6. What must be supported by the system and what need not be supported?

In a feasibility study, you may consult information sources such as the managers of the departments where the system will be used, software engineers who are familiar with the type of system that is proposed, technology experts and end-users of the system. Normally, you should try to complete a feasibility study in two or three weeks.

Once you have the information, you write the feasibility study report. You should make a recommendation about whether or not the system development should continue. In the report, you may propose changes to the scope, budget and schedule of the system and suggest further high-level requirements for the system.

7.2 Requirements elicitation and analysis

The next stage of the requirements engineering process is requirements elicitation and analysis. In this activity, software engineers work with customers and system end-users to find out about the application domain, what services the system should provide, the required performance of the system, hardware constraints, and so on.

Requirements elicitation and analysis may involve a variety of people in an organisation. The term *stakeholder* is used to refer to any person or group who will be affected by the system, directly or indirectly. Stakeholders include end-users who interact with the system and everyone else in an organisation that may be affected by its installation. Other system stakeholders may be engineers who are developing or maintaining related systems, business managers, domain experts and trade union representatives.

Eliciting and understanding stakeholder requirements is difficult for several reasons:

1. Stakeholders often don't know what they want from the computer system except in the most general terms. They may find it difficult to articulate what they want the system to do or make unrealistic demands because they are unaware of the cost of their requests.

2. Stakeholders naturally express requirements in their own terms and with implicit knowledge of their own work. Requirements engineers, without experience in the customer's domain, must understand these requirements.

3. Different stakeholders have different requirements, which they may express in different ways. Requirements engineers have to consider all potential sources of requirements and discover commonalities and conflict.

4. Political factors may influence the requirements of the system. For example, managers may demand specific system requirements that will increase their influence in the organisation.

5. The economic and business environment in which the analysis takes place is dynamic. It inevitably changes during the analysis process. Hence the importance of particular requirements may change. New requirements may emerge from new stakeholders who were not originally consulted.

A very general process model of the elicitation and analysis process is shown in Figure 7.3. Each organisation will have its own version or instantiation of this

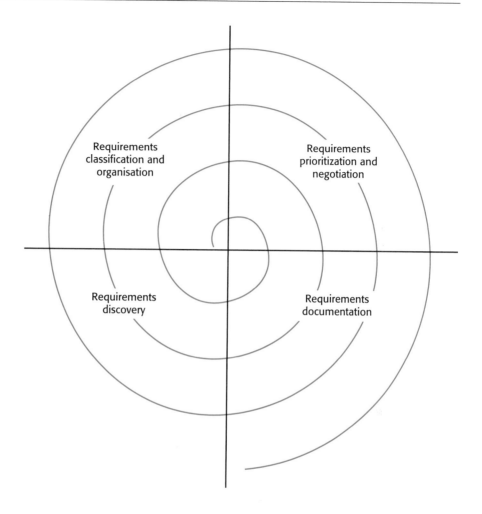

Figure 7.3 The requirements elicitation and analysis process

general model, depending on local factors such as the expertise of the staff, the type of system being developed and the standards used. Again, you can think of these activities within a spiral so that the activities are interleaved as the process proceeds from the inner to the outer rings of the spiral.

The process activities are:

1. *Requirements discovery* This is the process of interacting with stakeholders in the system to collect their requirements. Domain requirements from stakeholders and documentation are also discovered during this activity.

2. *Requirements classification and organisation* This activity takes the unstructured collection of requirements, groups related requirements and organises them into coherent clusters.

3. *Requirements prioritisation and negotiation* Inevitably, where multiple stakeholders are involved, requirements will conflict. This activity is concerned with

prioritising requirements, and finding and resolving requirements conflicts through negotiation.

4. *Requirements documentation* The requirements are documented and input into the next round of the spiral. Formal or informal requirements documents may be produced.

Figure 7.3 shows that requirements elicitation and analysis is an iterative process with continual feedback from each activity to other activities. The process cycle starts with requirements discovery and ends with requirements documentation. The analyst's understanding of the requirements improves with each round of the cycle.

In this chapter, I focus primarily on requirements discovery and the various techniques that have been developed to support this. Requirements classification and organization is primarily concerned with identifying overlapping requirements from different stakeholders and grouping related requirements. The most common way of grouping requirements is to use a model of the system architecture to identify subsystems and to associate requirements with each sub-system. This emphasises that requirements engineering and architectural design cannot always be separated.

Inevitably, stakeholders have different views on the importance and priority of requirements, and sometimes these views conflict. During the process, you should organise regular stakeholder negotiations so that compromises can be reached. It is impossible to completely satisfy every stakeholder, but if some stakeholders feel that their views have not been properly considered, they may deliberately attempt to undermine the RE process.

In the requirements documentation stage, the requirements that have been elicited are documented in such a way that they can be used to help with further requirements discovery. At this stage, an early version of the system requirements document may be produced, but it will have missing sections and incomplete requirements. Alternatively, the requirements may be documented as tables in a document or on cards. Writing requirements on cards (the approach used in extreme programming) can be very effective, as these are easy for stakeholders to handle, change and organise.

7.2.1   Requirements discovery

Requirements discovery is the process of gathering information about the proposed and existing systems and distilling the user and system requirements from this information. Sources of information during the requirements discovery phase include documentation, system stakeholders and specifications of similar systems. You interact with stakeholders through interviews and observation, and may use scenarios and prototypes to help with the requirements discovery. In this section, I discuss an approach that helps ensure you get broad stakeholder coverage when discovering requirements, and I describe techniques of requirements discovery including interviewing, scenarios and ethnography. Other requirements discovery techniques that may be used include structured analysis methods, covered in Chapter 8, and system prototyping, covered in Chapter 17.

Stakeholders range from system end-users through managers and external stakeholders such as regulators who certify the acceptability of the system. For example, system stakeholders for a bank ATM include:

1. *Current bank customers* who receive services from the system

2. *Representatives from other banks* who have reciprocal agreements that allow each other's ATMs to be used

3. *Managers of bank branches* who obtain management information from the system

4. *Counter staff at bank branches* who are involved in the day-to-day running of the system

5. *Database administrators* who are responsible for integrating the system with the bank's customer database

6. *Bank security managers* who must ensure that the system will not pose a security hazard

7. *The bank's marketing department* who are likely be interested in using the system as a means of marketing the bank

8. *Hardware and software maintenance engineers* who are responsible for maintaining and upgrading the hardware and software

9. *National banking regulators* who are responsible for ensuring that the system conforms to banking regulations

In addition to system stakeholders, we have already seen that requirements may come from the application domain and from other systems that interact with the system being specified. All of these must be considered during the requirements elicitation process.

These requirements sources (stakeholders, domain, systems) can all be represented as system viewpoints, where each viewpoint presents a sub-set of the requirements for the system. Each viewpoint provides a fresh perspective on the system, but these perspectives are not completely independent—they usually overlap so that they have common requirements.

Viewpoints

Viewpoint-oriented approaches to requirements engineering (Mullery, 1979; Finkelstein et al., 1992; Kotonya and Sommerville, 1992; Kotonya and Sommerville, 1996) organise both the elicitation process and the requirements themselves using viewpoints. A key strength of viewpoint-oriented analysis is that it recognises multiple perspectives and provides a framework for discovering conflicts in the requirements proposed by different stakeholders.

Viewpoints can be used as a way of classifying stakeholders and other sources of requirements. There are three generic types of viewpoint:

1. *Interactor viewpoints* represent people or other systems that interact directly with the system. In the bank ATM system, examples of interactor viewpoints are the bank's customers and the bank's account database.

2. *Indirect viewpoints* represent stakeholders who do not use the system themselves but who influence the requirements in some way. In the bank ATM system, examples of indirect viewpoints are the management of the bank and the bank security staff.

3. *Domain viewpoints* represent domain characteristics and constraints that influence the system requirements. In the bank ATM system, an example of a domain viewpoint would be the standards that have been developed for interbank communications.

Typically, these viewpoints provide different types of requirements. Interactor viewpoints provide detailed system requirements covering the system features and interfaces. Indirect viewpoints are more likely to provide higher-level organisational requirements and constraints. Domain viewpoints normally provide domain constraints that apply to the system.

The initial identification of viewpoints that are relevant to a system can sometimes be difficult. To help with this process, you should try to identify more specific viewpoint types:

1. Providers of services to the system and receivers of system services

2. Systems that should interface directly with the system being specified

3. Regulations and standards that apply to the system

4. The sources of system business and non-functional requirements

5. Engineering viewpoints reflecting the requirements of people who have to develop, manage and maintain the system

6. Marketing and other viewpoints that generate requirements on the product features expected by customers and how the system should reflect the external image of the organisation

Almost all organisational systems must interoperate with other systems in the organisation. When a new system is planned, the interactions with other systems must be planned. The interfaces offered by these other systems have already been designed. These may place requirements and constraints on the new system. Furthermore, new systems may have to conform to existing regulations and standards, and these constrain the system requirements.

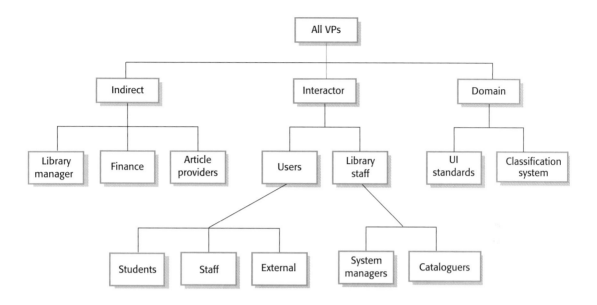

Figure 7.4
Viewpoints in LIBSYS

As I discussed earlier in the chapter, you should identify high-level business and non-functional requirements early in the RE process. The sources of these requirements may be useful viewpoints in a more detailed process. They may be able to expand and develop the high-level requirements into more specific system requirements.

Engineering viewpoints may be important for two reasons. Firstly, the engineers developing the system may have experience with similar systems and may be able to suggest requirements from that experience. Secondly, technical staff who have to manage and maintain the system may have requirements that will help simplify system support. System management requirements are increasingly important because system management costs are an increasing proportion of the total lifetime costs for a system.

Finally, viewpoints that provide requirements may come from the marketing and external affairs departments in an organisation. This is especially true for web-based systems, particularly e-commerce systems and shrink-wrapped software products. Web-based systems must present a favourable image of the organisation as well as deliver functionality to the user. For software products, the marketing department should know what system features will make the system more marketable to potential buyers.

For any non-trivial system, there are a huge number of possible viewpoints, and it is practically impossible to elicit requirements from all of them. Therefore, it is important that you organise and structure the viewpoints into a hierarchy. Viewpoints in the same branch are likely to share common requirements.

As an illustration, consider the viewpoint hierarchy shown in Figure 7.4. This is a relatively simple diagram of the viewpoints that may be consulted in deriving the requirements for the LIBSYS system. You can see that the classification of interactor, indirect and domain viewpoints helps identify sources of requirements apart from the immediate users of the system.

Once viewpoints have been identified and structured, you should try to identify the most important viewpoints and start with them when discovering system requirements.

Interviewing

Formal or informal interviews with system stakeholders are part of most requirements engineering processes. In these interviews, the requirements engineering team puts questions to stakeholders about the system that they use and the system to be developed. Requirements are derived from the answers to these questions. Interviews may be of two types:

1. Closed interviews where the stakeholder answers a predefined set of questions.

2. Open interviews where there is no predefined agenda. The requirements engineering team explores a range of issues with system stakeholders and hence develops a better understanding of their needs.

In practice, interviews with stakeholders are normally a mix of these. The answers to some questions may lead to other issues that are discussed in a less structured way. Completely open-ended discussions rarely work well; most interviews require some questions to get started and to keep the interview focused on the system to be developed.

Interviews are good for getting an overall understanding of what stakeholders do, how they might interact with the system and the difficulties that they face with current systems. People like talking about their work and are usually happy to get involved in interviews. However, interviews are not so good for understanding the requirements from the application domain.

It is hard to elicit domain knowledge during interviews for two reasons:

1. All application specialists use terminology and jargon that is specific to a domain. It is impossible for them to discuss domain requirements without using this terminology. They normally use terminology in a precise and subtle way that is easy for requirements engineers to misunderstand.

2. Some domain knowledge is so familiar to stakeholders that they either find it difficult to explain or they think it is so fundamental that it isn't worth mentioning. For example, for a librarian, it goes without saying that all acquisitions are catalogued before they are added to the library. However, this may not be obvious to the interviewer so it isn't taken into account in the requirements.

Interviews are not an effective technique for eliciting knowledge about organisational requirements and constraints because there are subtle power and influence relationships between the stakeholders in the organisation. Published organisational structures rarely match the reality of decision making in an organisation, but interviewees may not wish to reveal the actual rather than the theoretical structure to a stranger. In general, most people are reluctant to discuss political and organisational issues that may affect the requirements.

Effective interviewers have two characteristics:

1. They are open-minded, avoid preconceived ideas about the requirements and are willing to listen to stakeholders. If the stakeholder comes up with surprising requirements, they are willing to change their mind about the system.

2. They prompt the interviewee to start discussions with a question, a requirements proposal or by suggesting working together on a prototype system. Saying to people 'tell me what you want' is unlikely to result in useful information. Most people find it much easier to talk in a defined context rather than in general terms.

Information from interviews supplements other information about the system from documents, user observations, and so on. Sometimes, apart from information from documents, interviews may be the only source of information about the system requirements. However, interviewing on its own is liable to miss essential information, so it should be used alongside other requirements elicitation techniques.

Scenarios

People usually find it easier to relate to real-life examples than to abstract descriptions. They can understand and critique a scenario of how they might interact with a software system. Requirements engineers can use the information gained from this discussion to formulate the actual system requirements.

Scenarios can be particularly useful for adding detail to an outline requirements description. They are descriptions of example interaction sessions. Each scenario covers one or more possible interactions. Several forms of scenarios have been developed, each of which provides different types of information at different levels of detail about the system. Using scenarios to describe requirements is an integral part of agile methods, such as extreme programming, that I discuss in Chapter 17.

The scenario starts with an outline of the interaction, and, during elicitation, details are added to create a complete description of that interaction. At its most general, a scenario may include:

1. A description of what the system and users expect when the scenario starts

2. A description of the normal flow of events in the scenario

3. A description of what can go wrong and how this is handled

4. Information about other activities that might be going on at the same time

5. A description of the system state when the scenario finishes.

Figure 7.5 Scenario
for article
downloading in
LIBSYS

Initial assumption: The user has logged on to the LIBSYS system and has located the journal containing the copy of the article.

Normal: The user selects the article to be copied. The system prompts the user to provide subscriber information for the journal or to indicate a method of payment for the article. Payment can be made by credit card or by quoting an organisational account number.

The user is then asked to fill in a copyright form that maintains details of the transaction and submit it to the LIBSYS system.

The copyright form is checked and, if it is approved, the PDF version of the article is downloaded to the LIBSYS working area on the user's computer and the user is informed that it is available. The user is asked to select a printer and a copy of the article is printed. If the article has been flagged as 'print-only' it is deleted from the user's system once the user has confirmed that printing is complete.

What can go wrong: The user may fail to fill in the copyright form correctly. In this case, the form should be re-presented to the user for correction. If the resubmitted form is still incorrect, then the user's request for the article is rejected.

The payment may be rejected by the system, in which case the user's request for the article is rejected.

The article download may fail, causing the system to retry until successful or the user terminates the session.

It may not be possible to print the article. If the article is not flagged as 'print-only' it is held in the LIBSYS workspace. Otherwise, the article is deleted and the user's account credited with the cost of the article.

Other activities: Simultaneous downloads of other articles.

System state on completion: User is logged on. The downloaded article has been deleted from LIBSYS workspace if it has been flagged as print-only.

Scenario-based elicitation can be carried out informally, where the requirements engineer works with stakeholders to identify scenarios and to capture details of these scenarios. Scenarios may be written as text, supplemented by diagrams, screen shots, and so on. Alternatively, a more structured approach such as event scenarios or use-cases may be adopted.

As an example of a simple text scenario, consider how a user of the LIBSYS library system may use the system. This scenario is shown in Figure 7.5. The user wishes to print a personal copy of an article in a medical journal. This journal makes copies of articles available free to subscribers, but nonsubscribers have to pay a fee per article. The user knows the article, title and date of publication.

Use-cases

Use-cases are a scenario-based technique for requirements elicitation which were first introduced in the Objectory method (Jacobsen, et al., 1993). They have now

Figure 7.6 A simple use-case for article printing

Article printing

become a fundamental feature of the UML notation for describing object-oriented system models. In their simplest form, a use-case identifies the type of interaction and the actors involved . For example, Figure 7.6 shows the high-level use-case of the article printing facility in LIBSYS described in Figure 7.5.

Figure 7.6 illustrates the essentials of the use-case notation. Actors in the process are represented as stick figures, and each class of interaction is represented as a named ellipse. The set of use-cases represents all of the possible interactions to be represented in the system requirements. Figure 7.7 develops the LIBSYS example and shows other use-cases in that environment.

There is sometimes confusion about whether a use-case is a scenario on its own or, as suggested by Fowler (Fowler and Scott, 1997), a use-case encapsulates a set of scenarios, and each scenario is a single thread through the use-case. If a scenario includes multiple threads, there would be a scenario for the normal interaction plus scenarios for each possible exception.

Use-cases identify the individual interactions with the system. They can be documented with text or linked to UML models that develop the scenario in more detail. Sequence diagrams (introduced in Chapter 6) are often used to add information to a use-case. These sequence diagrams show the actors involved in the interaction, the objects they interact with and the operations associated with these objects.

As an illustration of this, Figure 7.8 shows the interactions involved in using LIBSYS for downloading and printing an article. In Figure 7.8, there are four objects of classes—Article, Form, Workspace and Printer—involved in this interaction. The sequence of actions is from top to bottom, and the labels on the arrows between the actors and objects indicate the names of operations. Essentially, a user request for an article triggers a request for a copyright form. Once the user has completed the form, the article is downloaded and sent to the printer. Once printing is complete, the article is deleted from the LIBSYS workspace.

The UML is a *de facto* standard for object-oriented modelling, so use-cases and use-case–based elicitation is increasingly used for requirements elicitation. Other types of UML models are discussed in Chapter 8, which covers system modelling, and in Chapter 14, which covers object-oriented design.

Scenarios and use-cases are effective techniques for eliciting requirements for interactor viewpoints, where each type of interaction can be represented as a use-case. They can also be used in conjunction with some indirect viewpoints where these viewpoints receive some results (such as a management report) from the system. However, because they focus on interactions, they are not as effective for eliciting constraints or high-level business and non-functional requirements from indirect viewpoints or for discovering domain requirements.

Figure 7.7 Use cases
for the library system

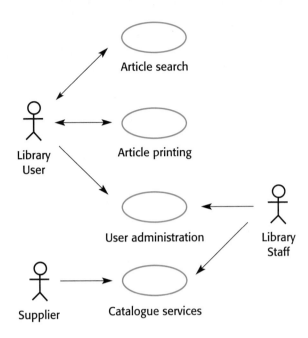

Article search

Library
User

Article printing

User administration

Library
Staff

Supplier

Catalogue services

Figure 7.8 System
interactions for
article printing

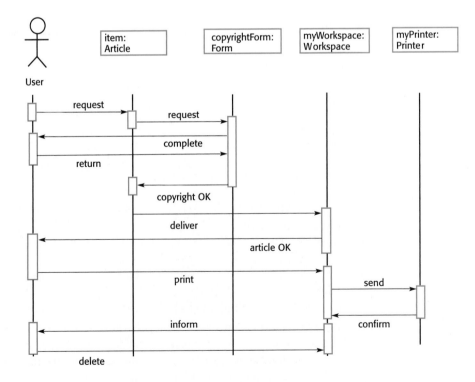

7.2.2   Ethnography

Software systems do not exist in isolation—they are used in a social and organisational context, and software system requirements may be derived or constrained by that context. Satisfying these social and organisational requirements is often critical for the success of the system. One reason why many software systems are delivered but never used is that they do not take proper account of the importance of these requirements.

Ethnography is an observational technique that can be used to understand social and organisational requirements. An analyst immerses him or herself in the working environment where the system will be used. He or she observes the day-to-day work and notes made of the actual tasks in which participants are involved. The value of ethnography is that it helps analysts discover implicit system requirements that reflect the actual rather than the formal processes in which people are involved.

People often find it very difficult to articulate details of their work because it is second nature to them. They understand their own work but may not understand its relationship with other work in the organisation. Social and organisational factors that affect the work but that are not obvious to individuals may only become clear when noticed by an unbiased observer.

Suchman (Suchman, 1987) used ethnography to study office work and found that the actual work practices were far richer, more complex and more dynamic than the simple models assumed by office automation systems. The difference between the assumed and the actual work was the most important reason why these office systems have had no significant effect on productivity. Other ethnographic studies for system requirements understanding have included work on air traffic control (Bentley, et al., 1992; Hughes, et al., 1993), underground railway control rooms (Heath and Luff, 1992), financial systems and various design activities (Heath, et al., 1993; Hughes, et al., 1994). In my own research, I have investigated methods of integrating ethnography into the software engineering process by linking it to requirements engineering methods (Viller and Sommerville, 1999; Viller and Sommerville, 1998; Viller and Sommerville, 2000) and by documenting patterns of interaction in cooperative systems (Martin, et al., 2001; Martin, et al., 2002; Martin and Sommerville, 2004).

Ethnography is particularly effective at discovering two types of requirements:

1. *Requirements that are derived from the way in which people actually work* rather than the way in which process definitions say they ought to work. For example, air traffic controllers may switch off an aircraft conflict alert system that detects aircraft with intersecting flight paths even though normal control procedures specify that it should be used. Their control strategy is designed to ensure that these aircraft are moved apart before problems occur and they find that the conflict alert alarm distracts them from their work.

2. *Requirements that are derived from cooperation and awareness of other people's activities.* For example, air traffic controllers may use an awareness of other controllers' work to predict the number of aircraft that will be entering

Figure 7.9
Ethnography and
prototyping for
requirements
analysis

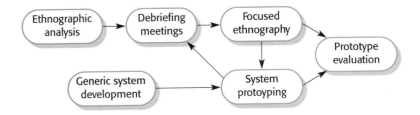

their control sector. They then modify their control strategies depending on that predicted workload. Therefore, an automated ATC system should allow controllers in a sector to have some visibility of the work in adjacent sectors.

Ethnography may be combined with prototyping (Figure 7.9). The ethnography informs the development of the prototype so that fewer prototype refinement cycles are required. Furthermore, the prototyping focuses the ethnography by identifying problems and questions that can then be discussed with the ethnographer. He or she should then look for the answers to these questions during the next phase of the system study (Sommerville, et al., 1993).

Ethnographic studies can reveal critical process details that are often missed by other requirements elicitation techniques. However, because of its focus on the end-user, this approach is not appropriate for discovering organisational or domain requirements. Ethnographic studies cannot always identify new features that should be added to a system. Ethnography is not, therefore, a complete approach to elicitation on its own, and it should be used to complement other approaches, such as use-case analysis.

7.3 Requirements validation

Requirements validation is concerned with showing that the requirements actually define the system that the customer wants. Requirements validation overlaps analysis in that it is concerned with finding problems with the requirements. Requirements validation is important because errors in a requirements document can lead to extensive rework costs when they are discovered during development or after the system is in service. The cost of fixing a requirements problem by making a system change is much greater than repairing design or coding errors. The reason for this is that a change to the requirements usually means that the system design and implementation must also be changed and then the system must be tested again.

During the requirements validation process, checks should be carried out on the requirements in the requirements document. These checks include:

1. *Validity checks* A user may think that a system is needed to perform certain functions. However, further thought and analysis may identify additional or different functions that are required. Systems have diverse stakeholders with distinct needs, and any set of requirements is inevitably a compromise across the stakeholder community.

2. *Consistency checks* Requirements in the document should not conflict. That is, there should be no contradictory constraints or descriptions of the same system function.

3. *Completeness checks* The requirements document should include requirements, which define all functions, and constraints intended by the system user.

4. *Realism checks* Using knowledge of existing technology, the requirements should be checked to ensure that they could actually be implemented. These checks should also take account of the budget and schedule for the system development.

5. *Verifiability* To reduce the potential for dispute between customer and contractor, system requirements should always be written so that they are verifiable. This means that you should be able to write a set of tests that can demonstrate that the delivered system meets each specified requirement.

A number of requirements validation techniques can be used in conjunction or individually:

1. *Requirements reviews* The requirements are analysed systematically by a team of reviewers. This process is discussed in the following section.

2. *Prototyping* In this approach to validation, an executable model of the system is demonstrated to end-users and customers. They can experiment with this model to see if it meets their real needs. I discuss prototyping and prototyping techniques in Chapter 17.

3. *Test-case generation* Requirements should be testable. If the tests for the requirements are devised as part of the validation process, this often reveals requirements problems. If a test is difficult or impossible to design, this usually means that the requirements will be difficult to implement and should be reconsidered. Developing tests from the user requirements before any code is written is an integral part of extreme programming.

You should not underestimate the problems of requirements validation. It is difficult to show that a set of requirements meets a user's needs. Users must picture the system in operation and imagine how that system would fit into their work. It is hard for skilled computer professionals to perform this type of abstract analysis and even harder for system users. As a result, you rarely find all requirements problems during the requirements validation process. It is inevitable that there will be further requirements changes to correct omissions and misunderstandings after the requirements document has been agreed upon.

7.3.1   Requirements reviews

A requirements review is a manual process that involves people from both client and contractor organisations. They check the requirements document for anomalies and omissions. The review process may be managed in the same way as program inspections (see Chapter 22). Alternatively, it may be organised as a broader activity with different people checking different parts of the document.

Requirements reviews can be informal or formal. Informal reviews simply involve contractors discussing requirements with as many system stakeholders as possible. It is surprising how often communication between system developers and stakeholders ends after elicitation and there is no confirmation that the documented requirements are what the stakeholders really said they wanted. Many problems can be detected simply by talking about the system to stakeholders before making a commitment to a formal review.

In a formal requirements review, the development team should 'walk' the client through the system requirements, explaining the implications of each requirement. The review team should check each requirement for consistency as well as check the requirements as a whole for completeness. Reviewers may also check for:

1. *Verifiability* Is the requirement as stated realistically testable?

2. *Comprehensibility* Do the procurers or end-users of the system properly understand the requirement?

3. *Traceability* Is the origin of the requirement clearly stated? You may have to go back to the source of the requirement to assess the impact of a change. Traceability is important as it allows the impact of change on the rest of the system to be assessed. I discuss it in more detail in the following section.

4. *Adaptability* Is the requirement adaptable? That is, can the requirement be changed without large-scale effects on other system requirements?

Conflicts, contradictions, errors and omissions in the requirements should be pointed out by reviewers and formally recorded in the review report. It is then up to the users, the system procurer and the system developer to negotiate a solution to these identified problems.

7.4 Requirements management

The requirements for large software systems are always changing. One reason for this is that these systems are usually developed to address 'wicked' problems (as discussed in Chapter 2). Because the problem cannot be fully defined, the software requirements are bound to be incomplete. During the software process, the stakeholders' understanding of the problem is constantly changing. These requirements must then evolve to reflect this changed problem view.

Furthermore, once a system has been installed, new requirements inevitably emerge. It is hard for users and system customers to anticipate what effects the new system will have on the organisation. Once end-users have experience of a system, they discover new needs and priorities:

1. Large systems usually have a diverse user community where users have different requirements and priorities. These may be conflicting or contradictory. The final system requirements are inevitably a compromise between them and, with experience, it is often discovered that the balance of support given to different users has to be changed.

2. The people who pay for a system and the users of a system are rarely the same people. System customers impose requirements because of organisational and budgetary constraints. These may conflict with end-user requirements and, after delivery, new features may have to be added for user support if the system is to meet its goals.

3. The business and technical environment of the system changes after installation, and these changes must be reflected in the system. New hardware may be introduced, it may be necessary to interface the system with other systems, business priorities may change with consequent changes in the system support, and new legislation and regulations may be introduced which must be implemented by the system.

Requirements management is the process of understanding and controlling changes to system requirements. You need to keep track of individual requirements and maintain links between dependent requirements so that you can assess the impact of requirements changes. You need to establish a formal process for making change proposals and linking these to system requirements. The process of requirements management should start as soon as a draft version of the requirements document is available, but you should start planning how to manage changing requirements during the requirements elicitation process.

7.4.1 Enduring and volatile requirements

Requirements evolution during the RE process and after a system has gone into service is inevitable. Developing software requirements focuses attention on software

Figure 7.10
Requirements
evolution

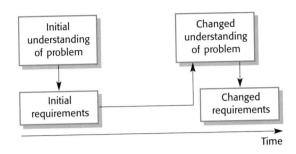

capabilities, business objectives and other business systems. As the requirements definition is developed, you normally develop a better understanding of users' needs. This feeds information back to the user, who may then propose a change to the requirements (Figure 7.10). Furthermore, it may take several years to specify and develop a large system. Over that time, the system's environment and the business objectives change, and the requirements evolve to reflect this.

From an evolution perspective, requirements fall into two classes:

1. *Enduring requirements* These are relatively stable requirements that derive from the core activity of the organisation and which relate directly to the domain of the system. For example, in a hospital, there will always be requirements concerned with patients, doctors, nurses and treatments. These requirements may be derived from domain models that show the entities and relations that characterise an application domain (Easterbrook, 1993; Prieto-Díaz and Arango, 1991).

2. *Volatile requirements* These are requirements that are likely to change during the system development process or after the system has been become operational. An example would be requirements resulting from government healthcare policies.

Harker and others (Harker, et al., 1993) have suggested that volatile requirements fall into five classes. Using these as a base, I have developed the classification shown in Figure 7.11.

7.4.2 Requirements management planning

Planning is an essential first stage in the requirements management process. Requirements management is very expensive. For each project, the planning stage establishes the level of requirements management detail that is required. During the requirements management stage, you have to decide on:

1. *Requirements identification* Each requirement must be uniquely identified so that it can be cross-referenced by other requirements and so that it may be used in traceability assessments.

Figure 7.11
Classification of
volatile requirements

Requirement Type	Description
Mutable requirements	Requirements which change because of changes to the environment in which the organisation is operating. For example, in hospital systems, the funding of patient care may change and thus require different treatment information to be collected.
Emergent requirements	Requirements which emerge as the customer's understanding of the system develops during the system development. The design process may reveal new emergent requirements.
Consequential requirements	Requirements which result from the introduction of the computer system. Introducing the computer system may change the organisation's processes and open up new ways of working which generate new system requirements.
Compatibility requirements	Requirements which depend on the particular systems or business processes within an organisation. As these change, the compatibility requirements on the commissioned or delivered system may also have to evolve.

2. *A change management process* This is the set of activities that assess the impact and cost of changes. I discuss this process in more detail in the following section.

3. *Traceability policies* These policies define the relationships between requirements, and between the requirements and the system design that should be recorded and how these records should be maintained.

4. *CASE tool support* Requirements management involves the processing of large amounts of information about the requirements. Tools that may be used range from specialist requirements management systems to spreadsheets and simple database systems.

There are many relationships among requirements and between the requirements and the system design. There are also links between requirements and the underlying reasons why these requirements were proposed. When changes are proposed, you have to trace the impact of these changes on other requirements and the system design. Traceability is the property of a requirements specification that reflects the ease of finding related requirements.

There are three types of traceability information that may be maintained:

1. *Source traceability* information links the requirements to the stakeholders who proposed the requirements and to the rationale for these requirements. When a change is proposed, you use this information to find and consult the stakeholders about the change.

Figure 7.12
A traceability matrix

Req. id	1.1	1.2	1.3	2.1	2.2	2.3	3.1	3.2
1.1		D	R					
1.2			D			R		D
1.3	R			R				
2.1			R		D			D
2.2								D
2.3		R		D				
3.1								R
3.2							R	

2. *Requirements traceability* information links dependent requirements within the requirements document. You use this information to assess how many requirements are likely to be affected by a proposed change and the extent of consequential requirements changes that may be necessary.

3. *Design traceability* information links the requirements to the design modules where these requirements are implemented. You use this information to assess the impact of proposed requirements changes on the system design and implementation.

Traceability information is often represented using traceability matrices, which relate requirements to stakeholders, each other or design modules. In a requirements traceability matrix, each requirement is entered in a row and in a column in the matrix. Where dependencies between different requirements exist, these are recorded in the cell at the row/column intersection.

Figure 7.12 shows a simple traceability matrix that records the dependencies between requirements. A 'D' in the row/column intersection illustrates that the requirement in the row depends on the requirement named in the column; an 'R' means that there is some other, weaker relationship between the requirements. For example, they may both define the requirements for parts of the same subsystem.

Traceability matrices may be used when a small number of requirements have to be managed, but they become unwieldy and expensive to maintain for large systems with many requirements. For these systems, you should capture traceability information in a requirements database where each requirement is explicitly linked to related requirements. You can then assess the impact of changes by using the database browsing facilities. Traceability matrices can be generated automatically from the database.

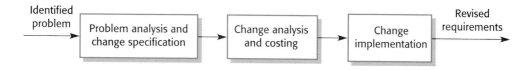

Figure 7.13
Requirements
change management

Requirements management needs automated support; the CASE tools for this should be chosen during the planning phase. You need tool support for:

1. *Requirements storage* The requirements should be maintained in a secure, managed data store that is accessible to everyone involved in the requirements engineering process.

2. *Change management* The process of change management (Figure 7.13) is simplified if active tool support is available.

3. *Traceability management* As discussed above, tool support for traceability allows related requirements to be discovered. Some tools use natural language processing techniques to help you discover possible relationships between the requirements.

For small systems, it may not be necessary to use specialised requirements management tools. The requirements management process may be supported using the facilities available in word processors, spreadsheets and PC databases. However, for larger systems, more specialised tool support is required. I have included links to information about requirements management tools such as DOORS and RequisitePro in the book's web pages.

7.4.3 Requirements change management

Requirements change management (Figure 7.13) should be applied to all proposed changes to the requirements. The advantage of using a formal process for change management is that all change proposals are treated consistently and that changes to the requirements document are made in a controlled way. There are three principal stages to a change management process:

1. *Problem analysis and change specification* The process starts with an identified requirements problem or, sometimes, with a specific change proposal. During this stage, the problem or the change proposal is analysed to check that it is valid. The results of the analysis are fed back to the change requestor, and sometimes a more specific requirements change proposal is then made.

2. *Change analysis and costing* The effect of the proposed change is assessed using traceability information and general knowledge of the system requirements. The cost of making the change is estimated in terms of modifications to the

requirements document and, if appropriate, to the system design and implementation. Once this analysis is completed, a decision is made whether to proceed with the requirements change.

3. *Change implementation* The requirements document and, where necessary, the system design and implementation are modified. You should organise the requirements document so that you can make changes to it without extensive rewriting or reorganisation. As with programs, changeability in documents is achieved by minimising external references and making the document sections as modular as possible. Thus, individual sections can be changed and replaced without affecting other parts of the document.

If a requirements change to a system is urgently required, there is always a temptation to make that change to the system and then retrospectively modify the

KEY POINTS

■ The requirements engineering process includes a feasibility study, requirements elicitation and analysis, requirements specification, requirements validation and requirements management.

■ Requirements elicitation and analysis is an iterative process that can be represented as a spiral of activities—requirements discovery, requirements classification and organisation, requirements negotiation and requirements documentation.

■ Different stakeholders in the system have different requirements. All complex systems should therefore be analysed from a number of viewpoints. Viewpoints can be people or other systems that interact with the system being specified, stakeholders who are affected by the system, or domain viewpoints that constrain the requirements.

■ Social and organisational factors have a strong influence on system requirements and may determine whether the software is actually used.

■ Requirements validation is the process of checking the requirements for validity, consistency, completeness, realism and verifiability. Requirements reviews and prototyping are the principal techniques used for requirements validation.

■ Business, organisational and technical changes inevitably lead to changes to the requirements for a software system. Requirements management is the process of managing and controlling these changes.

■ The requirements management process includes management planning, where policies and procedures for requirements management are designed, and change management, where you analyse proposed requirements changes and assess their impact.

requirements document. This almost inevitably leads to the requirements specification and the system implementation getting out of step. Once system changes have been made, requirements document changes may be forgotten or made in a way that is not consistent with the system changes.

Iterative development processes, such as extreme programming, have been designed to cope with requirements that change during the development process. In these processes, when a user proposes a requirements change, this does not go through a formal change management process. Rather, the user has to prioritise that change and, if it is high priority, decide what system features that were planned for the next iteration should be dropped.

FURTHER READING

'Requirements engineering'. This special issue includes two papers that focus on requirements engineering for particular domains (cars and medical devices) that offer interesting perspectives on the RE processes in these areas. (*IEEE Software*, 20 (1), January/February 2003.)

Mastering the Requirements Process. A readable book that is intended for practising requirements engineers. It gives specific guidance on developing an effective requirements engineering process. (S. Robertson and J. Robertson, 1999, Addison-Wesley.)

Requirements Engineering: Processes and Techniques. This book includes a more detailed look at the activities in the requirements engineering process and discusses the VORD method and its application. (G. Kotonya and I. Sommerville, 1999, John Wiley & Sons.)

EXERCISES

7.1 Suggest who might be stakeholders in a university student records system. Explain why it is almost inevitable that the requirements of different stakeholders will conflict in some way.

7.2 A software system is to be developed to manage the records of patients who enter a clinic for treatment. The records include records of all regular patient monitoring (temperature, blood pressure, etc.), treatments given, patient reactions and so on. After treatment, the records of their stay are sent to the patient's doctor who maintains their complete medical record. Identify the principal viewpoints which might be taken into account in the specification of this system and organise these using a viewpoint hierarchy diagram.

7.3 For three of the viewpoints identified in the library system, LIBSYS (Figure 7.4), suggest three requirements that could be suggested by stakeholders associated with that viewpoint.

7.4 The LIBSYS system has to include support for cataloguing new documents where the system catalog may be distributed across several machines. What are likely to be the most important types of non-functional requirements associated with the cataloguing facilities?

7.5   Using your knowledge of how an ATM is used, develop a set of use-cases that could serve as a basis for understanding the requirements for an ATM system.

7.6   Discuss an example of a type of system where social and political factors might strongly influence the system requirements. Explain why these factors are important in your example.

7.7   Who should be involved in a requirements review? Draw a process model showing how a requirements review might be organised.

7.8   Why do traceability matrices become difficult to manage when there are many system requirements? Design a requirements structuring mechanism, based on viewpoints, which might help reduce the scale of this problem.

7.9   When emergency changes have to be made to systems, the system software may have to be modified before changes to the requirements have been approved. Suggest a process model for making these modifications that ensures that the requirements document and the system implementation do not become inconsistent.

7.10   Your company uses a standard analysis method that is normally applied in all requirements analyses. In your work, you find that this method cannot represent social factors that are significant in the system you are analysing. You point this out to your manager, who makes it clear that the standard should be followed. Discuss what you should do in such a situation.

8

System models

Objectives

The objective of this chapter is to introduce a number of system models that may be developed during the requirements engineering process. When you have read the chapter, you will:

■ understand why it is important to establish the boundaries of a system and model its context;

■ understand the concepts of behavioural modelling, data modelling and object modelling;

■ have been introduced to some of the notations defined in the Unified Modeling Language (UML) and how these notations may be used to develop system models.

Contents

User requirements should be written in natural language because they have to be understood by people who are not technical experts. However, more detailed system requirements may be expressed in a more technical way. One widely used technique is to document the system specification as a set of system models. These models are graphical representations that describe business processes, the problem to be solved and the system that is to be developed. Because of the graphical representations used, models are often more understandable than detailed natural language descriptions of the system requirements. They are also an important bridge between the analysis and design processes.

You can use models in the analysis process to develop an understanding of the existing system that is to be replaced or improved or to specify the new system that is required. You may develop different models to represent the system from different perspectives. For example:

1. An external perspective, where the context or environment of the system is modelled

2. A behavioural perspective, where the behaviour of the system is modelled

3. A structural perspective, where the architecture of the system or the structure of the data processed by the system is modelled

I cover these three perspectives in this chapter and also discuss object modelling, which combines, to some extent, behavioural and structural modelling.

The most important aspect of a system model is that it leaves out detail. A system model is an abstraction of the system being studied rather than an alternative representation of that system. Ideally, a *representation* of a system should maintain all the information about the entity being represented. An *abstraction* deliberately simplifies and picks out the most salient characteristics. For example, in the very unlikely event of this book being serialised in a newspaper, the presentation there would be an abstraction of the book's key points. If it were translated from English into Italian, this would be an alternative representation. The translator's intention would be to maintain all the information as it is presented in English.

Different types of system models are based on different approaches to abstraction. A data-flow model (for example) concentrates on the flow of data and the functional transformations on that data. It leaves out details of the data structures. By contrast, a model of data entities and their relationships documents the system data structures rather than its functionality.

Examples of the types of system models that you might create during the analysis process are:

1. *A data- flow model* Data-flow models show how data is processed at different stages in the system.

2. *A composition model* A composition or *aggregation* model shows how entities in the system are composed of other entities.

3. *An architectural model* Architectural models show the principal sub-systems that make up a system.

4. *A classification model* Object class/inheritance diagrams show how entities have common characteristics.

5. *A stimulus-response model* A stimulus-response model, or *state transition diagram*, shows how the system reacts to internal and external events.

All these types of models are covered in this chapter. Wherever possible, I use notations from the Unified Modeling Language (UML), which has become a standard modelling language for object-oriented modelling (Booch, et al., 1999; Rumbaugh, et al., 1999a). Where UML does not include appropriate notations, I use simple intuitive notations for model description. A new version of UML (UML 2.0) is under development but was not available when I wrote this chapter. However, I understand that the UML notation that I have used here is likely to be compatible with UML 2.0.

8.1 Context models

At an early stage in the requirements elicitation and analysis process you should decide on the boundaries of the system. This involves working with system stakeholders to distinguish what is the system and what is the system's environment. You should make these decisions early in the process to limit the system costs and the time needed for analysis.

In some cases, the boundary between a system and its environment is relatively clear. For example, where an automated system is replacing an existing manual or computerised system, the environment of the new system is usually the same as the existing system's environment. In other cases, there is more flexibility, and you decide what constitutes the boundary between the system and its environment during the requirements engineering process.

For example, say you are developing the specification for the library system LIB-SYS. Recall that this system is intended to deliver electronic versions of copyrighted material to users' computers. The users may then print personal copies of the material. In developing the specification for this system, you have to decide whether other library database systems such as library catalogues are within the system boundary. If they are, then you may have to allow access to the system through the catalogue user interface; if they are not, then users may be inconvenienced by having to move from one system to another.

The definition of a system boundary is not a value-free judgement. Social and organisational concerns may mean that the position of a system boundary may be determined by non-technical factors. For example, a system boundary may be posi-

Figure 8.1 The
context of an ATM
system

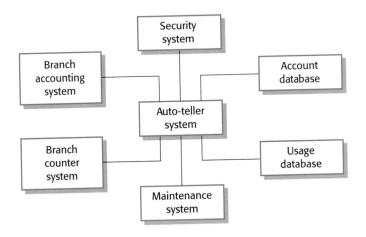

Figure 8.1 The
context of an ATM
system

tioned so that the analysis process can all be carried out on one site; it may be chosen so that a particularly difficult manager need not be consulted; it may be positioned so that the system cost is increased, and the system development division
must therefore expand to design and implement the system.

Once some decisions on the boundaries of the system have been made, part of
the analysis activity is the definition of that context and the dependencies that a
system has on its environment. Normally, producing a simple architectural model
is the first step in this activity.

Figure 8.1 is an architectural model that illustrates the structure of the information
system that includes a bank auto-teller network. High-level architectural models are
usually expressed as simple block diagrams where each sub-system is represented by
a named rectangle, and lines indicate associations between sub-systems.

From Figure 8.1, we see that each ATM is connected to an account database, a
local branch accounting system, a security system and a system to support machine
maintenance. The system is also connected to a usage database that monitors how
the network of ATMs is used and to a local branch counter system. This counter
system provides services such as backup and printing. These, therefore, need not
be included in the ATM system itself.

Architectural models describe the environment of a system. However, they do
not show the relationships between the other systems in the environment and the
system that is being specified. External systems might produce data for or consume
data from the system. They might share data with the system, or they might be connected directly, through a network or not at all. They might be physically co-located
or located in separate buildings. All of these relations might affect the requirements
of the system being defined and must be taken into account.

Therefore, simple architectural models are normally supplemented by other models, such as process models, that show the process activities supported by the system.
Data-flow models (described in the following section) may also be used to show the
data that is transferred between the system and other systems in its environment.

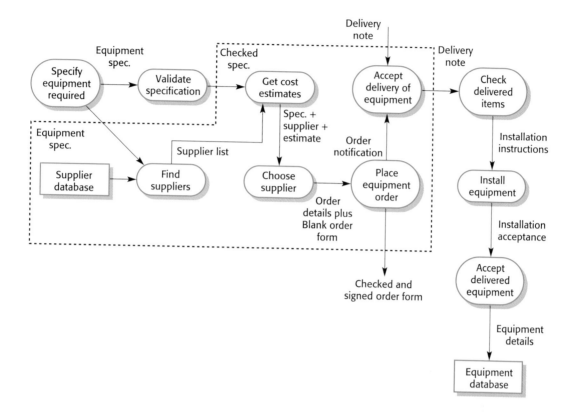

Figure 8.2 Process model of equipment procurement

Figure 8.2 illustrates a process model for the process of procuring equipment in an organisation. This involves specifying the equipment required, finding and choosing suppliers, ordering the equipment, taking delivery of the equipment and testing it after delivery. When specifying computer support for this process, you have to decide which of these activities will actually be supported. The other activities are outside the boundary of the system. In Figure 8.2, the dotted line encloses the activities that are within the system boundary.

8.2 Behavioural models

Behavioural models are used to describe the overall behaviour of the system. I discuss two types of behavioural model here: data-flow models, which model the data processing in the system, and state machine models, which model how the system reacts to events. These models may be used separately or together, depending on the type of system that is being developed.

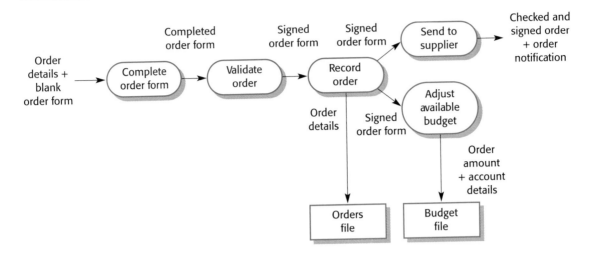

Figure 8.3 Data-flow
diagram of order
processing
Most business systems are primarily driven by data. They are controlled by the data inputs to the system with relatively little external event processing. A data-flow model may be all that is needed to represent the behaviour of these systems. By contrast, real-time systems are often event-driven with minimal data processing. A state machine model (discussed in Section 8.2.2) is the most effective way to represent their behaviour. Other classes of system may be both data and event driven. In these cases, you may develop both types of model.

8.2.1 Data-flow models

Data-flow models are an intuitive way of showing how data is processed by a system. At the analysis level, they should be used to model the way in which data is processed in the existing system. The use of data-flow models for analysis became widespread after the publication of DeMarco's book (DeMarco, 1978) on structured systems analysis. They are an intrinsic part of structured methods that have been developed from this work. The notation used in these models represents functional processing (rounded rectangles), data stores (rectangles) and data movements between functions (labelled arrows).

Data-flow models are used to show how data flows through a sequence of processing steps. For example, a processing step could be to filter duplicate records in a customer database. The data is transformed at each step before moving on to the next stage. These processing steps or transformations represent software processes or functions when data-flow diagrams are used to document a software design. However, in an analysis model, people or computers may carry out the processing.

A data-flow model, which shows the steps involved in processing an order for goods (such as computer equipment) in an organisation, is illustrated in Figure 8.3. This particular model describes the data processing in the **Place equipment order**

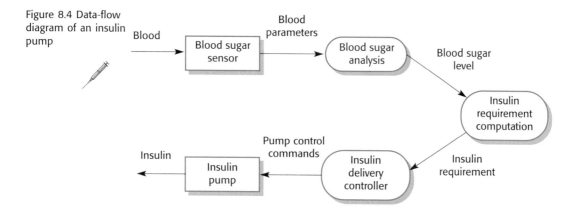

Figure 8.4 Data-flow diagram of an insulin pump

activity in the overall process model shown in Figure 8.2. The model shows how the order for the goods moves from process to process. It also shows the data stores (**Orders file** and **Budget file**) that are involved in this process.

Data-flow models are valuable because tracking and documenting how the data associated with a particular process moves through the system helps analysts understand what is going on. Data-flow diagrams have the advantage that, unlike some other modelling notations, they are simple and intuitive. It is usually possible to explain them to potential system users who can then participate in validating the analysis.

In principle, the development of models such as data-flow models should be a 'top-down' process. In this example, this would imply that you should start by analysing the overall procurement process. You then move on to the analysis of sub-processes such as ordering. In practice, analysis is never like that. You learn about several levels at the same time. Lower-level models may be developed first and then abstracted to create a more general model.

Data-flow models show a functional perspective where each transformation represents a single function or process. They are particularly useful during the analysis of requirements as they can be used to show end-to-end processing in a system. That is, they show the entire sequence of actions that take place from an input being processed to the corresponding output that is the system's response. Figure 8.4 illustrates this use of data flow diagrams. It is a diagram of the processing that takes place in the insulin pump system introduced in Chapter 3.

8.2.2 State machine models

A state machine model describes how a system responds to internal or external events. The state machine model shows system states and events that cause transitions from one state to another. It does not show the flow of data within the system. This type of model is often used for modelling real-time systems because these systems are often driven by stimuli from the system's environment. For example, the real-time

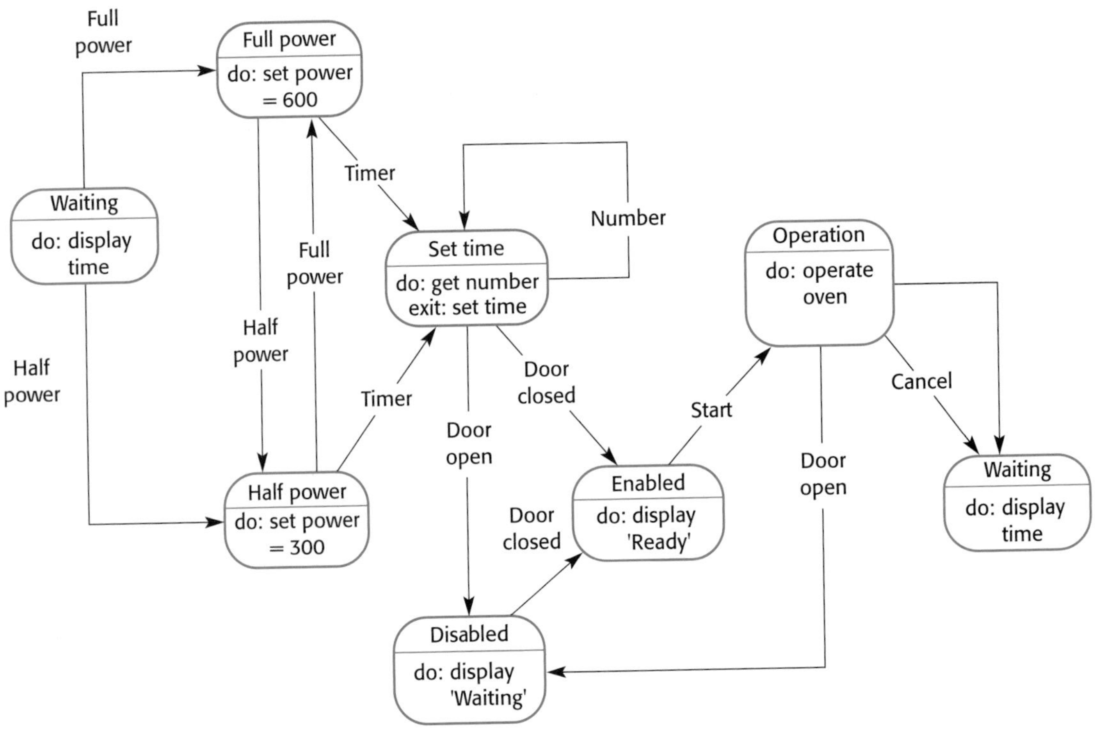

Figure 8.5 State machine model of a simple microwave oven

alarm system discussed in Chapter 13 responds to stimuli from movement sensors, door opening sensors, and so on.

State machine models are an integral part of real-time design methods such as that proposed by Ward and Mellor (Ward and Mellor, 1985) and Harel (Harel, 1987; Harel, 1988). Harel's method uses a notation called *Statecharts* and these were the basis for the state machine-modelling notation in the UML.

A state machine model of a system assumes that, at any time, the system is in one of a number of possible states. When a stimulus is received, this may trigger a transition to a different state. For example, a system controlling a valve may move from a state 'Valve open' to a state 'Valve closed' when an operator command (the stimulus) is received.

This approach to system modelling is illustrated in Figure 8.5. This diagram shows a state machine model of a simple microwave oven equipped with buttons to set the power and the timer and to start the system. Real microwave ovens are actually much more complex than the system described here. However, this model includes the essential features of the system. To simplify the model, I have assumed that the sequence of actions in using the microwave is:

1. Select the power level (either half-power or full-power).

2. Input the cooking time.

3.   Press Start, and the food is cooked for the given time.

For safety reasons, the oven should not operate when the door is open and, on completion of cooking, a buzzer is sounded. The oven has a very simple alphanumeric display that is used to display various alerts and warning messages.

The UML notation that I use to describe state machine models is designed for modelling the behaviour of objects. However, it is a general-purpose notation that can be used for any type of state machine modelling. The rounded rectangles in a model represent system states. They include a brief description (following 'do') of the actions taken in that state. The labelled arrows represent stimuli that force a transition from one state to another.

Therefore, from Figure 8.5, we can see that the system responds initially to either the full-power or the half-power button. Users can change their mind after selecting one of these and press the other button. The time is set and, if the door is closed, the Start button is enabled. Pushing this button starts the oven operation and cooking takes place for the specified time.

The UML notation lets you indicate the activity that takes place in a state. In a detailed system specification, you have to provide more detail about both the stimuli and the system states (Figure 8.6). This information may be maintained in a data dictionary or encyclopaedia (covered in Section 8.3) that is maintained by the CASE tools used to create the system model.

The problem with the state machine approach is that the number of possible states increases rapidly. For large system models, therefore, some structuring of these state models is necessary. One way to do this is by using the notion of a superstate that encapsulates a number of separate states. This superstate looks like a single state on a high-level model but is then expanded in more detail on a separate diagram. To illustrate this concept, consider the **Operation** state in Figure 8.5. This is a superstate that can be expanded, as illustrated in Figure 8.7.

The **Operation** state includes a number of sub-states. It shows that operation starts with a status check, and that if any problems are discovered, an alarm is indicated and operation is disabled. Cooking involves running the microwave generator for the specified time; on completion, a buzzer is sounded. If the door is opened during operation, the system moves to the disabled state, as shown in Figure 8.5.

8.3 Data models

Most large software systems make use of a large database of information. In some cases, this database is independent of the software system. In others, it is created for the system being developed. An important part of systems modelling is defin-

Figure 8.6 State and stimulus description for the microwave oven

State	Description
Waiting	The oven is waiting for input. The display shows the current time.
Half power	The oven power is set to 300 watts. The display shows 'Half power'.
Full power	The oven power is set to 600 watts. The display shows 'Full power'.
Set time	The cooking time is set to the user's input value. The display shows the cooking time selected and is updated as the time is set.
Disabled	Oven operation is disabled for safety. Interior oven light is on. Display shows 'Not ready'.
Enabled	Oven operation is enabled. Interior oven light is off. Display shows 'Ready to cook'.
Operation	Oven in operation. Interior oven light is on. Display shows the timer countdown. On completion of cooking, the buzzer is sounded for 5 seconds. Oven light is on. Display shows 'Cooking complete' while buzzer is sounding.

Stimulus	Description
Half power	The user has pressed the half power button.
Full power	The user has pressed the full power button.
Timer	The user has pressed one of the timer buttons.
Number	The user has pressed a numeric key.
Door open	The oven door switch is not closed.
Door closed	The oven door switch is closed.
Start	The user has pressed the start button.
Cancel	The user has pressed the cancel button.

ing the logical form of the data processed by the system. These are sometimes called *semantic data models*.

The most widely used data modelling technique is Entity-Relation-Attribute modelling (ERA modelling), which shows the data entities, their associated attributes and the relations between these entities. This approach to modelling was first proposed in the mid-1970s by Chen (Chen, 1976); several variants have been developed since then (Codd, 1979; Hammer and McLeod, 1981; Hull and King, 1987), all with the same basic form.

Figure 8.7 Microwave
oven operation

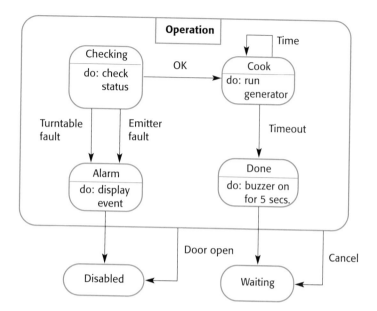

Figure 8.7 Microwave oven operation

Entity-relationship models have been widely used in database design. The relational database schemas derived from these models are naturally in third normal form, which is a desirable characteristic (Barker, 1989). Because of the explicit typing and the recognition of sub- and super-types, it is also straightforward to implement these models using object-oriented databases.

The UML does not include a specific notation for this database modelling, as it assumes an object-oriented development process and models data using objects and their relationships. However, you can use the UML to represent a semantic data model. You can think of entities in an ERA model as simplified object classes (they have no operations), attributes as class attributes and named associations between the classes as relations.

Figure 8.8 is an example of a data model that is part of the library system LIBSYS introduced in earlier chapters. Recall that LIBSYS is designed to deliver copies of copyrighted articles that have been published in magazines and journals and to collect payments for these articles. Therefore, the data model must include information about the article, the copyright holder and the buyer of the article. I have assumed that payments for articles are not made directly but through national copyright agencies.

Figure 8.8 shows that an **Article** has attributes representing the title, the authors, the name of the PDF file of the article and the fee payable. This is linked to the **Source**, where the article was published, and to the **Copyright Agency** for the country of publication. Both **Copyright Agency** and **Source** are linked to **Country**. The country of publication is important because copyright laws vary by country. The diagram also shows that **Buyers** place **Orders** for **Articles**.

Like all graphical models, data models lack detail, and you should maintain more detailed descriptions of the entities, relationships and attributes that are included in

Figure 8.8 Semantic
data model for the
LIBSYS system

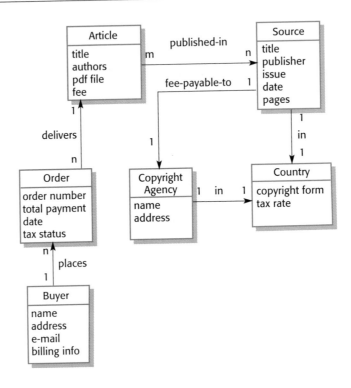

Figure 8.8 Semantic data model for the LIBSYS system

the model. You may collect these more detailed descriptions in a repository or data dictionary. Data dictionaries are generally useful when developing system models and may be used to manage all information from all types of system models.

A data dictionary is, simplistically, an alphabetic list of the names included in the system models. As well as the name, the dictionary should include an associated description of the named entity and, if the name represents a composite object, a description of the composition. Other information such as the date of creation, the creator and the representation of the entity may also be included depending on the type of model being developed.

The advantages of using a data dictionary are:

1. *It is a mechanism for name management.* Many people may have to invent names for entities and relationships when developing a large system model. These names should be used consistently and should not clash. The data dictionary software can check for name uniqueness where necessary and warn requirements analysts of name duplications.

2. *It serves as a store of organisational information.* As the system is developed, information that can link analysis, design, implementation and evolution is added to the data dictionary, so that all information about an entity is in one place.

Figure 8.9 Examples
of data dictionary
entries

Name	Description	Type	Date
Article	Details of the published article that may be ordered by people using LIBSYS.	Entity	30.12.2002
authors	The names of the authors of the article who may be due a share of the fee.	Attribute	30.12.2002
Buyer	The person or organisation that orders a copy of the article.	Entity	30.12.2002
fee-payable-to	A 1:1 relationship between Article and the Copyright Agency who should be paid the copyright fee.	Relation	29.12.2002
Address (Buyer)	The address of the buyer. This is used to any paper billing information that is required.	Attribute	31.12.2002

The data dictionary entries shown in Figure 8.9 define the names in the semantic data model for LIBSYS (Figure 8.8). I have simplified the presentation of this example by leaving out some names and by shortening the associated information.

All system names, whether they are names of entities, relations, attributes or services, should be entered in the dictionary. Software is normally used to create, maintain and interrogate the dictionary. This software might be integrated with other tools so that dictionary creation is partially automated. For example, CASE tools that support system modelling generally include support for data dictionaries and enter the names in the dictionary when they are first used in the model.

8.4 Object models

An object-oriented approach to the whole software development process is now commonly used, particularly for interactive systems development. This means expressing the systems requirements using an object model, designing using objects and developing the system in an object-oriented programming language such as Java or C++.

Object models that you develop during requirements analysis may be used to represent both system data and its processing. In this respect, they combine some of the uses of data-flow and semantic data models. They are also useful for showing how entities in the system may be classified and composed of other entities.

For some classes of system, object models are natural ways of reflecting the real-world entities that are manipulated by the system. This is particularly true when the system processes information about tangible entities, such as cars, aircraft or books, which have clearly identifiable attributes. More abstract, higher-level entities, such as the concept of a library, a medical record system or a word processor, are harder to model as object classes. They do not necessarily have a simple interface consisting of independent attributes and operations.

Developing object models during requirements analysis usually simplifies the transition to object-oriented design and programming. However, I have found that end-users of a system often find object models unnatural and difficult to understand. They may prefer to adopt a more functional, data-processing view. Therefore, it is sometimes helpful to supplement object models with data-flow models that show the end-to-end data processing in the system.

An object class is an abstraction over a set of objects that identifies common attributes (as in a semantic data model) and the services or operations that are provided by each object. Objects are executable entities with the attributes and services of the object class. Objects are instantiations of the object class, and many objects may be created from a class. Generally, the models developed using analysis focus on object classes and their relationships.

In object-oriented requirements analysis, you should model real-world entities using object classes. You should not include details of the individual objects (instantiations of the class) in the system. You may create different types of object models, showing how object classes are related to each other, how objects, are aggregated to form other objects, how objects interact with other objects and so on. These each present unique information about the system that is being specified.

The analysis process for identifying objects and object classes is recognised as one of the most difficult areas of object-oriented development. Object identification is basically the same for analysis and design. The methods of object identification covered in Chapter 14, which discusses object-oriented design, may be used. I concentrate here on some of the object models that might be generated during the analysis process.

Various methods of object-oriented analysis were proposed in the 1990s (Coad and Yourdon, 1990; Rumbaugh, et al., 1991; Jacobsen, et al., 1993; Booch, 1994). These methods had a great deal in common, and three of the key developers (Booch, Rumbaugh, and Jacobsen) decided to integrate their approaches to produce a unified method (Rumbaugh et al., 1999b). The Unified Modeling Language (UML) used in this unified method has become a standard for object modelling. The UML includes notations for different types of system models. We have already seen use-case models and sequence diagrams in earlier chapters and state machine models earlier in this chapter.

An object class in UML, as illustrated in the examples in Figure 8.10, is represented as a vertically oriented rectangle with three sections:

1. The name of the object class is in the top section.

2. The class attributes are in the middle section.

3. The operations associated with the object class are in the lower section of the rectangle.

I don't have space to cover all of the UML, so I focus here on object models that show how objects can be classified and can inherit attributes and operations from other objects, aggregation models that show how objects are composed, and simple behavioural models, which show object interactions.

8.4.1 Inheritance models

Object-oriented modelling involves identifying the classes of object that are important in the domain being studied. These are then organised into a taxonomy. A taxonomy is a classification scheme that shows how an object class is related to other classes through common attributes and services.

To display this taxonomy, the classes are organised into an inheritance hierarchy with the most general object classes at the top of the hierarchy. More specialised objects inherit their attributes and services. These specialised objects may have their own attributes and services.

Figure 8.10 illustrates part of a simplified class hierarchy for a model of a library. This hierarchy gives information about the items held in the library. The library holds various items, such as books, music, recordings of films, magazines and newspapers. In Figure 8.10, the most general item is at the top of the tree and has a set of attributes and services that are common to all library items. These are inherited by the classes **Published item** and **Recorded item**, which add their own attributes that are then inherited by lower-level items.

Figure 8.11 is an example of another inheritance hierarchy that might be part of the library model. In this case, the users of a library are shown. There are two classes of user: those who are allowed to borrow books, and those who may only read books in the library without taking them away.

In the UML notation, inheritance is shown 'upwards' rather than 'downwards' as it is in some other object-oriented notations or in languages such as Java, where sub-classes inherit from super-classes. That is, the arrowhead (shown as a triangle) points from the classes that inherit attributes and operations to the super-class. Rather than use the term *inheritance*, UML refers to the *generalisation relationship*.

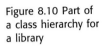

Figure 8.10 Part of
a class hierarchy for
a library

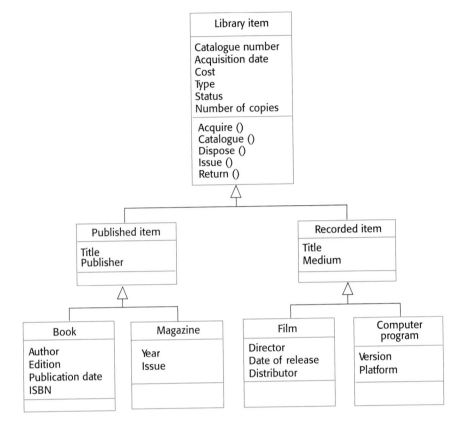

Figure 8.11 User
class hierarchy

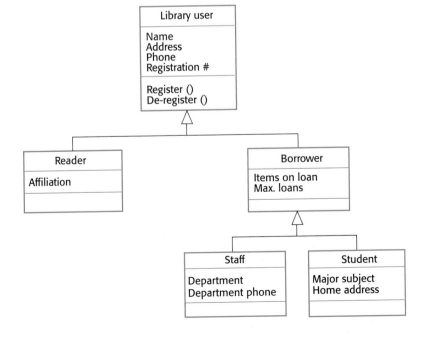

The design of class hierarchies is not easy, so the analyst needs to understand, in detail, the domain in which the system is to be installed. As an example of the subtlety of the problems that arise in practice, consider the library item hierarchy. It would seem that the attribute **Title** could be held in the most general item, then inherited by lower-level items.

However, while everything in a library must have some kind of identifier or registration number, it does not follow that everything must have a title. For example, a library may hold the personal papers of a retired politician. Many of these items, such as letters, may not be explicitly titled. These will be classified using some other class (not shown here) that has a different set of attributes.

Figure 8.10 and Figure 8.11 show class inheritance hierarchies where every object class inherits its attributes and operations from a single parent class. Multiple inheritance models may also be constructed where a class has several parents. Its inherited attributes and services are a conjunction of those inherited from each super-class. Figure 8.12 shows an example of a multiple inheritance model that may also be part of the library model.

The main problem with multiple inheritance is designing an inheritance graph where objects do not inherit unnecessary attributes. Other problems include the difficulty of reorganising the inheritance graph when changes are required and resolving name clashes where attributes of two or more super-classes have the same name but different meanings. At the system modelling level, such clashes are relatively easy to resolve by manually altering the object model. They cause more problems in object-oriented programming.

8.4.2 Object aggregation

As well as acquiring attributes and services through an inheritance relationship with other objects, some objects are groupings of other objects. That is, an object is an

Figure 8.12 Multiple inheritance

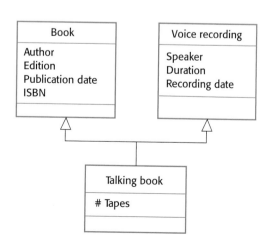

Figure 8.13
Aggregate object
representing a
course

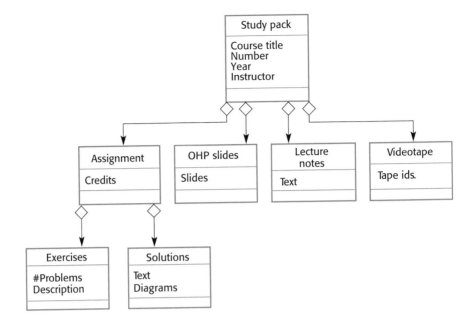

aggregate of a set of other objects. The classes representing these objects may be modelled using an object aggregation model, as shown in Figure 8.13. In this example, I have modelled a library item, which is a study pack for a university course. This study pack includes lecture notes, exercises, sample solutions, copies of transparencies used in lectures, and videotapes.

The UML notation for aggregation is to represent the composition by including a diamond shape on the source of the link. Therefore, Figure 8.13 can be read as 'A study pack is composed of one of more assignments, OHP slide packages, lecture notes and videotapes.'

8.4.3 Object behaviour modelling

To model the behaviour of objects, you have to show how the operations provided by the objects are used. In the UML, you model behaviours using scenarios that are represented as UML use-cases (discussed in Chapter 7). One way to model behaviour is to use UML sequence diagrams that show the sequence of actions involved in a use-case. As well as sequence diagrams, the UML also includes collaboration diagrams that show the sequence of messages exchanged by objects. These are similar to sequence diagrams so I do not cover them here.

You can see how sequence diagrams can be used for behaviour modelling in Figure 8.14 that expands a use-case from the LIBSYS system where users with-

Figure 8.14 The issue
of electronic items

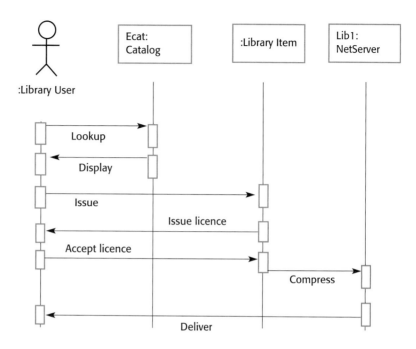

draw items from the library in electronic form. For example, imagine a situation where the study packs shown in Figure 8.13 could be maintained electronically and downloaded to the student's computer.

In a sequence diagram, objects and actors are aligned along the top of the diagram. Labelled arrows indicate operations; the sequence of operations is from top to bottom. In this scenario, the library user accesses the catalogue to see whether the item required is available electronically; if it is, the user requests the electronic issue of that item. For copyright reasons, this must be licensed so there is a transaction between the item and the user where the license is agreed. The item to be issued is then sent to a network server object for compression before being sent to the library user.

You can find another example of a sequence diagram that expands a LIBSYS use-case in Figure 7.8, which shows the sequence of actions involved in printing an article.

8.5 Structured methods

A structured method is a systematic way of producing models of an existing system or of a system that is to be built. They were first developed in the 1970s to support software analysis and design (Constantine and Yourdon, 1979; Gane and

Sarson, 1979; Jackson, 1983) and evolved in the 1980s and 1990s to support object-oriented development (Rumbaugh, et al., 1991; Robinson, 1992; Jacobsen, et al., 1993; Booch, 1994). These object-oriented methods coalesced, with the UML proposed as a standard modelling language (Booch, et al., 1999, Rumbaugh, et al., 1999a) and the Unified Process (Rumbaugh, et al., 1999b), and later with the Rational Unified Process (Krutchen, 2000), as an associated structured method. Budgen (Budgen, 2003) summarises and compares several of these structured methods.

Structured methods provide a framework for detailed system modelling as part of requirements elicitation and analysis. Most structured methods have their own preferred set of system models. They usually define a process that may be used to derive these models and a set of rules and guidelines that apply to the models. Standard documentation is produced for the system. CASE tools are usually available for method support. These tools support model editing and code and report generation, and provide some model-checking capabilities.

Structured methods have been applied successfully in many large projects. They can deliver significant cost reductions because they use standard notations and ensure that standard design documentation is produced. However, structured methods suffer from a number of weaknesses:

1. They do not provide effective support for understanding or modelling non-functional system requirements.

2. They are indiscriminate in that they do not usually include guidelines to help users decide whether a method is appropriate for a particular problem. Nor do they normally include advice on how they may be adapted for use in a particular environment.

3. They often produce too much documentation. The essence of the system requirements may be hidden by the mass of detail that is included.

4. The models that are produced are very detailed, and users often find them difficult to understand. These users therefore cannot check the realism of these models.

In practice, however, requirements engineers and designers don't restrict themselves to the models proposed in any particular method. For example, object-oriented methods do not usually suggest that data-flow models should be developed. However, in my experience, such models are often useful as part of a requirements analysis process because can present an overall picture of the end-to-end processing in the system. They may also contribute directly to object identification (the data which flows) and the identification of operations on these objects (the transformations).

Analysis and design CASE tools support the creation, editing and analysis of the graphical notations used in structured methods. Figure 8.15 shows the components that may be included method support environment.

Figure 8.15 The
components of a
CASE tool for
structured method
support

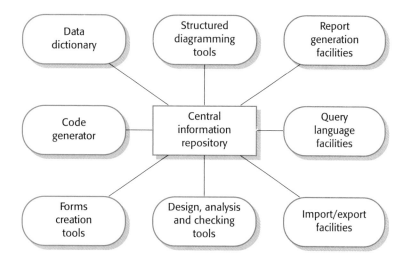

Comprehensive method support tools, as illustrated in Figure 8.15, normally include:

1. *Diagram editors* used to create object models, data models, behavioural models, and so on. These editors are not just drawing tools but are aware of the types of entities in the diagram. They capture information about these entities and save this information in the central repository.

2. *Design analysis and checking tools* that process the design and report on errors and anomalies. These may be integrated with the editing system so that user errors are trapped at an early stage in the process.

3. *Repository query languages* that allow the designer to find designs and associated design information in the repository.

4. A *data dictionary* that maintains information about the entities used in a system design.

5. *Report definition and generation tools* that take information from the central store and automatically generate system documentation.

6. *Forms definition tools* that allow screen and document formats to be specified.

7. *Import/export facilities* that allow the interchange of information from the central repository with other development tools.

8. *Code generators* that generate code or code skeletons automatically from the design captured in the central store.

Most comprehensive CASE toolsets allow the user to generate a program or a program fragment from the information provided in the system model. CASE tools often support different languages so the user can generate a program in C, C++ or Java from the same design model. Because models exclude low-level details, the code generator in a design workbench cannot usually generate the complete system. Some hand coding is usually necessary to add detail to the generated code.

KEY POINTS

■ A model is an abstract view of a system that ignores some system details. Complementary system models can be developed to present other information about the system.

■ Context models show how the system being modelled is positioned in an environment with other systems and processes. They define the boundaries of the system. Architectural models, process models and data-flow models may be used as context models.

■ Data-flow diagrams may be used to model the data processing carried out by a system. The system is modelled as a set of data transformations with functions acting on the data.

■ State machine models are used to model a system's behaviour in response to internal or external events.

■ Semantic data models describe the logical structure of the data that is imported to and exported by the system. These models show system entities, their attributes and the relationships in which they participate.

■ Object models describe the logical system entities and their classification and aggregation. They combine a data model with a processing model. Possible object models that may be developed include inheritance models, aggregation models and behavioural models.

■ Sequence models that show interactions between actors and objects in a system are used to model dynamic behaviour.

■ Structured methods provide a framework for supporting the development of system models. They normally have extensive case tool support, including model editing and checking and code generation.

FURTHER READING

Software Design, 2nd ed. Although this book is primarily focused on software design, the author discusses a number of structured methods that can also be used in the requirements engineering process. He does not just focus on object-oriented approaches. (D. Budgen, 2003, Addison-Wesley.)

Requirements Analysis and System Design. This book focuses on information systems analysis and discusses how different UML models can be used in the analysis process. (L. Maciaszek, 2001, Addison-Wesley.)

Software Engineering with Objects and Components. A short, readable introduction to the use of the UML in system specification and design. Although much less comprehensive than the full descriptions of the UML, this book is far better if you are trying to learn and understand the notation. (P. Stevens with R. Pooley, 1999, Addison-Wesley.)

EXERCISES

8.1   Draw a context model for a patient information system in a hospital. You may make any reasonable assumptions about the other hospital systems that are available, but your model must include a patient admissions system and an image storage system for X-rays, as well as other diagnostic records.

8.2   Based on your experience with a bank ATM, draw a data-flow diagram modelling the data processing involved when a customer withdraws cash from the machine.

8.3   Model the data processing that might take place in an e-mail system. You should model the mail-sending and mail-receiving processing separately.

8.4   Draw state machine models of the control software for:

    ■ An automatic washing machine that has different programs for different types of clothes

    ■ The software for a DVD player

    ■ A telephone answering system that records incoming messages and displays the number of accepted messages on an LED. The system should allow the telephone customer to dial in from any location, type a sequence of numbers (identified as tones) and play the recorded messages.

8.5   A software system model may be represented as a directed graph where nodes are the entities in the model and arcs are the relationships between these entities. Entities and relationships in the model may be labelled with a name and other information. Each entity in the model is typed and may be 'exploded' into a sub-model. Draw a data model that describes the structure of a software system model.

8.6   Model the object classes that might be used in an e-mail system. If you have tried Exercise 8.3, describe the similarities and differences between the data processing model and the object model.

8.7   Using the information about the system data shown in Figure 8.8, draw a sequence diagram that shows a possible sequence of actions that occur when a new article is catalogued by the LIBSYS system.

8.8   Develop an object model, including a class hierarchy diagram and an aggregation diagram showing the principal components of a personal computer system and its system software.

8.9 Develop a sequence diagram showing the interactions involved when a student registers for a course in a university. Courses may have limited enrolment, so the registration process must include checks that places are available. Assume that the student accesses an electronic course catalogue to find out about available courses.

8.10 Under what circumstances would you recommend against using structured methods for system development?

9

Critical systems specification

Objectives

The objective of this chapter is to explain how to specify functional and non-functional dependability requirements for critical systems. When you have read this chapter, you will:

■ understand how dependability requirements for critical systems can be identified by analysing the risks faced by these systems;

■ understand that safety requirements are generated from the system risk analysis rather than system stakeholders;

■ understand the process of deriving security requirements and how security requirements are generated to counter different types of threat to the system;

■ understand metrics for reliability specification and how these metrics may be used to specify reliability requirements.

Contents

In September 1993, a plane landed at Warsaw airport in Poland during a thunderstorm. For nine seconds after landing, the brakes on the computer-controlled braking system did not work. The plane ran off the end of the runway, hit an earth bank and caught fire. The subsequent enquiry showed that the braking system software had worked perfectly according to its specification. However, for reasons I won't go into here, the braking system did not recognise that the plane had landed. A safety feature on the aircraft had stopped the deployment of the braking system because this can be dangerous if the plane is in the air. The system failure was caused by an error in the system specification.

This illustrates the importance of specification for critical systems. Because of the high potential costs of system failure, it is important to ensure that the specification for critical systems accurately reflects the real needs of users of the system. If you don't get the specification right, then, irrespective of the quality of the software development, the system will not be dependable.

The need for dependability in critical systems generates both functional and non-functional system requirements:

1. System functional requirements may be generated to define error checking and recovery facilities and features that provide protection against system failures.

2. Non-functional requirements may be generated to define the required reliability and availability of the system.

In addition to these requirements, safety and security considerations can generate a further type of requirement that is difficult to classify as a functional or a non-functional requirement. They are high-level requirements that are perhaps best described as 'shall not' requirements. By contrast with normal functional requirements that define what the system shall do, 'shall not' requirements define system behaviour that is unacceptable. Examples of 'shall not' requirements are:

The system shall not allow users to modify access permissions on any files that they have not created. (security)

The system shall not allow reverse thrust mode to be selected when the aircraft is in flight. (safety)

The system shall not allow the simultaneous activation of more than three alarm signals. (safety)

These 'shall not' requirements are sometimes decomposed into more specific software functional requirements. Alternatively, implementation decisions may be deferred until the system is designed.

The user requirements for critical systems will always be specified using natural language and system models. However, as I discuss in Chapter 10, formal specification and associated verification are most likely to be cost-effective in critical systems development (Hall, 1996; Hall and Chapman, 2002; Wordsworth, 1996). Formal specifications are not just a basis for a verification of the design and implementation. They are the most precise way of specifying systems so reduce the scope for misunderstanding. Furthermore, constructing a formal specification forces a detailed analysis of the requirements, which is an effective way of discovering problems in the specification. In a natural language specification, errors can be concealed by the imprecision of the language. This is not the case if the system is formally specified.

9.1 Risk-driven specification

Critical systems specification is not an alternative to the normal requirements specification process. Rather, it supplements that process by focusing on the dependability of the system. Its objective is to understand the risks faced by the system and generate dependability requirements to cope with these risks. Risk-driven specification is an approach that has been widely used by safety and security critical systems developers. In safety-critical systems, the risks are hazards that can result in accidents; in security-critical systems, the risks are vulnerabilities that can lead to a successful attack on a system. However, a risk-driven approach is applicable to any system where dependability is a critical attribute.

The risk-driven specification process involves understanding the risks faced by the system, discovering their root causes and generating requirements to manage these risks. Figure 9.1 shows the iterative process of risk analysis:

1. *Risk identification* Potential risks that might arise are identified. These are dependent on the environment in which the system is to be used.

2. *Risk analysis and classification* The risks are considered separately. Those that are potentially serious and not implausible are selected for further analysis. At this stage, some risks may be eliminated simply because they are very unlikely ever to arise (e.g., simultaneous lightning strike and earthquake).

3. *Risk decomposition* Each risk is analysed individually to discover potential root causes of that risk. Techniques such as fault-tree analysis (discussed later in this chapter) may be used.

4. *Risk reduction assessment* Proposals for ways in which the identified risks may be reduced or eliminated are made. These then generate system dependability requirements that define the defences against the risk and how the risk will be managed if it arises.

For large systems, risk analysis may be structured into phases. Multiphase risk analysis is necessary for large systems such as chemical plants or aircraft. The phases of risk analysis include:

Figure 9.1 Risk-driven specification

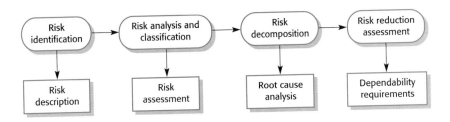

- Preliminary risk analysis where major risks are identified
- More detailed system and sub-system risk analysis
- Software risk analysis where the risks of software failure are considered
- Operational risk analysis that is concerned with the system user interface and risks that arise from operator errors.

Leveson (Leveson, 1995) discusses this multiphase risk analysis process in her book on safety-critical systems.

9.1.1 Risk identification

The objective of risk identification, the first stage of the risk analysis process, is to identify the risks that the critical system must cope with. This can be a complex and difficult process because risks often arise from interactions between the system and rare environmental conditions. The Warsaw accident that I discussed earlier happened when crosswinds generated during a thunderstorm caused the plane to tilt so that it landed on one rather than two wheels.

In safety-critical systems, the principal risks are hazards that can lead to an accident. You can tackle the hazard-identification problem by considering different classes of hazards, such as physical hazards, electrical hazards, biological hazards, radiation hazards, service failure hazards and so on. Each of these classes can then be analysed to discover associated hazards. Possible combinations of hazards must also be identified.

I introduced an example of an insulin pump system in Chapter 3. Like many medical devices, this is a safety-critical system. Some of the hazards or risks that might arise in this system are:

1. Insulin overdose (service failure)

2. Insulin underdose (service failure)

3. Power failure due to exhausted battery (electrical)

4. Electrical interference with other medical equipment such as a heart pacemaker (electrical)

5. Poor sensor and actuator contact caused by incorrect fitting (physical)

6. Parts of machine breaking off in patient's body (physical)

7. Infection caused by introduction of machine (biological)

8. Allergic reaction to the materials or insulin used in the machine (biological).

Software-related risks are normally concerned with failure to deliver a system service or with the failure of monitoring and protection systems. Monitoring systems may detect potentially hazardous conditions such as power failures.

Experienced engineers, working with domain experts and professional safety advisers, should identify system risks. Group working techniques such as brainstorming may be used to identify risks. Analysts with direct experience of previous incidents may also be able to identify risks.

9.1.2   Risk analysis and classification

The risk analysis and classification process is primarily concerned with understanding the likelihood that a risk will arise and the potential consequences if an accident or incident associated with that risk should occur. We need to make this analysis to understand whether a risk is a serious threat to the system or environment and to provide a basis for deciding the resources that should be used to manage the risk.

For each risk, the outcome of the risk analysis and classification process is a statement of acceptability. Risks can be categorised in three ways:

1. *Intolerable* The system must be designed in such a way so that either the risk cannot arise or, if it does arise, it will not result in an accident. Intolerable risks would, typically, be those that threaten human life or the financial stability of a business and which have a significant probability of occurrence. An example of an intolerable risk for an e-commerce system in an Internet bookstore, say, would be a risk of the system going down for more than a day.

2. *As low as reasonably practical (ALARP)* The system must be designed so that the probability of an accident arising because of the hazard is minimised, subject to other considerations such as cost and delivery. ALARP risks are those which have less serious consequences or which have a low probability of occurrence. An ALARP risk for an e-commerce system might be corruption of the web page images that presented the brand of the company. This is commercially undesirable but is unlikely to have serious short-term consequences.

3. *Acceptable* While the system designers should take all possible steps to reduce the probability of an 'acceptable' hazard arising, these should not increase costs, delivery time or other non-functional system attributes. An example of an acceptable risk for an e-commerce system is the risk that people using beta-release web browsers could not successfully complete orders.

Figure 9.2 Levels of
risk

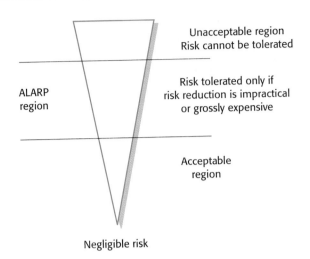

Unacceptable region
Risk cannot be tolerated

Risk tolerated only if
risk reduction is impractical
or grossly expensive

ALARP
region

Acceptable
region

Negligible risk

Figure 9.2 (Brazendale and Bell, 1994), developed for safety-critical systems, shows these three regions. The shape of the diagram reflects the costs of ensuring risks do not result in incidents or accidents. The cost of system design to cope with the risk is a function of the width of the triangle. The highest costs are incurred by risks at the top of the diagram, the lowest costs by risks at the apex of the triangle.

The boundaries between the regions in Figure 9.2 tend to move over time, due to public expectations of safety and political considerations. Although the financial costs of accepting risks and paying for any resulting accidents may be less than the costs of accident prevention, public opinion may demand that the additional costs must be accepted. For example, it may be cheaper for a company to clean up pollution on the rare occasion it occurs rather than install systems for pollution prevention. This may have been acceptable in the 1960s and 1970s but it is not likely to be publicly or politically acceptable now. The boundary between the intolerable region and the ALARP region has moved downwards so that risks that may have been accepted in the past are now intolerable.

Risk assessment involves estimating the risk probability and the risk severity. This is usually very difficult to do in an exact way and generally depends on making engineering judgements. Probabilities and severities are assigned using relative terms such as *probable*, *unlikely*, and *rare* and *high*, and *medium* and *low*. Previous system experience may allow some numeric value to be associated with these terms. However, because accidents are relatively uncommon, it is very difficult to validate the accuracy of this value.

Figure 9.3 shows a risk classification for the risks (hazards) identified in the previous section for the insulin delivery system. As I am not a physician, I have included the estimates to illustrate the principle. They are not necessarily the actual probabilities and severities that would arise in a real analysis of an insulin delivery system. Notice that an insulin overdose is potentially more serious than an insulin underdose in the short term. Insulin overdose can result in illness, coma and ultimately death.

Identified hazard	Hazard probability	Hazard severity	Estimated risk	Acceptability
1. Insulin overdose	Medium	High	High	Intolerable
2. Insulin underdose	Medium	Low	Low	Acceptable
3. Power failure	High	Low	Low	Acceptable
4. Machine incorrectly fitted	High	High	High	Intolerable
5. Machine breaks in patient	Low	High	Medium	ALARP
6. Machine causes infection	Medium	Medium	Medium	ALARP
7. Electrical interference	Low	High	Medium	ALARP
8. Allergic reaction	Low	Low	Low	Acceptable

Figure 9.3 Risk analysis of identified hazards in an insulin pump

Hazards 3–8 are not software related so I do not discuss them further here. To counter these hazards, the machine should have built-in self-checking software that should monitor the system state and warn of some of these hazards. The warning will often allow the hazard to be detected before it causes an accident. Examples of hazards that might be detected are power failure and incorrect placement of the machine. The monitoring software is, of course, safety-related as failure to detect a hazard could result in an accident.

9.1.3 Risk decomposition

Risk decomposition is the process of discovering the root causes of risks in a particular system. Techniques for risk decomposition have been primarily derived from safety-critical systems development where hazard analysis is a central part of the safety process. Risk analysis can be either deductive or inductive. Deductive, top-down techniques, which tend to be easier to use, start with the risk and work from that to the possible system failure; inductive, bottom-up techniques start with a proposed system failure and identify which hazards might arise that could lead to that failure.

Various techniques have been proposed as possible approaches to risk decomposition. These include reviews and checklists, as well as more formal techniques such as Petri net analysis (Peterson, 1981), formal logic (Jahanian and Mok, 1986) and fault-tree analysis (Leveson and Stolzy, 1987; Storey, 1996).

I cover fault-tree analysis here. This technique was developed for safety-critical systems and is relatively easy to understand without specialist domain knowledge. Fault-tree analysis involves identifying the undesired event and working backwards from that event to discover the possible causes of the hazard. You put the hazard at the root of the tree and identify the states that can lead to that hazard. For each

Figure 9.4 Fault tree
for insulin delivery
system

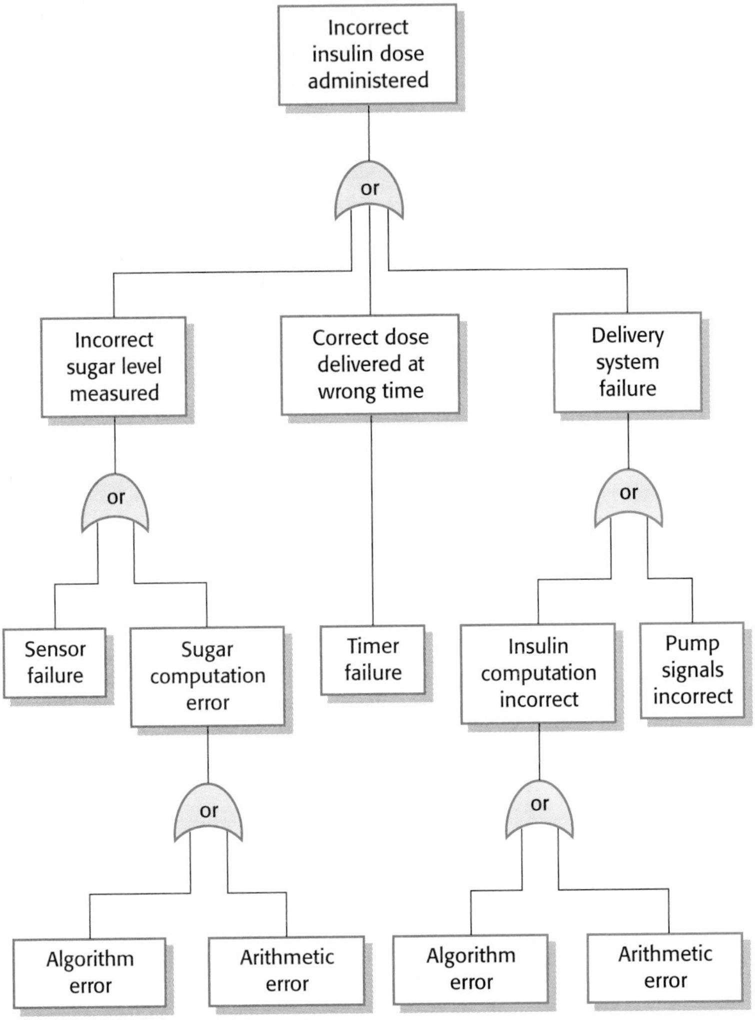

of these states, you then identify the states that can lead to that and continue this decomposition until you identify the root causes of the risk. States can be linked with 'and' and 'or' symbols. Risks that require a combination of root causes are usually less probable than risks that can result from a single root cause.

Figure 9.4 is the fault tree for the software-related hazards in the insulin delivery system. Insulin underdose and insulin overdose really represent a single hazard, namely, 'incorrect insulin dose administered', and a single fault tree can be drawn. Of course, when specifying how the software should react to hazards, you have to distinguish between an insulin underdose and an insulin overdose.

The fault tree in Figure 9.4 is incomplete. Only potential software faults have been fully decomposed. Hardware faults such as low battery power causing a sensor failure are not shown. At this level, further analysis is not possible. However, as a design and implementation and developed, more detailed fault trees may be developed. Leveson and Harvey (Leveson and Harvey, 1983) and Leveson (Leveson, 1985) show how fault trees can be developed throughout the software design down to the individual programming language statement level.

Fault trees are also used to identify potential hardware problems. A fault tree may provide insights into requirements for software to detect and, perhaps, correct these problems. For example, insulin doses are not administered at a very high frequency, no more than two or three times per hour and sometimes less often than this. Therefore, processor capacity is available to run diagnostic and self-checking programs. Hardware errors such as sensor, pump or timer errors can be discovered and warnings issued before they have a serious effect on the patient.

9.1.4 Risk reduction assessment

Once potential risks and their root causes have been identified, you should then derive system dependability requirements that manage the risks and ensure that incidents or accidents do not occur. There are three possible strategies that you can use:

1. *Risk avoidance* The system is designed so that the risk or hazard cannot arise.

2. *Risk detection and removal* The system is designed so that risks are detected and neutralised before they result in an accident.

3. *Damage limitation* The system is designed so that the consequences of an accident are minimised.

Normally, designers of critical systems use a combination of these approaches. In a safety-critical system, intolerable hazards may be handled by minimising their probability and adding a protection system that provides a safety backup. For example, in a chemical plant control system, the system will attempt to detect and avoid excess pressure in the reactor. However, there should also be an independent protection system that monitors the pressure and opens a relief valve if high pressure is detected.

In the insulin delivery system, a 'safe state' is a shutdown state where no insulin is injected. Over a short period this will not pose a threat to the diabetic's health. If the potential software problems identified in Figure 9.4 are considered, the following 'solutions' might be developed:

1. *Arithmetic error* This arises when some arithmetic computation causes a representation failure. The specification must identify all possible arithmetic errors that may occur. These depend on the algorithm used. The specification might state that an exception handler must be included for each identified arithmetic error. The specification should set out the action to be taken for each of these errors if they arise. A safe action is to shut down the delivery system and activate a warning alarm.

Figure 9.5 Examples
of safety
requirements for an
insulin pump

SR1:	The system shall not deliver a single dose of insulin that is greater than a specified maximum dose for a system user.
SR2:	The system shall not deliver a daily cumulative dose of insulin that is greater than a specified maximum for a system user.
SR3:	The system shall include a hardware diagnostic facility that shall be executed at least four times per hour.
SR4:	The system shall include an exception handler for all of the exceptions that are identified in Table 3.
SR5:	The audible alarm shall be sounded when any hardware or software anomaly is discovered and a diagnostic message as defined in Table 4 should be displayed.
SR6:	In the event of an alarm in the system, insulin delivery shall be suspended until the user has reset the system and cleared the alarm.

2. *Algorithmic error* This is a more difficult situation as no definite anomalous situation can be detected. It might be detected by comparing the required insulin dose computed with the previously delivered dose. If it is much higher, this may mean that the amount has been computed incorrectly. The system may also keep track of the dose sequence. After a number of above-average doses have been delivered, a warning may be issued and further dosage limited.

Some of the resulting safety requirements for the insulin pump system are shown in Figure 9.5 These are user requirements and, naturally, they would be expressed in more detail in a final system specification. In these requirements, the references to Tables 3 and 4 relate to tables that would be included in the requirements document.

9.2 Safety specification

The processes of risk management discussed so far have evolved from the processes developed for safety-critical systems. Until relatively recently, safety-critical systems were mostly control systems where failure of the equipment being controlled could cause injury. In the 1980s and 1990s, as computer control become widespread, the safety engineering community developed standards for safety-critical systems specification and development.

The process of safety specification and assurance is part of an overall safety life cycle that is defined in an international standard for safety management IEC 61508 (IEC, 1998). This standard was developed specifically for protection systems such as a system that stops a train if it passes a red signal. Although it can be used for

Figure 9.6 Control
system safety
requirements

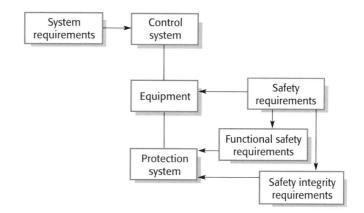

more general safety-critical systems, such as control systems, I think that its separation of safety specification from more general system specification is inappropriate for critical information systems. Figure 9.6 illustrates the system model that is assumed by the IEC 61508 standard.

Figure 9.7 is a simplified form of Redmill's presentation of the safety life cycle (Redmill, 1998). As you can see from Figure 9.7, this standard covers all aspects of safety management from initial scope definition through planning and system development to system decommissioning.

In this model, the control system controls some equipment that has associated high-level safety requirements. These high-level requirements generate two types of more detailed safety requirements that apply to the protection system for the equipment:

1. *Functional safety requirements* that define the safety functions of the system

2. *Safety integrity requirements* that define the reliability and availability of the protection system. These are based on the expected usage of the protection system and are intended to ensure that it will work when it is needed. Systems are classified using a safety integrity level (SIL) from 1 to 4. Each SIL level represents a higher level of reliability; the more critical the system, the higher the SIL required.

The first stages of the IEC 61508 safety life cycle define the scope of the system, assess the potential system hazards and estimate the risks they pose. This is followed by safety requirements specification and the allocation of these safety requirements to different sub-systems. The development activity involves planning and implementation. The safety-critical system itself is designed and implemented, as are related external systems that may provide additional protection. In parallel with this, the safety validation, installation, and operation and maintenance of the system are planned.

Safety management does not stop on delivery of the system. After delivery, the system must be installed as planned so that the hazard analysis remains valid. Safety

Figure 9.7 The IEC
61508 safety life
cycle

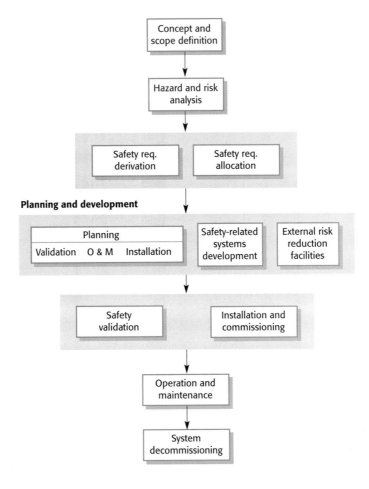

validation is then carried out before the system is put into use. Safety must also be managed during the operation and (particularly) the maintenance of the system. Many safety-related systems problems arise because of a poor maintenance process, so it is particularly important that the system is designed for maintainability. Finally, safety considerations that may apply during decommissioning (e.g., disposal of hazardous material in circuit boards) should also be taken into account.

9.3 Security specification

The specification of security requirements for systems has something in common with safety requirements. It is impractical to specify them quantitatively, and security requirements are often 'shall not' requirements that define unacceptable system behaviour rather than required system functionality. However, there are important differences between these types of requirements:

1. The notion of a safety life cycle that covers all aspects of safety management is well developed. The area of security specification and management is still immature and there is no accepted equivalent of a security life cycle.

2. Although some security threats are system specific, many are common to all types of system. All systems must protect themselves against intrusion, denial of service, and so on. By contrast, hazards in safety-critical systems are domain-specific.

3. Security techniques and technologies such as encryption and authentication devices are fairly mature. However, using this technology effectively often requires a high level of technical sophistication. It can be difficult to install, configure and stay up to date. Consequently, system managers make mistakes leaving vulnerabilities in the system.

4. The dominance of one software supplier in world markets means that a huge number of systems may be affected if security in their programs is breached. There is insufficient diversity in the computing infrastructure and consequently it is more vulnerable to external threats. Safety-critical systems are usually specialised, custom systems so this situation does not arise.

The conventional (non-computerised) approach to security analysis is based around the assets to be protected and their value to an organisation. Therefore, a bank will provide high security in an area where large amounts of money are stored compared to other public areas (say) where the potential losses are limited. The same approach can be used for specifying security for computer-based systems. A possible security specification process is shown in Figure 9.8.

The stages in this process are:

1. *Asset identification and evaluation* The assets (data and programs) and their required degree of protection are identified. The required protection depends on the asset value so that a password file (say) is normally more valuable than a set of public web pages as a successful attack on the password file has serious system-wide consequences.

2. *Threat analysis and risk assessment* Possible security threats are identified and the risks associated with each of these threats are estimated.

3. *Threat assignment* Identified threats are related to the assets so that, for each identified asset, there is a list of associated threats.

4. *Technology analysis* Available security technologies and their applicability against the identified threats are assessed.

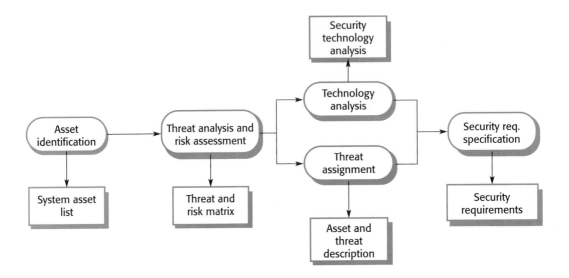

Figure 9.8 Security
specification

5. *Security requirements specification* The security requirements are specified. Where appropriate, they explicitly identify the security technologies that may be used to protect against threats to the system.

Security specification and security management are essential for all critical systems. If a system is insecure, then it is subject to infection with viruses and worms, corruption and unauthorised modification of data, and denial of service attacks. All of this means that we cannot be confident that the efforts made to ensure safety and reliability will be effective.

Different types of security requirements address the different threats faced by a system. Firesmith (Firesmith, 2003) identifies 10 types of security requirements that may be included in a system:

1. *Identification requirements* specify whether a system should identify its users before interacting with them.

2. *Authentication requirements* specify how users are identified.

3. *Authorisation requirements* specify the privileges and access permissions of identified users.

4. *Immunity requirements* specify how a system should protect itself against viruses, worms, and similar threats.

5. *Integrity requirements* specify how data corruption can be avoided.

6. *Intrusion detection requirements* specify what mechanisms should be used to detect attacks on the system.

7. *Non-repudiation requirements* specify that a party in a transaction cannot deny its involvement in that transaction.

Figure 9.9 Some
security requirements
for the LIBSYS
system

SEC1:   All system users shall be identified using their library card number and
personal password.

SEC2:   Users' privileges shall be assigned according to the class of user (student,
staff, library staff).

SEC3:   Before execution of any command, LIBSYS shall check that the user has
sufficient privileges to access and execute that command.

SEC4:   When a user orders a document, the order request shall be logged. The log
data maintained shall include the time of order, the user's identification and
the articles ordered.

SEC5:   All system data shall be backed up once per day and backups stored off-
site in a secure storage area.

SEC6:   Users shall not be permitted to have more than one simultaneous login
to LIBSYS.

8. *Privacy requirements* specify how data privacy is to be maintained.

9. *Security auditing requirements* specify how system use can be audited and
    checked.

10. *System maintenance security requirements* specify how an application can pre-
    vent authorised changes from accidentally defeating its security mechanisms.

Of course, not every system needs all of these security requirements. The particular requirements depend on the type of system, the situation of use and the expected
users. As an example, Figure 9.9 shows security requirements that might be
included in the LIBSYS system.

9.4 Software reliability specification

Reliability is a complex concept that should always be considered at the system
rather than the individual component level. Because the components in a system
are interdependent, a failure in one component can be propagated through the system and affect the operation of other components. In a computer-based system, you
have to consider three dimensions when specifying the overall system reliability:

1. *Hardware reliability* What is the probability of a hardware component failing
    and how long would it take to repair that component?

2. *Software reliability* How likely is it that a software component will produce an
    incorrect output? Software failures are different from hardware failures in that

software does not wear out: It can continue operating correctly after producing an incorrect result.

3. *Operator reliability* How likely is it that the operator of a system will make an error?

All of these are closely linked. Hardware failure can cause spurious signals to be generated that are outside the range of inputs expected by software. The software can then behave unpredictably. Unexpected system behaviour may confuse the operator and result in operator stress. The operator may then act incorrectly and choose inputs that are inappropriate for the current failure situation. These inputs further confuse the system and more errors are generated. A single sub-system failure that is recoverable can thus rapidly develop into a serious problem requiring a complete system shutdown.

Systems reliability should be specified as a non-functional requirement that, ideally, is expressed quantitatively using one of the metrics discussed in the next section. To meet the non-functional reliability requirements, it may be necessary to specify additional functional and design requirements on the system that specify how failures may be avoided or tolerated. Examples of these reliability requirements are:

1. A predefined range for all values that are input by the operator shall be defined, and the system shall check that all operator inputs fall within this predefined range.

2. As part of the initialisation process, the system shall check all disks for bad blocks.

3. N-version programming shall be used to implement the braking control system.

4. The system must be implemented in a safe subset of Ada and checked using static analysis.

There are no simple rules for deriving functional reliability requirements. In organisations that develop critical systems, there is usually organisational knowledge about possible reliability requirements and how these impact the actual reliability of a system. These organisations may specialise in specific types of system, such as railway control systems, so the reliability requirements, once derived, are reused across a range of systems. The higher the safety integrity level (discussed above) required in safety-critical systems, the more stringent the reliability requirements are likely to be.

9.4.1 Reliability metrics

Reliability metrics were first devised for hardware components. Hardware component failure is inevitable due to physical factors such as mechanical abrasion and electrical heating. Components have limited life spans, which is reflected in the most

Metric	Explanation
POFOD Probability of failure on demand	The likelihood that the system will fail when a service request is made. A POFOD of 0.001 means that one out of a thousand service requests may result in failure.
ROCOF Rate of failure occurrence	The frequency of occurrence with which unexpected behaviour is likely to occur. A ROCOF of 2/100 means that two failures are likely to occur in each 100 operational time units. This metric is sometimes called the failure intensity.
MTTF Mean time to failure	The average time between observed system failures. An MTTF of 500 means that one failure can be expected every 500 time units.
AVAIL Availability	The probability that the system is available for use at a given time. Availability of 0.998 means that the system is likely to be available for 998 of every 1,000 time units.

Figure 9.10 Reliability metrics

widely used hardware reliability metric, mean time to failure (MTTF). The MTTF is the mean time for which a component is expected to be operational. Hardware component failure is usually permanent, so the mean time to repair (MTTR), which reflects the time needed to repair or replace the component, is also significant.

However, these hardware metrics are not directly applicable to software reliability specification because software component failures are often transient rather than permanent. They show up only with some inputs. If the data is undamaged, the system can often continue in operation after a failure has occurred.

Metrics that have been used for specifying software reliability and availability are shown in Figure 9.10. The choice of which metric should be used depends on the type of system to which it applies and the requirements of the application domain. Some examples of the types of system where these different metrics may be used are:

1. *Probability of failure on demand* This metric is most appropriate for systems where services are demanded at unpredictable or at relatively long time intervals and where there are serious consequences if the service is not delivered. It might be used to specify protection systems such as the reliability of a pressure relief system in a chemical plant or an emergency shutdown system in a power plant.

2. *Rate of occurrence of failures* This metric should be used where regular demands are made on system services and where it is important that these services are correctly delivered. It might be used in the specification of a bank teller system that processes customer transactions or in a hotel reservation system.

3. *Mean time to failure* This metric should be used in systems where there are long transactions; that is, where people use the system for a long time. The MTTF should be longer than the average length of each transaction. Examples of systems where this metric may be used are word processor systems and CAD systems.

4. *Availability* This metric should be used in non-stop systems where users expect the system to deliver a continuous service. Examples of such systems are telephone switching systems and railway signalling systems.

There are three kinds of measurements that can be made when assessing the reliability of a system:

1. The number of system failures given a number of requests for system services. This is used to measure the POFOD.

2. The time (or number of transactions) between system failures. This is used to measure ROCOF and MTTF.

3. The elapsed repair or restart time when a system failure occurs. Given that the system must be continuously available, this is used to measure AVAIL.

Time units that may be used in these metrics are calendar time, processor time or some discrete unit such as number of transactions. In systems that spend much of their time waiting to respond to a service request, such as telephone switching systems, the time unit that should be used is processor time. If you use calendar time, then this includes the time when the system was doing nothing.

Calendar time is an appropriate time unit to use for systems that are in continuous operation. For example, monitoring systems such as alarm systems and other types of process control systems fall into this category. Systems that process transactions such as bank ATMs or airline reservation systems have variable loads placed on them depending on the time of day. In these cases, the unit of 'time' used should be the number of transactions; that is., the ROCOF would be number of failed transactions per N thousand transactions.

9.4.2 Non-functional reliability requirements

In many system requirements documents, reliability requirements are not carefully specified. The reliability specifications are subjective and unmeasurable. For example, statements such as 'The software shall be reliable under normal conditions of use' are meaningless. Quasi-quantitative statements such as 'The software shall exhibit no more than N faults/1000 lines' are equally useless. It is impossible to measure the number of faults/1000 lines of code as you can't tell when all faults have been discovered. Furthermore, the statement means nothing in terms of the dynamic behaviour of the system. It is software failures, not software faults, that affect the reliability of a system.

The types of failure that can occur are system specific, and the consequences of a system failure depend on the nature of that failure. When writing a reliability specification, you should identify different types of failure and think about whether these should be treated differently in the specification. Examples of different types of failure

Figure 9.11 Failure
classification

Failure class	Description
Transient	Occurs only with certain inputs
Permanent	Occurs with all inputs
Recoverable	System can recover without operator intervention
Unrecoverable	Operator intervention needed to recover from failure
Non-corrupting	Failure does not corrupt system state or data
Corrupting	Failure corrupts system state or data

are shown in Figure 9.11. Obviously combinations of these, such as a failure that is transient, recoverable and corrupting, can occur.

Most large systems are composed of several sub-systems with different reliability requirements. Because very high-reliability software is expensive, you should assess the reliability requirements of each sub-system separately rather than impose the same reliability requirement on all sub-systems. This avoids placing needlessly high demands for reliability on those sub-systems where it is unnecessary.

The steps involved in establishing a reliability specification are:

1. For each sub-system, identify the types of system failure that may occur and analyse the consequences of these failures.

2. From the system failure analysis, partition failures into appropriate classes. A reasonable starting point is to use the failure types shown in Figure 9.11.

3. For each failure class identified, define the reliability requirement using an appropriate reliability metric. It is not necessary to use the same metric for different classes of failure. If a failure requires some intervention to recover from it, the probability of that failure occurring on demand might be the most appropriate metric. When automatic recovery is possible and the effect of the failure is user inconvenience, ROCOF might be more appropriate.

4. Where appropriate, identify functional reliability requirements that define system functionality to reduce the probability of critical failures.

As an example, consider the reliability requirements for a bank ATM. Assume that each machine in the network is used about 300 times per day. The lifetime of the system hardware is 5 years and the software is normally upgraded every year. Therefore, during the lifetime of a software release, each machine will handle about 100,000 transactions. A bank has 1,000 machines in its network. This means that there are 300,000 transactions on the central database per day (say 100 million per year).

Figure 9.12 Reliability
specification for an
ATM

Failure class	Example	Reliability metric
Permanent, non-corrupting.	The system fails to operate with any card that is input. Software must be restarted to correct failure.	ROCOF 1 occurrence/1,000 days
Transient, non-corrupting	The magnetic stripe data cannot be read on an undamaged card that is input.	ROCOF 1 in 1,000 transactions
Transient, corrupting	A pattern of transactions across the network causes database corruption.	Unquantifiable! Should never happen in the lifetime of the system.

Figure 9.12 shows possible failure classes and possible reliability specifications for different types of system failure. The reliability requirements state that it is acceptable for a permanent failure to occur in a machine roughly once per three years. This means that, on average, one machine in the banking network might be affected each day. By contrast, faults that mean a transaction has to be cancelled can occur relatively frequently. Their only effect is to cause minor user inconvenience.

Ideally, faults that corrupt the database should never occur in the lifetime of the software. Therefore, the reliability requirement that might be placed on this is that the probability of a corrupting failure occurring when a demand is made is less than 1 in 200 million transactions. That is, in the lifetime of an ATM software release, there should never be an error that causes database corruption.

However, a reliability requirement like this cannot actually be tested. Say each transaction takes one second of machine time and a simulator can be built for the ATM network. Simulating the transactions which take place in a single day across the network will take 300,000 seconds. This is approximately 3.5 days. Clearly this period could be reduced by reducing the transaction time and using multiple simulators. Nevertheless, it is still very difficult to test the system to validate the reliability specification.

It is impossible to validate qualitative requirements that demand a very high level of reliability. For example, say a system was intended for use in a safety-critical application so it should never fail over the total lifetime of the system. Assume that 1,000 copies of the system are to be installed, and the system is 'executed' 1,000 times per second. The projected lifetime of the system is 10 years. The total estimated number of system executions is therefore approximately $3 * 10^{14}$. There is no point in specifying that the rate of occurrence of failure should be $1/10^{15}$ executions (this allows for some safety factor) as you cannot test the system for long enough to validate this level of reliability.

As a further example, consider the reliability requirements for the insulin pump system. This system delivers insulin a number of times per day and monitors the user's blood glucose several times per hour. Because the use of the system is intermittent and failure consequences are serious, the most appropriate reliability metric is POFOD (probability of failure on demand).

Failure to deliver insulin does not have immediate safety implications, so commercial factors rather than the safety factors govern the level of reliability required. Service costs are high because users need fast repair and replacement. It is in the manufacturer's interest to limit the number of permanent failures that require repair.

Again, two types of failure can be identified:

1. *Transient failures* that can be repaired by user actions such as resetting or recalibrating the machine. For these types of failures, a relatively low value of POFOD (say 0.002) may be acceptable. This means that one failure may occur in every 500 demands made on the machine. This is approximately once every 3.5 days.

2. *Permanent failures* that require the machine to be repaired by the manufacturer. The probability of this type of failure should be much lower. Roughly once a year is the minimum figure, so POFOD should be no more than 0.00002.

KEY POINTS

▨ Risk analysis is a key activity in the critical systems specification process. It involves identifying risks that can result in accidents or incidents. System requirements are then generated to ensure that these risks do not arise or, if they occur, they do not result in an incident.

▨ Risk analysis is the process of assessing the likelihood that a risk will result in an accident. Risk analysis identifies critical risks that must be avoided in the system and classifying risks according to their seriousness.

▨ To specify security requirements, you should identify the assets that are to be protected and define how security techniques and technology should be used to protect these assets.

▨ Reliability requirements should be defined quantitatively in the system requirements specification.

▨ There are several reliability metrics, such as probability of failure on demand (POFOD), rate of occurrence of failure, mean time to failure (MTTF) and availability. The most appropriate metric for a specific system depends on the type of system and application domain. Different metrics may be used for different sub-systems.

▨ Non-functional reliability specifications can lead to functional system requirements that define system features whose function is to reduce the number of system failures and hence increase reliability.

The cost of developing and validating a system reliability specification can be very high. Organisations must be realistic about whether these costs are worthwhile. They are clearly justified in systems where reliable operation is critical, such as telephone switching systems or where system failure may result in large economic losses. They are probably not justified for many types of business or scientific systems. These have modest reliability requirements, as the costs of failure are simply processing delays, and it is straightforward and relatively inexpensive to recover from these.

FURTHER READING

'Security use cases.' A good article, available on the web, that focuses on how use-cases can be used in security specification. The author also has a number of good articles on security specification that are referenced in this article. (D. G. Firesmith, *Journal of Object Technology*, 2 (3), May–June 2003.)

'Requirements Definition for survivable network systems.' Discusses the problems of defining requirements for survivable systems where survivability relates to both available and security. (R. C. Linger, et al., *Proc. ICRE' 98*, IEEE Press, 1998.)

Requirements Engineering: A Good Practice Guide. This book includes a section on the specification of critical systems and a discussion of the use of formal methods in critical systems specification (I. Sommerville and P. Sawyer, 1997, John Wiley & Sons.)

Safeware: System Safety and Computers. This is a thorough discussion of all aspects of safety-critical systems. It is particularly strong in its description of hazard analysis and the derivation of requirements from this. (N. Leveson, 1995, Addison-Wesley.)

EXERCISES

9.1 Explain why the boundaries in the risk triangle shown in Figure 9.2 are liable to change with time and with changing social attitudes.

9.2 In the insulin pump system, the user has to change the needle and insulin supply at regular intervals and may also change the maximum single dose and the maximum daily dose that may be administered. Suggest three user errors that might occur and propose safety requirements that would avoid these errors resulting in an accident.

9.3 A safety-critical software system for treating cancer patients has two principal components:

■ A radiation therapy machine that delivers controlled doses of radiation to tumour sites. This machine is controlled by an embedded software system.

■ A treatment database that includes details of the treatment given to each patient. Treatment requirements are entered in this database and are automatically downloaded to the radiation therapy machine.

Identify three hazards that may arise in this system. For each hazard, suggest a defensive requirement that will reduce the probability that these hazards will result in an accident. Explain why your suggested defence is likely to reduce the risk associated with the hazard.

9.4   Describe three important differences between the processes of safety specification and security specification.

9.5   Suggest how fault-tree analysis could be modified for use in security specification. Threats in a security-critical system are analogous to hazards in a safety-critical system.

9.6   What is the fundamental difference between hardware and software failures? Given this difference, explain why hardware reliability metrics are often inappropriate for measuring software reliability.

9.7   Explain why it is practically impossible to validate reliability specifications when these are expressed in terms of a very small number of failures over the total lifetime of a system.

9.8   Suggest appropriate reliability metrics for the following classes of software system. Give reasons for your choice of metric. Predict the usage of these systems and suggest appropriate values for the reliability metrics:

■ A system that monitors patients in a hospital intensive care unit

■ A word processor

■ An automated vending machine control system

■ A system to control braking in a car

■ A system to control a refrigeration unit

■ A management report generator.

9.9   You are responsible for writing the specification for a software system that controls a network of EPOS (electronic point of sale) terminals in a store. The system accepts bar code information from a terminal, queries a product database and returns the item name and its price to the terminal for display. The system must be continually available during the store's opening hours.

Giving reasons for your choice, choose appropriate metrics for specifying the reliability of such a system and write a plausible reliability specification that takes into account the fact that some faults are more serious than others.

Suggest four functional requirements that might be generated for this store system to help improve system reliability.

9.10   A train protection system automatically applies the brakes of a train if the speed limit for a segment of track is exceeded or if the train enters a track segment that is currently signalled with a red light (i.e., the segment should not be entered). Giving reasons for your answer, chose a reliability metric that might be used to specify the required reliability for such a system.

There are two essential safety requirements for such a system:

■ The train shall not enter a segment of track that is signalled with a red light.

■ The train shall not exceed the specified speed limit for a section of track.

Assuming that the signal status and the speed limit for the track segment are transmitted to on-board software on the train before it enters that track segment, propose five possible functional system requirements for the on-board software that may be generated from the system safety requirements.

9.11 Should software engineers working on the specification and development of safety-related systems be professionally certified in some way? Explain your reasoning.

9.12 As an expert in computer security, you have been approached by an organisation that campaigns for the rights of torture victims and have been asked to help them gain unauthorised access to the computer systems of a British company. This will help them confirm or deny that this company is selling equipment used directly in the torture of political prisoners. Discuss the ethical dilemmas that this request raises and how you would react to this request.

10

Formal specification

Objectives

The objective of this chapter is to introduce formal specification techniques that can be used to add detail to a system requirements specification. When you have read this chapter, you will:

■ understand why formal specification techniques help discover problems in system requirements;

■ understand the use of algebraic techniques of formal specification to define interface specifications;

■ understand how formal, model-based formal techniques are used for behavioural specification.

Contents

In 'traditional' engineering disciplines, such as electrical and civil engineering, progress has usually involved the development of better mathematical techniques. The engineering industry has had no difficulty accepting the need for mathematical analysis and in incorporating mathematical analysis into its processes. Mathematical analysis is a routine part of the process of developing and validating a product design.

However, software engineering has not followed the same path. Although there has now been more than 30 years of research into the use of mathematical techniques in the software process, these techniques have had a limited impact. So-called formal methods of software development are not widely used in industrial software development. Most software development companies do not consider it cost-effective to apply them in their software development processes.

The term *formal methods* is used to refer to any activities that rely on mathematical representations of software including formal system specification, specification analysis and proof, transformational development, and program verification. All of these activities are dependent on a formal specification of the software. A formal software specification is a specification expressed in a language whose vocabulary, syntax and semantics are formally defined. This need for a formal definition means that the specification languages must be based on mathematical concepts whose properties are well understood. The branch of mathematics used is discrete mathematics, and the mathematical concepts are drawn from set theory, logic and algebra.

In the 1980s, many software engineering researchers proposed that using formal development methods was the best way to improve software quality. They argued that the rigour and detailed analysis that are an essential part of formal methods would lead to programs with fewer errors and which were more suited to users' needs. They predicted that, by the 21st century, a large proportion of software would be developed using formal methods.

Clearly, this prediction has not come true. There are four main reasons for this:

1. *Successful software engineering* The use of other software engineering methods such as structured methods, configuration management and information hiding in software design and development processes have resulted in improvements in software quality. People who suggested that the only way to improve software quality was by using formal methods were clearly wrong.

2. *Market changes* In the 1980s, software quality was seen as the key software engineering problem. However, since then, the critical issue for many classes of software development is not quality but time to market. Software must be developed quickly, and customers are sometimes willing to accept software with some faults if rapid delivery can be achieved. Techniques for rapid software development do not work effectively with formal specifications. Of course, quality is still an important factor, but it must be achieved in the context of rapid delivery.

3. *Limited scope of formal methods* Formal methods are not well suited to specifying user interfaces and user interaction. The user interface component has

become a greater and greater part of most systems, so you can only really use formal methods when developing the other parts of the system.

4. *Limited scalability of formal methods* Formal methods still do not scale up well. Successful projects that have used these techniques have mostly been concerned with relatively small, critical kernel systems. As systems increase in size, the time and effort required to develop a formal specification grows disproportionately.

These factors mean that most software development companies have been unwilling to risk using formal methods in their development process. However, formal specification is an excellent way of discovering specification errors and presenting the system specification in an unambiguous way. Organisations that have made the investment in formal methods have reported fewer errors in the delivered software without an increase in development costs. It seems that formal methods can be cost-effective if their use is limited to core parts of the system and if companies are willing to make the high initial investment in this technology.

The use of formal methods is increasing in the area of critical systems development, where emergent system properties such as safety, reliability and security are very important. The high cost of failure in these systems means that companies are willing to accept the high introductory costs of formal methods to ensure that their software is as dependable as possible. As I discuss in Chapter 24, critical systems have very high validation costs, and the costs of system failure are large and increasing. Formal methods can reduce these costs.

Critical systems where formal methods have been applied successfully include an air traffic control information system (Hall, 1996), railway signalling systems (Dehbonei and Mejia, 1995), spacecraft systems (Easterbrook, et al., 1998) and medical control systems (Jacky, et al. 1997; Jacky, 1995). They have also been used for software tool specification (Neil, et al., 1998), the specification of part of IBM's CICS system (Wordsworth, 1991) and a real-time system kernel (Spivey, 1990). The Cleanroom method of software development (Prowell, et al., 1999) relies on formally based arguments that code conforms to its specification. Because reasoning about the security of a system is also possible if a formal specification is developed, it is likely that secure systems will be an important area for formal methods use (Hall and Chapman, 2002).

10.1 Formal specification in the software process

Critical systems development usually involves a plan-based software process that is based on the waterfall model of development discussed in Chapter 4. Both the system requirements and the system design are expressed in detail and carefully analysed and checked before implementation begins. If a formal specification of

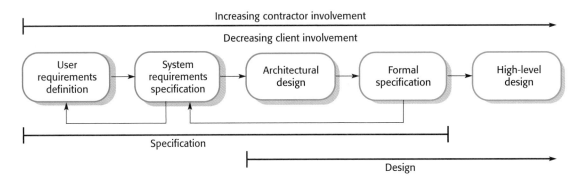

Increasing contractor involvement

Decreasing client involvement

Specification

Design

Figure 10.1
Specification and
design

the software is developed, this usually comes after the system requirements have been specified but before the detailed system design. There is a tight feedback loop between the detailed requirements specification and the formal specification. As I discuss later, one of the main benefits of formal specification is its ability to uncover problems and ambiguities in the system requirements.

The involvement of the client decreases and the involvement of the contractor increases as more detail is added to the system specification. In the early stages of the process, the specification should be 'customer-oriented'. You should write the specification so that the client can understand it, and you should make as few assumptions as possible about the software design. However, the final stage of the process, which is the construction of a complete, consistent and precise specification, is principally intended for the software contractor. It specifies the details of the system implementation. You may use a formal language at this stage to avoid ambiguity in the software specification.

Figure 10.1 shows the stages of software specification and its interface with the design process. The specification stages shown in Figure 10.1 are not independent nor are they necessarily developed in the sequence shown. Figure 10.2 shows specification and design activities that may be carried out in parallel streams. There is a two-way relationship between each stage in the process. Information is fed from the specification to the design process and vice versa.

Figure 10.2 Formal
specification in the
software process

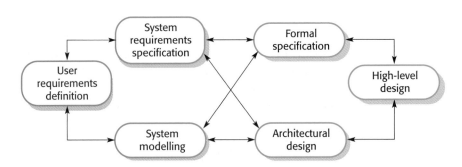

Figure 10.3 Software
development costs
with formal
specification

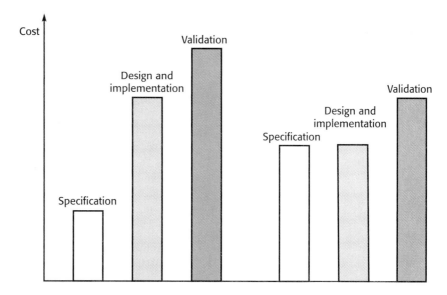

As you develop the specification in detail, your understanding of that specification increases. Creating a formal specification forces you to make a detailed systems analysis that usually reveals errors and inconsistencies in the informal requirements specification. This error detection is probably the most potent argument for developing a formal specification (Hall, 1990). It helps you discover requirements problems that can be very expensive to correct later.

Depending on the process used, specification problems discovered during formal analysis might influence changes to the requirements specification if this has not already been agreed. If the requirements specification has been agreed and is included in the system development contract, you should raise the problems that you have found with the customer. It is then up to the customer to decide how they should be resolved before you start the system design process.

Developing and analysing a formal specification front loads software development costs. Figure 10.3 shows how software process costs are likely to be affected by the use of formal specification. When a conventional process is used, validation costs are about 50% of development costs, and implementation and design costs are about twice the costs of specification. With formal specification, specification and implementation costs are comparable, and system validation costs are significantly reduced. As the development of the formal specification uncovers requirements problems, rework to correct these problems after the system has been designed is avoided.

Two fundamental approaches to formal specification have been used to write detailed specifications for industrial software systems. These are:

1. *An algebraic approach* where the system is described in terms of operations and their relationships

Figure 10.4 Formal
specification
languages

	Sequential	**Concurrent**
Algebraic	Larch (Guttag et al., 1993) OBJ (Futatsugi et al., 1985)	Lotos (Bolognesi and Brinksma, 1987)
Model-based	Z (Spivey, 1992) VDM (Jones, 1980) B (Wordsworth, 1996)	CSP (Hoare, 1985) Petri Nets (Peterson, 1981)

2. *A model-based approach* where a model of the system is built using mathematical constructs such as sets and sequences, and the system operations are defined by how they modify the system state

Different languages in these families have been developed to specify sequential and concurrent systems. Figure 10.4 shows examples of the languages in each of these classes. You can see from this table that most of these languages were developed in the 1980s. It takes several years to refine a formal specification language, so most formal specification research is now based on these languages and is not concerned with inventing new notations.

In this chapter, my aim is to introduce both algebraic and model-based approaches. The examples here should give you an idea of how formal specification results in a precise, detailed specification, but I don't discuss specification language details, specification techniques or methods of program verification. You can download a more detailed description of both algebraic and model-based techniques from the book's web site.

10.2 Sub-system interface specification

Large systems are usually decomposed into sub-systems that are developed independently. Sub-systems make use of other sub-systems, so an essential part of the specification process is to define sub-system interfaces. Once the interfaces are agreed and defined, the sub-systems can then be designed and implemented independently.

Sub-system interfaces are often defined as a set of objects or components (Figure 10.5). These describe the data and operations that can be accessed through the sub-system interface. You can therefore define a sub-system interface specification by combining the specifications of the objects that make up the interface.

Precise sub-system interface specifications are important because sub-system developers must write code that uses the services of other sub-systems before these have been implemented. The interface specification provides information for sub-system developers so that they know what services will be available in other sub-systems

Figure 10.5 Sub-system interface objects

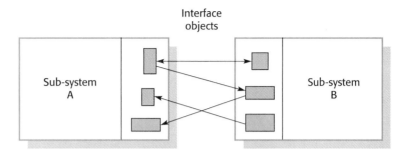

and how these can be accessed. Clear and unambiguous sub-system interface specifications reduce the chances of misunderstandings between a sub-system providing some service and the sub-systems using that service.

The algebraic approach was originally designed for the definition of abstract data type interfaces. In an abstract data type, the type is defined by specifying the type operations rather than the type representation. Therefore, it is similar to an object class. The algebraic method of formal specification defines the abstract data type in terms of the relationships between the type operations.

Guttag (Guttag, 1977) first discussed this approach in the specification of abstract data types. Cohen et al. (Cohen, et al., 1986) show how the technique can be extended to complete system specification using an example of a document retrieval system. Liskov and Guttag (Liskov and Guttag, 1986) also cover the algebraic specification of abstract data types.

The structure of an object specification is shown in Figure 10.6. The body of the specification has four components.

1. *An introduction* that declares the sort (the type name) of the entity being specified. A sort is the name of a set of objects with common characteristics. It is similar to a type in a programming language. The introduction may also include an 'imports' declaration, where the names of specifications defining other sorts are declared. Importing a specification makes these sorts available for use.

2. *A description* part, where the operations are described informally. This makes the formal specification easier to understand. The formal specification complements this description by providing an unambiguous syntax and semantics for the type operations.

3. *The signature* part defines the syntax of the interface to the object class or abstract data type. The names of the operations that are defined, the number and sorts of their parameters, and the sort of operation results are described in the signature.

4. *The axioms* part defines the semantics of the operations by defining a set of *axioms* that characterise the behaviour of the abstract data type. These axioms relate the operations used to construct entities of the defined sort with operations used to inspect its values.

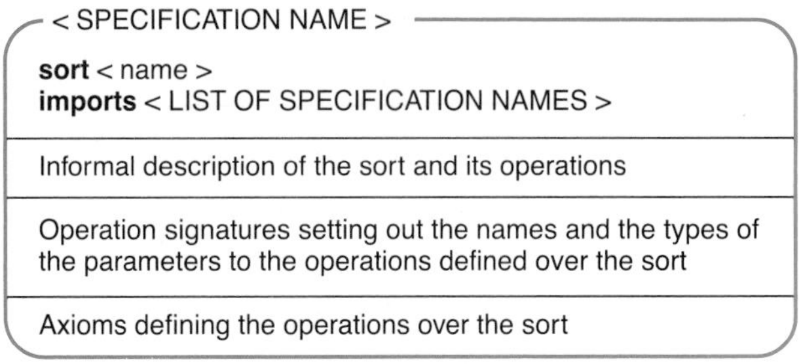

Figure 10.6 The
structure of an
algebraic
specification

```
< SPECIFICATION NAME >

  sort < name >
  imports < LIST OF SPECIFICATION NAMES >

  Informal description of the sort and its operations

  Operation signatures setting out the names and the types of
  the parameters to the operations defined over the sort

  Axioms defining the operations over the sort
```

The process of developing a formal specification of a sub-system interface includes the following activities:

1. *Specification structuring* Organise the informal interface specification into a set of abstract data types or object classes. You should informally define the operations associated with each class.

2. *Specification naming* Establish a name for each abstract type specification, decide whether they require generic parameters and decide on names for the sorts identified.

3. *Operation selection* Choose a set of operations for each specification based on the identified interface functionality. You should include operations to create instances of the sort, to modify the value of instances and to inspect the instance values. You may have to add functions to those initially identified in the informal interface definition.

4. *Informal operation specification* Write an informal specification of each operation. You should describe how the operations affect the defined sort.

5. *Syntax definition* Define the syntax of the operations and the parameters to each. This is the signature part of the formal specification. You should update the informal specification at this stage if necessary.

6. *Axiom definition* Define the semantics of the operations by describing what conditions are always true for different operation combinations.

To explain the technique of algebraic specification, I use an example of a simple data structure (a linked list), as shown in Figure 10.7. Linked lists are ordered data structures where each element includes a link to the following element in the structure. I have used a simple list with only a few associated operations so that the discussion here is not too long. In practice, object classes defining a list would probably have more operations

Assume that the first stage of the specification process, namely specification structuring, has been carried out and that the need for a list has been identified. The name of the specification and the name of the sort can be the same, although it is

Figure 10.7 A simple
list specification

LIST (Elem)

sort List
imports INTEGER

Defines a list where elements are added at the end and removed
from the front. The operations are Create, which brings an empty list
into existence, Cons, which creates a new list with an added member,
Length, which evaluates the list size, Head, which evaluates the front
element of the list, and Tail, which creates a list by removing the head
from its input list. Undefined represents an undefined value of type Elem.

Create → List
Cons (List, Elem) → List
Head (List) → Elem
Length (List) → Integer
Tail (List) → List

Head (Create) = Undefined **exception** (empty list)
Head (Cons (L, v)) = **if** L = Create **then** v **else** Head (L)
Length (Create) = 0
Length (Cons (L, v)) = Length (L) + 1
Tail (Create) = Create
Tail (Cons (L, v)) = **if** L = Create **then** Create **else** Cons (Tail (L), v)

useful to distinguish between these by using some convention. I use uppercase for
the specification name (**LIST**) and lowercase with an initial capital for the sort name
(**List**). As lists are collections of other types, the specification has a generic parameter (**Elem**). The name **Elem** can represent any type: integer, string, list, and so on.

In general, for each abstract data type, the required operations should include an
operation to bring instances of the type into existence (**Create**) and to construct the
type from its basic elements (**Cons**). In the case of lists, there should be an operation to evaluate the first list element (**Head**), an operation that returns the list created by removing the first element (**Tail**), and an operation to count the number of
list elements (**Length**).

To define the syntax of each of these operations, you must decide which parameters are required for the operation and the results of the operation. In general, input
parameters are either the sort being defined (**List**) or the generic sort (**Elem**). The
results of operations may be either of those sorts or some other sort such as **Integer**
or **Boolean**. In the list example, the **Length** operation returns an integer. Therefore,
you must include an 'imports' declaration, declaring that the specification of integer is used in the specification.

To create the specification, you define a set of axioms that apply to the abstract
type and these specify its semantics. You define the axioms using the operations
defined in the signature part. These axioms specify the semantics by setting out what
is always true about the behaviour of entities with that abstract type.

Operations on an abstract data type usually fall into two classes.

1. *Constructor operations* that create or modify entities of the sort defined in the
   specification. Typically, these are given names such as **Create**, **Update**, **Add** or,
   in this case, **Cons**, meaning construct.

2. *Inspection operations* that evaluate attributes of the sort defined in the specification. Typically, these are given names such as **Eval** or **Get**.

A good rule of thumb for writing an algebraic specification is to establish the constructor operations and write down an axiom for each inspection operation over each constructor. This suggests that if there are **m** constructor operations and n inspection operations, there should be **m * n** axioms defined.

However, the constructor operations associated with an abstract type may not all be primitive constructors. That is, it may be possible to define them using other constructors and inspection operations. If you define a constructor operation using other constructors, then you need only to define the inspection operations using the primitive constructors.

In the list specification, the constructor operations that build lists are **Create**, **Cons** and **Tail**. The inspection operations are **Head** (return the value of the first element in the list) and **Length** (return the number of elements in the list), which are used to discover list attributes. The **Tail** operation, however, is not a primitive constructor. There is therefore no need to define axioms over the **Tail** operation for **Head** and **Length** operations, but you do have to define **Tail** using the primitive constructor operations.

Evaluating the head of an empty list results in an undefined value. The specifications of **Head** and **Tail** show that **Head** evaluates the front of the list and **Tail** evaluates to the input list with its head removed. The specification of **Head** states that the head of a list created using **Cons** is either the value added to the list (if the initial list is empty) or is the same as the head of the initial list parameter to **Cons**. Adding an element to a list does not affect its head unless the list is empty.

Recursion is commonly used when writing algebraic specifications. The value of the **Tail** operation is the list that is formed by taking the input list and removing its head. The definition of **Tail** shows how recursion is used in constructing algebraic specifications. The operation is defined on empty lists, then recursively on non-empty lists with the recursion terminating when the empty list results.

It is sometimes easier to understand recursive specifications by developing a short example. Say we have a list [5, 7] where 5 is the front of the list and 7 the end of the list. The operation **Cons** ([5, 7], 9) should return a list [5, 7, 9] and a **Tail** operation applied to this should return the list [7, 9]. The sequence of equations that results from substituting the parameters in the above specification with these values is:

Tail ([5, 7, 9]) =
Tail (Cons ([5, 7], 9)) = Cons (Tail ([5, 7]), 9) =
   Cons (Tail (Cons ([5], 7)), 9) = Cons (Cons (Tail ([5]), 7), 9) =
   Cons (Cons (Tail (Cons ([], 5)), 7), 9) = Cons (Cons ([Create], 7), 9) =
   Cons ([7], 9) = [7, 9]

The systematic rewriting of the axiom for **Tail** illustrates that it does indeed produce the anticipated result. You can check that axiom for **Head** is correct using the same rewriting technique.

Now let us look at how you can use algebraic specification of an interface in a critical system specification. Assume that, in an air traffic control system, an object has been designed to represent a controlled sector of airspace. Each controlled sector may include a number of aircraft, each of which has a unique aircraft identifier. For safety reasons, all aircraft must be separated by at least 300 metres in height. The system warns the controller if an attempt is made to position an aircraft so that this constraint is breached.

To simplify the description, I have only defined a limited number of operations on the sector object. In a practical system, there are likely to be many more operations and more complex safety conditions related to the horizontal separation of the aircraft. The critical operations on the object are:

1. **Enter** This operation adds an aircraft (represented by an identifier) to the airspace at a specified height. There must not be other aircraft at that height or within 300 metres of it.

2. **Leave** This operation removes the specified aircraft from the controlled sector. This operation is used when the aircraft moves to an adjacent sector.

3. **Move** This operation moves an aircraft from one height to another. Again, the safety constraint that vertical separation of aircraft must be at least 300 metres is checked.

4. **Lookup** Given an aircraft identifier, this operation returns the current height of that aircraft in the sector.

It makes it easier to specify these operations if some other interface operations are defined. These are:

1. **Create** This is a standard operation for an abstract data type. It causes an empty instance of the type to be created. In this case, it represents a sector that has no aircraft in it.

2. **Put** This is a simpler version of the **Enter** operation. It adds an aircraft to the sector without any associated constraint checking.

3. **In-space** Given an aircraft call sign, this Boolean operation returns true if the aircraft is in the controlled sector, false otherwise.

4. **Occupied** Given a height, this Boolean operation returns true if there is an aircraft within 300 metres of that height, false otherwise.

The advantage of defining these simpler operations is that you can then use them as building blocks to define the more complex operations on the **Sector** sort. The algebraic specification of this sort is shown in Figure 10.8.

Essentially, the basic constructor operations are **Create** and **Put**, and I use these in the specification of the other operations. **Occupied** and **In-space** are checking oper-

Figure 10.8 The
specification of a
controlled sector

```
┌─ SECTOR ───────────────────────────────────────────────────────────────┐
│  sort Sector                                                             │
│  imports INTEGER, BOOLEAN                                                │
├─────────────────────────────────────────────────────────────────────────┤
│  Enter      – adds an aircraft to the sector if safety conditions are satisfed │
│  Leave      – removes an aircraft from the sector                        │
│  Move       – moves an aircraft from one height to another if safe to do so │
│  Lookup     – finds the height of an aircraft in the sector              │
│                                                                          │
│  Create     – creates an empty sector                                    │
│  Put        – adds an aircraft to a sector with no constraint checks     │
│  In-space   – checks if an aircraft is already in a sector               │
│  Occupied   – checks if a specified height is available                  │
├─────────────────────────────────────────────────────────────────────────┤
│  Enter (Sector, Call-sign, Height)  → Sector                            │
│  Leave (Sector, Call-sign)  → Sector                                    │
│  Move (Sector, Call-sign, Height)  → Sector                             │
│  Lookup (Sector, Call-sign) → Height                                    │
│                                                                          │
│  Create → Sector                                                         │
│  Put (Sector, Call-sign, Height)  → Sector                              │
│  In-space (Sector, Call-sign)  → Boolean                                │
│  Occupied (Sector, Height)  → Boolean                                   │
├─────────────────────────────────────────────────────────────────────────┤
```

Enter (S, CS, H) =
　　if　　In-space (S, CS) **then** S **exception** (Aircraft already in sector)
　　elsif　Occupied (S, H) **then** S **exception** (Height conflict)
　　else　Put (S, CS, H)

Leave (Create, CS) = Create **exception** (Aircraft not in sector)
Leave (Put (S, CS1, H1), CS) =
　　if CS = CS1 **then** S **else** Put (Leave (S, CS), CS1, H1)

Move (S, CS, H) =
　　if　　S = Create **then** Create **exception** (No aircraft in sector)
　　elsif　**not** In-space (S, CS) **then** S **exception** (Aircraft not in sector)
　　elsif　Occupied (S, H) **then** S **exception** (Height conflict)
　　else　Put (Leave (S, CS), CS, H)

-- NO-HEIGHT is a constant indicating that a valid height cannot be returned

Lookup (Create, CS) = NO-HEIGHT **exception** (Aircraft not in sector)
Lookup (Put (S, CS1, H1), CS) =
　　if CS = CS1 **then** H1 **else** Lookup (S, CS)

Occupied (Create, H) = false
Occupied (Put (S, CS1, H1), H) =
　　if　　(H1 > H **and** H1 - H ≤ 300) **or** (H > H1 **and** H - H1 ≤ 300) **then** true
　　else　Occupied (S, H)

In-space (Create, CS) = false
In-space (Put (S, CS1, H1), CS) =
　　if CS = CS1 **then** true **else** In-space (S, CS)

ations that I have defined using **Create** and **Put**, and I then use them in other specifications. I don't have space to explain all operations in detail here but I discuss
two of them (**Occupied** and **Move**). With this information, you should be able to
understand the other operation specifications.

1. The **Occupied** operation takes a sector and a parameter representing the height and checks whether any aircraft have been assigned to that height. Its specification states that:

    ■ In an empty sector (one that has been create by a **Create** operation), every level is vacant. The operation returns false irrespective of the value of the height parameter.

    ■ In a non-empty sector (one where there has been previous **Put** operations), the **Occupied** operation checks whether the specified height (parameter H) is within 300 metres of the height of aircraft that was last added to the sector by a **Put** operation. If so, that height is already occupied so the value of **Occupied** is true.

    ■ If it is not occupied, the operation checks the sector recursively. You can think of this check being carried out on the last aircraft put into the sector. If the height is not within range of the height of that aircraft, the operation then checks against the previous aircraft that has been put into the sector and so on. Eventually, if there are no aircraft within range of the specified height, the check is carried out against an empty sector and so returns false.

2. The **Move** operation moves an aircraft in a sector from one height to another. Its specification states that:

    ■ If a **Move** operation is applied to an empty airspace (the result of **Create**), the airspace is unchanged and an exception is raised to indicate that the specified aircraft is not in the airspace.

    ■ In a non-empty sector, the operation first checks (using **In-space**) whether the given aircraft is in the sector. If it is not, an exception is raised. If it is, the operation checks that the specified height is available (using **Occupied**), raising an exception if there is already an aircraft at that height.

    ■ If the specified height is available, the **Move** operation is equivalent to the specified aircraft leaving the airspace (so the operation **Leave** is used) and being put into the sector at the new height.

10.3 Behavioural specification

The simple algebraic techniques described in the previous section can be used to describe interfaces where the object operations are independent of the object state. That is, the results of applying an operation should not depend on the results of previous operations. Where this condition does not hold, algebraic techniques can become cumbersome. Furthermore, as they increase in size, I find that algebraic descriptions of system behaviour become increasingly difficult to understand.

An alternative approach to formal specification that has been more widely used in industrial projects is model-based specification. Model-based specification is an approach to formal specification where the system specification is expressed as a system state model. You can specify the system operations by defining how they affect the state of the system model. The combination of these specifications defines the overall behaviour of the system.

Mature notations for developing model-based specifications are VDM (Jones, 1980; Jones, 1986), B (Wordsworth, 1996) and Z (Hayes, 1987; Spivey, 1992). I use Z (pronounced Zed, not Zee) here. In Z, systems are modelled using sets and relations between sets. However, Z has augmented these mathematical concepts with constructs that specifically support software specification.

In an introduction to model-based specification, I can only give an overview of how a specification can be developed. A complete description of the Z notation would be longer than this chapter. Rather, I present some small examples to illustrate the technique and introduce notation as it is required. A full description of the Z notation is given in textbooks such as those by Diller (Potter, et al., 1996) and Jacky (Jacky, 1997).

Formal specifications can be difficult and tedious to read especially when they are presented as large mathematical formulae. The designers of Z have paid particular attention to this problem. Specifications are presented as informal text supplemented with formal descriptions. The formal description is included as small, easy-to-read chunks (called *schemas*) that are distinguished from associated text using graphical highlighting. Schemas are used to introduce state variables and to define constraints and operations on the state. Schemas can themselves be manipulated using operations such as schema composition, schema renaming and schema hiding.

To be most effective, a formal specification must be supplemented by supporting, informal description. The Z schema presentation has been designed so that it stands out from surrounding text (Figure 10.9).

The schema signature defines the entities that make up the state of the system and the schema predicate sets out conditions that must always be true for these entities. Where a schema defines an operation, the predicate may set out pre- and post-conditions. These define the state before and after the operation. The difference between these pre- and post-conditions defines the action specified in the operation schema.

Figure 10.9 The structure of a Z schema

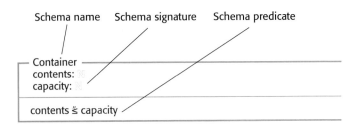

To illustrate the use of Z in the specification of a critical system, I have developed a formal specification of the control system of the insulin pump that I introduced in Chapter 3.

Recall that this system monitors the blood glucose level of diabetics and automatically injects insulin as required. Even for a small system like the insulin pump, the formal specification is fairly long. Although the basic operation of the system is simple, there are many possible alarm conditions that have to be considered. I include only some of the schemas defining the system here; the complete specification can be downloaded from the book's web site.

To develop a model-based specification, you have to define state variables and predicates that model the state of the system that you are specifying as well as define invariants (conditions that are always true) over these state variables.

The Z state schema that models the insulin pump state is shown in Figure 10.10. You can see how the two basic parts of the schema are used. In the top part, names and types are declared, and in the bottom part, the invariants are declared.

The names declared in the schema are used to represent system inputs, system outputs and internal state variables:

1. *System inpxuts* where the convention in Z is for all input variable names to be followed by a ? symbol. I have declared names to model the on/off switch on the pump (**switch?**), a button for manual delivery of insulin (**ManualDeliveryButton?**), the reading from the blood sugar sensor (**Reading?**), the result of running a hardware test program (**HardwareTest?**), sensors that detect the presence of the insulin reservoir and the needle (**InsulinReservoir?**, **Needle?**), and the value of the current time (**clock?**).

2. *System outputs* where the convention in Z is for all output variable names to be followed by a ! symbol. I have declared names to model the pump alarm (**alarm!**), two alphanumeric displays (**display1!** and **display2!**), a display of the current time (**clock!**), and the dose of insulin to be delivered (**dose!**).

3. *State variables used for dose computation* I have declared variables to represent the status of the device (**status**), to hold previous values of the blood sugar level (**r0, r1** and **r2**), the capacity of the insulin reservoir and the amount of insulin currently available (**capacity, insulin_available**), several variables used to impose limits on the dose of insulin delivered (**max_daily_dose, max_single_dose, minimim_dose, safemin, safemax**), and two variables used in the dose computation (**CompDose** and **cumulative_dose**). The type $\mathbb{N}$ means a non-negative number.

The schema predicate defines invariants that are always true. There is an implicit 'and' between each line of the predicate so all predicates must hold at all times. Some of these predicates simply set limits on the system, but others define fundamental operating conditions of the system. These include:

1. The dose must be less than or equal to the capacity of the insulin reservoir. That is, it is impossible to deliver more insulin than is in the reservoir.

Figure 10.10 State
schema for the
insulin pump

INSULIN_PUMP_STATE ──────────────────────────────

//Input device definition
switch?: (off, manual, auto)
ManualDeliveryButton?: $\mathbb{N}$
Reading?: $\mathbb{N}$
HardwareTest?: (OK, batterylow, pumpfail, sensorfail, deliveryfail)
InsulinReservoir?: (present, notpresent)
Needle?: (present, notpresent)
clock?: TIME

//Output device definition
alarm! = (on, off)
display1!, string
display2!: string
clock!: TIME
dose!: $\mathbb{N}$

// State variables used for dose computation
status: (running, warning, error)
r0, r1, r2: $\mathbb{N}$
capacity, insulin_available : $\mathbb{N}$
max_daily_dose, max_single_dose, minimum_dose: $\mathbb{N}$
safemin, safemax: $\mathbb{N}$
CompDose, cumulative_dose: $\mathbb{N}$

───

r2 = Reading?
dose! $\leq$ insulin_available
insulin_available $\leq$ capacity

*// The cumulative dose of insulin delivered is set to zero once every 24
hours*
clock? = 000000 $\Rightarrow$ cumulative_dose = 0

// If the cumulative dose exceeds the limit then operation is suspended
cumulative_dose $\geq$ max_daily_dose $\wedge$ status = error $\Rightarrow$
display1! = "Daily dose exceeded"

// Pump configuration parameters
capacity = 100 $\wedge$ safemin = 6 $\wedge$ safemax = 14
max_daily_dose = 25 $\wedge$ max_single_dose = 4 $\wedge$ minimum_dose = 1

display2! = nat_to_string (dose!)
clock! = clock?

2. The cumulative dose is reset at midnight each day. You can think of the Z phrase <logical expression 1> ⇒ <logical expression 2> as being the same as **if** <logical expression 1> **then** <logical expression 2>. In this case, <logical expression 1> is 'clock? = 000000' and <logical expression 2> is 'cumulative_dose = 0'.

3. The cumulative dose delivered over a 24-hour period may not exceed max_daily_dose. If this condition is false, then an error message is output.

4. display2! always shows the value of the last dose of insulin delivered and clock! always shows the current clock time.

The insulin pump operates by checking the blood glucose every 10 minutes, and (simplistically) insulin is delivered if the rate of change of blood glucose is increasing. The RUN schema, shown in Figure 10.11, models the normal operating condition of the pump.

If a schema name is included in the declarations part, this is equivalent to including all the names declared in that schema in the declaration and the conditions in the predicate part. The delta schema (Δ) in the first line in Figure 10.11 illustrates this. The delta means that the state variables defined in INSULIN_PUMP_STATE are in scope as are a set of other variables that represent state values before and after some operation. These are indicated by 'priming' the name defined in INSULIN_PUMP_STATE. Therefore, insulin_available represents the amount of insulin available before some operation, and insulin_available′ represents the amount of insulin available after some operation.

The RUN schema defines the operation of the system by specifying a set of predicates that are true in normal system use. Of course, these are in addition to the predicates defined in the INSULIN_PUMP_STATE schema that are invariant (always true). This schema also shows the use of a Z feature—schema composition—where the schemas SUGAR_LOW, SUGAR_OK and SUGAR_HIGH are included by giving their names. Notice that these schemas are 'ored' so that there is a schema for each of three possible conditions. The ability to compose schemas means that you can break down a specification into smaller parts in the same way that you can define functions and methods in a program.

I won't go into the details of the RUN schema here but, in essence, it starts by defining predicates that are true for normal operation. For example, it states that normal operation is only possible when the amount of insulin available is greater than the maximum single dose that may be delivered. Three schemas that represent different blood sugar levels are then ored and, as we shall see later, these define a value for the state variable CompDose.

The value of CompDose represents the amount of insulin that has been computed for delivery, based on the blood sugar level. The remainder of the predicates in this schema define various checks to be applied to ensure that the dose actually delivered (dose!) follows safety rules defined for the system. For example, one safety rule is that no single dose of insulin may exceed some defined maximum value.

Figure 10.11 The
RUN schema

RUN───
  ΔINSULIN_PUMP_STATE
  ───
  switch? = auto _
  status = running ∨ status = warning
  insulin_available ≥ max_single_dose
  cumulative_dose < max_daily_dose

  // The dose of insulin is computed depending on the blood sugar level

  (SUGAR_LOW ∨ SUGAR_OK ∨ SUGAR_HIGH)

  // 1. If the computed insulin dose is zero, don't deliver any insulin

  CompDose = 0 ⇒　dose! = 0

  ∨

  *// 2. The maximum daily dose would be exceeded if the computed dose was
  delivered so the insulin dose is set to the difference between the maximum
  allowed daily dose and the cumulative dose delivered so far*

  CompDose + cumulative_dose > max_daily_dose ⇒ alarm! = on ∧ status' =
  warning ∧ dose! = max_daily_dose−cumulative_dose

  ∨

  *// 3. The normal situation. If maximum single dose is not exceeded then
  deliver the computed dose. If the single dose computed is too high, restrict
  the dose delivered to the maximum single dose*

  CompDose + cumulative_dose < max_daily_dose ⇒
          (CompDose ≤ max_single_dose ⇒ dose! = CompDose

          ∨

          CompDose > max_single_dose ⇒　dose! = max_single_dose)
  insulin_available' = insulin_available−dose!
  cumulative_dose' = cumulative_dose + dose!

  insulin_available ≤ max_single_dose * 4 ⇒　status' = warning ∧
  display1! = "Insulin low"

  r1' = r2
  r0' = r1
  ───

Finally, the last two predicates define the changes to the value of **insulin_available**
and **cumulative_dose**. Notice how I have used the primed version of the names here.

The final schema example given in Figure 10.12 defines how the dose of insulin
is computed assuming that the level of sugar in the diabetic's blood lies within some
safe zone. In these circumstances, insulin is only delivered if the blood sugar level
is rising and the rate of change of blood sugar level is increasing. The other schemas,

Figure 10.12 The
SUGAR_OK schema

SUGAR_OK ──

r2 ≥ safemin ∨ r2 ∧ safemax

// sugar level stable or falling

r2 ≤ r1 ⇒ CompDose = 0

∨

// sugar level increasing but rate of increase falling
r2 > r1 ∧ (r2-r1) < (r1-r0) ⇒ CompDose = 0

∨

// sugar level increasing and rate of increase increasing compute dose
// a minimum dose must be delivered if rounded to zero

r2 > r1 ∧ (r2-r1) ≥ (r1-r0) ∧ (round ((r2-r1)/4) = 0) ⇒
                    CompDose = minimum_dose

∨

r2 > r1 ∧ (r2-r1) ≥ (r1-r0) ∧ (round ((r2-r1)/4) > 0) ⇒
                    CompDose = round ((r2-r1)/4)

──

SUGAR_LOW and SUGAR_HIGH define the dose to be delivered if the sugar level is outside the safe zone. The predicates in the schema are as follows:

1. The initial predicate defines the safe zone; that is, r2 must lie between **safemin** and **safemax**.

2. If the sugar level is stable or falling, indicated by r2 (the later reading) being equal to or less than r1 (an earlier reading), then the dose of insulin to be delivered is zero.

3. If the sugar level is increasing (r2 > r1) but the rate of increase is falling, then the dose to be delivered is zero.

4. If the sugar level is increasing and the rate of increase is stable, then a minimum dose of insulin is delivered.

5. If the sugar level is increasing and the rate of increase is increasing, then the dose of insulin to be delivered is derived by applying a simple formula to the computed values.

I don't model the temporal behaviour of the system (i.e., the fact that the glucose sensor is checked every 10 minutes) using Z. Although this is certainly possible, it is rather clumsy, and, in my view, an informal description actually communicates the specification more concisely than a formal specification.

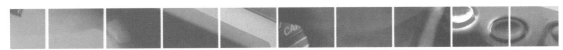

KEY POINTS

■ Methods of formal system specification complement informal requirements specification techniques. They may be used with a natural language requirements definition to clarify any areas of potential ambiguity in the specification.

■ Formal specifications are precise and unambiguous. They remove areas of doubt in a specification and avoid some of the problems of language misinterpretation. However, non-specialists may find formal specifications difficult to understand.

■ The principal value of using formal methods in the software process is that it forces an analysis of the system requirements at an early stage. Correcting errors at this stage is cheaper than modifying a delivered system.

■ Formal specification techniques are most cost-effective in the development of critical systems where safety, reliability and security are particularly important. They may also be used to specify standards.

■ Algebraic techniques of formal specification are particularly suited to specifying interfaces where the interface is defined as a set of object classes or abstract data types. These techniques conceal the system state and specify the system in terms of relationships between the interface operations.

■ Model-based techniques model the system using mathematical constructs such as sets and functions. They may expose the system state, which simplifies some types of behavioural specification.

■ You define the operations in a model-based specification by defining pre- and post-conditions on the system state.

FURTHER READING

'Correctness by construction: Developing a commercially secure system'. A good description of how formal methods can be used in the development of a security-critical system. (A. Hall and R. Chapman, *IEEE Software*, 19(1), January 2002.)

IEEE Transactions on Software Engineering, January 1998. This issue of the journal includes a special section on the practical uses of formal methods in software engineering. It includes papers on both Z and LARCH.

'Formal methods: Promises and problems'. This article is a realistic discussion of the potential gains from using formal methods and the difficulties of integrating the use of formal methods into practical software development (Luqi and J. Goguen. *IEEE Software,* 14 (1), January 1997.)

EXERCISES

10.1 Suggest why the architectural design of a system should precede the development of a formal specification.

10.2 You have been given the task of 'selling' formal specification techniques to a software development organisation. Outline how you would go about explaining the advantages of formal specifications to sceptical, practising software engineers.

10.3 Explain why it is particularly important to define sub-system interfaces in a precise way and why algebraic specification is particularly appropriate for sub-system interface specification.

10.4 An abstract data type representing a stack has the following operations associated with it:

New: Bring a stack into existence.
Push: Add an element to the top of the stack.
Top: Evaluate the element on top of the stack.
Retract: Remove the top element from the stack and return the modified stack.
Empty: True if there are no elements on the stack.

Define this abstract data type using an algebraic specification.

10.5 In the example of a controlled airspace sector, the safety condition is that aircraft may not be within 300 m of height in the same sector. Modify the specification shown in Figure 10.8 to allow aircraft to occupy the same height in the sector so long as they are separated by at least 8 km of horizontal difference. You may ignore aircraft in adjacent sectors. *Hint*: You have to modify the constructor operations so that they include the aircraft position as well as its height. You also have to define an operation that, given two positions, returns the separation between them.

10.6 Bank teller machines rely on using information on the user's card giving the bank identifier, the account number and the user's personal identifier. They also derive account information from a central database and update that database on completion of a transaction. Using your knowledge of ATM operation, write Z schemas defining the state of the system, card validation (where the user's identifier is checked) and cash withdrawal.

10.7 Modify the insulin pump schema, shown in Figure 10.10, to add a further safety condition that the ManualDeliveryButton? can only have a non-zero value if the pump switch is in the manual position.

10.8 Write a Z schema called SELF_TEST that tests the hardware components of the insulin pump and sets the value of the state variable HardwareTest?. Then modify the RUN schema to check that the hardware is operating successfully before any insulin is delivered. If not, the dose delivered should be zero and an error should be indicated on the insulin pump display.

10.9 Z supports the notion of sequences where a sequence is like an array. For example, for a sequence S, you can refer to its elements as S[1], S[2], and so on. It also allows you to determine the number of elements in a sequence using the # operator. That is, if a sequence S is [a, b, c, d] then #S is 4. You can add an element to the end of a sequence S by writing S + a, and to the beginning of the sequence by writing a + S. Using these constructs, write a Z specification of the LIST that is specified algebraically in Figure 10.7.

10.10 You are a systems engineer and are asked to suggest the best way to develop the safety-critical software for a heart pacemaker. You suggest formally specifying the system, but your manager rejects your suggestion. You think his reasons are weak and based on prejudice. Is it ethical to develop the system using methods that you think are inadequate?

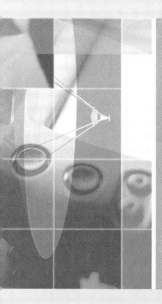

PART 3

DESIGN

The essence of software design is making decisions about the logical organisation of the software. Sometimes, you represent this logical organisation as a model in a defined modelling language such as the UML and sometimes you simply use informal notations and sketches to represent the design. Of course, you rarely start from scratch when making decisions about the software organisation but base your design on previous design experience.

Some authors think that the best way to encapsulate this design experience is in structured methods where you follow a defined design process and describe your design using different types of model. I have never been a great fan of structured methods as I have always found that they are too constraining. Design is a creative process and I strongly believe that we each tackle such creative processes in individual ways. There is no right or wrong way to design software and neither I nor anyone else can give you a 'recipe' for software design. You learn how to design by looking at examples of existing designs and by discussing your design with others.

Rather than represent experience as a 'design method', I prefer a more loosely structured approach. The chapters in this part encapsulate knowledge about software structures that have been successfully used in other systems, present some examples and give you some advice on design processes:

Chapters 11 to 13 are about the abstract structures of software. Chapter 11 discusses structural perspectives that have been found to be useful when designing software, Chapter 12 is about structuring software for distributed execution and Chapter 13 is about generic structures for various types of application. Chapter 13 is a new chapter that I have included in this edition because I have found many students of software engineering have no experience of applications software apart from the interactive systems that they use on an everyday basis on their own computers.

Chapters 14 to 16 are concerned with more specific software design issues. Chapter 14, which covers object-oriented design, concerns a way of thinking about software structures. Chapter 15, on real-time systems design, discusses the software structures that you need in systems where timely response is a critical requirement. Chapter 16 is a bit different because it focuses on the user interface design rather than on software structures. As an engineer, you have to think about systems—not just software—and the people in the system are an essential component. Design doesn't stop with the software structures but continues through to how the software is used.

11
Architectural design

Objectives

The objective of this chapter is to introduce the concepts of software architecture and architectural design. When you have read the chapter, you will:

■ understand why the architectural design of software is important;

■ understand the decisions that have to be made about the system architecture during the architectural design process;

■ have been introduced to three complementary architectural styles covering the overall system organisation, modular decomposition and control;

■ understand how reference architectures are used to communicate architectural concepts and to assess system architectures.

Contents

Large systems are always decomposed into sub-systems that provide some related set of services. The initial design process of identifying these sub-systems and establishing a framework for sub-system control and communication is called architectural design. The output of this design process is a description of the software architecture.

In the model presented in Chapter 4, architectural design is the first stage in the design process and represents a critical link between the design and requirements engineering processes. The architectural design process is concerned with establishing a basic structural framework that identifies the major components of a system and the communications between these components.

Bass et al. (Bass, et al., 2003) discuss three advantages of explicitly designing and documenting a software architecture:

1. *Stakeholder communication* The architecture is a high-level presentation of the system that may be used as a focus for discussion by a range of different stakeholders.

2. *System analysis* Making the system architecture explicit at an early stage in the system development requires some analysis. Architectural design decisions have a profound effect on whether the system can meet critical requirements such as performance, reliability and maintainability.

3. *Large-scale reuse* A system architecture model is a compact, manageable description of how a system is organised and how the components interoperate. The system architecture is often the same for systems with similar requirements and so can support large-scale software reuse. As I discuss in Chapter 18, it may be possible to develop product-line architectures where the same architecture is used across a range of related systems.

Hofmeister et al. (Hofmeister, et al., 2000) discuss how the architectural design stage forces software designers to consider key design aspects early in the process. They suggest that the software architecture can serve as a design plan that is used to negotiate system requirements and as a means of structuring discussions with clients, developers and managers. They also suggest that it is an essential tool for complexity management. It hides details and allows the designers to focus on the key system abstractions.

The system architecture affects the performance, robustness, distributability and maintainability of a system (Bosch, 2000). The particular style and structure chosen for an application may therefore depend on the non-functional system requirements:

1. *Performance* If performance is a critical requirement, the architecture should be designed to localise critical operations within a small number of sub-systems, with as little communication as possible between these sub-systems. This may mean using relatively large-grain rather than fine-grain components to reduce component communications.

2. *Security* If security is a critical requirement, a layered structure for the architecture should be used, with the most critical assets protected in the innermost layers and with a high level of security validation applied to these layers.

3. *Safety* If safety is a critical requirement, the architecture should be designed so that safety-related operations are all located in either a single sub-system or in a small number of sub-systems. This reduces the costs and problems of safety validation and makes it possible to provide related protection systems.

4. *Availability* If availability is a critical requirement, the architecture should be designed to include redundant components and so that it is possible to replace and update components without stopping the system. Fault-tolerant system architectures for high-availability systems are covered in Chapter 20.

5. *Maintainability* If maintainability is a critical requirement, the system architecture should be designed using fine-grain, self-contained components that may readily be changed. Producers of data should be separated from consumers and shared data structures should be avoided.

Obviously there is potential conflict between some of these architectures. For example, using large-grain components improves performance, and using fine-grain components improves maintainability. If both of these are important system requirements, then some compromise solution must be found. As I discuss later, this can sometimes be achieved by using different architectural styles for different parts of the system.

There is a significant overlap between the processes of requirements engineering and architectural design. Ideally, a system specification should not include any design information. In practice, this is unrealistic except for very small systems. Architectural decomposition is necessary to structure and organise the specification. An example of this was introduced in Chapter 2, where Figure 2.8 shows the architecture of an air traffic control system. You can use such an architectural model as the starting point for sub-system specification.

A sub-system design is an abstract decomposition of a system into large-grain components, each of which may be a substantial system in its own right. Block diagrams are often used to describe sub-system designs where each box in the diagram represents a sub-system. Boxes within boxes indicate that the sub-system has itself been decomposed to sub-systems. Arrows mean that data and or control signals are passed from sub-system to sub-system in the direction of the arrows. Block diagrams present a high-level picture of the system structure, which people from different disciplines who are involved in the system development process can readily understand.

For example, Figure 11.1 is an abstract model of the architecture for a packing robot system that shows the sub-systems that have to be developed. This robotic system can pack different kinds of object. It uses a vision sub-system to pick out

Figure 11.1 Block
diagram of a packing
robot control system

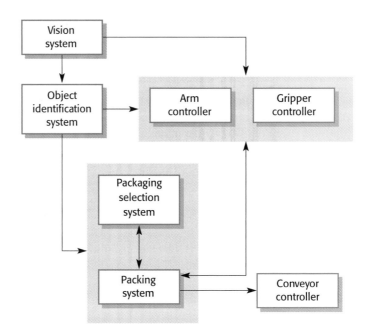

objects on a conveyor, identify the type of object and select the right kind of packaging. The system then moves objects from the delivery conveyor to be packaged. It places packaged objects on another conveyor. Other examples of architectural designs at this level are shown in Chapter 2 (Figures 2.6 and 2.8).

Bass et al. (Bass, et al., 2003) claim that simple box-and-line diagrams are not useful architectural representations because they do not show the nature of the relationships among system components nor do they show components' externally visible properties. From a software designer's perspective, this is absolutely correct. However, this type of model is effective for communication with system stakeholders and for project planning because it is not cluttered with detail. Stakeholders can relate to it and understand an abstract view of the system. The model identifies the key sub-systems that are to be independently developed so managers can start assigning people to plan the development of these systems. Box-and-line diagrams should certainly not be the only architectural representation that are used; however, they are one of a number of useful architectural models.

The general problem of deciding how to decompose a system into sub-systems is a difficult one. Of course, the system requirements are a major factor and you should try to create a design where there is a close match between requirements and sub-systems. This means that, if the requirements change, this change is likely to be localised rather than distributed across several sub-systems. In Chapter 13, I describe a number of generic application architectures that can be used as a starting point for sub-system identification.

11.1 Architectural design decisions

Architectural design is a creative process where you try to establish a system organisation that will satisfy the functional and non-functional system requirements. Because it is a creative process, the activities within the process differ radically depending on the type of system being developed, the background and experience of the system architect, and the specific requirements for the system. It is therefore more useful to think of the architectural design process from a decision perspective rather than from an activity perspective. During the architectural design process, system architects have to make a number of fundamental decisions that profoundly affect the system and its development process. Based on their knowledge and experience, they have to answer the following fundamental questions:

1. Is there a generic application architecture that can act as a template for the system that is being designed?

2. How will the system be distributed across a number of processors?

3. What architectural style or styles are appropriate for the system?

4. What will be the fundamental approach used to structure the system?

5. How will the structural units in the system be decomposed into modules?

6. What strategy will be used to control the operation of the units in the system?

7. How will the architectural design be evaluated?

8. How should the architecture of the system be documented?

Although each software system is unique, systems in the same application domain often have similar architectures that reflect the fundamental domain concepts. These application architectures can be fairly generic, such as the architecture of information management systems, or much more specific. For example, application product lines are applications that are built around a core architecture with variants that satisfy specific customer requirements. When designing a system architecture, you have to decide what your system and broader application classes have in common, and decide how much knowledge from these application architectures you can reuse. I discuss generic application architectures in Chapter 13 and application product lines in Chapter 18.

For embedded systems and systems designed for personal computers, there is usually only a single processor, and you will not have to design a distributed architecture for the system. However, most large systems are now distributed systems where the system software is distributed across many different computers. The choice of distribution architecture is a key decision that affects the performance and reliability of the system. This is a major topic in its own right and I cover it separately in Chapter 12.

The architecture of a software system may be based on a particular architectural model or style. An architectural style is a pattern of system organisation (Garlan and Shaw, 1993) such as a client–server organisation or a layered architecture. An awareness of these styles, their applications, and their strengths and weaknesses is important. However, the architectures of most large systems do not conform to a single style. Different parts of the system may be designed using different architectural styles. In some cases, the overall system architecture may be a composite architecture that is created by combining different architectural styles.

Garlan and Shaw's notion of an architectural style covers the next three design questions. You have to choose the most appropriate structure, such as client–server or layered structuring, that will allow you to meet the system requirements. To decompose structural system units into modules, you decide on the strategy for decomposing sub-systems into their components or modules. The approaches that you can use allow different types of architecture to be implemented. Finally, in the control modelling process, you make decisions about how the execution of sub-systems is controlled. You develop a general model of the control relationships between the parts of the system established. I cover these three topics in Sections 11.2 through 11.4.

Evaluating an architectural design is difficult because the true test of an architecture is in how well it meets its functional and non-functional requirements after it has been deployed. However, in some cases, you can do some evaluation by comparing your design against reference or generic architectural models. I cover reference architectures in Section 11.5 and other generic architectures in Chapter 13.

The product of the architectural design process is an architectural design document. This may include a number of graphical representations of the system along with associated descriptive text. It should describe how the system is structured into sub-systems, the approach adopted and how each sub-system is structured into modules. The graphical models of the system present different perspectives on the architecture. Architectural models that may be developed may include:

1. A *static structural model* that shows the sub-systems or components that are to be developed as separate units.

2. A *dynamic process model* that shows how the system is organised into processes at run-time. This may be different from the static model.

3. An *interface model* that defines the services offered by each sub-system through its public interface.

4. *Relationship models* that shows relationships, such as data flow, between the sub-systems.

5. A *distribution model* that shows how sub-systems may be distributed across computers.

A number of researchers have proposed the use of architectural description languages (ADLs) to describe system architectures. Bass et al. (Bass, et al., 2003) describe the main features of these languages. The basic elements of ADLs are components and connectors, and they include rules and guidelines for well-formed architectures. However, like all specialised languages, ADLs can only be understood by language experts and are inaccessible to domain and application specialists. This makes them difficult to analyse from a practical perspective. I think that they will only be used in a small number of applications. Informal models and notations such as the UML (Clements, et al., 2002) will remain the most commonly used notation for architectural description.

11.2 System organisation

The organisation of a system reflects the basic strategy that is used to structure a system. You have to make decisions on the overall organisational model of a system early in the architectural design process. The system organisation may be directly reflected in the sub-system structure. However, it is often the case that the sub-system model includes more detail than the organisational model, and there is not always a simple mapping from sub-systems to organisational structure.

In this section, I discuss three organisational styles that are very widely used. These are a shared data repository style, a shared services and servers style and an abstract machine or layered style where the system is organised as a tier of functional layers. These styles can be used separately or together. For example, a system may be organised around a shared data repository but may construct layers around this to present a more abstract view of the data.

11.2.1 The repository model

Sub-systems making up a system must exchange information so that they can work together effectively. There are two fundamental ways in which this can be done.

1. All shared data is held in a central database that can be accessed by all sub-systems. A system model based on a shared database is sometimes called a *repository model*.

2. Each sub-system maintains its own database. Data is interchanged with other sub-systems by passing messages to them.

The majority of systems that use large amounts of data are organised around a shared database or repository. This model is therefore suited to applications where data is generated by one sub-system and used by another. Examples of this type of

Figure 11.2 The
architecture of an
integrated CASE
toolset

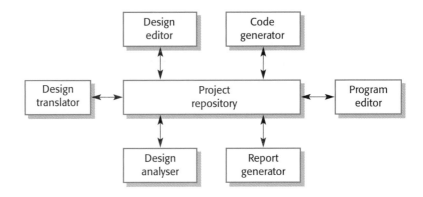

system include command and control systems, management information systems, CAD systems and CASE toolsets.

Figure 11.2 is an example of a CASE toolset architecture based on a shared repository. The first shared repository for CASE tools was probably developed in the early 1970s by a UK company called ICL to support their operating system development (McGuffin, et al., 1979). This model became more widely known when Buxton (Buxton, 1980) made proposals for the Stoneman environment to support the development of systems written in Ada. Since then, many CASE toolsets have been developed around a shared repository.

The advantages and disadvantages of a shared repository are as follows:

1. It is an efficient way to share large amounts of data. There is no need to transmit data explicitly from one sub-system to another.

2. However, sub-systems must agree on the repository data model. Inevitably, this is a compromise between the specific needs of each tool. Performance may be adversely affected by this compromise. It may be difficult or impossible to integrate new sub-systems if their data models do not fit the agreed schema.

3. Sub-systems that produce data need not be concerned with how that data is used by other sub-systems.

4. However, evolution may be difficult as a large volume of information is generated according to an agreed data model. Translating this to a new model will certainly be expensive; it may be difficult or even impossible.

5. Activities such as backup, security, access control and recovery from error are centralised. They are the responsibility of the repository manager. Tools can focus on their principal function rather than be concerned with these issues.

6. However, different sub-systems may have different requirements for security, recovery and backup policies. The repository model forces the same policy on all sub-systems.

7. The model of sharing is visible through the repository schema. It is straight-forward to integrate new tools given that they are compatible with the agreed data model.

8. However, it may be difficult to distribute the repository over a number of machines. Although it is possible to distribute a logically centralised repository, there may be problems with data redundancy and inconsistency.

In the above model, the repository is passive and control is the responsibility of the sub-systems using the repository. An alternative approach has been derived for AI systems that use a 'blackboard' model, which triggers sub-systems when particular data become available. This is appropriate when the form of the repository data is less well structured. Decisions about which tool to activate can only be made when the data has been analysed. This model is described by Nii (Nii, 1986), and Bosch (Bosch, 2000) includes a good discussion of how this style relates to system quality attributes.

11.2.2 The client–server model

The client–server architectural model is a system model where the system is organised as a set of services and associated servers and clients that access and use the services. The major components of this model are:

1. A set of servers that offer services to other sub-systems. Examples of servers are print servers that offer printing services, file servers that offer file management services and a compile server, which offers programming language compilation services.

2. A set of clients that call on the services offered by servers. These are normally sub-systems in their own right. There may be several instances of a client program executing concurrently.

3. A network that allows the clients to access these services. This is not strictly necessary as both the clients and the servers could run on a single machine. In practice, however, most client–server systems are implemented as distributed systems.

Clients may have to know the names of the available servers and the services that they provide. However, servers need not know either the identity of clients or how many clients there are. Clients access the services provided by a server through remote procedure calls using a request-reply protocol such as the http protocol used in the WWW. Essentially, a client makes a request to a server and waits until it receives a reply.

Figure 11.3 shows an example of a system that is based on the client–server model. This is a multi-user, web-based system to provide a film and photograph library. In this

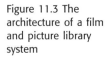

Figure 11.3 The architecture of a film and picture library system

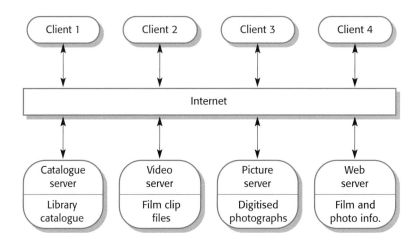

system, several servers manage and display the different types of media. Video frames need to be transmitted quickly and in synchrony but at relatively low resolution. They may be compressed in a store, so the video server may handle video compression and decompression into different formats. Still pictures, however, must be maintained at a high resolution, so it is appropriate to maintain them on a separate server.

The catalogue must be able to deal with a variety of queries and provide links into the web information system that includes data about the film and video clip, and an e-commerce system that supports the sale of film and video clips. The client program is simply an integrated user interface, constructed using a web browser, to these services.

The most important advantage of the client–server model is that it is a distributed architecture. Effective use can be made of networked systems with many distributed processors. It is easy to add a new server and integrate it with the rest of the system or to upgrade servers transparently without affecting other parts of the system. I discuss distributed architectures, including client–server architectures and distributed object architectures, in more detail in Chapter 12.

However, changes to existing clients and servers may be required to gain the full benefits of integrating a new server. There may be no shared data model across servers and sub-systems may organise their data in different ways. This means that specific data models may be established on each server to allow its performance to be optimised. Of course, if an XML-based representation of data is used, it may be relatively simple to convert from one schema to another. However, XML is an inefficient way to represent data, so performance problems can arise if this is used.

11.2.3 The layered model

The layered model of an architecture (sometimes called an abstract machine model) organises a system into layers, each of which provide a set of services. Each layer

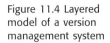

Figure 11.4 Layered model of a version management system

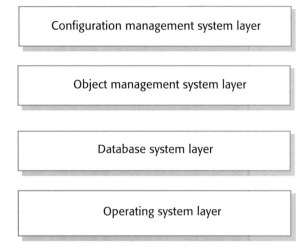

Configuration management system layer

Object management system layer

Database system layer

Operating system layer

can be thought of as an abstract machine whose machine language is defined by the services provided by the layer. This 'language' is used to implement the next level of abstract machine. For example, a common way to implement a language is to define an ideal 'language machine' and compile the language into code for this machine. A further translation step then converts this abstract machine code to real machine code.

An example of a layered model is the OSI reference model of network protocols (Zimmermann, 1980), discussed in Section 11.5. Another influential example was proposed by Buxton (Buxton, 1980), who suggested a three-layer model for an Ada Programming Support Environment (APSE). Figure 11.4 reflects the APSE structure and shows how a configuration management system might be integrated using this abstract machine approach.

The configuration management system manages versions of objects and provides general configuration management facilities, as discussed in Chapter 29. To support these configuration management facilities, it uses an object management system that provides information storage and management services for configuration items or objects. This system is built on top of a database system to provide basic data storage and services such as transaction management, rollback and recovery, and access control. The database management uses the underlying operating system facilities and filestore in its implementation. You can see other examples of layered architectural models in Chapter 13.

The layered approach supports the incremental development of systems. As a layer is developed, some of the services provided by that layer may be made available to users. This architecture is also changeable and portable. So long as its interface is unchanged, a layer can be replaced by another, equivalent layer. Furthermore, when layer interfaces change or new facilities are added to a layer, only the adjacent layer is affected. As layered systems localise machine dependencies in inner layers, this makes it easier to provide multi-platform implementations of an application system. Only the inner, machine-dependent layers need be reimplemented to take account of the facilities of a different operating system or database.

A disadvantage of the layered approach is that structuring systems in this way can be difficult. Inner layers may provide basic facilities, such as file management, that are required at all levels. Services required by a user of the top level may therefore have to 'punch through' adjacent layers to get access to services that are provided several levels beneath it. This subverts the model, as the outer layer in the system does not just depend on its immediate predecessor.

Performance can also be a problem because of the multiple levels of command interpretation that are sometimes required. If there are many layers, a service request from a top layer may have to be interpreted several times in different layers before it is processed. To avoid these problems, applications may have to communicate directly with inner layers rather than use the services provided by the adjacent layer.

11.3 Modular decomposition styles

After an overall system organisation has been chosen, you need to make a decision on the approach to be used in decomposing sub-systems into modules. There is not a rigid distinction between system organisation and modular decomposition. The styles discussed in Section 11.2 could be applied at this level. However, the components in modules are usually smaller than sub-systems, which allows alternative decomposition styles to be used.

There is no clear distinction between sub-systems and modules, but I find it useful to think of them as follows:

1. A sub-system is a system in its own right whose operation does not depend on the services provided by other sub-systems. Sub-systems are composed of modules and have defined interfaces, which are used for communication with other sub-systems.

2. A module is normally a system component that provides one or more services to other modules. It makes use of services provided by other modules. It is not normally considered to be an independent system. Modules are usually composed from a number of other simpler system components.

There are two main strategies that you can use when decomposing a sub-system into modules:

1. *Object-oriented decomposition* where you decompose a system into a set of communicating objects.

Figure 11.5 An object
model of an invoice
processing system

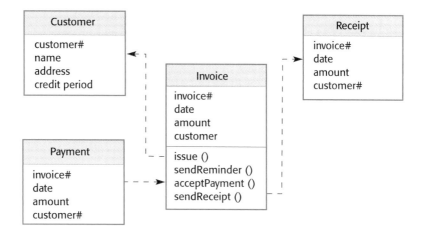

Figure 11.5 An object model of an invoice processing system

2. *Function-oriented pipelining* where you decompose a system into functional modules that accept input data and transform it into output data.

In the object-oriented approach, modules are objects with private state and defined operations on that state. In the pipelining model, modules are functional transformations. In both cases, modules may be implemented as sequential components or as processes.

You should avoid making premature commitments to concurrency in a system. The advantage of avoiding a concurrent system design is that sequential programs are easier to design, implement, verify and test than parallel systems. Time dependencies between processes are hard to formalise, control and verify. It is best to decompose systems into modules, then decide during implementation whether these need to execute in sequence or in parallel.

11.3.1 Object-oriented decomposition

An object-oriented, architectural model structures the system into a set of loosely coupled objects with well-defined interfaces. Objects call on the services offered by other objects. I have already introduced object models in Chapter 8, and I discuss object-oriented design in more detail in Chapter 14.

Figure 11.5 is an example of an object-oriented architectural model of an invoice processing system. This system can issue invoices to customers, receive payments, and issue receipts for these payments and reminders for unpaid invoices. I use the UML notation introduced in Chapter 8 where object classes have names and a set of associated attributes. Operations, if any, are defined in the lower part of the rectangle representing the object. Dashed arrows indicate that an object uses the attributes or services provided by another object.

An object-oriented decomposition is concerned with object classes, their attributes and their operations. When implemented, objects are created from these classes and some control model is used to coordinate object operations. In this particular example, the Invoice class has various associated operations that implement the system functionality. This class makes use of other classes representing customers, payments and receipts.

The advantages of the object-oriented approach are well known. Because objects are loosely coupled, the implementation of objects can be modified without affecting other objects. Objects are often representations of real-world entities so the structure of the system is readily understandable. Because these real-world entities are used in different systems, objects can be reused. Object-oriented programming languages have been developed that provide direct implementations of architectural components.

However, the object-oriented approach does have disadvantages. To use services, objects must explicitly reference the name and the interface of other objects. If an interface change is required to satisfy proposed system changes, the effect of that change on all users of the changed object must be evaluated. While objects may map cleanly to small-scale real-world entities, more complex entities are sometimes difficult to represent as objects.

11.3.2 Function-oriented pipelining

In a function-oriented pipeline or data-flow model, functional transformations process their inputs and produce outputs. Data flows from one to another and is transformed as it moves through the sequence. Each processing step is implemented as a transform. Input data flows through these transforms until converted to output. The transformations may execute sequentially or in parallel. The data can be processed by each transform item by item or in a single batch.

When the transformations are represented as separate processes, this model is sometimes called the pipe and filter style after the terminology used in the Unix system. The Unix system provides pipes that act as data conduits and a set of commands that are functional transformations. Systems that conform to this model can be implemented by combining Unix commands using pipes and the control facilities of the Unix shell. The term *filter* is used because a transformation 'filters out' the data it can process from its input data stream.

Variants of this pipelining model have been in use since computers were first used for automatic data processing. When transformations are sequential with data processed in batches, this architectural model is a batch sequential model. As I discuss in Chapter 13, this is a common architecture for data-processing systems such as billing systems. Data-processing systems usually generate many output reports that are derived from simple computations on a large number of input records.

An example of this type of system architecture is shown in Figure 11.6. An organisation has issued invoices to customers. Once a week, payments that have been

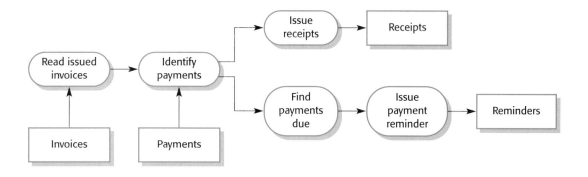

Figure 11.6 A
pipeline model of
an invoice processing
system
made are reconciled with the invoices. For those invoices that have been paid, a receipt is issued. For those invoices that have not been paid within the allowed payment time, a reminder is issued.

This is a model of only part of the invoice processing system; alternative transformations would be used for the issue of invoices. Notice the difference between this and its object-oriented equivalent discussed in the previous section. The object model is more abstract as it does not include information about the sequence of operations.

The advantages of this architecture are:

1. It supports the reuse of transformations.

2. It is intuitive in that many people think of their work in terms of input and output processing.

3. Evolving the system by adding new transformations is usually straightforward.

4. It is simple to implement either as a concurrent or a sequential system.

The principal problem with this style is that there has to be a common format for data transfer that can be recognised by all transformations. Each transformation must either agree with its communicating transformations on the format of the data that will be processed or with a standard format for all data communicated must be imposed. The latter is the only feasible approach when transformations are standalone and reusable. In Unix, the standard format is simply a character sequence. Each transformation must parse its input and unparse its output to the agreed form. This increases system overhead and may mean that it is impossible to integrate transformations that use incompatible data formats.

Interactive systems are difficult to write using the pipelining model because of the need for a stream of data to be processed. While simple textual input and output can be modelled in this way, graphical user interfaces have more complex I/O formats and control, which is based on events such as mouse clicks or menu selections. It is difficult to translate this into a form compatible with the pipelining model.

11.4 Control styles

The models for structuring a system are concerned with how a system is decomposed into sub-systems. To work as a system, sub-systems must be controlled so that their services are delivered to the right place at the right time. Structural models do not (and should not) include control information. Rather, the architect should organise the sub-systems according to some control model that supplements the structure model that is used. Control models at the architectural level are concerned with the control flow between sub-systems.

There are two generic control styles that are used in software systems:

1. *Centralised control* One sub-system has overall responsibility for control and starts and stops other sub-systems. It may also devolve control to another sub-system but will expect to have this control responsibility returned to it.

2. *Event-based control* Rather than control information being embedded in a sub-system, each sub-system can respond to externally generated events. These events might come from other sub-systems or from the environment of the system.

Control styles are used in conjunction with structural styles. All the structural styles that I have discussed may be realised using centralised or event-based control.

11.4.1 Centralised control

In a centralised control model, one sub-system is designated as the system controller and has responsibility for managing the execution of other sub-systems. Centralised control models fall into two classes, depending on whether the controlled sub-systems execute sequentially or in parallel.

1. *The call–return model* This is the familiar top-down subroutine model where control starts at the top of a subroutine hierarchy and, through subroutine calls, passes to lower levels in the tree. The subroutine model is only applicable to sequential systems.

2. *The manager model* This is applicable to concurrent systems. One system component is designated as a system manager and controls the starting, stopping and coordination of other system processes. A process is a sub-system or module that can execute in parallel with other processes. A form of this model may also be applied in sequential systems where a management routine calls particular sub-systems depending on the values of some state variables. This is usually implemented as a case statement.

Figure 11.7 The
call–return model of
control

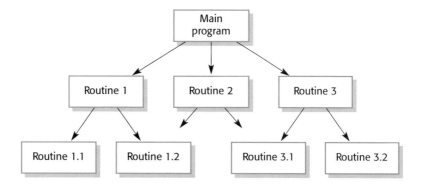

The call–return model is illustrated in Figure 11.7. The main program can call Routines 1, 2 and 3; Routine 1 can call Routines 1.2 or 1.2; Routine 3 can call Routines 3.1 or 3.2; and so on. This is a model of the program dynamics. It is *not* a structural model; there is no need for Routine 1.1, for example, to be part of Routine 1.

This familiar model is embedded in programming languages such as C, Ada and Pascal. Control passes from a higher-level routine in the hierarchy to a lower-level routine. It then returns to the point where the routine was called. The currently executing subroutine has responsibility for control and can either call other routines or return control to its parent. It is poor programming style to return to some other point in the program.

This call–return model may be used at the module level to control functions or objects. Subroutines in a programming language that are called by other subroutines are naturally functional. However, in many object-oriented systems, operations on objects (methods) are implemented as procedures or functions. For example, when a Java object requests a service from another object, it does so by calling an associated method.

The rigid and restricted nature of this model is both a strength and a weakness. It is a strength because it is relatively simple to analyse control flows and work out how the system will respond to particular inputs. It is a weakness because exceptions to normal operation are awkward to handle.

Figure 11.8 is an illustration of a centralised management model of control for a concurrent system. This model is often used in 'soft' real-time systems which do not have very tight time constraints. The central controller manages the execution of a set of processes associated with sensors and actuators. The building monitoring system discussed in Chapter 15 uses this model of control.

The system controller process decides when processes should be started or stopped depending on system state variables. It checks whether other processes have produced information to be processed or to pass information to them for processing. The controller usually loops continuously, polling sensors and other processes for events or state changes. For this reason, this model is sometimes called an event-loop model.

Figure 11.8 A
centralised control
model for a real-time
system

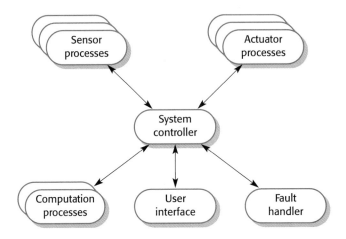

11.4.2 Event-driven systems

In centralised control models, control decisions are usually determined by the values of some system state variables. By contrast, event-driven control models are driven by externally generated events. The term *event* in this context does not just mean a binary signal. It may be a signal that can take a range of values or a command input from a menu. The distinction between an event and a simple input is that the timing of the event is outside the control of the process that handles that event.

There are many types of event-driven systems. These include editors where user interface events signify editing commands, rule-based production systems as used in AI where a condition becoming true causes an action to be triggered, and active objects where changing a value of an object's attribute triggers some actions. Garlan et al. (Garlan, et al., 1992) discuss these different types of system.

In this section, I discuss two event-driven control models:

1. *Broadcast models* In these models, an event is broadcast to all sub-systems. Any sub-system that has been programmed to handle that event can respond to it.

2. *Interrupt-driven models* These are exclusively used in real-time systems where external interrupts are detected by an interrupt handler. They are then passed to some other component for processing.

Broadcast models are effective in integrating sub-systems distributed across different computers on a network. Interrupt-driven models are used in real-time systems with stringent timing requirements.

In a broadcast model (Figure 11.9), sub-systems register an interest in specific events. When these events occur, control is transferred to the sub-system that can handle the event. The distinction between this model and the centralised model shown

Figure 11.9 A control
model based on
selective
broadcasting

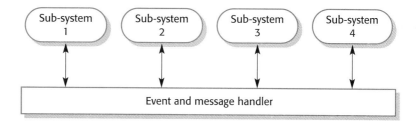

in Figure 11.8 is that the control policy is not embedded in the event and message handler. Sub-systems decide which events they require, and the event and message handler ensures that these events are sent to them.

All events could be broadcast to all sub-systems, but this imposes a great deal of processing overhead. More often, the event and message handler maintains a register of sub-systems and the events of interest to them. Sub-systems generate events indicating, perhaps, that some data is available for processing. The event handler detects the events, consults the event register and passes the event to those sub-systems who have declared an interest. In simpler systems, such as PC-based systems driven by user interface events, there are explicit event-listener sub-systems that listen for events from the mouse, the keyboard, and so on, and translate these into more specific commands.

The event handler also usually supports point-to-point communication. A sub-system can explicitly send a message to another sub-system. There have been a number of variations of this model, such as the Field environment (Reiss, 1990) and Hewlett-Packard's Softbench (Fromme and Walker, 1993). Both of these have been used to control tool interactions in software engineering environments. Object Request Brokers (ORBs), discussed in Chapter 12, also support this model of control for distributed object communications.

The advantage of this broadcast approach is that evolution is relatively simple. A new sub-system to handle particular classes of events can be integrated by registering its events with the event handler. Any sub-system can activate any other sub-system without knowing its name or location. The sub-systems can be implemented on distributed machines. This distribution is transparent to other sub-systems.

The disadvantage of this model is that sub-systems don't know if or when events will be handled. When a sub-system generates an event it does not know which other sub-systems have registered an interest in that event. It is quite possible for different sub-systems to register for the same events. This may cause conflicts when the results of handling the event are made available.

Real-time systems that require externally generated events to be handled very quickly must be event-driven. For example, if a real-time system is used to control the safety systems in a car, it must detect a possible crash and, perhaps, inflate an airbag before the driver's head hits the steering wheel. To provide this rapid response to events, you have to use interrupt-driven control.

Figure 11.10 An
interrupt-driven
control model

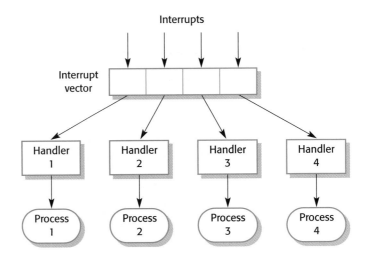

An interrupt-driven control model is illustrated in Figure 11.10. There are a known number of interrupt types with a handler defined for each type. Each type of interrupt is associated with the memory location where its handler's address is stored. When an interrupt of a particular type is received, a hardware switch causes control to be transferred immediately to its handler. This interrupt handler may then start or stop other processes in response to the event signalled by the interrupt.

This model is mostly used in real-time systems where an immediate response to some event is necessary. It may be combined with the centralised management model. The central manager handles the normal running of the system with interrupt-based control for emergencies.

The advantage of this approach is that it allows very fast responses to events to be implemented. Its disadvantages are that it is complex to program and difficult to validate. It may be impossible to replicate patterns of interrupt timing during system testing. It can be difficult to change systems developed using this model if the number of interrupts is limited by the hardware. Once this limit is reached, no other types of events can be handled. You can sometimes get around this limitation by mapping several types of events onto a single interrupt. The handler then works out which event has occurred. However, interrupt mapping may be impractical if a very fast response to individual interrupts is required.

11.5 Reference architectures

The above architectural models are general models: They can be applied to many classes of application. As well as these general models, architectural models that

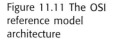
Figure 11.11 The OSI
reference model
architecture

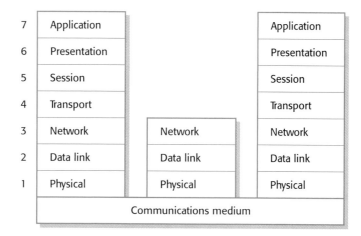

are specific to a particular application domain may also be used. Although instances of these systems differ in detail, the common architectural structure can be reused when developing new systems. These architectural models are called *domain-specific architectures*.

There are two types of domain-specific architectural model:

1. *Generic models* are abstractions from a number of real systems. They encapsulate the principal characteristics of these systems. For example, in real-time systems, there might be generic architectural models of different system types such as data collection systems or monitoring systems. I discuss a range of generic models in Chapter 13, which covers application architectures. In this section, I focus on architectural reference models.

2. *Reference models* are more abstract and describe a larger class of systems. They are a way of informing designers about the general structure of that class of system. Reference models are usually derived from a study of the application domain. They represent an idealised architecture that includes all the features that systems might incorporate.

There is not, of course, a rigid distinction between these types of model. Generic models can also serve as reference models. I distinguish between them here because generic models may be reused directly in a design. Reference models are normally used to communicate domain concepts and compare or evaluate possible architectures.

Reference architectures are not normally considered a route to implementation. Rather, their principal function is a means of discussing domain-specific architectures and comparing different systems in a domain. A reference model provides a vocabulary for comparison. It acts as a base, against which systems can be evaluated.

The OSI model is a seven-layer model for open systems interconnection. The model is illustrated in Figure 11.11. The exact functions of the layers are not important here.

Figure 11.12 The
ECMA reference
architecture for CASE
environments

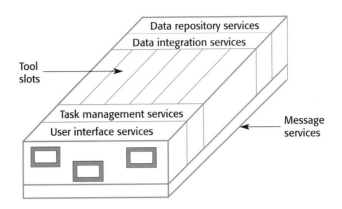

In essence, the lower layers are concerned with physical interconnection, the middle layers with data transfer and the upper layers with the transfer of semantically meaningful application information such as standardised documents.

The designers of the OSI model had the very practical objective of defining an implementation standard so that conformant systems could communicate with each other. Each layer should only depend on the layer beneath it. As technology developed, a layer could be transparently reimplemented without affecting the systems using other layers.

In practice, however, the performance problems of the layered approach to architectural modelling have compromised this objective. Because of the vast differences between networks, simple interconnection may be impossible. Although the functional characteristics of each layer are well defined, the non-functional characteristics are not defined. System developers have to implement their own higher-level facilities and skip layers in the model. Alternatively, they have to design non-standard features to improve system performance.

Consequently, the transparent replacement of a layer in the model is hardly ever possible. However, this does not negate the usefulness of the model as it provides a basis for the abstract structuring and the systematic implementation of communications between systems.

Another proposed reference model is a reference model for CASE environments (ECMA, 1991; Brown et al., 1992) that identifies five sets of services that a CASE environment should provide. It should also provide 'plug-in' facilities for individual CASE tools that use these services. The CASE reference model is illustrated in Figure 11.12. The five levels of service in the CASE reference model are:

1. *Data repository services* These provide facilities for the storage and management of data items and their relationships.

2. *Data integration services* These provide facilities for managing groups or the establishment of relationships between them. These services and data repository services are the basis of data integration in the environment.

3. *Task management services* These provide facilities for the definition and enactment of process models. They support process integration.

4. *Message services* These provide facilities for tool-tool, environment-tool and environment-environment communications. They support control integration.

5. *User interface services* These provide facilities for user interface development. They support presentation integration.

This reference model tells us what might be included in any particular CASE environment, although it is important to emphasise that not every feature of a reference architecture will be included in actual architectural designs. It means that we can ask questions of a system design such as 'how are the data repository services provided?' and 'does the system provide task management?'

KEY POINTS

■ The software architecture is the fundamental framework for structuring the system. Properties of a system such as performance, security and availability are influenced by the architecture used.

■ Architectural design decisions include decisions on the type of application, the distribution of the system, the architectural styles to be used and the ways in which the architecture should be documented and evaluated.

■ Different architectural models such as a structural model, a control model and a decomposition model may be developed during the architectural design process.

■ Organisational models of a system include repository models, client–server models and abstract machine models. Repository models share data through a common store. Client–server models usually distribute data. Abstract machine models are layered, with each layer implemented using the facilities provided by its foundation layer.

■ Decomposition styles include object-oriented and function-oriented decomposition. Pipelining models are functional, and object models are based on loosely coupled entities that maintain their own state and operations.

■ Control styles include centralised control and event-based control. In centralised models of control, control decisions are made depending on the system state; in event models, external events control the system.

■ Reference architectures may be used as a vehicle to discuss domain-specific architectures and to assess and compare architectural designs.

Again, the principal value of this reference architecture is as a means of classifying and comparing integrated CASE tools and environments. In addition, it can also be used in education to highlight the key features of these environments and to discuss them in a generic way.

FURTHER READING

Software Architecture in Practice, 2nd ed. This is a practical discussion of software architectures that does not oversell the approach and that provides a clear business rationale why architectures are important. (L. Bass, et al., 2003, Addison-Wesley.)

Design and Use of Software Architectures. Although this book focuses on product-line architectures, the first few chapters are an excellent introduction to general issues in software architecture design. (J. Bosch, 2000, Addison-Wesley.)

Software Architecture: Perspectives on an Emerging Discipline. This was the first book on software architecture and has a good discussion on different architectural styles. (M. Shaw and D. Garlan, 1996, Prentice-Hall.)

EXERCISES

11.1 Explain why it may be necessary to design the system architecture before the specifications are written.

11.2 Explain why design conflicts might arise when designing an architecture where availability and security requirements are the most important functional requirements.

11.3 Construct a table showing the advantages and disadvantages of the structural models discussed in this chapter.

11.4 Giving reasons for your answer, suggest an appropriate structural model for the following systems:

■ An automated ticket-issuing system used by passengers at a railway station

■ A computer-controlled video conferencing system that allows video, audio and computer data to be visible to several participants at the same time

■ A robot floor-cleaner that is intended to clean relatively clear spaces such as corridors. The cleaner must be able to sense walls and other obstructions.

11.5 Design an architecture for the above systems based on your choice of model. Make reasonable assumptions about the system requirements.

11.6   Real-time systems usually use event-driven models of control. Under what circumstances would you recommend the use of a call–return control model for a real-time system?

11.7   Giving reasons for your answer, suggest an appropriate control model for the following systems:

■ A batch processing system that takes information about hours worked and pay rates and prints salary slips and bank credit transfer information

■ A set of software tools that are produced by different vendors, but which must work together

■ A television controller that responds to signals from a remote control unit.

11.8   Discuss their advantages and disadvantages as far as distributability is concerned of the data-flow model and the object model. Assume that both single machine and distributed versions of an application are required.

11.9   You are given two integrated CASE toolsets and are asked to compare them. Explain how you could use a reference model for CASE (Brown, et al., 1992) to make this comparison.

11.10   Should there be a separate profession of 'software architect' whose role is to work independently with a customer to design a software system architecture? This system would then be implemented by some software company. What might be the difficulties of establishing such a profession?

12

Distributed systems architectures

Objectives

The objective of this chapter is to discuss models of the software architecture for distributed systems. When you have read this chapter, you will:

■ know the advantages and disadvantages of distributed systems architectures;

■ understand the two principal models of distributed systems architecture, namely client–server systems and distributed object systems;

■ understand the concept of an object request broker and the principles underlying the CORBA standards;

■ have been introduced to peer-to-peer and service-oriented architectures as ways to implement interorganisational distributed systems.

Contents

Virtually all large computer-based systems are now distributed systems. A distributed system is a system where the information processing is distributed over several computers rather than confined to a single machine. Obviously, the engineering of distributed systems has a great deal in common with the engineering of any other software, but there are specific issues that have to be taken into account when designing this type of system. I already introduced some of these issues in the introduction to client–server architectures in Chapter 11 and I cover them in more detail here.

Coulouris et al. (Coulouris, et al., 2001) discuss the important characteristics of distributed systems. They identify the following advantages of using a distributed approach to systems development:

1. *Resource sharing* A distributed system allows the sharing of hardware and software resources—such as disks, printers, files and compilers—that are associated with computers on a network.

2. *Openness* Distributed systems are normally open systems, which means they are designed around standard protocols that allow equipment and software from different vendors to be combined.

3. *Concurrency* In a distributed system, several processes may operate at the same time on separate computers on the network. These processes may (but need not) communicate with each other during their normal operation.

4. *Scalability* In principle at least, distributed systems are scalable in that the capabilities of the system can be increased by adding new resources to cope with new demands on the system. In practice, the network linking the individual computers in the system may limit the system scalability. If many new computers are added, then the network capacity may be inadequate.

5. *Fault tolerance* The availability of several computers and the potential for replicating information means that distributed systems can be tolerant of some hardware and software failures (see Chapter 20). In most distributed systems, a degraded service can be provided when failures occur; complete loss of service only tends to occur when there is a network failure.

For large-scale organisational systems, these advantages mean that distributed systems have largely replaced the centralised legacy systems that were developed in the 1980s and 1990s. However, compared to systems that run on a single processor or processor cluster, distributed systems have a number of disadvantages:

1. *Complexity* Distributed systems are more complex than centralised systems. This makes it more difficult to understand their emergent properties and to test these systems. For example, rather than the performance of the system being dependent on the execution speed of one processor, it depends on the network bandwidth and the speed of the processors on the network. Moving resources from one part of the system to another can radically affect the system's performance.

2. *Security* The system may be accessed from several different computers, and the traffic on the network may be subject to eavesdropping. This makes it more difficult to ensure that the integrity of the data in the system is maintained and that the system services are not degraded by denial-of-service attacks.

3. *Manageability* The computers in a system may be of different types and may run different versions of the operating system. Faults in one machine may propagate to other machines with unexpected consequences. This means that more effort is required to manage and maintain the system in operation.

4. *Unpredictability* As all users of the WWW know, distributed systems are unpredictable in their response. The response depends on the overall load on the system, its organisation and the network load. As all of these may change over a short period, the time taken to respond to a user request may vary dramatically from one request to another.

The design challenge is to design the software and hardware to provide desirable distributed system characteristics and, at the same time, minimise the problems that are inherent in these systems. To do so, you need to understand the advantages and disadvantages of different distributed systems architectures. I cover two generic types of distributed systems architecture here:

1. *Client–server architectures* In this approach, the system may be thought of as a set of services that are provided to clients that make use of these services. Servers and clients are treated differently in these systems.

2. *Distributed object architectures* In this case, there is no distinction between servers and clients, and the system may be thought of as a set of interacting objects whose location is irrelevant. There is no distinction between a service provider and a user of these services.

Both client–server and distributed object architectures are widely used in industry, but the distribution of the applications is generally within a single organisation. The distribution supported is therefore intra-organisational. I also discuss two other types of distributed architecture that are more suited to inter-organisational distribution: peer-to-peer (p2p) system architectures and service-oriented architectures. Peer-to-peer systems have mostly been used for personal systems but are starting to be used for business applications. At the time of this writing, service-oriented systems are just being introduced, but the service-oriented approach is likely to become a very significant distribution model by 2005.

The components in a distributed system may be implemented in different programming languages and may execute on completely different types of processors. Models of data, information representation and protocols for communication may all be different. A distributed system therefore requires software that can manage these diverse parts, and ensure that they can communicate and exchange data. The term *middleware* is used to refer to this software—it sits in the middle between the different distributed components of the system.

Bernstein (Bernstein, 1996) summarises types of middleware that are available to support distributed computing. Middleware is general-purpose software that is usually bought off-the-shelf rather than written specially by application developers. Examples of middleware are software for managing communications with databases, transaction managers, data converters and communication controllers. I describe object request brokers, a very important class of middleware for distributed systems, later in this chapter.

Distributed systems are usually developed using an object-oriented approach. These systems are made up of loosely integrated, independent parts, each of which may interact directly with users or with other parts of the system. Parts of the system may have to respond to independent events. Software objects reflect these characteristics, so are natural abstractions for distributed systems components.

12.1 Multiprocessor architectures

The simplest model of a distributed system is a multiprocessor system where the software system consists of a number of processes that may (but need not) execute on separate processors. This model is common in large real-time systems. As I discuss in Chapter 15, these systems collect information, make decisions using this information and send signals to actuators that modify the system's environment.

Logically, the processes concerned with information collection, decision making and actuator control could all run on a single processor under the control of a scheduler. Using multiple processors improves the performance and resilience of the system. The distribution of processes to processors may be pre-determined (this is common in critical systems) or may be under the control of a dispatcher that decides which process to allocate to each processor.

An example of this type of system is shown in Figure 12.1. This is a simplified model of a traffic control system. A set of distributed sensors collects information on the traffic flow and processes this locally before sending it to a control room. Operators make decisions using this information and give instructions to a separate traffic light control process. In this example, there are separate logical processes for managing the sensors, the control room and the traffic lights. These logical processes may be single processes or a group of processes. In this example, they run on separate processors.

Software systems composed of multiple processes are not necessarily distributed systems. If more than one processor is available, then distribution can be implemented, but the system designers need not always consider distribution issues during the design process. The design approach for this type of system is essentially that for real-time systems, as discussed in Chapter 15.

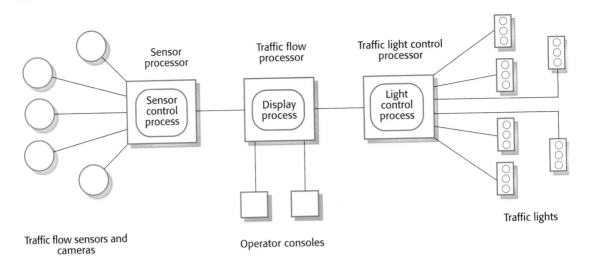

Figure 12.1 A
multiprocessor traffic
control system

12.2 Client–server architectures

I have already introduced the concept of client–server architectures in Chapter 11. In a client–server architecture, an application is modelled as a set of services that are provided by servers and a set of clients that use these services (Orfali and Harkey, 1998). Clients need to be aware of the servers that are available but usually do not know of the existence of other clients. Clients and servers are separate processes, as shown in Figure 12.2, which is a logical model of a distributed client–server architecture.

Several server processes can run on a single server processor so there is not necessarily a 1:1 mapping between processes and processors in the system. Figure 12.3 shows the physical architecture of a system with six client computers and two server computers. These can run the client and server processes shown in Figure 12.2. When I refer to *clients* and *servers,* I mean these logical processes rather than the physical computers on which they execute.

The design of client–server systems should reflect the logical structure of the application that is being developed. One way to look at an application is illustrated in Figure 12.4, which shows an application structured into three layers. The presentation layer is concerned with presenting information to the user and with all user interaction. The application processing layer is concerned with implementing the logic of the application, and the data management layer is concerned with all database operations. In centralised systems, these need not be clearly separated. However, when you are designing a distributed system, you should make a clear distinction between them, as it then becomes possible to distribute each layer to a different computer.

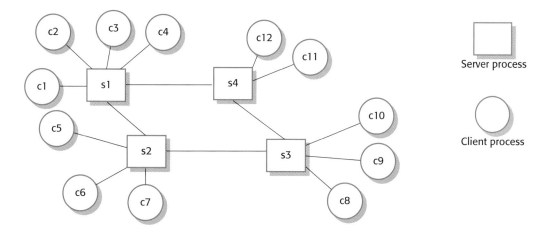

Figure 12.2 A
client–server system

The simplest client–server architecture is called a *two-tier client–server archi-tecture,* where an application is organised as a server (or multiple identical servers) and a set of clients. As illustrated in Figure 12.5, two-tier client–server architec-tures can take two forms:

1. *Thin-client model* In a thin-client model, all of the application processing and data management is carried out on the server. The client is simply responsible for running the presentation software.

2. *Fat-client model* In this model, the server is only responsible for data management. The software on the client implements the application logic and the interac-tions with the system user.

Figure 12.3
Computers in a
client–server network

A thin-client, two-tier architecture is the simplest approach to use when centralised legacy systems, as discussed in Chapter 2, are evolved to a client–server architecture.

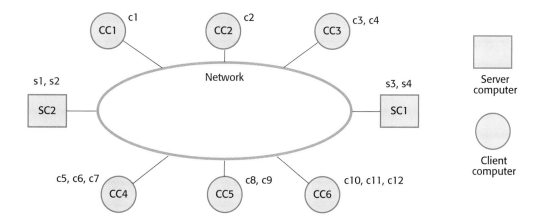

Figure 12.4
Application layers

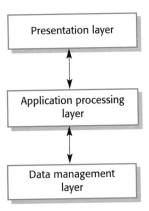

The user interface for these systems is migrated to PCs, and the application itself acts as a server and handles all application processing and data management. A thin-client model may also be implemented when the clients are simple network devices rather than PCs or workstations. The network device runs an Internet browser and the user interface implemented through that system.

A major disadvantage of the thin-client model is that it places a heavy processing load on both the server and the network. The server is responsible for all computation, and this may involve the generation of significant network traffic between the client and the server. There is a lot of processing power available in modern computing devices, which is largely unused in the thin-client approach.

The fat-client model makes use of this available processing power and distributes both the application logic processing and the presentation to the client. The server is essentially a transaction server that manages all database transactions. An example of this type of architecture is banking ATM systems, where the ATM is the client and the server is a mainframe running the customer account database. The hardware in the teller machine carries out a lot of the customer-related processing associated with a transaction.

Figure 12.5 Thin and
fat clients

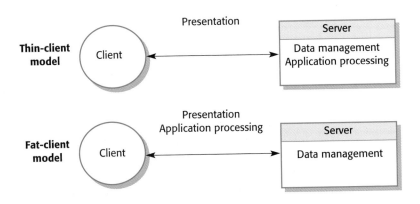

Figure 12.6 A
client–server ATM
system

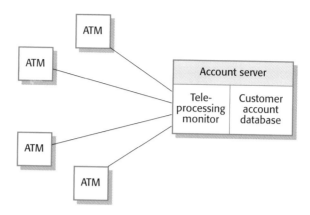

Figure 12.6 A
client–server ATM
system

This ATM distributed system is illustrated in Figure 12.6. Notice that the ATMs do not connect directly to the customer database but to a teleprocessing monitor. A teleprocessing monitor or transaction manager is a middleware system that organises communications with remote clients and serialises client transactions for processing by the database. Using serial transactions means that the system can recover from faults without corrupting the system data.

While the fat-client model distributes processing more effectively than a thin-client model, system management is more complex. Application functionality is spread across many computers. When the application software has to be changed, this involves reinstallation on every client computer. This can be a major cost if there are hundreds of clients in the system.

The advent of mobile code (such as Java applets and Active X controls), which can be downloaded from a server to a client, has allowed the development of client–server systems that are somewhere between the thin- and the fat-client model. Some of the application processing software may be downloaded to the client as mobile code, thus relieving the load on the server. The user interface is created using a web browser that has built-in facilities to run the downloaded code.

The problem with a two-tier client–server approach is that the three logical layers—presentation, application processing and data management—must be mapped onto two computer systems—the client and the server. There may either be problems with scalability and performance if the thin-client model is chosen, or problems of system management if the fat-client model is used. To avoid these issues, an alternative approach is to use a *three-tier client–server* architecture (Figure 12.7). In this architecture, the presentation, the application processing and the data management are logically separate processes that execute on different processors.

An Internet banking system (Figure 12.8) is an example of the three-tier client–server architecture. The bank's customer database (usually hosted on a mainframe computer) provides data management services; a web server provides the application services such as facilities to transfer cash, generate statements, pay bills and so on; and the user's own computer with an Internet browser is the client. This sys-

Figure 12.7 A three-tier client–server architecture

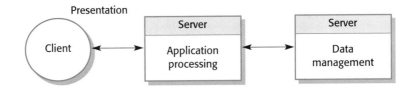

Figure 12.8 The distribution architecture of an Internet banking system

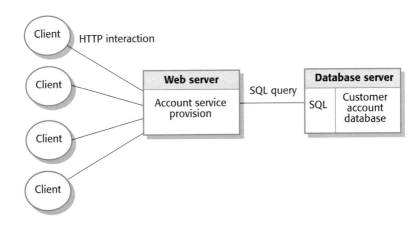

tem is scalable because it is relatively easy to add new web servers as the number of customers increase.

The use of a three-tier architecture in this case allows the information transfer between the web server and the database server to be optimised. The communications between these systems can use fast, low-level communications protocols. Efficient middleware that supports database queries in SQL (Structured Query Language) is used to handle information retrieval from the database.

In some cases, it is appropriate to extend the three-tier client–server model to a multi-tier variant where additional servers are added to the system. Multi-tier systems may be used where applications need to access and use data from different databases. In this case, an integration server is positioned between the application server and the database servers. The integration server collects the distributed data and presents it to the application as if it were from a single database.

Three-tier client–server architectures and multi-tier variants that distribute the application processing across several servers are inherently more scalable than two-tier architectures. Network traffic is reduced in contrast with thin-client two-tier architectures. The application processing is the most volatile part of the system, and it can be easily updated because it is centrally located. Processing, in some cases, may be distributed between the application logic and the data management servers, thus leading to more rapid response to client requests.

Designers of client–server architectures must take a number of factors into account when choosing the most appropriate architecture. Situations where the

Figure 12.9 Use of different client–server architectures

Architecture	Applications
Two-tier C/S architecture with thin clients	Legacy system applications where separating application processing and data management is impractical. Computationally-intensive applications such as compilers with little or no data management. Data-intensive applications (browsing and querying) with little or no application processing.
Two-tier C/S architecture with fat clients	Applications where application processing is provided by off-the-shelf software (e.g. Microsoft Excel) on the client. Applications where computationally-intensive processing of data (e.g. data visualisation) is required. Applications with relatively stable end-user functionality used in an environment with well-established system management.
Three-tier or multi-tier C/S architecture	Large-scale applications with hundreds or thousands of clients. Applications where both the data and the application are volatile. Applications where data from multiple sources are integrated.

client–server architectures that I have discussed are likely to be appropriate are shown in Figure 12.9.

12.3 Distributed object architectures

In the client–server model of a distributed system, clients and servers are different. Clients receive services from servers and not from other clients; servers may act as clients by receiving services from other servers but they do not request services from clients; clients must know the services that are offered by specific servers and must know how to contact these servers. This model works well for many types of applications. However, it limits the flexibility of system designers in that they must decide where services are to be provided. They must also plan for scalability and so provide some means for the load on servers to be distributed as more clients are added to the system.

A more general approach to distributed system design is to remove the distinction between client and server and to design the system architecture as a distributed object architecture. In a distributed object architecture (Figure 12.10), the fundamental system components are objects that provide an interface to a set of services that they provide. Other objects call on these services with no logical distinction between a client (a receiver of a service) and a server (a provider of a service).

Objects may be distributed across a number of computers on a network and communicate through middleware. This middleware is called an object request broker.

Figure 12.10
Distributed object
architecture

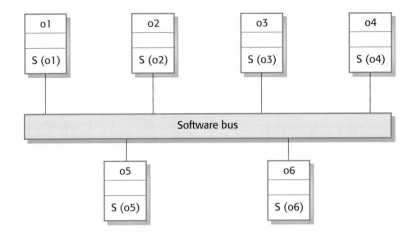

Its role is to provide a seamless interface between objects. It provides a set of services that allow objects to communicate and to be added to and removed from the system. I discuss object request brokers in Section 12.3.1.

The advantages of the distributed object model are:

- It allows the system designer to delay decisions on where and how services should be provided. Service-providing objects may execute on any node of the network. Therefore, the distinction between fat- and thin-client models becomes irrelevant, as there is no need to decide in advance where application logic objects are located.

- It is a very open system architecture that allows new resources to be added to it as required. As I discuss in the following section, object communication standards have been developed and implemented that allow objects written in different programming languages to communicate and to provide services to each other.

- The system is flexible and scalable. Different instances of the system with the same service provided by different objects or by replicated objects can be created to cope with different system loads. New objects can be added as the load on the system increases without disrupting other system objects.

- It is possible to reconfigure the system dynamically with objects migrating across the network as required. This may be important where there are fluctuating patterns of demand on services. A service-providing object can migrate to the same processor as service-requesting objects, thus improving the performance of the system.

A distributed object architecture can be used as a logical model that allows you to structure and organise the system. In this case, you think about how to provide application functionality solely in terms of services and combinations of services.

Figure 12.11 The
distribution
architecture of a data
mining system

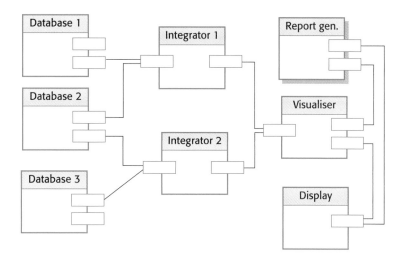

Figure 12.11 The distribution architecture of a data mining system

You then work out how to provide these services using a number of distributed objects. At this level, the objects that you design are usually large-grain objects (sometimes called *business objects*) that provide domain-specific services. For example, in a retail application, there may be business objects concerned with stock control, customer communications, goods ordering and so on. This logical model can, of course, then be realised as an implementation model.

Alternatively, you can use a distributed object approach to implement client–server systems. In this case, the logical model of the system is a client–server model, but both clients and servers are realised as distributed objects communicating through a software bus. This makes it possible to change the system easily, for example, from a two-tier to a multi-tier system. In this case, the server or the client may not be implemented as a single distributed object but may be composed from smaller objects that provide specialised services.

An example of a type of system where a distributed object architecture might be appropriate is a data mining system that looks for relationships between the data that is stored in a number of databases (Figure 12.11). An example of a data mining application might be where a retail business has, say, food stores and hardware stores, and wants to find relationships between a customer's food and hardware purchases. For instance, people who buy baby food may also buy particular types of wallpaper. With this knowledge, the business can then specifically target baby-food customers with combined offers.

In this example, each database can be encapsulated as a distributed object with an interface that provides read-only access to its data. Integrator objects are each concerned with specific types of relationships, and they collect information from all of the databases to try to deduce the relationships. There might be an integrator object that is concerned with seasonal variations in goods sold and another that is concerned with relationships between different types of goods.

Visualiser objects interact with integrator objects to produce a visualisation or a report on the relationships that have been discovered. Because of the large volumes of data that are handled, visualiser objects will normally use graphical presentations of the relationships that have been discovered. I discuss graphical information presentation in Chapter 16.

A distributed object architecture rather than a client–server architecture is appropriate for this type of application for three reasons:

1. Unlike a bank ATM system (say), the logical model of the system is not one of service provision where there are distinguished data management services.

2. You can add databases to the system without major disruption. Each database is simply another distributed object. The database objects can provide a simplified interface that controls access to the data. The databases that are accessed may reside on different machines.

3. It allows new types of relationships to be mined by adding new integrator objects. Parts of the business that are interested in specific relationships can extend the system by adding integrator objects that operate on their computers without requiring knowledge of any other integrators that are used elsewhere.

The major disadvantage of distributed object architectures is that they are more complex to design than client–server systems. Client–server systems appear to be a fairly natural way to think about systems. They reflect many human transactions where people request and receive services from other people who specialise in providing these services. It is more difficult to think about general service provision, and we do not yet have a great deal of experience with the design and development of large-grain business objects.

12.3.1 CORBA

As I indicated in the previous section, the implementation of a distributed object architecture requires middleware (object request brokers) to handle communications between the distributed objects. In principle, the objects in the system may be implemented using different programming languages, the objects may run on different platforms and their names need not be known to all other objects in the system. The middleware 'glue' therefore has to do a lot of work to ensure seamless object communications.

Middleware to support distributed object computing is required at two levels:

1. At the logical communication level, the middleware provides functionality that allows objects on different computers to exchange data and control information. Standards such as CORBA and COM (Pritchard, 1999) have been developed to facilitate logical object communications on different platforms.

Figure 12.12 The
structure of a
CORBA-based
distributed
application

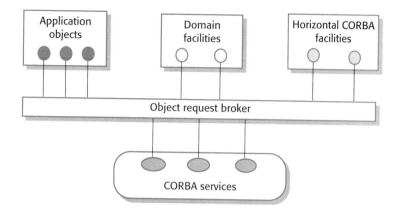

2. At the component level, the middleware provides a basis for developing compatible components. Standards such as EJB, CORBA components or Active X (Szyperski, 2002) provide a basis for implementing components with standard methods that can be queried and used by other components. I cover component standards in Chapter 19.

In this section, I focus on the middleware for logical object communication and discuss how this is supported by the CORBA standards. These were defined by the Object Management Group (OMG), which defines standards for object-oriented development. The OMG standards are available, free of charge, from their web site.

The OMG's vision of a distributed application is shown in Figure 12.12, which I have adapted from Siegel's diagram of the Object Management Architecture (Siegal, 1998). This proposes that a distributed application should be made up of a number of components:

1. Application objects that are designed and implemented for this application.

2. Standard objects that are defined by the OMG for a specific domain. These domain object standards cover finance/insurance, electronic commerce, healthcare, and a number of other areas.

3. Fundamental CORBA services that provide basic distributed computing services such as directories and security management.

4. Horizontal CORBA facilities such as user interface facilities, system management facilities, and so on. The term *horizontal facilities* suggests that these facilities are common to many application domains and the facilities are therefore used in many different applications.

The CORBA standards cover all aspects of this vision. There are four major elements to these standards:

1. An object model for application objects where a CORBA object is an encapsulation of state with a well-defined, language-neutral interface described in an IDL (Interface Definition Language).

2. An object request broker (ORB) that manages requests for object services. The ORB locates the object providing the service, prepares it for the request, sends the service request and returns the results to the requester.

3. A set of object services that are general services likely to be required by many distributed applications. Examples of services are directory services, transaction services and persistence services.

4. A set of common components built on top of these basic services that may be required by applications. These may be vertical domain-specific components or horizontal, general-purpose components that are used by many applications.

The CORBA object model considers an object to be an encapsulation of attributes and services, as is normal for objects. However, CORBA objects must have a separate interface definition that defines the public attributes and operations of the object. CORBA object interfaces are defined using a standard, language-independent interface definition language. If an object wishes to use services provided by another object, then it accesses these services through the IDL interface. CORBA objects have a unique identifier called an Interoperable Object Reference (IOR). This IOR is used when one object requests services from another.

The object request broker knows about the objects that are requesting services and their interfaces. The ORB handles the communication between the objects. The communicating objects do not need to know the location of other objects nor do they need to know anything about their implementation. As the IDL interface insulates the objects from the ORB, it is possible to change the object implementation in a completely transparent way. The object location can change between invocations, which is transparent to other objects in the system.

For example, in Figure 12.13, two objects o1 and o2 communicate through an ORB. The calling object (o1) has an associated IDL stub that defines the interface of the object providing the required service. The implementer of o1 embeds calls to this stub in their object implementation when a service is required. The IDL is a superset of C++, so it is very easy to access this stub if you are programming in C++, and it is fairly easy in C or Java. Language mappings to IDL have also been defined for other languages such as Ada and COBOL.

The object providing the service has an associated IDL skeleton that links the interface to the implementation of the services. In simple terms, when a service is called through the interface, the IDL skeleton translates this into a call to the service in whatever implementation language has been used. When the method or procedure has been executed, the IDL skeleton translates the results into IDL so that it can be accessed by the calling object. Where an object both provides services to other objects and uses services that are provided elsewhere, it needs both an IDL skeleton and IDL stubs. An IDL stub is required for every object that is used.

Figure 12.13 Object
communications
through an ORB

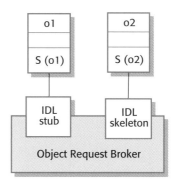

Object request brokers are not usually implemented as separate processes but are a set of libraries that can be linked with object implementations. Therefore, in a distributed system, each computer that is running distributed objects will have its own object request broker. This will handle all local invocations of objects. However, a request made for a service that is to be provided by a remote object requires inter-ORB communications.

This situation is illustrated in Figure 12.14. In this example, when object o1 or o2 requests a service from o3 or o4, the associated ORBs must communicate. A CORBA implementation supports ORB-to-ORB communication by providing all ORBs with access to IDL interface definitions and by implementing the OMG's standards Generic Inter-ORB Protocol (GIOP). This protocol defines standard messages that ORBs can exchange to implement remote object invocation and information transfer. When combined with lower-level Internet TCP/IP protocols, the GIOP allows ORBs to communicate across the Internet.

The CORBA initiative has been underway since the 1980s, and the early versions of CORBA were simply concerned with supporting distributed objects. However, as the standards have evolved they have become more extensive. As well as a mechanism for distributed object communications, the CORBA standards now define some standard services that may be provided to support distributed object-oriented applications.

You can think of CORBA services as facilities that are likely to be required by many distributed systems. The standards define approximately 15 common services. Some examples of these generic services are:

1. Naming and trading services that allow objects to refer to and discover other objects on the network. The naming service is a directory service that allows objects to be named and discovered by other objects. This is like the white pages of a phone directory. The trading services are like the yellow pages. Objects can find out what other objects have registered with the trader service and can access the specification of these objects.

2. Notification services that allow objects to notify other objects that some event has occurred. Objects may register their interest in a particular event with the

Figure 12.14
Inter-ORB
communications

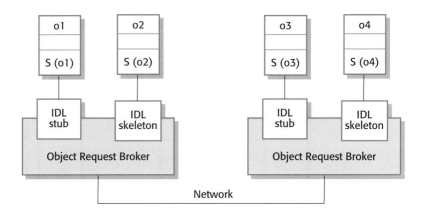

service and, when that event occurs, they are automatically notified. For example, say the system includes a print spooler that queues documents to be printed and a number of printer objects. The print spooler registers that it is interested in an 'end-of-printing' event from a printer object. The notification service informs it when printing is complete. It can then schedule the next document on that printer.

3. Transaction services that support atomic transactions and rollback on failure. Transactions are a fault-tolerance facility that supports recovery from errors during an update operation. If an object update operation fails, then the object state can be rolled back to its state before the update was started.

The CORBA standards include interface definitions for a wide range of horizontal and vertical components that may be used by distributed application builders. Vertical components are components that are specific to an application domain. Horizontal components are general-purpose components such as user interface components. The development of specifications for horizontal and vertical CORBA components is a long-term activity, and currently available specifications are published on the OMG website.

12.4 Inter-organisational distributed computing

For reasons of security and inter-operability, distributed computing has been primarily implemented at the organisational level. An organisation has a number of servers and spreads its computational load across these. Because these are all located within the same organisation, local standards and operational processes can be applied. Although, for web-based systems, client computers are often outside the organisational boundary, their functionality is limited to running user interface software.

Newer models of distributed computing, however, are now available that allow inter-organisational rather than intra-organisational distributed computing. I discuss two of these approaches in this section. Peer-to-peer computing is based around computations carried out by individual network nodes. Service-oriented systems rely on distributed services rather than distributed objects, and rely on XML-based standards for data exchange.

12.4.1 Peer-to-peer architectures

Peer-to-peer (p2p) systems are decentralised systems where computations may be carried out by any node on the network and, in principle at least, no distinctions are made between clients and servers. In peer-to-peer applications, the overall system is designed to take advantage of the computational power and storage available across a potentially huge network of computers. The standards and protocols that enable communications across the nodes are embedded in the application itself, and each node must run a copy of that application.

It the time of writing, peer-to-peer technologies have mostly been used for personal systems (Oram, 2001). For example, file-sharing systems based on the Gnutella and Kazaa protocols are used to share files on users' PCs, and instant messaging systems such as ICQ and Jabber provide direct communications between users without an intermediate server. SETI@home is a long-running project to process data from radio telescopes on home PCs to search for indications of extraterrestrial life, and Freenet is a decentralised database that has been designed to make it easier to publish information anonymously and to make it difficult for authorities to suppress this information.

However, there are indications that this technology is being increasingly used by businesses to harness the power in their PC networks (McDougall, 2000). Intel and Boeing have both implemented p2p systems for computationally intensive applications. For cooperative applications that support distributed working, this seems to be the most effective technology.

You can look at the architecture of p2p applications from two perspectives. The logical network architecture is the distribution architecture of the system, whereas the application architecture is the generic organisation of components in each application type. In this chapter, I focus on the two principal types of logical network architecture that may be used—decentralised architectures and semi-centralised architectures.

In principle, in peer-to-peer systems every node in the network could be aware of every other node, could make connections to it, and could exchange data with it. In practice, of course, this is impossible, so nodes are organised into 'localities' with some nodes acting as bridges to other node localities. Figure 12.15 shows this decentralised p2p architecture.

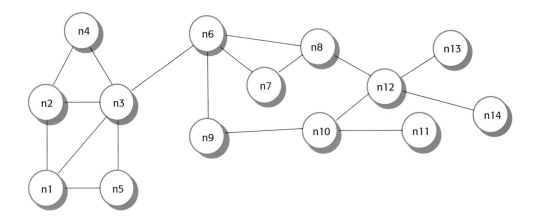

Figure 12.15
Decentralised
p2p architecture

In a decentralised architecture, the nodes in the network are not simply functional elements but are also communications switches that can route data and control signals from one node to another. For example, assume that Figure 12.15 represents a decentralised, document-management system. This system is used by a consortium of researchers to share documents, and each member of the consortium maintains his or her own document store. However, when a document is retrieved, the node retrieving that document also makes it available to other nodes. Someone who needs a document issues a search command that is sent to nodes in that 'locality'. These nodes check whether they have the document and, if so, return it to the requestor. If they do not have it, they route the search to other nodes; when the document is finally discovered, the node can route the document back to the original requestor. Therefore, if **n1** issues a search for a document that is stored at **n10**, this search is routed through nodes **n3**, **n6**, and **n9** to **n10**.

This decentralised architecture has obvious advantages in that it is highly redundant, and so is fault-tolerant and tolerant of nodes disconnecting from the network. However, there are obvious overheads in the system in that the same search may be processed by many different nodes and there is significant overhead in replicated peer communications. An alternative p2p architectural model that departs from a pure p2p architecture is a semi-centralised architecture where, within the network, one or more nodes act as servers to facilitate node communications. Figure 12.16 illustrates this model.

In a semi-centralised architecture, the role of a server is to help establish contact between peers in the network or to coordinate the results of a computation. For example, if Figure 12.16 represents an instant messaging system, then network nodes communicate with the server (indicated by dashed lines) to find out what other nodes are available. Once these are discovered, direct communications can be established and the connection to the server is unnecessary. Therefore nodes **n2**, **n3**, **n5** and **n6** are in direct communication.

In a computational p2p system where a processor-intensive computation is distributed across a large number of nodes, it is normal for some nodes to be

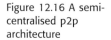

Figure 12.16 A semi-
centralised p2p
architecture

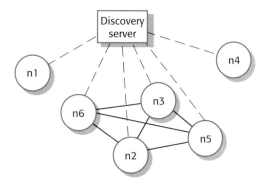

distinguished nodes whose role is to distribute work to other nodes and to collate
and check the results of the computation.

Although there are obvious overheads in peer-to-peer systems, it is a much more
efficient approach to inter-organisational computing than the service-based
approach that I discuss in the next section. There are still problems with using p2p
approaches for inter-organisational computing, as issues such as security and trust
are still unresolved. This means that p2p systems are most likely to be used either
for non-critical information systems or where there are already working relationships between organisations.

12.4.2 Service-oriented system architecture

The development of the WWW meant that client computers had access to remote
servers outside their own organisations. If these organisations converted their information to HTML, then this could be accessed by these computers. However, access
was solely through a web browser, and direct access to the information stores by
other programs was not practical. This meant that opportunistic connections
between servers where, for example, a program queried a number of catalogues,
was not possible.

To get around this problem, the notion of a web service was proposed. Using a
web service, organisations that want to make their information accessible to other
programs can do so by defining and publishing a web service interface. This interface defines the data available and how it can be accessed. More generally, a web
service is a standard representation for some computational or information resource
that can be used by other programs. Therefore, you could define a tax filing service where users could fill in their tax forms and have these automatically checked
and submitted to the tax authorities.

A web service is an instance of a more general notion of a service, which is
defined by (Lovelock, et al., 1996) as:

Figure 12.17 The
conceptual
architecture of a
service-oriented
system

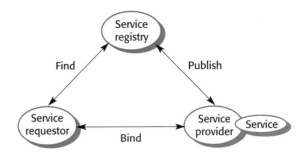

*an act or performance offered by one party to another. Although the process
may be tied to a physical product, the performance is essentially intangible
and does not normally result in ownership of any of the factors of production.*

The essence of a service, therefore, is that the provision of the service is independent of the application using the service (Turner, et al., 2003). Service providers can develop specialised services and offer these to a range of service users from different organisations. Applications may be constructed by linking services from various providers using either a standard programming language or a specialised service orchestration language such as BPEL4WS.

There are various service models, from the JINI model (Kumaran, 2001) through web services (Stal, 2002) and grid services (Foster, et al., 2002). Conceptually, all of these operate according to the model shown in Figure 12.17, which is a generalisation of the conceptual web service model described by Kreger (Kreger, 2001). A service provider offers a service by defining its interface and implementing the service functionality. A service requestor binds that service into its application. This means that the requestor's application includes code to call that service and process the results of the service call. To ensure that the service can be accessed by external service users, the service provider makes an entry in a service registry that includes information about the service and what it does.

The differences between this service model and the distributed object approach to distributed systems architectures are:

- Services can be offered by any service provider inside or outside of an organisation. Assuming these conform to certain standards (discussed below), organisations can create applications by integrating services from a range of providers. For example, a manufacturing company can link directly to services provided by its suppliers.

- The service provider makes information about the service public so that any authorised user can use it. The service provider and the service user do not need to negotiate about what the service does before it can be incorporated in an application program.

- Applications can delay the binding of services until they are deployed or until execution. Therefore, an application using a stock price service (say) could dynamically change service providers while the system was executing.

- Opportunistic construction of new services is possible. A service provider may recognise new services that can be created by linking existing services in innovative ways.

- Service users can pay for services according to their use rather than their provision. Therefore, instead of buying an expensive component that is rarely used, the application writer can use an external service that will be paid for only when required.

- Applications can be made smaller (which is important if they are to be embedded in other devices) because they can implement exception handling as external services.

- Applications can be reactive and adapt their operation according to their environment by binding to different services as their environment changes.

At the time of this writing, these advantages have sparked immense interest in web services as a basis for constructing loosely coupled, distributed applications. However, there is still limited practical experience with service-oriented architectures so we do not yet know that practical implications of this approach.

Software reuse has been a topic of research for many years; yet, as I discuss in Chapters 18 and 19, there remain many practical difficulties in reusing software. One of the major problems has been that standards for reusable components have been developed only relatively recently, and several standards are in use. However, the web services initiative has been driven by standards from its inception, and standards covering many aspects of web services are under development. The three fundamental standards that enable communications between web services are:

1. *SOAP (Simple Object Access Protocol)* This protocol defines an organisation for structured data exchange between web services.

2. *WSDL (Web Services Description Language)* This protocol defines how the interfaces of web services can be represented.

3. *UDDI (Universal Description, Discovery and Integration)* This is a discovery standard that defines how service description information, used by service requestors to discover services, can be organised.

All of these standards are based on XML—a human- and machine-readable markup language (Skonnard and Gudgin, 2002). You don't, however, need to know details of these standards to understand the web services concept.

Web service application architectures are loosely coupled architectures where service bindings can change during execution. Some systems will be solely built using

Figure 12.18 A
service-based in-car
information system

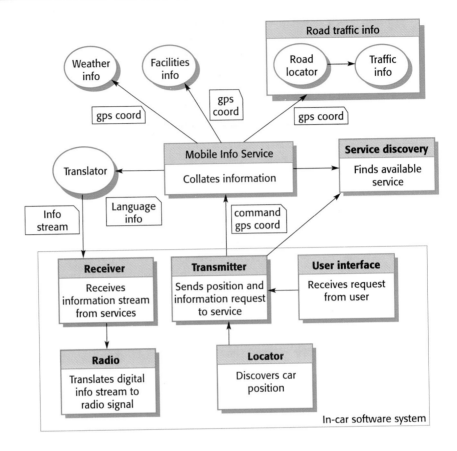

web services and others will mix web services with locally developed components.
To illustrate how applications may be organised, consider the following scenario:

> *An in-car information system provides drivers with information on weather,
> road traffic conditions, local information and so forth. This is linked to the
> car radio so that information is delivered as a signal on a specific radio chan-
> nel. The car is equipped with GPS receiver to discover its position and, based
> on that position, the system accesses a range of information services.
> Information may be delivered in the driver's specified language.*

Figure 12.18 illustrates a possible organisation for such a system. The in-car software includes five modules. These handle communications with the driver, with a
GPS receiver that reports the car's position and with the car radio. The Transmitter
and Receiver modules handle all communications with external services.

The car communicates with an externally provided mobile information service
which aggregates information from a range of other services that provide information on weather, traffic information and local facilities. Different providers in

different places provide this service, and the in-car system uses a discovery service to locate the appropriate information service and bind to it. The discovery service is also used by the mobile information service to bind to the appropriate weather, traffic and facilities services. Services exchange SOAP messages that include GPS position information used, by the services, to select the appropriate information. The aggregated information is passed back to the car through a service that translates the information language into the driver's language.

KEY POINTS

■ Distributed systems can support resource sharing, openness, concurrency, scalability, fault tolerance and transparency.

■ Client–server systems are distributed systems where the system is modelled as a set of services provided by servers to client processes.

■ In a client–server system, the user interface always runs on a client, and data management is always provided by a shared server. Application functionality may be implemented on the client computer or on the server.

■ In a distributed object architecture, there is no distinction between clients and servers. Objects provide general services that may be called on by other objects. This approach may be used for implementing client–server systems.

■ Distributed object systems require middleware to handle object communications and to allow objects to be added to and removed from the system.

■ The CORBA standards are a set of standards for middleware that supports distributed object architectures. They include object model definitions, definitions of an object request broker and common service definitions. Various implementations of the CORBA standards are available.

■ Peer-to-peer architectures are decentralised architectures where there are no distinguished clients and servers. Computations can be distributed over many systems in different organisations.

■ Service-oriented systems are created by linking software services provided by various service suppliers. An important aspect of service-oriented architectures is that binding of services to the architectural components can be delayed until the system is deployed or is executing.

This example illustrates one of the key advantages of the service-oriented approach. It is not necessary to decide when the system is programmed or deployed what service provider should be used and what specific services could be accessed. As the car moves around, the in-car software uses the service discovery service to find the most appropriate information service and binds to that. Because of the use of a translation service, it can move across borders and therefore make local information available to people who don't speak the local language.

This vision of service-oriented computing is not yet realisable with current web services, where the binding of services to applications is still fairly static. However, within the lifetime of this edition, it is likely that we will see more dynamic binding and application architectures. There is no question that the service-oriented model represents a very important new way to implement distributed, inter-organisational computing systems.

FURTHER READING

'Turning software into a service'. A good overview paper that discusses the principles of service-oriented computing. Unlike many papers on this topic, it does not conceal these principles behind a discussion of the standards involved. (M. Turner, et al., *IEEE Computer*, 36 (10), October 2003.)

Peer-to-Peer: Harnessing the Power of Disruptive Technologies. Although this book does not have a lot on p2p architectures, it is an excellent introduction to p2p computing and discusses the organisation and approach used in a number of p2p systems. (A. Oram (ed), 2001, O'Reilly and Associates, Inc.)

Distributed Systems: Concepts and Design, 3rd ed. A comprehensive textbook that discusses all aspects of distributed systems design and implementation. The first two chapters are particularly relevant to the material here. (G. Couloris, et al., 2001, Addison-Wesley.)

'Middleware: A model for distributed systems services'. This is an excellent overview paper that summarises the role of middleware in distributed systems and discusses the range of middleware services that may be provided. (P. A. Bernstein, *Comm. ACM*, 39 (2), February 1996.)

EXERCISES

12.1 Explain why distributed systems are inherently more scalable than centralised systems. What are the likely limits on the scalability of the system?

12.2 What is the fundamental difference between a fat-client and a thin-client approach to client–server systems development? Explain why the use of Java as an implementation language blurs the distinction between these approaches.

12.3   Your customer wants to develop a system for stock information where dealers can access information about companies and can evaluate various investment scenarios using a simulation system. Each dealer uses this simulation in a different way, according to his or her experience and the type of stocks in question. Suggest a client–server architecture for this system that shows where functionality is located. Justify the client–server system model that you have chosen.

12.4   By making reference to the application model shown in Figure 12.4, discuss problems that might arise when converting a 1980s mainframe legacy system for insurance policy processing to a client–server architecture.

12.5   What are the basic facilities that must be provided by an object request broker?

12.6   Explain why the use of distributed objects with an object request broker simplifies the implementation of scalable client–server systems. Illustrate your answer with an example.

12.7   How is the CORBA IDL used to support communications between objects that have been implemented in different programming languages? Explain why this approach may cause performance problems if there are radical differences between the languages used for object implementation.

12.8   Using a distributed object approach, propose an architecture for a national theatre booking system where users can check seat availability and book seats at a group of theatres. The system should support ticket returns so that people may return their tickets for last-minute resale to other customers.

12.9   Give two advantages and two disadvantages of decentralised and semi-centralised peer-to-peer architectures.

12.10 What are the advantages of dynamic binding in a service-oriented system?

12.11 For the in-car information system, explain why it is best that the in-car software communicates with an aggregation service rather than directly with the information services. You should consider issues such as communication reliability in formulating your answer.

12.12 The development of service-oriented computing has been based on the early specification and adoption of standards. Discuss the general role of standardisation in supporting and restricting competition and innovation in the software market.

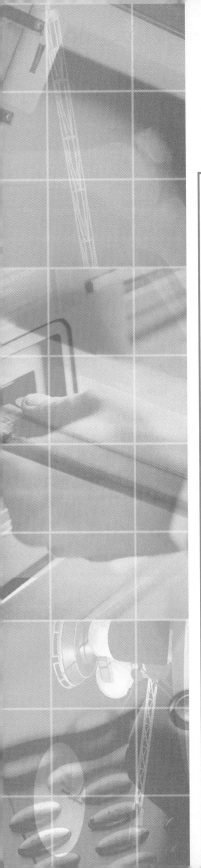

13

Application architectures

Objectives

The objective of this chapter is to introduce architectural models for specific classes of application software systems. When you have read this chapter, you will:

- be aware of two fundamental architectural organisations of business systems, namely batch and transaction-processing;

- understand the abstract architecture of information and resource management systems;

- understand how command-driven systems, such as editors, can be structured as event-processing systems;

- know the structure and organisation of language-processing systems.

Contents

As I explained in Chapter 11, you can look at system architectures from a range of perspectives. So far, the discussions of system architectures in Chapters 11 and 12 have concentrated on architectural perspectives and issues such as control, distribution and system structuring. In this chapter, however, I take an alternative approach and look at architectures from an application perspective.

Application systems are intended to meet some business or organisational need. All businesses have much in common—they need to hire people, issue invoices, keep accounts and so forth—and this is especially true of businesses operating in the same sector. Therefore, as well as general business functions, all phone companies need systems to connect calls, manage their network, issue bills to customers, etc. Consequently, the application systems that these businesses use also have much in common.

Usually, systems of the same type have similar architectures, and the differences between these systems are in the detailed functionality that is provided. This can be illustrated by the growth of Enterprise Resource Planning (ERP) systems such as the SAP/R3 system (Appelrath and Ritter, 2000) and vertical software packages for particular applications. In these systems, which I discuss briefly in Chapter 18, a generic system is configured and adapted to create a specific business application. For example, a system for supply chain management can be adapted for different types of suppliers, goods and contractual arrangements.

In the discussion of application architectures here, I present generic structural models of several types of application. I discuss the basic organisation of these application types and, where appropriate, break down the high-level architecture to show sub-systems that are normally included in applications.

As a software designer, you can use these generic application architectures in a number of ways:

1. *As a starting point for the architectural design process* If you are unfamiliar with this type of application, you can base your initial designs on the generic architectures. Of course, these will have to be specialised for specific systems, but they are a good starting point for your design.

2. *As a design checklist* If you have developed a system architectural design, you can check this against the generic application architecture to see whether you have missed any important design components.

3. *As a way of organising the work of the development team* The application architectures identify stable structural features of the system architectures and, in many cases, it is possible to develop these in parallel. You can assign work to group members to implement different sub-systems within the architecture.

4. *As a means of assessing components for reuse* If you have components you might be able to reuse, you can compare these with the generic structures to see whether reuse is likely in the application that you are developing.

5. *As a vocabulary for talking about types of applications* If you are discussing a specific application or trying to compare applications of the same types, then

you can use the concepts identified in the generic architecture to talk about the applications.

There are many types of application system and, on the surface, they may seem to be very different. However, when you examine the architectural organisation of applications, many of these superficially dissimilar applications have much in common. I illustrate this here by describing the architectures of four broad types of applications:

1. *Data-processing applications* Data-processing applications are applications that are data-driven. They process data in batches without explicit user interventions during the processing. The specific actions taken by the application depend on the data that it is processing. Batch-processing systems are commonly used in business applications where similar operations are carried out on a large amount of data. They handle a wide range of administrative functions such as payroll, billing, accounting, and publicity.

2. *Transaction-processing applications* Transaction-processing applications are database-centred applications that process user requests for information and that update the information in a database. These are the most common type of interactive business systems. They are organised in such a way that user actions can't interfere with each other and the integrity of the database is maintained. This class of system includes interactive banking systems, e-commerce systems, information systems and booking systems.

3. *Event-processing systems* This is a very large class of application where the actions of the system depend on interpreting events in the system's environment. These events might be the input of a command by a system user or a change in variables that are monitored by the system. Many PC-based applications, including games, editing systems such as word processors, spreadsheets, image editors and presentation systems are event-processing systems. Real-time systems, discussed in Chapter 15, also fall into this category.

4. *Language-processing systems* Language-processing systems are systems where the user's intentions are expressed in a formal language (such as Java). The language-processing system processes this language into some internal format and then interprets this internal representation. The best-known language-processing systems are compilers, which translate high-level language programs to machine code. However, language-processing systems are also used to interpret command languages for databases, information systems and markup languages such as XML (Harold and Means, 2002), which is extensively used to describe structured data items.

I have chosen these particular types of systems because they represent the majority of systems in use today. Business systems are generally either data- or transaction-processing systems, and most personal computer software is built around an event-processing architecture. Real-time systems are also event-processing systems; I cover these architectures in Chapter 15. All software development relies on language-processing systems such as compilers.

Batch-processing systems and transaction-processing systems are both database centric. Because of the central importance of data, it is common for applications of different types to share the same database. For example, a business data-processing system that prints bank statements uses the same customer account database as a transaction-processing system that provides web-based access to account information.

Of course, as I discussed in Chapter 11, complex applications rarely follow a single, simple architectural model. Rather, their architecture is more often a hybrid, with different parts of the application structured in different ways. When designing these systems, you therefore have to consider the architectures of individual sub-systems as well as how these are integrated within an overall system architecture.

13.1 Data-processing systems

Businesses rely on data-processing systems to support many aspects of their business such as paying salaries, calculating and printing invoices, maintaining accounts and issuing renewals for insurance policies. As the name implies, these systems focus on data and the databases that they rely on are usually orders of magnitude larger than the systems themselves. Data-processing systems are batch-processing systems where data is input and output in batches from a file or database rather than input from and output to a user terminal. These systems select data from the input records and, depending on the value of fields in the records, take some actions specified in the program. They may then write back the result of the computation to the database and format the input and computed output for printing.

The architecture of batch-processing systems has three major components, as illustrated in Figure 13.1. An input component collects inputs from one or more sources; a processing component makes computations using these inputs; and an output component generates outputs to be written back to the database and printed. For example, a telephone billing system takes customer records and telephone meter readings (inputs) from an exchange switch, computes the costs for each customer (process) and then prints bills (outputs) for each customer.

The input, processing and output components may themselves be further decomposed into an input-process-output structure. For example:

1. An input component may read some data (input) from a file or database, check the validity of that data and correct some errors (process), then queue the valid data for processing (output).

Figure 13.1 An input-
process-output
model of a data-
processing system

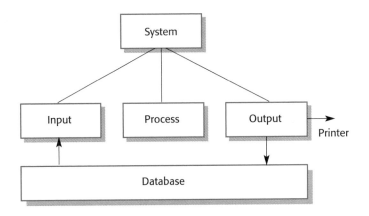

2. A processing component may take a transaction from a queue (input), perform some computations on the data and create a new data record recording the results of the computation (process), then queue this new record for printing (output). Sometimes the processing is done within the system database and sometimes it is a separate program.

3. An output component may read records from a queue (input), format these according to the output form (process), then send them to a printer or write new records back to the database (output).

The nature of data-processing systems where records or transactions are processed serially with no need to maintain state across transactions means that these systems are naturally function-oriented rather than object-oriented. Functions are components that do not maintain internal state information from one invocation to another. Data-flow diagrams, introduced in Chapter 8, are a good way to describe the architecture of business data-processing systems.

Data-flow diagrams are a way of representing function-oriented systems where each round-edged rectangle in the data flow represents a function that implements some data transformation, and each arrow represents a data item that is processed by the function. Files or data stores are represented as rectangles. The advantage of data-flow diagrams is that they show end-to-end processing. That is, you can see all of the functions that act on data as it moves through the stages of the system. The fundamental data-flow structure consists of an input function that passes data to a processing function and then to an output function.

Figure 13.2 illustrates how data-flow diagrams can be used to show a more detailed view of the architecture of a data-processing system. This figure shows the design of a salary payment system. In this system, information about employees in the organisation is read into the system, monthly salary and deductions are computed, and

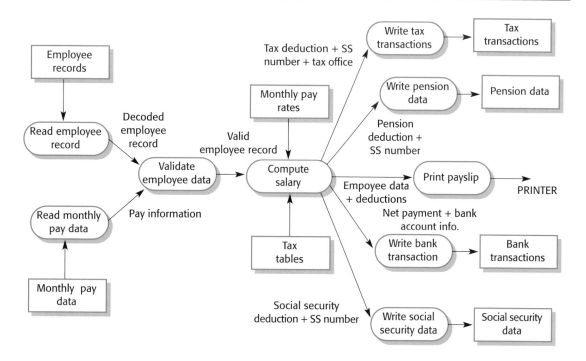

payments are made. You can see how this system follows the basic input-process-output structure:

1. The functions on the left of the diagram **Read employee record, Read monthly pay data** and **Validate employee data** input the data for each employee and check that data.

3. The **Compute salary** function works out the total gross salary for each employee and the various deductions that are made from that salary. The net monthly salary is then computed.

4. The output functions write a series of files that hold details of the deductions made and the salary to be paid. These files are processed by other programs once details for all employees have been computed. A payslip for the employee, recording the net pay and the deductions made, is printed by the system.

The architectural model of data-processing programs is relatively simple. However, in those systems the complexity of the application is often reflected in the data being processed. Designing the system architecture therefore involves thinking about the data architecture (Bracket, 1994) as well as the program architecture. The design of data architectures is outside the scope of this book.

Figure 13.3 The
structure of
transaction-
processing
applications

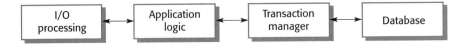

Figure 13.3 The
structure of
transaction-
processing
applications

13.2 Transaction-processing systems

Transaction-processing systems are designed to process user requests for information from a database or requests to update the database (Lewis et al., 2003).
Technically, a database transaction is sequence of operations that is treated as a
single unit (an atomic unit). All of the operations in a transaction have to be completed before the database changes are made permanent. This means that failure
of operations within the transaction do not lead to inconsistencies in the
database.

An example of a transaction is a customer request to withdraw money from a
bank account using an ATM. This involves getting details of the customer's
account, checking the balance, modifying the balance by the amount withdrawn and
sending commands to the ATM to deliver the cash. Until all of these steps have
been completed, the transaction is incomplete and the customer accounts database
is not changed.

From a user perspective, a transaction is any coherent sequence of operations
that satisfies a goal, such as 'find the times of flights from London to Paris'. If the
user transaction does not require the database to be changed then it may not be necessary to package this as a technical database transaction.

Transaction-processing systems are usually interactive systems where users make
asynchronous requests for service. Figure 13.3 illustrates the high-level architectural
structure of these applications. First a user makes a request to the system through
an I/O processing component. The request is processed by some application-specific
logic. A transaction is created and passed to a transaction manager, which is usually embedded in the database management system. After the transaction manager
has ensured that the transaction is properly completed, it signals to the application
that processing has finished.

The input-process-output structure that we can see in data-processing applications also applies to many transaction-processing systems. Some of these systems
are interactive versions of batch-processing systems. For example, at one time banks
input all customer transactions off-line then ran these transactions in a batch against
their accounts database every evening. This approach has mostly been replaced by
interactive, transaction-based systems that update accounts in real time.

An example of a transaction-processing system is a banking system that allows
customers to query their accounts and withdraw cash from an ATM. The system is
composed of two cooperating software sub-systems—the ATM software and the
account processing software in the bank's database server. The input and output

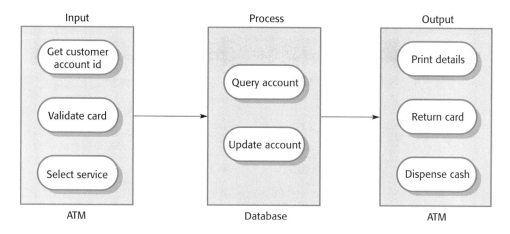

Figure 13.4 The software architecture of an ATM

sub-systems are implemented as software in the ATM, whereas the processing sub-system is in the bank's database server. Figure 13.4 shows the architecture of this system. I have added some detail to the basic input-process-output diagram to show components that may be involved in the input, processing and output activities. I have deliberately not suggested how these internal components interact, as the sequence of operation may differ from one machine to another.

In systems such as a bank customer accounting systems, there may be different ways to interact with the system. Many customers will interact through ATMs, but bank staff will use counter terminals to access the system. There may be several types of ATMs and counter terminals used, and some customers and staff may access the account data through web browsers.

To simplify the management of different terminal communication protocols, large-scale transaction-processing systems may include middleware that communicates with all types of terminal, organises and serialises the data from terminals, and sends that data for processing. This middleware, which I briefly discussed in Chapter 12, may be called a teleprocessing monitor or a transaction management system. IBM's CICS (Horswill and Miller, 2000) is a very widely used example of such a system.

Figure 13.5 shows another view of the architecture of a customer accounting system that handles personal account transactions from ATMs and counter terminals in a bank. The teleprocessing monitor handles the input and serialises transactions, which it converts to database queries. The query processing takes place in the database management system. Results are passed back to the teleprocessing monitor, which keeps track of terminals making the request. This system then organises the data into a form that can be handled by the terminal software and returns the results of the transaction to it.

13.2.1 Information and resource management systems

All systems that involve interaction with a shared database can be considered to be transaction-based information systems. An information system allows controlled access to a large base of information, such as a library catalogue, a flight timetable or the

Figure 13.5
Middleware for
transaction
management

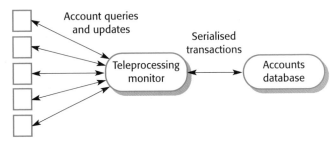

Figure 13.5
Middleware for
transaction
management

Account queries
and updates

Serialised
transactions

Teleprocessing
monitor

Accounts
database

ATMs and terminals

records of patients in a hospital. The development of the WWW meant that a huge number of information systems moved from being specialist organisational systems to universally accessible general-purpose systems.

Figure 13.6 is a very general model of an information system. The system is modelled using a layered or abstract machine approach (discussed in Section 11.2.3), where the top layer supports the user interface and the bottom layer the system database. The user communications layer handles all input and output from the user interface, and the information retrieval layer includes application-specific logic for accessing and updating the database. As we shall see later, the layers in this model can map directly onto servers in an Internet-based system.

As an example of an instantiation of this layered model, Figure 13.7 presents the architecture of the LIBSYS system. Recall that this system allows users to access documents in remote libraries and download these for printing. I have added detail to each layer in the model by identifying the components that support user communications and information retrieval and access. You should also notice that the database is a distributed database. Users actually connect, through the system, to the databases of the libraries that provide documents.

Figure 13.6 A layered
model of an
information system

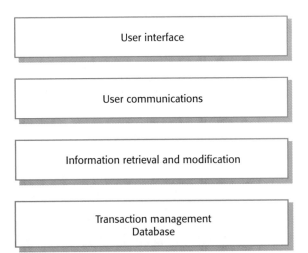

User interface

User communications

Information retrieval and modification

Transaction management
Database

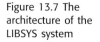

Figure 13.7 The
architecture of the
LIBSYS system

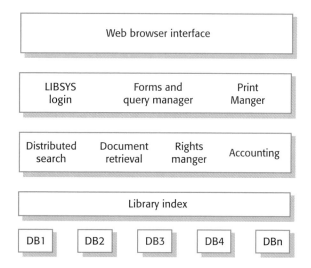

The user communication layer in Figure 13.7 includes three major components:

1. *The LIBSYS login component* identifies and authenticates users. All information systems that restrict access to a known set of users need to have user authentication as a fundamental part of their user communication systems. User authentication can be personal but, in e-commerce systems, may also require credit card details to be provided.

2. *The form and query manager component* manages the forms that may be presented to the user and provides query facilities allowing the user to request information from the system. Again, all information systems must include a component that provides these facilities.

3. *The print manager component* is specific to LIBSYS. It controls the printing of documents that, for copyright reasons, may be restricted. For example, some documents may only be printed once on printers of the registered library.

The information retrieval and modification layer in the LIBSYS system includes application-specific components that implement the system's functionality. These components are:

1. *Distributed search* This component searches for documents in response to user queries across all of the libraries that have registered with the system. The list of known libraries is maintained in the library index.

2. *Document retrieval* This component retrieves the document or documents that are required by the user to the server where the LIBSYS system is running.

3. *Rights manager* This component handles all aspects of digital rights management and copyright. It keeps track of who has requested documents and, for example, ensures that multiple requests for the same document cannot be made by the same person.

4. *Accounting* This component logs all requests and, if necessary, handles any charges that are made by the libraries in the system. It also produces management reports on the use of the system.

We can see the same, four-layer generic structure in another type of information system, namely systems that are designed to support resource allocation. Resource allocation systems manage a fixed amount of some given resource, such as tickets for a concert or a football game. These are allocated to users who request that resource from the supplier. Ticketing systems are an obvious example of a resource allocation system, but a large number of apparently dissimilar programs are also actually resource allocation systems. Some examples of this class of system are:

1. *Timetabling systems* that allocate classes to timetable slots. The resource being allocated here is a time period, and there are usually a large number of constraints associated with each demand for the resource.

2. *Library systems* that manage the lending and withdrawal of books or other items. In this case, the resources being allocated are the items that may be borrowed. In this type of system, the resources are not simply allocated but must sometimes be deallocated from the user of the resource.

3. *Air traffic management systems* where the resource that is being allocated is a segment of airspace so that separation is maintained between the planes that are being managed by the system. Again, this involves dynamic allocation and reallocation of resource, but the resource is a virtual rather than a physical resource.

Resource allocation systems are a very widely used class of application. If we look at their architecture in detail, we can see how it is aligned with the information system model shown in Figure 13.6. The components of a resource allocation system (shown in Figure 13.8) include:

1. *A resource database* that holds details of the resources being allocated. Resources may be added or removed from this database. For example, in a library system, the resource database includes details of all items that may be borrowed by users of the library. Normally, this is implemented using a database management system that includes a transaction-processing system. The database management system also includes resource-locking facilities so that the same resource cannot be allocated to users who make simultaneous requests.

2. *A rule set* that describes the rules of resource allocation. For example, a library system normally limits who may be allocated a resource (registered library users),

Figure 13.8 A layered
model of a resource
allocation system

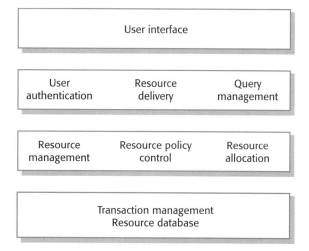

the length of time that a book or other item may be borrowed, the maximum
number of books that may be borrowed, and so on. This is encapsulated in the
resource policy control component.

3. A *resource management component* that allows the provider of the resources
    to add, edit or delete resources from the system.

4. A *resource allocation component* that updates the resource database when
    resources are assigned and that associates these resources with details of the
    resource requestor.

5. A *user authentication module* that allows the system to check that resources
    are being allocated to an accredited user. In a library system, this might be a
    machine-readable library card; in a ticket allocation system, it could be a credit
    card that verifies the user is able to pay for the resource.

6. A *query management module* that allows users to discover what resources are
    available. In a library system, this would typically be based around queries for
    particular items; in a ticketing system, it could involve a graphical display show-
    ing what tickets are available for particular dates.

7. A *resource delivery component* that prepares the resources for delivery to the
    requestor. In a ticketing system, this might involve preparing an e-mail con-
    firmation and sending a request to a ticket printer to print the tickets and the
    details of where these should be posted.

8. A *user interface component* (often a web browser) that is outside the system
    and allows the requester of the resource to issue queries and requests for the
    resource to be allocated.

This layered architecture can be realised in several ways. Information systems
software can be organised so that each layer is a large-scale component running on

Figure 13.9 A multi-tier Internet transaction-processing system

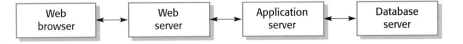

a separate server. Each layer defines its external interfaces and all communication takes place through these interfaces. Alternatively, if the entire information system executes on a single computer, then the middle layers are usually implemented as a single program that communicates with the database through its API. A third alternative is to implement finer-grain components as separate web services (discussed in Chapter 12) and compose these dynamically according to the user's requests.

Implementations of information and resource management systems based on Internet protocols are now the norm; the user interface in these systems is implemented using a web browser. The organisation of servers in these systems reflects the four-layer generic model presented in Figure 13.6. These systems are usually implemented as multi-tier client–server/architectures, as discussed in Chapter 12. The system organisation is shown in Figure 13.9. The web server is responsible for all user communications; the application server is responsible for implementing application-specific logic as well as information storage and retrieval requests; the database server moves information to and from the database. Using multiple servers allows high throughput and makes it possible to handle hundreds of transactions per minute.

E-commerce systems are Internet-based resource management systems that are designed to accept electronic orders for goods or services and then arrange delivery of these goods or services to the customer. There is a wide range of these systems now in use ranging from systems that allow services such as car-hire to be arranged to systems that support the order of tangible goods such as books or groceries. In an e-commerce system, the application-specific layer includes additional functionality supporting a 'shopping cart' in which users can place a number of items in separate transactions, then pay for them all together in a single transaction.

13.3 Event-processing systems

Event-processing systems respond to events in the system's environment or user interface. As I discussed in Chapter 11, the key characteristic of event-processing systems is that the timing of events is unpredictable and the system must be able to cope with these events when they occur.

We all use such event-based systems like this on our own computers—word processors, presentation systems and games are all driven by events from the user interface.

The system detects and interprets events. User interface events represent implicit commands to the system, which takes some action to obey that command. For example, if you are using a word processor and you double-click on a word, the double-click event means 'select that word'.

Real-time systems, which take action in 'real time' in response to some external stimulus, are also event-based processing systems. However, for real-time systems, events are not usually user interface events but events associated with servers or actuators in the system. Because of the need for real-time response to unpredictable events, these real-time systems are normally organised as a set of cooperating processes. I cover generic architectures for real-time systems in Chapter 15.

In this section, I focus on describing the generic architecture of editing systems. Editing systems are programs that run on PCs or workstations and that allow users to edit documents such as text documents, diagrams or images. Some editors focus on editing a single type of document, such as images from a digital camera or scanner. Others, including most word processors, are multi-editors and include support for editing different types including text and diagrams. You can even think of a spreadsheet as an editing system where you edit boxes on the sheet. Of course, spreadsheets have additional functionality to carry out computations.

Editing systems have a number of characteristics that distinguish them from other types of system and that influence their architectural design:

1. Editing systems are mostly single-user systems. They therefore don't have to deal with the problems of multiple concurrent access to data and have simpler data management than transaction-based systems. Even where data are shared, transaction management is not usually used because transactions take a long time and alternative methods of maintaining data integrity are used.

2. They have to provide rapid feedback on user actions such as 'select' and 'delete'. This means they have to operate on representations of data that is held in computer memory rather than on disk. Because the data is in volatile memory, it can be lost if there is a system fault, so editing systems should make some provision for error recovery.

3. Editing sessions are normally much longer than sessions involving ordering goods, or making some other transaction. This again means that there is a greater risk of loss if problems arise. Therefore, many editing systems include recovery facilities that automatically save work in progress and recover the work for the user in the event of a system failure.

A generic architecture for an editing system is shown in Figure 13.10 as a set of interacting objects. The objects in the system are active rather than passive (see Chapter 14) and can operate concurrently and autonomously. Essentially, screen events are processed and interpreted as commands. This updates a data structure, which is then redisplayed on the screen.

The responsibilities of the architectural components shown in Figure 13.10 are:

Figure 13.10 An
architectural model
of an editing system

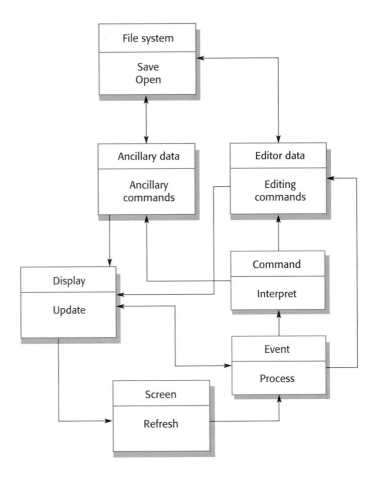

1. **Screen** This object monitors the screen memory segment and detects events that occur. These events are then passed to the event-processing object along with their screen coordinates.

2. **Event** This object is triggered by an event arriving from **Screen**. It uses knowledge of what is displayed to interpret this event and to translate this into the appropriate editing command. This command is then passed to the object responsible for command interpretation. For very common events, such as mouse clicks or key presses, the event object can communicate directly with the data structure. This allows faster updates of that structure.

3. **Command** This object processes a command from the event object and calls the appropriate method in the **Editor data object** to execute the command.

4. **Editor data** When the appropriate command method in Editor data object is called, it updates the data structure and calls the **Update** method in **Display** to display the modified data.

5. **Ancillary data** As well as the data structure itself, editors manage other data such as styles and preferences. In this simple architectural model, I have bundled this together under **Ancillary data**. Some editor commands, such as a command to initiate a spelling check, are implemented by a method in this object.

6. **File system** This object handles all opening and saving of files. These can be either editor data or ancillary data files. To avoid data loss, many editors have auto-save facilities that save the data structure automatically. This can then be retrieved in the event of system failure.

7. **Display** This object keeps track of the organisation of the screen display. It calls the **Refresh** method in **Screen** when the display has been changed.

Because of the need for a rapid response to user commands, editing systems do not have a central controller that calls the components to take action. Rather, the critical components in the system execute concurrently and can communicate directly (e.g., the event processor can communicate directly with the editor data structure) so that faster performance can be achieved.

13.4 Language-processing systems

Language-processing systems accept a natural or artificial language as an input and generate some other representation of that language as an output. In software engineering, the most widely used language-processing systems are compilers that translate an artificial high-level programming language into machine code, but other language-processing systems translate an XML data description into commands to query a database and natural language-processing systems that attempt to translate one natural language to another.

At the most abstract level, the architecture of a language-processing system is illustrated in Figure 13.11. The instructions describe what has to be done and are translated into some internal format by a translator. The instructions correspond to the machine instructions for an abstract machine. These instructions are then interpreted by another component that fetches the instructions for execution and executes them using, if necessary, data from the environment. The output of the process is the result of interpreting the instructions on the input data. Of course, for many compilers, the interpreter is a hardware unit that processes machine instructions and the abstract machine is a real processor. However, for languages such as Java, the interpreter is a software component.

Language-processing systems are used in situations where the easiest way to solve a problem is to specify that solution as an algorithm or as a description of the system data. For example, meta-CASE tools are program generators that are used to create specific CASE tools to support software engineering methods. Meta-CASE

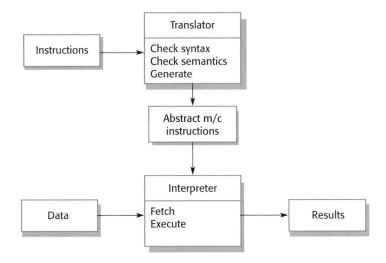

tools include a description of the method components, its rules and so on, written in a special-purpose language that is parsed and analysed to configure the generated CASE tool.

Translators in a language-processing system have a generic architecture (Figure 13.12) that includes the following components:

1. A lexical analyser, which takes input language tokens and converts them to an internal form

2. A symbol table, which holds information about the names of entities (variables, class names, object names, etc.) used in the text that is being translated

3. A syntax analyser, which checks the syntax of the language being translated. It uses a defined grammar of the language and builds a syntax tree

4. A syntax tree, which is an internal structure representing the program being compiled

5. A semantic analyser, which uses information from the syntax tree and the symbol table to check the semantic correctness of the input language text

6. A code generator, which 'walks' the syntax tree and generates abstract machine code

Other components might also be included that transform the syntax tree to improve efficiency and remove redundancy from the generated machine code. In other types of language-processing systems, such as a natural language translator, the generated code is actually the input text translated into another language.

The components that make up a language-processing system can be organised according to different architectural models. As Garlan and Shaw point out (Garlan

Figure 13.12 A data-
flow model of a
compiler

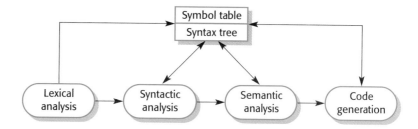

and Shaw, 1993), compilers can be implemented using a composite model. A data-
flow architecture may be used with the symbol table acting as a repository for shared
data. The phases of lexical, syntactic and semantic analysis are organised sequentially, as shown in Figure 13.12.

This data-flow model of compilation is still widely used. It is effective in batch
environments where programs are compiled and executed without user interaction.
It is less effective when the compiler is to be integrated with other language-processing
tools such as a structured editing system, an interactive debugger or a program pret-
typrinter. The generic system components can then be organised in a repository-
based model, as shown in Figure 13.13.

This figure illustrates how a language-processing system can be part of an integrated set of programming support tools. In this example, the symbol table and syntax tree act as a central information repository. Tools or tool fragments communicate
through it. Other information that is sometimes embedded in tools, such as the grammar definition and the definition of the output format for the program, have been
taken out of the tools and put into the repository. Therefore, a syntax-directed editor can check that the syntax of a program is correct as it is being typed, and a pret-
typrinter can create listings of the program in a format that is easy to read.

Figure 13.13 The
repository model of
a language-
processing system

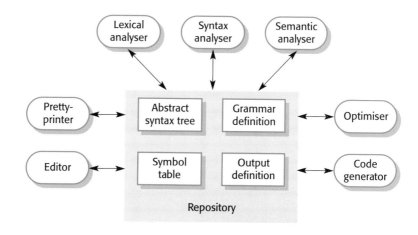

KEY POINTS

■ Generic models of application systems architectures help us understand the operation of applications, compare applications of the same type, validate application system designs and assess large-scale components for reuse.

■ Many applications either fall into one of four classes of generic application or are combinations of these generic applications. The four types of generic application covered here are data-processing systems, transaction-processing systems, event-processing systems and language-processing systems.

■ Data-processing systems operate in batch mode and generally have an input-process-output structure. Records are input into the system, the information is processed and outputs are generated.

■ Transaction-processing systems are interactive systems that allow information in a database to be remotely accessed and modified by a number of users. Information systems and resource management systems are examples of transaction-processing systems.

■ Event-processing systems include editing systems and real-time systems. In an editing system, user interface events are interpreted and an in-store data structure is modified. Word processors and presentation systems are examples of editing systems.

■ Language-processing systems are used to translate texts from one language into another and to carry out the instructions specified in the input language. They include a translator and an abstract machine that executes the generated language.

FURTHER READING

The topic of application architectures has been largely neglected; authors of books and articles on software architecture tend to focus on abstract principles or product line architectures.

Databases and Transaction Processing: An Application-oriented Approach. This is not really a book on software architecture, but it discusses the principles of transaction-processing and data-centric applications. (P. M. Lewis, et al., 2003, Addison-Wesley.)

Design and Use of Software Architectures. This book takes a product-line approach to software architectures and therefore discusses architecture from an application perspective. (J. Bosch, 2000, Addison-Wesley.)

EXERCISES

13.1 Explain how the generic applications architectures described here can be used to help the designer make decisions about software reuse.

13.2 Using the four basic application types introduced in this chapter, classify the following systems and explain your classification:

■ A point-of-sale system in a supermarket

■ A system that sends out reminders that magazine subscriptions are due to be paid

■ A photo album system that provides some facilities for restoring old photographs

■ A system that reads web pages to visually disabled users

■ An interactive game in which characters move around, cross obstacles and collect treasure

■ An inventory control system that keeps track of what items are in stock and automatically generates orders for new stock when the level falls below a certain value.

13.3 Based on an input-process-output model, expand the Compute salary function in Figure 13.2 and draw a data-flow diagram that shows the computations carried out in that function. You need the following information to do this:

■ The employee record identifies the grade of an employee. This grade is then used to look up the table of pay rates.

■ Employees below a particular grade may be paid overtime at the same rate as their normal hourly pay rate. The extra hours for which they are to be paid are indicated in their employee record.

■ The amount of tax deducted depends on the employee's tax code (indicated in the record) and their annual salary. Monthly deductions for each code and a standard salary are indicated in the tax tables. These are scaled up or down depending on the relationship between the actual salary and the standard salary used.

13.4 Explain why transaction management is necessary in systems where user inputs can result in database changes.

13.5 Using the basic model of an information system as presented in Figure 13.6, show the components of an information system that allows users to view information about flights arriving and departing from a particular airport.

13.6 Using the layered architecture shown in Figure 13.8, show the components of a resource management system that could be used to handle hotel room bookings.

13.7 In an editing system, all user interface events can be translated into implicit or explicit commands. Explain why, in Figure 13.10, the Event object therefore communicates directly with the editor data structure as well as the Command object.

13.8 Modify Figure 13.10 to show the generic architecture of a spreadsheet system. Base your design on the features of any spreadsheet system that you have used.

13.9 What is the function of the syntax tree component in a language-processing system?

13.10 Using the generic model of a language-processing system presented here, design the architecture of a system that accepts natural language commands and translates these into database queries in a language such as SQL.

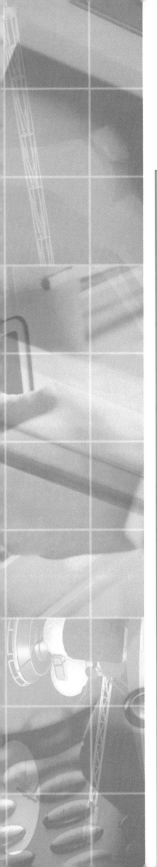

14

Object-oriented design

Objectives

The objective of this chapter is to introduce an approach to software design where the design is structured as interacting objects. When you have read this chapter, you will:

■ understand how a software design may be represented as a set of interacting objects that manage their own state and operations;

■ know the most important activities in a general object-oriented design process;

■ understand the different models that may be used to document an object-oriented design;

■ have been introduced to the representation of these models in the Unified Modeling Language (UML).

Contents

An object-oriented system is made up of interacting objects that maintain their own local state and provide operations on that state (Figure 14.1). The representation of the state is private and cannot be accessed directly from outside the object. Object-oriented design processes involve designing object classes and the relationships between these classes. These classes define the objects in the system and their interactions. When the design is realised as an executing program, the objects are created dynamically from these class definitions.

Object-oriented design is part of object-oriented development where an object-oriented strategy is used throughout the development process:

*   *Object-oriented analysis* is concerned with developing an object-oriented model of the application domain. The objects in that model reflect the entities and operations associated with the problem to be solved.

*   *Object-oriented design* is concerned with developing an object-oriented model of a software system to implement the identified requirements. The objects in an object-oriented design are related to the solution to the problem. There may be close relationships between some problem objects and some solution objects, but the designer inevitably has to add new objects and to transform problem objects to implement the solution.

*   *Object-oriented programming* is concerned with realising a software design using an object-oriented programming language, such as Java. An object-oriented programming language provides constructs to define object classes and a run-time system to create objects from these classes.

The transition between these stages of development should, ideally, be seamless, with compatible notations used at each stage. Moving to the next stage involves refining the previous stage by adding detail to existing object classes and devising new classes to provide additional functionality. As information is concealed within objects, detailed design decisions about the representation of data can be delayed until the system is implemented. In some cases, decisions on the distribution of objects and whether objects can be sequential or concurrent may also be delayed.

This means that software designers can devise designs that can be adapted to different execution environments. This is exemplified by the Model Driven Architecture (MDA) approach, which proposes that systems should be explicitly designed in two levels (Kleppe et al., 2003), an implementation-independent level and an implementation-dependent level. An abstract model of the system is designed at the implementation-independent level, and this is mapped to a more detailed platform-dependent model that can be used as a basis for code generation. At the time of this writing, the MDA approach is still experimental and it is not clear how widely it will be adopted.

Object-oriented systems are easier to change than systems developed using other approaches because the objects are independent. They may be understood and modified as standalone entities. Changing the implementation of an object or adding services should not affect other system objects. Because objects are associated with

Figure 14.1 A system
made up of
interacting objects

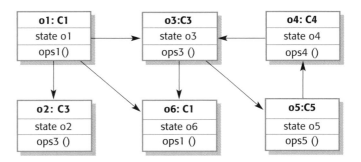

things, there is often a clear mapping between real-world entities (such as hardware components) and their controlling objects in the system. This improves the under-standability and hence the maintainability of the design.

Objects are, potentially, reusable components because they are independent encapsulations of state and operations. Designs can be developed using objects that have been created in previous designs. This reduces design, programming and val-idation costs. It may also lead to the use of standard objects (hence improving design understandability) and reduce the risks involved in software development. However, as I discuss in Chapters 18 and 19, reuse is sometimes best implemented using collections of objects (components or frameworks) rather than individual objects.

Several object-oriented design methods have been proposed (Coad and Yourdon, 1990; Robinson, 1992; Jacobson, et al., 1993; Graham, 1994; Booch, 1994). The UML is a unification of the notations used in these methods. The Rational Unified Process (RUP), which I discussed in Chapter 4, has been designed to exploit the models that can be expressed in the UML (Rumbaugh, et al., 1999). I use the UML throughout the chapter.

As I discuss in Chapter 17, system development based on extensive up-front design can be criticised because the extensive analysis and design effort is not well suited to incremental development and delivery. So-called agile methods have been devel-oped to address this problem, and these drastically reduce or completely eliminate the object-oriented design activity. My view on this is that extensive, 'heavyweight' design is unnecessary for small and medium-sized business systems. However, for large systems, particularly critical systems, it is essential to ensure that the teams working on different parts of the system are properly coordinated. For this reason, I have not used the previous examples of the library or the insulin pump system in this chapter, as these are relatively small systems. Rather, I use an example that is part of a much larger system where up-front object-oriented design is more useful.

This view is reflected, to some extent, in the Rational Unified Process that is geared to the iterative development and incremental delivery of large software sys-tems. This process is an iterative development process based around use-cases to express requirements and object-oriented design, with a particular focus on architecture-centric design.

The design process that I discuss in Section 14.2 has some things in common with the RUP but with less emphasis on use-case driven development. The use of use-cases means that the design is certainly user-centric and is based around user interactions with the system. However, representing the requirements of stakeholders who are not direct users of the system as use-cases is difficult. Use-cases certainly have a role in object-oriented analysis and design, but they need to be supplemented with other techniques to discover indirect and non-functional system requirements.

14.1 Objects and object classes

The terms *object* and *object-oriented* are applied to different types of entity, design methods, systems and programming languages. There is a general acceptance that an object is an encapsulation of information, and this is reflected in my definition of an object and an object class:

> *An object is an entity that has a state and a defined set of operations that operate on that state. The state is represented as a set of object attributes. The operations associated with the object provide services to other objects (clients) that request these services when some computation is required.*

> *Objects are created according to an object class definition. An object class definition is both a type specification and a template for creating objects. It includes declarations of all the attributes and operations that should be associated with an object of that class.*

In the UML, an object class is represented as a named rectangle with two sections. The object attributes are listed in the top section. The operations that are associated with the object are set out in the bottom section. Figure 14.2 illustrates this notation using an object class that models an employee in an organisation. The UML uses the term *operation* to mean the specification of an action; the term *method* is used to refer to the implementation of an operation.

The class **Employee** defines a number of attributes that hold information about employees including their name and address, social security number, tax code, and so on. The ellipsis (...) indicates that there are more attributes associated with the class than are shown. Operations associated with the object are **join** (called when an employee joins the organisation), **leave** (called when an employee leaves the organisation), **retire** (called when the employee becomes a pensioner of the organisation) and **changeDetails** (called when some employee information needs to be modified).

Objects communicate by requesting services (calling methods) from other objects and, if necessary, by exchanging the information required for service provision. The copies of information needed to execute the service and the results of service execution are passed as parameters. Some examples of this style of communication are:

Figure 14.2 An
employee object

Employee
name: string address: string dateOfBirth: date employeeNo: integer socialSecurityNo: string department: dept manager: employee salary: integer status: {current, left, retired} taxCode: integer . . .
join () leave () retire () changeDetails ()

```
// Call a method associated with a buffer object that returns the next value
// in the buffer
v = circularBuffer.Get () ;
// Call the method associated with a thermostat object that sets the
// temperature to be maintained
thermostat.setTemp (20) ;
```

In service-based systems, object communications are implemented directly as XML text messages that objects exchange. The receiving object parses the message, identifies the service and the associated data, and carries out the requested service. However, when the objects coexist in the same program, method calls are implemented as procedure or function calls in a language such as C.

When service requests are implemented in this way, communication between objects is synchronous. That is, the calling object waits for the service request to be completed. However, if objects are implemented as concurrent processes or threads, the object communication may be asynchronous. The calling object may continue in operation while the requested service is executing. I explain how objects may be implemented as concurrent processes later in this section.

As I discussed in Chapter 8, where I described a number of possible object models, object classes can be arranged in a generalisation or inheritance hierarchy that shows the relationship between general and more specific object classes. The more specific object class is completely consistent with its parent class but includes further information. In the UML, an arrow that points from a class entity to its parent class indicates generalisation. In object-oriented programming languages, generalisation is implemented using inheritance. The child class inherits attributes and operations from the parent class.

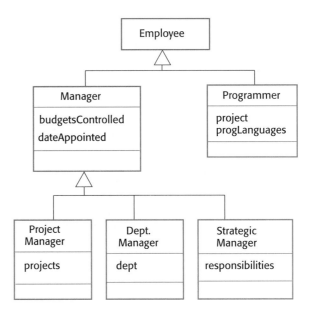

Figure 14.3 shows an example of an object class hierarchy where different classes
of employee are shown. Classes lower down the hierarchy have the same attributes
and operations as their parent classes but may add new attributes and operations or
modify some of those from their parent classes. This means that there is one-way
interchangability. If the name of a parent class is used in a model, the object in the
system may either be defined as of that class or of any of its descendants.

The class **Manager** in Figure 14.3 has all of the attributes and operations of the
class **Employee** but has, in addition, two new attributes that record the budgets controlled by the manager and the date that the manager was appointed to a particular
management role. Similarly, the class **Programmer** adds new attributes that define
the project that the programmer is working on and the programming language skills
that he or she has. Objects of class **Manager** or **Programmer** may therefore be used
anywhere an object of class **Employee** is required.

Objects that are members of an object class participate in relationships with other
objects. These relationships may be modelled by describing the associations
between the object classes. In the UML, associations are denoted by a line between
the object classes that may optionally be annotated with information about the association. This is illustrated in Figure 14.4, which shows the association between objects
of class **Employee** and objects of class **Department**, and between objects of class
Employee and objects of class **Manager**.

Association is a very general relationship and is often used in the UML to indicate that either an attribute of an object is an associated object or the implementation of an object method relies on the associated object. However, in principle at

Figure 14.4 An
association model

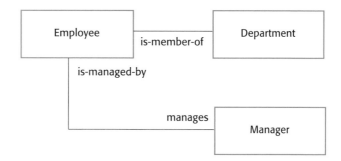

least, any kind of association is possible. One of the most common associations is aggregation, which illustrates how objects may be composed of other objects. See Chapter 8 for a discussion of this type of association.

14.1.1 Concurrent objects

Conceptually, an object requests a service from another object by sending a 'service request' message to that object. There is no requirement for serial execution where one object waits for completion of a requested service. Consequently, the general model of object interaction allows objects to execute concurrently as parallel processes. These objects may execute on the same computer or as distributed objects on different machines.

In practice, most object-oriented programming languages have as their default a serial execution model where requests for object services are implemented in the same way as function calls. Therefore, when an object called **theList** is created from a normal object class, you write in Java:

theList.append (17)

This calls the **append** method associated with **theList** object to add the element 17 to **theList**, and execution of the calling object is suspended until the append operation has been completed. However, Java includes a very simple mechanism (threads) that lets you create objects that execute concurrently. Threads are created in Java by using the built-in **Thread** class as a parent class in a class declaration. Threads must include a method called **run**, which is started by the Java run-time system when objects that are defined as threads are created. It is therefore easy to take an object-oriented design and produce an implementation where the objects are concurrent processes.

There are two kinds of concurrent object implementation:

1. *Servers* where the object is realised as a parallel process with methods corresponding to the defined object operations. Methods start up in response to an

external message and may execute in parallel with methods associated with other objects. When they have completed their operation, the object suspends itself and waits for further requests for service.

2. *Active objects* where the state of the object may be changed by internal operations executing within the object itself. The process representing the object continually executes these operations so never suspends itself.

Servers are most useful in a distributed environment where the calling and the called object may execute on different computers. The response time for the service that is requested is unpredictable, so, wherever possible, you should design the system so that the object that has requested a service does not have to wait for that service to be completed. They can also be used in a single machine where a service takes some time to complete (e.g., printing a document) and several objects may request the service.

Active objects are used when an object needs to update its own state at specified intervals. This is common in real-time systems where objects are associated with hardware devices that collect information about the system's environment. The object's methods allow other objects access to the state information.

Figure 14.5 shows how an active object may be defined and implemented in Java. The object class represents a transponder on an aircraft. The transponder keeps track of the aircraft's position using a satellite navigation system. It can respond to messages from air traffic control computers. It provides the current aircraft position in response to a request to the **givePosition** method. This object is implemented as a thread where a continuous loop in the run method includes code to compute the aircraft's position using signals from satellites.

14.2 An object-oriented design process

In this section, I illustrate the process of object-oriented design by developing an example design for the control software that is embedded in an automated weather station. As I discussed in the introduction, there are several methods of object-oriented design with no definitive 'best' method or design process. The process that I cover here is a general one that incorporates activities common to most OOD processes.

The general process that I use here for object-oriented design has a number of stages:

1. Understand and define the context and the modes of use of the system.

2. Design the system architecture.

3. Identify the principal objects in the system.

Figure 14.5
Implementation of
an active object
using Java threads

```
class Transponder extends Thread {

        Position currentPosition ;
        Coords c1, c2 ;
        Satellite sat1, sat2 ;
        Navigator theNavigator ;

        public Position givePosition ()
        {
            return currentPosition ;
        }

        public void run ()
        {
            while (true)
            {
                c1 = sat1.position () ;
                c2 = sat2.position () ;
                currentPosition = theNavigator.compute (c1, c2) ;
            }

        }

} //Transponder
```

4. Develop design models.

5. Specify object interfaces.

I have deliberately not illustrated this as a simple process diagram because that would imply there was a neat sequence of activities in this process. In fact, all of the above activities are interleaved and so influence each other. Objects are identified and the interfaces fully or partially specified as the architecture of the system is defined. As object models are produced, these individual object definitions may be refined, which leads to changes to the system architecture.

I discuss these as separate stages in the design process later in this section. However, you should not assume from this that design is a simple, well-structured process. In reality, you develop a design by proposing solutions and refining these solutions as information becomes available. You inevitably have to backtrack and retry when problems arise. Sometimes you explore options in detail to see if they work; at other times you ignore details until late in the process.

I illustrate these process activities by developing an example of an object-oriented design. This example is part of a system for creating weather maps using

Figure 14.6 Layered
architecture for
weather mapping
system

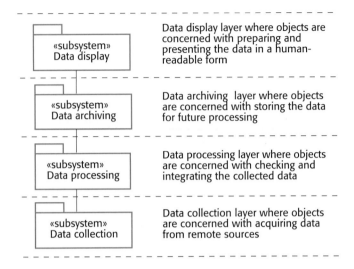

automatically collected meteorological data. The detailed requirements for such a weather mapping system would take up many pages. However, an overall system architecture can be developed from a relatively brief system description:

> *A weather mapping system is required to generate weather maps on a regular basis using data collected from remote, unattended weather stations and other data sources such as weather observers, balloons and satellites. Weather stations transmit their data to the area computer in response to a request from that machine.*

> *The area computer system validates the collected data and integrates the data from different sources. The integrated data is archived and, using data from this archive and a digitised map database, a set of local weather maps is created. Maps may be printed for distribution on a special-purpose map printer or may be displayed in a number of different formats.*

This description shows that part of the overall system is concerned with collecting data, part with integrating the data from different sources, part with archiving that data and part with creating weather maps. Figure 14.6 illustrates a possible system architecture that can be derived from this description. This is a layered architecture (discussed in Chapter 11) that reflects the stages of processing in the system, namely data collection, data integration, data archiving and map generation. A layered architecture is appropriate in this case because each stage relies only on the processing of the previous stage for its operation.

In Figure 14.6, I have shown the layers and have included the layer name in a UML package symbol that has been denoted as a sub-system. A UML package rep-

Figure 14.7
Subsystems in the
weather mapping
system

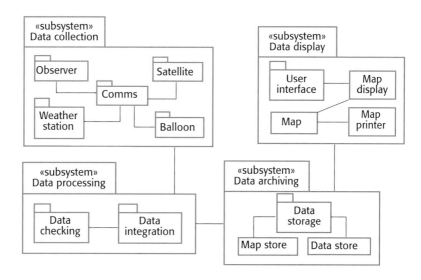

resents a collection of objects and other packages. I have used it here to show that each layer includes a number of other components.

In Figure 14.7, I have expanded on this abstract architectural model by showing the components of the sub-systems. These are still abstract and have been derived from the information in the description of the system. I continue the design example by focusing on the weather station sub-system that is part of the data collection layer.

14.2.1 System context and models of use

The first stage in any software design process is to develop an understanding of the relationships between the software that is being designed and its external environment. You need this understanding to help you decide how to provide the required system functionality and how to structure the system to communicate with its environment.

The system context and the model of system use represent two complementary models of the relationships between a system and its environment:

1. The system context is a static model that describes the other systems in that environment.

2. The model of the system use is a dynamic model that describes how the system actually interacts with its environment.

The context model of a system may be represented using associations (see Figure 14.4) where a simple block diagram of the overall system architecture is produced.

Figure 14.8 Use-
cases for the
weather station

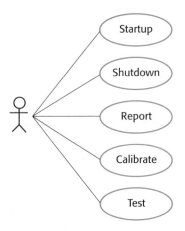

You then develop this by deriving a sub-system model using UML packages as shown in Figure 14.7. This model shows that the context of the weather station system is within a sub-system concerned with data collection. It also shows other sub-systems that make up the weather mapping system.

When you model the interactions of a system with its environment you should use an abstract approach that does not include too much detail. The approach that is proposed in the RUP is to develop a use-case model where each use-case represents an interaction with the system. In use-case models (also discussed in Chapter 7), each possible interaction is named in an ellipse and the external entity involved in the interaction is represented by a stick figure. In the case of the weather station system, this external entity is not a human but is the data-processing system for the weather data.

The use-case model for the weather station is shown in Figure 14.8. This shows that weather station interacts with external entities for startup and shutdown, for reporting the weather data that has been collected, and for instrument testing and calibration.

Each of these use-cases can be described in structured natural language. This helps designers identify objects in the system and gives them an understanding of what the system is intended to do. I use a standard form for this description that clearly identifies what information is exchanged, how the interaction is initiated and so on. This is shown in Figure 14.9, which describes the **Report** use-case from Figure 14.8.

The use-case description helps to identify objects and operations in the system. From the description of the **Report** use-case, it is obvious that objects representing the instruments that collect weather data will be required, as will an object representing the summary of the weather data. Operations to request weather data and to send weather data are required.

Figure 14.9 Report
use-case description

System	Weather station
Use-case	Report
Actors	Weather data collection system, Weather station
Data	The weather station sends a summary of the weather data that has been collected from the instruments in the collection period to the weather data collection system. The data sent are the maximum, minimum and average ground and air temperatures, the maximum, minimum and average air pressures, the maximum, minimum and average wind speeds, the total rainfall, and the wind direction as sampled at five-minute intervals.
Stimulus	The weather data collection system establishes a modem link with the weather station and requests transmission of the data.
Response	The summarised data is sent to the weather data collection system.
Comments	Weather stations are usually asked to report once per hour but this frequency may differ from one station to another and may be modified in future.

14.2.2 Architectural design

Once the interactions between the software system that is being designed and the system's environment have been defined, you can use this information as a basis for designing the system architecture. Of course, you need to combine this with your general knowledge of the principles of architectural design and with more detailed domain knowledge.

The automated weather station is a relatively simple system, and its architecture can again be represented as a layered model. I have illustrated this in Figure 14.10 as three UML packages within the more general Weather station package. Notice how I have used UML annotations (text in boxes with a folded corner) to provide additional information here.

The three layers in the weather station software are:

1. The *interface layer* that is concerned with all communications with other parts of the system and with providing the external interfaces of the system;

2. The *data collection layer* that is concerned with managing the collection of data from the instruments and with summarising the weather data before transmission to the mapping system;

3. The *instruments layer* that is an encapsulation of all of the instruments used to collect raw data about the weather conditions.

Figure 14.10 The
weather station
architecture

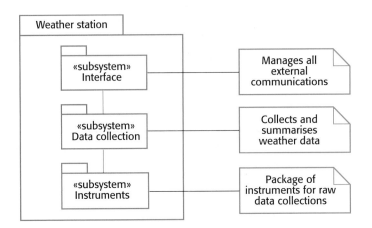

In general, you should try to decompose a system so that architectures are as simple as possible. A good rule of thumb is that there should be no more than seven fundamental entities included in an architectural model. Each of these entities can be described separately but, of course, you may choose to reveal the structure of the entities as I have done in Figure 14.7.

14.2.3 Object identification

By this stage in the design process, you should have some ideas about the essential objects in the system that you are designing. In the weather station system, it is clear that the instruments should be objects, and you need at least one object at each of the architectural levels. This reflects a general principle that objects tend to emerge during the design process. However, you usually also have to look for and document other objects that may be relevant.

Although I have headed this section 'object identification', in practice this process is actually concerned with identifying object classes. The design is described in terms of these classes. Inevitably, you have to refine the object classes that you initially identify and revisit this stage of the process as you develop a deeper understanding of the design.

There have been various proposals made about how to identify object classes:

1. Use a grammatical analysis of a natural language description of a system. Objects and attributes are nouns; operations or services are verbs (Abbott, 1983). This approach has been embodied in the HOOD method for object-oriented design (Robinson, 1992) that was widely used in the European aerospace industry.

2. Use tangible entities (things) in the application domain such as aircraft, roles such as manager, events such as request, interactions such as meetings,

locations such as offices, organisational units such as companies, and so on (Shlaer and Mellor, 1988; Coad and Yourdon, 1990; Wirfs-Brock, et al., 1990). Support this by identifying storage structures (abstract data structures) in the solution domain that might be required to support these objects.

3. Use a behavioural approach where the designer first understands the overall behaviour of the system. The various behaviours are assigned to different parts of the system and an understanding is derived of who initiates and participates in these behaviours. Participants who play significant roles are recognised as objects (Rubin and Goldberg, 1992).

4. Use a scenario-based analysis where various scenarios of system use are identified and analysed in turn. As each scenario is analysed, the team responsible for the analysis must identify the required objects, attributes and operations. A method of analysis called CRC cards where analysts and designers take on the role of objects is effective in supporting this scenario-based approach (Beck and Cunningham, 1989).

These approaches help you get started with object identification. In practice, you may have to use several knowledge sources to discover object classes. Object classes, attributes and operations that are initially identified from the informal system description can be a starting point for the design. Further information from application domain knowledge or scenario analysis may then be used to refine and extend the initial objects. This information may be collected from requirements documents, from discussions with users and from an analysis of existing systems.

I have used a hybrid approach here to identify the weather station objects. I don't have space to describe all the objects, but I have shown five object classes in Figure 14.11. **Ground thermometer**, **Anemometer** and **Barometer** represent application domain objects, and **WeatherStation** and **WeatherData** have been identified from the system description and the scenario (use-case) description.

These objects are related to the levels in the system architecture.

1. The **WeatherStation** object class provides the basic interface of the weather station with its environment. Its operations therefore reflect the interactions shown in Figure 14.8. In this case, I use a single object class to encapsulate all of these interactions, but in other designs you may chose to design the system interface as several different classes.

2. The **WeatherData** object class encapsulates the summarised data from the instruments in the weather station. Its associated operations are concerned with collecting and summarising the data that is required.

3. The **Ground thermometer**, **Anemometer** and **Barometer** object classes are directly related to instruments in the system. They reflect tangible hardware entities in the system and the operations are concerned with controlling that hardware.

Figure 14.11
Examples of object
classes in the
weather station
system

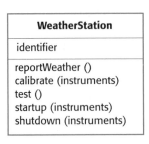

WeatherStation
identifier
reportWeather ()   calibrate (instruments)   test ()   startup (instruments)   shutdown (instruments)

WeatherData
airTemperatures   groundTemperatures   windSpeeds   windDirections   pressures   rainfall
collect ()   summarise ()

Ground thermometer
temperature
test ()   calibrate ()

Anemometer
windSpeed   windDirection
test ()

Barometer
pressure   height
test ()   calibrate ()

At this stage in the design process, you use knowledge of the application domain to identify further objects and services. We know that weather stations are often located in remote places and include various instruments that sometimes go wrong. Instrument failures should be reported automatically. This implies that you need attributes and operations to check the correct functioning of the instruments. Obviously, there are many remote weather stations. You need to identify the data collected from each station so each weather station should have its own identifier.

In this example, I have decided that the objects associated with each instrument should not be active objects. The collect operation in **WeatherData** calls on instrument objects to make readings when required. Active objects include their own control and, in this case, it would mean that each instrument would decide when to make readings. The disadvantage of this is that, if a decision was made to change the timing of the data collection or if different weather stations collected data differently, then new object classes would have to be introduced. By making the instrument objects make readings on request, any changes to collection strategy can be easily implemented without changing the objects associated with the instruments.

14.2.4 Design models

Design models show the objects or object classes in a system and, where appropriate, the relationships between these entities. Design models essentially are the design. They are the bridge between the requirements for the system and the system implementation. This means that there are conflicting requirements on these models. They have to be abstract so that unnecessary detail doesn't hide the relationships between them and the system requirements. However, they also have to include enough detail for programmers to make implementation decisions.

In general, you get around this conflict by developing models at different levels of detail. Where there are close links between requirements engineers, designers and programmers, then abstract models may be all that are required. Specific design decisions may be made as the system is implemented. When the links between system specifiers, designers and programmers are indirect (e.g., where a system is being designed in one part of an organisation but implemented elsewhere), then more detailed models may be required.

An important step in the design process, therefore, is to decide which design models that you need and the level of detail of these models. This depends on the type of system that is being developed. A sequential data processing system will be designed in a different way from an embedded real-time system, and different design models will therefore be used. There are very few systems where all models are necessary. Minimising the number of models that are produced reduces the costs of the design and the time required to complete the design process.

There are two types of design models that should normally be produced to describe an object-oriented design:

1. *Static models* describe the static structure of the system using object classes and their relationships. Important relationships that may be documented at this stage are generalisation relationships, uses/used-by relationships and composition relationships.

2. *Dynamic models* describe the dynamic structure of the system and show the interactions between the system objects (not the object classes). Interactions that may be documented include the sequence of service requests made by objects and the way in which the state of the system is related to these object interactions.

The UML provides for 12 different static and dynamic models that may be produced to document a design. I don't have space to go into all of these and not all are appropriate for the weather station example. The models that I discuss in this section are:

1. *Subsystem models* that show logical groupings of objects into coherent sub-systems. These are represented using a form of class diagram where each sub-system is shown as a package. Subsystem models are static models.

2. *Sequence models* that show the sequence of object interactions. These are represented using a UML sequence or a collaboration diagram. Sequence models are dynamic models.

3. *State machine models* that show how individual objects change their state in response to events. These are represented in the UML using statechart diagrams. State machine models are dynamic models.

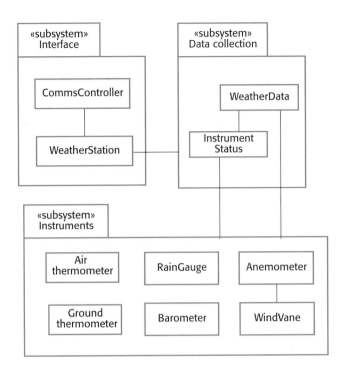

I have already discussed other models that may be developed for object-oriented design and analysis. Use-case models show interactions with the system (Figure 14.8; Figures 7.6 and 7.7, Chapter 7); object models describe the object classes (Figure 14.2); generalisation or inheritance models (Figures 8.10, 8.11 and 8.12, Chapter 8) show how classes may be generalisations of other classes; and aggregation models (Figure 8.13) show how collections of objects are related.

Figure 14.12 shows the objects in the sub-systems in the weather station. I also show some associations in this model. For example, the **CommsController** object is associated with the **WeatherStation** object, and the **WeatherStation** object is associated with the **Data collection** package. This means that this object is associated with one or more objects in this package. A package model plus an object class model should describe the logical groupings in the system.

A sub-system model is a useful static model as it shows how the design may be organised into logically related groups of objects. I have already used this type of model in Figure 14.7 to show the sub-systems in the weather mapping system. The UML packages contain encapsulation constructs and do not reflect directly on entities in the system that is developed. However, they may be reflected in structuring constructs such as Java libraries.

Sequence models are dynamic models that document, for each mode of interaction, the sequence of object interactions that take place. Figure 14.13 is an example of a sequence model that shows the operations involved in collecting the data from a weather station. In a sequence model:

Figure 14.13
Sequence of
operations—data
collection

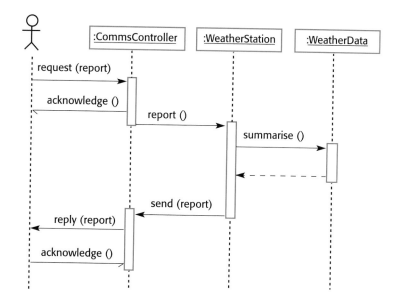

1. The objects involved in the interaction are arranged horizontally with a vertical line linked to each object.

2. Time is represented vertically so that time progresses down the dashed vertical lines. Therefore, the sequence of operations can be read easily from the model.

3. Labelled arrows linking the vertical lines represent interactions between objects. These are *not* data flows but represent messages or events that are fundamental to the interaction.

4. The thin rectangle on the object lifeline represents the time when the object is the controlling object in the system. An object takes over control at the top of this rectangle and relinquishes control to another object at the bottom of the rectangle. If there is a hierarchy of calls, control is not relinquished until the last return to the initial method call has been completed.

When documenting a design, you should produce a sequence model for each significant interaction. If you have developed a use-case model then there should be a sequence model for each use-case that you have identified.

Figure 14.13 shows the sequence of interactions when the external mapping system requests the data from the weather station. You read sequence diagrams from top to bottom:

1. An object that is an instance of **CommsController** (**:CommsController**) receives a request from its environment to send a weather report. It acknowledges receipt of this request. The half-arrowhead on the acknowledge message indicates that the message sender does not expect a reply.

2. This object sends a message to an object that is an instance of **WeatherStation** to create a weather report. The instance of **CommsController** then suspends itself (its control box ends). The style of arrowhead used indicates that the **CommsController** object instance and the **WeatherStation** object instance are objects that may execute concurrently.

3. The object that is an instance of **WeatherStation** sends a message to a **WeatherData** object to summarise the weather data. In this case, the squared-off style of arrowhead indicates that the instance of **WeatherStation** waits for a reply.

4. This summary is computed and control returns to the **WeatherStation** object. The dotted arrow indicates a return of control.

5. This object sends a message to **CommsController** requesting it to transfer the data to the remote system. The **WeatherStation** object then suspends itself.

6. The **CommsController** object sends the summarised data to the remote system, receives an acknowledgement, and then suspends itself waiting for the next request.

From the sequence diagram, we can see that the **CommsController** object and the **WeatherStation** object are actually concurrent processes, where execution can be suspended and resumed. Essentially, the **CommsController** object instance listens for messages from the external system, decodes these messages and initiates weather station operations.

Sequence diagrams are used to model the combined behaviour of a group of objects, but you may also want to summarise the behaviour of a single object in response to the messages it can process. To do this, you can use a state machine model that shows how the object instance changes state depending on the messages that it receives. The UML uses statecharts, initially invented by Harel (Harel, 1987), to describe state machine models.

Figure 14.14 is a statechart for the **WeatherStation** object that shows how it responds to requests for various services.

You can read this diagram as follows:

1. If the object state is **Shutdown** then it can only respond to a **startup()** message. It then moves into a state where it is waiting for further messages. The unlabelled arrow with the black blob indicates that the **Shutdown** state is the initial state.

2. In the **Waiting** state, the system expects further messages. If a **shutdown()** message is received, the object returns to the shutdown state.

3. If a **reportWeather()** message is received, the system moves to the **Summarising** state. When the summary is complete, the system moves to a **Transmitting** state where the information is transmitted through the **CommsController**. It then returns to the **Waiting** state.

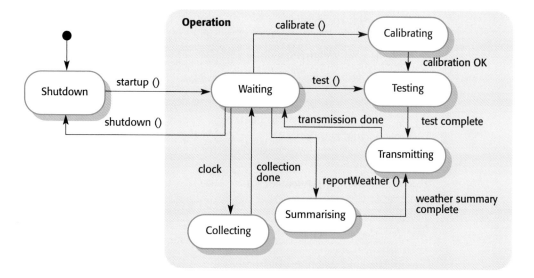

Figure 14.14 State diagram for WeatherStation

4. If a **calibrate()** message is received, the system moves to the **Calibrating** state, then the **Testing** state, and then the **Transmitting** state, before returning to the **Waiting** state. If a **test()** message is received, the system moves directly to the **Testing** state.

5. If a signal from the clock is received, the system moves to the **Collecting** state, where it is collecting data from the instruments. Each instrument is instructed in turn to collect its data.

You don't usually have to draw a statechart for all of the objects that you have defined. Many of the objects in a system are relatively simple and a state machine model would not help implementers to understand these objects.

14.2.5 Object interface specification

An important part of any design process is the specification of the interfaces between the components in the design. You need to specify interfaces so that objects and sub-systems can be designed in parallel. Once an interface has been specified, the developers of other objects may assume that interface will be implemented.

You should try to avoid including details of the interface representation in an interface design. The representation should be hidden and object operations provided to access and update the data. If the representation is hidden, it can be changed without affecting the objects that use these attributes. This leads to a design that is inherently more maintainable. For example, an array representation of a stack may be changed to a list representation without affecting other objects that use the stack. By contrast, it often makes sense to expose the attributes in a static design model, as this is the most compact way of illustrating essential characteristics of the objects.

Figure 14.15 Java
description of
weather station
interface

```
interface WeatherStation {

    public void WeatherStation () ;

    public void startup () ;
    public void startup (Instrument i) ;

    public void shutdown () ;
    public void shutdown (Instrument i) ;

    public void reportWeather ( ) ;

    public void test () ;
    public void test ( Instrument i ) ;

    public void calibrate ( Instrument i) ;

    public int getID () ;

} //WeatherStation
```

There is not necessarily a simple 1:1 relationship between objects and interfaces. The same object may have several interfaces, each of which is a viewpoint on the methods that it provides. This is supported directly in Java, where interfaces are declared separately from objects, and objects 'implement' interfaces. Equally, a group of objects may all be accessed through a single interface.

Object interface design is concerned with specifying the detail of the interface to an object or to a group of objects. This means defining the signatures and semantics of the services that are provided by the object or by a group of objects. Interfaces can be specified in the UML using the same notation as in a class diagram. However, there is no attribute section, and the UML stereotype <interface> should be included in the name part.

An alternative approach, one that I prefer, is to use a programming language to define the interface. This is illustrated in Figure 14.15, which shows the interface specification in Java of the weather station. As interfaces become more complex, this approach becomes more effective because the syntax-checking facilities in the compiler may be used to discover errors and inconsistencies in the interface description. The Java description can show that some methods can take different numbers of parameters. Therefore, the shutdown method can be applied either to the station as a whole if it has no parameters or to a single instrument.

Figure 14.16 New
objects to support
pollution monitoring

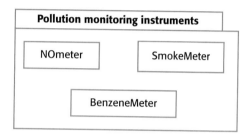

14.3 Design evolution

After a decision has been made to develop a system such as a weather data collection system, it is inevitable that proposals for system changes will be made. An important advantage of an object-oriented approach to design is that it simplifies the problem of making changes to the design. The reason for this is that object state representation does not influence the design. Changing the internal details of an object is unlikely to affect any other system objects. Furthermore, because objects are loosely coupled, it is usually straightforward to introduce new objects without significant effects on the rest of the system.

To show how an object-oriented approach to design makes change easier, assume that pollution-monitoring capabilities are to be added to each weather station. This involves adding an air quality meter to compute the amount of various pollutants in the atmosphere. The pollution readings are transmitted at the same time as the weather data. To modify the design, the following changes must be made:

1. An object class called **Air quality** should be introduced as part of **WeatherStation** at the same level as **WeatherData**.

2. An operation **reportAirQuality** should be added to **WeatherStation** to send the pollution information to the central computer. The weather station control software must be modified so that pollution readings are automatically collected when requested by the top-level **WeatherStation** object.

3. Objects representing the types of pollution monitoring instruments should be added. In this case, levels of nitrous oxide, smoke and benzene can be measured.

The pollution monitoring objects are encapsulated in a separate package called **Pollution monitoring instruments**. This has associations with **Air quality** and **WeatherStation** but not with any of the objects used to collect weather data. Figure 14.16 shows **WeatherStation** and the new objects added to the system. Apart from at the highest level of the system (**WeatherStation**), no software changes are required in the original objects in the weather station. The addition of pollution data collection does not affect weather data collection in any way.

KEY POINTS

■ Object-oriented design is an approach to software design where the fundamental components in the design represent objects with their own private state as well as represent operations rather than functions.

■ An object should have constructor and inspection operations allowing its state to be inspected and modified. The object provides services (operations using state information) to other objects. Objects are created at run-time using a specification in an object class definition.

■ Objects may be implemented sequentially or concurrently. A concurrent object may be a passive object whose state is only changed through its interface or an active object that can change its own state without outside intervention.

■ The Unified Modeling Language (UML) provides a range of notations that can be used to document an object-oriented design.

■ The process of object-oriented design includes activities to design the system architecture, identify objects in the system, describe the design using different object models and document the object interfaces.

■ A range of different models may be produced during an object-oriented design process. These include static models (class models, generalisation models, association models) and dynamic models (sequence models, state machine models).

■ Object interfaces must be defined precisely so that other objects can use them. A programming language such as Java may be used to document object interfaces.

■ An important advantage of object-oriented design is that it simplifies the evolution of the system.

FURTHER READING

Applying UML and Patterns: An Introduction to Object-Oriented Analysis and Design and the Unified Process, 2nd ed. A good introduction to the use of the UML within an object-oriented design process. Its coverage of design patterns is also relevant reading for Chapter 18. (C. Larman, 2001, Prentice Hall.)

The Unified Modeling Language User Guide. The definitive text on UML and its use for describing object-oriented designs. There are two associated texts—one is a UML reference manual, the other proposes an object-oriented development process. (G. Booch, et al., 1999, Addison-Wesley.)

A new standard for UML (UML 2.0) was finalised in mid-2003 but, at the time of this writing, these books had not been updated to reflect this. I expect that editions incorporating this new standard will be available in 2004.

There is also an immense amount of introductory and tutorial UML material on the web. I have included some links in the book's web pages.

EXERCISES

14.1   Explain why adopting an approach to design that is based on loosely coupled objects that hide information about their representation should lead to a design that may be readily modified.

14.2   Using examples, explain the difference between an object and an object class.

14.3   Under what circumstances might you develop a design where objects execute concurrently?

14.4   Using the UML graphical notation for object classes, design the following object classes identifying attributes and operations. Use your own experience to decide on the attributes and operations that should be associated with these objects:

   ■ A telephone

   ■ A printer for a personal computer

   ■ A personal stereo system

   ■ A bank account

   ■ A library catalogue.

14.5   Develop the design of the weather station in detail by proposing interface descriptions of the objects shown in Figure 14.11. These may be expressed in Java, in C++ or in the UML.

14.6   Develop the design of the weather station to show the interaction between the data collection sub-system and the instruments that collect weather data. Use sequence charts to show this interaction.

14.7 Identify possible objects in the following systems and develop an object-oriented design for them. You may make any reasonable assumptions about the systems when deriving the design.

■ A group diary and time management system is intended to support the timetabling of meetings and appointments across a group of coworkers. When an appointment is to be made that involves a number of people, the system finds a common slot in each of their diaries and arranges the appointment for that time. If no common slots are available, it interacts with the user to rearrange his or her personal diary to make room for the appointment.

■ A petrol (gas) station is to be set up for fully automated operation. Drivers swipe their credit card through a reader connected to the pump; the card is verified by communication with a credit company computer; and a fuel limit is established. The driver may then take the fuel required. When fuel delivery is complete and the pump hose is returned to its holster, the driver's credit card account is debited with the cost of the fuel taken. The credit card is returned after debiting. If the card is invalid, the pump returns it before fuel is dispensed.

14.8 Write precise interface definitions in Java or C++ for the objects you have defined in Exercise 14.7.

14.9 Draw a sequence diagram showing the interactions of objects in a group diary system when a group of people arrange a meeting.

14.10 Draw a statechart showing the possible state changes in one or more of the objects that you have defined in Exercise 14.7.

15

Real-time
software design

Objectives

The objectives of this chapter are to introduce techniques that are used in the design of real-time systems and to describe some generic real-time system architectures. When you have read this chapter, you will:

■ understand the concept of a real-time system and why real-time systems are usually implemented as a set of concurrent processes;

■ have been introduced to a design process for real-time systems;

■ understand the role of a real-time operating system;

■ know the generic process architectures for monitoring and control systems and data acquisition systems.

Contents

Computers are used to control a wide range of systems from simple domestic machines to entire manufacturing plants. These computers interact directly with hardware devices. The software in these systems is *embedded real-time software* that must react to events generated by the hardware and issue control signals in response to these events. It is embedded in some larger hardware system and must respond, in real time, to events from the system's environment.

Real-time embedded systems are different from other types of software systems. Their correct functioning is dependent on the system responding to events within a short time interval. I define a real-time system as follows:

A real-time system is a software system where the correct functioning of the system depends on the results produced by the system and the time at which these results are produced. A soft real-time system is a system whose operation is degraded if results are not produced according to the specified timing requirements. A hard real-time system is a system whose operation is incorrect if results are not produced according to the timing specification.

Timely response is an important factor in all embedded systems but, in some cases, very fast response is not necessary. For example, the insulin pump system that I use as an example in several chapters in this book is an embedded system. However, while it needs to check the glucose level at periodic intervals, it does not need to respond very quickly to external events. I therefore use different examples in this chapter to illustrate the fundamentals of real-time systems design.

One way of looking at a real-time system is as a stimulus/response system. Given a particular input stimulus, the system must produce a corresponding response. You can therefore define the behaviour of a real-time system by listing the stimuli received by the system, the associated responses and the time at which the response must be produced.

Stimuli fall into two classes:

1. *Periodic stimuli* These occur at predictable time intervals. For example, the system may examine a sensor every 50 milliseconds and take action (respond) depending on that sensor value (the stimulus).

2. *Aperiodic stimuli* These occur irregularly. They are usually signalled using the computer's interrupt mechanism. An example of such a stimulus would be an interrupt indicating that an I/O transfer was complete and that data was available in a buffer.

Periodic stimuli in a real-time system are usually generated by sensors associated with the system. These provide information about the state of the system's environment. The responses are directed to a set of actuators that control some equipment, such as a pump, that then influences the system's environment. Aperiodic stimuli may be generated either by the actuators or by sensors. They often indicate some exceptional condition, such as a hardware failure, that must be

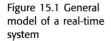

Figure 15.1 General
model of a real-time
system

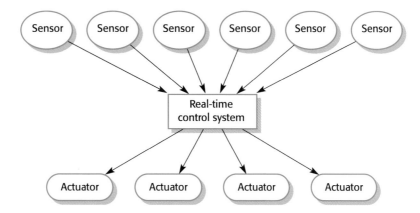

handled by the system. This sensor-system-actuator model of an embedded real-time system is illustrated in Figure 15.1.

A real-time system has to respond to stimuli that occur at different times. You therefore have to organise its architecture so that, as soon as a stimulus is received, control is transferred to the correct handler. This is impractical in sequential programs. Consequently, real-time systems are normally designed as a set of concurrent, cooperating processes. To support the management of these processes, the execution platform for most real-time systems includes a *real-time operating system*. The facilities in this operating system are accessed through the run-time support system for the real-time programming language that is used.

The generality of this stimulus-response model of a real-time system leads to a generic, abstract architectural model where there are three types of processes. For each type of sensor, there is a sensor management process; computational processes compute the required response for the stimuli received by the system; actuator control processes manage actuator operation. This model allows data to be collected quickly from the sensor (before the next input becomes available) and allows processing and the associated actuator response to be carried out later.

This generic architecture can be instantiated into a number of different application architectures that extend the set of architectures discussed in Chapter 13. Real-time application architectures are instances of event-driven architecture in which the stimuli, either directly or indirectly, cause events to be generated. In this chapter, I introduce two further application architectures: the architecture for monitoring and control systems (in Section 15.3), and the architecture for data acquisition systems (in Section 15.4).

Programming languages for real-time systems development have to include facilities to access the system hardware, and it should be possible to predict the timing of particular operations in these languages. Hard real-time systems are still sometimes programmed in assembly language so that tight deadlines can be met. Systems-level languages, such as C, that allow efficient code to be generated are also widely used.

The advantage of using a low-level systems programming language such as C is that it allows the development of very efficient programs. However, these languages do not include constructs to support concurrency or the management of shared resources. These are implemented through calls to the real-time operating system that cannot be checked by the compiler, so programming errors are more likely. Programs are also often more difficult to understand because real-time features are not explicit in the program.

Over the past few years, there has been extensive work to extend Java for real-time systems development (Nilsen, 1998; Higuera-Toledano and Issarny, 2000; Hardin, et al., 2002). This work involves modifying the language to address fundamental real-time problems:

1. It is not possible to specify the time at which threads should execute.

2. Garbage collection is uncontrollable—it may be started at any time. Therefore, the timing behaviour of threads is unpredictable.

3. It is not possible to discover the sizes of queue associated with shared resources.

4. The implementation of the Java Virtual Machine varies from one computer to another, so the same program can have different timing behaviours.

5. The language does not allow for detailed run-time space or processor analysis.

6. There are no standard ways to access the hardware of the system.

Real-time versions of Java, such as Sun's J2ME (Java 2 Micro Edition), are now available. A number of vendors supply implementations of the Java Virtual Machine adapted for real-time systems development. These developments mean that Java will be become increasingly used as a real-time programming language.

15.1 System design

As discussed in Chapter 2, part of the system design process involves deciding which system capabilities are to be implemented in software and which in hardware. For many real-time systems embedded in consumer products, such as the systems in cell phones, the costs and power consumption of the hardware are critical. Specific processors designed to support embedded systems may be used and, for some systems, special-purpose hardware may have to be designed and built.

This means that a top-down design process—where the design starts with an abstract model that is decomposed and developed in a series of stages—is impractical for

Figure 15.2
Sensor/actuator
control processes

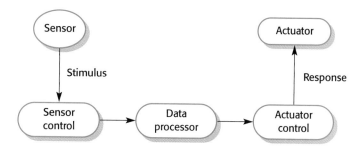

most real-time systems. Low-level decisions on hardware, support software and system timing must be considered early in the process. These limit the flexibility of system designers and may mean that additional software functionality, such as battery and power management, is required.

Events (the stimuli) rather than objects or functions should be central to the real-time software design process. There are several interleaved stages in this design process:

1. Identify the stimuli that the system must process and the associated responses.

2. For each stimulus and associated response, identify the timing constraints that apply to both stimulus and response processing.

3. Choose an execution platform for the system: the hardware and the real-time operating system to be used. Factors that influence these choices include the timing constraints on the system, limitations on power available, the experience of the development team and the price target for the delivered system.

4. Aggregate the stimulus and response processing into a number of concurrent processes. A good rule of thumb in real-time systems design is to associate a process with each class of stimulus and response as shown in Figure 15.2.

5. For each stimulus and response, design algorithms to carry out the required computations. Algorithm designs often have to be developed relatively early in the design process to give an indication of the amount of processing required and the time required to complete that processing.

6. Design a scheduling system that will ensure that processes are started in time to meet their deadlines.

The order of these activities in the process depends on the type of system being developed and its process and platform requirements. In some cases, you may be able to follow a fairly abstract approach where you start with the stimuli and associated processing and decide on the hardware and execution platforms late in the process. In other cases, the choice of hardware and operating system is made before the software design starts and you have to orient your design around the hardware capabilities.

Processes in a real-time system have to be coordinated. Process coordination mechanisms ensure mutual exclusion to shared resources. When one process is modifying a shared resource, other processes should not be able to change that resource. Mechanisms for ensuring mutual exclusion include semaphores (Dijkstra, 1968), monitors (Hoare, 1974) and critical regions (Brinch-Hansen, 1973). These mechanisms are described in most operating system texts (Tanenbaum, 2001; Silberschatz, et al., 2002).

Once you have chosen the execution platform for the system, designed a process architecture, and decided on a scheduling policy, you may need to check that the system will meet its timing requirements. You can do this through static analysis of the system using knowledge of the timing behaviour of components or through simulation. This analysis may reveal that the system will not perform adequately. The process architecture, the scheduling policy, the execution platform or all of these may then have to be redesigned to improve the performance of the system.

Timing analysis for real-time systems is difficult. Because aperiodic stimuli are unpredictable, designers have to make assumptions about the probability of these stimuli occurring (and therefore requiring service) at any particular time. These assumptions may be incorrect, and system performance after delivery may not be adequate. Cooling's book (Cooling, 2003) discusses techniques for real-time system performance analysis.

Because real-time systems must meet their timing constraints, you may not be able to use object-oriented development for hard real-time systems. Object-oriented development involves hiding data representations and accessing attribute values through operations defined with the object. This means that there is a significant performance overhead in object-oriented systems because extra code is required to mediate access to attributes and handle calls to operations. The consequent loss of performance may make it impossible to meet real-time deadlines.

Timing constraints or other requirements may sometimes mean that it is best to implement some system functions, such as signal processing, in hardware rather than in software. Hardware components deliver much better performance than the equivalent software. System-processing bottlenecks can be identified and replaced by hardware, thus avoiding expensive software optimisation.

15.1.1 Real-time system modelling

Real-time systems have to respond to events occurring at irregular intervals. These events (or stimuli) often cause the system to move to a different state. For this reason, state machine modelling, described in Chapter 8, is often used to model real-time systems.

State machine models are a good, language-independent way of representing the design of a real-time system and are therefore an integral part of real-time system

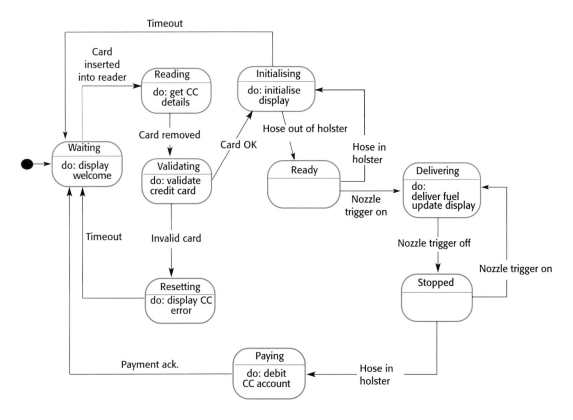

Figure 15.3 State machine model of a petrol (gas) pump

design methods (Gomaa, 1993). The UML supports the development of state models based on Statecharts (Harel, 1987; Harel, 1988). Statecharts structure state models so that groups of states can be considered a single entity. Douglass discusses the use of the UML in real-time systems development (Douglass, 1999).

A state model of a system assumes that, at any time, the system is in one of a number of possible states. When a stimulus is received, this may cause a transition to a different state. For example, a system controlling a valve may move from a state 'Valve open' to a state 'Valve closed' when an operator command (the stimulus) is received.

I have already illustrated this approach to system modelling in Chapter 8 using the model of a simple microwave oven. Figure 15.3 is another example of a state machine model that shows the operation of a fuel delivery software system embedded in a petrol (gas) pump. The rounded rectangles represent system states, and the arrows represent stimuli that force a transition from one state to another. The names chosen in the state machine diagram are descriptive and the associated information indicates actions taken by the system actuators or information that is displayed.

The fuel delivery system is designed to allow unattended operation. The buyer inserts a credit card into a card reader built into the pump. This causes a transition to a **Reading** state where the card details are read and the buyer is asked to remove the card. The system moves to a **Validating** state where the card is validated. If the card is valid, the system initialises the pump and, when the fuel hose is removed from its holster, is ready to deliver fuel. Activating the trigger on the nozzle causes fuel to be pumped; this stops when the trigger is released (for simplicity, I have ignored the pressure switch that is designed to stop fuel spillage). After the fuel delivery is complete and the buyer has replaced the hose in its holster, the system moves to a **Paying** state where the user's account is debited.

15.2 Real-time operating systems

All but the very simplest embedded systems now work in conjunction with a real-time operating system (RTOS). A real-time operating system manages processes and resource allocation in a real-time system. It starts and stops processes so that stimuli can be handled and allocates memory and processor resources. There are many RTOS products available, from very small, simple systems for consumer devices to complex systems for cell phones and mobile devices and operating systems specially designed for process control and telecommunications.

The components of an RTOS (Figure 15.4) depend on the size and complexity of the real-time system being developed. For all except the simplest systems, they usually include:

1. *A real-time clock* This provides information to schedule processes periodically.

2. *An interrupt handler* This manages aperiodic requests for service.

3. *A scheduler* This component is responsible for examining the processes that can be executed and choosing one of these for execution.

4. *A resource manager* Given a process that is scheduled for execution, the resource manager allocates appropriate memory and processor resources.

5. *A despatcher* This component is responsible for starting the execution of a process.

Real-time operating systems for large systems, such as process control or telecommunication systems, may have additional facilities, such as disk storage management and fault management facilities, that detect and report system faults and a configuration manager that supports the dynamic reconfiguration of real-time applications.

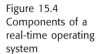

Figure 15.4
Components of a
real-time operating
system

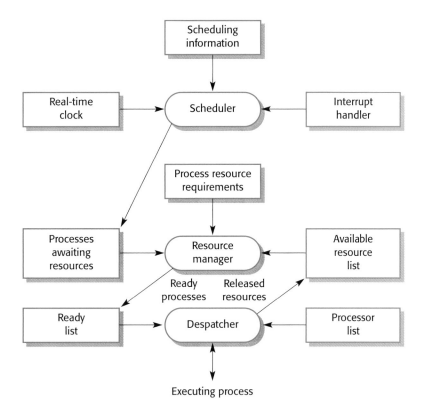

15.2.1 Process management

Real-time systems have to handle external events quickly and, in some cases, meet deadlines for processing these events. This means that the event-handling processes must be scheduled for execution in time to detect the event and must be allocated sufficient processor resources to meet their deadline. The process manager in an RTOS is responsible for choosing processes for execution, allocating processor and memory resources, and starting and stopping process execution on a processor.

The process manager has to manage processes with different priorities. For some stimuli, such as those associated with certain exceptional events, it is essential that their processing should be completed within the specified time limits. Other processes may be safely delayed if a more critical process requires service. Consequently, the RTOS has to be able to manage at least two priority levels for system processes:

1. *Interrupt level* This is the highest priority level. It is allocated to processes that need a very fast response. One of these processes will be the real-time clock process.

2. *Clock level* This level of priority is allocated to periodic processes.

Figure 15.5 RTOS
actions required to
start a process

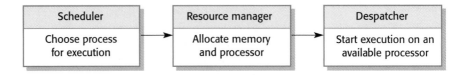

There may be a further priority level allocated to background processes (such as a self-checking process) that do not need to meet real-time deadlines. These processes are scheduled for execution when processor capacity is available.

Within each of these priority levels, different classes of process may be allocated different priorities. For example, there may be several interrupt lines. An interrupt from a very fast device may have to pre-empt processing of an interrupt from a slower device to avoid information loss. The allocation of process priorities so that all processes are serviced in time usually requires extensive analysis and simulation.

Periodic processes are processes that must be executed at specified time intervals for data acquisition and actuator control. In most real-time systems, there will be several types of periodic processes. These will have different periods (the time between process executions), execution times and deadlines (the time by which processing must be complete). Using the timing requirements specified in the application program, the RTOS arranges the execution of periodic processes so that they can all meet their deadlines.

The actions taken by the operating system for periodic process management are shown in Figure 15.5. The scheduler examines the list of periodic processes and selects a process to be executed. The choice depends on the process priority, the process periods, the expected execution times and the deadlines of the ready processes. Sometimes, two processes with different deadlines should be executed at the same clock tick. In such a situation, one process must be delayed so long as its deadline can still be met.

Processes that have to respond to asynchronous events are usually interrupt-driven. The computer's interrupt mechanism causes control to transfer to a predetermined memory location. This location contains an instruction to jump to a simple and fast interrupt service routine. The service routine first disables further interrupts to avoid being interrupted itself. It then discovers the cause of the interrupt and initiates, with a high priority, a process to handle the stimulus causing the interrupt. In some high-speed data acquisition systems, the interrupt handler saves the data that the interrupt signalled was available in a buffer for later processing. Interrupts are then enabled again and control is returned to the operating system.

At any one time, there may be several processes, with different priorities, that could be executed. The process scheduler implements system-scheduling policies that determine the order of process execution. There are two basic scheduling strategies:

1. *Non pre-emptive scheduling* Once a process has been scheduled for execution, it runs to completion or until it is blocked for some reason, such as waiting for input. This can cause problems, however, when there are processes with different priorities and a high-priority process has to wait for a low-priority process to finish.

2. *Pre-emptive scheduling* The execution of an executing process may be stopped if a higher-priority process requires service. The higher-priority process preempts the execution of the lower-priority process and is allocated to a processor.

Within these strategies, different scheduling algorithms have been developed. These include round-robin scheduling where each process is executed in turn, rate monotonic scheduling where the process with the shortest period is given priority and shortest deadline first scheduling (Burns and Wellings, 2001).

Information about the process to be executed is passed to the resource manager. The resource manager allocates memory and, in a multiprocessor system, a processor to this process. The process is then placed on the ready list, a list of processes that are ready for execution. When a processor finishes executing a process and becomes available, the dispatcher is invoked. It scans the ready list to find a process that can be executed on the available processor and starts its execution.

15.3 Monitoring and control systems

Monitoring and control systems are an important class of real-time system. They check sensors providing information about the system's environment and take actions depending on the sensor reading. Monitoring systems take action when some exceptional sensor value is detected. Control systems continuously control hardware actuators depending on the value of associated sensors.

The characteristic architecture of monitoring and control systems is shown in Figure 15.6. Each type of sensor being monitored has its own monitoring process, as does each type of actuator that is being controlled. A monitoring process collects and integrates the data before passing it to a control process, which makes decisions based on this data and sends appropriate control commands to the equipment control processes. In simple systems, the monitoring and control responsibilities may be integrated into a single process. I have also shown two other processes that may be included in monitoring and control systems. These are a testing process that can run hardware test programs and a control panel process that manages the system control panels or operator console.

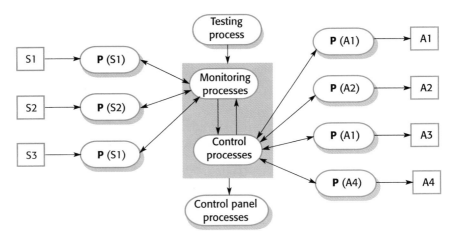

Figure 15.6 Generic
architecture for a
monitoring and
control system

To illustrate the design of monitoring and control systems, I use an example of a burglar alarm system that might be installed in an office building:

A software system is to be implemented to control a burglar alarm system for installation in commercial buildings. This uses several different types of sensors. These include movement detectors in individual rooms, window sensors on ground-floor windows that detect when a window has been broken, and door sensors that detect corridor doors opening. There are up to 50 window sensors, up to 30 door sensors and up to 200 movement detectors in the system.

When a sensor detects the presence of an intruder, the system automatically calls the local police and, using a voice synthesiser, reports the location of the alarm. It switches on lights in the rooms around the active sensor and sets off an audible alarm. The sensor system is normally powered by the mains but is equipped with a battery backup. Power loss is detected using a separate power circuit monitor that monitors the mains voltage. It interrupts the alarm system when a voltage drop is detected.

This system is a 'soft' real-time system that does not have stringent timing requirements. The sensors do not need to detect high-speed events, so they need only be polled twice per second. To make the example easier to understand, I have simplified the design by leaving out the testing and display processes.

The design process follows the steps discussed in Section 15.1, so you start by identifying the aperiodic stimuli that the system receives and the associated responses. Because of the design simplifications that I proposed, stimuli generated by system testing procedures and external signals to switch it off in the event of a false alarm can be ignored. This means there are only two classes of stimulus to be processed:

1. *Power failure* This is generated by the circuit monitor. The required response is to switch the circuit to backup power by signalling an electronic power-switching device.

Stimulus/Response	Timing requirements
Power fail interrupt	The switch to backup power must be completed within a deadline of 50 ms.
Door alarm	Each door alarm should be polled twice per second.
Window alarm	Each window alarm should be polled twice per second.
Movement detector	Each movement detector should be polled twice per second.
Audible alarm	The audible alarm should be switched on within half a second of an alarm being raised by a sensor.
Lights switch	The lights should be switched on within half a second of an alarm being raised by a sensor.
Communications	The call to the police should be started within 2 seconds of an alarm being raised by a sensor.
Voice synthesiser	A synthesised message should be available within 4 seconds of an alarm being raised by a sensor.

2. *Intruder alarm* This is a stimulus generated by one of the system sensors. The response to this stimulus is to compute the room number of the active sensor, set up a call to the police, initiate the voice synthesiser to manage the call, and switch on the audible intruder alarm and the building lights in the area.

The next step in the design process is to consider the timing constraints associated with each stimulus and associated response. These timing constraints are shown in Figure 15.7. You should normally list the timing constraints for each class of sensor separately, even when, as in this case, they are the same. By handling them separately, you leave scope for future change and make it easier to compute the number of times the controlling process has to be executed each second.

Allocation of the system functions to concurrent processes is the next design stage. There are three types of sensor that must be polled periodically, each with an associated process. There is an interrupt-driven system to handle power failure and switching, a communications system, a voice synthesiser, an audible alarm system and a light-switching system to switch on lights around the sensor. An independent process controls each of these systems. This results in the system architecture shown in Figure 15.8.

In Figure 15.8, annotated arrows join processes, indicating data flows between them with the annotation indicating the type of data flow. Not all processes receive data from other processes. For example, the process responsible for managing a power failure has no need for data from elsewhere in the system.

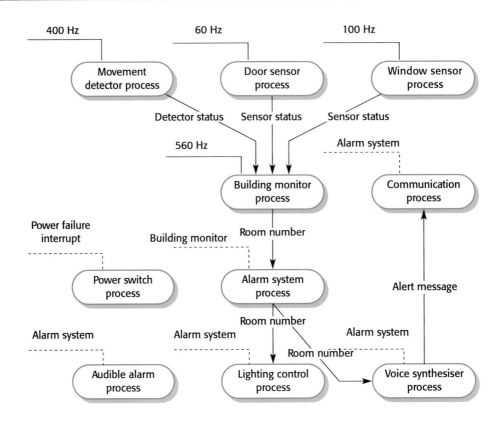

Figure 15.8 Process
architecture of the
intruder alarm
system

The line associated with each process on the top left is used to indicate how the process is controlled. The lines on a periodic process are solid lines with the minimum number of times a process should be executed per second as an annotation. Aperiodic processes have dashed lines on their top-left corner, which are annotated with the event that causes the process to be scheduled.

The number of sensors to be polled and the timing requirements of the system are used to calculate how often each process has to be scheduled. For example, there are 30 door sensors that must be checked twice per second. This means that the associated door sensor process must run 60 times per second (60 Hz). The movement detector process must run 400 times per second because there may be up to 200 movement sensors in the system. The control information on the actuator processes (i.e., the audible alarm controller, the lighting controller, etc.) indicates that they are started by an explicit command from the **Alarm** system process or by a **Power failure interrupt**.

These processes may be implemented in Java using threads. Figure 15.9 shows the Java code that implements the **BuildingMonitor** process, which polls the system sensors. If these signal an intruder, the software activates the associated alarm system. I use standard Java here and assume that the timing requirements (included as comments) can be met. As I discussed earlier, standard Java does not include facilities to allow thread execution frequency to be specified.

Figure 15.9 Java
implementation of
the BuildingMonitor
process

```java
// See http://www.software-engin.com/ for links to the complete Java code for this
// example

class BuildingMonitor extends Thread {

    BuildingSensor win, door, move ;

    Siren    siren = new Siren () ;
    Lights    lights = new Lights () ;
    Synthesizer synthesizer = new Synthesizer () ;
    DoorSensors doors = new DoorSensors (30) ;
    WindowSensors   windows = new WindowSensors (50) ;
    MovementSensors movements = new MovementSensors (200) ;
    PowerMonitor pm = new PowerMonitor () ;

    BuildingMonitor()
    {
        // initialise all the sensors and start the processes
        siren.start () ; lights.start () ;
        synthesizer.start () ; windows.start () ;
        doors.start () ; movements.start () ; pm.start () ;
    {}

    {public void run ()
    {{
        int room = 0 ;
        while (true)
        {
            // poll the movement sensors at least twice per second (400 Hz)
            move = movements.getVal () ;
            // poll the window sensors at least twice/second (100 Hz)
            win = windows.getVal () ;
            // poll the door sensors at least twice per second (60 Hz)
            door = doors.getVal () ;
            if (move.sensorVal == 1 | door.sensorVal == 1 | win.sensorVal == 1)
                {
                    // a sensor has indicated an intruder
                    if (move.sensorVal == 1)        room = move.room ;
                    if (door.sensorVal == 1)        room = door.room ;
                    if (win.sensorVal == 1 )        room = win.room ;

                    lights.on (room) ; siren.on () ; synthesizer.on (room) ;
                    break ;
                }
        }
        lights.shutdown () ; siren.shutdown () ; synthesizer.shutdown () ;
        windows.shutdown () ; doors.shutdown () ; movements.shutdown () ;

    } // run
} //BuildingMonitor
```

Figure 15.10 Process
architecture of a
temperature control
system

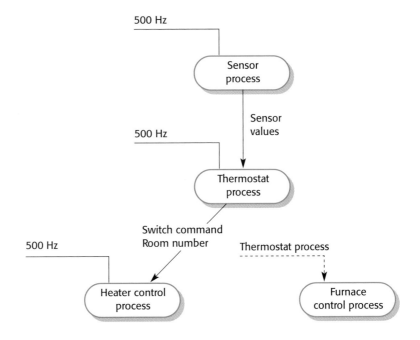

Once the system process architecture has been established, the algorithms for
stimulus processing and response generation should be designed. As I discussed in
Section 15.1, this detailed design stage is necessary early in the design process to
ensure that the system can meet its specified timing constraints. If the associated
algorithms are complex, changes to the timing constraints may be required.
However, unless signal processing is required, real-time system algorithms are often
quite simple. They may only require a memory location to be checked, some simple computations to be carried out or a signal to be despatched. As you can see
from Figure 15.9, the processing required in the burglar alarm system follows this
simple model.

The final step in the design process is to design a scheduling system that ensures
a process will always be scheduled to meet its deadlines. In this example, deadlines
are not tight. Process priorities should be organised so that all sensor-polling processes have the same priority. The process for handling a power failure should be
a higher-priority interrupt level process. The priorities of the processes managing
the alarm system should be the same as the sensor processes.

The burglar alarm system is a monitoring system rather than a control system,
as it does not include actuators that are directly affected by sensor values. An example of a control system would be a building heating control system. This system
monitors temperature sensors in different rooms in the building and switches a heater
unit off and on depending on the actual temperature and the temperature set on the
room thermostat. The thermostat also controls the switching of the furnace in the
system.

Figure 15.11 The
generic architecture
of data acquisition
systems

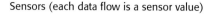

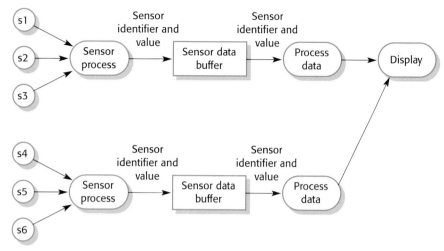

Figure 15.11 The generic architecture of data acquisition systems

The process architecture of this system is shown in Figure 15.10. It is clear that its general form is similar to the burglar alarm system. I leave it to you to develop the design of this system in more detail.

15.4 Data acquisition systems

Data acquisition systems collect data from sensors for subsequent processing and analysis. These systems are used in circumstances where the sensors are collecting lots of data from the system's environment and it isn't possible or necessary to process the data collected in real-time. Data acquisition systems are commonly used in scientific experiments and process control systems where physical processes, such as a chemical reaction, happen very quickly.

In data acquisition systems, the sensors may be generating data very quickly, and the key problem is to ensure that a sensor reading is collected before the sensor value changes. This leads to a generic architecture, as shown in Figure 15.11. The essential feature of the architecture of data acquisition systems is that each group of sensors has three processes associated with it. These are the sensor process that interfaces with the sensor and converts analogue data to digital values if necessary, a buffer process, and a process that consumes the data and carries out further processing.

Sensors, of course, can be of different types, and the number of sensors in a group depends on the rate at which data arrives from the environment. In Figure 15.11, I have shown two groups of sensors, s1–s3 and s4–s6. I have also shown, on the right, a further process that displays the sensor data. Most data acquisition systems

Neutron flux sensors

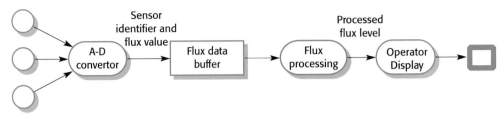

Figure 15.12 Neutron flux data acquisition

include display and reporting processes that aggregate the collected data and carry out further processing.

As an example of a data acquisition system, consider the system model shown in Figure 15.12. This represents a system that collects data from sensors monitoring the neutron flux in a nuclear reactor. The sensor data is placed in a buffer from which it is extracted and processed, and the average flux level is displayed on an operator's display.

Each sensor has an associated process that converts the analogue input flux level into a digital signal. It passes this flux level, with the sensor identifier, to the sensor data buffer. The process responsible for data processing takes the data from this buffer, processes it and passes it to a display process for output on an operator console.

In real-time systems that involve data acquisition and processing, the execution speeds and periods of the acquisition process (the producer) and the processing process (the consumer) may be out of step. When significant processing is required, the data acquisition may go faster than the data processing. If only simple computations need be carried out, the processing may be faster than the data acquisition.

To smooth out these speed differences, data acquisition systems buffer input data using a circular buffer. The process producing the data (the producer) adds information to this buffer, and the process using the data (the consumer) takes information from the buffer (Figure 15.13).

Obviously, mutual exclusion must be implemented to prevent the producer and consumer processes from accessing the same element in the buffer at the same time. The system must also ensure that the producer does not try to add information to a full buffer and the consumer does not take information from an empty buffer.

In Figure 15.14 (p. 358) I show a possible implementation of the data buffer as a Java object. The values in the buffer are of type **SensorRecord**, and there are two operations that are defined—namely, **get** and **put**. The **get** operation takes an item from the buffer and the **put** operation adds an item to the buffer. The constructor for the buffer sets the size when objects of type **CircularBuffer** are declared.

The **synchronized** modifier associated with the **get** and **put** methods indicates that these methods should not run concurrently. When one of these methods is invoked, the run-time system obtains a lock on the object instance to ensure that the other method can't change the same entry in the buffer. The **wait** and **notify** method invocations are used to ensure that entries can't be put into a full buffer or taken from an empty buffer. The **wait** method causes the invoking thread to suspend itself until

Figure 15.13 A ring buffer for data acquisition

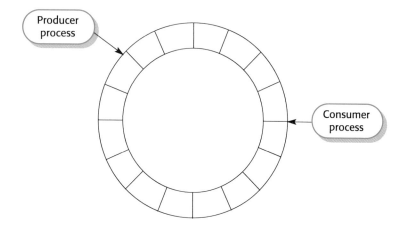

another thread tells it to stop waiting. It does this by calling the **notify** method. When **wait** is called, the lock on the protected object is released. The **notify** method wakes up one of the threads that is waiting and causes it to restart execution.

KEY POINTS

■ A real-time system is a software system that must respond to events in real time. Its correctness does not just depend on the results it produces but also on the time when these results are produced.

■ A general model for real-time systems architecture involves associating a process with each class of sensor and actuator device. Other coordination processes may also be required.

■ The architectural design of a real-time system usually involves organising the system as a set of interacting, concurrent processes.

■ A real-time operating system is responsible for process and resource management. It always includes a scheduler, which is the component responsible for deciding which process should be scheduled for executing. Scheduling decisions are made using process priorities.

■ Monitoring and control systems periodically poll a set of sensors that capture information from the system's environment. They take actions, depending on the sensor readings, by issuing commands to actuators.

■ Data acquisition systems are usually organised according to a producer-consumer model. The producer process puts the data into a circular buffer, where it is consumed by the consumer process. The buffer is also implemented as a process so that conflicts between the producer and consumer are eliminated.

```
class CircularBuffer
{
    int bufsize ;
    SensorRecord [] store ;
    int numberOfEntries = 0 ;
    int front = 0, back = 0 ;

    CircularBuffer (int n) {
        bufsize = n ;
        store = new SensorRecord [bufsize] ;
    } // CircularBuffer

    synchronized void put (SensorRecord rec ) throws InterruptedException
    {
        if ( numberOfEntries == bufsize)
            wait () ;
        store [back] = new SensorRecord (rec.sensorId, rec.sensorVal) ;
        back = back + 1 ;
        if (back == bufsize)
            back = 0 ;
        numberOfEntries = numberOfEntries + 1 ;
        notify () ;
    } // put

    synchronized SensorRecord get () throws InterruptedException
    {
        SensorRecord result = new SensorRecord (-1, -1) ;
        if (numberOfEntries == 0)
                wait () ;
        result = store [front] ;
        front = front + 1 ;
        if (front == bufsize)
            front = 0 ;
        numberOfEntries = numberOfEntries−1 ;
        notify () ;
        return result ;
    } // get
} // CircularBuffer
```

FURTHER READING

Software Engineering for Real-Time Systems. Written from an engineering rather than a computer science perspective, this book is a good practical guide to real-time systems engineering. It has better coverage of hardware issues than Burns and Wellings' book, so is an excellent complement to it. (J. Cooling, 2003, Addison- Wesley.)

Real-time Systems and Programming Languages, 3rd edition. An excellent and comprehensive text that provides broad coverage of all aspects of real-time systems. (A. Burns and A. Wellings, 2001, Addison-Wesley.)

Doing Hard Time: Developing Real-time Systems with UML, Objects, Frameworks and Patterns. This book discusses how object-oriented techniques can be used in the design of real-time systems. As hardware speeds increase, this is becoming an increasingly viable approach to real-time systems design. (B. P. Douglass, 1999, Addison-Wesley.)

EXERCISES

15.1 Using examples, explain why real-time systems usually have to be implemented using concurrent processes.

15.2 Explain why an object-oriented approach to software development may not be suitable for real-time systems.

15.3 Draw state machine models of the control software for the following systems:

■ An automatic washing machine that has different programs for different types of clothes.

■ The software for a compact disk player.

■ A telephone answering machine that records incoming messages and displays the number of accepted messages on an LED display. The system should allow the telephone owner to dial in, type a sequence of numbers (identified as tones) and have the recorded messages replayed over the phone.

■ A vending machine that can dispense coffee with and without milk and sugar. The user deposits a coin and makes his or her selection by pressing a button on the machine. This causes a cup with powdered coffee to be output. The user places this cup under a tap, presses another button and hot water is dispensed.

15.4 Using the real-time system design techniques discussed in this chapter, redesign the weather station data collection system covered in Chapter 14 as a stimulus-response system.

Figure 15.15 Train
protection system
description

- The system acquires information on the speed limit of a segment from a trackside transmitter, which continually broadcasts the segment identifier and its speed limit. The same transmitter also broadcasts information on the status of the signal controlling that track segment. The time required to broadcast track segment and signal information is 50 milliseconds.

- The train can receive information from the trackside transmitter when it is within 10 m of a transmitter.

- The maximum train speed is 180 kph.

- Sensors on the train provide information about the current train speed (updated every 250 milliseconds) and the train brake status (updated every 100 milliseconds).

- If the train speed exceeds the current segment speed limit by more than 5 kph, a warning is sounded in the driver's cabin. If the train speed exceeds the current segment speed limit by more than 10 kph, the train's brakes are automatically applied until the speed falls to the segment speed limit. Train brakes should be applied within 100 milliseconds of the time when the excessive train speed has been detected.

- If the train enters a track segment that is signalled with a red light, the train protection system applies the train brakes and reduces the speed to zero. Train brakes should be applied within 100 milliseconds of the time when the red light signal is received.

- The system continually updates a status display in the driver's cabin.

15.5 Design a process architecture for an environmental monitoring system that collects data from a set of air quality sensors situated around a city. There are 5000 sensors organised into 100 neighbourhoods. Each sensor must be interrogated four times per second. When more than 30% of the sensors in a particular neighbourhood indicate that the air quality is below an acceptable level, local warning lights are activated. All sensors return the readings to a central computer, which generates reports every 15 minutes on the air quality in the city.

15.6 Discuss the strengths and weaknesses of Java as a programming language for real-time systems. To what extent will the problems of real-time programming on Java disappear when faster processors are used?

15.7 A train protection system automatically applies the brakes of a train if the speed limit for a segment of track is exceeded or if the train enters a track segment that is currently signalled with a red light (i.e., the segment should not be entered). Details are shown in Figure 15.15. Identify the stimuli that must be processed by the on-board train control system and the associated responses to these stimuli.

15.8 Suggest a possible process architecture for this system. Document this process architecture using the rotation shown in Figure 15.8, clearly indicating if stimuli are periodic or aperiodic.

15.9   If a periodic process in the on-board train protection system is used to collect data from the trackside transmitter, how often must it be scheduled to ensure that the system is guaranteed to collect information from the transmitter? Explain how you arrived at your answer.

15.10 You are asked to work on a real-time development project for a military application but have no previous experience of projects in that domain. Discuss what you, as a professional software engineer, should do before starting work on the project.

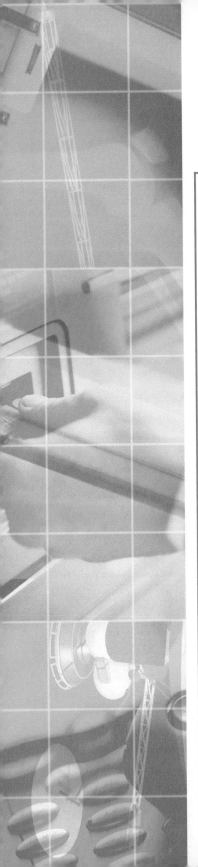

16

User interface design

Objectives

The objective of this chapter is to introduce some aspects of user interface design that are important for software engineers. When you have read this chapter, you will:

■ understand a number of user interface design principles;

■ have been introduced to several interaction styles and understand when these are most appropriate;

■ understand when to use graphical and textual presentation of information;

■ know what is involved in the principal activities in the user interface design process;

■ understand usability attributes and have been introduced to different approaches to interface evaluation.

Contents

Computer system design encompasses a spectrum of activities from hardware design to user interface design. While specialists are often employed for hardware design and for the graphic design of web pages, only large organisations normally employ specialist interface designers for their application software. Therefore, software engineers must often take responsibility for user interface design as well as for the design of the software to implement that interface.

Even when software designers and programmers are competent users of interface implementation technologies, such as Java's Swing classes (Elliott et al., 2002) or XHTML (Musciano and Kennedy, 2002), the user interfaces they develop are often unattractive and inappropriate for their target users. I focus, therefore, on the design process for user interfaces rather than the software that implements these facilities. Because of space limitations, I consider only graphical user interfaces. I don't discuss interfaces that require special (perhaps very simple) displays such as cell phones, DVD players, televisions, copiers and fax machines. Naturally, I can only introduce the topic here and I recommend texts such as those by Dix et al. (Dix, et al., 2004), Weiss (Weiss, 2002) and Shneiderman (Shneiderman, 1998) for more information on user interface design.

Careful user interface design is an essential part of the overall software design process. If a software system is to achieve its full potential, it is essential that its user interface should be designed to match the skills, experience and expectations of its anticipated users. Good user interface design is critical for system dependability. Many so-called 'user errors' are caused by the fact that user interfaces do not consider the capabilities of real users and their working environment. A poorly designed user interface means that users will probably be unable to access some of the system features, will make mistakes and will feel that the system hinders rather than helps them in achieving whatever they are using the system for.

When making user interface design decisions, you should take into account the physical and mental capabilities of the people who use software. I don't have space to discuss human issues in detail here but important factors that you should consider are:

1. People have a limited short-term memory—we can instantaneously remember about seven items of information (Miller, 1957). Therefore, if you present users with too much information at the same time, they may not be able to take it all in.

2. We all make mistakes, especially when we have to handle too much information or are under stress. When systems go wrong and issue warning messages and alarms, this often puts more stress on users, thus increasing the chances that they will make operational errors.

3. We have a diverse range of physical capabilities. Some people see and hear better than others, some people are colour-blind, and some are better than others at physical manipulation. You should not design for your own capabilities and assume that all other users will be able to cope.

Figure 16.1 User
interface design
principles

Principle	Description
User familiarity	The interface should use terms and concepts drawn from the experience of the people who will make most use of the system.
Consistency	The interface should be consistent in that, wherever possible, comparable operations should be activated in the same way.
Minimal surprise	Users should never be surprised by the behaviour of a system.
Recoverability	The interface should include mechanisms to allow users to recover from errors.
User guidance	The interface should provide meaningful feedback when errors occur and provide context-sensitive user help facilities.
User diversity	The interface should provide appropriate interaction facilities for different types of system users.

4. We have different interaction preferences. Some people like to work with pictures, others with text. Direct manipulation is natural for some people, but others prefer a style of interaction that is based on issuing commands to the system.

These human factors are the basis for the design principles shown in Figure 16.1. These general principles are applicable to all user interface designs and should normally be instantiated as more detailed design guidelines for specific organisations or types of system. User interface design principles are covered in more detail by Dix, et al. (Dix, et al., 2004). Shneiderman (Shneiderman, 1998) gives a longer list of more specific user interface design guidelines.

The principle of *user familiarity* suggests that users should not be forced to adapt to an interface because it is convenient to implement. The interface should use terms that are familiar to the user, and the objects manipulated by the system should be directly related to the user's working environment. For example, if a system is designed for use by air traffic controllers, the objects manipulated should be aircraft, flight paths, beacons, and so on. Associated operations might be to increase or reduce aircraft speed, adjust heading and change height. The underlying implementation of the interface in terms of files and data structures should be hidden from the end-user.

The principle of *user interface consistency* means that system commands and menus should have the same format, parameters should be passed to all commands in the same way, and command punctuation should be similar. Consistent interfaces reduce user learning time. Knowledge learned in one command or application is therefore applicable in other parts of the system or in related applications.

Interface consistency across applications is also important. As far as possible, commands with similar meanings in different applications should be expressed in the same way. Errors are often caused when the same keyboard command, such as 'Control-b' means different things in different systems. For example, in the word processor that I normally use, 'Control-b' means embolden text, but in the graphics program that I use to draw diagrams, 'Control-b' means move the selected object behind another object. I make mistakes when using them together and sometimes try to embolden text in a diagram using the key combination. I then get confused when the text disappears behind the enclosing object. You can normally avoid this kind of error if you follow the command key shortcuts defined by the operating system that you use.

This level of consistency is low-level. Interface designers should always try to achieve this in a user interface. Consistency at a higher level is also sometimes desirable. For example, it may be appropriate to support the same operations (print, copy, etc.) on all types of system entities. However, Grudin (Grudin, 1989) points out that complete consistency is neither possible nor desirable. It may be sensible to implement deletion from a desktop by dragging entities into a trash can. It would be awkward to delete text in a word processor in this way.

Unfortunately, the principles of user familiarity and user consistency are sometimes conflicting. Ideally, applications with common features should always use the same commands to access these features. However, this can conflict with user practice when systems are designed to support a particular type of user, such as graphic designers. These users may have evolved their own styles of interactions, terminology and operating conventions. These may clash with the interaction 'standards' that are appropriate to more general applications such as word processors.

The principle of *minimal surprise* is appropriate because people get very irritated when a system behaves in an unexpected way. As a system is used, users build a mental model of how the system works. If an action in one context causes a particular type of change, it is reasonable to expect that the same action in a different context will cause a comparable change. If something completely different happens, the user is both surprised and confused. Interface designers should therefore try to ensure that comparable actions have comparable effects.

Surprises in user interfaces are often the result of the fact that many interfaces are moded. This means that there are several modes of working (e.g., viewing mode and editing mode), and the effect of a command is different depending on the mode. It is very important that, when designing an interface, you include a visual indicator showing the user the current mode.

The principle of *recoverability* is important because users inevitably make mistakes when using a system. The interface design can minimise these mistakes (e.g., using menus means avoids typing mistakes), but mistakes can never be completely eliminated. Consequently, you should include interface facilities that allow users to recover from their mistakes. These can be of three kinds:

1. *Confirmation of destructive actions* If a user specifies an action that is potentially destructive, the system should ask the user to confirm that this is really what is wanted before destroying any information.

2.   *The provision of an undo facility* Undo restores the system to a state before the action occurred. Multiple levels of undo are useful because users don't always recognise immediately that a mistake has been made.

3.   *Checkpointing* Checkpointing involves saving the state of a system at periodic intervals and allowing the system to restart from the last checkpoint. Then, when mistakes occur, users can go back to a previous state and start again. Many systems now include checkpointing to cope with system failures but, paradoxically, they don't allow system users to use them to recover from their own mistakes.

A related principle is the principle of *user assistance*. Interfaces should have built-in user assistance or help facilities. These should be integrated with the system and should provide different levels of help and advice. Levels should range from basic information on getting started to a full description of system facilities. Help systems should be structured so that users are not overwhelmed with information when they ask for help.

The principle of *user diversity* recognises that, for many interactive systems, there may be different types of users. Some will be casual users who interact occasionally with the system while others may be power users who use the system for several hours each day. Casual users need interfaces that provide guidance, but power users require shortcuts so that they can interact as quickly as possible. Furthermore, users may suffer from disabilities of various types and, if possible, the interface should be adaptable to cope with these. Therefore, you might include facilities to display enlarged text, to replace sound with text, to produce very large buttons and so on. This reflects the notion of Universal Design (UD) (Preiser and Ostoff, 2001), a design philosophy whose goal is to avoid excluding users because of thoughtless design choices.

The principle of recognising user diversity can conflict with the other interface design principles, since some users may prefer very rapid interaction over, for example, user interface consistency. Similarly, the level of user guidance required can be radically different for different users, and it may be impossible to develop support that is suitable for all types of users. You therefore have to make compromises to reconcile the needs of these users.

16.1 Design issues

Before going on to discuss the process of user interface design, I discuss some general design issues that have to be considered by UI designers. Essentially, the designer of a user interface to a computer is faced with two key questions:

1.   How should the user interact with the computer system?

2. How should information from the computer system be presented to the user?

A coherent user interface must integrate user interaction and information presentation. This can be difficult because the designer has to find a compromise between the most appropriate styles of interaction and presentation for the application, the background and experience of the system users, and the equipment that is available.

16.1.1 User interaction

User interaction means issuing commands and associated data to the computer system. On early computers, the only way to do this was through a command-line interface, and a special-purpose language was used to communicate with the machine. However, this was geared to expert users and a number of approaches have now evolved that are easier to use. Shneiderman (Shneiderman, 1998) has classified these forms of interaction into five primary styles:

1. *Direct manipulation* The user interacts directly with objects on the screen. Direct manipulation usually involves a pointing device (a mouse, a stylus, a trackball or, on touch screens, a finger) that indicates the object to be manipulated and the action, which specifies what should be done with that object. For example, to delete a file, you may click on an icon representing that file and drag it to a trash can icon.

2. *Menu selection* The user selects a command from a list of possibilities (a menu). The user may also select another screen object by direct manipulation, and the command operates on that object. In this approach, to delete a file, you would select the file icon then select the delete command.

3. *Form fill-in* The user fills in the fields of a form. Some fields may have associated menus, and the form may have action 'buttons' that, when pressed, cause some action to be initiated. You would not normally use this approach to implement the interface to operations such as file deletion. Doing so would involve filling in the name of the file on the form then 'pressing' a delete button.

4. *Command language* The user issues a special command and associated parameters to instruct the system what to do. To delete a file, you would type a delete command with the filename as a parameter.

5. *Natural language* The user issues a command in natural language. This is usually a front end to a command language; the natural language is parsed and translated to system commands. To delete a file, you might type 'delete the file named xxx'.

Each of these styles of interaction has advantages and disadvantages and is best suited to a particular type of application and user (Shneiderman, 1998). Figure 16.2

Figure 16.2
Advantages and
disadvantages of
interaction styles

Interaction style	Main advantages	Main disadvantages	Application examples
Direct manipulation	Fast and intuitive interaction Easy to learn	May be hard to implement Only suitable where there is a visual metaphor for tasks and objects	Video games CAD systems
Menu selection	Avoids user error Little typing required	Slow for experienced users Can become complex if many menu options	Most general-purpose systems
Form fill-in	Easy to learn Checkable	Simple data entry Takes up a lot of screen space Causes problems where user options do not match the form fields	Stock control Personal loan processing
Command language	Powerful and flexible	Hard to learn Poor error management	Operating systems Command and control systems
Natural language	Accessible to casual users Easily extended	Requires more typing Natural language understanding systems are unreliable	Information retrieval systems

shows the main advantages and disadvantages of these styles and suggests types of applications where they might be used.

Of course, these interaction styles may be mixed, with several styles used in the same application. For example, Microsoft Windows supports direct manipulation of the iconic representation of files and directories, menu-based command selection, and for commands such as configuration commands, the user must fill in a special-purpose form that is presented to them.

In principle, it should be possible to separate the interaction style from the underlying entities that are manipulated through the user interface. This was the basis of the Seeheim model (Pfaff and ten Hagen, 1985) of user interface management. In this model, the presentation of information, the dialogue management and the application are separate. In reality, this model is more of an ideal than practical, but it is certainly possible to have separate interfaces for different classes of users (casual users and experienced users, say) that interact with the same underlying system. This is illustrated in Figure 16.3, which shows a command language interface and a graphical interface to an underlying operating system such as Linux.

Web-based user interfaces are based on the support provided by HTML or XHTML (the page description languages used for web pages) along with languages such as

Figure 16.3 Multiple
user interfaces

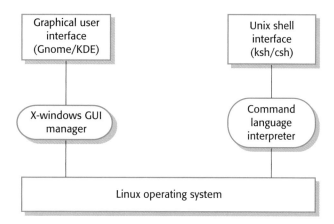

Figure 16.3 Multiple
user interfaces

Java, which can associate programs with components on a page. Because these web-based interfaces are usually designed for casual users, they mostly use forms-based interfaces. It is possible to construct direct manipulation interfaces on the web, but this is a complex programming task. Furthermore, because of the range of experience of web users and the fact that they come from many different cultures, it is difficult to establish a user interface metaphor for direct interaction that is universally acceptable.

To illustrate the design of web-based user interaction, I discuss the approach used in the LIBSYS system where users can access documents from other libraries. There are two fundamental operations that need to be supported:

1. *Document search* where users use the search facilities to find the documents that they need

2. *Document request* where users request that the document be delivered to their local machine or server for printing

The LIBSYS user interface is implemented using a web browser, so, given that users must supply information to the system such as the document identifier, their name and their authorisation details, it makes sense to use a forms-based interface. Figure 16.4 shows a possible interface design for the search component of the system.

In forms-based interfaces, the user supplies all of the information required then initiates the action by pressing a button. Forms fields can be menus, free-text input fields or radio buttons. In the LIBSYS example, a user chooses the collection to search from a menu of collections that can be accessed ('All' is the default, meaning search all collections) and types the search phrase into a free-text input field. The user chooses the field of the library record from a menu ('Title' is the default) and selects a radio button to indicate whether the search terms should be adjacent in the record.

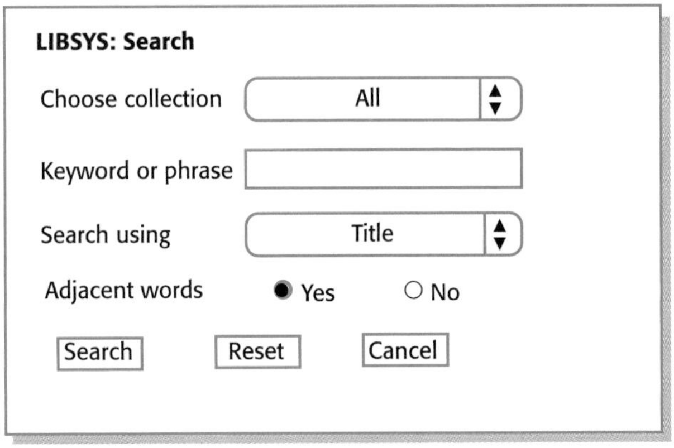

Figure 16.4 A forms-based interface to the LIBSYS system

LIBSYS: Search

Choose collection   All

Keyword or phrase

Search using   Title

Adjacent words   ● Yes   ○ No

[Search]   [Reset]   [Cancel]

16.1.2 Information presentation

All interactive systems have to provide some way of presenting information to users. The information presentation may simply be a direct representation of the input information (e.g., text in a word processor) or it may present the information graphically. A good design guideline is to keep the software required for information presentation separate from the information itself. Separating the presentation system from the data allows us to change the representation on the user's screen without having to change the underlying computational system. This is illustrated in Figure 16.5.

The MVC approach (Figure 16.6), first made widely available in Smalltalk (Goldberg and Robson, 1983), is an effective way to support multiple presentations of data. Users can interact with each presentation in a style that is appropriate to the presentation. The data to be displayed is encapsulated in a model object. Each model object may have a number of separate view objects associated with it where each view is a different display representation of the model.

Each view has an associated controller object that handles user input and device interaction. Therefore, a model that represents numeric data may have a view that represents the data as a histogram and a view that presents the data as a table. The model may be edited by changing the values in the table or by lengthening or shortening the bars in the histogram. I discuss this in more detail in Chapter 18, where I explain how you can use the Observer pattern to implement the MVC framework.

To find the best presentation of information, you need to know the users' background and how they use the system. When you are deciding how to present information, you should bear the following questions in mind:

1. Is the user interested in precise information or in the relationships between data values?

2. How quickly do the information values change? Should the change in a value be indicated immediately to the user?

Figure 16.5
Information
presentation

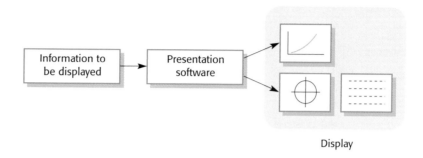

Display

Figure 16.6
The MVC model of
user interaction

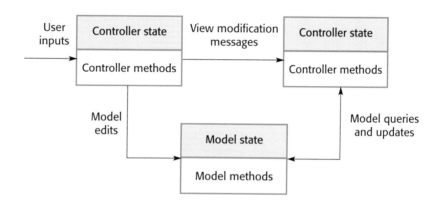

3. Must the user take some action in response to a change in information?

4. Does the user need to interact with the displayed information via a direct manipulation interface?

5. Is the information to be displayed textual or numeric? Are relative values of information items important?

You should not assume that using graphics makes your display more interesting. Graphics take up valuable screen space (a major issue with portable devices) and can take a long time to download if the user is working over a slow, dial-up connection.

Information that does not change during a session may be presented either graphically or as text depending on the application. Textual presentation takes up less screen space but cannot be read at a glance. You should distinguish information that does not change from dynamic information by using a different presentation style. For example, you could present all static information in a particular font or colour, or you could associate a 'static information' icon with it.

You should use text to present information when precise information is required and the information changes relatively slowly. If the data changes quickly or if the

Figure 16.7
Alternative
information
presentations

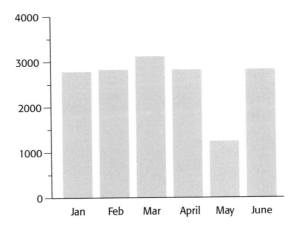

relationships between data rather than the precise data values are significant, then you should present the information graphically.

For example, consider a system that records and summarises the sales figures for a company on a monthly basis. Figure 16.7 illustrates how the same information can be presented as text or in a graphical form. Managers studying sales figures are usually more interested in trends or anomalous figures rather than precise values. Graphical presentation of this information, as a histogram, makes the anomalous figures in March and May stand out from the others. Figure 16.7 also illustrates how textual presentation takes less space than a graphical representation of the same information.

In control rooms or instrument panels such as those on a car dashboard, the information that is to be presented represents the state of some other system (e.g., the altitude of an aircraft) and is changing all the time. A constantly changing digital display can be confusing and irritating as readers can't read and assimilate the information before it changes. Such dynamically varying numeric information is therefore best presented graphically using an analogue representation. The graphical display can be supplemented if necessary with a precise digital display. Different ways of presenting dynamic numeric information are shown in Figure 16.8.

Continuous analogue displays give the viewer some sense of relative value. In Figure 16.9, the values of temperature and pressure are approximately the same. However, the graphical display shows that temperature is close to its maximum value whereas pressure has not reached 25% of its maximum. With only a digital value, the viewer must know the maximum values and mentally compute the relative state of the reading. The extra thinking time required can lead to human errors in stressful situations when problems occur and operator displays may be showing abnormal readings.

Figure 16.8 Methods of presenting dynamically varying numeric information

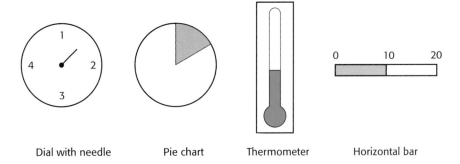

Dial with needle   Pie chart   Thermometer   Horizontal bar

Figure 16.9 Graphical information display showing relative values

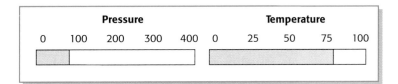

When large amounts of information have to be presented, abstract visualisations that link related data items may be used. This can expose relationships that are not obvious from the raw data. You should be aware of the possibilities of visualisation, especially when the system user interface must represent physical entities. Examples of data visualisations are:

1. Weather information, gathered from a number of sources, is shown as a weather map with isobars, weather fronts, and so on.

2. The state of a telephone network is displayed graphically as a linked set of nodes in a network management centre.

3. The state of a chemical plant is visualised by showing pressures and temperatures in a linked set of tanks and pipes.

4. A model of a molecule is displayed and manipulated in three dimensions using a virtual reality system.

5. A set of web pages is displayed as a hyperbolic tree (Lamping et al., 1995).

Shneiderman (Shneiderman, 1998) offers a good overview of approaches to visualisation as well as identifies classes of visualisation that may be used. These include visualising data using two- and three-dimensional presentations and as trees or networks. Most of these are concerned with the display of large amounts of information managed on a computer. However, the most common use of visualisation in user interfaces is to represent some physical structure such as the molecular structure of a new drug, the links in a telecommunications network and so on. Three-dimensional presentations that may use special virtual reality equipment are particularly effective in product visualisations. Direct manipulation of these visualisations is a very effective way to interact with the data.

In addition to the style of information presentation, you should think carefully about how colour is used in the interface. Colour can improve user interfaces by helping users understand and manage complexity. However, it is easy to misuse colour and to create user interfaces that are visually unattractive and error-prone. Shneiderman gives 14 key guidelines for the effective use of colour in user interfaces. The most important of these are:

1. *Limit the number of colours employed and be conservative how these are used*
    You should not use more than four or five separate colours in a window and no more than seven in a system interface. If you use too many, or if they are too bright, the display may be confusing. Some users may find masses of colour disturbing and visually tiring. User confusion is also possible if colours are used inconsistently.

2. *Use colour change to show a change in system status* If a display changes colour, this should mean that a significant event has occurred. Thus, in a fuel gauge, you could use a change of colour to indicate that fuel is running low. Colour highlighting is particularly important in complex displays where hundreds of distinct entities may be displayed.

3. *Use colour coding to support the task users are trying to perform* If they have to identify anomalous instances, highlight these instances; if similarities are also to be discovered, highlight these using a different colour.

4. *Use colour coding in a thoughtful and consistent way* If one part of a system displays error messages in red (say), all other parts should do likewise. Red should not be used for anything else. If it is, the user may interpret the red display as an error message.

5. *Be careful about colour pairings* Because of the physiology of the eye, people cannot focus on red and blue simultaneously. Eyestrain is a likely consequence of a red on blue display. Other colour combinations may also be visually disturbing or difficult to read.

In general, you should use colour for highlighting, but you should not associate meanings with particular colours. About 10% of men are colour-blind and may misinterpret the meaning. Human colour perceptions are different, and there are different conventions in different professions about the meaning of particular colours. Users with different backgrounds may unconsciously interpret the same colour in different ways. For example, to a driver, red usually means *danger*. However, to a chemist, red means *hot*.

As well as presenting application information, systems also communicate with users through messages that give information about errors and the system state. A user's first experience of a software system may be when the system presents an

Factor	Description
Context	Wherever possible, the messages generated by the system should reflect the current user context. As far as is possible, the system should be aware of what the user is doing and should generate messages that are relevant to their current activity.
Experience	As users become familiar with a system they become irritated by long, 'meaningful' messages. However, beginners find it difficult to understand short, terse statements of a problem. You should provide both types of message and allow the user to control message conciseness.
Skill level	Messages should be tailored to the users' skills as well as their experience. Messages for the different classes of users may be expressed in different ways depending on the terminology that is familiar to the reader.
Style	Messages should be positive rather than negative. They should use the active rather than the passive mode of address. They should never be insulting or try to be funny.
Culture	Wherever possible, the designer of messages should be familiar with the culture of the country where the system is sold. There are distinct cultural differences between Europe, Asia and America. A suitable message for one culture might be unacceptable in another.

error message. Inexperienced users may start work, make an initial error and immediately have to understand the resulting error message. This can be difficult enough for skilled software engineers. It is often impossible for inexperienced or casual system users. Factors that you should take into account when designing system messages are shown in Figure 16.10.

You should anticipate the background and experience of users when designing error messages. For example, say a system user is a nurse in an intensive-care ward in a hospital. Patient monitoring is carried out by a computer system. To view a patient's current state (heart rate, temperature, etc.), the nurse selects 'display' from a menu and inputs the patient's name in the box, as shown in Figure 16.11.

In this case, let's assume that the nurse has misspelled the patient's name and has typed 'MacDonald' instead of 'McDonald'. The system generates an error message. Error messages should always be polite, concise, consistent and constructive. They must not be abusive and should not have associated beeps or other noises that might embarrass the user. Wherever possible, the message should suggest how the error might be corrected. The error message should be linked to a context-sensitive online help system.

Figure 16.12 shows examples of good and bad error messages. The left-hand message is badly designed. It is negative (it accuses the user of making an error), it is not tailored to the user's skill and experience level, and it does not take context

Figure 16.11 An
input text box used
by a nurse

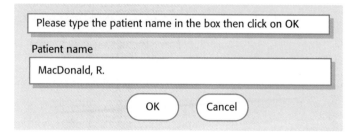

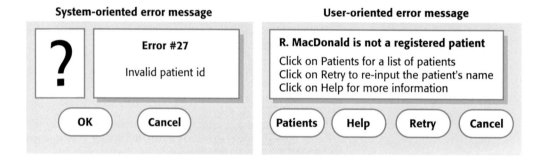

Figure 16.12 System
and user-oriented
error messages

information into account. It does not suggest how the situation might be rectified. It uses system-specific terms (patient id) rather than user-oriented language. The right-hand message is better. It is positive, implying that the problem is a system rather than a user problem. It identifies the problem in the nurse's terms and offers an easy way to correct the mistake by pressing a single button. The help system is available if required.

16.2 The UI design process

User interface (UI) design is an iterative process where users interact with designers and interface prototypes to decide on the features, organisation and the look and feel of the system user interface. Sometimes, the interface is separately prototyped in parallel with other software engineering activities. More commonly, especially where iterative development is used, the user interface design proceeds incrementally as the software is developed. In both cases, however, before you start programming, you should have developed and, ideally, tested some paper-based designs.

The overall UI design process is illustrated in Figure 16.13. There are three core activities in this process:

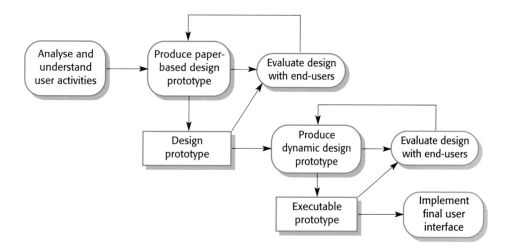

Figure 16.13 The UI design process

1. *User analysis* In the user analysis process, you develop an understanding of the tasks that users do, their working environment, the other systems that they use, how they interact with other people in their work and so on. For products with a diverse range of users, you have to try to develop this understanding through focus groups, trials with potential users and similar exercises.

2. *System prototyping* User interface design and development is an iterative process. Although users may talk about the facilities they need from an interface, it is very difficult for them to be specific until they see something tangible. Therefore, you have to develop prototype systems and expose them to users, who can then guide the evolution of the interface.

3. *Interface evaluation* Although you will obviously have discussions with users during the prototyping process, you should also have a more formalised evaluation activity where you collect information about the users' actual experience with the interface.

I focus on user analysis and interface evaluation in this section with only a brief discussion of specific user interface prototyping techniques. I cover more general issues in prototyping and prototyping techniques in Chapter 17.

The scheduling of UI design within the software process depends, to some extent, on other activities. As I discuss in Chapter 7, prototyping may be used as part of the requirements engineering process and, in this case, it makes sense to start the UI design process at that stage. In iterative processes, discussed in Chapter 17, UI design is integrated with the software development. Like the software itself, the UI may have to be refactored and redesigned during development.

Figure 16.14 A library
interaction scenario

> Jane is a religious studies student writing an essay on Indian architecture and how it has been influenced by religious practices. To help her understand this, she would like to access pictures of details on notable buildings but can't find anything in her local library. She approaches the subject librarian to discuss her needs and he suggests search terms that she might use. He also suggests libraries in New Delhi and London that might have this material, so he and Jane log on to the library catalogues and search using these terms. They find some source material and place a request for photocopies of the pictures with architectural details, to be posted directly to Jane.

16.3 User analysis

A critical UI design activity is the analyses of the user activities that are to be supported by the computer system. If you don't understand what users want to do with a system, then you have no realistic prospect of designing an effective user interface. To develop this understanding, you may use techniques such as task analysis, ethnographic studies, user interviews and observations or, commonly, a mixture of all of these.

A challenge for engineers involved in user analysis is to find a way to describe user analyses so that they communicate the essence of the tasks to other designers and to the users themselves. Notations such as UML sequence charts may be able to describe user interactions and are ideal for communicating with software engineers. However, other users may think of these charts as too technical and will not try to understand them. Because it is very important to engage users in the design process, you therefore usually have to develop natural language scenarios to describe user activities.

Figure 16.14 is an example of a natural language scenario that might have been developed during the specification and design process for the LIBSYS system. It describes a situation where LIBSYS does not exist and where a student needs to retrieve information from another library. From this scenario, the designer can see a number of requirements:

1. Users might not be aware of appropriate search terms. They may need to access ways of helping them choose search terms.

2. Users have to be able to select collections to search.

3. Users need to be able to carry out searches and request copies of relevant material.

You should not expect user analysis to generate very specific user interface requirements. Normally, the analysis helps you understand the needs and concerns of the

Figure 16.15
Hierarchical task
analysis

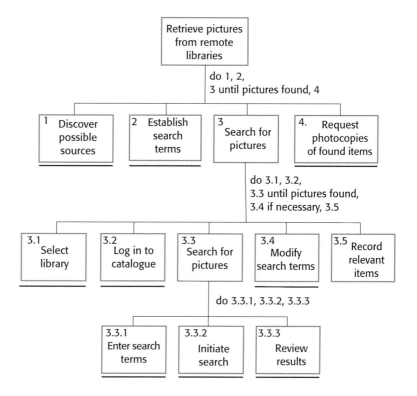

system users. As you become more aware of how they work, their concerns and their constraints, your design can take these into account. This means that your initial designs (which you will refine through prototyping anyway) are more likely to be acceptable to users and so convince them to become engaged in the process of design refinement.

16.3.1 Analysis techniques

As I suggested in the previous section, there are three basis user analysis techniques: task analysis, interviewing and questionnaires, and ethnography. Task analysis and interviewing focus on the individual and the individual's work, whereas ethnography takes a broader perspective and looks at how people interact with each other, how they arrange their working environment and how they cooperate to solve problems.

There are various forms of task analysis (Diaper, 1989), but the most commonly used is Hierarchical Task Analysis (HTA). HTA was originally developed to help with writing user manuals, but it can also be used to identify what users do to achieve some goal. In HTA, a high-level task is broken down into subtasks, and plans are identified that specify what might happen in a specific situation. Starting with a user goal, you draw a hierarchy showing what has to be done to achieve that goal. Figure

16.15 illustrates this approach using the library scenario introduced in Figure 16.14. In the HTA notation, a line under a box normally indicates that it will not be decomposed into more detailed subtasks.

The advantage of HTA over natural language scenarios is that it forces you to consider each of the tasks and to decide whether these should be decomposed. With natural language scenarios, it is easy to miss important tasks. Scenarios also become long and boring to read if you want to add a lot of detail to them.

The problem with this approach to describing user tasks is that it is best suited to tasks that are sequential processes. The notation becomes awkward when you try to model tasks that involve interleaved or concurrent activities or that involve a very large number of subtasks. Furthermore, HTA does not record why tasks are done in a particular way or constraints on the user processes. You can get a partial view of user activities from HTA, but you need additional information to develop a fuller understanding of the UI design requirements.

Normally, you collect information for HTA through observing and interviewing users. In this interviewing process, you can collect some of this additional information and record it alongside the task analyses. When interviewing to discover what users actually do, you should design interviews so that users can provide any information that they (rather than you) feel is relevant. This means you should not stick rigidly to prepared list of questions. Rather, your questions should be open-ended and should encourage users to tell you why they do things as well as what they actually do.

Interviewing, of course, is not just a way of gathering information for task analysis—it is a general information-gathering technique. You may decide to supplement individual interviews with group interviews or focus groups. The advantage of using focus groups is that users stimulate each other to provide information and may end up discussing different ways that they have developed of using systems.

Task analysis focuses on how individuals work but, of course, most work is actually cooperative. People work together to achieve a goal, and users find it difficult to discuss how this cooperation actually takes place. Therefore, direct observation of how users work and use computer-based systems is an important additional technique of user analysis.

One approach to direct observation that has been used in a wide variety of settings is ethnography (Suchman, 1983; Hughes, et al., 1997; Crabtree, 2003). I discussed ethnography in Chapter 7 as a technique that supports requirements engineering. Ethnographers closely observe how people work, how they interact with others and how features in the workplace are used to support their work. The advantage of ethnography is that the ethnographer can observe intuitive actions and informal collaborations that can then spark further discussions about the work.

As an example of how ethnography can influence user interface design, Figure 16.16 is a fragment from a report of an ethnographic study on air traffic controllers in which I was involved (Bentley, et al., 1992). We were interested in the interface design for a more automated ATC system and we learned two important things from these observations:

Figure 16.16 A report
of observations of air
traffic control

Air traffic control involves a number of control 'suites' where the suites
controlling adjacent sectors of airspace are physically located next to each
other. Flights in a sector are represented by paper strips that are fitted into
wooden racks in an order that reflects their position in the sector. If there
are not enough slots in the rack (i.e. when the airspace is very busy),
controllers spread the strips out on the desk in front of the rack. When we
were observing controllers, we noticed that controllers regularly glanced at
the strip racks in the adjacent sector. We pointed this out to them and
asked them why they did this. They replied that, when the adjacent
controller has strips on his or her desk, then this means that a lot of flights
will be entering their sector. They therefore tried to increase the speed of
aircraft in the sector to 'clear space' for the incoming aircraft.

1. Controllers had to be able to see all flights in a sector (this was why they spread strips out on the desk). Therefore, we should avoid using scrolling displays where flights disappeared off the top or bottom of the display.

2. The interface should have some way of telling controllers how many flights are in adjacent sectors so that controllers can plan their work load.

Checking adjacent sectors was an automatic controller action and it is very likely that they would not have mentioned this in discussions of the ATC process. It was only through direct observation that we discovered these important requirements.

None of these user analysis techniques, on their own, give you a complete picture of what users actually do. They are complementary approaches that you should use together to help you understand what users do and get insights into what might be an appropriate user interface design.

16.4 User interface prototyping

Because of the dynamic nature of user interfaces, textual descriptions and diagrams are not good enough for expressing user interface requirements. Evolutionary or exploratory prototyping with end-user involvement is the only practical way to design and develop graphical user interfaces for software systems. Involving the user in the design and development process is an essential aspect of *user-centred design* (Norman and Draper, 1986), a design philosophy for interactive systems.

The aim of prototyping is to allow users to gain direct experience with the interface. Most of us find it difficult to think abstractly about a user interface and to explain exactly what we want. However, when we are presented with examples, it is easy to identify the characteristics that we like and dislike.

Ideally, when you are prototyping a user interface, you should adopt a two-stage prototyping process:

1. Very early in the process, you should develop paper prototypes—mock-ups of screen designs—and walk through these with end-users.

2. You then refine your design and develop increasingly sophisticated automated prototypes, then make them available to users for testing and activity simulation.

Paper prototyping is a cheap and surprisingly effective approach to prototype development (Snyder, 2003). You don't need to develop any executable software and the designs don't have to be drawn to professional standards. You can draw paper versions of the system screens that users interact with and design a set of scenarios describing how the system might be used. As a scenario progresses, you sketch the information that would be displayed and the options available to users.

You then work through these scenarios with users to simulate how the system might be used. This is an effective way to get users' initial reactions to an interface design, the information they need from the system and how they would normally interact with the system.

Alternatively, you can use a storyboarding technique to present the interface design. A *storyboard* is a series of sketches that illustrate a sequence of interactions. This is less hands-on but can be more convenient when presenting the interface proposals to groups rather than individuals.

After initial experiments with a paper prototype, you should implement a software prototype of the interface design. The problem, of course, is that you need to have some system functionality with which the users can interact. If you are prototyping the UI very early in the system development process, this may not be available. To get around this problem, you can use 'Wizard of Oz' prototyping (see the web page for an explanation if you haven't seen the film). In this approach, users interact with what appears to be a computer system, but their inputs are actually channelled to a hidden person who simulates the system's responses. They can do this directly or by using some other system to compute the required responses. In this case, you don't need to have any executable software apart from the proposed user interface.

Further prototyping experiments may then be carried out using either an evolutionary or a throw-away approach. I discuss these approaches to prototyping in Chapter 17, where I also describe a range of techniques that can be used for prototyping and rapid application development. There are three approaches that you can use for user interface prototyping:

1. *Script-driven approach* If you simply need to explore ideas with users, you can use a script-driven approach such as you'd find in Macromedia Director. In this approach, you create screens with visual elements, such as buttons and menus, and associate a script with these elements. When the user interacts with these

screens, the script is executed and the next screen is presented, showing them the results of their actions. There is no application logic involved.

2. *Visual programming languages* Visual programming languages, such as Visual Basic, incorporate a powerful development environment, access to a range of reusable objects and a user-interface development system that allows interfaces to be created quickly, with components and scripts associated with interface objects. I describe visual development systems in Chapter 17.

3. *Internet-based prototyping* These solutions, based on web browsers and languages such as Java, offer a ready-made user interface. You add functionality by associating segments of Java programs with the information to be displayed. These segments (called applets) are executed automatically when the page is loaded into the browser. This approach is a fast way to develop user interface prototypes, but there are inherent restrictions imposed by the browser and the Java security model.

Prototyping is obviously closely associated with interface evaluation. Formal evaluation is unlikely to be cost-effective for early prototypes, so what you are trying to achieve at this stage is a 'formative evaluation' where you look for ways in which the interface can be improved. As the prototype becomes more complete, you can use systematic evaluation techniques, as discussed in the following section.

16.5 Interface evaluation

Interface evaluation is the process of assessing the usability of an interface and checking that it meets user requirements. Therefore, it should be part of the normal verification and validation process for software systems. Neilsen (Neilsen, 1993) includes a good chapter on this topic in his book on usability engineering.

Ideally, an evaluation should be conducted against a usability specification based on usability attributes, as shown in Figure 16.17. Metrics for these usability attributes can be devised. For example, in a learnability specification, you might state that an operator who is familiar with the work supported should be able to use 80% of the system functionality after a three-hour training session. However, it is more common to specify usability (if it is specified at all) qualitatively rather than using metrics. You therefore usually have to use your judgement and experience in interface evaluation.

Systematic evaluation of a user interface design can be an expensive process involving cognitive scientists and graphics designers. You may have to design and carry out a statistically significant number of experiments with typical users. You may need to use specially constructed laboratories fitted with monitoring equipment. A user interface evaluation of this kind is economically unrealistic for systems developed by small organisations with limited resources.

Figure 16.17
Usability attributes

Attribute	Description
Learnability	How long does it take a new user to become productive with the system?
Speed of operation	How well does the system response match the user's work practice?
Robustness	How tolerant is the system of user error?
Recoverability	How good is the system at recovering from user errors?
Adaptability	How closely is the system tied to a single model of work?

There are a number of simpler, less expensive techniques of user interface evaluation that can identify particular user interface design deficiencies:

1. Questionnaires that collect information about what users thought of the interface;

2. Observation of users at work with the system and 'thinking aloud' about how they are trying to use the system to accomplish some task;

3. Video 'snapshots' of typical system use;

4. The inclusion in the software of code which collects information about the most-used facilities and the most common errors.

Surveying users by questionnaire is a relatively cheap way to evaluate an interface. The questions should be precise rather than general. It is no use asking questions such as 'Please comment on the usability of the interface' as the responses will probably vary so much that you won't see any common trend. Rather, specific questions such as 'Please rate the understandability of the error messages on a scale from 1 to 5. A rating of 1 means very clear and 5 means incomprehensible' are better. They are both easier to answer and more likely to provide useful information to improve the interface.

Users should be asked to rate their own experience and background when filling in the questionnaire. This allows the designer to find out whether users from any particular background have problems with the interface. Questionnaires can even be used before any executable system is available if a paper mock-up of the interface is constructed and evaluated.

Observation-based evaluation simply involves watching users as they use a system, looking at the facilities used, the errors made and so on. This can be supplemented by 'think aloud' sessions where users talk about what they are trying to achieve, how they understand the system and how they are trying to use the system to accomplish their objectives.

Relatively low-cost video equipment means that you can record user sessions for later analysis. Complete video analysis is expensive and requires a specially equipped evaluation suite with several cameras focused on the user and on the screen. However, video recording of selected user operations can be helpful in detecting problems. Other evaluation methods must be used to find out which operations cause user difficulties.

Analysis of recordings allows the designer to find out whether the interface requires too much hand movement (a problem with some systems is that users must regularly move their hand from keyboard to mouse) and to see whether unnatural eye movements are necessary. An interface that requires many shifts of focus may mean that the user makes more errors and misses parts of the display.

Instrumenting code to collect usage statistics allows interfaces to be improved in a number of ways. The most common operations can be detected. The interface can be reorganised so that these are the fastest to select. For example, if pop-up or pull-down menus are used, the most frequent operations should be at the top of the

KEY POINTS

- User interface principles covering user familiarity, consistency, minimal surprise, recoverability, user guidance and user diversity help guide the design of user interfaces.

- Styles of interaction with a software system include direct manipulation, menu systems, form fill-in, command languages and natural language.

- Graphical information display should be used when it is intended to present trends and approximate values. Digital display should only be used when precision is required.

- Colour should be used sparingly and consistently in user interfaces. Designers should take account of the fact that a significant number of people are colour-blind.

- The user interface design process includes sub-processes concerned with user analysis, interface prototyping and interface evaluation.

- The aim of user analysis is to sensitise designers to the ways in which users actually work. You should use different techniques—task analysis, interviewing and observation—during user analysis.

- User interface prototype development should be a staged process with early prototypes based on paper versions of the interface that, after initial evaluation and feedback, are used as a basis for automated prototypes.

- The goals of user interface evaluation are to obtain feedback on how a UI design can be improved and to assess whether an interface meets its usability requirements.

menu and destructive operations towards the bottom. Code instrumentation also allows error-prone commands to be detected and modified.

Finally, it is easy to give users a 'gripe' command that they can use to pass messages to the tool designer. This makes users feel that their views are being considered. The interface designer and other engineers can gain rapid feedback about individual problems.

None of these relatively simple approaches to user interface evaluation is foolproof and they are unlikely to detect all user interface problems. However, the techniques can be used with a group of volunteers before a system is released without a large outlay of resources. Many of the worst problems of the user interface design can then be discovered and corrected.

FURTHER READING

Human-Computer Interaction, 3rd ed. A good general text whose strengths are a focus on design issues and cooperative work. (A. Dix, et al., 2004, Prentice Hall.)

Interaction Design. The focus of this book is on designing interaction with computer-based systems. It presents much of the same material as *Human-Computer Interaction* but in a quite different way. Both books are well written and worth reading. (J. Preece, et al., 2002, John Wiley & Sons.)

'Usability Engineering'. This special issue of *IEEE Software* includes a number of articles on usability that have been written specifically for readers with a software engineering background. (*IEEE Software*, 18(1), January 2001.)

EXERCISES

16.1 I suggested in Section 16.1 that the objects manipulated by users should be drawn from their domain rather than from a computer domain. Suggest appropriate objects for the following users and systems.

■ A warehouse assistant using an automated parts catalogue

■ An airline pilot using an aircraft safety monitoring system

■ A manager manipulating a financial database

■ A policeman using a patrol car control system

16.2 Suggest situations where it is unwise or impossible to provide a consistent user interface.

16.3 What factors have to be taken into account in the design of a menu-based interface for 'walk-up' systems such as bank ATMs? Write a critical commentary on the interface of an ATM that you use.

16.4 Suggest ways in which the user interface to an e-commerce system such as an online bookstore or music retailer might be adapted for users who have a visual impairment or problems with muscular control.

16.5 Discuss the advantages of graphical information display and suggest four applications where it would be more appropriate to use graphical rather than digital displays of numeric information.

16.6 What are the guidelines that should be followed when using colour in a user interface? Suggest how colour might be used more effectively in the interface of an application system that you use.

16.7 Consider the error messages produced by MS-Windows, Linux, Mac OS or some other operating system. Suggest how these might be improved.

16.8 Write possible interaction scenarios for the following systems:

■ Using a web-based theatre booking service to order theatre tickets and pay for them by credit card

■ Ordering the same tickets using an interface on a cell phone

■ Using a CASE toolset to create an object model of a software system (see Chapters 8 and 14) and generating code automatically from that model.

16.9 Under what circumstances could you use 'Wizard of Oz' prototyping? For what type of systems is this approach unsuitable?

16.10 Design a questionnaire to gather information about the user interface of some tool (such as a word processor) with which you are familiar. If possible, distribute this questionnaire to a number of users and try to evaluate the results. What do these tell you about the user interface design?

16.11 Discuss whether it is ethical to instrument software to monitor its use without telling end-users that their work is being monitored.

16.12 What ethical issues might user interface designers face when trying to reconcile the needs of end-users of a system with the needs of the organisation that is paying for the system to be developed.

PART 4 DEVELOPMENT

When software engineering was first established as a discipline, the development process for most systems was a process of writing a program based on a design specification. Imperative programming languages such as C, FORTRAN or Ada were used. In software engineering texts, the chapters on software development mostly focused on good programming practice.

Now there are many different ways to develop software. These include original programming in languages such as C++ or Java, scripting, database programming, program generation from CASE tools, and reuse-based software engineering. Furthermore, the fact that there is no real distinction between development and maintenance is finally being recognised, and we are starting to think of development as the first stage in a process of program evolution. To reflect these developments, I have included this new part in the book, focusing on development techniques. There are five chapters in this part:

1. Chapter 17 is a new chapter describing techniques for rapid software development. In today's business environment means companies need their software to be delivered quickly so that they can respond to new challenges and opportunities. In this chapter, I discuss agile methods of development, with a particular focus on extreme programming. I also describe environments for rapid application development and the appropriate use of system prototyping.

2. The topic of Chapters 18 and 19 is reuse-based software engineering. Over the past few years, software reuse has become more and more common and reuse-based development is now a mainstream approach to software engineering. Chapter 18 presents an overview of software reuse and development with reuse. Chapter 19 focuses on component-based software engineering, including component composition and the CBSE process.

3. Chapter 20 continues the discussion of critical systems that runs through the book. I cover a range of development approaches for achieving system dependability, including fault avoidance and fault tolerance, and I discuss how programming constructs and techniques may be used to achieve dependability. In the final part of this chapter, I return to the topic of software architectures and describe architectural approaches to fault tolerance.

4. Chapter 21 is concerned with software evolution. Change is inevitable for all software systems and, rather than consider the change process as a separate activity, I think it makes sense to consider it as a continuation of the initial software development. In this chapter, I discuss the inevitability of evolution, software maintenance, evolution processes and decision making for legacy systems evolution.

17
Rapid software development

Objectives

The objective of this chapter is to describe a number of approaches to software development that are geared to rapid software delivery. When you have read the chapter, you will:

■ understand how an iterative, incremental software development approach leads to faster delivery of more useful software;

■ understand the differences between agile development methods and software development methods that rely on documented specifications and designs;

■ know the principles, practices and some of the limitations of extreme programming;

■ understand how prototyping can be used to help resolve requirements and design uncertainties when a specification-based approach to development has to be used.

Contents

Businesses now operate in a global, rapidly changing environment. They have to respond to new opportunities and markets, changing economic conditions and the emergence of competing products and services. Software is part of almost all business operations so it is essential that new software is developed quickly to take advantage of new opportunities and to respond to competitive pressure. Rapid development and delivery is therefore now often the most critical requirement for software systems. In fact, many businesses are willing to trade-off software quality and compromise on requirements against rapid software delivery.

Because these businesses are operating in a changing environment, it is often practically impossible to derive a complete set of stable software requirements. The requirements that are proposed inevitably change because customers find it impossible to predict how a system will affect working practices, how it will interact with other systems and what user operations should be automated. It may be only after a system has been delivered and users gain experience with it that the real requirements become clear.

Software development processes that are based on completely specifying the requirements then designing, building and testing the system are not geared to rapid software development. As the requirements change or as requirements problems are discovered, the system design or implementation has to be reworked and retested. As a consequence, a conventional waterfall or specification-based process is usually prolonged and the final software is delivered to the customer long after it was originally specified.

In a fast-moving business environment, this can cause real problems. By the time the software is available for use, the original reason for its procurement may have changed so radically that the software is effectively useless. Therefore, for business systems in particular, development processes that focus on rapid software development and delivery are essential.

Rapid software development processes are designed to produce useful software quickly. Generally, they are iterative processes where specification, design, development and testing are interleaved. The software is not developed and deployed in its entirety but in a series of increments, with each increment including new system functionality. Although there are many approaches to rapid software development, they share some fundamental characteristics:

1. The processes of specification, design and implementation are concurrent. There is no detailed system specification, and design documentation is minimised or generated automatically by the programming environment used to implement the system. The user requirements document defines only the most important characteristics of the system.

2. The system is developed in a series of increments. End-users and other system stakeholders are involved in specifying and evaluating each increment. They may propose changes to the software and new requirements that should be implemented in a later increment of the system.

3. System user interfaces are often developed using an interactive development system that allows the interface design to be quickly created by drawing and placing icons on the interface. The system may then generate a web-based interface for a browser or an interface for a specific platform such as Microsoft Windows.

Incremental development, introduced in Chapter 4, involves producing and delivering the software in increments rather than in a single package. Each process iteration produces a new software increment. The two main advantages to adopting an incremental approach to software development are:

1. *Accelerated delivery of customer services* Early increments of the system can deliver high-priority functionality so that customers can get value from the system early in its development. Customers can see their requirements in practice and specify changes to be incorporated in later releases of the system.

2. *User engagement with the system* Users of the system have to be involved in the incremental development process because they have to provide feedback to the development team on delivered increments. Their involvement does not just mean that the system is more likely to meet their requirements; it also means that the system end-users have made a commitment to it and are likely to want to make it work.

A general process model for incremental development is illustrated in Figure 17.1. Notice that the early stages of this process focus on architectural design. If you do not consider the architecture at the beginning of the process, the overall structure of the system is likely to be unstable and to degrade as new increments are released.

Incremental software development, in my view, is a far better approach to development for most business, e-commerce and personal systems because it reflects the fundamental way that we all tend to solve problems. We rarely work out a complete problem solution in advance but move towards a solution in a series of steps, backtracking when we realise that we have made a mistake.

However, there can be real difficulties with this approach, particularly in large companies with fairly rigid procedures and in organisations where software development is usually outsourced to an external contractor. The major difficulties with iterative development and incremental delivery are:

1. *Management problems* Software management structures for large systems are set up to deal with a software process model that generates regular deliverables to assess progress. Incrementally developed systems change so quickly that it is not cost-effective to produce lots of system documentation. Furthermore, incremental development may sometimes require unfamiliar technologies to be used to ensure the most rapid delivery of the software. Managers may find it difficult to use existing staff in incremental development processes because they lack these skills.

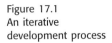

Figure 17.1
An iterative
development process

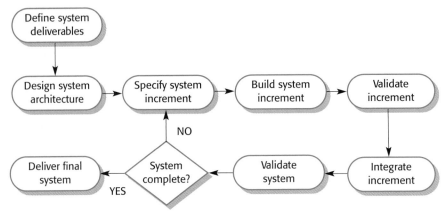

2. *Contractual problems* The normal contractual model between a customer and a software developer is based around a system specification. When there is no such specification, it may be difficult to design a contract for the system development. Customers may be unhappy with a contract that simply pays developers for the time spent on the project, as this can lead to function creep and budget overruns; developers are unlikely to accept a fixed-price contract because they cannot control the changes requested by the end-users.

3. *Validation problems* In a specification-based process, verification and validation are geared towards demonstrating that the system meets its specification. An independent V & V team can start work as soon as the specification is available and can prepare tests in parallel with the system implementation. Iterative development processes try to minimise documentation and interleave specification and development. Hence, independent validation of incrementally developed systems is difficult.

4. *Maintenance problems* Continual change tends to corrupt the structure of any software system. This means that anyone apart from the original developers may find the software difficult to understand. One way to reduce this problem is to use refactoring, where software structures are continually improved during the development process. I discuss this in Section 17.2, where I cover extreme programming. Furthermore, if specialised technology, such as RAD environments (discussed in Section 17.3), is used to support rapid development, the RAD technology may become obsolete. Therefore, finding people who have the required knowledge to maintain the system may be difficult.

Of course, there are some types of systems where incremental development and delivery is not the best approach. These are very large systems where development may involve teams working in different locations, some embedded systems where the software depends on hardware development and some critical systems where all the requirements must be analysed to check for interactions that may compromise the safety or security of the system.

Figure 17.2
Incremental
development and
prototyping

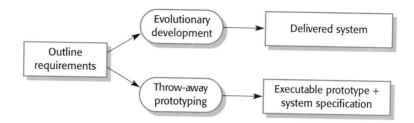

These systems, of course, suffer from the same problems of uncertain and changing requirements. Therefore, to address these problems and to get some of the benefits of incremental development, a hybrid process may be used where a system prototype is developed iteratively and used as a platform for experiments with the system requirements and design. With the experience gained from the prototype, you can have increased confidence that the requirements meet the real needs of the system stakeholders.

I use the term *prototyping* here to mean an iterative process of developing an experimental system that is *not* intended for deployment by the customer. A system prototype is developed to help the software developer and the customer understand what to implement. However, the term *evolutionary prototyping* is sometimes used as a synonym for incremental software development. The prototype is not discarded but evolves to meet the customer's requirements.

Figure 17.2 shows that incremental development and prototyping have different objectives:

1. The objective of incremental development is to deliver a working system to end-users. This means that you should normally start with the user requirements that are best understood and that have the highest priority. Lower-priority and vaguer requirements are implemented when and if the users demand them.

2. The objective of throw-away prototyping is to validate or derive the system requirements. You should start with requirements that are not well understood because you need to find out more about them. Requirements that are straightforward may never need to be prototyped.

Another important distinction between these approaches is in the management of the quality of the systems. Throw-away prototypes have a very short lifetime. It must be possible to change them rapidly during development, but long-term maintainability is not required. Poor performance and reliability may be acceptable in a throw-away prototype so long as it helps everyone understand the requirements.

By contrast, incremental development systems where early versions evolve into the final system should be developed to the same organisational quality standards as any other software. They should have a robust structure so that they are maintainable for many years. They should be reliable and efficient, and they should conform to appropriate organisational standards.

Agile methods

In the 1980s and early 1990s, there was a widespread view that the best way to achieve better software was through careful project planning, formalised quality assurance, the use of analysis and design methods supported by CASE tools, and controlled and rigorous software development processes. This view came, essentially, from the software engineering community concerned with developing large, long-lived software systems that were usually made up of a large number of individual programs.

Some or all of these programs were often critical systems, as discussed in Chapter 3. This software was developed by large teams who sometimes worked for different companies. They were often geographically dispersed and worked on the software for long periods of time. An example of this type of software is the control systems for a modern aircraft, which might take up to 10 years from initial specification to deployment. These approaches, some of which I cover in this book, involve a significant overhead in planning, designing and documenting the system. This overhead is justified when the work of multiple development teams has to be coordinated, when the system is a critical system and when many different people will be involved in maintaining the software over its lifetime.

However, when this heavyweight, plan-based development approach was applied to small and medium-sized business systems, the overhead involved was so large that it sometimes dominated the software development process. More time was spent on how the system should be developed than on program development and testing. As the system requirements changed, rework was essential and, in principle at least, the specification and design had to change with the program.

Dissatisfaction with these heavyweight approaches led a number of software developers in the 1990s to propose new agile methods. These allowed the development team to focus on the software itself rather than on its design and documentation. Agile methods universally rely on an iterative approach to software specification, development and delivery, and were designed primarily to support business application development where the system requirements usually changed rapidly during the development process. They are intended to deliver working software quickly to customers, who can then propose new and changed requirements to be included in later iterations of the system.

Probably the best-known agile method is extreme programming (Beck, 1999; Beck, 2000), which I describe later in this chapter. However, other agile approaches include Scrum (Schwaber and Beedle, 2001), Crystal (Cockburn, 2001), Adaptive Software Development (Highsmith, 2000), DSDM (Stapleton, 1997) and Feature Driven Development (Palmer and Felsing, 2002). The success of these methods has led to some integration with more traditional development methods based on system modelling, resulting in the notion of agile modelling (Ambler and Jeffries, 2002) and agile instantiations of the Rational Unified Process (Larman, 2002).

Although these agile methods are all based around the notion of incremental development and delivery, they propose different processes to achieve this. However, they

Figure 17.3 The principles of agile methods

Principle	Description
Customer involvement	Customers should be closely involved throughout the development process. Their role is provide and prioritise new system requirements and to evaluate the iterations of the system.
Incremental delivery	The software is developed in increments with the customer specifying the requirements to be included in each increment.
People not process	The skills of the development team should be recognised and exploited. Team members should be left to develop their own ways of working without prescriptive processes.
Embrace change	Expect the system requirements to change, so design the system to accommodate these changes.
Maintain simplicity	Focus on simplicity in both the software being developed and in the development process. Wherever possible, actively work to eliminate complexity from the system.

share a set of principles and therefore have much in common. These principles are shown in Figure 17.3.

Supporters of agile methods have been evangelical in promoting their use and have tended to overlook their shortcomings. This has prompted an equally extreme response, which, in my view, exaggerates the problems with this approach (Stephens and Rosenberg, 2003). More reasoned critics such as DeMarco and Boehm (DeMarco and Boehm, 2002) highlight both the advantages and disadvantages of agile methods. They propose a hybrid approach where agile methods incorporate some techniques from plan-based development may be the best way forward.

In practice, however, the principles underlying agile methods are sometimes difficult to realise:

1. While the idea of customer involvement in the development process is an attractive one, its success depends on having a customer who is willing and able to spend time with the development team and who can represent all system stakeholders. Frequently, the customer representatives are subject to other pressures and cannot take full part in the software development.

2. Individual team members may not have suitable personalities for the intense involvement that is typical of agile methods. They may therefore not interact well with other team members.

3. Prioritising changes can be extremely difficult, especially in systems where there are many stakeholders. Typically, each stakeholder gives different priorities to different changes.

4. Maintaining simplicity requires extra work. Under pressure from delivery schedules, the team members may not have time to carry out desirable system simplifications.

Another, nontechnical problem, which is a general problem with incremental development and delivery, occurs when the system customer uses an outside organisation for system development. As I discussed in Chapter 6, the software requirements document is usually part of the contract between the customer and the supplier. Because incremental specification is inherent in agile methods, writing contracts for this type of development may be difficult.

Consequently, agile methods have to rely on contracts where the customer pays for the time required for system development rather than the development of a specific set of requirements. So long as all goes well, this benefits both the customer and the developer. However, if problems arise there may be difficult disputes over who is to blame and who should pay for the extra time and resources required to resolve the problems.

All methods have limits, and agile methods are only suitable for some types of system development. In my view, they are best suited to the development of small or medium-sized business systems and personal computer products. They are not well suited to large-scale systems development with the development teams in different places and where there may be complex interactions with other hardware and software systems. Nor should agile methods be used for critical systems development where a detailed analysis of all of the system requirements is necessary to understand their safety or security implications.

17.2 Extreme programming

Extreme programming (XP) is perhaps the best known and most widely used of the agile methods. The name was coined by Beck (Beck, 2000) because the approach was developed by pushing recognised good practice, such as iterative development, and customer involvement to 'extreme' levels.

In extreme programming, all requirements are expressed as scenarios (called user stories), which are implemented directly as a series of tasks. Programmers work in pairs and develop tests for each task before writing the code. All tests must be successfully executed when new code is integrated into the system. There is a short time gap between releases of the system. Figure 17.4 illustrates the XP process to produce an increment of the system that is being developed.

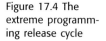
Figure 17.4 The extreme programming release cycle

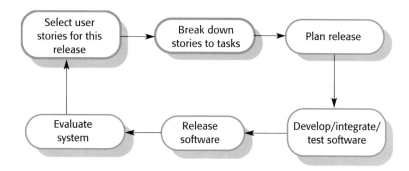

Extreme programming involves a number of practices, summarised in Figure 17.5, that fit into the principles of agile methods:

1. Incremental development is supported through small, frequent releases of the system and by an approach to requirements description based on customer stories or scenarios that can be the basis for process planning.

2. Customer involvement is supported through the full-time engagement of the customer in the development team. The customer representative takes part in the development and is responsible for defining acceptance tests for the system.

3. People, not process, are supported through pair programming, collective ownership of the system code, and a sustainable development process that does not involve excessively long working hours.

4. Change is supported through regular system releases, test-first development and continuous integration.

5. Maintaining simplicity is supported through constant refactoring to improve code quality and using simple designs that do not anticipate future changes to the system.

In an XP process, customers are intimately involved in specifying and prioritising system requirements. The requirements are not specified as lists of required system functions. Rather, the system customer is part of the development team and discusses scenarios with other team members. Together, they develop a 'story card' that encapsulates the customer needs. The development team then aims to implement that scenario in a future release of the software. An example of a story card for the LIBSYS system, based on a scenario in Chapter 6, is illustrated in Figure 17.6.

Once the story cards have been developed, the development team breaks these down into tasks and estimates the effort and resources required for implementation. The customer then prioritises the stories for implementation, choosing those stories that can be used immediately to deliver useful business support. Of course, as require-

Figure 17.5 Extreme
programming
practices

Principle or practice	Description
Incremental planning	Requirements are recorded on Story Cards and the Stories to be included in a release are determined by the time available and their relative priority. The developers break these Stories into development 'Tasks'. See Figure 17.6 and Figure 17.7.
Small releases	The minimal useful set of functionality that provides business value is developed first. Releases of the system are frequent and incrementally add functionality to the first release.
Simple design	Enough design is carried out to meet the current requirements and no more.
Test-first development	An automated unit test framework is used to write tests for a new piece of functionality before that functionality itself is implemented.
Refactoring	All developers are expected to refactor the code continuously as soon as possible code improvements are found. This keeps the code simple and maintainable.
Pair programming	Developers work in pairs, checking each other's work and providing the support to always do a good job.
Collective ownership	The pairs of developers work on all areas of the system, so that no islands of expertise develop and all the developers own all the code. Anyone can change anything.
Continuous integration	As soon as work on a task is complete it is integrated into the whole system. After any such integration, all the unit tests in the system must pass.
Sustainable pace	Large amounts of overtime are not considered acceptable as the net effect is often to reduce code quality and medium-term productivity
On-site customer	A representative of the end-user of the system (the Customer) should be available full time for the use of the XP team. In an extreme programming process, the customer is a member of the development team and is responsible for bringing system requirements to the team for implementation.

ments change, the unimplemented stories change or may be discarded. If changes are required for a system that has already been delivered, new story cards are developed and, again, the customer decides whether these changes should have priority over new functionality.

Figure 17.6 Story
card for document
downloading

Downloading and printing an article
First, you select the article that you want from a displayed list. You then have to tell the system how you will pay for it—this can either be through a subscription, though a company account or by credit card.
After this, you get a copyright form from the system to fill in. When you have submitted this, the article you want is downloaded onto your computer.
You then choose a printer and a copy of the article is printed. You tell the system printing has been successful.
If the article is a print-only article, you can't keep the PDF version, so it is automatically deleted from your computer.

Extreme programming takes an 'extreme' approach to iterative development. New versions of the software may be built several times per day and increments are delivered to customers roughly every two weeks. When a programmer builds the system to create a new version, he or she must run all existing automated tests as well as the tests for the new functionality. The new build of the software is accepted only if all tests execute successfully.

A fundamental precept of traditional software engineering is that you should design for change. That is, you should anticipate future changes to the software and design it so that these changes can be easily implemented. Extreme programming, however, has discarded this principle on the basis that designing for change is often wasted effort. The changes anticipated often never materialise and completely different change requests are actually made.

The problem with unanticipated change implementation is that it tends to degrade the software structure, so changes become harder and harder to implement. Extreme programming tackles this problem by suggesting that the software should be constantly refactored. This means that the programming team looks for possible improvements to the software and implements them immediately. Therefore, the software should always be easy to understand and change as new stories are implemented.

17.2.1 Testing in XP

As I discussed in the introduction to this chapter, one of the important differences between iterative development and plan-based development is in the way that the system is tested. With iterative development, there is no system specification that can be used by an external testing team to develop system tests. As a consequence, some approaches to iterative development have a very informal testing process.

To avoid some of the problems of testing and system validation, XP places more emphasis than other agile methods on the testing process. System testing is central to XP where an approach has been developed that reduces the likelihood that producing new system increments will introduce errors into the existing software.

The key features of testing in XP are:

1. Test-first development

2. Incremental test development from scenarios

3. User involvement in the test development and validation

4. The use of automated test harnesses

Test-first development is one of the most important innovations in XP. Writing tests first implicitly defines both an interface and a specification of behaviour for the functionality being developed. Problems of requirements and interface misunderstandings are reduced. This approach can be adopted in any process where there is a clear relationship between a system requirement and the code implementing that requirement. In XP, you can always see this link because the story cards representing the requirements are broken down into tasks, and the tasks are the principal unit of implementation.

As I have discussed, user requirements in XP are expressed as scenarios or stories and the user prioritises these for development. The development team assesses each scenario and breaks it down into tasks. Each task represents a discrete feature of the system and a unit test can then be designed for that task. For example, some of the task cards developed from the story card for document downloading (Figure 17.6) are shown in Figure 17.7.

Each task generates one or more unit tests that check the implementation described in that task. For example, Figure 17.8 is a shortened description of a test case that has been developed to check that a valid credit card number has been implemented.

The role of the customer in the testing process is to help develop acceptance tests for the stories that are to be implemented in the next release of the system. As I discuss in Chapter 23, acceptance testing is the process where the system is tested using customer data to check that it meets the customer's real needs. In XP, acceptance testing, like development, is incremental. For this particular story, the acceptance test would involve making several document selections, paying for them in different ways and printing them on different printers. In practice, a series of acceptance tests rather than a single test would probably be developed.

Test-first development and the use of automated test harnesses are major strengths of the XP approach. Rather than writing the program code, then writing the tests of that code, test-first development means that the test is written before the code. Critically, the test is written as an executable component before the task is implemented. Once the software has been implemented, the test can be executed immediately. This testing component should be standalone, should simulate the submission of input to be tested and should check that the result meets the output spec-

Figure 17.7 Task
cards for document
downloading

Task 1: Implement principal work flow

Task 2: Implement article catalog and selection

Task 3: Implement payment collection

Payment may be made in 3 different ways. The user
selects which way they wish to pay. If the user
has a library subscription, then they can input the
subscriber key which should be checked by the
system. Alternatively, they can input an organizational
account number. If this is valid, a debit of the cost
of the article is posted to this account. Finally, they
may input a 16 digit credit card number and expiry
date. This should be checked for validity and, if
valid a debit is posted to that credit card account.

Figure 17.8 Test case
description for credit
card validity

Test 4: Test credit card validity

Input:
A string representing the credit card number and two integers
representing the month and year when the card expires
Tests:
Check that all bytes in the string are digits
Check that the month lies between 1 and 12 and the
year is greater than or equal to the current year.
Using the first 4 digits of the credit card number,
check that the card issuer is valid by looking up the
card issuer table. Check credit card validity by submitting the
card number and expire date information to the card issuer
Output:
OK or error message indicating that the card is invalid

ification. The automated test harness is a system that submits these automated tests
for execution.

With test-first development, there is always a set of tests that can be quickly and
easily executed. This means that whenever any functionality is added to the system, the tests can be run and problems that the new code has introduced can be
caught immediately.

In test-first development, the task implementers have to thoroughly understand
the specification so that they can write the test for the system. This means that ambiguities and omissions in the specification have to be clarified before implementation begins. Furthermore, it also avoids the problem of 'test-lag' where, because
the developer of the system works at a faster pace than the tester, the implementation gets further and further ahead of the testing and there is a tendency to skip
tests so that the schedule can be maintained.

However, test-first development does not always work as intended. Programmers prefer programming to testing and sometimes write incomplete tests that do not check for exceptional situations. Furthermore, some tests can be very difficult to write. For example, in a complex user interface, it is often difficult to write unit tests for the code that implements the 'display logic' and workflow between screens. Finally, it is difficult to judge the completeness of a set of tests. Although you may have a lot of system tests, your test set may not provide complete coverage. Crucial parts of the system may not be executed and so remain untested.

Relying on the customer to support acceptance test development is sometimes a major difficulty in the XP testing process. People adopting the customer role have very limited available time and may not be able to work full-time with the development team. The customer may feel that providing the requirements was enough of a contribution and be reluctant to get involved in the testing process.

17.2.2 Pair programming

Another innovative practice that has been introduced is that programmers work in pairs to develop the software. They actually sit together at the same workstation to develop the software. Development does not always involve the same pair of people working together. Rather, the idea is that pairs are created dynamically so that all team members may work with other members in a programming pair during the development process.

The use of pair programming has a number of advantages:

1. It supports the idea of common ownership and responsibility for the system. This reflects Weinberg's idea of egoless programming (Weinberg, 1971) where the software is owned by the team as a whole and individuals are not held responsible for problems with the code. Instead, the team has collective responsibility for resolving these problems.

2. It acts as an informal review process because each line of code is looked at by at least two people. Code inspections and reviews (covered in Chapter 22) are very successful in discovering a high percentage of software errors. However, they are time consuming to organise and, typically, introduce delays into the development process. While pair programming is a less formal process that probably doesn't find so many errors, it is a much cheaper inspection process than formal program inspections.

3. It helps support refactoring, which is a process of software improvement. A principle of XP is that the software should be constantly refactored. That is, parts of the code should be rewritten to improve their clarity or structure. The difficulty of implementing this in a normal development environment is that this is effort that is expended for long-term benefit, and an individual who practices refactoring may be judged less efficient than one who simply carries on developing code. Where pair programming and collective ownership are used,

others gain immediately from the refactoring so they are likely to support the process.

You might think that pair programming is less efficient that individual programming and that a pair of developers would produce half as much code as two individuals working alone. Studies of XP developments, however, do not bear this out. Development productivity with pair programming seems to be comparable with that of two people working independently (Williams, et al., 2000). The reasons for this are that pairs discuss the software before development so probably have fewer false starts and less rework, and that the number of errors avoided by the informal inspection is such that less time is spent repairing bugs discovered during the testing process.

17.3 Rapid application development

Although agile methods as an approach to iterative development have received a great deal of attention in the last few years, business systems have been developed iteratively for many years using rapid application development techniques. Rapid application development (RAD) techniques evolved from so-called fourth-generation languages in the 1980s and are used for developing applications that are data-intensive. Consequently, they are usually organised as a set of tools that allow data to be created, searched, displayed and presented in reports. Figure 17.9 illustrates a typical organisation for a RAD system.

The tools that are included in a RAD environment are:

1. *A database programming language* that embeds knowledge of the database structures and includes fundamental database manipulation operations. SQL (Groff et al., 2002) is the standard database programming language. The SQL commands may be input directly or generated automatically from forms filled in by an end-user.

2. *An interface generator,* which is used to create forms for data input and display.

3. *Links to office applications* such as a spreadsheet for the analysis and manipulation of numeric information or a word processor for report template creation.

4. *A report generator,* which is used to define and create reports from information in the database.

RAD systems are successful because, as I explained in Chapter 13, there is a great deal of commonality across business applications. In essence, these applications are often concerned with updating a database and producing reports from the informa-

Figure 17.9 A rapid
application
development
environment

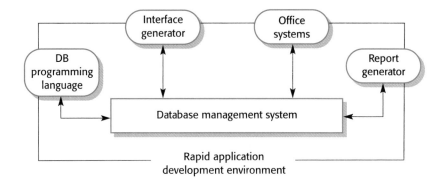

tion in the database. Standard forms are used for input and output. RAD systems are geared towards producing interactive applications that rely on abstracting information from an organisational database, presenting it to end-users on their terminal or workstation, and updating the database with changes made by users.

Many business applications rely on structured forms for input and output, so RAD environments provide powerful facilities for screen definition and report generation. Screens are often defined as a series of linked forms (in one application we studied, there were 137 form definitions) so the screen generation system must provide for:

1. *Interactive form definition* where the developer defines the fields to be displayed and how these are to be organised.

2. *Form linking* where the developer can specify that particular inputs cause further forms to be displayed.

3. *Field verification* where the developer defines allowed ranges for values input to form fields.

All RAD environments now support the development of database interfaces based on web browsers. These allow the database to be accessed from anywhere with a valid Internet connection. This reduces training and software costs and allows external users to have access to a database. However, the inherent limitations of web browsers and Internet protocols mean that this approach may be unsuitable for systems where very fast, interactive responses are required.

Most RAD systems now also include visual programming tools that allow the system to be developed interactively. Rather than write a sequential program, the system developer manipulates graphical icons representing functions, data or user interface components, and associates processing scripts with these icons. An executable program is generated automatically from the visual representation of the system.

Visual development systems such as Visual Basic support this approach to application development. Application programmers build the system interactively by defining the interface in terms of screens, fields, buttons and menus. These are

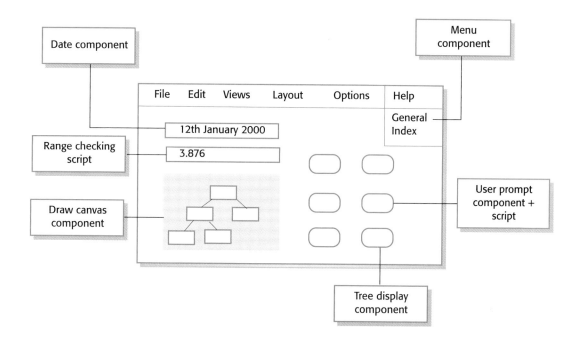

Figure 17.10 Visual
programming with
reuse
named and processing scripts are associated with individual parts of the interface
(e.g., a button named Simulate). These scripts may be calls to reusable components,
special-purpose code or a mixture of both.

I illustrate this approach in Figure 17.10, which shows an application screen including menus along the top, input fields (the white fields on the left of the display),
output fields (the grey field on the left of the display) and buttons (the rounded rectangles on the right of the display). When these entities are positioned on the display by the visual programming system, the developer defines which reusable
component should be associated with them or writes a program fragment to carry
out the required processing. Figure 17.10 also shows the components that are associated with some of the display elements.

Visual Basic is a very sophisticated example of a scripting language
(Ousterhout, 1998). Scripting languages are typeless, high-level languages that are
designed to help you integrate components to create systems. An early example of
a scripting language was the Unix shell (Bourne, 1978; Gordon and Bieman, 1995);
since its development, a number of more powerful scripting languages have been
created (Ousterhout, 1994; Lutz, 1996; Wall, et al., 1996). Scripting languages include
control structures and graphical toolkits, which as Ousterhout (Ousterhout, 1998)
illustrates can radically reduce the time required for system development.

This approach to system development allows for the rapid development of relatively simple applications that can be built by a small team of people. For larger systems that must be developed by larger teams, this approach is more difficult to organise.
There is no explicit system architecture and there are often complex dependencies
between parts of the system, which can cause difficulties when changes are

Figure 17.11
Application linking

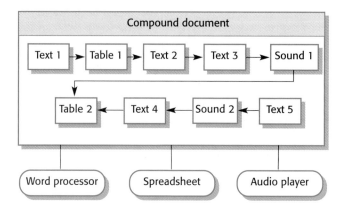

required. In addition, because scripting languages are limited to a specific set of interaction objects, implementing nonstandard user interfaces can be difficult.

Visual development is an approach to RAD that relies on integrating fine-grain, reusable software components. An alternative reuse-based approach reuses 'components' that are complete application systems. This is sometimes called COTS-based development, where COTS means 'Commercial Off-the-Shelf'—the applications are already available. For example, if a system requires a text-processing capability, you may use a standard word-processing system such as Microsoft Word. I discuss COTS-based development from a reuse perspective in Chapter 18.

To illustrate the type of application that might be developed using a COTS-based approach, consider the process of requirements management discussed in Chapter 7. A requirements management support system needs a way to capture requirements, store these requirements, produce reports, discover requirements relationships and manage these relationships as traceability tables. In a COTS-based approach, a prototype could be created by linking a database (to store requirements), a word processor (to capture requirements and format reports), a spreadsheet (to manage traceability tables) and specially written code to find relationships between the requirements.

COTS-based development gives the developer access to all of the functionality of an application. If the application also provides scripting or tailoring facilities (e.g., Excel macros) these may be used to develop some application functionality. A compound document metaphor is helpful to understand this approach to application development. The data processed by the system may be organised into a compound document that acts as a container for several objects. These objects contain different types of data (such as a table, a diagram, a form) that can be processed by different applications. Objects are linked and typed so that accessing an object results in the associated application being initiated.

Figure 17.11 illustrates an application system made up of a compound document that includes text elements, spreadsheet elements and sound files. Text elements are processed by the word processor, tables by the spreadsheet application and sound files by an audio player. When a system user accesses an object of a particular type, the associated application is called to provide user functionality. For example, when objects of type sound are accessed, the audio player is called to process them.

The main advantage of this approach is that a lot of application functionality can be implemented quickly at a very low cost. Users who are already familiar with the applications making up the system do not have to learn how to use new features. However, if they do not know how to use the applications, learning may be difficult, especially as they may be confused by application functionality that isn't necessary. There may also be performance problems with the application because of the need to switch from one application system to another. The switching overhead depends on the operating system support that is provided.

17.4 Software prototyping

As I discussed in the introduction to this chapter, there are some circumstances where, for practical or contractual reasons, an incremental software delivery process cannot be used. In those situations, a statement of the system requirements is completed and is used by the development team as the basis for the system software. As I explained, you can get some of the benefits of an incremental development process by creating a prototype of the software. This approach is sometimes called throwaway prototyping because the prototype is not delivered to the customer or maintained by the developer.

A prototype is an initial version of a software system that is used to demonstrate concepts, try out design options and, generally, to find out more about the problem and its possible solutions. Rapid, iterative development of the prototype is essential so that costs are controlled and system stakeholders can experiment with the prototype early in the software process.

A software prototype can be used in a software development process in several ways:

1. In the requirements engineering process, a prototype can help with the elicitation and validation of system requirements.

2. In the system design process, a prototype can be used to explore particular software solutions and to support user interface design.

3. In the testing process, a prototype can be used to run back-to-back tests with the system that will be delivered to the customer.

System prototypes allow users to see how well the system supports their work. They may get new ideas for requirements and find areas of strength and weakness in the software. They may then propose new system requirements. Furthermore, as the prototype is developed, it may reveal errors and omissions in the requirements that have been proposed. A function described in a specification may seem useful

Figure 17.12 Back-to-back testing

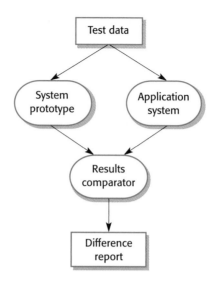

Figure 17.12 Back-to-back testing

and well-defined. However, when that function is combined with other functions, users often find that their initial view was incorrect or incomplete. The system specification may then be modified to reflect their changed understanding of the requirements.

A system prototype may be used while the system is being designed to carry out design experiments to check the feasibility of a proposed design. For example, a database design may be prototyped and tested to check that it allows for the most efficient data access for the most common user queries. Prototyping is also an essential part of the user interface design process. Because of the dynamic nature of user interfaces, textual descriptions and diagrams are not good enough for expressing the user interface requirements. Therefore, rapid prototyping with end-user involvement is the only sensible way to develop graphical user interfaces for software systems.

A major problem in system testing is test validation where you have to check whether the results of a test are what you expect. When a system prototype is available, you can reduce the effort involved in result checking by running back-to-back tests (Figure 17.12). The same test cases are submitted to the prototype and to the system under test. If both systems give the same result, the test case has probably not detected a fault. If the results differ, it may mean that there is a system fault and the reasons for the difference should be investigated.

Finally, as well as supporting software process activities, prototypes can be used to reduce the time required to develop user documentation and to train users with the system. A working, albeit limited, system is available quickly to demonstrate the feasibility and usefulness of the application to management.

In a study of 39 prototyping projects, Gordon and Bieman (Gordon and Bieman, 1995) found that the benefits of using prototyping were:

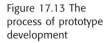

Figure 17.13 The
process of prototype
development

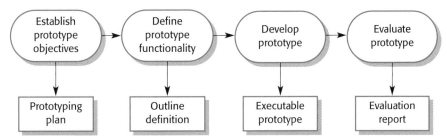

1. Improved system usability

2. A closer match of the system to users' needs

3. Improved design quality

4. Improved maintainability

5. Reduced development effort

Their study suggests that the improvements in usability and better user requirements that stem from using a prototype do not necessarily mean an overall increase in system development costs. Prototyping usually increases costs in the early stages of the software process but reduces costs later in the development process. The main reason for this is that rework during development is avoided because customers request fewer system changes. However, Gordon and Bieman found that overall system performance is sometimes degraded if inefficient prototype code is reused.

A process model for prototype development is shown in Figure 17.13. The objectives of prototyping should be made explicit from the start of the process. These may be to develop a system to prototype the user interface, to develop a system to validate functional system requirements or to develop a system to demonstrate the feasibility of the application to management. The same prototype cannot meet all objectives. If the objectives are left unstated, management or end-users may misunderstand the function of the prototype. Consequently, they may not get the benefits that they expected from the prototype development.

The next stage in the process to is decide what to put into and, perhaps more importantly, what to leave out of the prototype system. To reduce prototyping costs and accelerate the delivery schedule, you may leave some functionality out of the prototype. You may decide to relax non-functional requirements such as response time and memory utilisation. Error handling and management may be ignored or may be rudimentary unless the objective of the prototype is to establish a user interface. Standards of reliability and program quality may be reduced.

The final stage of the process is prototype evaluation. Provision must be made during this stage for user training, and the prototype objectives should be used to derive a plan for evaluation. Users need time to become comfortable with a new system and to settle into a normal pattern of usage. Once they are using the system normally, they then discover requirements errors and omissions.

A general problem with developing an executable, throw-away prototype is that the mode of use of the prototype may not correspond with how the final delivered system is used. The tester of the prototype may not be typical of system users. The training time during prototype evaluation may be insufficient. If the prototype is slow, the evaluators may adjust their way of working and avoid those system features that have slow response times. When provided with better response in the final system, they may use it in a different way.

Developers are sometimes pressured by managers to deliver throw-away prototypes, particularly when there are delays in delivering the final version of the software. Rather than face up to delays in the project the manager may believe that delivering an incomplete or poor quality system is better than nothing. However, this is usually unwise for the following reasons:

KEY POINTS

■ As pressure grows for the rapid delivery of software, an iterative approach to software development is becoming increasingly used as the standard development technique for small and medium-sized systems, especially in the business domain.

■ Agile methods are iterative development methods that focus on incremental specification, design and system implementation. They involve the customer directly in the development process. Reducing development overhead can make faster software development possible.

■ Extreme programming is a well-known agile method that integrates a range of good programming practices such as systematic testing, continuous software improvement and customer participation in the development team.

■ A particular strength of extreme programming is the development of automated tests before a program feature is created. All tests must successfully execute when an increment is integrated into a system.

■ Rapid application development involves using development environments that include powerful tools to support system production. These include database programming languages, form and report generators, and links to office applications.

■ Throw-away prototyping is an iterative development process where a prototype system is used to explore the requirements and design options. This prototype is not intended for deployment by the system customer.

■ When implementing a throw-away prototype, you first develop the parts of the system you understand least; by contrast, in an incremental development approach, you begin by developing the parts of the system you understand best.

1. It may be impossible to tune the prototype to meet non-functional requirements that were ignored during prototype development, such as performance, security, robustness and reliability.

2. Rapid change during development inevitably means that the prototype is undocumented. The only design specification is the prototype code. This is not good enough for long-term maintenance.

3. The changes made during prototype development will probably have degraded the system structure. The system will be difficult and expensive to maintain.

4. Organisational quality standards are normally relaxed for prototype development.

Throw-away prototypes do not have to be executable to be useful in the requirements engineering process. As I discuss in Chapter 16, paper-based mock-ups of the system user interface (Rettig, 1994) can be effective in helping users refine an interface design and work through usage scenarios. These are very cheap to develop and can be constructed in a few days. An extension of this technique is a Wizard of Oz prototype where only the user interface is developed. Users interact with this interface, but their requests are passed to a person who interprets them and outputs the appropriate response.

FURTHER READING

Extreme Programming Explained. This was the first book on XP and is still, perhaps, the most readable. It explains the approach from the perspective of one its inventors, and his enthusiasm comes through very clearly. (Kent Beck, 2000, Addison-Wesley.)

'Get ready for agile methods, with care'. A thoughtful critique of agile methods that discusses their strengths and weaknesses, written by a vastly experienced software engineer. (B. Boehm, *IEEE Computer*, January 2002.)

'Scripting: Higher-level programming for the 21st century'. An overview of scripting languages by the inventor of Tcl/Tk, who discusses the advantages of this approach for rapid application development. (J. K. Ousterhout, *IEEE Computer*, March 1998.)

DSDM: Dynamic Systems Development Method. A description of an approach to rapid application development that some people consider to be an early instance of an agile method. (J. Stapleton, 1997, Addison-Wesley.)

EXERCISES

17.1   Explain why the rapid delivery and deployment of new systems is often more important to businesses than the detailed functionality of these systems.

17.2   Explain how the principles underlying agile methods lead to the accelerated development and deployment of software.

17.3   When would you recommend *against* the use of an agile method for developing a software system?

17.4   Extreme programming expresses user requirements as stories, with each story written on a card. Discuss the advantages and disadvantages of this approach to requirements description.

17.5   Explain why test-first development helps the programmer develop a better understanding of the system requirements. What are the potential difficulties with test-first development?

17.6   Suggest four reasons why the productivity rate of programmers working as a pair is roughly the same as two programmers working individually.

17.7   You have been asked to investigate the feasibility of prototyping in the software development process in your organisation. Write a report for your manager discussing the classes of project for which prototyping should be used, and setting out the expected costs and benefits of prototyping.

17.8   A software manager is involved in the project development of a software design support system that supports the translation of software requirements to a formal software specification. Comment on the advantages and disadvantages of the following development strategies:

   a. Develop a throw-away prototype, evaluate, it then review the system requirements. Develop the final system using C.

   b. Develop the system from the existing requirements using Java, then modify it to adapt to any changed user requirements.

   c. Develop the system using incremental development with a user involved in the development team.

17.9   A charity has asked you to prototype a system that keeps track of all donations they have received. This system has to maintain the names and addresses of donors, their particular interests, the amount donated and when the donation was made. If the donation is over a certain amount, the donor may attach conditions to the donation (e.g., it must be spent on a particular project), and the system must keep track of these and how the donation was spent. Discuss how you would prototype this system, bearing in mind that the charity has a mixture of paid workers and volunteers. Many of the volunteers are retirees who have had little or no computer experience.

17.10   You have developed a throw-away prototype system for a client who is very happy with it. However, she suggests that there is no need to develop another system but that you should deliver the prototype, and she offers you an excellent price for the system. You know that there may be future problems with maintaining the system. Discuss how you might respond to this customer.

18

Software reuse

Objectives

The objectives of this chapter are to introduce software reuse and to explain how reuse contributes to the software development process. When you have read this chapter, you will:

- understand the benefits and problems of reusing software when developing new systems;

- have learned several ways to implement software reuse;

- understand concept reuse and how reusable concepts can be represented as patterns or embedded in program generators;

- have learned how systems can be developed quickly by composing large, off-the-shelf applications;

- have been introduced to software product lines that are made up of a common core architecture and configurable, reusable components.

Contents

The design process in most engineering disciplines is based on reuse of existing systems or components. Mechanical or electrical engineers do not normally specify a design where every component has to be manufactured specially. They base their design on components that have been tried and tested in other systems. These are not just small components such as flanges and valves but include major subsystems such as engines, condensers or turbines.

Reuse-based software engineering is a comparable software engineering strategy where the development process is geared to reusing existing software. Although the benefits of reuse have been recognised for many years (McIlroy, 1968), it is only in the past 10 years that there has been a gradual transition from original software development to reuse-based development. The move to reuse-based development has been in response to demands for lower software production and maintenance costs, faster delivery of systems and increased software quality. More and more companies see their software as a valuable asset and are promoting reuse to increase their return on software investments.

Reuse-based software engineering is an approach to development that tries to maximise the reuse of existing software. The software units that are reused may be of radically different sizes. For example:

1. *Application system reuse* The whole of an application system may be reused by incorporating it without change into other systems, by configuring the application for different customers or by developing application families that have a common architecture but are tailored for specific customers. I cover application system reuse in Section 18.5.

2. *Component reuse* Components of an application ranging in size from sub-systems to single objects may be reused. For example, a pattern-matching system developed as part of a text-processing system may be reused in a database management system. This is covered in Chapter 19.

3. *Object and function reuse* Software components that implement a single function, such as a mathematical function or an object class, may be reused. This form of reuse, based around standard libraries, has been common for the past 40 years. Many libraries of functions and classes for different types of application and development platform are available. These can be easily used by linking them with other application code. In areas such as mathematical algorithms and graphics, where specific expertise is needed to develop objects and functions, this is a particularly effective approach.

Software systems and components are specific reusable entities, but their specific nature sometimes means that it is expensive to modify them for a new situation. A complementary form of reuse is *concept reuse* where, rather than reuse a component, the reused entity is more abstract and is designed to be configured and adapted for a range of situations. Concept reuse can be embodied in approaches such as design patterns, configurable system products and program generators. The reuse process, when concepts are reused, includes an instantiation activity where the abstract concepts are

Figure 18.1 Benefits
of software reuse

Benefit	Explanation
Increased dependability	Reused software, which has been tried and tested in working systems, should be more dependable than new software because its design and implementation faults have already been found and fixed.
Reduced process risk	The cost of existing software is already known, while the costs of development are always a matter of judgement. This is an important factor for project management because it reduces the margin of error in project cost estimation. This is particularly true when relatively large software components such as sub-systems are reused.
Effective use of specialists	Instead doing the same work over and over, these application specialists can develop reusable software that encapsulates their knowledge.
Standards compliance	Some standards, such as user interface standards, can be implemented as a set of standard reusable components. For example, if menus in a user interface are implemented using reusable components, all applications present the same menu formats to users. The use of standard user interfaces improves dependability because users are less likely to make mistakes when presented with a familiar interface.
Accelerated development	Bringing a system to market as early as possible is often more important than overall development costs. Reusing software can speed up system production because both development and validation time should be reduced.

configured for a specific situation. I cover two of these approaches to concept reuse—design patterns and program generation—later in this chapter.

An obvious advantage of software reuse is that overall development costs should be reduced. Fewer software components need be specified, designed, implemented and validated. However, cost reduction is only one advantage of reuse. In Figure 18.1, I have listed other advantages of reusing software assets.

However, there are also costs and problems associated with reuse (Figure 18.2). In particular, there is a significant cost associated with understanding whether a component is suitable for reuse in a particular situation and in testing that component to ensure its dependability. These additional costs may inhibit the introduction of reuse and may mean that the reductions in overall development cost through reuse may be less than anticipated.

Systematic reuse does not just happen—it must be planned and introduced through an organisation-wide reuse programme. This has been recognised for many years in Japan (Matsumoto, 1984), where reuse is an integral part of the Japanese

Figure 18.2 Problems with reuse

Problem	Explanation
Increased maintenance costs	If the source code of a reused software system or component is not available then maintenance costs may be increased because the reused elements of the system may become increasingly incompatible with system changes.
Lack of tool support	CASE toolsets may not support development with reuse. It may be difficult or impossible to integrate these tools with a component library system. The software process assumed by these tools may not take reuse into account.
Not-invented-here syndrome	Some software engineers prefer to rewrite components because they believe they can improve on them. This is partly to do with trust and partly to do with the fact that writing original software is seen as more challenging than reusing other people's software.
Creating and maintaining a component library	Populating a reusable component library and ensuring the software developers can use this library can be expensive. Our current techniques for classifying, cataloguing and retrieving software components are immature.
Finding, understanding and adapting reusable components	Software components have to be discovered in a library, understood and, sometimes, adapted to work in a new environment. Engineers must be reasonably confident of finding a component in the library before they will make include a component search as part of their normal development process.

'factory' approach to software development (Cusamano, 1989). Companies such as Hewlett-Packard have also been very successful in their reuse programs (Griss and Wosser, 1995), and their experience has been incorporated in a general book by Jacobsen et al. (Jacobsen, et al., 1997).

18.1 The reuse landscape

Over the past 20 years, many techniques have been developed to support software reuse. These exploit the facts that systems in the same application domain are similar and have potential for reuse, that reuse is possible at different levels (from simple functions to complete applications), and that standards for reusable components

Figure 18.3 The
reuse landscape

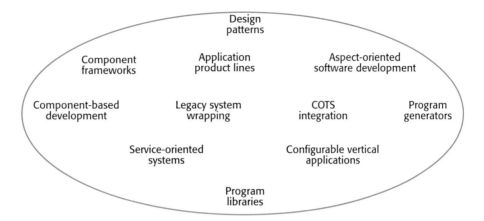

Figure 18.3 The
reuse landscape

facilitate reuse. Figure 18.3 shows a number of ways to support software reuse, each
of which is briefly described in Figure 18.4.

Given this array of techniques for reuse, the key question is which is the most
appropriate technique to use? Obviously, this depends on the requirements for the
system being developed, the technology and reusable assets available, and the expertise of the development team. Key factors that you should consider when planning
reuse are:

1. *The development schedule for the software* If the software has to be developed
    quickly, you should try to reuse off-the-shelf systems rather than individual com-
    ponents. These are large-grain reusable assets. Although the fit to requirements
    may be imperfect, this approach minimises the amount of development
    required.

2. *The expected software lifetime* If you are developing a long-lifetime system, you
    should focus on the maintainability of the system. In those circumstances, you
    should not just think about the immediate possibilities of reuse but also the long-
    term implications. You will have to adapt the system to new requirements, which
    will probably mean making changes to components and how they are used. If
    you do not have access to the source code, you should probably avoid using com-
    ponents and systems from external suppliers; you cannot be sure that these sup-
    pliers will be able to continue supporting the reused software.

3. *The background, skills and experience of the development team* All reuse tech-
    nologies are fairly complex and you need quite a lot of time to understand and
    use them effectively. Therefore, if the development team has skills in a par-
    ticular area, this is probably where you should focus.

4. *The criticality of the software and its non-functional requirements* For a criti-
    cal system that has to be certified by an external regulator, you may have to
    create a dependability case for the system (discussed in Chapter 24). This is

Approach	Description
Design patterns	Generic abstractions that occur across applications are represented as design patterns showing abstract and concrete objects and interactions.
Component-based development	Systems are developed by integrating components (collections of objects) that conform to component-model standards. This is covered in Chapter 19.
Application frameworks	Collections of abstract and concrete classes can be adapted and extended to create application systems.
Legacy system wrapping	Legacy systems (see Chapter 2) that can be 'wrapped' by defining a set of interfaces and providing access to these legacy systems through these interfaces.
Service-oriented systems	Systems are developed by linking shared services, which may be externally provided.
Application product lines	An application type is generalised around a common architecture so that it can be adapted for different customers.
COTS integration	Systems are developed by integrating existing application systems.
Configurable vertical applications	A generic system is designed so that it can be configured to the needs of specific system customers.
Program libraries	Class and function libraries implementing commonly used abstractions are available for reuse.
Program generators	A generator system embeds knowledge of a particular type of application and can generate systems or system fragments in that domain.
Aspect-oriented software development	Shared components are woven into an application at different places when the program is compiled.

difficult if you don't have access to the source code of the software. If your software has stringent performance requirements, it may be impossible to use strategies such as reuse through program generators. These systems tend to generate relatively inefficient code.

5. *The application domain* In some application domains, such as manufacturing and medical information systems, there are several generic products that may be reused by configuring them to a local situation. If you are working in such a domain, you should always consider these an option.

6. *The platform on which the system will run* Some components models, such as COM/Active X, are specific to Microsoft platforms. If you are developing on such a platform, this may be the most appropriate approach. Similarly, generic application systems may be platform-specific and you may only be able to reuse these if your system is designed for the same platform.

The range of available reuse techniques is such that, in most situations, there is the possibility of some software reuse. Whether or not reuse is achieved is often a managerial rather than a technical issue. Managers may be unwilling to compromise their requirements to allow reusable components to be used, or they may decide that original component development would help create a software asset base. They may not understand the risks associated with reuse as well as they understand the risks of original development. Therefore, although the risks of new software development may be higher, some managers may prefer known to unknown risks.

18.2 Design patterns

When you try to reuse executable components, you are inevitably constrained by detailed design decisions that have been made by the implementers of these components. These range from the particular algorithms that have been used to implement the components to the objects and types in the component interfaces. When these design decisions conflict with your particular requirements, reusing the component is either impossible or introduces inefficiencies into your system.

One way around this is to reuse abstract designs that do not include implementation detail. You can implement these to fit your specific application requirements. The first instances of this approach to reuse came in the documentation and publication of fundamental algorithms (Knuth, 1971) and, later, in the documentation of abstract data types such as stacks, trees and lists (Booch, 1987). More recently, this approach to reuse has been embodied in design patterns.

Design patterns were derived from ideas put forward by Christopher Alexander (Alexander, et al., 1977), who suggested that there were certain patterns of building design that were common and that were inherently pleasing and effective. The pattern is a description of the problem and the essence of its solution, so that the solution may be reused in different settings. The pattern is not a detailed specification. Rather, you can think of it as a description of accumulated wisdom and experience, a well-tried solution to a common problem. A quote from the hillside.net web site, which is dedicated to maintaining information about patterns, encapsulates their role in reuse:

> *Patterns and Pattern Languages are ways to describe best practices, good designs, and capture experience in a way that it is possible for others to reuse this experience.*

Most designers think of design patterns as a way of supporting object-oriented design. Patterns often rely on object characteristics such as inheritance and polymorphism to provide generality. However, the general principle of encapsulating experience in a pattern is one that is equally applicable to all software design approaches.

Gamma et al. (Gamma, et al., 1995) define the four essential elements of design patterns:

1. A name that is a meaningful reference to the pattern

2. A description of the problem area that explains when the pattern may be applied

3. A solution description of the parts of the design solution, their relationships and their responsibilities. This is not a concrete design description. It is a template for a design solution that can be instantiated in different ways. This is often expressed graphically and shows the relationships between the objects and object classes in the solution.

4. A statement of the consequences—the results and trade-offs—of applying the pattern. This can help designers understand whether a pattern can be effectively applied in a particular situation.

These essential elements of a pattern description may be decomposed, as shown in the example in Figure 18.5. For example, Gamma and his co-authors break down the problem description into motivation (a description of why the pattern is useful) and applicability (a description of situations where the pattern may be used). Under the description of the solution, they describe the pattern structure, participants, collaborations and implementation.

To illustrate pattern description, I use the Observer pattern, taken from the book by Gamma et al. This pattern can be used in a variety of situations where different presentations of an object's state are required. It separates the object that must be displayed from the different forms of presentation. This is illustrated in Figure 18.6, which shows two graphical presentations of the same data set. In my description, I use the four essential description elements and supplement these with a brief statement of what the pattern can do.

Graphical representations are normally used to illustrate the object classes that are used in patterns and their relationships. These supplement the pattern description and add detail to the solution description. Figure 18.7 is the representation in UML of the Observer pattern.

A huge number of published patterns are now available (see the book web pages for links) covering a range of application domains and languages. The notion of a pattern as a reusable concept has been developed in a number of areas apart from software design, including configuration management, user interface design and interaction scenarios (Berczuk and Appleton, 2002; Borchers, 2001; Martin, et al., 2001; Martin, et al., 2002).

The use of patterns is an effective form of reuse. However, I am convinced that only experienced software engineers who have a deep knowledge of patterns can use them effectively. These developers can recognise generic situations where a pattern

Figure 18.5 A
description of the
Observer pattern

Pattern name: Observer

Description: Separates the display of the state of an object from the object itself
and allows alternative displays to be provided. When the object state changes, all
displays are automatically notified and updated to reflect the change.

Problem description: In many situations, it is necessary to provide multiple displays
of some state information, such as a graphical display and a tabular display. Not all
of these may be known when the information is specified. All alternative
presentations may support interaction and, when the state is changed, all displays
must be updated.

This pattern may be used in all situations where more than one display format for
state information may be required and where it is not necessary for the object that
maintains the state information to know about the specific display formats used.

Solution description: The structure of the pattern is shown in Figure 18.7. This
defines two abstract objects, Subject and Observer, and two concrete objects,
ConcreteSubject and ConcreteObject, which inherit the attributes of the related
abstract objects. The state to be displayed is maintained in ConcreteSubject, which
also inherits operations from Subject allowing it to add and remove Observers and
to issue a notification when the state has changed.

The ConcreteObserver maintains a copy of the state of ConcreteSubject and
implements the Update () interface of Observer that allows these copies to be kept
in step. The ConcreteObserver automatically displays its state—this is not normally an
interface operation.

Consequences: The subject only knows the abstract Observer and does not know
details of the concrete class. Therefore there is minimal coupling between these
objects. Because of this lack of knowledge, optimisations that enhance display
performance are impractical. Changes to the subject may cause a set of linked
updates to observers to be generated some of which may not be necessary.

can be applied. Inexperienced programmers, even if they have read the pattern books,
will always find it hard to decide whether they can reuse a pattern or need to develop
a special-purpose solution.

18.3 Generator-based reuse

Concept reuse through patterns relies on describing the concept in an abstract way
and leaving it up to the software developer to create an implementation. An alternative approach to this is generator-based reuse (Biggerstaff, 1998). In this
approach, reusable knowledge is captured in a program generator system that can
be programmed by domain experts using either a domain-oriented language or an
interactive CASE tool that supports system generation. The application description
specifies, in an abstract way, which reusable components are to be used, how they

Figure 18.6 Multiple
displays

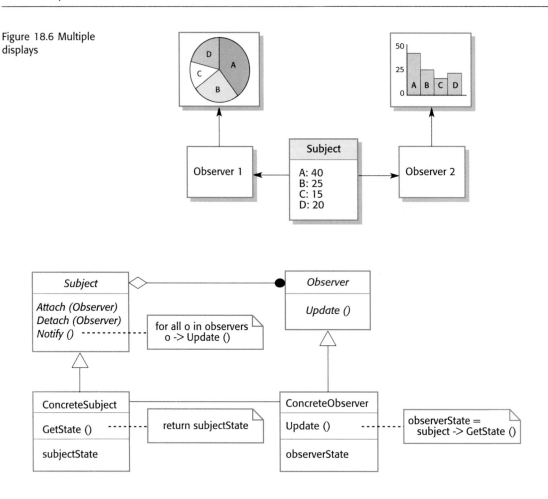

Figure 18.7 The
Observer pattern

are to be combined and their parameterisation. Using this information, an operational software system can be generated (Figure 18.8).

Generator-based reuse takes advantage of the fact that applications in the same domain, such as business systems, have common architectures and carry out comparable functions. For example, as I discussed in Chapter 13, data-processing systems normally follow an input-process-output model and usually include operations such as data verification and report generation. Therefore, generic components for selecting items from a database, checking that these are within range and creating reports can be created and incorporated in an application generator. To reuse these components, the programmer simply has to select the data items to be used, the checks to be applied and the format of reports.

Generator-based reuse has been particularly successful for business application systems, and there are many different business application generator products available. These may generate complete applications or may partially automate application creation and leave the programmer to fill in specific details. The generator-based approach to reuse is also used in other areas, including:

Figure 18.8
Generator-based
reuse

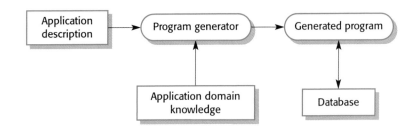

1. *Parser generators for language processing* The generator input is a grammar describing the language to be parsed, and the output is a language parser. This approach is embodied in systems such as lex and yacc for C and JavaCC, a compiler for Java.

2. *Code generators in CASE tools* The input to these generators is a software design and the output is a program implementing the designed system. These may be based on UML models and, depending on the information in the UML models, generate either a complete program or component, or a code skeleton. The software developer then adds detail to complete the code.

These approaches to generator-based reuse take advantage of the common structure of applications in these areas. The technique has also been used in more specific application domains such as command and control systems (O'Connor, et al., 1994) and scientific instrumentation (Butler, 1994) where libraries of components have been developed. Domain experts then use a domain-specific language to compose these components and create applications. However, there is a high initial cost in defining and implementing the domain concepts and composition language. This has meant that many companies are reluctant to take the risks of adopting this approach.

Generator-based reuse is cost-effective for applications such as business data processing. It is much easier for end-users to develop programs using generators compared to other component-based approaches to reuse. Inevitably, however, there are inefficiencies in generated programs. This means that it may not be possible to use this approach in systems with high-performance or throughput requirements.

Generative programming is a key component of emerging techniques of software development that combine program generation with component-based development. Czarnecki and Eisenecher's book (Czarnecki and Eisenecher, 2000) describes these newer approaches.

The most developed of these approaches is aspect-oriented software development (AOSD) (Elrad, et al., 2001). Aspect-oriented software development addresses one of the major problems in software design—the problem of separation of concerns. Separation of concerns is a basic design principle; you should design your software so that each unit or component does one thing and one thing only. For example, in the LIBSYS system, there should be a component concerned with searching for documents, a component concerned with printing documents, a component concerned with managing downloads, and so on.

Figure 18.9 Aspect
weaving

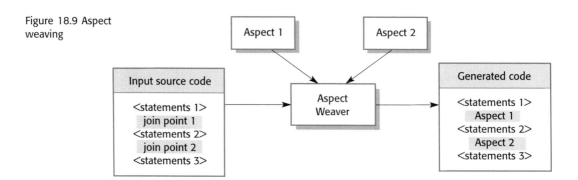

However, in many situations, concerns are not associated with clearly defined application functions but are cross-cutting—that is, they affect all of the components in the system. For example, say you want to keep track of the usage of each of the system modules by each system user. You therefore have a monitoring concern that has to be associated with all components. This can't be simply implemented as an object that is referenced by these components. The specific monitoring that is carried out needs context information from the system function that is being monitored.

In aspect-oriented programming, these cross-cutting concerns are implemented as aspects and, within the program, you define where an aspect should be associated. These are called the *join points*. Aspects are developed separately; then, in a precompilation step called *aspect weaving*, they are linked to the join points (Figure 18.9). Aspect weaving is a form of program generation—the output from the weaver is a program where the aspect code has been integrated. A development of Java called AspectJ (Kiczales, et al., 2001) is the best-known language for aspect-oriented development.

AOSD is currently a very important research topic but it has not yet been widely used for industrial software development. There are problems with this approach—generated code is never as efficient as handwritten code, and we need a better understanding of the relationship between aspects and non-functional properties of the system. However, over the next few years, I expect AOSD to become an important approach to software reuse, where aspects can be reused across applications.

18.4 Application frameworks

The early proponents of object-oriented development suggested that objects were the most appropriate abstraction for reuse. However, experience has shown that objects are often too fine-grain and too specialised to a particular application. Instead, it has become clear that object-oriented reuse is best supported in an object-oriented development process through larger-grain abstractions called *frameworks.*

A framework (or application framework) is a sub-system design made up of a collection of abstract and concrete classes and the interface between them (Wirfs-Brock and Johnson, 1990). Particular details of the application sub-system are implemented by adding components and by providing concrete implementations of abstract classes in the framework. Frameworks are rarely applications in their own right. Applications are normally constructed by integrating a number of frameworks.

Fayad and Schmidt (Fayad and Schmidt, 1997) discuss three classes of framework:

1. *System infrastructure frameworks* These frameworks support the development of system infrastructures such as communications, user interfaces and compilers (Schmidt, 1997).

2. *Middleware integration frameworks* These consist of a set of standards and associated object classes that support component communication and information exchange. Examples of this type of framework include CORBA, Microsoft's COM+, and Enterprise Java Beans. These frameworks provide support for standardised component models, as discussed in Chapter 19.

3. *Enterprise application frameworks* These are concerned with specific application domains such as telecommunications or financial systems (Baumer, et al., 1997). These embed application domain knowledge and support the development of end-user applications.

As the name suggests, a framework is a generic structure that can be extended to create a more specific sub-system or application. It is implemented as a collection of concrete and abstract object classes. To extend the framework, you may have to add concrete classes that inherit operations from abstract classes in the framework. In addition, you may have to define *callbacks*. Callbacks are methods that are called in response to events recognised by the framework.

One of the best-known and most widely used frameworks for GUI design is the Model-View-Controller (MVC) framework (Figure 18.10). The MVC framework was originally proposed in the 1980s as an approach to GUI design that allowed for multiple presentations of an object and separate styles of interaction with each of these presentations. The MVC framework supports the presentation of data in different ways (see Figure 18.6) and separate interaction with each of these presentations. When the data is modified through one of the presentations, all of the other presentations are updated.

Frameworks are often instantiations of a number of patterns, as discussed in Section 18.2. For example, the MVC framework includes the Observer pattern that is described in Figure 18.5, the Strategy pattern that is concerned with updating the model, the Composite pattern and a number of others that are discussed by Gamma et al. (Gamma, et al., 1995).

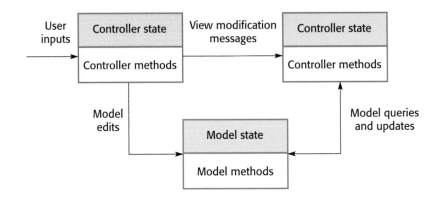

Figure 18.10 The
Model-View-
Controller framework

Applications that are constructed using frameworks can be the basis for further reuse through the concept of software product lines or application families, as discussed in Section 18.5.2. Because these applications are constructed using a framework, modifying family members to create new family members is simplified. However, frameworks are usually more abstract than generic products and thus allow a wider range of applications to be created.

The fundamental problem with frameworks is their inherent complexity and the time it takes to learn to use them. Several months may be required to completely understand a framework, so it is likely that, in large organisations, some software engineers will become framework specialists. There is no doubt that this is an effective approach to reuse, but it is very expensive to introduce into software development processes.

18.5 Application system reuse

Application system reuse involves reusing entire application systems either by configuring a system for a specific environment or by integrating two or more systems to create a new application. As I suggested in Section 18.1, application system reuse is often the most effective reuse technique. It involves the reuse of large-grain assets that can be quickly configured to create a new system.

In this section, I discuss two types of application reuse: the creation of new systems by integrating two or more off-the-shelf applications and the development of product lines. A product line is a set of systems based around a common core architecture and shared components. The core system is specifically designed to be configured and adapted to suit the specific needs of different system customers.

18.5.1 COTS product reuse

A commercial-off-the-shelf (COTS) product is a software system that can be used without change by its buyer. Virtually all desktop software and a wide variety of server products are COTS software. Because this software is designed for general use, it usually includes many features and functions so has the potential to be reused in different applications and environments. Although there can be problems with this approach to system construction (Tracz, 2001), there is an increasing number of success stories that demonstrate its viability (Baker, 2002; Balk and Kedia, 2000; Pfarr and Reis, 2002).

Some types of COTS product have been reused for many years. Database systems are perhaps the best example of this. Very few developers would consider implementing their own database management system. However, until the mid-1990s, there were only a few large systems such as database management systems and teleprocessing monitors, that were routinely reused. Most large systems were designed as standalone systems, and there were often many problems in making these systems work together.

It is now common for large systems to have defined Application Programming Interfaces (APIs) that allow program access to system functions. This means that creating large systems such as e-commerce systems by integrating a range of COTS systems should always be considered as a serious design option. Because of the functionality that these COTS products offer, it is possible to reduce costs and delivery times by orders of magnitude compared to the development of new software. Furthermore, risks may be reduced as the product is already available and managers can see whether it meets their requirements.

To develop systems using COTS products, you have to make a number of design choices:

1. *Which COTS products offer the most appropriate functionality?* If you don't already have experience with a COTS product, it can be difficult to decide which product is the most suitable.

2. *How will data be exchanged?* In general, individual products use unique data structures and formats, and you have to write adaptors that convert from one representation to another.

3. *What features of a product will actually be used?* Most COTS products have more functionality than you need, and functionality is often duplicated across different products. You have to decide which features in what product are most appropriate for your requirements. If possible, you should also deny access to unused functionality because this can interfere with normal system operation. The failure of the first flight of the Ariane 5 rocket, discussed in Chapter 19 (Nuseibeh, 1997), was a consequence of failure in unused functionality in a reused sub-system.

As an illustration of COTS integration, assume that a large organisation wishes to develop a procurement system that allows staff to place orders from their desktop. By introducing this system across the organisation, the company estimates that

Figure 18.11 A
COTS-based
procurement system

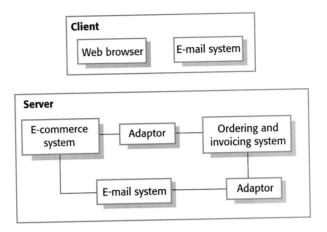

it can save $5 million per year. By centralizing buying, the new procurement system can ensure that orders are always made from suppliers who offer the best prices and should reduce the paperwork costs associated with orders. As with manual systems, this involves choosing the goods available from a supplier, creating an order, having the order approved, sending the order to a supplier, receiving the goods and confirming that payment should be made.

The company has an existing ordering system that is used by the procurement office. This is already integrated with their invoicing and delivery system. To create the new ordering system, they integrate the old one with a web-based e-commerce platform and an electronic mail system that handles communications with users. The structure of the final procurement system constructed using COTS is shown in Figure 18.11.

This procurement system is client–server based, and on the client, standard web browsing and e-mail software are used. These are already integrated by the software suppliers. On the server, the e-commerce platform has to integrate with the existing ordering system through an adaptor. The e-commerce system has its own format for orders, conformations of delivery, and so forth, which have to be converted into the format used by the ordering system. The e-commerce system has built-in integration with the e-mail system to send notifications to users, but the ordering system was never designed for this. Therefore, another adaptor has to be written to convert the notifications into e-mail messages.

In principle, using a large-scale COTS system is the same as using any other more specific component. You have to understand the system interfaces and use them exclusively to communicate with the component; you have to trade-off specific requirements against rapid development and reuse; and you have to design a system architecture that allows the COTS systems to operate together.

However, the fact that these products are usually large systems in their own right and are often sold as separate standalone systems introduces additional problems. Boehm and Abts (Boehm and Abts, 1999) discuss four problems with COTS system integration:

1. *Lack of control over functionality and performance* Although the published interface of a product may appear to offer the required facilities, these may not be properly implemented or may perform poorly. The product may have hidden operations that interfere with its use in a specific situation. Fixing these problems may be a priority for the COTS product integrator but may not be of real concern to the product vendor. Users may simply have to find workarounds to problems if they wish to reuse the COTS product.

2. *Problems with COTS system interoperability* It is sometimes difficult to get COTS products to work together because each product embeds its own assumptions about how it will be used. Garlan et al. (Garlan, et al., 1995), reporting on their experience of trying to integrate four COTS products, found that three of these products were event-based but each used a different model of events and assumed that it had exclusive access to the event queue. As a consequence, the project required five times as much effort as originally predicted and the schedule grew to two years rather than the predicted six months.

3. *No control over system evolution* Vendors of COTS products make their own decisions on system changes in response to market pressures. For PC products in particular, new versions are often produced frequently and may not be compatible with all previous versions. New versions may have additional unwanted functionality, and previous versions may become unavailable and unsupported.

4. *Support from COTS vendors* The level of support available from COTS vendors varies widely. Because these are off-the-shelf systems, vendor support is particularly important when problems arise because developers do not have access to the source code and detailed documentation of the system. While vendors may commit to providing support, changing market and economic circumstances may make it difficult for them to deliver this commitment. For example, a COTS system vendor may decide to discontinue a product because of limited demand or may be taken over by another company that does not wish to support all of its current products.

Of course, it is unlikely that all of these problems will arise in every case, but my guess is that at least one of them should be expected in most COTS integration projects. Consequently, the cost and schedule benefits from COTS reuse are likely to be less than they might first appear.

Furthermore, Boehm and Abts reckon that, in many cases, the cost of system maintenance and evolution may be greater when COTS products are used. All of the above difficulties are lifecycle problems; they don't just affect the initial development of the system. The further removed from the original system developers the people involved in the system maintenance become, the more likely it is that real difficulties will arise with the integrated COTS products.

In spite of these problems, the benefits of COTS product reuse are potentially large because these systems offer so much functionality to the reuser. Months and sometimes years of implementation effort can be saved if an existing system is reused and system development times drastically reduced. For example, the procurement system that I described in Figure 18.11 was implemented and deployed in a very large company in nine months rather than the three years that they originally estimated for a new system. If rapid system delivery is essential and you have some requirements flexibility, then COTS product integration is often the most effective reuse strategy to adopt.

18.5.2 Software product lines

One of the most effective approaches to reuse is creating software product lines or application families. A product line is a set of applications with a common application-specific architecture, as discussed in Chapter 13. Each specific application is specialised in some way. The common core of the application family is reused each time a new application is required. The new development may involve specific component configuration, implementing additional components and adapting some of the components to meet new demands.

Various types of specialisation of a software product line may be developed:

1. *Platform specialisation* Versions of the application are developed for different platforms. For example, versions of the application may exist for Windows, Solaris and Linux platforms. In this case, the functionality of the application is normally unchanged; only those components that interface with the hardware and operating system are modified.

2. *Environment specialisation* Versions of the application are created to handle particular operating environments and peripheral devices. For example, a system for the emergency services may exist in different versions depending on the type of radio system used. In this case, the system components are changed to reflect the functionality of the communications equipment used.

3. *Functional specialisation* Versions of the application are created for specific customers who have different requirements. For example, a library automation system may be modified depending on whether it is used in a public library, a reference library or a university library. In this case, components that implement functionality may be modified and new components added to the system.

4. *Process specialisation* The system is adapted to cope with specific business processes. For example, an ordering system may be adapted to cope with a centralised ordering process in one company and a distributed process in another.

Software product lines are designed to be reconfigured. This reconfiguration may involve adding or removing components from the system, defining parameters and constraints for system components, and including knowledge of business processes. Software product lines can be configured at two points in the development process:

Figure 18.12
Configuration of an
ERP system

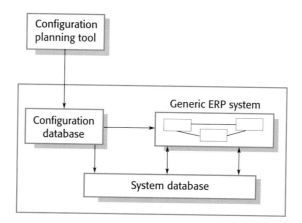

- *Deployment-time configuration* where a generic system is designed for configuration by a customer or consultants working with the customer. Knowledge of the customer's specific requirements and the system's operating environment is embedded in a set of configuration files that are used by the generic system.

- *Design-time configuration* where the organisation that is developing the software modifies a common product line core by developing, selecting or adapting components to create a new system for a customer.

Deployment-time configuration is the approach used in vertical software packages that are designed for a specific application such as a hospital information management system. It is also used in Enterprise Resource Planning (ERP) systems (O'Leary, 2000) such as those produced by SAP and BEA. These are large-scale, integrated systems designed to support business processes such as ordering and invoicing, inventory management and manufacturing scheduling. The configuration process for these systems involves gathering detailed information about the customer's business and business processes and then embedding this information in a configuration database. This often requires detailed knowledge of configuration notations and tools and is usually carried out by consultants working alongside system customers. Figure 18.12 illustrates the organisation of an ERP system.

The generic ERP system includes a large number of modules that may be composed in different ways to create a specific system. The configuration process involves choosing which modules are to be included, configuring these individual modules, defining business processes and business rules, and defining the structure and organisation of the system database.

ERP systems are perhaps the most widespread example of software reuse. The majority of large companies use these systems to support some or all of their functions. However, there is the obvious limitation that the functionality of the system is restricted to the functionality of the generic core. Furthermore, a company's processes

Figure 18.13 The
architecture of a
resource allocation

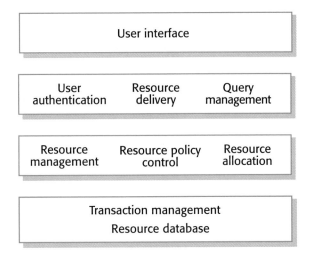

and operations have to be expressed in the system configuration language, and there
may be a mismatch between the concepts in the business and the concepts supported
in the configuration language. For example, in an ERP system that was sold to a
university, the concept of a customer had to be defined. This caused real problems
because universities have multiple types of customer (students, research-funding agencies, educational charities, etc.) and none of these are comparable to a commercial
customer. A serious mismatch between the business model used by the system and
that of the customer makes it highly probable that the ERP system will not meet
the customer's real needs (Scott, 1999).

The alternative approach to application family reuse is configuration by the system supplier before delivery to the customer. The supplier starts with a generic system and then, by modifying and extending modules in this system, creates a
specific system that delivers the required customer functionality. This approach usually involves changing and extending the source code of the core system so greater
flexibility is possible than with deployment-time configuration.

Software product lines usually emerge from existing applications. That is, an organisation develops an application and, when a new application is required, uses this as a
basis for the new application. Further demands for new applications cause the process
to continue. However, because change tends to corrupt application structure, at some
stage a specific decision to design a generic product line is made. This design is based
on reusing the knowledge gained from developing the initial set of applications.

You can think of software product lines as instantiations and specialisations of
more general application architectures, as discussed in Chapter 13. An application
architecture is very general; software product lines specialise the architecture for a
specific type of application. For example, consider a product line system that is
designed to handle vehicle despatching for emergency services. Operators of this
system take calls about incidents, find the appropriate vehicle to respond to the incident

Figure 18.14 The
product line
architecture of a
vehicle-dispatching
system

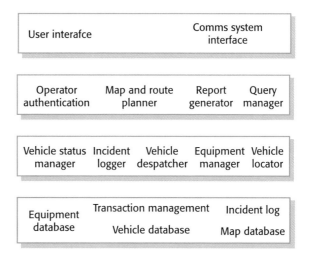

and despatch the vehicle to the incident site. The developers of such a system may market versions of this for police, fire and ambulance services.

This vehicle-despatching system is an example of a resource management system whose application architecture is shown in Figure 18.13. You can see how this four-layer structure is instantiated in Figure 18.14, which shows the modules that might be included in a vehicle-despatching system product line. The components at each level in the product line system are:

1. At the user interface level, there are components providing an operator display interface and an interface with the communications systems used.

2. At the I/O management level (level 2), there are components that handle operator authentication, generate reports of incidents and vehicles despatched, support map output and route planning, and provide a mechanism for operators to query the system databases.

3. At the resource management level (level 3), there are components that allow vehicles to be located and despatched, components to update the status of vehicles and equipment, and a component to log details of incidents.

4. At the database level, as well as the usual transaction management support, there are separate databases of vehicles, equipment and maps.

To create a specific version of this system, you may have to modify individual components. For example, the police have a large number of vehicles but a small number of vehicle types, whereas the fire service has many types of specialised vehicles, so a different vehicle database structure may need to be incorporated into the system.

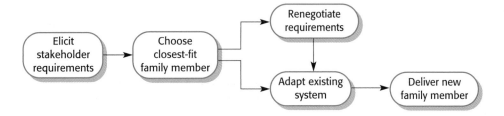

Figure 18.15
Product instance
development

Figure 18.15 shows the steps involved in adapting an application family to create a new application. The steps involved in this general process are:

1. *Elicit stakeholder requirements* You may start with a normal requirements engineering process. However, because a system already exists, you will need to demonstrate and have stakeholders experiment with that system, expressing their requirements as modifications to the functions provided.

2. *Choose closest-fit family member* The requirements are analysed and the family member that is the closest fit is chosen for modification. This need not be the system that was demonstrated.

3. *Renegotiate requirements* As more details of required changes emerge and the project is planned, there may be some requirements renegotiation to minimise the changes that are needed.

4. *Adapt existing system* New modules are developed for the existing system, and existing system modules are adapted to meet the new requirements.

5. *Deliver new family member* The new instance of the product line is delivered to the customer. At this stage, you should document its key features so that it may be used as a basis for other system developments in the future.

When you create a new member of an application family, you may have to find a compromise between reusing as much of the generic application as possible and satisfying detailed stakeholder requirements. The more detailed the system requirements, the less likely it is that the existing components will meet these requirements. However, if stakeholders are willing to be flexible and to limit the system modifications that are required, you can usually deliver the system more quickly and at a lower cost.

In general, developing applications by adapting a generic version of the application means that a very high proportion of the application code is reused. Furthermore, application experience is often transferable from one system to another, so that when software engineers join a development team, their learning process is shortened. Testing is simplified because tests for large parts of the application may also be reused, reducing the overall application development time.

KEY POINTS

■ The advantages of software reuse are lower costs, faster software development and lower risks. System dependability is increased and specialists can be used more effectively by concentrating their expertise on the design of reusable components.

■ Design patterns are high-level abstractions that document successful design solutions. They are fundamental to design reuse in object-oriented development. A pattern description should include a pattern name, a problem and solution description, and a statement of the results and trade-offs of using the pattern.

■ Program generators are an alternative approach to concept reuse where the reusable concepts are embedded in a generator system. The designer specifies the abstractions required using a domain-specific language, and an executable program is generated.

■ Applications frameworks are collections of concrete and abstract objects that are designed to be reused through specialisation and the addition of new objects.

■ COTS product reuse is concerned with the reuse of large-scale, off-the-shelf systems. These provide a lot of functionality, and their reuse can radically reduce costs and development time.

■ Potential problems with COTS-based reuse include lack of control over functionality and performance, lack of control over system evolution, the need for support from external vendors and difficulties in ensuring that systems can interoperate.

■ Enterprise Resource Planning systems are very widely used. Specific ERP systems are created by configuring a generic system at deployment time with information about the customer's business.

■ Software product lines are related applications that are developed from one or more base applications. A generic system is adapted and specialised to meet specific requirements for functionality, target platform or operational configuration.

FURTHER READING

Reuse-based Software Engineering. A comprehensive discussion of different approaches to software reuse. The authors cover technical reuse issues and managing reuse processes. (H. Mili, et al., 2002, John Wiley & Sons.)

'A Lifecycle Process for the effective reuse of commercial off-the-shelf software'. This is a good general introduction, covering the advantages and disadvantages of using COTS in software engineering. (C. L. Braun, *Proc. Symposium on Software Reusability*, Los Angeles, 1999. ACM Press. Available from the ACM Digital Library.)

Design Patterns: Elements of Reusable Object-oriented Software. This is the original software patterns handbook that introduced software patterns to a wide community. (E. Gamma, et al., 1995, Addison-Wesley.)

'Aspect-oriented programming'. This special issue of the *CACM* has a number of articles on aspect-oriented software development. It is an excellent starting point for reading on this topic. (*Comm. ACM*, 44(10), October 2001.)

EXERCISES

18.1   What are the major technical and nontechnical factors that hinder software reuse? Do you reuse much software, and if not, why?

18.2   Suggest why the savings in cost from reusing existing software is not simply proportional to the size of the components that are reused.

18.3   Give four circumstances where you might recommend against software reuse.

18.4   Why are patterns an effective form of design reuse? What are the disadvantages to this approach to reuse?

18.5   Apart from the application domains discussed here, suggest two other domains where generator-based reuse could be successful. Explain why you think that this approach to reuse will be cost-effective in these domains.

18.6   Explain why adaptors are usually needed when systems are constructed by integrating COTS products.

18.7   Identify six possible risks that can arise when systems are constructed using COTS. What steps can a company take to reduce these risks?

18.8   Using a general information system architecture (discussed in Chapter 13) as a starting point, design an application family of library information systems that could be used in book, film, music and newspaper cutting libraries.

18.9   Using the example of the weather station system described in Chapter 14, suggest an architecture for a family of applications that are concerned with remote monitoring and data collection.

18.10 The reuse of software raises a number of copyright and intellectual property issues. If a customer pays a software contractor to develop a system, who has the right to reuse the developed code? Does the software contractor have the right to use that code as a basis for a generic component? What payment mechanisms might be used to reimburse providers of reusable components? Discuss these and other ethical issues associated with the reuse of software.

19

Component-based software engineering

Objectives

The objective of this chapter is to describe a software development process based on the composition of reusable, standardised components. When you have read this chapter, you will:

■ know that component-based software engineering is concerned with developing standardised components based on a component model and composing these into application systems;

■ understand what is meant by a component and a component model;

■ know the principal activities in the CBSE process and understand why you have to make requirements compromises so that components can be reused;

■ understand some of the difficulties and problems that arise during the process of component composition.

Contents

As I suggested in Chapter 18, reuse-based software engineering is becoming the main development approach for business and commercial systems. The entities that are reused range from fine-grain functions to entire application systems. However, until relatively recently, it was difficult to reuse medium-grain program components. Medium-grain components are significantly larger than individual objects or procedures, with more functionality, but they are smaller and more specific than application systems. Fortunately, developments in standardisation promoted by major software vendors now mean that components can interoperate within a framework such as CORBA. This has opened up opportunities for systematic reuse through component-based software engineering.

Component-based software engineering (CBSE) emerged in the late 1990s as a reuse-based approach to software systems development. Its creation was motivated by designers' frustration that object-oriented development had not led to extensive reuse, as originally suggested. Single object classes were too detailed and specific, and often had to be bound with an application at compile-time. You had to have detailed knowledge of the classes to use them, which usually meant that you had to have the component source code. This made marketing objects as reusable components difficult. In spite of early optimistic predictions, no significant market for individual objects has ever developed.

CBSE is the process of defining, implementing and integrating or composing loosely coupled independent components into systems. It has become as an important software development approach because software systems are becoming larger and more complex and customers are demanding more dependable software that is developed more quickly. The only way that we can cope with complexity and deliver better software more quickly is to reuse rather than re-implement software components.

The essentials of component-based software engineering are:

1. *Independent components* that are completely specified by their interfaces. There should be a clear separation between the component interface and its implementation so that one implementation of a component can be replaced by another without changing the system.

2. *Component standards* that facilitate the integration of components. These standards are embodied in a component model and define, at the very minimum, how component interfaces should be specified and how components communicate. Some models define interfaces that should be implemented by all conformant components. If components conform to standards, then their operation is independent of their programming language. Components written in different languages can be integrated into the same system.

3. *Middleware* that provides software support for component integration. To make independent, distributed components work together, you need middleware support that handles component communications. Middleware such as CORBA (Pope, 1998), discussed in Chapter 12, handles low-level level issues efficiently and allows you to focus on application-related problems. In addition, middleware

to implement a component model may provide support for resource allocation, transaction management, security and concurrency.

4. *A development process* that is geared to component-based software engineering. If you try to add a component-based approach to a development process that is geared to original software production, you will find that the assumptions inherent in the process limit the potential of CBSE. I discuss CBSE development processes in Section 19.2.

Component-based development is being increasingly adopted as a mainstream approach to software engineering even if reusable components are not available. Underlying CBSE are sound design principles that support the construction of understandable and maintainable software. Components are independent so they do not interfere with each other's operation. Implementation details are hidden, so the component's implementation can be changed without affecting the rest of the system. The components communicate through well-defined interfaces, so if these interfaces are maintained, one component can be replaced by another that provides additional or enhanced functionality. In addition, component infrastructures provide high-level platforms that reduce the costs of application development.

Although CBSE is developing rapidly into a mainstream approach to software development, a number of problems remain:

1. *Component trustworthiness* Components are black-box program units, and the source code of the component may not be available to component users. In such cases, how does a user know that a component is to be trusted? The component may have undocumented failure modes that compromise the system where the component is used. Its non-functional behaviour may not be as expected and, most seriously, the black-box component could be a Trojan horse that conceals malicious code that breaches system security.

2. *Component certification* Closely related to trustworthiness is the issue of certification. It has been proposed that independent assessors should certify components to assure users that the components could be trusted. However, it is not clear how this can be made to work. Who would pay for certification, who would be responsible if the component did not operate as certified, and how could the certifiers limit their liability? In my view, the only viable solution is to certify that components conform to a formal specification. However, the industry does not appear to be willing to pay for this.

3. *Emergent property prediction* As I discussed in Chapter 2, all systems have emergent properties, and trying to predict and control these emergent properties is important in the system development process. Because components are opaque, predicting their emergent properties is particularly difficult. Consequently, you may find that when components are integrated, the resulting system has undesirable properties that limit its use.

4. *Requirements trade-offs* You usually have to make trade-offs between ideal requirements and available components in the system specification and design process. At the moment, making these trade-offs is an intuitive process. We need a more structured, systematic trade-off analysis method to help designers select and configure components.

The main use of CBSE so far has been to build enterprise information systems, such as e-commerce systems. The components that are reused are internally developed or are procured from known, trusted suppliers. Although some vendors sell components online, most companies are still reluctant to trust externally procured, binary components. It is unlikely that the complete vision of CBSE with specialised component suppliers will be realised until these major problems have been solved.

19.1 Components and component models

There is general agreement in the community that a component is an independent software unit that can be composed with other components to create a software system. Beyond that, however, different people have proposed definitions of a software component. Councill and Heineman (Councill and Heineman, 2001) define a *component* as:

> *a software element that conforms to a component model and can be independently deployed and composed without modification according to a composition standard.*

This definition is essentially based on standards—a software unit that conforms to these standards is a component. Szyperski (Szyperski, 2002), however, does not mention standards in his definition of a component but focuses instead on the key characteristics of components:

> *A software component is a unit of composition with contractually specified interfaces and explicit context dependencies only. A software component can be deployed independently and is subject to composition by third parties.*

Szyperski also states that a component has no externally observable state. This means that copies of components are indistinguishable. However, some component models, such as the Enterprise Java Beans model, allow stateful components, so these clearly do not correspond with Szyperski's definition of a component. While stateless components are certainly simpler to use, I think that CBSE should accommodate both stateless and stateful components.

Figure 19.1
Component
characteristics

Component characteristic	Description
Standardised	Component standardisation means that a component used in a CBSE process has to conform to some standardised component model. This model may define component interfaces, component metadata, documentation, composition and deployment.
Independent	A component should be independent—it should be possible to compose and deploy it without having to use other specific components. In situations where the component needs externally provided services, these should be explicitly set out in a 'requires' interface specification.
Composable	For a component to be composable, all external interactions must take place through publicly defined interfaces. In addition, it must provide external access to information about itself, such as its methods and attributes.
Deployable	To be deployable, a component has to be self-contained and must be able to operate as a standalone entity on a component platform that implements the component model. This usually means that the component is binary and does not have to be compiled before it is deployed.
Documented	Components have to be fully documented so that potential users can decide whether or not the components meet their needs. The syntax and, ideally, the semantics of all component interfaces have to be specified.

What these definitions have in common is that they agree that components are independent and that they are the fundamental unit of composition in a system. In my view, a complete definition of a component can be derived from both of these proposals. Figure 19.1 shows what I consider to be the essential characteristics of a component as used in CBSE.

These formal component definitions are rather abstract and do not really give you a clear picture of what a component does. One of the most useful ways to consider a component is as a standalone service provider. When a system needs some service, it calls on a component to provide that service without caring about where that component is executing or the programming language used to develop the component. For example, a component in a library system might provide a search service that allows users to search different library catalogues; a component that converts from one graphical format to another (e.g., TIFF to JPEG) provides a data-conversion service.

Viewing a component as a service provider emphasises two critical characteristics of a reusable component:

1.   The component is an independent executable entity. Source code is not available, so the component does not have to be compiled before it is used with other system components.

Figure 19.2
Component
interfaces

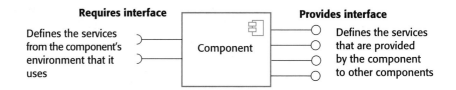

2.   The services offered by a component are made available through an interface, and all interactions are through that interface. The component interface is expressed in terms of parameterised operations and its internal state is never exposed.

Components are defined by their interfaces and, in the most general cases, can be thought of as having two related interfaces, as shown in Figure 19.2.

1.   A *provides* interface defines the services provided by the component. The provides interface, essentially, is the component API. It defines the methods that can be called by a user of the component. Provides interfaces are indicated by a circle at the end of a line from the component icon.

2.   A *requires* interface specifies what services must be provided by other components in the system. If these are not available, then the component will not work. This does not compromise the independence or deployability of the component because it is not required that a specific component should be used to provide the services. Requires interfaces are indicated by a semi-circle at the end of a line from the component icon. Notice that provides and required interface icons can fit together like a ball and socket.

For example, Figure 19.3 shows a model of a component that has been designed to collect and collate information from an array of sensors. It runs autonomously to collect data over a period of time and, on request, provides collated data to a calling component. The provides interface includes methods to add, remove, start, stop and test sensors. It also includes reporting methods (**report** and **listAll**) that report the data collected and the sensor configuration. Although I have not shown this here, these methods naturally have associated parameters specifying the sensor locations and so on.

The collector component requires that sensors provide a management interface and a data interface. These have parameters that specify the operation and the data to be collected. I have deliberately designed the required interface so that it does not include specific operations such as **Test**. The more abstract requires interface allows the collector component to be used with sensors with different interfaces. An adaptor component is used as an interface between the collector and the hardware-specific sensor interface.

Object classes have associated methods that are clearly similar to the methods defined in component interfaces. What, then, is the distinction between components and objects? Components are usually developed using an object-oriented approach, but they differ from objects in a number of important ways:

Figure 19.3 A model
of a data collector
component

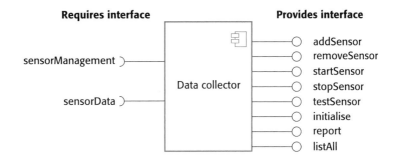

1. *Components are deployable entities* That is, they are not compiled into an application program but are installed directly on an execution platform. The methods and attributes defined in their interfaces can then be accessed by other components.

2. *Components do not define types* A class definition defines an abstract data type and objects are instances of that type. A component is an instance, not a template that is used to define an instance.

3. *Component implementations are opaque* Components are, in principle at least, completely defined by their interface specification. The implementation is hidden from component users. Components are often delivered as binary units so the buyer of the component does not have access to the implementation.

4. *Components are language-independent* Object classes have to follow the rules of a particular object-oriented programming language and, generally, can only interoperate with other classes in that language. Although components are usually implemented using object-oriented languages such as Java, you can implement them in non-object-oriented programming languages.

5. *Components are standardised* Unlike object classes that you can implement in any way, components must conform to some component model that constrains their implementation.

19.1.1 Component models

A component model is a definition of standards for component implementation, documentation and deployment. These standards are for component developers to ensure that components can interoperate. They are also for providers of component execution infrastructures who provide middleware to support component operation. Many component models have been proposed, but the most important models are the CORBA component model from the OMG, Sun's Enterprise Java Beans model and Microsoft's COM+ model (Blevins, 2001; Ewald, 2001; Wang, et al., 2001).

The specific infrastructure technologies such as COM+ and EJB that are used in CBSE are very complex. Consequently, it is difficult to describe these technologies

Figure 19.4 Basic
elements of a
component model

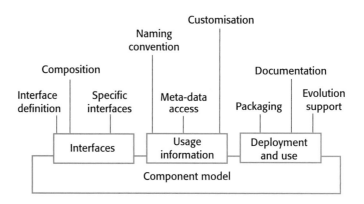

without going into a lot of implementation detail about the assumptions that underlie each approach and the interfaces that are used. Rather than go into this detail here, I focus on the fundamental elements of component models.

The basic elements of an ideal component model are discussed by Weinreich and Sametinger (Weinreich and Sametinger, 2001). I summarise these model elements in Figure 19.4. This diagram shows that the elements in a component model can be classified as elements relating to the component interfaces, elements relating to information that you need to use the component in a program and elements concerned with component deployment.

The defining elements of a component are its interfaces. The component model specifies how the interfaces should be defined and the elements, such as operation names, parameters and exceptions, that should be included in an interface definition. The model should also specify the language used to define the interfaces (the IDL). In CORBA and COM+, this is a specific interface definition language; EJB is Java-specific so Java is used as the IDL. Some component models require specific interfaces that must be defined by a component. These are used to compose the component with the component model infrastructure that provides standardised services such as security and transaction management.

In order for components to be distributed and accessed remotely, they need to have a unique name or handle associated with them. In COM+, this is a unique 128-bit identifier. In the CORBA component model and in EJB, it is a hierarchical name with the root based on an Internet domain name. Component metadata is data about the component itself, such as information about its interfaces and attributes. The metadata is important so that users of the component can find out what services are provided and required. Component model implementations normally include specific ways (such as the use of a reflection interface in Java) to access this component metadata.

Components are generic entities and, when deployed, they have to be customised to their particular application environment. For example, the **Data collector** component shown in Figure 19.3 might be customised with the maximum number of sensors in a sensor array. The component model should therefore specify how the binary components can be configured for a particular deployment environment.

An important part of a component model is a definition of how components should be packaged for deployment as independent, executable entities. Because components are independent entities, they have to be packaged with everything that is not provided by the component infrastructure or not defined in a requires interface. Deployment information includes information about the contents of a package and its binary organisation.

Inevitably, as new requirements emerge, components will have to be changed or replaced. The component model should therefore include rules governing when and how component replacement is allowed. Finally, the component model should define the component documentation that should be produced. This is used to find the component and to decide whether it is appropriate.

Component models are not just standards; they are also the basis for system middleware that provides support for executing components. Weinreich and Sametinger (Weinreich and Sametinger, 2001) use the analogy of an operating system to explain component models. An operating system provides a set of generic services that can be used by applications. A component model implementation provides comparable shared services for components. Figure 19.5 shows some of the services that may be provided by an implementation of a component model.

The services provided by a component model implementation fall into two categories:

1. *Platform services* These fundamental services enable components to communicate with each other. CORBA is an example of a component model platform. I have described the platform services in Chapter 12.

2. *Horizontal services* These application-independent services are likely to be used by many different components. The availability of these services reduces the costs of component development and means that potential component incompatibilities can be avoided.

To make use of the services provided by a component model infrastructure, components are deployed in a predefined, standardised container. A *container* is a set of interfaces used to access the implementations of the support services. Including the component in the container automatically provides service access. The component interfaces themselves are not accessed directly by other components; they are accessed through the container.

19.1.2 Component development for reuse

The long-term vision of CBSE is that there will be component suppliers whose business is based on the development and sale of reusable components. As I have said, the problems of trust mean that an open market for components has not yet developed, and most components that are reused are developed within a company. The

Figure 19.5 Services
provided by a
component model

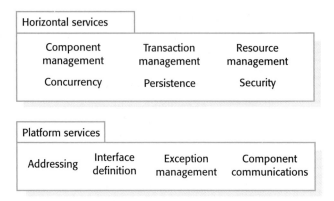

Horizontal services		
Component management	Transaction management	Resource management
Concurrency	Persistence	Security

Platform services			
Addressing	Interface definition	Exception management	Component communications

reusable components are not developed specially but are based on existing components that have already been implemented and used in application systems.

Generally, internally developed components are not immediately reusable. They include
application-specific features and interfaces that are unlikely to be required in other applications. Therefore, you have to adapt and extend these components to create a more
generic and hence more reusable version. Obviously, this has an associated cost. You
have to decide, first, whether a component is likely to be reused and second, whether
the cost savings of reuse justify the costs of making the component reusable.

To answer the first of these questions, you have to decide whether the component implements one or more stable domain abstractions. Stable domain abstractions are fundamental concepts in the application domain that change slowly. For
example, in a banking system, domain abstractions might include accounts, account
holders and statements. In a hospital management system, domain abstractions might
include patients, treatments and nurses. These domain abstractions are sometimes
called business objects. If the component is an implementation of a commonly used
business object or group of related objects, it can probably be reused.

To answer the question about the cost-effectiveness, you have to assess the costs
of changes that are required to make the component reusable. These costs are the
costs of component documentation, of component validation and of making the component more generic. Changes that you may make to a component to make it more
reusable include:

- Removing application-specific methods
- Changing names to make them more general
- Adding methods to provide more complete functional coverage
- Making exception handling consistent for all methods
- adding a 'configuration' interface to allow the component to be adapted to dif-
  ferent situations of use
- Integrating required components to increase independence.

The problem of exception handling is a particularly difficult one. In principle, all exceptions should be part of the component interface. Components should not handle exceptions themselves, because each application will have its own requirements for exception handling. Rather, the component should define what exceptions can arise and should publish these as part of the interface. For example, a simple component implementing a stack data structure should detect and publish stack overflow and stack underflow exceptions. In practice, however, a component may provide some local exception handling, and changing this may have serious implications for the functionality of the component.

Mili et al. (Mili, et al., 2002) discuss ways of estimating the costs of making a component reusable and estimating the returns from that investment. The benefits of reusing rather than redeveloping a component are not simply productivity gains. They also include quality gains, because a reused component should be more dependable, and time-to-market gains. These are the increased returns that accrue from deploying the software more quickly. Mili et al. present various formulae for estimating these gains, as does the COCOMO model discussed in Chapter 26 (Boehm, et al., 2000). However, the parameters of these formulae are difficult to estimate accurately, and the formulae must be adapted to local circumstances. I suspect that these factors mean very few software project managers would be willing to trust them.

Obviously, whether a component is reusable depends on its application domain and functionality. As you add generality to a component, you increase its reusability. However, this normally means that the component has more operations and is more complex, which makes the component harder to understand and use.

There is an inevitable trade-off between the reusability and the usability of a component. Making the component reusable involves providing a set of generic interfaces with operations that cater to all ways in which the component could be used. Making the component usable means providing a simple, minimal interface that is easy to understand. Reusability adds complexity and hence reduces component understandability. It is therefore more difficult to decide when and how to reuse that component. When designing a reusable component, you must find a compromise between generality and understandability.

Another important source of components is existing legacy systems. As I discussed in Chapter 2, these are systems that fulfil an important business function but are written using obsolete software technologies. Because of this, it may be difficult to use them with new systems. However, if you convert these old systems to components, their functionality can be reused in new applications.

Of course, these legacy systems do not normally have clearly defined requires and provides interfaces. To make these components reusable, you have to conduct a wrapper that defines the component interfaces. The wrapper hides the complexity of the underlying code and provides an interface for external components to access services that are provided. Naturally, this wrapper is a fairly complex piece of software as it has to access the legacy system functionality. However, the cost of wrapper development is often much less than the cost of re-implementing the legacy system.

Figure 19.6 The
CBSE process

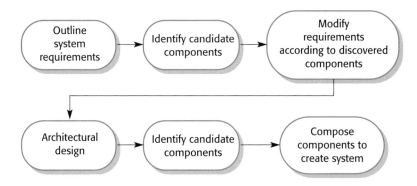

19.2 The CBSE process

I suggested in the introduction that the successful reuse of components requires a development process tailored to CBSE. The structure of such a process was discussed in Chapter 4; Figure 19.6 shows the principal sub-activities within a CBSE process. Some of the activities within this process, such as the initial discovery of user requirements, are carried out in the same way as in other software processes. However, the essential differences between this process and software processes based on original software development are:

1. The user requirements are initially developed in outline rather than in detail, and stakeholders are encouraged to be as flexible as possible in defining their requirements. The reason for this is that very specific requirements limit the number of components that might meet these requirements. Unlike incremental development, however, you need a complete set of requirements so that you can identify as many components as possible for reuse.

2. Requirements are refined and modified early in the process depending on the components available. If the user requirements cannot be satisfied from available components, you should discuss the related requirements that can be supported. Users may be willing to change their minds if this means cheaper or quicker system delivery.

3. There is a further component search and design refinement activity after the system architecture has been designed. Some apparently usable components may turn out to be unsuitable or do not work properly with other chosen components. Although not shown in Figure 19.6, this implies that further requirements changes may be necessary.

2. Development is a composition process where the discovered components are integrated. This involves integrating the components with the component model infrastructure and, often, developing 'glue code' to reconcile the interfaces of

incompatible components. Of course, additional functionality may be required over and above that provided by usable components. Naturally, you should develop this as components that can be reused in future systems.

The architectural design stage is particularly important. During the architectural design, you may finally decide on a component model, although, for many systems, this decision will be made before the search for components begins. As covered in Chapters 11 through 13, you also establish the high-level organisation of the system and make decisions about system distribution and control. Jacobsen et al. (Jacobsen, et al., 1997) have found that defining a robust architecture is critical for successful reuse.

One activity that is unique to the CBSE process is component identification. This involves a number of sub-activities, as shown in Figure 19.7. There are two stages in the CBSE process where you have to identify components for possible use in the system. In the early stage, your focus should be on search and selection. You need to convince yourself that there are components available to meet your requirements. Obviously, you should do some initial checking that the component is suitable but detailed testing may not be required. In the later stage, after the system architecture has been designed, you should spend more time on component validation. You need to be confident that the identified components are really suited to your application; if not, then you have to repeat the search and selection processes.

The first stage in identifying components is to look for components that are available locally or from trusted suppliers. The vision of advocates of CBSE such as Szyperski (Szyperski, 2002) is that there should be a viable component marketplace where external vendors compete to provide components. At the time of this writing, this has not emerged to any significant extent. The main reason for this is that users of external components face risks that these components will not work as advertised. If this is the case, the costs of reuse exceed the benefits, and few project managers believe that the risks are worth taking. Another important reason why component markets have not developed is that many components are in specialised application domains. There is not a sufficiently large market in these domains for external component suppliers to establish a viable, long-term business.

As a consequence, component search is often confined to a software development organisation. Software development companies can build their own database of reusable components without the risks inherent in using components from external suppliers.

Once the component search process has identified candidate components, specific components from this list have to be selected. In some cases, this will be a straightforward task. Components on the list will map directly onto the user requirements, and there will not be competing components that match these requirements. In other cases, however, the selection process is much more complex. There will not be a clean mapping of requirements to components, and you will find that several components have to be used to meet a specific requirement or group of requirements. Unfortunately, it is likely that different requirements will require different groups of components, so you have to decide which component compositions provide the best coverage of the requirements.

Once you have selected components for possible inclusion in a system, you should validate them to check that they behave as advertised. The extent of the validation required depends on the source of the components. If you are using a component that has been developed by a known and trusted source, you may decide that separate component testing is unnecessary and you test the component when it is integrated with other components. On the other hand, if you are using a component from an unknown source, you should always check and test that component before including it in your system.

Component validation involves developing a set of test cases for the component (or, possibly, extending test cases supplied with the component) and developing a test harness to run the component tests. The major problem with component validation is that the component specification may not be sufficiently detailed to allow you to develop a complete set of component tests. Components are usually specified informally, with the only formal documentation being their interface specification. This may not include enough information for you to develop a complete set of tests that would convince you that the component's advertised interface is what you require.

A further validation problem, which may arise at this stage, is that the component may have features that could interfere with your use of the component. Reusable components will often have more functionality than you need. You can simply ignore the unwanted functionality, but it can sometimes interfere with other components or with the system as a whole. In some cases, the unwanted functionality can even cause serious system failures. Figure 19.8 briefly describes a situation where unnecessary functionality in a reused system caused a catastrophic software failure.

The problem in the Ariane 5 launcher arose because the assumptions made about the software for Ariane 4 were invalid for Ariane 5. This is a general problem with reusable components. They are originally implemented for an application environment and, naturally, embed assumptions about that environment. These assumptions are rarely documented so, when the component is reused, it is impossible to derive tests to check whether the assumptions are still valid.

19.3 Component composition

Component composition is the process of assembling components to create a system. If we assume a situation where reusable components are available, then most systems will be constructed by composing these reusable components with each other, with specially written components and with the component support infrastructure

Figure 19.8 A
component
validation failure

The Ariane 5 launcher failure

While developing the Ariane 5 space launcher, the designers decided to reuse the inertial reference software that had performed successfully in the Ariane 4 launcher. The inertial reference software maintains the stability of the rocket. They decided to reuse this without change (as you would do with components), although it included additional functionality over and above that required in Ariane 5.

In the first launch of Ariane 5, the inertial navigation software failed after 37 seconds and the rocket could not be controlled. Ground controllers instructed the launcher to self-destruct and the rocket payload was destroyed. A subsequent enquiry found that the cause of the problem was an unhandled exception when a conversion of a fixed-point number to an integer resulted in a numeric overflow. This caused the run-time system to shut down the inertial reference system and launcher stability could not be maintained. The fault had never occurred in Ariane 4 because it had less powerful engines and the value that was converted could not be large enough for the conversion to overflow.

The fault occurred in code that was not required for Ariane 5. The validation tests for the reused software were based on Ariane 5 requirements. Because there were no requirements for the function that failed, no tests were developed. Consequently, the problem with the software was never discovered during launch simulation tests.

provided by the model framework. As I discussed in Section 19.1, this infrastructure provides facilities to support component communication and horizontal services such as user interface services, transaction management, concurrency and security. The ways in which components are integrated with this infrastructure are documented for each component model and are not discussed in this section.

Composition is not a simple operation; there are a number of types (Figure 19.9):

1. *Sequential composition* This occurs when, in the composite component, the constituent components are executed in sequence. It corresponds to situation (a) in Figure 19.9, where the provides interfaces of each component are composed. Some extra code is required to make the link between the components.

2. *Hierarchical composition* This occurs when one component calls directly on the services provided by another component. It corresponds to a situation where the provides interface of one component is composed with the requires interface of another component. This is situation (b) in Figure 19.9.

3. *Additive composition* This occurs when the interfaces of two or more components are put together (added) to create a new component. The interfaces of the composite component are created by putting together all of the interfaces of the constituent components, with duplicate operations removed if necessary. This corresponds to situation (c) in Figure 19.9.

Figure 19.9 Types of
component
composition

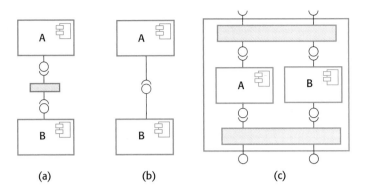

    (a)   (b)   (c)

You might use all the forms of component composition when creating a system. In all cases, you may have to write 'glue code' that links the components. For example, for sequential composition, the output of component A typically becomes the input to component B. You need intermediate statements that call component A, collect the result and then call component B with that result as a parameter.

When you write components especially for composition, you design the interfaces of these components so that they are compatible. You can therefore easily compose these components into a single unit. However, when components are developed independently for reuse, you will often be faced with interface incompatibilities where the interfaces of the components that you wish to compose are not the same. Three types of incompatibility can occur:

1. *Parameter incompatibility* The operations on each side of the interface have the same name but their parameter types or the number of parameters are different.

2. *Operation incompatibility* The names of the operations in the provides and requires interfaces are different.

3. *Operation incompleteness* The provides interface of a component is a subset of the requires interface of another component or vice versa.

In all cases, you tackle the problem of incompatibility by writing an adaptor component that reconciles the interfaces of the two components being reused. When you know the interfaces of the components that you want to use, you write an adaptor component that converts one interface to another. The precise form of the adaptor depends on the type of composition. Sometimes, as in the next example, the adaptor simply takes a result from one component and converts it into a form where it can be used as an input to another. In other cases, the adaptor may be called by component A, and itself calls component B. This latter situation would arise if A and B were compatible but the number of parameters in their interfaces was different.

Figure 19.10
Incompatible
components

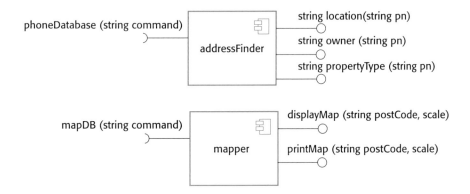

Figure 19.10
Incompatible
components

To illustrate adaptors, consider the components shown in Figure 19.10. These might be part of a system used by the emergency services. When the emergency operator takes a call, the phone number is input to the **addressFinder** component to locate the address. Then, using the **mapper** component, they print a map to be sent to the vehicle despatched to the emergency. In fact, the components would have more complex interfaces than those shown here, but the simplified version illustrates the concept of an adaptor.

The first component, **addressFinder**, finds the address that matches a phone number. It can also return the owner of the property associated with the phone number and the type of property. The **mapper** component takes a post code (in the United States, a standard ZIP code with the additional four digits identifying property location) and displays or prints a street map of the area around that code at a specified scale.

These components are composable in principle because the property location includes the post or ZIP code. However, you have to write an adaptor component called **postCodeStripper** that takes the location data from **addressFinder** and strips out the post code. This post code is then used as an input to **mapper**, and the street map is displayed at a scale of 1:10,000. The following code illustrates the sequence of calls that is required to implement this:

```
address = addressFinder.location (phonenumber) ;
postCode = postCodeStripper.getPostCode (address) ;
mapper.displayMap(postCode, 10000) ;
```

Another case in which an adaptor component may be used is where one component wishes to make use of another, but there is an incompatibility between the provides and requires interfaces of these components. I have illustrated this in Figure 19.11, where the data collector component is connected to a sensor component using an adaptor. It reconciles the requires interfaces of the data collection component with the provides interfaces of the sensor component. The data collection component was designed with a generic requires mechanism that was not based on a specific

Figure 19.11 Adaptor
for the data collector
component

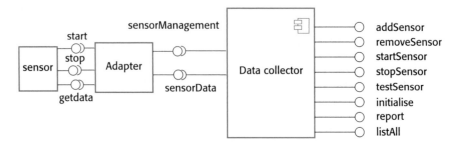

sensor interface. I anticipated that an adaptor would always be used to connect the data collector to a specific sensor interface.

The discussion of component composition assumes you can tell from the component documentation whether interfaces are compatible. Of course, the interface definition includes the operation name and parameter types, so you can make some assessment of the compatibility from this. However, you depend on the component documentation to decide whether the interfaces are semantically compatible.

For example, consider the composition shown in Figure 19.12. These components are used to implement a system that downloads images from a digital camera and stores them in a photograph library. The system user can provide additional information to describe and catalogue the photograph. To avoid clutter, I have not shown all interface methods here but simply show the methods that are needed to illustrate the component documentation problem. The methods in the interface of **Photo Library** are:

```
public void addItem (Identifier pid ; Photograph p; CatalogEntry photodesc) ;
public Photograph retrieve (Identifier pid) ;
public CatalogEntry catEntry (Identifier pid) ;
```

Assume that the documentation for the **addItem** method in **Photo Library** is:

This method adds a photograph to the library and associates the photograph identifier and catalogue descriptor with the photograph.

This description appears to be comprehensive, but consider the following questions:

What happens if the photograph identifier is already associated with a photograph in the library?

Is the photograph descriptor associated with the catalogue entry as well as the photograph? That is, if I delete the photograph, do I also delete the catalogue information?

Figure 19.12 Photo
Library composition

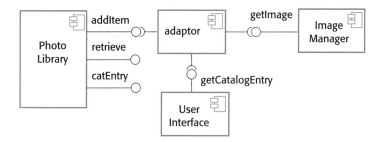

There is not enough information in the informal description of **addItem** to answer these questions. Of course, it is possible to add more information to the natural language description of the method, but, in general, the best way to resolve ambiguities is to use a formal language to describe the interface. In Chapter 10, I suggested that interface description was one area where formal specifications are most useful. The specification shown in Figure 19.13 is part of the description of the interface of **Photo Library** that adds information to the informal description.

The specification in Figure 19.13 uses pre- and post-conditions, and I have used a notation based on the object constraint language (OCL) that is part of the UML (Warmer and Kleppe, 1998). OCL is designed to describe constraints in UML object models; it allows you to express predicates that must always be true, that must be true before a method has executed, and that must be true after a method has executed. These are invariants, pre-conditions and post-conditions. To access the value of a variable before an operation, you add **@pre** after its name. Therefore:

age = age@pre + 1

means that the value of age after an operation is one more than it was before that operation.

OCL-based approaches are being increasingly used to add semantic information to UML models. The general approach has been derived from Meyer's Design by Contract approach (Meyer, 1992), in which the interfaces and obligations of communicating objects are formally specified and enforced by the run-time system. Meyer suggests that using Design by Contract is essential if we are to develop trusted components (Meyer, 2003).

Figure 19.13 includes a specification for the **addItem** and the **delete** methods in **Photo Library**. The method being specified is indicated by the keyword context and the pre- and post-conditions by the keywords **pre** and **post**. The pre-conditions for **addItem** state that:

- There must not be a photograph in the library with the same identifier as the photograph to be entered.
- The library must exist—assume that creating a library adds a single item to it so that the size of a library is always greater than zero.

Figure 19.13 Formal
description of the
Photo Library
interface

— The context keyword names the component to which the conditions apply
context addItem

— The preconditions specify what must be true before execution of addItem
pre: PhotoLibrary.libSize() > 0
         PhotoLibrary.retrieve(pid) = null

— The postconditions specify what is true after execution
post: libSize () = libSize()@pre + 1
         PhotoLibrary.retrieve(pid) = p
         PhotoLibrary.catEntry(pid) = photodesc

context delete

pre: PhotoLibrary.retrieve(pid) null ;

post   PhotoLibrary.retrieve(pid) = null
         PhotoLibrary.catEntry(pid) = PhotoLibrary.catEntry(pid)@pre
         PhotoLibrary.libSize() = libSize()@pre[em]1

The post-conditions for **addItem** state that:

- The size of the library has increased by 1 (so only a single entry has been made).
- If you retrieve using the same identifier, then you get back the photograph that you added.
- If you look up the catalogue using that identifier, you get back the catalogue entry that you made.

The specification of **delete** provides further information. The pre-condition states that to delete an item, it must be in the library and, after deletion, the photo can no longer be retrieved and the size of the library is reduced by 1. However, **delete** does not delete the catalogue entry—you can still retrieve it after the photo has been deleted. The reason for this is that you may wish to maintain information in the catalogue about why a photo was deleted, its new location, and so on.

When you create a system by composing components, you may find that there are potential conflicts between functional and non-functional requirements, the need to deliver a system as quickly as possible, and the need to create a system that can evolve as requirements change. The decisions where you may have to make trade-offs are:

Figure 19.14 Data
collection and report
generation
components

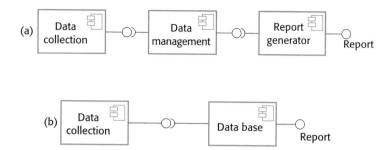

1. What composition of components is most effective in delivering the functional requirements for the system?

2. What composition of the components will allow adaptations for future changes to the requirements?

3. What will be the emergent properties of the composed system? These emergent properties are properties such as performance and dependability. You can only assess these once the complete system is implemented.

Unfortunately, there are many situations where the solutions to the composition problems are mutually conflicting. For example, consider a situation such as that illustrated in Figure 19.14, where a system can be created through two alternative compositions. The system is a data collection and reporting system where data is collected from different sources, stored in a database, and a different report summarising that data is produced.

The advantages of composition (a) are that reporting and data management are separate, so there is more flexibility for future change. The data management system could be replaced and, if reports are required that the current reporting component cannot produce, that component can also be replaced. In composition (b), a database component with built-in reporting facilities (e.g., Microsoft Access) is used. The advantages of composition (b) are that there are fewer components, so this will probably be faster because there are no component communication overheads. Furthermore, data integrity rules that apply to the database will also apply to reports. These reports will not be able to combine data in incorrect ways. In composition (a), there are no such constraints, so errors in reports are more likely.

In general, a good composition principle to follow is the principle of separation of concerns. That is, you should try to design your system in such a way that each component has a clearly defined role and that, ideally, these roles should not overlap. However, it may be cheaper to buy one multifunctional component rather than two or three separate components. Furthermore, there may be dependability or performance penalties when multiple components are used.

KEY POINTS

■ Component-based software engineering is a reuse-based approach to defining, implementing and composing loosely coupled independent components into systems.

■ A component is a software unit whose functionality and dependencies are completely defined by a set of public interfaces. Components can be combined with other components without reference to their implementation and can be deployed as an executable unit.

■ A component model defines a set of standards for components, including interface standards, usage standards and deployment standards. The implementation of the component model provides a set of horizontal services that may be used by all components.

■ During the CBSE process, you have to interleave the processes of requirements engineering and system design. You have to trade-off desirable requirements against the services that are available from existing reusable components.

■ Component composition is the process of 'wiring' components together to create a system. Types of composition include sequential composition, hierarchical composition and additive composition.

■ When composing reusable components that have not been written for your application, you normally need to write adaptors or 'glue code' to reconcile the different component interfaces.

■ When choosing compositions, you have to consider the required functionality of the system, the non-functional requirements and the ease with which one component can be replaced by another when the system is changed.

FURTHER READING

Component-based Software Engineering: Putting the Pieces Together. This book is a collection of papers from various authors on different aspects of CBSE. Like all collections, it is rather mixed, but it has better coverage of general issues of software engineering with components than Szyperski's book. (G. T. Heineman and W. T. Councill, 2001, Addison-Wesley.)

Component Software: Beyond Object-Oriented Programming, 2nd ed. This updated edition of the first book on CBSE covers technical and nontechnical issues in CBSE. It includes more detail on specific technologies than Heineman and Councill's book and a thorough discussion of market issues. (C. Szyperski, 2002, Addison-Wesley.)

'Specification, implementation and deployment of components'. A good introduction to the fundamentals of CBSE. The same issue of the CACM includes articles on components and component-based development. (I. Crnkovic, et al., *Comm. ACM,* 45(10), October 2002.)

EXERCISES

19.1 Why is it important that all component interactions are defined through requires and provides interfaces?

19.2 The principle of component independence means that it ought to be possible to replace one component with another that is implemented in a completely different way. Using an example, discuss how such component replacement might have undesired consequences and may lead to system failure.

19.3 What are the fundamental differences between components and web services (see Chapter 12).

19.4 Why is it important that components should be based on a standard component model?

19.5 Using an example of a component that implements an abstract data type such as a stack or a list, show why it is usually necessary to extend and adapt components for reuse.

19.6 Explain why it is very difficult to validate a reusable component without the component source code. In what ways would a formal component specification simplify the problems of validation?

19.7 Design a reusable component that implements the search feature of the LIBSYS system discussed in previous chapters. This is not a simple keyword search of web pages. You have to be able to search the catalogues of several libraries, as specified by the user.

19.8 Using examples, illustrate the different types of adaptors needed to support sequential composition, hierarchical composition and additive composition.

19.9 Design the interfaces of components that might be used in a system in an emergency control room. You should design interfaces for a call-logging component that records calls made, and a vehicle-discovery component that, given a post code and an incident type, finds the nearest suitable vehicle to be despatched to the incident.

19.10 It has been suggested that an independent certification authority should be established. Vendors would submit their components to this authority, which would validate that the component was trustworthy. What would be the advantages and disadvantages of such a certification authority?

20

Critical systems development

Objectives

The objective of this chapter is to introduce implementation techniques that are used in the development of critical systems. When you have read this chapter, you will:

■ understand how fault avoidance and fault tolerance contribute to the development of dependable systems;

■ know the characteristics of and activities in dependable software processes;

■ have been introduced to programming techniques for fault avoidance;

■ understand the stages involved in implementing fault tolerance and the ways in which diversity and redundancy are used in fault-tolerant architectures.

Contents

Improved software engineering techniques, better programming languages and better quality management have led to significant improvements in dependability for most software. However, critical systems, such as those that control unattended machinery, medical systems, telecommunications switches or aircraft engines need higher levels of dependability. In these cases, special development techniques may be used to ensure that the system is safe, secure and reliable.

There are three complementary approaches to developing dependable software:

1. *Fault avoidance* The design and implementation process for the system should use approaches to software development that help avoid programming errors and so minimise the number of faults in a program.

2. *Fault detection* The verification and validation processes are designed to discover and remove faults in a program before it is deployed for operational use.

3. *Fault tolerance* The system is designed so that faults or unexpected system behaviour during execution are detected and managed in such a way that system failure does not occur.

This chapter focuses on processes and techniques that support fault avoidance and fault tolerance. Fault detection is a major topic in its own right and is covered in Part 5. I discuss static techniques for fault detection in Chapter 22, program testing in Chapter 23 and verification and validation techniques that are specific to critical systems in Chapter 24.

Fundamental to the achievement of dependability in any system are the basic notions of redundancy and diversity. Diversity and redundancy are everyday coping strategies for avoiding failure. If you are investing in the stock market, you should not place all your investments in a single company because you could lose everything if the company fails (diversity). People keep spare batteries and light bulbs in their homes so that they can recover quickly from failures (redundancy). We all should back up our computers regularly in case of disk failure (redundancy) and, to secure our homes, we often have more than one type of lock on the door (diversity).

Critical systems may include components that replicate the functionality of other components (redundancy) or additional checking code that is not strictly necessary for the system to function (redundancy). Faults can therefore be detected before they cause failures, and the system may be able to continue operating if individual components fail. If the redundant components are not the same as other components (diversity), a common failure in the same, replicated component will not result in a complete system failure.

In systems where availability is a critical requirement, redundant servers are normally made available. These automatically come into operation if a designated server fails. Sometimes, to ensure that attacks on the system cannot exploit a common vulnerability, these servers may be of different types and may run different operating systems. Using different operating systems is one example of software diversity and redundancy. In other cases, as I discuss later, diversity and redundancy may be built into the software by including redundant software components that have been deliberately programmed using different techniques.

Diversity and redundancy are also used to achieve dependable processes. As well as testing a program, you may use program inspections and static analysis as fault-finding techniques. These validation techniques are complementary: One can find faults that are missed by the other. Furthermore, the same process activity (e.g., a program inspection) may be carried out by several team members—people tackle tasks in different ways depending on their personality, experience and education, so this kind of redundancy provides a diverse perspective on the system.

Unfortunately, adding diversity and redundancy to systems makes them more complex, and thus harder to understand. It is therefore more likely that programmers will make errors and less likely that people checking the program will find errors. As a consequence, some people think that it is best to avoid redundancy and diversity in software, to design the system to be as simple as possible and to have extremely rigorous verification and validation procedures (Parnas, et al., 1990). Both approaches are used in commercial, safety-critical systems. The Airbus 340 flight control system is diverse and redundant (Storey, 1996), whereas the flight control system on the Boeing 777 is based on a single version of the software.

A goal of software engineering research has been to develop tools, techniques and methods that lead to the production of fault-free software. Fault-free software is software that conforms exactly to its specification. This does not, however, mean that the software will never fail. There may be errors in the specification that are reflected in the software, or the users may misunderstand or misuse the software system. However, eliminating software faults certainly has a huge impact on the number of system failures.

For small and medium-sized systems, our software engineering techniques are such that it is probably possible to develop fault-free software. To achieve this goal, you need to use a range of software engineering techniques:

1. *Dependable software processes* The use of a dependable software process (discussed in Section 20.1) with appropriate verification and validation activities is essential if the number of faults in a program is to be minimised, and those that do slip through are to be detected.

2. *Quality management* The organisation developing the system must have a culture in which quality drives the software process. The culture should encourage programmers to write bug-free programs. Design and development standards should be established, and procedures should be in place to check that these have been followed.

3. *Formal specification* There must be a precise (preferably formal) system specification that defines the system to be implemented. Many design and programming mistakes are a result of misinterpretation of an ambiguous or poorly worded specification.

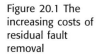

Figure 20.1 The
increasing costs of
residual fault
removal

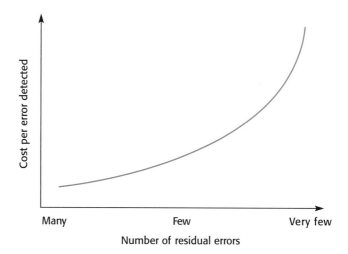

4. *Static verification* Static verification techniques, such as the use of static analysers, can find anomalous program features that could be faults. Formal verification, based on the system specification, may also be used.

5. *Strong typing* A strongly typed programming language such as Java or Ada must be used for development. If the language has strong typing, the language compiler can detect many programming errors before they can be introduced into the delivered program.

6. *Safe programming* Some programming language constructs are more complex and error-prone than others, and you are more likely to make mistakes if you use them. Safe programming means avoiding or at least minimising the use of these constructs.

7. *Protected information* An approach to software design and implementation based on information hiding and encapsulation should be used. Object-oriented languages such as Java obviously satisfy this condition. The development of programs that are designed for readability and understandability should be encouraged.

I have discussed several of these techniques in other chapters of this book. In this chapter, I concentrate on describing dependable software processes and programming techniques that contribute to fault avoidance.

However, there are hardly any situations where it is economically practical to deploy all these techniques to create fault-free software. The cost of finding and removing remaining faults rises exponentially as faults in the program are discovered and removed (Figure 20.1). As the software becomes more reliable, you need to spend more and more time and effort to find fewer and fewer faults. At some stage, the costs of this additional effort become unjustifiable.

Figure 20.2
Characteristics of
dependable
processes

Process characteristic	Description
Documentable	The process should have a defined process model that sets out the activities in the process and the documentation that is to be produced during these activities.
Standardised	A comprehensive set of software development standards that define how the software is to be produced and documented should be available.
Auditable	The process should be understandable by people apart from process participants who can check that process standards are being followed and make suggestions for process improvement.
Diverse	The process should include redundant and diverse verification and validation activities.
Robust	The process should be able to recover from failures of individual process activities.

As a result, software development companies accept that their software will always contain some residual faults. The level of faults depends on the type of system. Shrink-wrapped products have a relatively high level of faults (although they are much better than they were 10 years ago), whereas critical systems usually have a much lower fault density.

The rationale for accepting faults is that, if and when the system fails, it is cheaper to pay for the consequences of failure than it would be to discover and remove the faults before system delivery. However, as discussed in Chapter 3, the decision to release faulty software is not simply economic. The social and political acceptability of system failure must also be taken into account.

20.1 Dependable processes

Dependable software processes are processes that are geared to fault avoidance and fault detection. Dependable processes are well defined and repeatable, and include a spectrum of verification and validation activities. A well-defined process is a process that has been standardised and documented. A repeatable process is one that does not rely on individual interpretation and judgement. Irrespective of the people involved in the process, the organisation can be confident that the process will be successful. I discuss the importance of processes in achieving software quality and process improvement in Chapter 28. The essential characteristics of dependable processes are shown in Figure 20.2.

A dependable process should always include well-planned, comprehensive verification and validation activities whose aim is to ensure residual faults in the software are discovered before it is deployed. Process activities that are geared to fault avoidance and fault detection include:

1. *Requirements inspections* As I discussed in Chapter 7, these are intended to discover problems with the system specification. A high proportion of faults in delivered software result from requirements errors. If these can be discovered and eliminated from the specification, then this class of faults will be minimised.

2. *Requirements management* Requirements management, discussed in Chapter 7, is concerned with keeping track of changes to requirements and tracing these through to the design and implementation. Many errors in delivered systems are a result of failing to ensure that a requirements change has actually been included in the design and implementation of the system.

3. *Model checking* Model checking involves CASE tools automatically analysing system models to ensure internal and external consistency. *Internal consistency* means that a single model is consistent; *external consistency* means that different models of the system (e.g. a state model and an object model) are consistent.

4. *Design and code inspections* As I discuss in Chapter 22, design and code inspections are often based on checklists of common faults and are intended to discover and remove these faults before system testing.

5. *Static analysis* Static analysis is an automated technique of program analysis where the program is analysed in detail to find potentially erroneous conditions. I discuss this in Chapter 22.

6. *Test planning and management* A comprehensive set of tests for the system should be designed and the testing process carefully managed to ensure complete test coverage and traceability between the system tests and the system requirements and design. I discuss testing in Chapter 23.

A possible source of error in critical systems is to include the wrong component or the wrong version of a component in a system. To avoid this, you need to use strict configuration management. *Configuration management* is concerned with managing software change and keeping track of the versions of a system and its components. I cover this topic in Chapter 29.

20.2 Dependable programming

Dependable programming involves using programming constructs and techniques that contribute to fault avoidance and fault tolerance. Faults in programs arise because programmers make mistakes. While some mistakes are due to misunderstanding the specification, others arise from over-complex programs or the use of inherently error-prone constructs. To achieve dependability, therefore, you should design for simplicity, protect information from unauthorised access and minimise the use of potentially unsafe programming constructs.

Programming techniques for fault tolerance rely on the fact that there is a distinction between faults and failures. A *failure* is something that is observable to the users of a system, whereas a *fault* is an internal system characteristic. If a fault arises in an executing program, you may be able to tolerate it by detecting it and taking recovery action before it results in a system failure. In this section, I discuss the use of exception handling constructs to make programs more fault tolerant and easier to understand.

20.2.1 Protected information

A security principle that is adopted by military organisations is the 'need to know' principle. Only those individuals who need to know a particular piece of information in order to carry out their duties are given that information. Information that is not directly relevant to their work is withheld.

When programming, you should adopt an analogous principle to control access to system data. Program components should only be allowed access to data that they need for their implementation. You can protect other data by using the scope rules of the programming language to hide it from other parts of the program. If you hide information, it cannot be corrupted by program components that are not supposed to use it. If the interface remains the same, the data representation may be changed without affecting other components in the system.

Protecting information is much simpler in Java than in older programming languages such as C or Pascal. Because these languages do not have encapsulation constructs such as object classes, details of the implementation of data structures cannot be protected. Other parts of the program can access the structure directly, which can lead to unexpected side effects when changes are made.

It is generally good practice when programming in an object-oriented language to provide methods that access and update attribute values rather than allow other objects to access these attributes directly. This means that you can change the representation of the attribute without worrying about how other objects use the attribute. It is particularly important that you use this approach for data structures and other complex attributes.

Java's interface definition construct makes it possible to use this approach and to declare the interface to an object without reference to its implementation. This is illustrated in Figure 20.3. Users of objects of type Queue can put objects onto the queue, remove them from the queue and query the size of the queue. However, in the class that implements this interface, the actual implementation of the queue should be concealed by declaring the attributes and methods to be private to that object class. Separating interfaces and their implementation is an essential part of component-based software engineering.

Figure 20.3 A Queue
specification using a
Java interface
declaration

```
interface Queue {

    public void put (Object o) ;
    public void remove (Object o) ;
    public int size () ;

} //Queue
```

Figure 20.4 A Signal
declaration in Java
that hides the type
representation

```
class Signal {

    static public final int red = 1 ;
    static public final int amber = 2 ;
    static public final int green = 3 ;

    public int sigState ;
}
```

A related type of information protection is illustrated in Figure 20.4. In situations where a limited set of values may be assigned to some variable, these values should be declared as constants. Language such as C++ support enumerated types, but in Java this must be implemented by associating these constraints with the class declaration.

For example, consider a signalling system, implemented in Java, that supports red, amber and green lights. A **Signal** type should be defined that includes constant declarations reflecting these colours. It is therefore possible to refer to **Signal.red**, **Signal.green** and so on. This avoids the accidental assignment of incorrect values to variables of type **Signal**. You are therefore protecting variables of type **Signal** from incorrect assignments and, at the same time, hiding the representation of red, amber and green. You can change these constant values later without having to make any other program changes.

20.2.2 Safe programming

Faults in programs, and therefore many program failures, are usually a consequence of human error. Programmers make mistakes because they lose track of all of the relationships between the state variables. They write program statements that result in unexpected behaviour and system state changes. People will always make mistakes, but it became clear in the late 1960s that some approaches to programming were more error-prone than others.

Dijkstra (Dijkstra, 1968) recognised that the goto statement or unconditional branch was an inherently error-prone programming construct. It made it difficult to localise state changes. This observation led to the development of structured programming. Structured programming is programming without goto statements, using only while loops and if-statements as control constructs and designing using a top-down approach. Structured programming was an important milestone in the development of software engineering because it was the first step away from an undisciplined approach to software development.

Other programming language constructs and programming techniques are also inherently error-prone. Faults are less likely to be introduced into programs if you avoid these or, at least, use them as little as possible. Potentially error-prone constructs include:

1. *Floating-point numbers* Floating-point numbers are inherently imprecise. This is a particular problem when they are compared because representation imprecision may lead to invalid comparisons. For example, 3.00000000 may sometimes be represented as 2.99999999 and sometimes as 3.00000001. A comparison would show these to be unequal. Fixed-point numbers where a number is represented to a given number of decimal places are safer because exact comparisons are possible.

2. *Pointers* Pointers are low-level constructs that hold addresses that refer directly to areas of the machine memory. Errors in their use can be devastating, because they allow aliasing (discussed later in this list) and because they make bound checking of arrays and other structures harder to implement.

3. *Dynamic memory allocation* Program memory may be allocated at run-time rather than at compile-time. The danger with this is that the memory may not be deallocated, so eventually the system runs out of available memory. This can be a very difficult error to detect because the system may run successfully for a long time before the problem occurs.

4. *Parallelism* Parallelism is dangerous because of the difficulties of predicting the subtle effects of timing interactions between parallel processes. Timing problems cannot usually be detected by program inspection, and the peculiar combination of circumstances that cause a timing problem may not occur during system testing. Parallelism may be unavoidable, but its use should be carefully controlled to minimise interprocess dependencies. Programming language facilities such as Java threads help manage parallelism so that some programming errors can be avoided.

5. *Recursion* Recursion is when a procedure or method calls itself or calls another procedure that then calls the original calling procedure. Its use can result in concise programs but it can be difficult to follow the logic of recursive programs. Programming errors are therefore more difficult to detect. Recursion errors may result in the allocation of all the system's memory as temporary stack variables are created.

6. *Interrupts* These are a means of forcing control to transfer to a section of code irrespective of the code currently executing. The dangers of this are obvious: The interrupt may cause a critical operation to be terminated.

7. *Inheritance* The problem with inheritance in object-oriented programming is that the code associated with an object is not all in one place. This makes it more difficult to understand the behaviour of the object. Hence, it is more likely that programming errors will be missed. Furthermore, inheritance when combined with dynamic binding can cause timing problems at run-time. At different times, different instances of a specific method could be called and different amounts of time will be spent searching for the correct method instance.

8. *Aliasing* This occurs when more than one name is used to refer to the same entity in a program. It is easy for program readers to miss statements that change the entity when they have several names to consider.

9. *Unbounded arrays* In languages such asC, arrays are simply ways of accessing memory, and you can make assignments beyond the end of an array. The run-time system does not check that assignments actually refer to elements in the array. Buffer overflow, where an attacker deliberately constructs a program to write memory beyond the end of a buffer that is implemented as an array, is a known security vulnerability.

10. *Default input processing* Some systems provide a default for input processing irrespective of the input that is presented to the system. This is a security loophole that an attacker may exploit by presenting the program with unexpected inputs that are not rejected by the system.

Some standards for safety-critical systems development completely prohibit the use of these constructs. However, this extreme position is not normally practical. All of these constructs and techniques are useful, but they must be used with care. Wherever possible, their potentially dangerous effects should be controlled by using them within abstract data types or objects. These act as natural 'firewalls' limiting the damage caused if errors occur.

The designers of Java have recognised some of the problems of error-prone constructs. The language does not include goto statements, it has built-in garbage collection so has no need of dynamic memory allocation, and it does not support pointers or unbounded arrays. However, Java's numeric representation is such that overflow is not detected by the run-time system, and failures due to floating-point errors are still possible.

20.2.3 Exception handling

During program execution, errors or unexpected events inevitably occur. These may arise because of a program fault or may be a result of unpredictable external circumstances. An error or an unexpected event that occurs during the execution of a program is called an *exception*. Exceptions may be caused by hardware or software conditions. Examples of exceptions might be a system power failure, an attempt to access non-existent data, and numeric overflow or underflow.

When an exception occurs, it must be managed by the system. This can be done within the program itself or may involve transferring control to a system exception-handling mechanism. Typically, the system's exception management mechanism simply reports the error and shuts down execution. Therefore, to ensure that program exceptions do not cause system failure, you should define an exception handler for all possible exceptions that may arise and make sure that all exceptions are explicitly handled.

In programming languages such as C, if-statements must be used to detect the exception and to transfer control to the exception-handling code. This means that you have to explicitly check for exceptions wherever in the program they may occur. However, this adds complexity and so increases the chances that you will make mistakes and that the exception will not be correctly handled.

Some programming languages, such as Java, C++ and Ada, include constructs that support exception handling so that you do not need extra conditional statements to check for exceptions. Rather, the programming language includes a special built-in type (often called **Exception**) and different exceptions may be declared to be of this type. When an exceptional situation occurs, the exception is signalled and the language run-time system transfers control to an exception handler. This is a code section that states exception names and appropriate actions to handle each exception.

In Java, new types of exception may be declared by extending the built-in **Exception** class. Exceptions are signalled in Java using a **throw** statement. The handler of an exception is indicated by the keyword **catch**, which is followed by a block of code that can handle the exception.

Figure 20.5 illustrates the use of exceptions in Java. This example, part of the software for the insulin pump introduced in Chapter 3, is a sensor controller that reads a blood glucose value from a sensor. The first declaration in Figure 20.5 shows how exceptions in Java are declared. The built-in object class called **Exception** is extended, and the constructor method defines the code to be implemented when the exception is thrown. In this case, an alarm is activated.

The **Sensor** class provides a single method, called **readVal**, that includes a throw statement in its declaration. This means that a **SensorFailureException** may be thrown from within the method, but that the calling method is expected to provide a handler for **SensorFailureException**. It is usually best for exceptions to be handled by the calling method because that method knows what it intended to do with the result of the called method. However, as I show later, there are some situations where exceptions are locally handled to ensure that the result of a method call is always valid.

The **try** keyword indicates that an exception may be thrown in the following block of code. The exception **SensorFailureException** is thrown if a value of less than zero is returned when the sensor is checked. **DeviceIO.readInteger** can throw an exception called **deviceIOException**, so a handler for this must also be included following the

Figure 20.5
Exceptions to handle
failure in the insulin
pump

```
class SensorFailureException extends Exception {

    SensorFailureException (String msg) {
        super (msg) ;
        Alarm.activate (msg) ;
    }
}  // SensorFailureException

class Sensor {

    int readVal () throws SensorFailureException {

    try {
        int theValue = DeviceIO.readInteger () ;
        if (theValue < 0)
            throw new SensorFailureException ("Sensor failure") ;
        return theValue ;
    }
    catch (deviceIOException e)
        {
            throw new SensorFailureException (" Sensor read error ") ;
        }
    }  // readVal
}  // Sensor
```

catch keyword. In this case, the handler simply throws a sensor failure exception to indicate that the calling object should handle the exception.

Exception handling can also be used to simplify programs and make them easier to read and understand. This reduces the probability of programmer error and increases the chances that program inspectors will find any problems that exist. You use exception handling to separate error-handling code from code that handles normal processing. You can therefore read and understand each of these code sections in isolation.

I have illustrated this in Figure 20.6. This Java class is an implementation of a temperature controller on a food freezer. The required temperature may be set between -18 and -40 degrees Celsius. Frozen food may start to defrost and bacteria become active at temperatures over -18 degrees. The control system maintains this temperature by switching a refrigerant pump on and off according to the value of a temperature sensor. If the required temperature cannot be maintained, the controller sets off an alarm.

In the Java implementation, the temperature of the freezer is discovered by interrogating an object called **tempSensor**, and the required temperature is discovered

Figure 20.6
Exceptions in a
freezer temperature
controller

```
class FreezerController {

    Sensor tempSensor = new Sensor () ;
    Dial tempDial = new Dial () ;
    float freezerTemp = tempSensor.readVal () ;
    final float dangerTemp = (float) -18.0 ;
    final long coolingTime = (long) 200000.0 ;

    public void run ( ) throws InterruptedException {
    try {
        Pump.switchIt (Pump.on) ;
        do {
            if (freezerTemp > tempDial.setting ())
                if (Pump.status == Pump.off)
                {
                    Pump.switchIt (Pump.on) ;
                    Thread.sleep (coolingTime) ;
                }
            else
                    if (Pump.status == Pump.on)
                        Pump.switchIt (Pump.off) ;

            if (freezerTemp > dangerTemp)
                throw new FreezerTooHotException () ;
            freezerTemp = tempSensor.readVal () ;

        } while (true) ;

    } // try block
    catch (FreezerTooHotException f)
    { Alarm.activate ( ) ; }
    catch (InterruptedException e)
    {
        System.out.println ("Thread exception") ;
        throw new InterruptedException ( ) ;
    }

    } //run
} // FreezerController
```

by inspecting an object called **tempDial**. A pump object (**Pump**) responds to signals to switch its state. Once the pump has been switched on, the system waits for some time (by calling **Thread.sleep**) for the temperature to fall. If it has not fallen sufficiently, an exception called **FreezerTooHotException** is thrown.

The exception handler (located at the end of the code) catches this exception and activates the **Alarm** object. A handler is also included for the built-in exception **InterruptedException**, which can be thrown by **Thread.sleep**. This logs the exception, then re-throws it for handling by the main method.

20.3 Fault tolerance

A fault-tolerant system can continue in operation after some system faults have occurred. The fault-tolerance mechanisms in the system ensure that these system faults do not cause system failure. You may need fault tolerance in situations where system failure could cause a catastrophic accident or where a loss of system operation would cause large economic losses. For example, the computers in an aircraft must carry on working until the aircraft has landed; the computers in an air traffic control system must be continuously available while planes are in the air.

There are four aspects to fault-tolerance:

1. *Fault detection* The system must detect a fault that could lead to a system failure. Generally, this involves checking that the system state is consistent.

2. *Damage assessment* The parts of the system state that have been affected by the fault must be detected.

3. *Fault recovery* The system must restore its state to a known 'safe' state. This may be achieved by correcting the damaged state (forward error recovery) or by restoring the system to a known 'safe' state (backward error recovery).

4. *Fault repair* This involves modifying the system so that the fault does not recur. However, many software faults manifest themselves as transient states. They are due to a peculiar combination of system inputs. No repair is necessary and normal processing can resume immediately after fault recovery.

You might think that fault-tolerance facilities are unnecessary in systems that have been developed using techniques that avoid the introduction of faults. If there are no faults in the system, there would not seem to be any chance of system failure. However, 'fault-free' does not mean 'failure-free'. It can only mean that the program corresponds to its specification. The specification may contain errors or omissions and may be based on incorrect assumptions about the system's environment. And, of course, we can never conclusively demonstrate that a system is completely fault-free. In systems that have the highest reliability and availability requirements, you need to use the redundant and diverse approaches of fault avoidance and fault tolerance.

Figure 20.7 State constraints that apply in the insulin pump

```
// The dose of insulin to be delivered must always be greater
// than zero and less that some defined maximum single dose

insulin_dose >= 0 & insulin_dose <= insulin_reservoir_contents

// The total amount of insulin delivered in a day must be less
// than or equal to a defined daily maximum dose

cumulative_dose <= maximum_daily_dose
```

20.3.1 Fault detection and damage assessment

The first stage of fault tolerance is to detect that a fault (an erroneous system state) either has occurred or will occur unless some action is taken immediately. To do this, you need to know when the value of a state variable is illegal or when relationships between state variables are not maintained. Therefore, you need to define state constraints that define the conditions that must always hold for all legal states. If these predicates are false, then a fault has occurred. Some examples of state constraints that apply to the insulin pump software are shown in Figure 20.7. I have deliberately not written these as Java assert statements for reasons that I explain later.

There are two types of fault detection that you can use:

1. *Preventative fault detection* In this case, the fault detection mechanism is initiated before a state change is committed. If a potentially erroneous state is detected, then the state change is not made.

2. *Retrospective fault detection* In this case, the fault detection mechanism is initiated after the system state has been changed to check whether a fault has occurred. If a fault is discovered, an exception is signalled and a repair mechanism is used to recover from the fault.

You can use preventative fault detection when the state constraints that have been defined apply only to individual state variables. For example, you can use this approach when the value of a state variable must fall within a defined range. Preventative fault detection avoids the overhead of damage repair, as the system state will always be valid—although not necessarily correct. However, the system must have a mechanism for continuing operation in the presence of an incorrect state if a system failure is to be avoided.

In Java, the safest way to implement preventative fault detection is to explicitly check for faults and use the exception-handling mechanism in the language to signal that an erroneous system state has been detected. This is illustrated in Figure 20.8. This is an implementation of a class where the values of instances of the class

Figure 20.8
PositiveEven number
class in Java

```
class PositiveEvenInteger {

    int val = 0 ;

    PositiveEvenInteger (int n) throws NumericException
    {
        if (n < 0 | n%2 == 1)
            throw new NumericException () ;
        else
            val = n ;

    }// PositiveEvenInteger

    public void assign (int n) throws NumericException
    {
        if (n < 0 | n%2 == 1)
            throw new NumericException ();
        else
            val = n ;
    } // assign

    int toInteger ()
    {
        return val ;
    } //to Integer

    boolean equals (PositiveEvenInteger n)
    {
        return (val == n.val) ;
    } // equals

} //PositiveEven
```

are restricted to positive, even numbers. If an attempt is made to assign a number that is odd or less than 0, then an exception is thrown.

In Java 1.4, an assertion facility was introduced where state constraints could be defined in an assert statement. Therefore, to specify that a number should be positive and even, you would write:

```
assert n >= 0 & n%2 == 0: "Value must be positive and even"
```

The run-time system checks that the condition holds and, if not, raises an error and causes the associated message to be printed.

However, Java's assertion facility was really designed to help discover state inconsistencies during development and debugging rather than to support fault-tolerant programming. It is possible to switch assertion checking on and off, so you cannot rely on assertions always being checked. Furthermore, it is not possible to associate a specific type of exception with each assertion, so you cannot identify individual assertion failure. This was a deliberate design decision—the designers did not intend that it should be possible to take recovery action after an assertion failure.

Preventative fault detection is possible when you know the range of values that may be assigned to a state variable. However, when a valid value depends on the value assigned to other values in the state, preventative fault detection may be impossible. For example, say your program reads three values, A, B and C, in that order. The state constraint is:

A < B & B < C

You cannot apply preventative fault detection when reading the value of A because you don't know what the value of B and C will be. Similarly, when reading B, you can't check that it is less than C. You therefore need to use retrospective fault detection, checking the state constraint after all of the values have been read. If the constraint is false, then you may take some action to restore consistency to the system.

One way to implement retrospective fault detection in Java is to associate a checking function with an object. This function can be called after state changes have been made to ensure that the state constraints hold. You can call these when necessary—the state may not need to be checked after every change has been made. The following interface can be used for checking functions:

```
interface CheckableObject {
    public boolean check () ;
}
```

Objects to be checked are instantiations of an object class that implements this interface, so each object has an associated check function. Each object class implements its own checking function that defines the particular constraints that apply to objects of that class. When the state as a whole is checked, dynamic binding is used to ensure that the check function appropriate for the class of object being checked is applied. We can see an example of this in Figure 20.9, where the check function checks that the elements of an array satisfy some constraint.

Retrospective fault detection, which uses state constraints that apply to more than one state variable, is illustrated in Figure 20.10. In this example, the fault detection check is applied to consecutive elements of an array and checks that the array is ordered.

Damage assessment involves analysing the system state to estimate the extent of the state corruption. Damage assessment is needed when you can't avoid making a state change or when a fault is caused by an invalid sequence of individually correct state changes.

Figure 20.9 An array
class with damage
assessment

```
class RobustArray {

    // Checks that all the objects in an array of objects
    // conform to some defined constraint

    boolean [] checkState ;
    CheckableObject [] theRobustArray ;

    RobustArray (CheckableObject [] theArray)
    {
        checkState = new boolean [theArray.length] ;
        theRobustArray = theArray ;
    } //RobustArray

    public void assessDamage () throws ArrayDamagedException
    {
        boolean hasBeenDamaged = false ;

        for (int i= 0; i <this.theRobustArray.length ; i ++)
        {
            if (! theRobustArray [i].check ())
                {
                    checkState [i] = true ;
                    hasBeenDamaged = true ;
                }
            else
                checkState [i] = false ;
        }
        if (hasBeenDamaged)
            throw new ArrayDamagedException () ;
    } //assessDamage

} // RobustArray
```

The role of the damage assessment procedures is not to recover from the fault but to assess what parts of the state space have been affected by the fault. Damage can only be assessed if it is possible to apply some 'validity function' that checks whether the state is consistent. If inconsistencies are found, these are highlighted or signalled in some way.

Figure 20.9 shows one way of implementing damage assessment in Java. The data structure called **RobustArray** is a collection of objects of type **CheckableObject**. The class that implements the **CheckableObject** type must include a method called **check** that can test whether the value of the object satisfies some constraint. This checking method is associated with this object rather than with the **RobustArray** object because the details of the check depend on the use of the type **CheckableObject**.

The **assessDamage** method in the **RobustArray** class examines every element of the array and checks that its state is correct. If one or more elements of the array do not meet the state constraints defined in the check function, then the elements that are damaged are recorded in the **checkState** array. An exception called **ArrayDamagedException** is then thrown. A handler for this exception that manages the damage must be included in the calling method. This can use the information in **checkState** to decide what to do.

Other fault detection and damage assessment techniques depend on the system state representation and on the type of application. These damage assessment techniques include:

1. The use of coding checks and checksums in data communications and check digits in numeric data

2. The use of redundant links in data structures that contain pointers

3. The use of watchdog timers in concurrent systems

Coding checks (Fujiwara and Pradhan, 1990) can be used when data is exchanged where a checksum is associated with numeric data. A checksum is a unique value that is computed by applying some mathematical function to data. This checksum is computed by the sender, which applies the checksum function to the data and appends that function value to the data to be transferred. The receiver applies the same function to the data and compares the computed value to the appended checksum. As the functions are the same, if these values differ, then the data itself must have changed. This technique can be used to detect security intrusions as well as deliberate and accidental corruption of data.

When linked data structures are used, the representation can be made redundant by including backward references. That is, for every reference from A to B, there exists a comparable reference from B to A. You can also count the number of elements in the structure. Checking can determine whether backward and forward references are consistent (they should refer to each other) and whether the stored size and the computed structure size are the same.

When processes must react within a specific time period, a watchdog timer may be installed. A watchdog timer is a timer that must be reset by the executing process after its action is complete. It is started at the same time as a process, and it times the process execution. A controller may interrogate it at regular intervals. If, for some reason, the process fails to terminate, the watchdog timer is not reset. The controller can therefore detect that a problem has arisen and take action to force process termination.

20.3.2 Fault recovery and repair

Fault recovery is the process of modifying the state space of the system so that the effects of the fault are eliminated or reduced. The system can continue to operate, perhaps in some degraded form. **Forward recovery** involves trying to correct the damaged system state and to create the intended state. **Backward recovery** restores the system state to a known 'correct' state.

Forward error recovery is only possible in situations where the state information includes built-in redundancy. There are two general situations (both discussed in the previous section) where this error recovery technique can be applied:

1. *When coded data is corrupted* The use of coding techniques that add redundancy to the data allows errors to be corrected as well as detected.

2. *When linked structures are corrupted* When forward and backward pointers are included in the data structure, the structure can be recreated—if enough pointers remain uncorrupted. This technique is frequently used for file system and database repair.

Backward error recovery is a simpler technique that restores the state to a known safe state after an error has been detected. Most database systems include backward error recovery. When a user initiates a database computation, a transaction is initiated. Changes made during that transaction are not immediately incorporated in the database. The database is only updated after the transaction is finished and no problems are detected. If the transaction fails, the database is not updated.

Transactions allow error recovery because they do not commit changes to the database until they have completed. However, they do not permit recovery from state changes that are valid but incorrect. Checkpointing is a technique that can recover from this situation. The system state is duplicated periodically. When a problem is discovered, a correct state may be restored from one of these copies.

As an example of how backward recovery can be implemented using checkpointing, consider the Java class **SafeSort** shown in Figure 20.10, which includes code for error detection and backward recovery.

The method creates a checkpoint by copying the array before the sort operation. In this example, I use a bubble sort for simplicity, but obviously any sorting algorithm may be used. If there is an error in the sorting algorithm and the array is not properly sorted, this is detected by explicit checks on the order of the elements in the array. If the array is not properly sorted, a **SortError** exception is thrown. The exception handler does not try to repair the problem, but restores the original value of the array and rethrows **SortError** to indicate to the calling method that the sort has not been successful. It is then the calling method's responsibility to decide how to continue execution.

As I suggested earlier, many software faults are transient, and no explicit repair is required to correct the conditions that caused these faults. They disappear in a subsequent execution of the system. Where this is not the case, it may be possible to take some repair actions. The most common software repair action is to re-initialise the system,

```
class SafeSort {

    static void sort ( int [] intarray, int order ) throws SortError
    {
        int [] copy = new int [intarray.length];

        // copy the input array

        for (int i = 0; i < intarray.length ; i++)
            copy [i] = intarray [i] ;
        try {
            Sort.bubblesort (intarray, intarray.length, order) ;
            if (order == Sort.ascending)
                for (int i = 0; i <= intarray.length-2 ; i++)
                    if (intarray [i] > intarray [i+1])
                        throw new SortError () ;
            else
                for (int i = 0; i <= intarray.length-2 ; i++)
                    if (intarray [i+1] > intarray [i])
                        throw new SortError () ;
        } // try block
        catch (SortError e )
        {
            for (int i = 0; i < intarray.length ; i++)
                intarray [i] = copy [i] ;
            throw new SortError ("Array not sorted") ;
        } //catch
    } // sort
} // SafeSort
```

resetting the state to its initial, safe values (Huang and Kintala, 1993). This can sometimes be done without stopping the system if initialisation is fast and service requests
can be delayed. Other repair alternatives, such as dynamic reconfiguration, are normally only possible when you have made explicit provision, for this in the system design.

20.4 Fault-tolerant architectures

In many systems, it is possible to implement software fault tolerance by explicitly
including checks and recovery actions in the software. This is called defensive programming. However, this approach cannot cope effectively with system faults that

Figure 20.11 Triple-
modular redundancy
to cope with
hardware failure

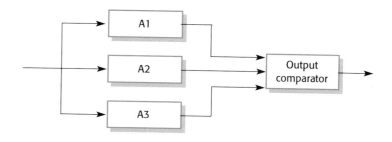

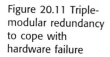

Figure 20.11 Triple-
modular redundancy
to cope with
hardware failure

arise from interactions between the hardware and the software. Furthermore, misunderstandings of the requirements may mean that both the system code and the
associated defence are incorrect.

For the most critical systems, particularly those with stringent availability
requirements, a specific system architecture designed to support fault tolerance may
be required. Examples of systems that use this approach to fault tolerance are systems in aircraft that must be in operation throughout the duration of the flight, telecommunication systems, and critical command and control systems. Pullum (Pullum,
2001) describes different types of fault-tolerant architecture that have been proposed.

There has been a need for many years to build fault-tolerant hardware. The most
commonly used hardware fault-tolerant technique is based around the notion of triple-
modular redundancy (TMR). The hardware unit is replicated three (or sometimes
more) times. The output from each unit is passed to an output comparator that is
usually implemented as a voting system. If one of the units fails and does not produce the same output as the other units, its output is ignored. A fault manager may
try to repair the faulty unit automatically, but, if this is impossible, the system is
automatically reconfigured to take the unit out of service. The system then continues to function with two working units (Figure 20.11).

This approach to fault tolerance relies on most hardware failures being the result
of component failure rather than design faults. The components are therefore likely
to fail independently. It assumes that, when fully operational, all hardware units perform to specification. There is therefore a low probability of simultaneous component failure in all hardware units.

Of course, the components could all have a common design fault and thus all
produce the same (wrong) answer. Using hardware units that have a common specification, but which are designed and built by different manufacturers, reduces the
chances of such a common mode failure. It is assumed that the probability of different teams making the same design or manufacturing error is small.

If the availability and reliability requirements for a system are such that you need
to use fault-tolerant hardware, then you may also need fault-tolerant software. There
are two related approaches to the provision of software fault tolerance (Figures 20.12
and 20.13). Both of these techniques have been derived from the hardware model
where redundant components (or perhaps redundant systems) are included and faulty
components may be taken out of service.

Figure 20.12
N-version
programming

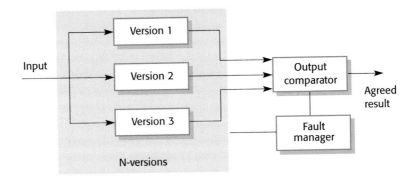

The two approaches to software fault tolerance are:

1. *N-version programming* Using a common specification, the software system is implemented in a number of versions by a number of teams. These versions are executed in parallel on separate computers. Their outputs are compared using a voting system, and inconsistent outputs or outputs that are not produced in time are rejected. At least three versions of the system should be available so that two versions should be consistent in the event of a single failure. This is the most commonly used approach to software fault tolerance. It has been used in railway signalling systems, in aircraft systems and in reactor protection systems. Avizienis (Avizienis, 1985; Avizienis, 1995) describes this approach.

2. *Recovery blocks* In this approach, each program component includes a test to check that the component has executed successfully. It also includes alternative code that allows the system to back up and repeat the computation if the test detects a failure. The implementations are deliberately different interpretations of the same specification. They are executed in sequence rather than in parallel, so replicated hardware is not required. In N-version programming, the implementations may be different

Figure 20.13
Recovery blocks

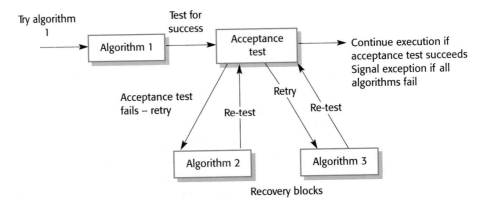

but it is not uncommon for two or more development teams to chose the same algorithms to implement the specification. Randell (Randell, 1975) and Randell and Xu (Randell and Xu, 1995) describe the recovery block method.

The provision of software fault tolerance requires the software to be executed under the control of a fault-tolerant controller that will ensure that the steps involved in tolerating a fault are executed. This controller examines the outputs and compares them. If they differ, some recovery actions may be initiated. Laprie et al. (Laprie, et al., 1995) describe fault-tolerant systems architectures.

Both of these approaches to fault tolerance make use of design and implementation diversity. When diverse approaches are used to implement the same specification, it is a reasonable assumption that the different versions of the software will not include the same faults, so common failures are unlikely. Diversity can be achieved in a number of ways:

1. By including requirements that different approaches to design should be used. For example, one team may be required to produce an object-oriented design and another team may produce a function-oriented design.

2. By requiring that the implementations should be written in different programming languages. For example, in a three-version system, Ada, C++ and Java could be used to write the software versions.

3. By requiring the use of different tools and development environments for the system.

4. By explicitly requiring different algorithms to be used in some parts of the implementation. However, this limits the freedom of the design team and may be difficult to reconcile with system performance requirements.

Each development team should work with a system specification—the V-spec— that has been derived from the system requirements specification (Avizienis, 1995). As well as specifying the functionality of the system, the V-spec should define where system outputs for comparison should be generated. The development teams for each version should work in isolation to reduce the likelihood of them developing common misunderstanding about the system.

Design diversity certainly increases the overall reliability of the system. However, a number of experiments have suggested that the assumption that independent design teams do not make the same mistakes may not always be valid (Knight and Leveson, 1986; Brilliant, et al., 1990; Leveson, 1995). Development teams may make the same mistakes because of common misinterpretations of the specification or because they independently arrive at the same algorithms to solve the problem. Recovery blocks reduce the probability of common errors because different algorithms are explicitly used for each recovery block.

The weakness of both approaches to fault tolerance is that they are based on the assumption that the specification is correct. They do not tolerate specification errors. In many cases, however, the specification is incorrect or incomplete, so the system behaves in an unexpected way. One way to reduce the possibility of common specification errors is to develop the V-specs for the system independently and to define the specifications in different languages. One development team might work from a formal specification, another from a state-based system model and the third from a natural language specification. This helps avoid some errors of specification interpretation, but does not get round the problem of specification errors.

KEY POINTS

■ Dependability in a program can be achieved by avoiding the introduction of faults, by detecting and removing faults before system deployment and by including fault tolerance facilities that allow the system to remain operational after a fault has caused a system failure.

■ The use of redundancy and diversity in both software processes and software systems is essential to the development of dependable systems.

■ The use of a well-defined, repeatable process is important if faults in a system are to be minimised. The process should include verification and validation activities at all stages, from requirements definition through system implementation.

■ Some programming constructs and techniques, such as goto statements, pointers, recursion, inheritance and floating-point numbers, are inherently error-prone. These should not be used when developing dependable systems.

■ Exceptions are used to support error management in dependable systems. All exceptions should be explicitly handled in a dependable system.

■ The four aspects of program fault tolerance are failure detection, damage assessment, fault recovery and fault repair.

■ N-version programming and recovery blocks are alternative approaches to fault-tolerant architectures where redundant copies of the hardware and software are maintained. Both rely on design diversity and the use of a fault-tolerance controller to coordinate the execution of redundant program units.

FURTHER READING

Software Fault Tolerance Techniques and Implementation. A comprehensive discussion of techniques to achieve software fault tolerance and fault-tolerant architectures. The book also covers general issues of software dependability. (L. L. Pullum, 2001, Artech House.)

Handbook of Software Reliability Engineering. This collection includes several articles discussing recovery blocks and N-version programming. It also includes a good article on fault-tolerant system architectures. (M. R. Lyu (ed.), 1996, McGraw-Hill.)

EXERCISES

20.1   Give four reasons why it is hardly ever cost-effective for companies to ensure that their software is free of faults.

20.2   Give two examples of diverse, redundant activities that might be incorporated into dependable processes.

20.3   Explain why inheritance is a potentially error-prone construct and why its use should be minimised when developing critical systems in an object-oriented language.

20.4   Discuss the problems of developing and maintaining 'nonstop' systems such as telephone exchange software. How might exceptions be used in the development of such systems?

20.5   Explain why you should explicitly handle all exceptions in a fault-tolerant system.

20.6   Briefly describe forward and backward fault recovery strategies. Why is backward fault recovery used more often than forward error recovery? Give two examples of classes of systems where backward error recovery might be used.

20.7   What is essential for forward error recovery to be implemented in a fault-tolerant system? Is forward error recovery possible in interactive systems?

20.8   Design an abstract data type or object class called RobustList that implements forward error recovery in a linked list. You should include operations to check the list for corruption and to re-build the list if corruption has occurred. Assume that you can check corruption by maintaining forward and backward references to and from adjacent members of the list.

20.9   Suggest circumstances where it is appropriate to use a fault-tolerant architecture when implementing a software-based control system and explain why this approach is required.

20.10 It has been suggested that the control software for a radiation therapy machine (used to treat patients with cancer) should be implemented using N-version programming. Comment on whether you think this is a good suggestion.

20.11 Give two reasons why all the system versions in an N-version system may fail in a similar way.

20.12 Using the techniques discussed here to produce safe software obviously involves considerable extra costs. What extra costs can be justified if 100 lives would be saved over the 15-year lifetime of a system? Would the same costs be justified if 10 lives were saved? How much is a life worth? Do the earning capabilities of the people affected make a difference to this judgement?

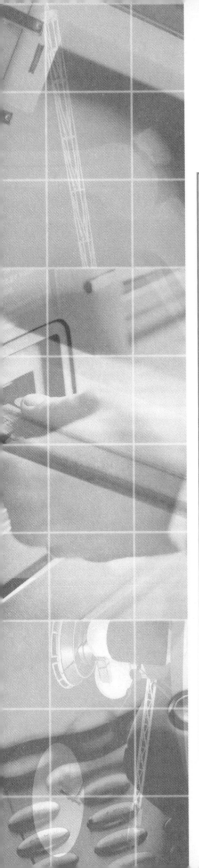

21

Software evolution

Objectives

The objectives of this chapter are to introduce software evolution and to describe a number of ways to modify software. When you have read this chapter, you will:

■ understand that change is inevitable if software systems are to remain useful and that software development and software evolution may be integrated in a spiral model;

■ have learned about different types of software maintenance and the factors that affect maintenance costs;

■ be aware of the processes involved in software evolution, including the process of software re-engineering;

■ understand how legacy systems can be assessed to decide whether they should be scrapped, maintained, re-engineered or replaced.

Contents

After systems have been deployed, they inevitably have to change if they are to remain useful. Once software is put into use, new requirements emerge and existing requirements change. Business changes often generate new requirements for existing software. Parts of the software may have to be modified to correct errors that are found in operation, to adapt it for a new platform and to improve its performance or other non-functional characteristics. Software development, therefore, does not stop when a system is delivered but continues throughout the lifetime of the system.

Software evolution is important because organisations are now completely dependent on their software systems and have invested millions of dollars in these systems. Their systems are critical business assets and they must invest in system change to maintain the value of these assets. The majority of the software budget in large companies is therefore devoted to maintaining existing systems, and we should not be surprised by figures such as those by Erlikh (Erlikh, 2000) that suggest that 90% of software costs are evolution costs. There is quite a lot of uncertainty in this percentage, however, as people mean different things when they refer to evolution or maintenance costs.

As I discuss later, post-deployment changes are not simply concerned with repairing faults in the software. The majority of changes are a consequence of new requirements that are generated in response to changing business and user needs. Consequently, you can think of software engineering as a spiral process with requirements, design, implementation and testing going on throughout the lifetime of the system. This is illustrated in Figure 21.1. You start by creating Release 1 of the system. Once delivered, changes are proposed and the development of Release 2 starts almost immediately. In fact, the need for evolution may become obvious even before the system is deployed so that later releases of the software may be under development before the initial version has been released.

This is an idealised model of software evolution that can be applied in situations where a single organisation is responsible for both the initial software development and the evolution of the software. Most generic software products are developed using this approach. However, custom software may be developed externally but the evolution may be the responsibility of the customer's software development staff. Alternatively, the software user might issue a separate contract to an external company for system support and evolution.

In this case, there are often discontinuities in the spiral process. Requirements and design documents may not be passed from one company to another. Companies may merge or reorganise and inherit software from other companies, and then find that this has to be changed. When the transition from development to evolution is not seamless, the process of changing the software after delivery is often called *software maintenance*. As I discuss later in this chapter, maintenance involves extra process activities, such as program understanding, in addition to the normal activities of software development.

Figure 21.1 A spiral model of development and evolution

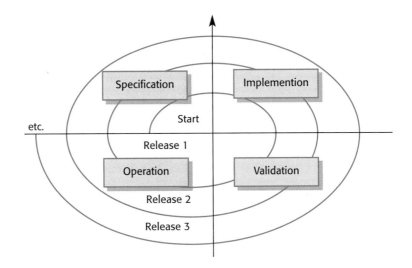

21.1 Program evolution dynamics

Program evolution dynamics is the study of system change. The majority of work in this area has been carried out by Lehman and Belady, initially in the 1970s and 1980s (Lehman and Belady, 1985). The work continued in the 1990s as Lehman and others investigated the significance of feedback in evolution processes (Lehman, 1996; Lehman, et al., 1998; Lehman, et al., 2001). From these studies, they proposed a set of laws (Lehman's laws) concerning system change. They claim these laws (hypotheses, really) are invariant and widely applicable. Lehman and Belady examined the growth and evolution of a number of large software systems. The proposed laws, shown in Figure 21.2, were derived from these measurements.

The first law states that system maintenance is an inevitable process. As the system's environment changes, new requirements emerge and the system must be modified. When the modified system is re-introduced to the environment, this promotes more environmental changes, so the evolution process recycles.

The second law states that, as a system is changed, its structure is degraded. The only way to avoid this happening is to invest in preventative maintenance where you spend time improving the software structure without adding to its functionality. Obviously, this means additional costs, over and above those of implementing required system changes.

The third law is, perhaps, the most interesting and the most contentious of Lehman's laws. It suggests that large systems have a dynamic of their own that is established at an early stage in the development process. This determines the gross trends of the system maintenance process and limits the number of possible system changes.

Figure 21.2 Lehman's laws

Law	Description
Continuing change	A program that is used in a real-world environment necessarily must change or become progressively less useful in that environment.
Increasing complexity	As an evolving program changes, its structure tends to become more complex. Extra resources must be devoted to preserving and simplifying the structure.
Large program evolution	Program evolution is a self-regulating process. System attributes such as size, time between releases and the number of reported errors is approximately invariant for each system release.
Organisational stability	Over a program's lifetime, its rate of development is approximately constant and independent of the resources devoted to system development.
Conservation of familiarity	Over the lifetime of a system, the incremental change in each release is approximately constant.
Continuing growth	The functionality offered by systems has to continually increase to maintain user satisfaction.
Declining quality	The quality of systems will appear to be declining unless they are adapted to changes in their operational environment.
Feedback system	Evolution processes incorporate multi-agent, multi-loop feedback systems and you have to treat them as feedback systems to achieve significant product improvement.

Lehman and Belady suggest that this law is a consequence of structural factors that influence and constrain system change, as well as organisational factors that affect the evolution process.

Once a system exceeds some minimal size it becomes more difficult to change. Because it is large and complex, the system is hard to understand, and programmers are more likely to make errors and introduce faults into the system. Therefore, making small changes avoids reducing the dependability of the system. A large change will probably introduce many new faults that will limit the useful change delivered in the new version of the system.

Large systems are usually produced by large organisations, which have internal bureaucracies that set the change budget for each system and control the decision-making process. Organisations have to make decisions on the risks and value of the changes and the costs involved. Such decisions take time to make. During that time, other, higher-priority system changes may be proposed. It may be necessary to shelve the original changes until a later date. The organisation's decision-making processes therefore govern the rate of change of the system.

Lehman's fourth law suggests that most large programming projects work in what he terms a *saturated* state. That is, a change to resources or staffing has imperceptible effects on the long-term evolution of the system. This is consistent with the third law, which suggests that program evolution is largely independent of management decisions. This law confirms that large software development teams are often unproductive because communication overheads dominate the work of the team.

Lehman's fifth law is concerned with the change increments in each system release. Adding new functionality to a system inevitably introduces new system faults. The more functionality added in each release, the more faults there will be. Therefore, a large increment in functionality in one system release means that this will have to be followed by a further release where the new system faults are repaired. Relatively little new functionality will be included in this release. The law suggests that you should not budget for large functionality increments in each release without taking into account the need for fault repair.

The first five laws were in Lehman's initial proposals; the remaining laws were added after further work. The sixth and seventh laws are similar and essentially say that users of software will become increasingly unhappy with it unless it is maintained and new functionality is added to it. The final law reflects the most recent work on feedback processes, although it is not yet clear how this can be applied in practical software development.

Lehman's observations seem generally sensible. They should be taken into account when planning the maintenance process. It may be that business considerations require them to be ignored at any one time. For example, for marketing reasons, it may necessary to make several major system changes in a single release. The probable consequences of this are that one or more releases devoted to error repair are likely to be required.

It may appear that the radical differences that are obvious between releases of program products violate Lehman's laws. For example, Microsoft Word has been transformed from a simple word processor that operated in 256K of memory to a gigantic, feature-laden system. It now needs many megabytes of memory and a fast processor to operate. Its evolution seems to contradict the fourth and fifth of Lehman's laws. However, I suspect that this program is not really a sequence of revisions of a common core program. Rather, the name has been retained for marketing reasons, but the program itself has been rewritten and re-structured more than once since it was originally released.

21.2 Software maintenance

Software maintenance is the general process of changing a system after it has been delivered. The term is usually applied to custom software where separate development groups are involved before and after delivery. The changes made to the software may be simple changes to correct coding errors, more extensive changes to correct design errors or significant enhancements to correct specification errors or accommodate new requirements. Changes are implemented by modifying existing system components and, where necessary, by adding new components to the system.

There are three different types of software maintenance:

1. *Maintenance to repair software faults* Coding errors are usually relatively cheap to correct; design errors are more expensive as they may involve rewriting several program components. Requirements errors are the most expensive to repair because of the extensive system redesign that may be necessary.

2. *Maintenance to adapt the software to a different operating environment* This type of maintenance is required when some aspect of the system's environment such as the hardware, the platform operating system or other support software changes. The application system must be modified to adapt it to cope with these environmental changes.

3. *Maintenance to add to or modify the system's functionality* This type of maintenance is necessary when the system requirements change in response to organisational or business change. The scale of the changes required to the software is often much greater than for the other types of maintenance.

In practice, there isn't a clear-cut distinction between these types of maintenance. When you adapt the system to a new environment, you may add functionality to take advantage of new environmental features. Software faults are often exposed because users use the system in unanticipated ways. Changing the system to accommodate their way of working is the best way to fix these faults.

These types of maintenance are generally recognised, but different people sometimes give them different names. *Corrective maintenance* is universally used to refer to maintenance for fault repair. However, *adaptive maintenance* sometimes means adapting to a new environment and can mean adapting the software to new requirements. *Perfective maintenance* can mean perfecting the software by implementing new requirements; in other cases it means maintaining the functionality of the system but improving its structure and its performance. Because of this naming uncertainty, I have avoided the use of all of these terms in this chapter.

Surveys by Lientz and Swanson (Lientz and Swanson, 1980) and Nosek and Palvia (Nosek and Palvia, 1990) suggest that about 65% of maintenance is concerned with implementing new requirements, 18% with changing the system to adapt it to a new operating environment and 17% to correcting system faults (Figure 21.3). For custom systems, this distribution of costs is still roughly correct. The important point is not the specific percentages but the fact that repairing system faults is not the most expensive maintenance activity. Evolving the system to cope with new environments and new or changed requirements consumes most maintenance effort.

Maintenance costs as a proportion of development costs vary from one application domain to another. Guimaraes (Guimaraes, 1983) suggests that the maintenance

Figure 21.3
Maintenance effort
distribution

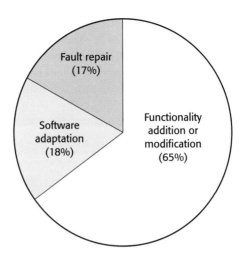

costs for business application systems are broadly comparable with system development costs. For embedded real-time systems, maintenance costs may be up to four times higher than development costs. The high reliability and performance requirements of these systems often mean that modules have to be tightly linked and hence difficult to change.

It is usually cost-effective to invest effort in designing and implementing a system to reduce maintenance costs. Adding new functionality after delivery is expensive because you have to spend time understanding the system and analysing the impact of the proposed changes. Therefore, work done during development to make the software easier to understand and change is likely to reduce maintenance costs. Good software engineering techniques such as precise specification, the use of object-oriented development and configuration management contribute to maintenance cost reduction.

Figure 21.4 shows how overall lifetime costs may decrease as more effort is expended during system development to produce a maintainable system. Because of the potential reduction in costs of understanding, analysis and testing, there is a significant multiplier effect when the system is developed for maintainability. For System 1, extra development costs of $25,000 are invested in making the system more maintainable. This results in a savings of $100,000 in maintenance costs over the lifetime of the system. This assumes that a percentage increase in development costs results in a comparable percentage decrease in overall system costs.

One important reason why maintenance costs are high is that it is more expensive to add functionality after a system is in operation than it is to implement the same functionality during development. The key factors that distinguish development and maintenance, and which lead to higher maintenance costs, are:

1. *Team stability* After a system has been delivered, it is normal for the development team to be broken up and people work on new projects. The new team

Figure 21.4
Development and
maintenance costs

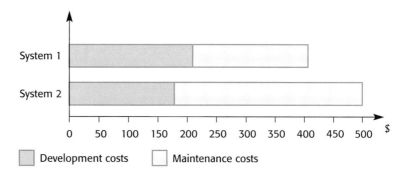

or the individuals responsible for system maintenance do not understand the system or the background to system design decisions. A lot of the effort during the maintenance process is taken up with understanding the existing system before implementing changes to it.

2. *Contractual responsibility* The contract to maintain a system is usually separate from the system development contract. The maintenance contract may be given to a different company rather than the original system developer. This factor, along with the lack of team stability, means that there is no incentive for a development team to write the software so that it is easy to change. If a development team can cut corners to save effort during development, it is worthwhile for them to do so even if it means increasing maintenance costs.

3. *Staff skills* Maintenance staff are often relatively inexperienced and unfamiliar with the application domain. Maintenance has a poor image among software engineers. It is seen as a less skilled process than system development and is often allocated to the most junior staff. Furthermore, old systems may be written in obsolete programming languages. The maintenance staff may not have much experience of development in these languages and must learn these languages to maintain the system.

4. *Program age and structure* As programs age, their structure tends to be degraded by change, so they become harder to understand and modify. Some systems have been developed without modern software engineering techniques. They may never have been well structured and were perhaps optimised for efficiency rather than understandability. System documentation may be lost or inconsistent. Old systems may not have been subject to configuration management, so time is often wasted finding the right versions of system components to change.

The first three of these problems stem from the fact that many organisations still consider development and maintenance to be separate activities. Maintenance is seen as a second-class activity, and there is no incentive to spend money during development to reduce the costs of system change. The only long-term solution to this problem is to accept that systems rarely have a defined lifetime but continue in use, in some form, for an indefinite period. As I suggested in the introduction, you should think of systems as evolving throughout their lifetime through a continual development process.

The fourth issue, the problem of degraded system structure, is in some ways the easiest problem to address. Software re-engineering techniques (briefly described later in this chapter) may be applied to improve the system structure and understandability. Architectural transformations can adapt the system to new hardware. Preventative maintenance work (essentially incremental re-engineering) can be supported to improve the system and make it easier to change.

21.2.1 Maintenance prediction

Managers hate surprises, especially if these result in unexpectedly high costs. You should therefore try to predict what system changes are likely and what parts of the system are likely to be the most difficult to maintain. You should also try to estimate the overall maintenance costs for a system in a given time period. Figure 21.5 illustrates these predictions and associated questions.

These predictions are obviously closely related:

1. Whether a system change should be accepted depends, to some extent, on the maintainability of the system components affected by that change.

2. Implementing system changes tends to degrade the system structure and hence reduce its maintainability.

3. Maintenance costs depend on the number of changes, and the costs of change implementation depend on the maintainability of system components.

Predicting the number of change requests for a system requires an understanding of the relationship between the system and its external environment. Some systems have a very complex relationship with their external environment and changes to that environment inevitably result in changes to the system. To evaluate the relationships between a system and its environment, you should assess:

1. *The number and complexity of system interfaces* The larger the number of interfaces and the more complex they are, the more likely it is that demands for change will be made.

2. *The number of inherently volatile system requirements* As I discussed in Chapter 7, requirements that reflect organisational policies and procedures are likely to be more volatile than requirements that are based on stable domain characteristics.

3. *The business processes in which the system is used* As business processes evolve, they generate system change requests. The more business processes that use a system, the more the demands for system change.

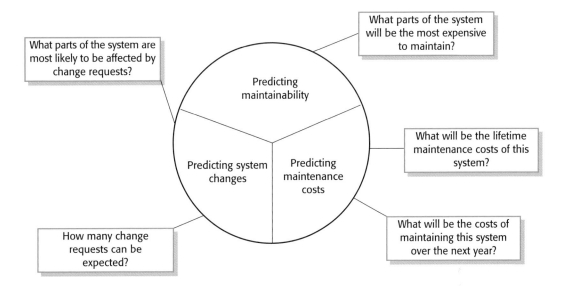

What parts of the system will be the most expensive to maintain?

What parts of the system are most likely to be affected by change requests?

Predicting maintainability

What will be the lifetime maintenance costs of this system?

Predicting system changes

Predicting maintenance costs

How many change requests can be expected?

What will be the costs of maintaining this system over the next year?

Figure 21.5
Maintenance
prediction

To predict system maintainability, you need to understand the number and the types of relationship between the system components as well as the inherent complexity of these components. There have been various studies of the different types of complexity in a system (McCabe, 1976; Halstead, 1977) and of the relationships between complexity and maintainability (Kafura and Reddy, 1987; Banker, et al., 1993). It is not surprising that these studies have found that the more complex a system or component, the more expensive it is to maintain.

Complexity measurements have been found to be particularly useful in identifying individual program components that are likely to be particularly expensive to maintain. Kafura and Reddy (Kafura and Reddy, 1987) examined a number of system components and found that maintenance effort tended to be focused on a small number of complex components. They suggest that, to reduce maintenance costs, you should replace particularly complex system components with simpler alternatives.

After a system has been put into service, you may be able to use process data to help predict maintainability. Examples of process metrics that can be used for assessing maintainability are:

1. *Number of requests for corrective maintenance* An increase in the number of failure reports may indicate that more errors are being introduced into the program than are being repaired during the maintenance process. This may indicate a decline in maintainability.

2. *Average time required for impact analysis* This reflects the number of program components that are affected by the change request. If this time increases, it implies that more and more components are affected and maintainability is decreasing.

3. *Average time taken to implement a change request* This is not the same as the time for impact analysis although it may correlate with it. This is the amount

of time that you need to actually modify the system and its documentation, after you have assessed which components are affected. An increase in the time needed to implement a change may indicate a decline in maintainability.

4. *Number of outstanding change requests* An increase in this number over time may imply a decline in maintainability.

You use predicted information about change requests and about system maintainability to predict maintenance costs. Most managers combine this information with intuition and experience to estimate costs. The COCOMO 2 model of cost estimation (Boehm, et al., 2000), discussed in Chapter 26, suggests that an estimate for software maintenance effort can be based on the effort to understand existing code and the effort to develop the new code.

21.3 Evolution processes

Software evolution processes vary considerably depending on the type of software being maintained, the development processes used in an organisation and the people involved in the process. In some organisations, evolution may be an informal process where change requests mostly come from conversations between the system users and developers. In other companies, it is a formalised process with structured documentation produced at each stage in the process.

System change proposals are the driver for system evolution in all organisations. These change proposals may involve existing requirements that have not been implemented in the released system, requests for new requirements and bug repairs from system stakeholders, and new ideas and proposals for software improvement from the system development team. As illustrated in Figure 21.6, the processes of change identification and system evolution are cyclical and continue throughout the lifetime of a system.

The evolution process includes the fundamental activities of change analysis, release planning, system implementation and releasing a system to customers. The cost and impact of these changes are assessed to see how much of the system is affected by the change and how much it might cost to implement the change. If the proposed changes are accepted, a new release of the system is planned. During release planning, all proposed changes (fault repair, adaptation and new functionality) are considered. A decision is then made on which changes to implement in the next version of the system. The changes are implemented and validated, and a new version of the system is released. The process then iterates with a new set of changes proposed for the next release. Figure 21.7, adapted from Arthur (Arthur, 1988), shows an overview of this process.

The process of change implementation is, essentially, an iteration of the development process where the revisions to the system are designed, implemented and

Figure 21.6 Change identification and evolution processes

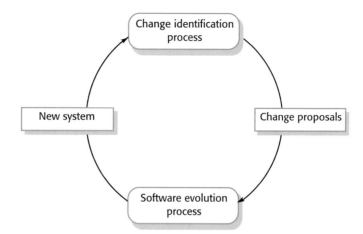

tested. However, a critical difference is that the initial stage of change implementation is program understanding. During this phase, you have to understand how the program is structured and how it delivers its functionality. When implementing a change, you use this understanding to make sure that the implemented change does not adversely affect the existing system.

Ideally, the change implementation stage of this process should modify the system specification, design and implementation to reflect the changes to the system (Figure 21.8). New requirements that reflect the system changes are proposed, analysed and validated. System components are redesigned and implemented and the system is re-tested. If appropriate, prototyping of the proposed changes may be carried out as part of the change analysis process.

As you change software, you develop succeeding releases of the system. These are composed from versions of the system's components. You have to keep track of these versions to ensure that you use the right versions of components in each system release. Configuration management is covered in Chapter 29.

During the evolution process, the requirements are analysed in detail and, frequently, implications of the changes emerge that were not apparent in the earlier

Figure 21.7 The system evolution process

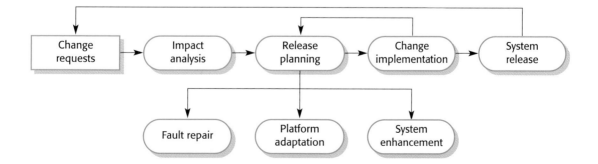

Figure 21.8 Change
implementation

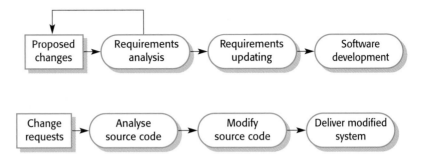

Figure 21.9 The
emergency repair
process

change analysis process. This means that the proposed changes may be modified
and further customer discussions may be required before they are implemented.

Change requests sometimes relate to system problems that have to be tackled
very urgently. These urgent changes can arise for three reasons:

1. If a serious system fault occurs that has to be repaired to allow normal operation to continue

2. If changes to the system's operating environment have unexpected effects that
   disrupt normal operation

3. If there are unanticipated changes to the business running the system, such as
   the emergence of new competitors or the introduction of new legislation

In these cases, the need to make the change quickly means that you may not be
able to follow the formal change analysis process. Rather than modify the requirements
and design, you make an emergency fix to the program to solve the immediate problem (Figure 21.9). However, the danger is that the requirements, the software design
and the code gradually become inconsistent. While you may intend to document the
change in the requirements and design, additional emergency fixes to the software may
then be needed. These take priority over documentation. Eventually, the original
change is forgotten and the system documentation and code never become consistent.

A further problem with emergency system repairs is that they have to be completed as quickly as possible. You chose a quick and workable solution rather than
the best solution as far as system structure is concerned. This accelerates the process of software ageing so that future changes become progressively more difficult
and maintenance costs increase.

Ideally, when emergency code repairs are made, the change request should remain
outstanding after the code faults have been fixed. It can then be re-implemented
more carefully after further analysis. Of course, the code of the repair may be reused.
An alternative, better solution to the problem may be discovered when more time
is available for analysis. In practice, however, it is almost inevitable that these changes
will have a low priority and, after further system changes are made, it is unrealistic to re-do the emergency repairs.

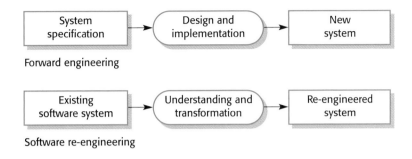

Figure 21.10 Forward engineering and re-engineering

21.3.1 System re-engineering

As discussed in the previous section, the process of system evolution involves understanding the program that has to be changed, then implementing these changes. However, many systems, especially older legacy systems (discussed in Chapter 2), are difficult to understand and change. The programs may have been originally optimised for performance or space utilisation at the expense of understandability, or, over time, the initial program structure may have been corrupted by a series of changes.

To simplify the problems of changing its legacy systems, a company may decide to re-engineer these systems to improve their structure and understandability. Software re-engineering is concerned with re-implementing legacy systems to make them more maintainable. Re-engineering may involve re-documenting the system, organising and restructuring the system, translating the system to a more modern programming language, and modifying and updating the structure and values of the system's data. The functionality of the software is not changed and, normally, the system architecture also remains the same.

Re-engineering a software system has two key advantages over more radical approaches to system evolution:

1. *Reduced risk* There is a high risk in re-developing business-critical software. Errors may be made in the system specification, or there may be development problems. Delays in introducing the new software may mean that business is lost and extra costs are incurred. For example, in 1999 a large US food company encountered delays in introducing a new ordering system, which led to delays in delivering $100 million worth of goods during a peak sales season.

2. *Reduced cost* The cost of re-engineering is significantly less than the cost of developing new software. Ulrich (Ulrich, 1990) quotes an example of a commercial system where the re-implementation costs were estimated at $50 million. The system, was successfully re-engineered for $12 million. I suspect that, with modern software technology, the relative cost of re-implementation is probably less than this but will still considerably exceed the costs of re-engineering.

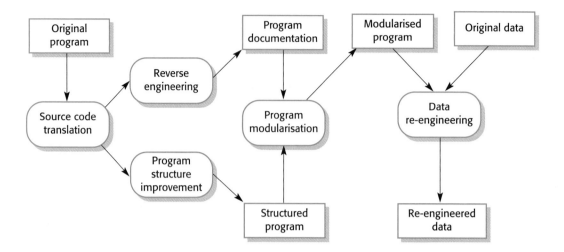

Figure 21.11 The re-
engineering process
The critical distinction between re-engineering and new software development is the starting point for the development. Rather than starting with a written specification, the old system acts as a specification for the new system. Chikofsky and Cross (Chikofsky and Cross, 1990) call conventional development *forward engineering* to distinguish it from software re-engineering. This distinction is illustrated in Figure 21.10. Forward engineering starts with a system specification and involves the design and implementation of a new system. Re-engineering starts with an existing system and the development process for the replacement is based on understanding and transforming the original system.

Figure 21.11 illustrates the re-engineering process. The input to the process is a legacy program and the output is a structured, modularised version of the same program. During program re-engineering, the data for the system may also be re-engineered. The activities in this re-engineering process are:

1. *Source code translation* The program is converted from an old programming language to a more modern version of the same language or to a different language.

2. *Reverse engineering* The program is analysed and information extracted from it. This helps to document its organisation and functionality.

2. *Program structure improvement* The control structure of the program is analysed and modified to make it easier to read and understand.

3. *Program modularisation* Related parts of the program are grouped together and, where appropriate, redundancy is removed. In some cases, this stage may involve architectural transformation where a centralised system intended for a single computer is modified to run on a distributed platform.

4. *Data re-engineering* The data processed by the program is changed to reflect program changes.

Figure 21.12
Re-engineering
approaches

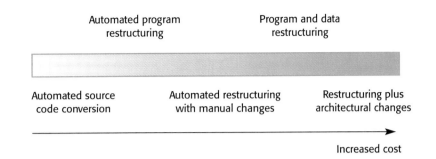

System re-engineering may not necessarily require all of the steps in Figure 21.11. Source code translation may not be needed if the programming language used to develop the system is still supported by the compiler supplier. If the re-engineering relies completely on automated tools, then recovering documentation through reverse engineering may be unnecessary. Data re-engineering is only required if the data structures in the program change during system re-engineering. However, software re-engineering always involves some program re-structuring.

To make the re-engineered system interoperate with the new software, you may have to develop adaptor components, as discussed in Chapter 19. These hide the original interfaces of the software system and present new, better-structured interfaces that can be used by other components. This process of legacy system wrapping is an important technique for developing large-scale reusable components.

The costs of re-engineering obviously depend on the extent of the work that is carried out. There is a spectrum of possible approaches to re-engineering, as shown in Figure 21.12. Costs increase from left to right so that source code translation is the cheapest option. Re-engineering as part of architectural migration is the most expensive.

Apart from the extent of the re-engineering, the principal factors that affect re-engineering costs are:

1. *The quality of the software to be re-engineered* The lower the quality of the software and its associated documentation (if any), the higher the re-engineering costs.

2. *The tool support available for re-engineering* It is not normally cost-effective to re-engineer a software system unless you can use CASE tools to automate most of the program changes.

3. *The extent of data conversion required* If re-engineering requires large volumes of data to be converted, the process cost increases significantly.

4. *The availability of expert staff* If the staff responsible for maintaining the system cannot be involved in the re-engineering process, the costs will increase because system re-engineers will have to spend a great deal of time understanding the system.

The main disadvantage of software re-engineering is that there are practical limits to the extent that a system can be improved by re-engineering. It isn't possible, for example, to convert a system written using a functional approach to an object-oriented system. Major architectural changes or radical re-organisation of the system data management cannot be carried out automatically, so they incur high additional costs. Although re-engineering can improve maintainability, the re-engineered system will probably not be as maintainable as a new system developed using modern software engineering methods.

21.4 Legacy system evolution

For new software systems developed using modern software engineering processes such as iterative development and CBSE, it is possible to plan how to integrate system development and evolution. More and more companies are starting to understand that the system development process is a whole life-cycle process and that an artificial separation between software development and software maintenance is unhelpful. However, there are still many legacy systems that are critical business systems. These have to be extended and adapted to changing e-business practices.

Organisations that have a limited budget for maintaining and upgrading their legacy systems have to decide how to get the best return on their investment. This means that they have to make a realistic assessment of their legacy systems and then decide what is the most appropriate strategy for evolving these systems. There are four strategic options:

1. *Scrap the system completely* This option should be chosen when the system is not making an effective contribution to business processes. This occurs when business processes have changed since the system was installed and are no longer completely dependent on the system. This situation is most common when mainframe terminals have been replaced by PCs, and off-the-shelf software on these machines has been adapted to provide much of the computer support that the business process needs.

2. *Leave the system unchanged and continue with regular maintenance* This option should be chosen when the system is still required but is fairly stable and the system users make relatively few change requests.

3. *Re-engineer the system to improve its maintainability* This option should be chosen when the system quality has been degraded by regular change and where regular change to the system is still required. As I discussed, this process may include developing new interface components so that the original system can work with other, newer systems.

4. *Replace all or part of the system with a new system* This option should be chosen when other factors such as new hardware mean that the old system cannot continue in operation or where off-the-shelf systems would allow the new system to be developed at a reasonable cost. In many cases, an evolutionary replacement strategy can be adopted where major system components are replaced by off-the-shelf systems with other components reused wherever possible.

Naturally, these options are not exclusive, so when a system is composed of several programs, different options may be applied to different parts of the system.

When you are assessing a legacy system, you have to look at it from both a business perspective and a technical perspective (Warren, 1998). From a business perspective, you have to decide whether the business really needs the system. From a technical perspective, you have to assess the quality of the application software and the system's support software and hardware. You then use a combination of the business value and the system quality to inform your decision on what to do with the legacy system.

To illustrate, let's assume that an organisation has 10 legacy systems. The quality and the business value of each of these systems is assessed and compared with others by plotting it on a chart showing relative business value and system quality. This is illustrated in Figure 21.13.

From Figure 21.13, you can see that there are four clusters of systems:

1. *Low quality, low business value* Keeping these systems in operation will be expensive and the rate of the return to the business will be fairly small. These systems should be scrapped.

2. *Low quality, high business value* These systems are making an important business contribution so they cannot be scrapped. However, their low quality means that it is expensive to maintain them. These systems should be re-engineered to improve their quality or replaced, if a suitable off-the-shelf system is available.

3. *High quality, low business value* These are systems that don't contribute much to the business but that may not be very expensive to maintain. It is not worth replacing these systems so normal system maintenance may be continued so long as no expensive changes are required and the system hardware is operational. If expensive changes become necessary, they should be scrapped.

4. *High quality, high business value* These systems have to be kept in operation, but their high quality means that you don't have to invest in transformation or system replacement. Normal system maintenance should be continued.

To assess the business value of a system, you have to identify system stakeholders, such as end-users of the system and their managers, and ask a series of questions about the system. There are four basic issues that you have to discuss:

Figure 21.13 Legacy
system assessment

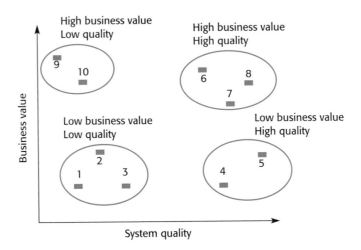

1. *The use of the system* If systems are only used occasionally or by a small number of people, they may have a low business value. A legacy system may have been developed to meet a business need that has either changed or that can now be met more effectively in other ways.

2. *The business processes that are supported* When a system is introduced, business processes to exploit that system may be designed. However, changing these processes may be impossible because the legacy system can't be adapted. Therefore, a system may have a low business value because new processes can't be introduced.

3. *The system dependability* System dependability is not only a technical problem but also a business problem. If a system is not dependable and the problems directly affect the business customers or mean that people in the business are diverted from other tasks to solve these problems, the system has a low business value.

4. *The system outputs* The key issue here is the importance of the system outputs to the successful functioning of the business. If the business depends on these outputs, then the system has a high business value. Conversely, if these outputs can be easily generated in some other way or if the system produces outputs that are rarely used, then its business value may be low.

For example, let's assume that a company provides a travel ordering system where the staff responsible for arranging travel can place orders with an approved travel agent. Tickets are then delivered and the company is invoiced for these. However, a business value assessment may reveal that this system is only used for a fairly small percentage of travel orders placed. People making travel arrangements find

Figure 21.14 Factors
used in environment
assessment

Factor	Questions
Supplier stability	Is the supplier is still in existence? Is the supplier financially stable and likely to continue in existence? If the supplier is no longer in business, does someone else maintain the systems?
Failure rate	Does the hardware have a high rate of reported failures? Does the support software crash and force system restarts?
Age	How old is the hardware and software? The older the hardware and support software, the more obsolete it will be. It may still function correctly but there could be significant economic and business benefits to moving to more modern systems.
Performance	Is the performance of the system adequate? Do performance problems have a significant effect on system users?
Support requirements	What local support is required by the hardware and software? If there are high costs associated with this support, it may be worth considering system replacement.
Maintenance costs	What are the costs of hardware maintenance and support software licences? Older hardware may have higher maintenance costs than modern systems. Support software may have high annual licensing costs.
Interoperability	Are there problems interfacing the system to other systems? Can compilers, for example, be used with current versions of the operating system? Is hardware emulation required?

it cheaper and more convenient to deal directly with travel suppliers through their web sites. This system may still be used, but there is no real point in keeping it. The same functionality is available from external systems.

Conversely, say a company has developed a system that keeps track of all previous customer orders and automatically generates reminders for customers to reorder goods. This results in a large number of repeat orders and keeps customers satisfied because they feel that their supplier is aware of their needs. The outputs from such a system are very important to the business, this system therefore has a high business value.

To assess a software system from a technical perspective, you need to consider both the application system itself and the environment in which the system operates. The environment includes the hardware and all associated support software, such as compilers and linkers, that is required to maintain the system. The environment is important because many system changes result from changes to the environment, such as upgrades to the hardware or operating system.

If possible, in the process of environmental assessment, you should make measurements of the system and its maintenance processes. Examples of data that may be useful include the costs of maintaining the system hardware and support soft-

Figure 21.15 Factors
used in application
assessment

Factor	Questions
Understandability	How difficult is it to understand the source code of the current system? How complex are the control structures that are used? Do variables have meaningful names that reflect their function?
Documentation	What system documentation is available? Is the documentation complete, consistent and current?
Data	Is there an explicit data model for the system? To what extent is data duplicated across files? Is the data used by the system up-to-date and consistent?
Performance	Is the performance of the application adequate? Do performance problems have a significant effect on system users?
Programming language	Are modern compilers available for the programming language used to develop the system? Is the programming language still used for new system development?
Configuration management	Are all versions of all parts of the system managed by a configuration management system? Is there an explicit description of the versions of components that are used in the current system?
Test data	Does test data for the system exist? Is there a record of regression tests carried out when new features have been added to the system?
Personnel skills	Are there people available who have the skills to maintain the application? Are there only a limited number of people who understand the system?

ware, the number of hardware faults that occur over some time period and the frequency of patches and fixes applied to the system support software.

Factors that you should consider during the environment assessment are shown in Figure 21.14. Notice that these are not all technical characteristics of the environment. You also have to consider the reliability of the suppliers of the hardware and support software. If these suppliers are no longer in business, there may not be maintenance support for their systems.

To assess the technical quality of an application system, you have to assess a range of factors (Figure 21.15) that are primarily related to the system dependability, the difficulties of maintaining the system and the system documentation. You may also collect quantitative system data that will help you judge the quality of the system. Examples of quantitative data that might be collected are:

1. *The number of system change requests* System changes tend to corrupt the system structure and make further changes more difficult. The higher this value, the lower the quality of the system.

2. *The number of user interfaces* This is an important factor in forms-based systems where each form can be considered as a separate user interface. The more interfaces, the more likely that there will be inconsistencies and redundancies in these interfaces.

3. *The volume of data used by the system* The higher the volume of data (number of files, size of database, etc.), the more complex the system.

Although this data is often useful, collecting it can be very expensive and therefore impractical. Furthermore, there are no absolute values that may be used. The age and size of the system have to be taken into account when making quality judgements based on measurements.

Ideally, objective assessment should be used to inform decisions about what to do with a legacy system. However, in many cases, these decisions are not really objective but are based on organisational or political considerations. For example, if two businesses merge, the most politically powerful partner will usually keep its systems and scrap the other systems. If senior management in an organisation decide to move to a new hardware platform, then this may require applications to be replaced. If there is no budget available for system transformation in a particular year, then system maintenance may be continued even although this will result in higher long-term costs.

KEY POINTS

■ Software development and evolution should be a single, integrated, iterative process that can be represented using a spiral model.

■ Lehman's laws, such as the notion that change is continuous, describe a number of insights derived from long-term studies of system evolution.

■ There are three types of software maintenance: bug fixing, modifying the software to work in a new environment, and implementing new or changed requirements.

■ For custom systems, the costs of software maintenance generally exceed the software development costs.

■ The process of software evolution is driven by requests for changes and includes change impact analysis, release planning and change implementation.

■ Software re-engineering is concerned with re-structuring and re-documenting software to make it more understandable and easier to change.

■ The business value of a legacy system and the quality of the application software and its environment should be assessed to determine whether the system should be replaced, transformed or maintained.

FURTHER READING

Modernizing Legacy Systems: Software Technologies, Engineering Processes, and Business Practices. This excellent book covers general issues of software maintenance and evolution as well as legacy system migration. The book is based on a large case study of the transformation of a COBOL system to a Java-based client-server system. (R. C. Seacord, et al., 2003, Addison-Wesley.)

The Renaissance of Legacy Systems. This book is mostly concerned with a method for evolving legacy systems. However, it includes a good general discussion of these systems, case studies that illustrate legacy system structures and a chapter on system assessment. (I. Warren, 1998, Springer.)

EXERCISES

21.1   Explain why a software system that is used in a real-world environment must change or become progressively less useful.

21.2   Explain the rationale underlying Lehman's laws. Under what circumstances might the laws break down?

21.3   Briefly describe the three types of software maintenance. Why is it sometimes difficult to distinguish between them?

21.4   As a software project manager in a company that specialises in the development of software for the offshore oil industry, you have been given the task of discovering the factors that affect the maintainability of the systems developed by your company. Suggest how you might set up a programme to analyse the maintenance process and discover appropriate maintainability metrics for your company.

21.5   From Figure 21.7, you can see that impact analysis is an important sub-process in the software evolution process. Using a diagram, suggest what activities might be involved in change impact analysis.

21.6   What are the principal factors that affect the costs of system re-engineering?

21.7   What are the essential conditions for software re-engineering to be successful?

21.8   Under what circumstances might an organisation decide to scrap a system when the system assessment suggests that it is of high quality and high business value.

21.9   What are the strategic options for legacy system evolution? When would you normally replace all or part of a system rather than continue maintenance of the software (with or without re-engineering)?

21.10 Explain why problems with support software might mean that an organisation has to replace its legacy systems.

21.11 Do software engineers have a professional responsibility to produce code that can be readily evolved even if this is not explicitly requested by their employer?

21.12 The management of an organisation has asked you to carry out a system assessment and suggested that they would like the results of that assessment to show that the system is obsolete and that it should be replaced by a new system. This will mean that a number of system maintainers will lose their jobs. Your assessment actually shows that the system is well maintained and is of high quality and high business value. How would you report these results to the management of the organisation?

PART **5** VERIFICATION AND VALIDATION

Testing a program is the most common way of checking that it meets its specification and does what the customer wants. However, testing is only one of a range of verification and validation techniques. Some of these techniques, such as program inspections, have been used for almost thirty years but have still not become part of mainstream software engineering.

In this part of the book, I cover approaches to verifying that software meets its specification and validating that it also meets the needs of the software customer. This part of the book has three chapters that are each concerned with different aspects of verification and validation:

1. Chapter 22 is a general look at approaches to program verification and validation. I explain the distinction between verification and validation, and the V & V planning process. I then go on to describe static techniques of system verification. These are techniques where you check the source code of the program rather than test it. I discuss program inspections, the use of automated static analysis and, finally, the role of formal methods in the verification process.

2. Program testing is the topic of Chapter 23. I explain how testing is usually carried out at different levels and explain the differences between component testing and system testing. Using simple examples, I introduce a number of techniques that you can use to design test cases for programs and, finally, briefly discuss test automation. Test automation is the use of software tools to help reduce the time and effort involved in testing processes.

3. Chapter 24 looks at the more specialised topic of critical systems validation. For critical systems, you may have to prove to a customer or external regulator that the system meets its specification and dependability requirements. I describe approaches to reliability, safety and security assessment and explain how evidence about the system V & V processes may be used in the development of a system dependability case.

22

Verification and validation

Objectives

The objective of this chapter is to introduce software verification and validation with a particular focus on static verification techniques. When you have read this chapter, you will:

■ understand the distinctions between software verification and software validation;

■ have been introduced to program inspections as a method of discovering defects in programs;

■ understand what automated static analysis is and how it is used in verification and validation;

■ understand how static verification is used in the Cleanroom development process.

Contents

During and after the implementation process, the program being developed must be checked to ensure that it meets its specification and delivers the functionality expected by the people paying for the software. *Verification and validation* (V &V) is the name given to these checking and analysis processes. Verification and activities take place at each stage of the software process. V & V starts with requirements reviews and continues through design reviews and code inspections to product testing.

Verification and validation are not the same thing, although they are often confused. Boehm (Boehm, 1979) succinctly expressed the difference between them:

- 'Validation: Are we building the right product?'
- 'Verification: Are we building the product right?'

These definitions tell us that the role of verification involves checking that the software conforms to its specification. You should check that it meets its specified functional and non-functional requirements. Validation, however, is a more general process. The aim of validation is to ensure that the software system meets the customer's expectations. It goes beyond checking that the system conforms to its specification to showing that the software does what the customer expects it to do. As I discussed in Part 2, software system specifications do not always reflect the real wishes or needs of users and system owners.

The ultimate goal of the verification and validation process is to establish confidence that the software system is 'fit for purpose'. This means that the system must be good enough for its intended use. The level of required confidence depends on the system's purpose, the expectations of the system users and the current marketing environment for the system:

1. *Software function* The level of confidence required depends on how critical the software is to an organisation. For example, the level of confidence required for software that is used to control a safety-critical system is very much higher than that required for a prototype software system that has been developed to demonstrate some new ideas.

2. *User expectations* It is a sad reflection on the software industry that many users have low expectations of their software and are not surprised when it fails during use. They are willing to accept these system failures when the benefits of use outweigh the disadvantages. However, user tolerance of system failures has been decreasing since the 1990s. It is now less acceptable to deliver unreliable systems, so software companies must devote more effort to verification and validation.

3. *Marketing environment* When a system is marketed, the sellers of the system must take into account competing programs, the price those customers are willing to pay for a system and the required schedule for delivering that system. Where a company has few competitors, it may decide to release a program before it has

Figure 22.1 Static
and dynamic
verification and
validation

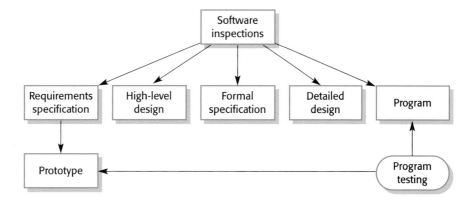

been fully tested and debugged because they want to be the first into the market. Where customers are not willing to pay high prices for software, they may be willing to tolerate more software faults. All of these factors must be considered when deciding how much effort should be spent on the V & V process.

Within the V & V process, there are two complementary approaches to system checking and analysis:

1. *Software inspections or peer reviews* analyse and check system representations such as the requirements document, design diagrams and the program source code. You can use inspections at all stages of the process. Inspections may be supplemented by some automatic analysis of the source text of a system or associated documents. Software inspections and automated analyses are static V & V techniques, as you don't need to run the software on a computer.

2. *Software testing* involves running an implementation of the software with test data. You examine the outputs of the software and its operational behaviour to check that it is performing as required. Testing is a dynamic technique of verification and validation.

Figure 22.1 shows that software inspections and testing play complementary roles in the software process. The arrows indicate the stages in the process where the techniques may be used. Therefore, you can use software inspections at all stages of the software process. Starting with the requirements, any readable representations of the software can be inspected. As I have discussed, requirements and design reviews are the main techniques used for error detection in the specification and design.

You can only test a system when a prototype or an executable version of the program is available. An advantage of incremental development is that a testable version of the system is available at a fairly early stage in the development process. Functionality can be tested as it is added to the system so you don't have to have a complete implementation before testing begins.

Inspection techniques include program inspections, automated source code analysis and formal verification. However, static techniques can only check the correspondence between a program and its specification (verification); they cannot demonstrate that the software is operationally useful. You also can't use static techniques to check emergent properties of the software such as its performance and reliability.

Although software inspections are now widely used, program testing will always be the main software verification and validation technique. Testing involves exercising the program using data like the real data processed by the program. You discover program defects or inadequacies by examining the outputs of the program and looking for anomalies. There are two distinct types of testing that may be used at different stages in the software process:

1. *Validation testing* is intended to show that the software is what the customer wants—that it meets its requirements. As part of validation testing, you may use statistical testing to test the program's performance and reliability, and to check how it works under operational conditions. I discuss statistical testing and reliability estimation in Chapter 24.

2. *Defect testing* is intended to reveal defects in the system rather than to simulate its operational use. The goal of defect testing is to find inconsistencies between a program and its specification. I cover defect testing in Chapter 23.

Of course, there is no hard-and-fast boundary between these approaches to testing. During validation testing, you will find defects in the system; during defect testing, some of the tests will show that the program meets its requirements.

The processes of V & V and debugging are normally interleaved. As you discover faults in the program that you are testing, you have to change the program to correct these faults. However, testing (or, more generally verification and validation) and debugging have different goals:

1. Verification and validation processes are intended to establish the existence of defects in a software system.

2. Debugging is a process (Figure 22.2) that locates and corrects these defects.

There is no simple method for program debugging. Skilled debuggers look for patterns in the test output where the defect is exhibited and use their knowledge of the type of defect, the output pattern, the programming language and the programming process to locate the defect. When you are debugging, you can use your knowledge of common programmer errors (such as failing to increment a counter) and match these against the observed patterns. You should also look for characteristic programming language errors, such as pointer misdirection in C.

Locating the faults in a program is not always a simple process, since the fault may not be close to the point where the program failed. To locate a program fault,

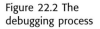
Figure 22.2 The
debugging process

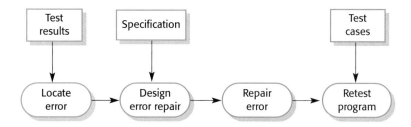

you may have to design additional tests that reproduce the original fault and that pinpoint its location in the program. You may have to trace the program manually, line by line. Debugging tools that collect information about the program's execution may also help you locate the source of a problem.

Interactive debugging tools are generally part of a set of language support tools that are integrated with a compilation system. They provide a specialised run-time environment for the program that allows access to the compiler symbol table and, from there, to the values of program variables. You can control execution by 'stepping' through the program statement by statement. After each statement has been executed, you can examine the values of variables and so discover the location of the fault.

After a defect in the program has been discovered, you have to correct it and revalidate the system. This may involve re-inspecting the program or regression testing where existing tests are executed again. Regression testing is used to check that the changes made to a program have not introduced new faults. Experience has shown that a high proportion of fault 'repairs' are either incomplete or introduce new faults into the program.

In principle, you should repeat all tests after every defect repair; in practice, this is usually too expensive. As part of the test plan, you should identify dependencies between components and the tests associated with each component. That is, there should be traceability from the test cases to the components that are tested. If this traceability is documented, you may then run a subset of the system test cases to check the modified component and its dependents.

22.1 Planning verification and validation

Verification and validation is an expensive process. For some systems, such as real-time systems with complex non-functional constraints, more than half the system development budget may be spent on V & V. Careful planning is needed to get the most out of inspections and testing and to control the costs of the verification and validation process.

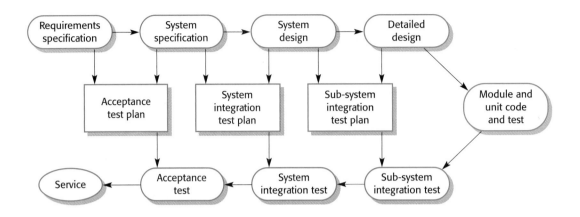

Figure 22.3 Test
plans as a link
between develop-
ment and testing

You should start planning system validation and verification early in the development process. The software development process model shown in Figure 22.3 is sometimes called the V-model (turn Figure 22.3 on end to see the V). It is an instantiation of the generic waterfall model (see Chapter 4) and shows that test plans should be derived from the system specification and design. This model also breaks down system V & V into a number of stages. Each stage is driven by tests that have been defined to check the conformance of the program with its design and specification.

As part of the V & V planning process, you should decide on the balance between static and dynamic approaches to verification and validation, draw up standards and procedures for software inspections and testing, establish checklists to drive program inspections (see Section 22.3) and define the software test plan.

The relative effort devoted to inspections and testing depends on the type of system being developed and the organisational expertise with program inspection. As a general rule, the more critical a system, the more effort should be devoted to static verification techniques.

Test planning is concerned with establishing standards for the testing process, not just with describing product tests. As well as helping managers allocate resources and estimate testing schedules, test plans are intended for software engineers involved in designing and carrying out system tests. They help technical staff get an overall picture of the system tests and place their own work in this context. A good description of test plans and their relation to more general quality plans is given in Frewin and Hatton (Frewin and Hatton, 1986). Humphrey (Humphrey, 1989) and Kit (Kit, 1995) also include discussions on test planning.

The major components of a test plan for a large and complex system are shown in Figure 22.4. As well as setting out the testing schedule and procedures, the test plan defines the hardware and software resources that are required. This is useful for system managers who are responsible for ensuring that these resources are available to the testing team. Test plans should normally include significant amounts of contingency so that slippages in design and implementation can be accommodated and staff redeployed to other activities.

Figure 22.4 The
structure of a
software test plan

The testing process
A description of the major phases of the testing process. These might be as
described earlier in this chapter.

Requirements traceability
Users are most interested in the system meeting its requirements and testing should
be planned so that all requirements are individually tested.

Tested items
The products of the software process that are to be tested should be specified.

Testing schedule
An overall testing schedule and resource allocation for this schedule is, obviously,
linked to the more general project development schedule.

Test recording procedures
It is not enough simply to run tests; the results of the tests must be systematically
recorded. It must be possible to audit the testing process to check that it has been
carried out correctly.

Hardware and software requirements
This section should set out the software tools required and estimated hardware
utilisation.

Constraints
Constraints affecting the testing process such as staff shortages should be anticipated
in this section.

For smaller systems, a less formal test plan may be used, but there is still a need
for a formal document to support the planning of the testing process. For some agile
processes such as extreme programming, testing is inseparable from development. Like
other planning activities, test planning is also incremental. In XP, the customer is ultimately responsible for deciding how much effort should be devoted to system testing.

Test plans are not a static documents but evolve during the development process. Test plans change because of delays at other stages in the development process. If part of a system is incomplete, the system as a whole cannot be tested. You
then have to revise the test plan to redeploy the testers to some other activity and
bring them back when the software is once again available.

22.2 Software inspections

Software inspection is a static V & V process in which a software system is reviewed
to find errors, omissions and anomalies. Generally, inspections focus on source code,

but any readable representation of the software such as its requirements or a design model can be inspected. When you inspect a system, you use knowledge of the system, its application domain and the programming language or design model to discover errors.

There are three major advantages of inspection over testing:

1. During testing, errors can mask (hide) other errors. Once one error is discovered, you can never be sure if other output anomalies are due to a new error or are side effects of the original error. Because inspection is a static process, you don't have to be concerned with interactions between errors. Consequently, a single inspection session can discover many errors in a system.

2. Incomplete versions of a system can be inspected without additional costs. If a program is incomplete, then you need to develop specialised test harnesses to test the parts that are available. This obviously adds to the system development costs.

3. As well as searching for program defects, an inspection can also consider broader quality attributes of a program such as compliance with standards, portability and maintainability. You can look for inefficiencies, inappropriate algorithms and poor programming style that could make the system difficult to maintain and update.

Inspections are an old idea. There have been several studies and experiments that have demonstrated that inspections are more effective for defect discovery than program testing. Fagan (Fagan, 1986) reported that more than 60% of the errors in a program can be detected using informal program inspections. Mills et al. (Mills, et al., 1987) suggest that a more formal approach to inspection based on correctness arguments can detect more than 90% of the errors in a program. This technique is used in the Cleanroom process described in Section 22.4. Selby and Basili (Selby, et al., 1987) empirically compared the effectiveness of inspections and testing. They found that static code reviewing was more effective and less expensive than defect testing in discovering program faults. Gilb and Graham (Gilb and Graham, 1993) have also found this to be true.

Reviews and testing each have advantages and disadvantages and should be used together in the verification and validation process. Indeed, Gilb and Graham suggest that one of the most effective uses of reviews is to review the test cases for a system. Reviews can discover problems with these tests and can help design more effective ways to test the system. You can start system V & V with inspections early in the development process, but once a system is integrated, you need testing to check its emergent properties and that the system's functionality is what the owner of the system really wants.

In spite of the success of inspections, it has proven to be difficult to introduce formal inspections into many software development organisations. Software engineers with experience of program testing are sometimes reluctant to accept that inspections can be more effective for defect detection than testing. Managers may be suspicious because inspections require additional costs during design and development. They may not wish to take the risk that there will be no corresponding savings during program testing.

There is no doubt that inspections 'front-load' software V & V costs and result in cost savings only after the development teams become experienced in their use. Furthermore, there are the practical problems of arranging inspections: Inspections take time to arrange and appear to slow down the development process. It is difficult to convince a hard-pressed manager that this time can be made up later because less time will be spent on program debugging.

22.2.1 The program inspection process

Program inspections are reviews whose objective is program defect detection. The notion of a formalised inspection process was first developed at IBM in the 1970s (Fagan, 1976; Fagan, 1986). It is now a fairly widely used method of program verification, especially in critical systems engineering. From Fagan's original method, a number of alternative approaches to inspection have been developed (Gilb and Graham, 1993). These are all based on a team with members from different backgrounds making a careful, line-by-line review of the program source code.

The key difference between program inspections and other types of quality review is that the specific goal of inspections is to find program defects rather than to consider broader design issues. Defects may be logical errors, anomalies in the code that might indicate an erroneous condition or noncompliance with organisational or project standards. By contrast, other types of review may be more concerned with schedule, costs, progress against defined milestones or assessing whether the software is likely to meet organisational goals.

The program inspection is a formal process that is carried out by a team of at least four people. Team members systematically analyse the code and point out possible defects. In Fagan's original proposals, he suggested roles such as author, reader, tester and moderator. The reader reads the code aloud to the inspection team, the tester inspects the code from a testing perspective and the moderator organises the process.

As organisations have gained experience with inspection, other proposals for team roles have emerged. In a discussion of how inspection was successfully introduced in Hewlett-Packard's development process, Grady and Van Slack (Grady and Van Slack, 1994) suggest six roles, as shown in Figure 22.5. They do not think that reading the program aloud is necessary. The same person can take more than one role so the team size may vary from one inspection to another. Gilb and Graham suggest that inspectors should be selected to reflect different viewpoints such as testing, end-user and quality management.

The activities in the inspection process are shown in Figure 22.6. Before a program inspection process begins, it is essential that:

Figure 22.5 Roles in the inspection process

Role	Description
Author or owner	The programmer or designer responsible for producing the program or document. Responsible for fixing defects discovered during the inspection process.
Inspector	Finds errors, omissions and inconsistencies in programs and documents. May also identify broader issues that are outside the scope of the inspection team.
Reader	Presents the code or document at an inspection meeting.
Scribe	Records the results of the inspection meeting.
Chairman or moderator	Manages the process and facilitates the inspection. Reports process results to the chief moderator.
Chief moderator	Responsible for inspection process improvements, checklist updating, standards development, etc.

1. You have a precise specification of the code to be inspected. It is impossible to inspect a component at the level of detail required to detect defects without a complete specification.

2. The inspection team members are familiar with the organisational standards.

3. An up-to-date, compilable version of the code has been distributed to all team members. There is no point in inspecting code that is 'almost complete' even if a delay causes schedule disruption.

The inspection team moderator is responsible for inspection planning. This involves selecting an inspection team, organising a meeting room and ensuring that the material to be inspected and its specifications are complete. The program to be inspected is presented to the inspection team during the overview stage when the author of the code describes what the program is intended to do. This is followed by a period of individual preparation. Each inspection team member studies the specification and the program and looks for defects in the code.

The inspection itself should be fairly short (no more than two hours) and should focus on defect detection, standards conformance and poor-quality programming. The inspection team should not suggest how these defects should be corrected nor should it recommend changes to other components.

Following the inspection, the program's author should make changes to it to correct the identified problems. In the follow-up stage, the moderator should decide whether a reinspection of the code is required. He or she may decide that a complete reinspection is not required and that the defects have been successfully fixed. The program is then approved by the moderator for release.

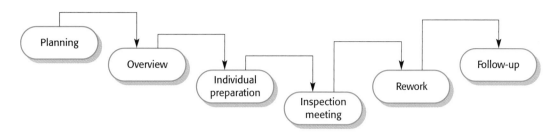

Figure 22.6 The
inspection process

During an inspection, a checklist of common programmer errors is often used to focus the discussion. This checklist can be based on checklist examples from books or from knowledge of defects that are common in a particular application domain. You need different checklists for different programming languages because each language has its own characteristic errors. Humphrey (Humphrey, 1989), in a comprehensive discussion of inspections, gives a number of examples of inspection checklists.

This checklist varies according to programming language because of the different levels of checking provided by the language compiler. For example, a Java compiler checks that functions have the correct number of parameters, a C compiler does not. Possible checks that might be made during the inspection process are shown in Figure 22.7. Gilb and Graham (Gilb and Graham, 1993) emphasise that each organisation should develop its own inspection checklist based on local standards and practices. Checklists should be regularly updated as new types of defects are found.

The time needed for an inspection and the amount of code that can be covered depends on the experience of the inspection team, the programming language and the application domain. Both Fagan at IBM and Barnard and Price (Barnard and Price, 1994), who assessed the inspection process for telecommunications software, came to similar conclusions:

1. About 500 source code statements per hour can be presented during the overview stage.

2. During individual preparation, about 125 source code statements per hour can be examined.

3. From 90 to 125 statements per hour can be inspected during the inspection meeting.

With four people involved in an inspection team, the cost of inspecting 100 lines of code is roughly equivalent to one person-day of effort. This assumes that the inspection itself takes about an hour and that each team member spends one to two hours preparing for the inspection. Testing costs vary widely and depend on the number of faults in the program. However, the effort required for the program inspection is probably less than half the effort that would be required for equivalent defect testing.

Figure 22.7
Inspection checks

Fault class	Inspection check
Data faults	Are all program variables initialised before their values are used? Have all constants been named? Should the upper bound of arrays be equal to the size of the array or Size -1? If character strings are used, is a delimiter explicitly assigned? Is there any possibility of buffer overflow?
Control faults	For each conditional statement, is the condition correct? Is each loop certain to terminate? Are compound statements correctly bracketed? In case statements, are all possible cases accounted for? If a break is required after each case in case statements, has it been included?
Input/output faults	Are all input variables used? Are all output variables assigned a value before they are output? Can unexpected inputs cause corruption?
Interface faults	Do all function and method calls have the correct number of parameters? Do formal and actual parameter types match? Are the parameters in the right order? If components access shared memory, do they have the same model of the shared memory structure?
Storage management faults	If a linked structure is modified, have all links been correctly reassigned? If dynamic storage is used, has space been allocated correctly? Is space explicitly de-allocated after it is no longer required?
Exception management faults	Have all possible error conditions been taken into account?

Some organisations (Gilb and Graham, 1993) have now abandoned component testing in favour of inspections. They have found that program inspections are so effective at finding errors that the costs of component testing are not justifiable. These organisations found that inspections of components, combined with system testing, were the most cost-effective V & V strategy. As I discuss later in the chapter, this approach is used in the Cleanroom software development process.

The introduction of inspections has implications for project management. Sensitive management is important if inspections are to be accepted by software development teams. Program inspection is a public process of error detection compared with the more private component testing process. Inevitably, mistakes that are made by individuals are revealed to the whole programming team. Inspection team leaders must be trained to manage the process carefully and to develop a culture that provides support without blame when errors are discovered.

As an organisation gains experience of the inspection process, it can use the results of inspections to help with process improvement. Inspections are an ideal way to collect data on the type of defects that occur. The inspection team and the authors of the code that was inspected can suggest reasons why these defects were introduced. Wherever possible, the process should then be modified to eliminate the reasons for defects so they can be avoided in future systems.

22.3 Automated static analysis

Inspections are one form of static analysis—you examine the program without executing it. As I discussed, inspections are often driven by checklists of errors and heuristics that identify common errors in different programming languages. For some errors and heuristics, it is possible to automate the process of checking programs against this list, which has resulted in the development of automated static analysers for different programming languages.

Static analysers are software tools that scan the source text of a program and detect possible faults and anomalies. They parse the program text and thus recognise the types of statements in the program. They can then detect whether statements are well formed, make inferences about the control flow in the program and, in many cases, compute the set of all possible values for program data. They complement the error-detection facilities provided by the language compiler. They can be used as part of the inspection process or as a separate V & V process activity.

The intention of automatic static analysis is to draw an inspector's attention to anomalies in the program, such as variables that are used without initialisation, variables that are unused or data whose value could go out of range. Some of the checks that can be detected by static analysis are shown in Figure 22.8. Anomalies are often a result of programming errors or omissions, so they highlight things that could go wrong when the program is executed. However, you should understand that these anomalies are not necessarily program faults. They may be deliberate or may have no adverse consequences.

The stages involved in static analysis include:

1. *Control flow analysis* This stage identifies and highlights loops with multiple exit or entry points and unreachable code. Unreachable code is code that is surrounded by unconditional goto statements or that is in a branch of a conditional statement where the guarding condition can never be true.

2. *Data use analysis* This stage highlights how variables in the program are used. It detects variables that are used without previous initialisation, variables that

Figure 22.8
Automated static
analysis checks

Fault class	Static analysis check
Data faults	Variables used before initialisation Variables declared but never used Variables assigned twice but never used between assignments Possible array bound violations Undeclared variables
Control faults	Unreachable code Unconditional branches into loops
Input/output faults	Variables output twice with no intervening assignment
Interface faults	Parameter type mismatches Parameter number mismatches Non-usage of the results of functions Uncalled functions and procedures
Storage management faults	Unassigned pointers Pointer arithmetic

are written twice without an intervening assignment and variables that are declared but never used. Data use analysis also discovers ineffective tests where the test condition is redundant. Redundant conditions are conditions that are either always true or always false.

3. *Interface analysis* This analysis checks the consistency of routine and procedure declarations and their use. It is unnecessary if a strongly typed language such as Java is used for implementation as the compiler carries out these checks. Interface analysis can detect type errors in weakly typed languages like FORTRAN and C. Interface analysis can also detect functions and procedures that are declared and never called or function results that are never used.

4. *Information flow analysis* This phase of the analysis identifies the dependencies between input and output variables. While it does not detect anomalies, it shows how the value of each program variable is derived from other variable values. With this information, a code inspection should be able to find values that have been wrongly computed. Information flow analysis can also show the conditions that affect a variable's value.

5. *Path analysis* This phase of semantic analysis identifies all possible paths through the program and sets out the statements executed in that path. It essentially unravels the program's control and allows each possible predicate to be analysed individually.

Static analysers are particularly valuable when a programming language such as C is used. C does not have strict type rules, and the checking that the C compiler can do is limited. Therefore, it is easy for programmers to make mistakes, and the static analysis tool can automatically discover some of the resulting program faults. This is particularly important when C (and to a lesser extent, C++) is used for critical systems development. In this case, static analysis can discover a large number of potential errors and can significantly reduce testing costs.

There is no doubt that, for languages such as C, static analysis is an effective technique for discovering program errors. It compensates for weaknesses in the programming language design. However, the designers of modern programming languages such as Java have removed some error-prone language features. All variables must be initialised, there are no goto statements so unreachable code is less likely to be created accidentally, and storage management is automatic. This approach of error avoidance rather than error detection is more effective in improving program reliability. Although static analysers for Java are available, they are not widely used. It is not clear whether the number of errors detected justifies the time required to analyse their output.

Therefore, to illustrate static analysis I use a small C program rather than a Java program. Unix and Linux systems include a static analyser called LINT for C programs. LINT provides static checking, which is equivalent to that provided by the compiler in a strongly typed language such as Java. An example of the output produced by LINT is shown in Figure 22.9. In this transcript of a Unix terminal session, commands are shown in italics. The first command (line 138) lists the (nonsensical) program. It defines a function with one parameter, called **printarray**, and then calls this function with three parameters. Variables i and c are declared but are never assigned values. The value returned by the function is never used.

The line numbered 139 shows the C compilation of this program with no errors reported by the C compiler. This is followed by a call of the LINT static analyser, which detects and reports program errors.

The static analyser shows that the variables c and i have been used but not initialised, and that **printarray** has been called with a different number of arguments than are declared. It also identifies the inconsistent use of the first argument in **printarray** and the fact that the function value is never used.

Tool-based analysis cannot replace inspections, as there are some types of error that static analysers cannot detect. For example, they can detect uninitialised variables, but they cannot detect initialisations that are incorrect. In weakly typed languages such as C, static analysers can detect functions that have the wrong numbers and types of arguments, but they cannot detect situations where an incorrect argument of the correct type has been passed to a function.

To address some of these problems, static analysers such as LCLint (Orcero, 2000; Evans and Larochelle, 2002) support the use of annotations where users define constraints as stylised comments in the program. These constraints allow a programmer to specify that variables in a function should not be changed, the global variables used, and so on. The static analyser can then check the program against these constraints and highlight code sections that appear to be incorrect.

Figure 22.9 LINT
static analysis

```
138% more lint_ex.c

#include <stdio.h>
printarray (Anarray)
int Anarray;
{
printf("%d",Anarray);
}
main ()
{
int Anarray[5]; int i; char c;
printarray (Anarray, i, c);
printarray (Anarray) ;
}

139% cc lint_ex.c
140% lint lint_ex.c

lint_ex.c(10): warning: c may be used before set
lint_ex.c(10): warning: i may be used before set
printarray: variable # of args. lint_ex.c(4) :: lint_ex.c(10)
printarray, arg. 1 used inconsistently lint_ex.c(4) :: lint_ex.c(10)
printarray, arg. 1 used inconsistently lint_ex.c(4) :: lint_ex.c(11)
printf returns value which is always ignored
```

22.4 Verification and formal methods

Formal methods of software development are based on mathematical representations of the software, usually as a formal specification. These formal methods are mainly concerned with a mathematical analysis of the specification; with transforming the specification to a more detailed, semantically equivalent representation; or with formally verifying that one representation of the system is semantically equivalent to another representation.

You can think of the use of formal methods as the ultimate static verification technique. They require very detailed analyses of the system specification and the program, and their use is often time consuming and expensive. Consequently, the use of formal methods is mostly confined to safety- and security-critical software development processes. The use of formal mathematical specification and associated verification was mandated in UK defence standards for safety-critical software (MOD, 1995).

Formal methods may be used at different stages in the V & V process:

1. A formal specification of the system may be developed and mathematically analysed for inconsistency. This technique is effective in discovering specification errors and omissions, as discussed in Chapter 10.

2. You can formally verify, using mathematical arguments, that the code of a software system is consistent with its specification. This requires a formal specification and is effective in discovering programming and some design errors. A transformational development process where a formal specification is transformed through a series of more detailed representations or a Cleanroom process may be used to support the formal verification process.

The argument for the use of formal specification and associated program verification is that formal specification forces a detailed analysis of the specification. It may reveal potential inconsistencies or omissions that might not otherwise be discovered until the system is operational. Formal verification demonstrates that the developed program meets its specification so implementation errors do not compromise dependability.

The argument against the use of formal specification is that it requires specialised notations. These can only be used by specially trained staff and cannot be understood by domain experts. Hence, problems with the system requirements can be concealed by formality. Software engineers cannot recognise potential difficulties with the requirements because they don't understand the domain; domain experts cannot find these problems because they don't understand the specification. Although the specification may be mathematically consistent, it may not specify the system properties that are really required.

Verifying a nontrivial software system takes a great deal of time and requires specialised tools such as theorem provers and mathematical expertise. It is therefore an extremely expensive process and, as the system size increases, the costs of formal verification increase disproportionately. Many people therefore think that formal verification is not cost-effective. The same level of confidence in the system can be achieved more cheaply by using other validation techniques such as inspections and system testing.

It is sometimes claimed that the use of formal methods for system development leads to more reliable and safer systems. There is no doubt that a formal system specification is less likely to contain anomalies that must be resolved by the system designer. However, formal specification and proof do not guarantee that the software will be reliable in practical use. The reasons for this are:

1. *The specification may not reflect the real requirements of system users.* Lutz (Lutz, 1993) discovered that many failures experienced by users were a consequence of specification errors and omissions that could not be detected by formal system specification. Furthermore, system users rarely understand formal notations so they cannot read the formal specification directly to find errors and omissions.

2. *The proof may contain errors*. Program proofs are large and complex, so, like large and complex programs, they usually contain errors.

3. *The proof may assume a usage pattern which is incorrect*. If the system is not used as anticipated, the proof may be invalid.

In spite of their disadvantages, my view (discussed in Chapter 10) is that formal methods have an important role to play in the development of critical software systems. Formal specifications are very effective in discovering specification problems that are the most common causes of system failure. Formal verification increases confidence in the most critical components of these systems. The use of formal approaches is increasing as procurers demand it and as more and more engineers become familiar with these techniques.

22.4.1 Cleanroom software development

Formal methods have been integrated with a number of software development processes. In the B method (Wordsworth, 1996) a formal specification is transformed through a series of correctness-preserving transformations to a program. SDL (Mitschele-Thiel, 2001) is used for telecommunications systems development and VDM (Jones, 1986) and Z (Spivey, 1992) have been used in waterfall-type processes. Another well-documented approach that uses formal methods is the Cleanroom development process. Cleanroom software development (Mills, et al., 1987; Cobb and Mills, 1990; Linger, 1994; Prowell, et al., 1999) is a software development philosophy that uses formal methods to support rigorous software inspection.

A model of the Cleanroom process is shown in Figure 22.10. The objective of this approach to software development is zero-defect software. The name 'Cleanroom' was derived by analogy with semiconductor fabrication units where defects are avoided by manufacturing in an ultra-clean atmosphere. Cleanroom development is particularly relevant to this chapter because it has replaced the unit testing of system components by inspections to check the consistency of these components with their specifications.

The Cleanroom approach to software development is based on five key strategies:

1. *Formal specification* The software to be developed is formally specified. A state-transition model that shows system responses to stimuli is used to express the specification.

2. *Incremental development* The software is partitioned into increments that are developed and validated separately using the Cleanroom process. These increments are specified, with customer input, at an early stage in the process.

3. *Structured programming* Only a limited number of control and data abstraction constructs are used. The program development process is a process of stepwise

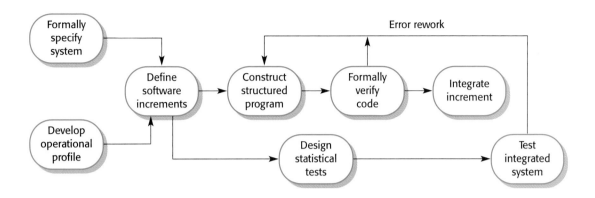

Figure 22.10 The
Cleanroom develop-
ment process

refinement of the specification. A limited number of constructs are used and the
aim is to systematically transform the specification to create the program code.

4. *Static verification* The developed software is statically verified using rigorous
   software inspections. There is no unit or module testing process for code
   components.

5. *Statistical testing of the system* The integrated software increment is tested statistically, as discussed in Chapter 24, to determine its reliability. These statistical tests are based on an operational profile, which is developed in parallel
   with the system specification as shown in Figure 22.10.

There are three teams involved when the Cleanroom process is used for large
system development:

1. *The specification team* This group is responsible for developing and maintaining the system specification. This team produces customer-oriented specifications (the user requirements definition) and mathematical specifications for
   verification. In some cases, when the specification is complete, the specification team also takes responsibility for development.

2. *The development team* This team has the responsibility of developing and verifying the software. The software is not executed during the development process. A structured, formal approach to verification based on inspection of code
   supplemented with correctness arguments is used.

3. *The certification team* This team is responsible for developing a set of statistical tests to exercise the software after it has been developed. These tests are
   based on the formal specification. Test case development is carried out in parallel with software development. The test cases are used to certify the software
   reliability. Reliability growth models (Chapter 24) may be used to decide when
   to stop testing.

Use of the Cleanroom approach has generally led to software with very few errors. Cobb and Mills discuss several successful Cleanroom development projects that had a uniformly low failure rate in delivered systems (Cobb and Mills, 1990). The costs of these projects were comparable with other projects that used conventional development techniques.

The approach to incremental development in the Cleanroom process is to deliver critical customer functionality in early increments. Less important system functions are included in later increments. The customer therefore has the opportunity to try these critical increments before the whole system has been delivered. If requirements problems are discovered, the customer feeds back this information to the development team and requests a new release of the increment.

As with extreme programming, this means that the most important customer functions receive the most validation. As new increments are developed, they are combined with the existing increments and the integrated system is tested. Therefore, existing increments are retested with new test cases as new system increments are added.

Rigorous program inspection is a fundamental part of the Cleanroom process. A state model of the system is produced as a system specification. This is refined through a series of more detailed system models to an executable program. The approach used for development is based on well-defined transformations that attempt to preserve the correctness at each transformation to a more detailed representation. At each stage, the new representation is inspected, and mathematically rigorous arguments are developed that demonstrate that the output of the transformation is consistent with its input.

The mathematical arguments used in the Cleanroom process are not, however, formal proofs of correctness. Formal mathematical proofs that a program is correct with respect to its specification are too expensive to develop. They depend on using knowledge of the formal semantics of the programming language to construct theories that relate the program and its formal specification. These theories must then be proven mathematically, often with the assistance of large and complex theorem-prover programs. Because of their high cost and the specialist skills that are needed, proofs are usually developed only for the most safety- or security-critical applications.

Inspection and formal analysis has been found to be very effective in the Cleanroom process. The vast majority of defects are discovered before execution and are not introduced into the developed software. Linger (Linger, 1994) reports that, on average, only 2.3 defects per thousand lines of source code were discovered during testing for Cleanroom projects. Overall development costs are not increased because less effort is required to test and repair the developed software.

Selby et al., (Selby, et al., 1987), using students as developers, carried out an experiment that compared Cleanroom development with conventional techniques. They found that most teams could successfully use the Cleanroom method. The programs produced were of higher quality than those developed using traditional techniques—the source code had more comments and a simpler structure. More of the Cleanroom teams met the development schedule.

Cleanroom development works when practised by skilled and committed engineers. Reports of the success of the Cleanroom approach in industry have mostly, though not exclusively, come from people already committed to it. We don't know whether this process can be transferred effectively to other types of software development organisations. These organisations may have less committed and less skilled engineers. Transferring the Cleanroom approach or, indeed, any other approach where formal methods are used, to less technically advanced organisations still remains a challenge.

KEY POINTS

■ Verification and validation are not the same thing. Verification is intended to show that a program meets its specification. Validation is intended to show that the program does what the user requires.

■ Test plans should include a description of the items to be tested, the testing schedule, the procedures for managing the testing process, the hardware and software requirements, and any testing problems that are likely to arise.

■ Static verification techniques involve examination and analysis of the program source code to detect errors. They should be used with program testing as part of the V & V process.

■ Program inspections are effective in finding program errors. The aim of an inspection is to locate faults. A fault checklist should drive the inspection process.

■ In a program inspection, a small team systematically checks the code. Team members include a team leader or moderator, the author of the code, a reader who presents the code during the inspection and a tester who considers the code from a testing perspective.

■ Static analysers are software tools that process a program source code and draw attention to anomalies such as unused code sections and uninitialised variables. These anomalies may be the result of faults in the code.

■ Cleanroom software development relies on static techniques for program verification and statistical testing for system reliability certification. It has been successful in producing systems that have a high level of reliability.

FURTHER READING

Software Quality Assurance: From Theory to Implementation. This book provides good general background reading on verification and validation, with a particularly good chapter on reviews and inspections. (D. Galin, 2004, Addison-Wesley.)

'Software inspection'. A special issue of a journal that contains a number of articles on program inspection, including a discussion on using this technique with object-oriented development. (*IEEE Software,* 20(4), July/August 2003.)

'Software debugging, testing and verification'. This is a general article on verification and validation and one of the few articles that addresses both testing and static verification techniques. (B. Hailpern and P. Santhanam, *IBM Systems Journal,* 41(1), January 2002.)

Cleanroom Software Engineering: Technology and Process. A good book on the Cleanroom approach that has sections on the basics of the technique, the process and a practical case study. (S. J. Powell, et al., 1999, Addison-Wesley.)

EXERCISES

22.1 Discuss the differences between verification and validation, and explain why validation is a particularly difficult process.

22.2 Explain why it is not necessary for a program to be completely free of defects before it is delivered to its customers. To what extent can testing be used to validate that the program is fit for its purpose?

22.3 The test plan in Figure 22.4 has been designed for custom systems that have a separate requirements document. Suggest how the test plan structure might be modified for testing shrink-wrapped software products.

22.4 Explain why program inspections are an effective technique for discovering errors in a program. What types of error are unlikely to be discovered through inspections?

22.5 Suggest why an organisation with a competitive, elitist culture would probably find it difficult to introduce program inspections as a V & V technique.

22.6 Using your knowledge of Java, C++, C or some other programming language, derive a checklist of common errors (not syntax errors) that could not be detected by a compiler but that might be detected in a program inspection.

22.7 Produce a list of conditions that could be detected by a static analyser for Java, C++ or another programming language that you use. Comment on this list compared to the list given in Figure 22.7.

22.8 Explain why it may be cost-effective to use formal methods in the development of safety-critical software systems. Why do you think that some developers of this type of system are against the use of formal methods?

22.9 A manager decides to use the reports of program inspections as an input to the staff appraisal process. These reports show who made and who discovered program errors. Is this ethical managerial behaviour? Would it be ethical if the staff were informed in advance that this would happen? What difference might it make to the inspection process?

22.10 One approach that is commonly adopted to system testing is to test the system until the testing budget is exhausted and then deliver the system to customers. Discuss the ethics of this approach.

23
Software testing

Objectives

The objective of this chapter is to describe the processes of software testing and introduce a range of testing techniques. When you have read the chapter, you will:

■ understand the distinctions between validation testing and defect testing;

■ understand the principles of system testing and component testing;

■ understand three strategies that may be used to generate system test cases;

■ understand the essential characteristics of software tools that support test automation.

Contents

In Chapter 4, I discussed a general testing process that started with the testing of individual program units such as functions or objects. These were then integrated into sub-systems and systems, and the interactions of these units were tested. Finally, after delivery of the system, the customer may carry out a series of acceptance tests to check that the system performs as specified.

This model of the testing process is appropriate for large system development—but for smaller systems, or for systems that are developed through scripting or reuse, there are often fewer distinct stages in the process. A more abstract view of software testing is shown in Figure 23.1. The two fundamental testing activities are component testing—testing the parts of the system—and system testing—testing the system as a whole.

The aim of the component testing stage is to discover defects by testing individual program components. These components may be functions, objects or reusable components as described in Chapter 19. During system testing, these components are integrated to form sub-systems or the complete system. At this stage, system testing should focus on establishing that the system meets its functional and non-functional requirements, and does not behave in unexpected ways. Inevitably, defects in components that have been missed during earlier testing are discovered during system testing.

As I explained in Chapter 22, the software testing process has two distinct goals:

1. *To demonstrate to the developer and the customer that the software meets its requirements.* For custom software, this means that there should be at least one test for every requirement in the user and system requirements documents. For generic software products, it means that there should be tests for all of the system features that will be incorporated in the product release. As discussed in Chapter 4, some systems may have an explicit acceptance testing phase where the customer formally checks that the delivered system conforms to its specification.

2. *To discover faults or defects in the software where the behaviour of the software is incorrect, undesirable or does not conform to its specification.* Defect testing is concerned with rooting out all kinds of undesirable system behaviour, such as system crashes, unwanted interactions with other systems, incorrect computations and data corruption.

The first goal leads to validation testing, where you expect the system to perform correctly using a given set of test cases that reflect the system's expected use. The second goal leads to defect testing, where the test cases are designed to expose

Figure 23.1 Testing phases

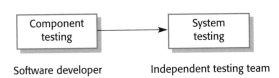

Software developer   Independent testing team

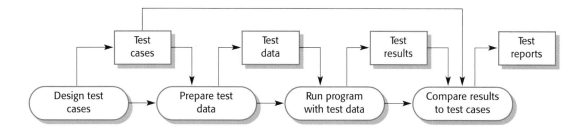

Figure 23.2 A model of the software testing process

defects. The test cases can be deliberately obscure and need not reflect how the system is normally used. For validation testing, a successful test is one where the system performs correctly. For defect testing, a successful test is one that exposes a defect that causes the system to perform incorrectly.

Testing cannot demonstrate that the software is free of defects or that it will behave as specified in every circumstance. It is always possible that a test that you have overlooked could discover further problems with the system. As Edsger Dijkstra, a leading early figure in the development of software engineering, eloquently stated (Dijkstra, et al., 1972), 'Testing can only show the presence of errors, not their absence.'

Overall, therefore, the goal of software testing is to convince system developers and customers that the software is good enough for operational use. Testing is a process intended to build confidence in the software.

A general model of the testing process is shown in Figure 23.2. Test cases are specifications of the inputs to the test and the expected output from the system plus a statement of what is being tested. Test data are the inputs that have been devised to test the system. Test data can sometimes be generated automatically. Automatic test case generation is impossible. The output of the tests can only be predicted by people who understand what the system should do.

Exhaustive testing, where every possible program execution sequence is tested, is impossible. Testing, therefore, has to be based on a subset of possible test cases. Ideally, software companies should have policies for choosing this subset rather than leave this to the development team. These policies might be based on general testing policies, such as a policy that all program statements should be executed at least once. Alternatively, the testing policies may be based on experience of system usage and may focus on testing the features of the operational system. For example:

1. All system functions that are accessed through menus should be tested.

2. Combinations of functions (e.g., text formatting) that are accessed through the same menu must be tested.

3. Where user input is provided, all functions must be tested with both correct and incorrect input.

It is clear from experience with major software products such as word processors or spreadsheets that comparable guidelines are normally used during product testing. When features of the software are used in isolation, they normally work.

Problems arise, as Whittaker explains (Whittaker, 2002), when combinations of features have not been tested together. He gives the example of how, in a commonly used word processor, using footnotes with multicolumn layout causes incorrect layout of the text.

As part of the V & V planning process, managers have to make decisions on who should be responsible for the different stages of testing. For most systems, programmers take responsibility for testing the components that they have developed. Once this is completed, the work is handed over to an integration team, which integrates the modules from different developers, builds the software and tests the system as a whole. For critical systems, a more formal process may be used where independent testers are responsible for all stages of the testing process. In critical system testing, the tests are developed separately and detailed records are maintained of the test results.

Component testing by developers is usually based on an intuitive understanding of how the components should operate. System testing, however, has to be based on a written system specification. This can be a detailed system requirements specification, as discussed in Chapter 6, or it can be a higher-level user-oriented specification of the features that should be implemented in the system. A separate team is normally responsible for system testing. As discussed in Chapter 4, the system testing team works from the user and system requirements documents to develop system-testing plans (see Figure 4.10).

Most discussions of testing start with component testing and then move on to system testing. I have deliberately reversed the order of discussion in this chapter because more and more software development involves integrating reusable components and configuring and adapting existing software to meet specific requirements. All testing in such cases is system testing, and there is no separate component testing process.

23.1 System testing

System testing involves integrating two or more components that implement system functions or features and then testing this integrated system. In an iterative development process, system testing is concerned with testing an increment to be delivered to the customer; in a waterfall process, system testing is concerned with testing the entire system.

For most complex systems, there are two distinct phases to system testing:

1. *Integration testing,* where the test team have access to the source code of the system. When a problem is discovered, the integration team tries to find the source of the problem and identify the components that have to be debugged. Integration testing is mostly concerned with finding defects in the system.

2. *Release testing,* where a version of the system that could be released to users is tested. Here, the test team is concerned with validating that the system meets its requirements and with ensuring that the system is dependable. Release testing is usually 'black-box' testing where the test team is simply concerned with demonstrating that the system does or does not work properly. Problems are reported to the development team whose job is to debug the program. Where customers are involved in release testing, this is sometimes called *acceptance testing*. If the release is good enough, the customer may then accept it for use.

Fundamentally, you can think of integration testing as the testing of incomplete systems composed of clusters or groupings of system components. Release testing is concerned with testing the system release that is intended for delivery to customers. Naturally, these overlap, especially when incremental development is used and the system to be released is incomplete. Generally, the priority in integration testing is to discover defects in the system and the priority in system testing, is to validate that the system meets its requirements. However, in practice, there is some validation testing and some defect testing during both of these processes.

23.1.1 Integration testing

The process of system integration involves building a system from its components (see Chapter 29) and testing the resultant system for problems that arise from component interactions. The components that are integrated may be off-the-shelf components, reusable components that have been adapted for a particular system or newly developed components. For many large systems, all three types of components are likely to be used. Integration testing checks that these components actually work together, are called correctly and transfer the right data at the right time across their interfaces.

System integration involves identifying clusters of components that deliver some system functionality and integrating these by adding code that makes them work together. Sometimes, the overall skeleton of the system is developed first, and components are added to it. This is called *top-down integration*. Alternatively, you may first integrate infrastructure components that provide common services, such as network and database access, then add the functional components. This is *bottom-up integration*. In practice, for many systems, the integration strategy is a mixture of these, with both infrastructure components and functional components added in increments. In both top-down and bottom-up integration, you usually have to develop additional code to simulate other components and allow the system to execute.

A major problem that arises during integration testing is localising errors. There are complex interactions between the system components and, when an anomalous output is discovered, you may find it hard to identify where the error occurred. To make it easier to locate errors, you should always use an incremental approach to system integration and testing. Initially, you should integrate a minimal system

Figure 23.3
Incremental
integration testing

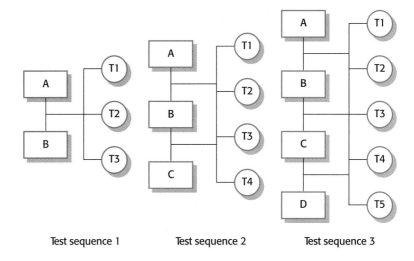

Test sequence 1   Test sequence 2   Test sequence 3

configuration and test this system. You then add components to this minimal configuration and test after each added increment.

In the example shown in Figure 23.3, A, B, C and D are components and T1 to T5 are related sets of tests of the features incorporated in the system. T1, T2 and T3 are first run on a system composed of component A and component B (the minimal system). If these reveal defects, they are corrected. Component C is integrated and T1, T2 and T3 are repeated to ensure that there have not been unexpected interactions with A and B. If problems arise in these tests, this probably means that they are due to interactions with the new component. The source of the problem is localised, thus simplifying defect location and repair. Test set T4 is also run on the system. Finally, component D is integrated and tested using existing and new tests (T5).

When planning integration, you have to decide the order of integration of components. In a process such as XP, the customer is involved in the development process and decides which functionality should be included in each system increment. Therefore, system integration is driven by customer priorities. In other approaches to development when off-the-shelf components and specially developed components are integrated, the customer may not be involved and the integration team decides on the integration priorities.

In such cases, a good rule of thumb is to integrate the components that implement the most frequently used functionality first. This means that the components that are most used receive the most testing. For example, in the library system, LIB-SYS, you should start by integrating the search facility so that, in a minimal system, users can search for documents that they need. You should then add the functionality to allow users to download a document, then progressively add the components that implement other system features.

Of course, reality is rarely as simple as this model suggests. The implementation of system features may be spread across a number of components. To test a new feature, you may have to integrate several different components. The testing may reveal errors in the interactions between these individual components and other parts of the system. Repairing errors may be difficult because a group of components that implement the system feature may have to be changed. Furthermore, integrating and testing a new component can change the pattern of already tested component interactions. Errors may be revealed that were not exposed in the tests of the simpler configuration.

These problems mean that when a new increment is integrated, it is important to rerun the tests for previous increments as well as the new tests that are required to verify the new system functionality. Rerunning an existing set of tests is called *regression testing*. If regression testing exposes problems, then you have to check whether these are problems in the previous increment that the new increment has exposed or whether these are due to the added increment of functionality.

Regression testing is clearly an expensive process and is impractical without some automated support. In extreme programming, as discussed in Chapter 17, all tests are written as executable code where the test input and the expected outputs are specified and automatically checked. When used with an automated testing framework such as JUnit (Massol and Husted, 2003), this means that tests can be automatically rerun. It is a basic principle of extreme programming that the complete test set is executed whenever new code is integrated and that this new code is not accepted until all tests run successfully.

23.1.2 Release testing

Release testing is the process of testing a release of the system that will be distributed to customers. The primary goal of this process is to increase the supplier's confidence that the system meets its requirements. If so, it can be released as a product or delivered to the customer. To demonstrate that the system meets its requirements, you have to show that it delivers the specified functionality, performance and dependability, and that it does not fail during normal use.

Release testing is usually a black-box testing process where the tests are derived from the system specification. The system is treated as a black box whose behaviour can only be determined by studying its inputs and the related outputs. Another name for this is *functional testing* because the tester is only concerned with the functionality and not the implementation of the software.

Figure 23.4 illustrates the model of a system that is assumed in black-box testing. The tester presents inputs to the component or the system and examines the corresponding outputs. If the outputs are not those predicted (i.e., if the outputs are in set O_e) then the test has detected a problem with the software.

When testing system releases, you should try to 'break' the software by choosing test cases that are in the set I_e in Figure 23.4. That is, your aim should be to select inputs that have a high probability of generating system failures (outputs in set O_e). You use previous experience of what are likely to be successful defect tests and testing guidelines to help you make your choice.

Figure 23.4 Black-
box testing

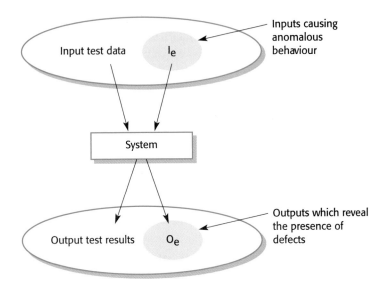

Authors such as Whittaker (Whittaker, 2002) have encapsulated their testing experience in a set of guidelines that increase the probability that the defect tests will be successful. Some examples of these guidelines are:

1. Choose inputs that force the system to generate all error messages.

2. Design inputs that cause input buffers to overflow.

3. Repeat the same input or series of inputs numerous times.

4. Force invalid outputs to be generated.

5. Force computation results to be too large or too small.

To validate that the system meets its requirements, the best approach to use is scenario-based testing, where you devise a number of scenarios and develop test cases from these scenarios. For example, the following scenario might describe how the library system LIBSYS, discussed in previous chapters, might be used:

A student in Scotland studying American history has been asked to write a paper on 'Frontier mentality in the American West from 1840 to 1880'. To do this, she needs to find sources from a range of libraries. She logs on to the LIBSYS system and uses the search facility to discover whether she can access original documents from that time. She discovers sources in various US university libraries and downloads copies of some of these. However, for one document, she needs to have confirmation from her university that she is a genuine student and that use is for non-commercial purposes. The student then uses the facility in LIBSYS that can request such permission and registers her request. If granted, the document will be downloaded to the registered library's server and printed for her. She receives a message from LIBSYS telling her that she will receive an e-mail message when the printed document is available for collection.

From this scenario, it is possible to device a number of tests that can be applied to the proposed release of LIBSYS:

1. Test the login mechanism using correct and incorrect logins to check that valid users are accepted and invalid users are rejected.

2. Test the search facility using queries against known sources to check that the search mechanism is actually finding documents.

3. Test the system presentation facility to check that information about documents is displayed properly.

4. Test the mechanism to request permission for downloading.

5. Test the e-mail response indicating that the downloaded document is available.

For each of these tests, you should design a set of tests that include valid and invalid inputs and that generate valid and invalid outputs. You should also organise scenario-based testing so that the most likely scenarios are tested first, and unusual or exceptional scenarios considered later, so your efforts are devoted to those parts of the system that receive the most use.

If you have used use-cases to describe the system requirements, these use-cases and associated sequence diagrams can be a basis for system testing. The use-cases and sequence charts can be used during both integration and release testing. To illustrate this, I use an example from the weather station system described in Chapter 14.

Figure 23.5 shows the sequence of operations in the weather station when it responds to a request to collect data for the mapping system. You can use this diagram to identify operations that will be tested and to help design the test cases to execute the tests. Therefore issuing a request for a report will result in the execution of the following thread of methods:

CommsController:request → **WeatherStation:report** → **WeatherData:summarise**

The sequence diagram can also be used to identify inputs and outputs that have to be created for the test:

1. An input of a request for a report should have an associated acknowledgement and a report should ultimately be returned from the request. During the testing, you should create summarised data that can be used to check that the report is correctly organised.

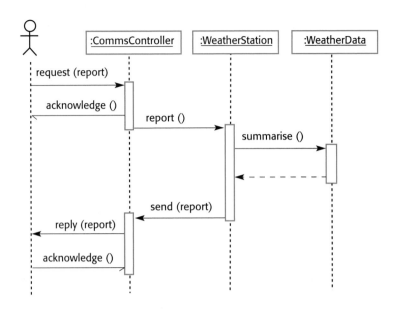

Figure 23.5 Collect
weather data
sequence chart

2. An input request for a report to **WeatherStation** results in a summarised report being generated. You can test this in isolation by creating raw data corresponding to the summary that you have prepared for the test of **CommsController** and checking that the **WeatherStation** object correctly produces this summary.

3. This raw data is also used to test the **WeatherData** object.

Of course, I have simplified the sequence diagram in Figure 23.5 so that it does not show exceptions. A complete scenario test must also take these into account and ensure that objects correctly handle exceptions.

23.1.3 Performance testing

Once a system has been completely integrated, it is possible to test the system for emergent properties (see Chapter 2) such as performance and reliability. Performance tests have to be designed to ensure that the system can process its intended load. This usually involves planning a series of tests where the load is steadily increased until the system performance becomes unacceptable.

As with other types of testing, performance testing is concerned both with demonstrating that the system meets its requirements and discovering problems and defects in the system. To test whether performance requirements are being achieved, you may have to construct an operational profile. An operational profile is a set of tests that reflect the actual mix of work that will be handled by the system. Therefore, if 90% of the transactions in a system are of type A, 5% of type B and the remainder of types C, D, and E, then you have to design the operational profile so that the vast majority of tests are of type A. Otherwise, you will not get an accurate test of the operational performance of the system. I discuss operational profiles and their use in reliability testing in Chapter 24.

This approach, of course, is not necessarily the best approach for defect testing. As I discuss later, experience has shown that an effective way to discover defects is to design tests around the limits of the system. In performance testing, this means stressing the system (hence the name *stress testing*) by making demands that are outside the design limits of the software.

For example, a transaction processing system may be designed to process up to 300 transactions per second; an operating system may be designed to handle up to 1,000 separate terminals. Stress testing continues these tests beyond the maximum design load of the system until the system fails. This type of testing has two functions:

1. It tests the failure behaviour of the system. Circumstances may arise through an unexpected combination of events where the load placed on the system exceeds the maximum anticipated load. In these circumstances, it is important that system failure should not cause data corruption or unexpected loss of user services. Stress testing checks that overloading the system causes it to 'fail-soft' rather than collapse under its load.

2. It stresses the system and may cause defects to come to light that would not normally be discovered. Although it can be argued that these defects are unlikely to cause system failures in normal usage, there may be unusual combinations of normal circumstances that the stress testing replicates.

Stress testing is particularly relevant to distributed systems based on a network of processors. These systems often exhibit severe degradation when they are heavily loaded. The network becomes swamped with coordination data that the different processes must exchange, so the processes become slower and slower as they wait for the required data from other processes.

23.2 Component testing

Component testing (sometimes called *unit testing*) is the process of testing individual components in the system. This is a defect testing process so its goal is to expose faults in these components. As I discussed in the introduction, for most systems, the developers of components are responsible for component testing.

There are different types of component that may be tested at this stage:

1. Individual functions or methods within an object

2. Object classes that have several attributes and methods

Figure 23.6 The
weather station
object interface

WeatherStation
identifier
reportWeather ()   calibrate (instruments)   test ()   startup (instruments)   shutdown (instruments)

3. Composite components made up of several different objects or functions. These composite components have a defined interface that is used to access their functionality.

Individual functions or methods are the simplest type of component and your tests are a set of calls to these routines with different input parameters. You can use the approaches to test case design, discussed in the next section, to design the function or method tests.

When you are testing object classes, you should design your tests to provide coverage of all of the features of the object. Therefore, object class testing should include:

1. The testing in isolation of all operations associated with the object

2. The setting and interrogation of all attributes associated with the object

3. The exercise of the object in all possible states. This means that all events that cause a state change in the object should be simulated.

Consider, for example, the weather station from Chapter 14 whose interface is shown in Figure 23.6. It has only a single attribute, which is its identifier. This is a constant that is set when the weather station is installed. You therefore only need a test that checks whether it has been set up. You need to define test cases for **reportWeather, calibrate, test, startup** and **shutdown**. Ideally, you should test methods in isolation but, in some cases, some test sequences are necessary. For example, to test **shutdown** you need to have executed the **startup** method.

To test the states of the weather station, you use a state model as shown in Figure 14.14. Using this model, you can identify sequences of state transitions that have to be tested and define event sequences to force these transitions. In principle, you should test every possible state transition sequence, although in practice this may be too expensive. Examples of state sequences that should be tested in the weather station include:

Shutdown → Waiting → Shutdown
Waiting → Calibrating → Testing → Transmitting → Waiting
Waiting → Collecting → Waiting → Summarising → Transmitting → Waiting

Figure 23.7 Interface
testing

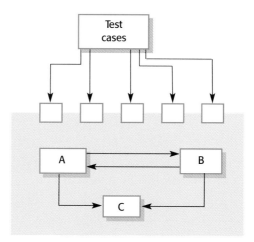

If you use inheritance, this makes it more difficult to design object class tests. Where a superclass provides operations that are inherited by a number of subclasses, all of these subclasses should be tested with all inherited operations. The reason for this is that the inherited operation may make assumptions about other operations and attributes, which these may have been changed when inherited. Equally, when a superclass operation is overridden then the overwriting operation must be tested.

The notion of equivalence classes, discussed in Section 23.3.2, may also be applied to object classes. Tests that fall into the same equivalence class might be those that use the same attributes of the objects. Therefore, equivalence classes should be identified that initialise, access and update all object class attributes.

23.1.1 Interface testing

Many components in a system are not simple functions or objects but are composite components that are made up of several interacting objects. As I discussed in Chapter 19, which covered component-based software engineering, you access the functionality of these components through their defined interface. Testing these composite components then is primarily concerned with testing that the component interface behaves according to its specification.

Figure 23.7 illustrates this process of interface testing. Assume that components A, B and C have been integrated to create a larger component or sub-system. The test cases are not applied to the individual components but to the interface of the composite component created by combining these components.

Interface testing is particularly important for object-oriented and component-based development. Objects and components are defined by their interfaces and may be reused in combination with other components in different systems. Interface errors in the composite component cannot be detected by testing the individual objects or components. Errors in the composite component may arise because of interactions between its parts.

There are different types of interfaces between program components and, consequently, different types of interface errors that can occur:

1. *Parameter interfaces* These are interfaces where data or sometimes function references are passed from one component to another.

2. *Shared memory interfaces* These are interfaces where a block of memory is shared between components. Data is placed in the memory by one sub-system and retrieved from there by other sub-systems.

3. *Procedural interfaces* These are interfaces where one component encapsulates a set of procedures that can be called by other components. Objects and reusable components have this form of interface.

4. *Message passing interfaces* These are interfaces where one component requests a service from another component by passing a message to it. A return message includes the results of executing the service. Some object-oriented systems have this form of interface, as do client-server systems.

Interface errors are one of the most common forms of error in complex systems (Lutz, 1993). These errors fall into three classes:

1. *Interface misuse* A calling component calls some other component and makes an error in the use of its interface. This type of error is particularly common with parameter interfaces where parameters may be of the wrong type, may be passed in the wrong order or the wrong number of parameters may be passed.

2. *Interface misunderstanding* A calling component misunderstands the specification of the interface of the called component and makes assumptions about the behaviour of the called component. The called component does not behave as expected and this causes unexpected behaviour in the calling component. For example, a binary search routine may be called with an unordered array to be searched. The search would then fail.

3. *Timing errors* These occur in real-time systems that use a shared memory or a message-passing interface. The producer of data and the consumer of data may operate at different speeds. Unless particular care is taken in the interface design, the consumer can access out-of-date information because the producer of the information has not updated the shared interface information.

Testing for interface defects is difficult because some interface faults may only manifest themselves under unusual conditions. For example, say an object implements a queue as a fixed-length data structure. A calling object may assume that the queue is implemented as an infinite data structure and may not check for queue overflow when an item is entered. This condition can only be detected during testing by designing test cases that force the queue to overflow and cause that overflow to corrupt the object behaviour in some detectable way.

A further problem may arise because of interactions between faults in different modules or objects. Faults in one object may only be detected when some other object behaves in an unexpected way. For example, an object may call some other object to receive some service and may assume that the response is correct. If there has been a misunderstanding about the value computed, the returned value may be valid but incorrect. This will only manifest itself when some later computation goes wrong.

Some general guidelines for interface testing are:

1. Examine the code to be tested and explicitly list each call to an external component. Design a set of tests where the values of the parameters to the external components are at the extreme ends of their ranges. These extreme values are most likely to reveal interface inconsistencies.

2. Where pointers are passed across an interface, always test the interface with null pointer parameters.

3. Where a component is called through a procedural interface, design tests that should cause the component to fail. Differing failure assumptions are one of the most common specification misunderstandings.

4. Use stress testing, as discussed in the previous section, in message-passing systems. Design tests that generate many more messages than are likely to occur in practice. Timing problems may be revealed in this way.

5. Where several components interact through shared memory, design tests that vary the order in which these components are activated. These tests may reveal implicit assumptions made by the programmer about the order in which the shared data is produced and consumed.

Static validation techniques are often more cost-effective than testing for discovering interface errors. A strongly typed language such as Java allows many interface errors to be trapped by the compiler. Where a weaker language, such as C, is used, a static analyser such as LINT (see Chapter 22) can detect interface errors. Program inspections can concentrate on component interfaces and questions about the assumed interface behaviour asked during the inspection process.

23.3 Test case design

Test case design is a part of system and component testing where you design the test cases (inputs and predicted outputs) that test the system. The goal of the test case design process is to create a set of test cases that are effective in discovering program defects and showing that the system meets its requirements.

To design a test case, you select a feature of the system or component that you are testing. You then select a set of inputs that execute that feature, document the expected outputs or output ranges and, where possible, design an automated check that tests that the actual and expected outputs are the same.

There are various approaches that you can take to test case design:

1. *Requirements-based testing* where test cases are designed to test the system requirements. This is mostly used at the system-testing stage as system requirements are usually implemented by several components. For each requirement, you identify test cases that can demonstrate that the system meets that requirement.

2. *Partition testing* where you identify input and output partitions and design tests so that the system executes inputs from all partitions and generates outputs in all partitions. Partitions are groups of data that have common characteristics such as all negative numbers, all names less than 30 characters, all events arising from choosing items on a menu, and so on.

3. *Structural testing* where you use knowledge of the program's structure to design tests that exercise all parts of the program. Essentially, when testing a program, you should try to execute each statement at least once. Structural testing helps identify test cases that can make this possible.

In general, when designing test cases, you should start with the highest-level tests from the requirements then progressively add more detailed tests using partition and structural testing.

23.3.1 Requirements-based testing

A general principle of requirements engineering, discussed in Chapter 6, is that requirements should be testable. That is, the requirement should be written in such a way that a test can be designed so that an observer can check that the requirement has been satisfied. Requirements-based testing, therefore, is a systematic approach to test case design where you consider each requirement and derive a set of tests for it. Requirements-based testing is validation rather than defect testing—you are trying to demonstrate that the system has properly implemented its requirements.

For example, consider the requirements for the LIBSYS system introduced in Chapter 6.

1. The user shall be able to search either all of the initial set of databases or select a subset from it.

2. The system shall provide appropriate viewers for the user to read documents in the document store.

3. Every order shall be allocated a unique identifier (ORDER_ID) that the user shall be able to copy to the account's permanent storage area.

Possible tests for the first of these requirements, assuming that a search function has been tested, are:

*   Initiate user searches for items that are known to be present and known not to be present, where the set of databases includes one database.

*   Initiate user searches for items that are known to be present and known not to be present, where the set of databases includes two databases.

*   Initiate user searches for items that are known to be present and known not to be present where the set of databases includes more than two databases.

*   Select one database from the set of databases and initiate user searches for items that are known to be present and known not to be present.

*   Select more than one database from the set of databases and initiate searches for items that are known to be present and known not to be present.

You can see from this that testing a requirement does not mean just writing a single test. You normally have to write several tests to ensure that you have coverage of the requirement.

Tests for the other requirements in the LIBSYS system can be developed in the same way. For the second requirement, you would write tests that delivered documents of all types that could be processed by the system and check that these are properly displayed. The third requirement is simpler. To test this, you simulate placing several orders and then check that the order identifier is present in the user confirmation and is unique in each case.

23.3.2 Partition testing

The input data and output results of a program usually fall into a number of different classes that have common characteristics such as positive numbers, negative numbers and menu selections. Programs normally behave in a comparable way for all members of a class. That is, if you test a program that does some computation and requires two positive numbers, then you would expect the program to behave in the same way for all positive numbers.

Because of this equivalent behaviour, these classes are sometimes called *equivalence partitions* or *domains* (Bezier, 1990). One systematic approach to test case design is based on identifying all partitions for a system or component. Test cases are designed so that the inputs or outputs lie within these partitions. Partition testing can be used to design test cases for both systems and components.

In Figure 23.8, each equivalence partition is shown as an ellipse. Input equivalence partitions are sets of data where all of the set members should be processed

Figure 23.8
Equivalence
partitioning

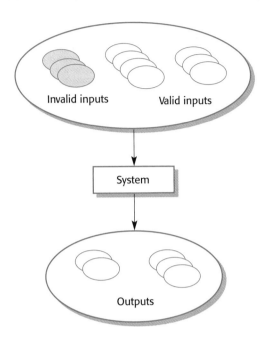

Figure 23.8
Equivalence
partitioning

in an equivalent way. Output equivalence partitions are program outputs that have common characteristics, so they can be considered as a distinct class. You also identify partitions where the inputs are outside the other partitions that you have chosen. These test whether the program handles invalid input correctly. Valid and invalid inputs also form equivalence partitions.

Once you have identified a set of partitions, you can chose test cases from each of these partitions. A good rule of thumb for test case selection is to choose test cases on the boundaries of the partitions plus cases close to the mid-point of the partition. The rationale for this is that designers and programmers tend to consider typical values of inputs when developing a system. You test these by choosing the mid-point of the partition. Boundary values are often atypical (e.g., zero may behave differently from other nonnegative numbers) so are overlooked by developers. Program failures often occur when processing these atypical values.

You identify partitions by using the program specification or user documentation and, from experience, where you predict the classes of input value that are likely to detect errors. For example, say a program specification states that the program accepts 4 to 8 inputs that are five-digit integers greater than 10,000. Figure 23.9 shows the partitions for this situation and possible test input values.

To illustrate the derivation of test cases, I use the specification of a search component, shown in Figure 23.10. This component searches a sequence of elements for a given element (the key). It returns the position of that element in the sequence. I have specified this in an abstract way by defining pre-conditions, which are true before the component is called, and post-conditions, which are true after execution.

Figure 23.9
Equivalence
partitions

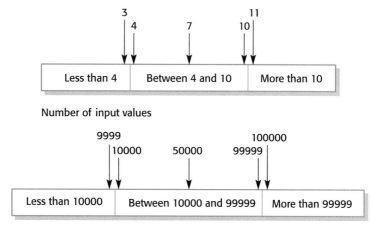

The pre-condition states that the search routine will only work with sequences that are not empty. The post-condition states that the variable **Found** is set if the key element is in the sequence. The position of the key element is the index L. The index value is undefined if the element is not in the sequence.

From this specification, you can see two equivalence partitions:

1. Inputs where the key element is a member of the sequence **(Found = true)**

2. Inputs where the key element is not a sequence member **(Found = false)**

When you are testing programs with sequences, arrays or lists, there are a number of guidelines that are often useful in designing test cases:

Figure 23.10 The
specification of a
search routine

```
procedure Search (Key : ELEM ; T: SEQ of ELEM ;
Found : in out BOOLEAN; L: in out ELEM_INDEX) ;


Pre-condition
    – the sequence has at least one element
    T'FIRST <= T'LAST
Post-condition
    – the element is found and is referenced by L
    ( Found and T (L) = Key)
or
    – the element is not in the sequence
    ( not Found and
    not (exists i, T'FIRST >= i <= T'LAST, T (i) = Key ))
```

Figure 23.11
Equivalence
partitions for search
routine

Sequence	Element
Single value	In sequence
Single value	Not in sequence
More than 1 value	First element in sequence
More than 1 value	Last element in sequence
More than 1 value	Middle element in sequence
More than 1 value	Not in sequence

Input sequence (T)	Key (Key)	Output (Found, L)
17	17	true, 1
17	0	false, ??
17, 29, 21, 23	17	true, 1
41, 18, 9, 31, 30, 16, 45	45	true, 7
17, 18, 21, 23, 29, 41, 38	23	true, 4
21, 23, 29, 33, 38	25	false, ??

1. Test software with sequences that have only a single value. Programmers naturally think of sequences as made up of several values, and sometimes they embed this assumption in their programs. Consequently, the program may not work properly when presented with a single-value sequence.

2. Use different sequences of different sizes in different tests. This decreases the chances that a program with defects will accidentally produce a correct output because of some accidental characteristics of the input.

3. Derive tests so that the first, middle and last elements of the sequence are accessed. This approach reveals problems at partition boundaries.

From these guidelines, two more equivalence partitions can be identified:

1. The input sequence has a single value.

2. The number of elements in the input sequence is greater than 1.

You then identify further partitions by combining these partitions—for example, the partition where the number of elements in the sequence is greater than 1 and the element is not in the sequence. Figure 23.11 shows the partitions that I have identified to test the search component.

A set of possible test cases based on these partitions is also shown in Figure 23.11. If the key element is not in the sequence, the value of L is undefined ('??'). The guideline that different sequences of different sizes should be used has been applied in these test cases.

The set of input values used to test the search routine is not exhaustive. The routine may fail if the input sequence happens to include the elements 1, 2, 3 and 4.

Figure 23.12
Structural testing

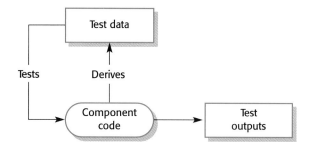

However, it is reasonable to assume that if the test fails to detect defects when one member of a class is processed, no other members of that class will identify defects. Of course, defects may still exist. Some equivalence partitions may not have been identified, errors may have been made in equivalence partition identification or the test data may have been incorrectly prepared.

23.3.3 Structural testing

Structural testing (Figure 23.12) is an approach to test case design where the tests are derived from knowledge of the software's structure and implementation. This approach is sometimes called 'white-box', 'glass-box' testing, or ''clear-box' testing to distinguish it from black-box testing.

   Understanding the algorithm used in a component can help you identify further partitions and test cases. To illustrate this, I have implemented the search routine specification (Figure 23.10) as a binary search routine (Figure 23.14). Of course, this has stricter pre-conditions. The sequence is implemented as an array that array must be ordered and the value of the lower bound of the array must be less than the value of the upper bound.

   By examining the code of the search routine, you can see that binary searching involves splitting the search space into three parts. Each of these parts makes up an equivalence partition (Figure 23.13). You then design test cases where the key lies at the boundaries of each of these partitions.

Figure 23.13 Binary search equivalence classes

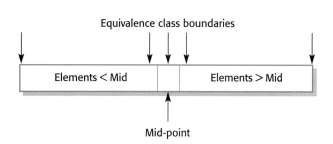

Figure 23.14 Java
implementation of a
binary search routine

```
class BinSearch {

// This is an encapsulation of a binary search function that takes an array of
// ordered objects and a key and returns an object with 2 attributes namely
// index - the value of the array index
// found - a boolean indicating whether or not the key is in the array
// An object is returned because it is not possible in Java to pass basic types by
// reference to a function and so return two values
// the key is -1 if the element is not found

       public static void search ( int key, int [] elemArray, Result r )
       {
1.         int bottom = 0 ;
2.         int top = elemArray.length - 1 ;
           int mid ;
3.         r.found = false ;
4.         r.index = -1 ;
5.         while ( bottom <= top )
           {
6.             mid = (top + bottom) / 2 ;
7.             if (elemArray [mid] == key)
               {
8.                 r.index = mid ;
9.                 r.found = true ;
10.                return ;
               } // if part
               else
               {
11.                if (elemArray [mid] < key)
12.                    bottom = mid + 1 ;
                   else
13.                    top = mid - 1 ;
               }
           } //while loop
14.    } // search
} //BinSearch
```

This leads to a revised set of test cases for the search routine, as shown in Figure
23.15. Notice that I have modified the input array so that it is arranged in ascend-
ing order and have added further tests where the key element is adjacent to the mid-
point of the array.

Figure 23.15 Test
cases for search
routine

Input array (T)	Key (Key)	Output (Found, L)
17	17	true, 1
17	0	false, ??
17, 21, 23, 29	17	true, 1
9, 16, 18, 30, 31, 41, 45	45	true, 7
17, 18, 21, 23, 29, 38, 41	23	true, 4
17, 18, 21, 23, 29, 33, 38	21	true, 3
12, 18, 21, 23, 32	23	true, 4
21, 23, 29, 33, 38	25	false, ??

23.3.4 Path testing

Path testing is a structural testing strategy whose objective is to exercise every independent execution path through a component or program. If every independent path is executed, then all statements in the component must have been executed at least once. Furthermore, all conditional statements are tested for both true and false cases. In an object-oriented development process, path testing may be used when testing methods associated with objects.

The number of paths through a program is usually proportional to its size. As modules are integrated into systems, it becomes unfeasible to use structural testing techniques. Path testing techniques are therefore mostly used during component testing.

Path testing does not test all possible combinations of all paths through the program. For any components apart from very trivial ones without loops, this is an impossible objective. There are an infinite number of possible path combinations in programs with loops. Even when all program statements have been executed at least once, program defects may still show up when particular paths are combined.

The starting point for path testing is a program flow graph. This is a skeletal model of all paths through the program. A flow graph consists of nodes representing decisions and edges showing flow of control. The flow graph is constructed by replacing program control statements by equivalent diagrams. If there are no goto statements in a program, it is a simple process to derive its flow graph. Each branch in a conditional statement (if-then-else or case) is shown as a separate path. An arrow looping back to the condition node denotes a loop. I have drawn the flow graph for the binary search method in Figure 23.16. To make the correspondence between this and the program in Figure 23.14 more obvious, I have shown each statement as a separate node where the node number corresponds to the line number in the program.

The objective of path testing is to ensure that each independent path through the program is executed at least once. An independent program path is one that traverses at least one new edge in the flow graph. In program terms, this means exercising one or more new conditions. Both the true and false branches of all conditions must be executed.

Figure 23.16 Flow
graph for a binary
search routine

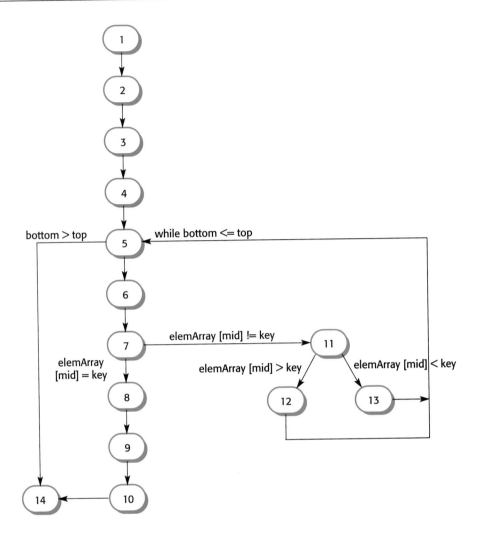

The flow graph for the binary search procedure is shown in Figure 23.16 where
each node represents a line in the program with an executable statement. By tracing the flow, therefore, you can see that the paths through the binary search flow
graph are:

1, 2, 3, 4, 5, 6, 7, 8, 9, 10, 14
1, 2, 3, 4, 5, 14
1, 2, 3, 4, 5, 6, 7, 11, 12, 5, ...
1, 2, 3, 4, 6, 7, 2, 11, 13, 5, ...

If all of these paths are executed, we can be sure that every statement in the
method has been executed at least once and that every branch has been exercised
for true and false conditions.

You can find the number of independent paths in a program by computing the *cyclomatic complexity* (McCabe, 1976) of the program flow graph. For programs without goto statements, the value of the cyclomatic complexity is one more than the number of conditions in the program. A simple condition is logical expression without 'and' or 'or' connectors. If the program includes compound conditions, which are logical expressions including 'and' or 'or' connectors, then you count the number of simple conditions in the compound conditions when calculating the cyclomatic complexity.

Therefore, if there are six if-statements and a while loop and all conditional expressions are simple, the cyclomatic complexity is 8. If one conditional expression is a compound expression such as 'if A and B or C', then you count this as three simple conditions. The cyclomatic complexity is therefore 10. The cyclomatic complexity of the binary search algorithm (Figure 23.14) is 4 because there are three simple conditions at lines 5, 7 and 11.

After discovering the number of independent paths through the code by computing the cyclomatic complexity, you next design test cases to execute each of these paths. The minimum number of test cases that you need to test all program paths is equal to the cyclomatic complexity.

Test case design is straightforward in the case of the binary search routine. However, when programs have a complex branching structure, it may be difficult to predict how any particular test case will be processed. In these cases, a dynamic program analyser can be used to discover the program's execution profile.

Dynamic program analysers are testing tools that work in conjunction with compilers. During compilation, these analysers add extra instructions to the generated code. These count the number of times each program statement has been executed. After the program has been run, an execution profile can be printed. This shows which parts of the program have and have not been executed using particular test cases. This execution profile therefore reveals untested program sections.

23.4 Test automation

Testing is an expensive and laborious phase of the software process. As a result, testing tools were among the first software tools to be developed. These tools now offer a range of facilities and their use can significantly reduce the costs of testing.

I have already discussed one approach to test automation (Mosley and Posey, 2002) where a testing framework such as JUnit (Massol and Husted, 2003) is used for regression testing. JUnit is a set of Java classes that the user extends to create an automated testing environment. Each individual test is implemented as an object and a test runner runs all of the tests. The tests themselves should be written in such a way that they indicate whether the tested system has behaved as expected.

Figure 23.17 A
testing workbench

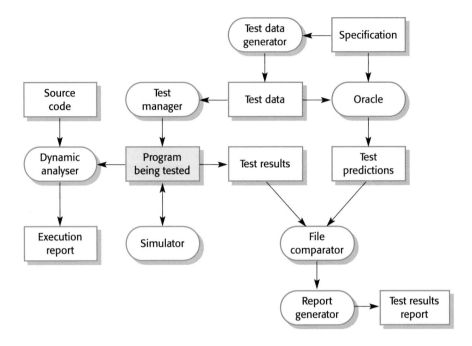

A software testing workbench is an integrated set of tools to support the testing process. In addition to testing frameworks that support automated test execution, a workbench may include tools to simulate other parts of the system and to generate system test data. Figure 23.17 shows some of the tools that might be included in such a testing workbench:

1. *Test manager* Manages the running of program tests. The test manager keeps track of test data, expected results and program facilities tested. Test automation frameworks such as JUnit are examples of test managers.

2. *Test data generator* Generates test data for the program to be tested. This may be accomplished by selecting data from a database or by using patterns to generate random data of the correct form.

3. *Oracle* Generates predictions of expected test results. Oracles may either be previous program versions or prototype systems. Back-to-back testing (discussed in Chapter 17) involves running the oracle and the program to be tested in parallel. Differences in their outputs are highlighted.

4. *File comparator* Compares the results of program tests with previous test results and reports differences between them. Comparators are used in regression testing where the results of executing different versions are compared. Where automated tests are used, this may be called from within the tests themselves.

5. *Report generator* Provides report definition and generation facilities for test results.

6. *Dynamic analyser* Adds code to a program to count the number of times each statement has been executed. After testing, an execution profile is generated showing how often each program statement has been executed.

7. *Simulator* Different kinds of simulators may be provided. Target simulators simulate the machine on which the program is to execute. User interface simulators are script-driven programs that simulate multiple simultaneous user interactions. Using simulators for I/O means that the timing of transaction sequences is repeatable.

When used for large system testing, tools have to be configured and adapted for the specific system that is being tested. For example:

KEY POINTS

■ Testing can only show the presence of errors in a program. It cannot demonstrate that there are no remaining faults.

■ Component testing is the responsibility of the component developer. A separate testing team usually carries out system testing.

■ Integration testing is the initial system testing activity where you test integrated components for defects. Release testing is concerned with testing customer releases and should validate that the system to be released meets its requirements.

■ When testing systems, you should try to 'break' the system by using experience and guidelines to choose types of test cases that have been effective in discovering defects in other systems.

■ Interface testing is intended to discover defects in the interfaces of composite components. Interface defects may arise because of errors made in reading the specification, specification misunderstandings or errors or invalid timing assumptions.

■ Equivalence partitioning is a way of deriving test cases. It depends on finding partitions in the input and output data sets and exercising the program with values from these partitions. Often, the value that is most likely to lead to a successful test is a value at the boundary of a partition.

■ Structural testing relies on analysing a program to determine paths through it and using this analysis to assist with the selection of test cases.

■ Test automation reduces the costs of testing by supporting the testing process with a range of software tools.

1. New tools may have to be added to test specific application characteristics, and some existing testing tools may not be required.

2. Scripts may have to be written for user interface simulators and patterns defined for test data generators. Report formats may also have to be defined.

3. Sets of expected test results may have to be prepared manually if no previous program versions are available to serve as an oracle.

4. Special-purpose file comparators may have to be written that include knowledge of the structure of the test results on file.

A significant amount of effort and time is usually needed to create a comprehensive testing workbench. Complete test workbenches, as shown in Figure 23.17, are therefore only used when large systems are being developed. For these systems, the overall testing costs may be up to 50% of the total development costs, so it is cost-effective to invest on high-quality CASE tool support for testing. However, because different types of systems require different types of testing support, off-the-shelf testing tools may not be available. Rankin (Rankin, 2002) discusses such a situation in IBM and describes the design of the testing support system that they developed for an e-business server.

FURTHER READING

How to Break Software: A Practical Guide to Testing. This is a practical rather than theoretical book on software testing where the author presents a set of experience-based guidelines on designing tests that are likely to be effective in discovering system faults. (J. A. Whittaker, 2002, Addison-Wesley.)

'Software Testing and Verification'. This special issue of the *IBM Systems Journal* includes a number of papers on testing, including a good overview, papers on test metrics and test automation. (*IBM Systems Journal*, 41(1), January 2002.)

Testing Object-oriented Systems: Models, Patterns and Tools. This immense book provides complete coverage of object-oriented testing. Its length means that this shouldn't be the first thing that you read on object-oriented testing (most books on object-oriented development have a testing chapter) but it is clearly the definitive book on object-oriented testing. (R. V. Binder, 1999, Addison-Wesley.)

'How to design practical test cases'. A how-to article on test case design by an author from a Japanese company that has a very good reputation for delivering software with very few faults. (T. Yamaura, *IEEE Software,* 15(6), November 1998.)

EXERCISES

23.1   Explain why testing can only detect the presence of errors, not their absence.

23.2   Compare top-down and bottom-up integration and testing by discussing their advantages and disadvantages for architectural testing, demonstrating a version of the system to users and for the practical implementation and observation of tests. Explain why most large system integration, in practice, has to use a mixture of top-down and bottom-up approaches.

23.3   What is regression testing? Explain how the use of automated tests and a testing framework such as JUnit simplifies regression testing.

23.4   Write a scenario that could be used as the basis for deriving tests for the weather station system that was used as an example in Chapter 14.

23.5   Using the sequence diagram in Figure 8.14 as a scenario, propose tests for the issue of electronic items in the LIBSYS system.

23.6   What are the problems in developing performance tests for a distributed database system such as the LIBSYS system?

23.7   Explain why interface testing is necessary even when individual components have been extensively validated through component testing and program inspections.

23.8   Using the approach discussed here for object testing, design test cases to test the states of the microwave oven whose state model is defined in Figure 8.5.

23.9   You have been asked to test a method called catWhiteSpace in a Paragraph object that, within the paragraph, replaces sequences of blank characters with a single blank character. Identify testing partitions for this example and derive a set of tests for the catWhiteSpace method.

23.10 Give three situations where the testing of all independent paths through a program may not detect program errors.

24

Critical systems validation

Objectives

The objective of this chapter is to discuss verification and validation techniques that are used in the development of critical systems. When you have read this chapter, you will:

■ understand how the reliability of a software system can be measured and how reliability growth models can be used to predict when a required level of reliability will be achieved;

■ understand the principles of safety arguments and how these may be used along with other V & V methods in system safety assurance;

■ understand the problems of assuring the security of a system;

■ have been introduced to safety cases that present arguments and evidence of system safety.

Contents

The verification and validation of a critical system has, obviously, much in common with the validation of any other system. The V & V processes should demonstrate that the system meets its specification, and that the system services and behaviour support the customer's requirements. However, for critical systems, where a high level of dependability is required, additional testing and analysis are required to produce evidence that the system is trustworthy. There are two reasons why you should do this:

1. *Costs of failure* The costs and consequences of critical systems failure are potentially much greater than for noncritical systems. You lower the risks of system failure by spending more on system verification and validation. It is usually cheaper to find and remove faults before the system is delivered than to pay for the consequent costs of accidents or disruptions to system service.

2. *Validation of dependability attributes* You may have to make a formal case to customers that the system meets its specified dependability requirements (availability, reliability, safety and security). Assessing these dependability characteristics requires specific V & V activities discussed later in this chapter. In some cases, external regulators such as national aviation authorities may have to certify that the system is safe before it can be deployed. To obtain this certification, you may have to design and carry out special V & V procedures that collect evidence about the system's dependability.

For these reasons, the costs of V & V for critical systems are usually much higher than for other classes of system. It is normal for V & V to take up more than 50% of the total development costs for critical software systems. This cost is, of course, justified, if an expensive system failure is avoided. For example, in 1996 a mission-critical software system on the Ariane 5 rocket failed and several satellites were destroyed. The losses were in the hundreds of millions of dollars. The subsequent enquiry discovered that deficiencies in system V & V were partly responsible for this failure.

Although the critical systems validation process mostly focuses on validating the system, related activities should verify that defined system development processes have been followed. As I discuss in Chapters 27 and 28, system quality is affected by the quality of processes used to develop the system. In short, good processes lead to good systems. Therefore, to produce dependable systems, you need to be confident that a sound development process has been followed.

This process assurance is an inherent part of the ISO 9000 standards for quality management, discussed briefly in Chapter 27. These standards require documentation of the processes that are used and associated activities that ensure that these processes have been followed. This normally requires the generation of process records, such as signed forms, that certify the completion of process activities and product quality checks. ISO 9000 standards specify what tangible process outputs should be produced and who is responsible for producing them. In Section 24.2.2, I give an example of a process record for a hazard analysis process.

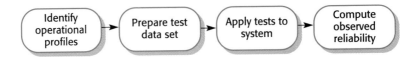

Figure 24.1 The
reliability
measurement
process

24.1 Reliability validation

As I explained in Chapter 9, a number of metrics have been developed to specify a system's reliability requirements. To validate that the system meets these requirements, you have to measure the reliability of the system as seen by a typical system user.

The process of measuring the reliability of a system is illustrated in Figure 24.1. This process involves four stages:

1. You start by studying existing systems of the same type to establish an operational profile. An operational profile identifies classes of system inputs and the probability that these inputs will occur in normal use.

2. You then construct a set of test data that reflect the operational profile. This means that you create test data with the same probability distribution as the test data for the systems that you have studied. Normally, you use a test data generator to support this process.

3. You test the system using these data and the count the number and type of failures that occur. The times of these failures are also logged. As discussed in Chapter 9, the time units that you choose should be appropriate for the reliability metric used.

4. After you have observed a statistically significant number of failures, you can compute the software reliability and work out the appropriate reliability metric value.

This approach is sometimes called *statistical testing*. The aim of statistical testing is to assess system reliability. This contrasts with defect testing, discussed in Chapter 23, where the aim is to discover system faults. Prowell et al. (Prowell, et al., 1999) give a good description of statistical testing in their book on Cleanroom software engineering.

This conceptually attractive approach to reliability measurement is not easy to apply in practice. The principal difficulties that arise are due to:

1. *Operational profile uncertainty* The operational profiles based on experience with other systems may not be an accurate reflection of the real use of the system.

2. *High costs of test data generation* It can be very expensive to generate the large volume of data required in an operational profile unless the process can be totally automated.

3. *Statistical uncertainty when high reliability is specified* You have to generate a statistically significant number of failures to allow accurate reliability measurements. When the software is already reliable, relatively few failures occur and it is difficult to generate new failures.

Developing an accurate operational profile is certainly possible for some types of systems, such as telecommunication systems, that have a standardised pattern of use. For other system types, however, there are many different users who each have their own ways of using the system. As I discussed in Chapter 3, different users can get quite different impressions of reliability because they use the system in different ways.

By far the best way to generate the large data set required for reliability measurement is to use a test data generator that can be set up to automatically generate inputs matching the operational profile. However, it is not usually possible to automate the production of all test data for interactive systems because the inputs are often a response to system outputs. Data sets for these systems have to be generated manually, with correspondingly higher costs. Even where complete automation is possible, writing commands for the test data generator may take a significant amount of time.

Statistical uncertainty is a general problem in measuring the reliability of a system. To make an accurate prediction of reliability, you need to do more than simply cause a single system failure. You have to generate a reasonably large, statistically significant number of failures to be confident that your reliability measurement is accurate. The better you get at minimising the number of faults in a system, the harder it becomes to measure the effectiveness of fault minimisation techniques. If very high levels of reliability are specified, it is often impractical to generate enough system failures to check these specifications.

24.1.1 Operational profiles

The operational profile of the software reflects how it will be used in practice. It consists of a specification of classes of input and the probability of their occurrence. When a new software system replaces an existing manual or automated system, it is reasonably easy to assess the probable pattern of usage of the new software. It should correspond to the existing usage, with some allowance made for the new functionality that is (presumably) included in the new software. For example, an operational profile can be specified for telecommunication switching systems because telecommunication companies know the call patterns that these systems have to handle.

Figure 24.2 An
operational profile

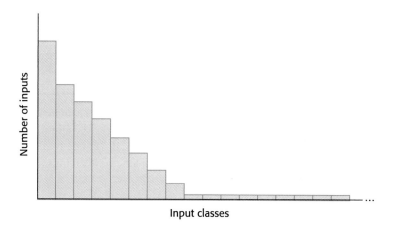

Typically, the operational profile is such that the inputs that have the highest probability of being generated fall into a small number of classes, as shown on the left of Figure 24.2. There is an extremely large number of classes where inputs are highly improbable but not impossible. These are shown on the right of Figure 24.2. The ellipsis (...) means that there are many more of these unusual inputs than are shown.

Musa (Musa, 1993; Musa, 1998) suggests guidelines for the development of operational profiles. He worked in telecommunication systems engineering, and there is a long history of collecting usage data in that domain. Consequently, the process of operational profile development is relatively straightforward. For a system that required about 15 person-years of development effort, an operational profile was developed in about 1 person-month. In other cases, operational profile generation took longer (2–3 person-years), but the cost was spread over a number of system releases. Musa reckons that his company (a telecommunications company) had at least a 10-fold return on the investment required to develop an operational profile.

However, when a software system is new and innovative, it is difficult to anticipate how it will be used and, therefore, to generate an accurate operational profile. Many different users with different expectations, backgrounds and experience may use the new system. There is no historical usage database. These users may make use of systems in ways that were not anticipated by the system developers.

The problem is further compounded because operational profiles may change as the system is used. As users learn about a new system and become more confident with it, they often use it in more sophisticated ways. Because of these difficulties, Hamlet (Hamlet, 1992) suggests that it is often impossible to develop a trustworthy operational profile. If you are not sure that your operational profile is correct, then you cannot be confident about the accuracy of your reliability measurements.

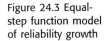

Figure 24.3 Equal-step function model of reliability growth

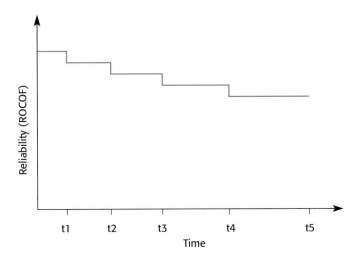

24.1.2 Reliability prediction

During software validation, managers have to assign effort to system testing. As testing is very expensive, it is important to stop testing as soon as possible and not 'over-test' the system. Testing can stop when the required level of system reliability has been achieved. Sometimes, of course, reliability predictions may reveal that the required level of reliability will never be achieved. In this case, the manager must make difficult decisions about rewriting parts of the software or renegotiating the system contract.

A reliability growth model is a model of how the system reliability changes over time during the testing process. As system failures are discovered, the underlying faults causing these failures are repaired so that the reliability of the system should improve during system testing and debugging. To predict reliability, the conceptual reliability growth model must then be translated into a mathematical model. I do not go into this level of detail here but simply discuss the principle of reliability growth.

There are various reliability growth models that have been derived from reliability experiments in a number of different application domains. As Kan (Kan, 2003) discusses, most of these models are exponential, with reliability increasing quickly as defects are discovered and removed (see Figure 24.5). The increase then tails off and reaches a plateau as fewer and fewer defects are discovered and removed in the later stages of testing.

The simplest model that illustrates the concept of reliability growth is a step function model (Jelinski and Moranda, 1972). The reliability increases by a constant increment each time a fault (or a set of faults) is discovered and repaired (Figure 24.3) and a new version of the software is created. This model assumes that soft-

Figure 24.4 Random-
step function model
of reliability growth

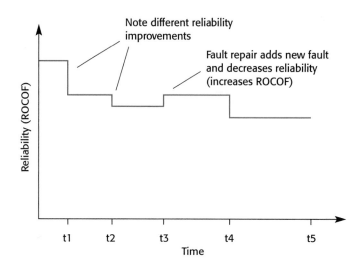

Note different reliability
improvements

Fault repair adds new fault
and decreases reliability
(increases ROCOF)

Reliability (ROCOF)

t1   t2   t3   t4   t5

Time

ware repairs are always correctly implemented so that the number of software faults
and associated failures decreases in each new version of the system. As repairs are
made, the rate of occurrence of software failures (ROCOF) should therefore
decrease, as shown in Figure 24.3. Note that the time periods on the horizontal axis
reflect the time between releases of the system for testing so they are normally of
unequal length.

In practice, however, software faults are not always fixed during debugging, and
when you change a program, you sometimes introduce new faults into it. The probability of occurrence of these faults may be higher than the occurrence probability
of the fault that has been repaired. Therefore, the system reliability may sometimes
worsen in a new release rather than improve.

The simple equal-step reliability growth model also assumes that all faults contribute equally to reliability and that each fault repair contributes the same amount
of reliability growth. However, not all faults are equally probable. Repairing the
most common faults contributes more to reliability growth than does repairing faults
that occur only occasionally. You are also likely to find these probable faults early
in the testing process, so reliability may increase more than when later, less probable, faults are discovered.

Later models, such as that suggested by Littlewood and Verrall (Littlewood and
Verrall, 1973) take these problems into account by introducing a random element
into the reliability growth improvement effected by a software repair. Thus, each
repair does not result in an equal amount of reliability improvement but varies depending on the random perturbation (Figure 24.4).

Littlewood and Verrall's model allows for negative reliability growth when a software repair introduces further errors. It also models the fact that as faults are repaired,
the average improvement in reliability per repair decreases. The reason for this is
that the most probable faults are likely to be discovered early in the testing process. Repairing these contributes most to reliability growth.

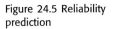

Figure 24.5 Reliability prediction

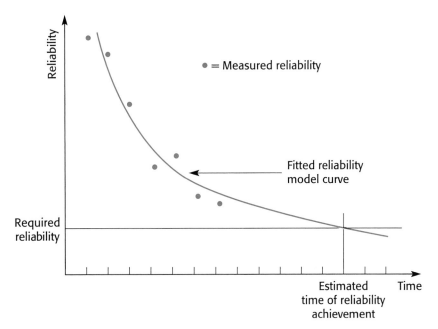

The above models are discrete models that reflect incremental reliability growth. When a new version of the software with repaired faults is delivered for testing, it should have a lower rate of failure occurrence than the previous version. However, to predict the reliability that will be achieved after a given amount of testing, continuous mathematical models are needed. Many models, derived from different application domains, have been proposed and compared (Littlewood, 1990).

Simplistically, you can predict reliability by matching the measured reliability data to a known reliability model. You then extrapolate the model to the required level of reliability and observe when the required level of reliability will be reached (Figure 24.5). Therefore, testing and debugging must continue until that time.

Predicting system reliability from a reliability growth model has two main benefits:

1. *Planning of testing* Given the current testing schedule, you can predict when testing will be completed. If this is after the planned delivery date for the system, then you may have to deploy additional resources for testing and debugging to accelerate the rate of reliability growth.

2. *Customer negotiations* Sometimes the reliability model shows that the growth of reliability is very slow and that a disproportionate amount of testing effort is required for relatively little benefit. It may be worth renegotiating the reliability requirements with the customer. Alternatively, it may be that the model predicts that the required reliability will probably never be reached. In this case, you will have to renegotiate the reliability requirements with the customer for the system.

I have simplified reliability growth modelling here to give you a basic understanding of the concept. If you wish to use these models, you have to go into much more depth and develop an understanding of the mathematics underlying these models and their practical problems. Littlewood and Musa (Littlewood, 1990; Abdel-Ghaly, et al., 1986; Musa, 1998) have written extensively on reliability growth models and Kan (Kan, 2003) has an excellent summary in his book. Various authors have described their practical experience of the use of reliability growth models (Ehrlich, et al., 1993; Schneidewind and Keller, 1992; Sheldon, et al., 1992).

24.2 Safety assurance

The processes of safety assurance and reliability validation have different objectives. You can specify reliability quantitatively using some metric and then measure the reliability of the completed system. Within the limits of the measurement process, you know whether the required level of reliability has been achieved. Safety, however, cannot be meaningfully specified in a quantitative way and so cannot be measured when a system is tested.

Safety assurance is therefore concerned with establishing a confidence level in the system that might vary from 'very low' to 'very high'. This is a matter for professional judgement based on a body of evidence about the system, its environment and its development processes. In many cases, this confidence is partly based on the experience of the organisation developing the system. If a company has previously developed a number of control systems that have operated safely, then it is reasonable to assume that they will continue to develop safe systems of this type.

However, such an assessment must be backed up by tangible evidence from the system design, the results of system V& V, and the system development processes that have been used. For some systems, this tangible evidence is assembled in a safety case (see Section 24.4) that allows an external regulator to come to a conclusion of the developer's confidence in the system's safety is justified.

The V & V processes for safety-critical systems have much in common with the comparable processes of any other systems with high reliability requirements. There must be extensive testing to discover as many defects as possible, and where appropriate, statistical testing may be used to assess the system reliability. However, because of the ultra-low failure rates required in many safety-critical systems, statistical testing cannot always provide a quantitative estimate of the system reliability. The tests simply provide some evidence, which is used with other evidence such as the results of reviews and static checking (see Chapter 22), to make a judgement about the system safety.

Extensive reviews are essential during a safety-oriented development process to expose the software to people who will look at it from different perspectives. Parnas et al. (Parnas, et al., 1990) suggest five types of review that should be mandatory for safety-critical systems:

1. review for correct intended function;

2. review for maintainable, understandable structure;

3. review to verify that the algorithm and data structure design are consistent with the specified behaviour;

4. review the consistency of the code and the algorithm and data structure design;

5. review the adequacy of the system test cases.

An assumption that underlies work in system safety is that the number of system faults that can lead to safety-critical hazards is significantly less than the total number of faults that may exist in the system. Safety assurance can concentrate on these faults with hazard potential. If it can be demonstrated that these faults cannot occur or, if they do, the associated hazard will not result in an accident, then the system is safe. This is the basis of safety arguments that I discuss in the next section.

24.2.1 Safety arguments

Proofs of program correctness, as discussed in Chapter 22, have been proposed as a software verification technique for more than 30 years. Formal program proofs can certainly be constructed for small systems. However, the practical difficulties of proving that a system meets its specifications are so great that few organisations consider correctness proofs to be a cost. Nevertheless, for some critical applications, it may be economical to develop correctness proofs to increase confidence that the system meets its safety or security requirements. This is particularly the case where safety-critical functionality can be isolated in a fairly small sub-system that can be formally specified.

Although it may not be cost-effective to develop correctness proofs for most systems, it is sometimes possible to develop simpler safety arguments that demonstrate that the program meets its safety obligations. In a safety argument, it is not necessary to prove that the program's functionality is as specified. It is only necessary to demonstrate that program execution cannot result in an unsafe state.

The most effective technique for demonstrating the safety of a system is proof by contradiction. You start by assuming that an unsafe state, which was identified by the system hazard analysis, can be reached by executing the program. You write a predicate that defines this unsafe state. You then systematically analyse the code and show that, for all program paths leading to that state, the terminating condition of these paths contradicts the unsafe state predicate. If this is the case, the initial assumption of an unsafe state is incorrect. If you then repeat this for all identified hazards, then the software is safe.

Figure 24.6 Insulin
delivery code

```
– The insulin dose to be delivered is a function of
– blood sugar level, the previous dose delivered and
– the time of delivery of the previous dose

    currentDose = computeInsulin () ;

    // Safety check—adjust currentDose if necessary

    // if-statement 1

    if (previousDose == 0)
    {
         if (currentDose > 16)
                 currentDose = 16 ;
    }
    else
         if (currentDose > (previousDose * 2) )
                 currentDose = previousDose * 2 ;

    // if-statement 2

    if ( currentDose < minimumDose )
                 currentDose = 0 ;
    else if ( currentDose > maxDose )
                 currentDose = maxDose ;
administerInsulin (currentDose) ;
```

As an example, consider the code in Figure 24.6, which might be part of the implementation of the insulin delivery system. Developing a safety argument for this code involves demonstrating that the dose of insulin administered is never greater than some maximum level that is established for each individual diabetic. Therefore, it is not necessary to prove that the system delivers the correct dose, merely that it never delivers an overdose to the patient.

To construct the safety argument, you identify the pre-condition for the unsafe state which, in this case, is that currentDose > maxDose. You then demonstrate that all program paths lead to a contradiction of this unsafe assertion. If this is the case, the unsafe condition cannot be true. Therefore, the system is safe. You can structure and present the safety arguments graphically as shown in Figure 24.7.

Safety arguments, such as that shown in Figure 24.7, are much shorter than formal system verifications. You first identify all possible paths that lead to the potentially unsafe state. You work backwards from this unsafe state and consider the last assignment to all state variables on each path leading to it. You can ignore previous

Figure 24.7 Informal safety argument based on demonstrating contradictions

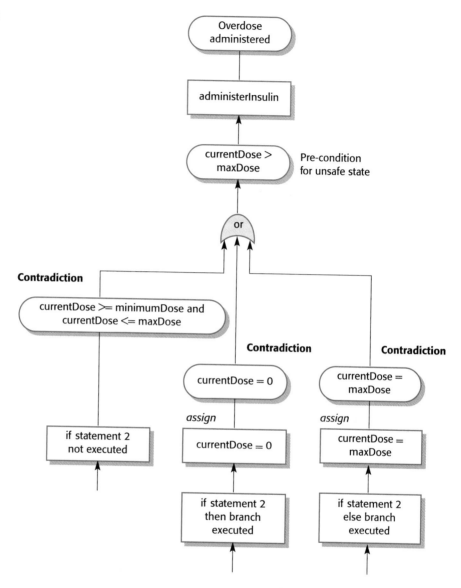

computations (such as if-statement 1 in Figure 24.7) in the safety argument. In this example, all you need be concerned with are the set of possible values of **currentDose** immediately before the **administerInsulin** method is executed.

In the safety argument shown in Figure 24.7, there are three possible program paths that lead to the call to the **administerInsulin** method. We wish to demonstrate that the amount of insulin delivered never exceeds **maxDose**. All possible program paths to **administerInsulin** are considered:

1. Neither branch of if-statement 2 is executed. This can only happen if currentDose is either greater than or equal to minimumDose and less than or equal to maxDose.

2. The then-branch of if-statement 2 is executed. In this case, the assignment setting currentDose to zero is executed. Therefore, its post-condition is currentDose = 0.

3. The else-if-branch of if-statement 2 is executed. In this case, the assignment setting currentDose to maxDose is executed. Therefore, its post-condition is currentDose = maxDose.

In all three cases, the post-conditions contradict the unsafe pre-condition that the dose administered is greater than maxDose, so the system is safe.

24.2.2 Process assurance

I have already discussed the importance of assuring the quality of the system development process in the introduction to this chapter. This is important for all critical systems but it is particularly important for safety-critical systems. There are two reasons for this:

1. Accidents are rare events in critical systems and it may be practically impossible to simulate them during the testing of a system. You can't rely on extensive testing to replicate the conditions that can lead to an accident.

2. Safety requirements, as I discussed in Chapter 9, are sometimes 'shall not' requirements that exclude unsafe system behaviour. It is impossible to demonstrate conclusively through testing and other validation activities that these requirements have been met.

The life-cycle model for safety-critical systems development (Chapter 9, Figure 9.7) makes it clear that explicit attention should be paid to safety during all stages of the software process. This means that specific safety assurance activities must be included in the process. These include:

1. The creation of a hazard-logging and monitoring system that traces hazards from preliminary hazard analysis through to testing and system validation.

2. The appointment of project safety engineers who have explicit responsibility for the safety aspects of the system.

3. The extensive use of safety reviews throughout the development process.

4. The creation of a safety certification system whereby the safety of critical components is formally certified.

5. The use of a very detailed configuration management system (see Chapter 29), which is used to track all safety-related documentation and keep it in step with

Figure 24.8 A
simplified hazard log
page

Hazard Log   **Page 4: Printed 20.02.2003**
System: Insulin Pump System   *File:* InsulinPump/Safety/HazardLog
Safety Engineer: James Brown   *Log version:* 1/3
Identified Hazard   Insulin overdose delivered to patient
Identified by   Jane Williams
Criticality class   1
Identified risk   High
Fault tree identified   YES   *Date*   24.01.99   *Location*   Hazard Log, Page 5
Fault tree creators   Jane Williams and Bill Smith
Fault tree checked   YES   *Date*   28.01.99   *Checker*   James Brown

System safety design requirements

1. The system shall include self-testing software that will test the sensor system, the clock and the insulin delivery system.
2. The self-checking software shall be executed once per minute.
3. In the event of the self-checking software discovering a fault in any of the system components, an audible warning shall be issued and the pump display should indicate the name of the component where the fault has been discovered. The delivery of insulin should be suspended.
4. The system shall incorporate an override system that allows the system user to modify the computed dose of insulin that is to be delivered by the system.
5. The amount of override should be limited to be no greater than a pre-set value that is set when the system is configured by medical staff.

the associated technical documentation. There is little point in having stringent validation procedures if a failure of configuration management means that the wrong system is delivered to the customer.

To illustrate safety assurance, I use the hazard analysis process that is an essential part of safety-critical systems development. Hazard analysis is concerned with identifying hazards, their probability, and the probability that these hazards will lead to an accident. If the development process includes clear traceability from hazard identification through to the system itself, then an argument can be made why these hazards will not result in accidents. This may be supplemented by safety arguments, as discussed in Section 24.2.1. Where external certification is required before a system is used (e.g., in an aircraft), it is usually a condition of certification that this traceability can be demonstrated.

The central safety document is the hazard log, where hazards identified during the specification process are documented and traced. This hazard log is then used at each stage of the software development process to assess how that development stage has taken the hazards into account. A simplified example of a hazard log entry for the insulin delivery system is shown in Figure 24.8. This form documents the process of hazard analysis and shows design requirements that have been generated during this process. These design requirements are intended to ensure that the control system can never deliver an insulin overdose to a user of the insulin pump.

As shown in Figure 24.8, individuals who have safety responsibilities should be explicitly identified. Safety-critical systems development projects should always appoint a project safety engineer who is not be involved in the system development. The engineer's responsibility is to ensure that appropriate safety checks have been made and documented. The system may also require an independent safety assessor to be appointed from an outside organisation, who reports directly to the client on safety matters.

In some domains, system engineers who have safety responsibilities must be certified. In the UK, this means that they have to have been accepted as a member of one of the engineering institutes (civil, electrical, mechanical, etc.) and have to be chartered engineers. Inexperienced, poorly qualified engineers may not take responsibility for safety.

This does not currently apply to software engineers, although there has been extensive discussion on the licensing of software engineers in several states in the United States (Knight and Leveson, 2002; Bagert, 2002). However, future process standards for safety-critical software development may require that project safety engineers should be formally certified engineers with a defined minimum level of training.

24.2.3 Run-time safety checking

I described defensive programming in Chapter 20, where you add redundant statements to a program to monitor its operation and check for possible system faults. The same technique can be used for the dynamic monitoring of safety-critical systems. Checking code can be added to the system that checks a safety constraint. It throws an exception if that constraint is violated. The safety constraints that should always hold at particular points in a program may be expressed as *assertions*. Assertions are predicates that describe conditions that must hold before the following statement can be executed. In safety-critical systems, the assertions should be generated from the safety specification. They are intended to assure safe behaviour rather than behaviour that conforms to the specification.

Assertions can be particularly valuable in assuring the safety of communications between components of the system. For example, in the insulin delivery system, the dose of insulin administered involves generating signals to the insulin pump to deliver a specified number of insulin increments (Figure 24.9). The number of insulin increments associated with the allowed maximum insulin dose can be pre-computed and included as an assertion in the system.

If there has been an error in the computation of currentDose, which is the state variable that holds the amount of insulin to be delivered, or if this value has been corrupted in some way, then this will be trapped at this stage. An excessive dose of insulin will not be delivered, as the check in the method ensures that the pump will not deliver more than maxDose.

From the safety assertions that are included as program comments, code to check these assertions can be generated. You can see this in Figure 24.9, where the if-statement after the assert comment checks the assertion. In principle, much of this code

Figure 24.9 Insulin
administration with
run-time checking

```
static void administerInsulin ( ) throws SafetyException {

        int maxIncrements = InsulinPump.maxDose / 8 ;
        int increments = InsulinPump.currentDose / 8 ;

        // assert currentDose <= InsulinPump.maxDose

        if (InsulinPump.currentDose > InsulinPump.maxDose)
            throw new SafetyException (Pump.doseHigh);
        else
            for (int i=1; i<= increments; i++)
            {
                generateSignal () ;
                if (i > maxIncrements)
                    throw new SafetyException ( Pump.incorrectIncrements);
            } // for loop

    } //administerInsulin
```

generation could be automated using an assertion preprocessor. However, these tools usually have to be specially written and assertion code is normally generated by hand.

24.3 Security assessment

The assessment of system security is becoming increasingly important as more and more critical systems are Internet-enabled and can be accessed by anyone with a network connection. There are daily stories of attacks on web-based systems, and viruses and worms are regularly distributed using Internet protocols.

All of this means that the verification and validation processes for web-based systems must focus on security assessment, where the ability of the system to resist different types of attack is tested. However, as Anderson explains (Anderson, 2001), this type of security assessment is very difficult to carry out. Consequently, systems are often deployed with security loopholes that attackers use to gain access to or damage these systems.

Fundamentally, the reason why security is so difficult to assess is that security requirements, like some safety requirements, are 'shall not' requirements. That is, they specify what should not happen rather than system functionality or required behaviour. It is not usually possible to define this unwanted behaviour as simple constraints that may be checked by the system.

Figure 24.10
Examples of entries
in a security checklist

Security checklist
1. Do all files that are created in the application have appropriate access permissions? The wrong access permissions may lead to these files being accessed by unauthorised users.
2. Does the system automatically terminate user sessions after a period of inactivity? Sessions that are left active may allow unauthorised access through an unattended computer.
3. If the system is written in a programming language without array bound checking, are there situations where buffer overflow may be exploited? Buffer overflow may allow attackers to send code strings to the system and then execute them.
4. If passwords are set, does the system check that passwords are 'strong'? Strong passwords consist of mixed letters, numbers and punctuation, and are not normal dictionary entries. They are more difficult to break than simple passwords.

If resources are available, you can always demonstrate that a system meets its functional requirements. However, it is impossible to prove that a system does not do something, so, irrespective of the amount of testing, security vulnerabilities may remain in a system after it has been deployed. Even in systems that have been in use for many years, an ingenious attacker can discover a new form of attack and penetrate what was thought to be a secure system. For example, the RSA algorithm for data encryption that was thought, for many years, to be secure was cracked in 1999.

There are four complementary approaches to security checking:

1. *Experience-based validation* In this case, the system is analysed against types of attack that are known to the validation team. This type of validation is usually carried out in conjunction with tool-based validation. Checklists of known security problems (Figure 24.10) may be created to assist with the process. This approach may use all system documentation and could be part of other system reviews that check for errors and omissions.

2. *Tool-based validation* In this case, various security tools such as password checkers are used to analyse the system. Password checkers detect insecure passwords such as common names or strings of consecutive letters. This is really an extension of experience-based validation, where the experience is embodied in the tools used.

3. *Tiger teams* In this case, a team is set up and given the objective of breaching the system security. They simulate attacks on the system and use their ingenuity to discover new ways to compromise the system security. This approach can be very effective, especially if team members have previous experience with breaking into systems.

4. *Formal verification* A system can be verified against a formal security specification. However, as in other areas, formal verification for security is not widely used.

It is very difficult for end-users of a system to verify its security. Consequently, as discussed by Gollmann (Gollmann, 1999), bodies in North America and in Europe have established sets of security evaluation criteria that can be checked by specialised evaluators. Software product suppliers can submit their products for evaluation and certification against these criteria.

Therefore, if you have a requirement for a particular level of security, you can choose a product that has been validated to that level. However, many products are not security-certified or their certification applies only to individual products. When the certified system is used in conjunction with other uncertified systems, such as locally developed software, the security level of the overall system cannot be assessed.

24.4 Safety and dependability cases

Safety cases and, more generically, dependability cases are structured documents setting out detailed arguments and evidence that a system is safe or that a required level of dependability has been achieved. For many types of critical systems, the production of a safety case is a legal requirement, and the case must satisfy some certification body before the system can be deployed.

Regulators are created by government to ensure that private industry does not profit by failing to following national standards for safety, security, and so on. There are regulators in many different industries. For example, airlines are regulated by national aviation authorities such as the FAA (in the US) and the CAA (in the UK). Railway regulators exist to ensure the safety of railways, and nuclear regulators must certify the safety of a nuclear plant before it can go on line. In the banking sector, national banks serve as regulators, establishing procedures and practices to reduce the probability of fraud and to protect banking customers from risky banking practices. As software systems have become increasingly important in the critical infrastructure of countries, these regulators have become more and more concerned with safety and dependability cases for software systems.

The role of a regulator is to check that a completed system is as safe as practicable, so they are mainly involved when a development project is complete. However, regulators and developers rarely work in isolation; they communicate with the development team to establish what has to be included in the safety case. The regulator and developers jointly examine processes and procedures to make sure that these are being enacted and documented to the regulator's satisfaction.

Of course, software itself is not dangerous. It is only when it is embedded in a large, computer-based or socio-technical system that software failures can result in failures of other equipment or processes that can cause injury or death. Therefore, a software safety case is always part of a wider system safety case that demonstrates the safety of the overall system. When constructing a software safety case, you have to relate software failures to wider system failures and demonstrate that either these

Figure 24.11
Components of a
software safety case

Component	Description
System description	An overview of the system and a description of its critical components
Safety requirements	The safety requirements abstracted from the system requirements specification
Hazard and risk analysis	Documents describing the hazards and risks that have been identified and the measures taken to reduce risk
Design analysis	A set of structured arguments that justify why the design is safe
Verification and validation	A description of the V & V procedures used and, where appropriate, the test plans for the system
Review reports	Records of all design and safety reviews
Team competences	Evidence of the competence of all of the team involved in safety-related systems development and validation
Process QA	Records of the quality assurance processes carried out during system development
Change management processes	Records of all changes proposed, actions taken and, where appropriate, justification of the safety of these changes
Associated safety cases	References to other safety cases that may impact on this safety case

software failures will not occur or that they will not be propagated in such a way
that dangerous system failures may occur.

A safety case is a set of documents that include a description of the system, that
has to be certified, information about the processes used to develop the system and,
critically, logical arguments that demonstrate that the system is likely to be safe.
More succinctly, Bishop and Bloomfield (Bishop and Bloomfield, 1998; Bishop and
Bloomfield, 1995) define a safety case as:

> *A documented body of evidence that provides a convincing and valid argument*
> *that a system is adequately safe for a given application in a given environment.*

The organisation and contents of a safety case depends on the type of system
that is to be certified and its context of operation. Figure 24.11 shows one possible
organisation for a software safety case.

A key component of a safety case is a set of logical arguments for system safety.
These may be absolute arguments (event X will or will not happen) or probabilistic
arguments (the probability of event X is 0.Y); when combined, these should demonstrate safety. As shown in Figure 24.12, an argument is a relationship between what

Figure 24.12 The
structure of an
argument

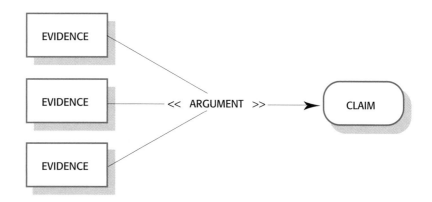

is thought to be the case (a claim) and a body of evidence that has been collected. The argument essentially explains why the claim (which is generally that something is safe) can be inferred from the available evidence. Naturally, given the multilevel nature of systems, claims are organised in a hierarchy. To demonstrate that a high-level claim is valid, you first have to work through the arguments for lower-level claims. Figure 24.13 shows part of this claim hierarchy for the insulin pump.

As a medical device, the insulin pump system may have to be externally certified. For example, in the UK, the Medical Devices Directorate have to issue a safety certificate for any medical device that is sold in the UK Various arguments may have to be produced to demonstrate the safety of this system. For example, the following argument could be part of a safety case for the insulin pump.

Claim:	The maximum single dose computed by the insulin pump will not exceed **maxDose**.
Evidence:	Safety argument for insulin pump (Figure 24.7)
Evidence:	Test data sets for insulin pump
Evidence:	Static analysis report for insulin pump software
Argument:	The safety argument presented shows that the maximum dose of insulin that can be computed is equal to **maxDose**.
	In 400 tests, the value of **Dose** was correctly computed and never exceeded **maxDose**.
	The static analysis of the control software revealed no anomalies.
	Overall, it is reasonable to assume that the claim is justified.

Of course, this is a very simplified argument, and in a real safety case detailed references to the evidence would be presented. Because of their detailed nature, safety cases are therefore very long and complex documents. Various software tools are available to help with their construction, and I have included links to these tools in the book's web pages.

Figure 24.13 The
claim hierarchy in
the insulin pump
safety case

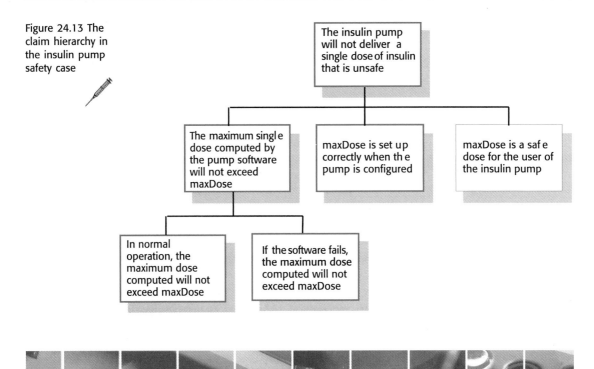

KEY POINTS

■ Statistical testing is used to estimate software reliability. It relies on testing the system
with a test data set that reflects the operational profile of the software. Test data may be
generated automatically.

■ Reliability growth models display the change in reliability as faults are removed from
software during the testing process. Reliability models can be used to predict when the
required reliability will be achieved.

■ Safety proofs are an effective product safety assurance technique. They show that an
identified hazardous condition can never occur. They are usually simpler than proving that a
program meets its specification.

■ It is important to have a well-defined, certified process for safety-critical systems
development. The process must include the identification and monitoring of potential
hazards.

■ Security validation may be carried out using experience-based analysis, tool-based analysis,
or 'tiger teams' that simulate attacks on the system.

■ Safety cases collect all of the evidence that demonstrates a system is safe. These safety
cases are required when an external regulator must certify the system before it is used.

FURTHER READING

'Best practices in code inspection for safety-critical software'. This practical paper presents a checklist of guidelines for inspecting and reviewing safety-critical software. (J. R. de Almeida, et al., *IEEE Software*, 20(3), May/June 2003.)

'Statically scanning Java code: Finding security vulnerabilities'. This is a good paper on avoiding security vulnerabilities in general. It discusses how these vulnerabilities arise and how they can be detected using a static analyser. (J. Viega, et al., *IEEE Software*, 17(5), September/October 2000.)

Software Reliability Engineering: More Reliable Software, Faster Development and Testing. This is probably the definitive book on the use of operational profiles and reliability models for reliability assessment. It includes details of experiences with statistical testing. (J. D. Musa, 1998, McGraw-Hill.)

Safety-critical Computer Systems. This excellent textbook includes a particularly good chapter on the place of formal methods in the development of safety-critical systems. (N. Storey, 1996, Addison-Wesley.)

Safeware: System Safety and Computers. This includes a good chapter on the validation of safety-critical systems with more detail than I have given here on the use of safety arguments based around fault trees. (N. Leveson, 1995, Addison-Wesley.)

EXERCISES

24.1 Describe how you would go about validating the reliability specification for a supermarket system that you specified in Exercise 9.8. Your answer should include a description of any validation tools that might be used.

24.2 Explain why it is practically impossible to validate reliability specifications when these are expressed in terms of a very small number of failures over the total lifetime of a system.

24.3 Using the literature as background information, write a report for management (who have no previous experience in this area) on the use of reliability growth models.

24.4 Is it ethical for an engineer to agree to deliver a software system with known faults to a customer? Does it make any difference if the customer is told of the existence of these faults in advance? Would it be reasonable to make claims about the reliability of the software in such circumstances?

24.5 Explain why ensuring system reliability is not a guarantee of system safety.

24.6 The door lock control mechanism in a nuclear waste storage facility is designed for safe operation. It ensures that entry to the storeroom is only permitted when radiation shields are in place or when the radiation level in the room falls below some given value (dangerLevel). That is:

(i) If remotely controlled radiation shields are in place within a room, the door may be opened by an authorised operator.

(ii) If the radiation level in a room is below a specified value, the door may be opened by an authorised operator.

(iii) An authorised operator is identified by the input of an authorised door entry code.

The Java code shown in Figure 24.14 controls the door-locking mechanism. Note that the safe state is that entry should not be permitted. Develop a safety argument that shows that this code is potentially unsafe. Modify the code to make it safe.

24.7 Using the specification for the dosage computation given in Chapter 10 (Figure 10.11), write the Java method computeInsulin as used in Figure 24.6. Construct an informal safety argument that this code is safe.

24.8 Suggest how you would go about validating a password protection system for an application that you have developed. Explain the function of any tools that you think may be useful.

24.9 Why is it necessary to include details of system changes in a software safety case?

24.10 List four types of systems that would require system software safety cases.

24.11 Assume you were part of a team that developed software for a chemical plant, which failed in some way, causing a serious pollution incident. Your boss is interviewed on television and states that the validation process is comprehensive and that there are no faults in the software. She asserts that the problems must be due to poor operational procedures. A newspaper approaches you for your opinion. Discuss how you should handle such an interview.

24.12 What are the arguments for and against the licensing of software engineers?

Figure 24.14 Door lock controller

```
1       entryCode = lock.getEntryCode () ;
2       if (entryCode == lock.authorisedCode)
3       {
4           shieldStatus = Shield.getStatus ();
5           radiationLevel = RadSensor.get ();
6           if (radiationLevel < dangerLevel)
7               state = safe;
8           else
9               state = unsafe;
10          if (shieldStatus == Shield.inPlace() )
11              state = safe;
12          if (state == safe)
13              {
14                  Door.locked = false ;
15                  Door.unlock ();
16              }
17          else
18          {
19              Door.lock ( );
20              Door.locked := true ;
21          }
22      }
```

PART 6

MANAGING
PEOPLE

It is sometimes suggested that the key difference between software engineers and other programmers is that software engineering is a managed process. By this, I mean that the software development takes place within an organisation and is subject to a range of schedule, budget and organisational constraints. You can contrast this with open-source development, which is largely a voluntary activity. Open-source developers make their own decisions on when and how they work on the software, and the quality of their work illustrates that successful software development does not have to be strictly managed.

However, most software projects can't be developed using an open source approach—that development model is only suitable for infrastructure systems such as operating systems, web servers, compilers, etc. More specialised application development is always a managed process. The chapters in this part of the book extend the introductory management chapter in the Overview (Chapter 5) and discuss a number of management topics:

1. Chapter 25 is concerned with people management. This is not a technical topic so it is not normally covered in software engineering textbooks. However, in my experience, people management is the critical management activity in software development projects. My aim here is to introduce the issues and problems of people management; I cover selecting and motivating staff, managing project groups and, finally, the SEI's people capability maturity model.

2. In Chapter 26 I focus on software cost estimation. I discuss software productivity and a range of software cost estimation techniques. There is a lot of uncertainty in this area and some people believe that the best way to tackle this is through algorithmic cost modelling. I cover the COCOMO II model here, but as this is a very comprehensive model, I can only give a brief introduction to its fundamental features.

3. Chapters 27 and 28 are concerned with issues of quality management. Quality management is concerned with processes and techniques for ensuring and improving the quality of software and Chapter 27 introduces the topic. Chapter 28 backs this up with a discussion of software process improvement—how can processes be changed so that both product and process attributes are improved.

4. Finally, Chapter 29 discusses configuration management. This is an issue that is important for all large systems that are developed by teams. However, the need for configuration management is not always obvious to students who have only been concerned with personal software development so I introduce the various aspects of this topic here including configuration planning, version management, system building and change management.

25

Managing people

Objectives

The objective of this chapter is to discuss the importance of people in the software engineering process. When you have read the chapter, you will:

■ understand some of the issues involved in selecting and retaining staff in a software development organisation;

■ understand factors that influence individual motivation and their implications for software project managers;

■ understand key issues of team working, including team composition, team cohesiveness, team communications and team organisation;

■ be aware of the structure of the People Capability Maturity Model—a model that is a framework for enhancing the capabilities of software engineers in an organisation.

Contents

The people working in a software organisation are its greatest assets. They represent intellectual capital, and it is up to software managers to ensure that the organisation gets the best possible return on its investment in people. In successful companies and economies, this is achieved when people are respected by the organisation. They should have a level of responsibility and reward that reflects their skills.

Effective management is therefore about managing the people in an organisation. Project managers have to solve technical and nontechnical problems by using the people in their team in the most effective way possible. They have to motivate people, plan and organise their work and ensure that the work is being done properly. Poor management of people is one of the most significant contributors to project failure.

Unfortunately, poor leadership is all too common in the software industry. Managers fail to take into account the limitations of individuals and impose unrealistic deadlines on project teams. They equate management with meetings yet fail to allow people in these meetings to contribute to the project. They may accept new requirements without proper analysis of what this means for the project team. They sometimes see their role as one of exploiting their staff rather than working with them to identify how their work can contribute to both organisational and personal goals.

There are, in my view, four critical factors in people management:

1. *Consistency* People in a project team should all be treated in a comparable way. While no one expects all rewards to be identical, people should not feel that their contribution to the organisation is undervalued.

2. *Respect* Different people have different skills and managers should respect these differences. All members of the team should be given an opportunity to make a contribution. In some cases, of course, you will find that people simply don't fit into a team and cannot continue, but it is important not to jump to conclusions about this.

3. *Inclusion* People contribute effectively when they feel that others listen to them and take account of their proposals. It is important to develop a working environment where all views, even those of the most junior staff, are considered.

4. *Honesty* As a manager, you should always be honest about what is going well and what is going badly in the team. You should also be honest about your level of technical knowledge and be willing to defer to staff with more knowledge when necessary. If you are less than honest, you will eventually be found out and will lose the respect of the group.

My aim in this chapter is to introduce some of the issues that software engineering managers may have to face and to provide background information that helps you understand these issues. Management, in my view, is something that can only be learned through experience, so the role of a book is to help you learn from previous experience. You will not become a good manager of people simply by reading this chapter.

However, I hope the material here will help you understand the problems that managers face when dealing with teams of technically talented individuals.

25.1 Selecting staff

One of the most important project management tasks is team selection. In exceptional cases, project managers can appoint the people who are best suited to the job irrespective of their other responsibilities or budget considerations. More often, however, project managers do not have a free choice of staff. They may have to use whoever is available in an organisation, they may have to find people very quickly and they may have a limited budget. Budget limitations may constrain the number of expensive experienced engineers available to work on the project.

The decision on who to appoint to a project is usually made using three types of information:

1. Information provided by candidates about their background and experience (their résumé or CV). This is usually the most reliable evidence that you have available to judge whether candidates are likely to be suitable.

2. Information gained by interviewing candidates. Interviews can give you a good impression of whether a candidate is a good communicator and whether he or she has good social skills. However, tests have shown that interviewers are liable to accept or reject candidates on the basis of rapid subjective judgements. Consequently, interviews are not a reliable method for making judgements of technical capabilities.

3. Recommendations from people who have worked with the candidates. This can be effective when you know the people making the recommendation. Otherwise, the recommendations cannot be trusted and, in my view, are of little use in making decisions about staff.

Figure 25.1 presents a short case study of issues that can arise when appointing staff. Some characteristic lessons from this case study are:

1. If you are looking for people with specific skills from inside the company, the manager of the project where they are already working may not wish to lose them. Sometimes, you have to accept that people will only be able to work for part of the time on your project.

2. Skills such as user interface design and hardware interfacing are in short supply. You may not have a wide choice of applicants for these posts, especially if the company is not located near other software industries.

Figure 25.1 Staff
selection

Case study 1: Choosing team members

Alice is a software project manager working in a company that develops alarm systems. This company wishes to enter the growing market of assistive technology to help elderly and disabled people live independently. Alice has been asked to lead a team of 6 developers than can develop new products based around the company's alarm technology. Her first role is to select team members either from software engineers already in the company or from outside.

To help select a team, Alice first assesses the skills that she will need: These are:

- Experience with existing alarm technology, as it is reused.
- User interface design experience because the users are untrained and may be disabled and hence need facilities such as variable font sizes, etc.
- Ideally, someone who has experience of designing assistive technology systems. Otherwise, someone with experience of interfacing to hardware units as all systems being developed involve some hardware control.
- General-purpose development skills.

The next stage is to try and find people from within the company with the necessary skills. However, the company has expanded significantly and has few staff available. The best that Alice can negotiate is to have help from an alarm expert (Fred) for 2 days/week. She therefore decides to advertise for new project staff, listing the attributes that she'd like:

- Programming experience in C. She has decided to develop all the assistive technology control software in C.
- Experience in user interface design. A UI designer is essential but there may not be a need for a full-time appointment.
- Experience in hardware interfacing with C and using remote development systems. All the devices used have complex hardware interfaces.
- Experience of working with hardware engineers. At times, it will be necessary to build completely new hardware.
- A sympathetic personality so that they can relate to and work with elderly people who are providing requirements for and are testing the system.

Alice gets 30 responses to the advert and, from the applicants, is able to identify suitable candidates with hardware interfacing (Dorothy) and user interface design experience (Ed). She also decides to hire two new graduates (Brian and Bob) who have some C programming experience but who will essentially have to be trained in the company. All that remains then is to appoint a more senior programmer to join the development team and Alice has two choices. Carol has several years C programming experience and has recently taken a short career break to have children. Dave has a comparable amount of programming experience and is a programming enthusiast. He spends most of his spare time working on open source development projects and has encyclopaedic knowledge of C and C++.

After interviewing both Carol and Dave, Alice decides to offer the job to Carol although Dave has deeper programming knowledge.

3.   Recent graduates may not have the specific skills you need but they are normally enthusiastic and may have been exposed to up-to-date technology.

4.   It doesn't always make sense to employ the most technically proficient person for a technical development job. In this job, interaction with elderly users may be required and Alice decides that Carol is likely to be more sympathetic to their problems.

Figure 25.2 Factors
governing staff
selection

Factor	Explanation
Application domain experience	For a project to develop a successful system, the developers must understand the application domain. It is essential that some members of a development team have some domain experience.
Platform experience	This may be significant if low-level programming is involved. Otherwise, this is not usually a critical attribute.
Programming language experience	This is normally only significant for short-duration projects where there is not enough time to learn a new language. While learning a language itself is not difficult, it takes several months to become proficient in using the associated libraries and components.
Problem solving ability	This is very important for software engineers who constantly have to solve technical problems. However, it is almost impossible to judge without knowing the work of the potential team member.
Educational background	This may provide an indicator of what the candidate knows and his or her ability to learn. This factor becomes increasingly irrelevant as engineers gain experience across a range of projects.
Communication ability	Project staff must be able to communicate orally and in writing with other engineers, managers and customers.
Adaptability	Adaptability may be judged by looking at the experience that candidates have had. This is an important attribute, as it indicates an ability to learn.
Attitude	Project staff should have a positive attitude toward their work and should be willing to learn new skills. This is an important attribute but often very difficult to assess.
Personality	This is an important attribute but difficult to assess. Candidates must be reasonably compatible with other team members. No particular type of personality is more or less suited to software engineering.

If you have some choice of staff, the factors that may influence your decision are shown in Figure 25.2. The most important factors vary depending on the application domain, the type of project and the skills of other members of the project team.

As a project manager, you may be faced with problems finding people with appropriate skills and experience. You may have to build your team using relatively inexperienced engineers. This may lead to problems because the team members don't understand the application domain or the technology. However, in a long-term project, understanding of concepts and the application domain is more important than specific knowledge, particularly of programming languages and methods. Therefore, unless you need specific knowledge of a programming language for a short-term assignment, it is best to select staff who have problem-solving or domain experience. It is relatively easy to learn a new language but much more difficult to develop deeper conceptual knowledge required for complex problem solving.

Some companies test candidate team members. These include programming aptitude tests and psychometric tests that rely on candidates completing a number of small exercises in a relatively short time. Psychometric tests are intended to produce a psychological profile of the candidate indicating attitude and suitability for certain types of task. Some managers consider these tests to be useless; others think they provide helpful information for staff selection. I doubt whether aptitude tests provide useful information about problem-solving ability. Solving complex software problems is a long-term, iterative process. I don't believe that the skills needed for complex problem solving are comparable to the skills needed to complete simple aptitude test puzzles.

A lack of experienced technical people may be a result of organisational policy where technically skilled staff quickly reach a career plateau. To progress further, they have to become managers, and this promotion inevitably means that useful technical skills are lost. To avoid this skill leakage, some large companies have developed parallel technical and managerial career structures of equal worth. Experienced technical people are rewarded at the same level as managers. As an individual's career develops, he or she may specialise in either technical or managerial activities and move between them without losing status or salary.

25.2 Motivating people

One of the roles of project managers is to motivate the people who work for them. Motivation means organising the work and the working environment so that people are stimulated to work as effectively as possible. If people are not motivated, they will not be interested in the work they are doing. They will work slowly, be more likely to make mistakes and will not contribute to the broader goals of the team or the organisation.

Maslow (Maslow 1954) suggests that people are motivated by satisfying their needs and that needs are arranged in a series of levels, as shown in Figure 25.3. The lower levels of this hierarchy represent fundamental needs for food, sleep, and so on, as well as the need to feel secure in an environment. Social needs are concerned with the need to feel part of a social grouping. Esteem needs are the need to feel respected by others, and self-realisation needs are concerned with personal development. Human priorities are to satisfy lower-level needs such as hunger before the more abstract, higher-level needs.

Figure 25.3 Human
needs hierarchy

People working in software development organisations are not usually hungry or thirsty and generally do not feel physically threatened by their environment. Therefore, ensuring the satisfaction of social, esteem and self-realisation needs is most significant from a management point of view.

1. To satisfy social needs, you need to give people time to meet their co-workers and to provide places for them to meet. This is relatively easy when all of the members of a development team work in the same place but, increasingly, team members are not located in the same building or even the same town or state. They may work for different organisations or from home most of the time. Electronic communications such as e-mail and teleconferencing may be used to support this remote working. However, my experience with electronic communications is that they do not really satisfy social needs. If your team is distributed, you should arrange periodic face-to-face meetings so that people experience direct interaction with other members of the team. Through this direct interaction, people become part of a social group and may be motivated by the goals and priorities of that group.

2. To satisfy esteem needs, you need to show people that they are valued by the organisation. Public recognition of achievements is a simple yet effective way of doing this. Obviously, people must also feel that they are paid at a level that reflects their skills and experience.

3. Finally, to satisfy self-realisation needs, you need to give people responsibility for their work, assign them demanding (but not impossible) tasks and provide a training programme where people can develop their skills.

In Figure 25.4, I illustrate a problem of motivation that managers often have to face. In this example, a competent group member loses interest in the work and in the group as a whole. The quality of her work falls and becomes unacceptable. This situation has to be dealt with quickly. If you don't sort out the problem, the other group members will become dissatisfied and feel that they are doing an unfair share of the work.

Figure 25.4
Individual motivation

Case study 2: Motivation

Alice's assistive technology project starts well. Good working relationships develop within the team and creative new ideas are developed. The company decides to develop a peer-to-peer messaging system using digital televisions linked to the alarm network for communications. However, some months into the project, Alice notices that Dorothy, the hardware design expert, starts coming into work late, the quality of her work deteriorates and, increasingly, she does not appear to be communicating with other members of the team.

Alice talks about the problem informally with other team members to try to find out if Dorothy's personal circumstances have changed and if this might be affecting her work. They don't know of anything, so Alice decides to talk with Dorothy to try to understand the problem.

After some initial denials that there is a problem, Dorothy admits that she has lost interest in the job. She expected she would be able to develop and use her hardware interfacing skills. However, because of the product direction that has been chosen, she has little opportunity for this. Basically, she is working as a C programmer with other team members. While she admits that the work is challenging, she is concerned that she is not developing her interfacing skills. She is worried that finding a job that involves hardware interfacing will be difficult after this project. Because she does not want to upset the team by revealing that she is thinking about the next project, she has decided that it is best to minimise conversation with them.

In this example, Alice tries to find out if Dorothy's personal circumstances could be the problem. Personal difficulties commonly affect motivation because people cannot concentrate on their work. You may have to give people time and support to resolve these issues, although you also have to make it clear that the people concerned still have a responsibility to their employer.

In fact, Dorothy's motivation problem is one that arises frequently when projects develop in an unanticipated direction. People who expected to do one type of work may end up doing something completely different. This becomes a problem when people want to develop their skills in some way that is different from that taken by the project. In those circumstances, you may decide that the team member should leave the team and find opportunities elsewhere. In this circumstance, however, Alice decides to try to convince Dorothy that broadening her experience is a positive career step. She gives Dorothy more design autonomy and organises training courses in software engineering that will provide her with more opportunities after her current project has finished.

The principal problem with Maslow's model of motivation is that it takes an exclusively personal viewpoint on motivation. It does not take adequate account of the fact that people feel themselves to be part of an organisation, a professional group and, usually, some culture. This is not simply a question of satisfying social needs—people can be motivated through helping a group achieve shared goals.

Being a member of a cohesive group is highly motivating to most people. People with fulfilling jobs often like to go to work because they are motivated by the people they work with and by the work that they do. Therefore, as well as thinking about individual motivation, you also have to think about how the group as a whole can be motivated to achieve the organisation's goals. I discuss group management issues in the next section.

In a psychological study of motivation, Bass and Dunteman (Bass and Dunteman, 1963) classified professionals into three types:

1. *Task-oriented* people are motivated by the work they do. In software engineering, they are technicians who are motivated by the intellectual challenge of software development.

2. *Self-oriented* people are principally motivated by personal success and recognition. They are interested in software development as a means of achieving their own goals. This does not mean that these people are selfish and think only of their own concerns. Rather, they often have longer-term goals such as career progression, that motivate them. They wish to be successful in their work to help realise these goals.

3. *Interaction-oriented* people are motivated by the presence and actions of coworkers. As software development becomes more user-centered, interaction-oriented individuals are becoming more involved in software engineering.

Interaction-oriented personalities usually like to work as part of a group, whereas task-oriented and self-oriented people often prefer to work alone. Women are more likely to be interaction-oriented than men. They are often more effective communicators. I discuss the mix of these different personality types in groups in Section 25.3.2.

Each individual's motivation is made up of elements of each class but one type of motivation is usually dominant at any one time. However, personalities are not static and individuals can change. For example, technical people who feel they are not being properly rewarded can become self-oriented and put personal interests before technical concerns.

25.3 Managing Groups

Most professional software is developed by project teams ranging in size from two to several hundred people. However, as it is clearly impossible for all these people to work together on a single problem, these large teams are usually split into a number of groups. Each group is responsible for part of the overall system. As a general rule, software engineering project groups should normally have no more than eight or ten members. When small groups are used, communication problems are reduced. The whole group can get round a table for a meeting and can meet in each other's offices.

Putting together a group that works effectively is therefore a critical manage-ment task. It is obviously important that the group should have the right balance of technical skills, experience and personalities. However, successful groups are more than simply a collection of individuals with the right balance of skills. A good group has a team spirit so that the people involved are motivated by the success of the group as well as by their own personal goals.

There are a number of factors that influence group working:

1. *Group composition* Is there the right balance of skills, experience and person-alities in the team?

2. *Group cohesiveness* Does the group think of itself as a team rather than as a collection of individuals who are working together?

3. *Group communications* Do the members of the group communicate effectively with each other?

4. *Group organisation* Is the team organised in such a way that everyone feels valued and is satisfied with his or her role in the group?

25.3.1 Group composition

As I discussed in Section 25.2, many software engineers are motivated primarily by their work. Software development groups, therefore, are often composed of peo-ple who have their own ideas about how technical problems should be solved. This is borne out by regularly reported problems of interface standards being ignored, systems being redesigned as they are coded, unnecessary system embellishments and so on. You should try, if possible, to select group members so that these kinds of problems are avoided.

A group that has complementary personalities may work better than a group selected solely on technical ability. People who are motivated by the work are likely to be the strongest technically. People who are self-oriented will probably be best at pushing the work forward to finish the job. People who are interaction-oriented help facilitate communications within the group. I think that it is particularly important to have interaction-oriented people in a group. They like to talk to peo-ple and can detect tensions and disagreements at an early stage, before they have a serious impact on the group.

In the case study example shown in Figure 25.5, I have shown how Alice, the project manager, has tried to create a group with complementary personalities. This particular group has a good mix of interaction and task-oriented people, but I have already discussed in Figure 25.4 how Dorothy's self-oriented personality can cause problems. Fred's part-time role in the group as a domain expert might also be a problem here. He is mostly interested in technical challenges, so he may not inter-act well with other group members. The fact that he is not always part of the team means that he may not relate well to the team's goals.

Figure 25.5 Group
composition

Case study 3: Group composition
In creating a group for assistive technology development, Alice is aware of the
importance of selecting members with complementary personalities. When
interviewing people, she tried to assess whether they were task-oriented, self-
oriented or interaction-oriented. She felt that she was primarily a self-oriented type
as she felt that this project was a way in which she would be noticed by senior
management and promoted. She therefore looked for one or perhaps two
interaction-oriented personalities and wanted to task-oriented individuals to complete
the team. The final assessment that she arrived at was:

> Alice—self-oriented
> Brian—task-oriented
> Bob—task-oriented
> Carol—interaction-oriented
> Dorothy—self-oriented
> Ed—interaction-oriented
> Fred—task-oriented

It is sometimes impossible to choose a group with complementary personalities.
In this case, the project manager has to control the group so that individual goals
do not transcend organisational and group objectives. This control is easier to achieve
if all group members participate in each stage of the project. Individual initiative
is most likely when group members are given instructions without being aware of
the part that their task plays in the overall project.

For example, say an engineer is given a program design for coding and notices
possible design improvements. If he implements these improvements without
understanding the rationale for the original design, they might have adverse implications for other parts of the system. If all the members of the group are involved
in the design from the start, they will understand why design decisions have been
made. They may identify with these decisions rather than oppose them.

The group leader has an important role. He or she may be responsible for providing technical direction and project administration. Group leaders must keep track
of the day-to-day work of their group, ensure that people are working effectively
and work closely with project managers on project planning.

Leaders are normally appointed and report to the overall project manager.
However, the appointed leader may not be the real leader of the group as far as
technical matters are concerned. The group members may look to another group
member for leadership. He or she may be the most technically competent engineer
or may be a better motivator than the appointed group leader.

Sometimes, it is effective to separate technical leadership and project administration. People who are technically competent are not always the best administrators. Being
given an administrative role can reduce their overall value to the group. It is best to
support them with an administrator who can relieve them of day-to-day tasks.

Imposing an unwanted leader on a group is likely to cause tensions. The team
members will not respect the leader and may reject group loyalty in favour of individual

goals. This is a particular problem in a fast-changing field such as software engineering, where new members may be more up-to-date and better educated than experienced group leaders. Some people with experience may resent the imposition of a young leader with new ideas.

25.3.2 Group cohesiveness

In a cohesive group, members think of the group as more important than the individual in it. Members of a well-led, cohesive group are loyal to the group. They identify with group goals and with other group members. They attempt to protect the group, as an entity, from outside interference. This makes the group robust and able to cope with problems and unexpected situations. The group can cope with change by providing mutual support and help.

The advantages of a cohesive group are:

1. *A group quality standard can be developed* Because this standard is established by consensus, it is more likely to be observed than external standards imposed on the group.

2. *Group members work closely together* People in the group learn from each other. Inhibitions caused by ignorance are minimised as mutual learning is encouraged.

2. *Group members can get to know each other's work* Continuity can be maintained if a group member leaves. Others in the group can take over critical tasks and ensure that the project is not unduly disrupted.

3. *Egoless programming can be practised* Programs are regarded as group property rather than personal property.

Egoless programming (Weinberg, 1971) is a style of group working where designs, programs and other documents are considered to be the common property of the group rather than the individual who wrote them. In a culture of egoless programming, people are more likely to offer their work for inspection by other group members, to accept criticism and to work with the group to improve the program. Group cohesiveness is improved because all members feel that they have a shared responsibility for the software. The idea of egoless programming is fundamental to extreme programming (Beck, 2000), discussed in Chapter 17. In extreme programming, constant improvement of the code in the system, irrespective of who wrote that code, is one of the basic tenets.

As well as improving the quality of designs, programs and documents, egoless programming also improves communications within the group. It encourages uninhibited discussion without regard to status, experience or gender. Individual members actively cooperate with other group members throughout the course of the project. This draws the members of the group together and makes them feel part of a team.

Figure 25.6 Group
cohesion

Case study 4: Team spirit

Alice, an experienced project manager, understands the importance of creating a
cohesive group. As the product development is new, she takes the opportunity of
involving all group members in the product specification and design by getting them
to discuss possible technology with elderly members of their families and to bring
family members to the weekly group lunch. The group lunch is an opportunity for all
team members to meet informally, talk around issues of concern and get to know
each other.

At the lunch Alice tells the group members what she knows about organisational
news, policies, strategies and so forth. Each team member then briefly summarises
what they have been doing and the group discusses a general topic such as new
product ideas from elderly relatives.

Every few months, Alice organises an 'away day' for the group where the team
spend two days on 'technology updating'. Each team member prepares an update
on a relevant technology and presents it to the group. This is an off-site meeting in a
good hotel and plenty time is scheduled for discussion and social interaction.

Group cohesiveness depends on many factors, including the organisational culture and the personalities in the group. Managers can encourage cohesiveness in a
number of ways: They may organise social events for group members and their families; they may try to establish a sense of group identity by naming the group and
establishing a group identity and territory; or they may get involved in explicit group-
building activities such as sports and games.

One of the most effective ways to promote cohesion is to be inclusive and ensure
that group members are treated as responsible and trustworthy and are given access to
information. Often, managers feel that they cannot reveal certain information to everyone in the group. This invariably creates a climate of mistrust. Simple information exchange
is a cheap and efficient way of making people feel that they are part of a team.

We see an example of this in the case study fragment shown in Figure 25.6. Alice
arranges regular informal meetings where she tells the other group members what
is going on. She makes a point of involving people in the product development by
asking them to come up with new ideas derived from their own family experiences.
The 'away days' are also good ways of promoting cohesion—people relax together
while they help each other learn about new technologies.

Strong, cohesive groups, however, can sometimes suffer from two problems:

1. *Irrational resistance to a leadership change* If the leader of a cohesive group
    has to be replaced by someone outside of the group, the group members may
    band together against the new leader. Group members may spend time resist-
    ing changes proposed by the new group leader with a consequent loss of pro-
    ductivity. Whenever possible, new leaders are therefore best appointed from
    within the group.

2. *Groupthink* Groupthink (Janis, 1972) is when the critical abilities of group mem-
    bers are eroded by group loyalties. Consideration of alternatives is replaced by

loyalty to group norms and decisions. Any proposal favoured by the majority of the group may be adopted without proper consideration of alternatives.

To avoid groupthink, you should organise formal sessions in which group members are encouraged to question decisions that have been made. Outside experts may be introduced to review the group's decisions. People who are naturally argumentative, questioning and disrespectful of the *status quo* may be appointed as discussion leaders. They act as a devil's advocate, constantly questioning group decisions and thus forcing other group members to think about and evaluate their activities.

25.3.3 Group communications

Good communication between members of a software development group is essential. The group members must exchange information on the status of their work, the design decisions that have been made and changes to previous decisions that are necessary. Good communication also strengthens group cohesiveness as group members come to understand the motivations, strengths and weaknesses of other people in the group.

Some key factors that influence the effectiveness of communication are:

1. *Group size* As a group increases in size, ensuring that all members communicate effectively with each other becomes more difficult. The number of one-way communication links is $n * (n - 1)$, where n is the group size, so, with a group of seven or eight members, it is quite possible that some people will rarely communicate. Status differences between group members means that communications are often one-way. Higher-status members tend to dominate communications with lower-status members, who are often reluctant to start a conversation or make critical remarks.

2. *Group structure* People in informally structured groups communicate more effectively than people in groups with a formal, hierarchical structure. In hierarchical groups, communications tend to flow up and down the hierarchy. People at the same level may not talk to each other. This is a particular problem in a large project with several development groups. When people working on different sub-systems communicate only through their managers, the project may suffer delays and misunderstandings.

3. *Group composition* People with the same personality types may clash and communications may be inhibited. Communication is also usually better in mixed-sex groups (Marshall and Heslin, 1975) than in single-sex groups. Women tend to be more interaction-oriented than men and may act as interaction controllers and facilitators for the group.

4. *The physical work environment* The organisation of the workplace is a major factor in facilitating or inhibiting communications. I discuss this later in Section 25.3.5.

25.3.4 Group organisation

Small programming groups are usually organised in a fairly informal way. The group leader gets involved in the software development with the other group members. A technical leader may emerge who effectively controls software production. In an informal group, the work to be carried out is discussed by the group as a whole, and tasks are allocated according to ability and experience. More senior group members may be responsible for the architectural design. However, detailed design and implementation is the responsibility of the team member who is allocated to a particular task.

Informal groups can be very successful, particularly when the majority of group members are experienced and competent. Such a group makes decisions by consensus, which improves group spirit, cohesiveness and performance. If a group is composed mostly of inexperienced or incompetent members, informality can be a hindrance because no definite authority exists to direct the work, causing a lack of coordination between group members and, possibly, eventual project failure.

An interesting organisational variant of democratic group organisation is described by Beck in his book on extreme programming (Beck, 2000). In this approach, many decisions that are usually seen as management decisions, such as decisions on schedule, are devolved to group members. Programmers work together in pairs to develop code and take joint responsibility for the programs that are developed.

As I discuss in Chapter 26, individual ability has the most significant influence on programmer productivity. The best programmers may be up to 25 times as productive as the worst programmers. It therefore makes sense to use the best people in the most effective way and to provide them with as much support as possible.

To make the most effective use of highly skilled programmers, Baker (Baker, 1972) and others (Aron, 1974; Brooks, 1975) suggest that teams should be built around an individual, highly skilled chief programmer. The underlying principle of the chief programmer team is that skilled and experienced staff should be responsible for all software development. They should not be concerned with routine matters and should have good technical and administrative support for their work. They should focus on the software to be developed and should not get involved in external meetings.

But the chief programmer team organisation has serious problems because it is over-dependent on the chief programmer and their assistant. Other team members, who are not given sufficient responsibility, become unmotivated because they feel their skills are underused.

However, the general principle of augmenting a programming team with specialists is a good one. When choosing team members, you can focus on people who have generic skills such as communication and problem solving, and then bring in experts as required during the project. Using experts as required also means that relatively inexperienced developers have opportunities to learn and develop their expertise as the project progresses.

25.3.5 Working environments

The workplace has important effects on people's performance and their job satisfaction. Psychological experiments have shown that behaviour is affected by room size, furniture, equipment, temperature, humidity, brightness and quality of light, noise and the degree of privacy available. Group behaviour is affected by architectural organisation and telecommunication facilities. Communications within a group are affected by the building architecture and the structure of the workspace.

There is a real and significant cost in failing to provide good working conditions. When people are unhappy about their working conditions, staff turnover increases. More costs must therefore be expended on recruitment and training. Software projects may be delayed because of lack of qualified staff (DeMarco and Lister, 1999).

Software development staff often work in large, open-plan office areas, sometimes with cubicles, and only senior management have individual offices. McCue (McCue, 1978) carried out a study that showed the open-plan architecture favoured by many organisations was neither popular nor productive. The most important environmental factors identified in that design study were:

1. *Privacy* Programmers require an area where they can concentrate and work without interruption.

2. *Outside awareness* People prefer to work in natural light and with a view of the outside environment.

3. *Personalisation* Individuals adopt different working practices and have different opinions on decor. The ability to rearrange the workplace to suit working practices and to personalise that environment is important.

In short, people like individual offices that they can organise to their taste and needs. Individual offices mean less disruption and fewer interruptions than open-plan workspaces. In open-plan offices, people are denied privacy and a quiet working environment. They are limited in the ways that they can personalise their own workspace. Concentration can be difficult and performance is degraded.

Providing individual offices for software engineering staff can make a significant difference to productivity. DeMarco and Lister (DeMarco and Lister, 1985) compared the productivity of programmers in different types of workplace. They found that factors such as a private workspace and the ability to cut off interruptions had a significant effect. Programmers who had good working conditions were more than twice as productive than equally skilled programmers who had to work in poorer conditions.

Development groups need areas where all members of the group can get together and discuss their project, both formally and informally. Meeting rooms must be able to accommodate the whole group in privacy. Individual privacy requirements and group communication requirements seem to be exclusive objectives. McCue suggested grouping individual offices round larger group meeting rooms (Figure 25.7) was the best way to reconcile these conflicting requirements.

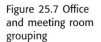
Figure 25.7 Office
and meeting room
grouping

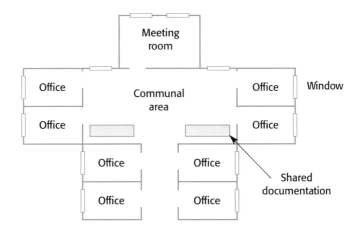

A similar model is suggested by Beck in his description of an environment for extreme programming. However, he suggests retaining an open-plan area with all programming activities taking place in the communal area and individual cubicles for the group members when they wish to work alone. Clearly, the key requirement is to provide both individual and group space so that people can work alone or as a group when necessary.

Facilitating communications by providing communal meeting areas helps people solve their problems and exchange information in an informal but effective way. Weinberg (Weinberg, 1971) cites an anecdotal example of how an organisation wanted to stop programmers wasting time talking to each other around a coffee machine. They removed the machine, then immediately had a dramatic increase in requests for formal programming assistance. As well as gossiping around the machine, people were solving each other's problems. This illustrates that companies need informal meeting places as well as formal conference rooms.

The case study in Figure 25.8 illustrates that you often have to work within the constraints of existing buildings. You can't necessarily adapt these or have as much space as you would like. In this example, Alice has used a single office as a space for concentrated work and confined development work, where people will be discussing what to do, to a single room. Shared desks are increasingly common for team members who are not always working in the office. As each member of the team have a laptop, they can work anywhere—at their desk, in the quiet room or in the shared social spaces in the building.

25.4 The People Capability Maturity Model

The Software Engineering Institute (SEI) in the United States is engaged in a long-term programme of software process improvement. Part of this programme is the

Figure 25.8 Office
organisation

Case study 5: Office organisation

Alice understands the importance of working environments but her company is based in a 1970s building that can't be adapted to an ideal structure. She is assigned three offices for her team—a small, separate individual office and two adjacent larger offices that can each hold four desks. Two team members (Carol and Brian) often work from home and Fred, the alarm expert, only works with the team two days per week. The team has access to a meeting room shared by other groups, and each floor in the building has a coffee space for informal interaction.

Rather than use the small office as her personal office, as intended by management, Alice decides that this should be a quiet 'thinking' space that can be used by any team member who needs to work without distraction. She sets up one of the offices as a development office with tables for hardware and paper prototypes of user interfaces. This room also has a desk that is mostly used by Fred when he is working with the team but is also shared by Carol and Brian when they are working in the office. Alice shares the other office with Bob, Dorothy and Ed. The building has a wireless network and all team members have laptops.

Capability Maturity Model (CMM) for software processes, which I discuss in Chapter 28. This is concerned with best practice in software engineering. To support this model, they have also proposed a People Capability Maturity Model (P-CMM) (Curtis, et al., 2001). The P-CMM can be used as a framework for improving the way in which an organisation manages its human assets.

Like the CMM, the P-CMM is a five-level model, as shown in Figure 25.9. The five levels are:

1. *Initial* Ad hoc, informal people management practices

2. *Repeatable* Establishment of policies for developing the capability of the staff

3. *Defined* Standardisation of best people management practice across the organisation

4. *Managed* Quantitative goals for people management

5. *Optimizing* Continuous focus on improving individual competence and workforce motivation

Curtis et al. (Curtis, et al., 2001) state that the strategic objectives of the P-CMM are:

1. To improve the capability of software organisations by increasing the capability of their workforce

2. To ensure that software development capability is an attribute of the organisation rather than of a few individuals

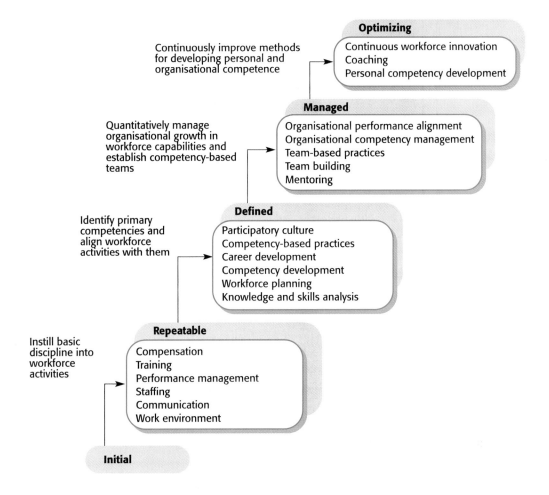

Optimizing

Continuously improve methods
for developing personal and
organisational competence

Continuous workforce innovation
Coaching
Personal competency development

Managed

Quantitatively manage
organisational growth in
workforce capabilities and
establish competency-based
teams

Organisational performance alignment
Organisational competency management
Team-based practices
Team building
Mentoring

Defined

Identify primary
competencies and
align workforce
activities with them

Participatory culture
Competency-based practices
Career development
Competency development
Workforce planning
Knowledge and skills analysis

Repeatable

Instill basic
discipline into
workforce
activities

Compensation
Training
Performance management
Staffing
Communication
Work environment

Initial

Figure 25.9 The
People Capability
Maturity Model

3. To align the motivation of individuals with that of the organisation

4. To retain valuable human assets (i.e., people with critical knowledge and
    skills) within the organisation.

The P-CMM is a practical tool for improving the management of people in an
organisation because it provides a framework for motivating, recognising, standardising and improving good practice. However, like all capability models created by
the SEI, it is designed for large rather than small companies. It reinforces the need
to recognise the importance of people as individuals and to develop their capabilities. Of course, the complete application of this model is very expensive and probably unnecessary for most organisations. However, it is a helpful guide that can
lead to significant improvements in the capability of organisations to produce high-
quality software.

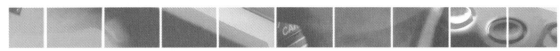

KEY POINTS

■ Selecting staff to work on a project is an important task for project managers. Factors that might be used to select staff include application domain experience, adaptability and personality.

■ People are motivated by interaction with other people, by the recognition of management and their peers, and by being given opportunities for personal development.

■ Software development groups should be small and cohesive. Group leaders should be technically competent and should have administrative and technical support.

■ Communications within a group are influenced by factors such as the status of group members, the size of the group, the gender composition of the group, personalities and available communication channels.

■ Working environments for teams should include spaces where the team can interact and where individual team members can quietly concentrate on their work.

■ The People Capability Maturity Model provides a framework and associated advice for improving the capabilities of people in an organisation and improving the organisation's capability to gain benefits from its human assets.

FURTHER READING

A Handbook of Software and Systems Engineering: Empirical Observations, Laws and Theories. This book is concerned with empirical findings, hypotheses and theories that are relevant to software engineering. Chapter 10 covers user skills, motivation and satisfaction, and discusses theories from psychology that back up the material in this chapter. (A. Andres and D. Rombach, 2003, Addison-Wesley)

Software Management, 6th ed. This is an IEEE tutorial text that has several articles about managing and motivating people. (D. J. Reifer, 2002, Wiley-IEEE Press.)

The People Capability Maturity Model: Guidelines for Improving the Workforce. This book is a comprehensive description of the P-CMM, including guidance on improving individual capability, developing a strong organisational culture, measuring performance and creating a flexible workforce. (B. Curtis, et al., 2001, Addison-Wesley.)

Peopleware: Productive Projects and Teams, 2nd ed. This is a classic book on the importance of treating people properly when managing software projects. It's easy to read and one of the few books that recognises the importance of the place where people work. Strongly recommended. (T. DeMarco and T. Lister, 1999, Dorset House.)

EXERCISES

25.1 Explain why consistency, respect, inclusion and honesty are factors that contribute to effective people management.

25.2 What factors should be taken into account when selecting staff to work on a software development project? Giving reasons for your answer, suggest which of these would be most important in choosing staff for an embedded real-time systems development project to develop a controller for an eye surgery machine.

25.3 Develop the case study example on motivation in Figure 25.4 to include general activities that Alice could introduce to ensure that other members of the team remain motivated.

25.4 Explain why keeping all members of a group informed about progress and technical decisions in a project can improve group cohesiveness.

25.5 Explain what you understand by groupthink. Describe the dangers of this phenomenon and explain how it might be avoided.

25.6 What problems do you think might arise in extreme programming teams where many management decisions are devolved to the team members themselves?

25.7 Why are open-plan and communal offices sometimes less suitable for software development than individual offices? Under what circumstances do you think that open-plan environments might be better?

25.8 Why is the P-CMM an effective framework for improving the management of people in an organisation? Suggest how it may have to be modified if it is to be used in small companies.

25.9 Should managers become friendly and mix socially with more junior members of their group?

25.10 Is it ethical to provide the answers that you think the tester wants rather than saying what you really feel when taking psychological or aptitude tests?

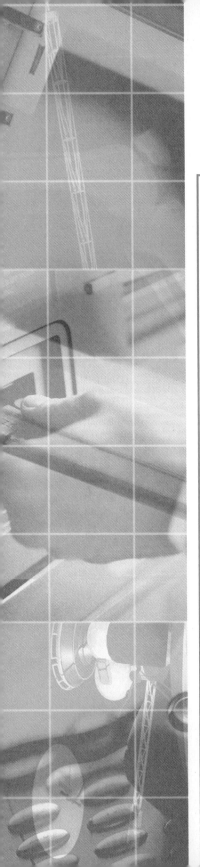

26

Software cost estimation

Objectives

The objective of this chapter is to introduce techniques for estimating the cost and effort required for software production. When you have read this chapter, you will:

■ understand the fundamentals of software costing and reasons why the price of the software may not be directly related to its development cost;

■ have been introduced to three metrics that are used for software productivity assessment;

■ appreciate why a range of techniques should be used when estimating software costs and schedule;

■ understand the principles of the COCOMO II model for algorithmic cost estimation.

Contents

26.1 Software productivity
26.2 Estimation techniques
26.3 Algorithmic cost modelling
26.4 Project duration and staffing

In Chapter 5, I introduced the project planning process where the work in a project is split into a number of separate activities. This earlier discussion of project planning concentrated on ways to represent these activities, their dependencies and the allocation of people to carry out these tasks. In this chapter, I turn to the problem of associating estimates of effort and time with the project activities. Estimation involves answering the following questions:

1. How much effort is required to complete each activity?

2. How much calendar time is needed to complete each activity?

3. What is the total cost of each activity?

Project cost estimation and project scheduling are normally carried out together. The costs of development are primarily the costs of the effort involved, so the effort computation is used in both the cost and the schedule estimate. However, you may have to do some cost estimation before detailed schedules are drawn up. These initial estimates may be used to establish a budget for the project or to set a price for the software for a customer.

There are three parameters involved in computing the total cost of a software development project:

• Hardware and software costs including maintenance

• Travel and training costs

• Effort costs (the costs of paying software engineers).

For most projects, the dominant cost is the effort cost. Computers that are powerful enough for software development are relatively cheap. Although extensive travel costs may be needed when a project is developed at different sites, the travel costs are usually a small fraction of the effort costs. Furthermore, using electronic communications systems such as e-mail, shared web sites and videoconferencing can significantly reduce the travel required. Electronic conferencing also means that travelling time is reduced and time can be used more productively in software development. In one project where I worked, making every other meeting a videoconference rather than a face-to-face meeting reduced travel costs and time by almost 50%.

Effort costs are not just the salaries of the software engineers who are involved in the project. Organisations compute effort costs in terms of overhead costs where they take the total cost of running the organisation and divide this by the number of productive staff. Therefore, the following costs are all part of the total effort cost:

1. Costs of providing, heating and lighting office space

2. Costs of support staff such as accountants, administrators, system managers, cleaners and technicians

3. Costs of networking and communications

4. Costs of central facilities such as a library or recreational facilities

5. Costs of Social Security and employee benefits such as pensions and health insurance.

This overhead factor is usually at least twice the software engineer's salary, depending on the size of the organisation and its associated overheads. Therefore, if a company pays a software engineer $90,000 per year, its total costs are at least $180,000 per year or $15,000 per month.

Once a project is underway, project managers should regularly update their cost and schedule estimates. This helps with the planning process and the effective use of resources. If actual expenditure is significantly greater than the estimates, then the project manager must take some action. This may involve applying for additional resources for the project or modifying the work to be done.

Software costing should be carried out objectively with the aim of accurately predicting the cost of developing the software. If the project cost has been computed as part of a project bid to a customer, a decision then has to be made about the price quoted to the customer. Classically, price is simply cost plus profit. However, the relationship between the project cost and the price to the customer is not usually so simple.

Software pricing must take into account broader organisational, economic, political and business considerations, such as those shown in Figure 26.1. Therefore, there may not be a simple relationship between the price to the customer for the software and the development costs. Because of the organisational considerations involved, project pricing should involve senior management (i.e., those who can make strategic decisions), as well as software project managers.

For example, say a small oil services software company employs 10 engineers at the beginning of a year, but only has contracts in place that require 5 members of the development staff. However, it is Bidding for a very large contract with a major oil company that requires 30 person years of effort over 2 years. The project will not start up for at least 12 months but, if granted, it will transform the finances of the small company. The oil services company gets an opportunity to bid on a project that requires 6 people and has to be completed in 10 months. The costs (including overheads of this project) are estimated at $1.2 million. However, to improve its competitive position, the oil services company bids a price to the customer of $0.8 million. This means that, although it loses money on this contract, it can retain specialist staff for more profitable future projects.

26.1 Software productivity

You can measure productivity in a manufacturing system by counting the number of units that are produced and dividing this by the number of person-hours required

Figure 26.1 Factors
affecting software
pricing

Factor	Description
Market opportunity	A development organisation may quote a low price because it wishes to move into a new segment of the software market. Accepting a low profit on one project may give the organisation the opportunity to make a greater profit later. The experience gained may also help it develop new products.
Cost estimate uncertainty	If an organisation is unsure of its cost estimate, it may increase its price by some contingency over and above its normal profit.
Contractual terms	A customer may be willing to allow the developer to retain ownership of the source code and reuse it in other projects. The price charged may then be less than if the software source code is handed over to the customer.
Requirements volatility	If the requirements are likely to change, an organisation may lower its price to win a contract. After the contract is awarded, high prices can be charged for changes to the requirements.
Financial health	Developers in financial difficulty may lower their price to gain a contract. It is better to make a smaller than normal profit or break even than to go out of business.

to produce them. However, for any software problem, there are many different solutions, each of which has different attributes. One solution may execute more efficiently while another may be more readable and easier to maintain. When solutions with different attributes are produced, comparing their production rates is not really meaningful.

Nevertheless, as a project manager, you may be faced with the problem of estimating the productivity of software engineers. You may need these productivity estimates to help define the project cost or schedule, to inform investment decisions or to assess whether process or technology improvements are effective.

Productivity estimates are usually based on measuring attributes of the software and dividing this by the total effort required for development. There are two types of metric that have been used:

1. *Size-related metrics* These are related to the size of some output from an activity. The most commonly used size-related metric is lines of delivered source code. Other metrics that may be used are the number of delivered object code instructions or the number of pages of system documentation.

2. *Function-related metrics* These are related to the overall functionality of the delivered software. Productivity is expressed in terms of the amount of useful

functionality produced in some given time. Function points and object points are the best-known metrics of this type.

Lines of source code per programmer-month (LOC/pm) is a widely used software productivity metric. You can compute LOC/pm by counting the total number of lines of source code that are delivered, then divide the count by the total time in programmer-months required to complete the project. This time therefore includes the time required for all other activities (requirements, design, coding, testing and documentation) involved in software development.

This approach was first developed when most programming was in FORTRAN, assembly language or COBOL. Then, programs were typed on cards, with one statement on each card. The number of lines of code was easy to count: It corresponded to the number of cards in the program deck. However, programs in languages such as Java or C++ consist of declarations, executable statements and commentary. They may include macro instructions that expand to several lines of code. There may be more than one statement per line. There is not, therefore, a simple relationship between program statements and lines on a listing.

Comparing productivity across programming languages can also give misleading impressions of programmer productivity. The more expressive the programming language, the lower the apparent productivity. This anomaly arises because all software development activities are considered together when computing the development time, but the LOC metric applies only to the programming process. Therefore, if one language requires more lines than another to implement the same functionality, productivity estimates will be anomalous.

For example, consider an embedded real-time system that might be coded in 5,000 lines of assembly code or 1,500 lines of C. The development time for the various phases is shown in Figure 26.2. The assembler programmer has a productivity of 714 lines/month and the high-level language programmer less than half of this—300 lines/month. Yet the development costs for the system developed in C are lower and it is delivered earlier.

An alternative to using code size as the estimated product attribute is to use some measure of the functionality of the code. This avoids the above anomaly, as functionality is independent of implementation language. MacDonell (MacDonell, 1994) briefly describes and compares several function-based measures. The best known of these measures is the function-point count. This was proposed by Albrecht (Albrecht, 1979) and refined by Albrecht and Gaffney (Albrecht and Gaffney, 1983). Garmus and Herron (Garmus and Herron, 2000) describe the practical use of function points in software projects.

Productivity is expressed as the number of function points that are implemented per person-month. A function point is not a single characteristic but is computed by combining several different measurements or estimates. You compute the total number of function points in a program by measuring or estimating the following program features:

Figure 26.2 System development times

	Analysis	Design	Coding	Testing	Documentation
Assembly code	3 weeks	5 weeks	8 weeks	10 weeks	2 weeks
High-level language	3 weeks	5 weeks	4 weeks	6 weeks	2 weeks

	Size	Effort	Productivity
Assembly code	5000 lines	28 weeks	714 lines/month
High-level language	1500 lines	20 weeks	300 lines/month

- external inputs and outputs;
- user interactions;
- external interfaces;
- files used by the system.

Obviously, some inputs and outputs, interactions. and so on are more complex than others and take longer to implement. The function-point metric takes this into account by multiplying the initial function-point estimate by a complexity-weighting factor. You should assess each of these features for complexity and then assign the weighting factor that varies from 3 (for simple external inputs) to 15 for complex internal files. Either the weighting values proposed by Albrecht or values based on local experience may be used.

You can then compute the so-called unadjusted function-point count (UFC) by multiplying each initial count by the estimated weight and summing all values.

$$\text{UFC} = \sum (\text{number of elements of given type}) \times (\text{weight})$$

You then modify this unadjusted function-point count by additional complexity factors that are related to the complexity of the system as a whole. This takes into account the degree of distributed processing, the amount of reuse, the performance, and so on. The unadjusted function-point count is multiplied by these project complexity factors to produce a final function-point count for the overall system.

Symons (Symons, 1988) notes that the subjective nature of complexity estimates means that the function-point count in a program depends on the estimator. Different people have different notions of complexity. There are therefore wide variations in function-point count depending on the estimator's judgement and the type of system being developed. Furthermore, function points are biased towards data-processing systems that are dominated by input and output operations. It is harder to estimate function-point counts for event-driven systems. For this reason, some people think that function points are not a very useful way to measure software productivity (Furey and Kitchenham, 1997; Armour, 2002). However, users of function points argue that, in spite of their flaws, they are effective in practical situations (Banker, et al., 1993; Garmus and Herron, 2000).

Object points (Banker, et al., 1994) are an alternative to function points. They can be used with languages such as database programming languages or scripting languages. Object points are not object classes that may be produced when an object-oriented approach is taken to software development. Rather, the number of object points in a program is a weighted estimate of:

1. *The number of separate screens that are displayed* Simple screens count as 1 object point, moderately complex screens count as 2, and very complex screens count as 3 object points.

2. *The number of reports that are produced* For simple reports, count 2 object points, for moderately complex reports, count 5, and for reports that are likely to be difficult to produce, count 8 object points.

3. *The number of modules in imperative programming languages such as Java or C++ that must be developed to supplement the database programming code* Each of these modules counts as 10 object points.

Object points are used in the COCOMO II estimation model (where they are called application points) that I cover later in this chapter. The advantage of object points over function points is that they are easier to estimate from a high-level software specification. Object points are only concerned with screens, reports and modules in conventional programming languages. They are not concerned with implementation details, and the complexity factor estimation is much simpler.

If function points or object points are used, they can be estimated at an early stage in the development process before decisions that affect the program size have been made. Estimates of these parameters can be made as soon as the external interactions of the system have been designed. At this stage, it is very difficult to produce an accurate estimate of the size of a program in lines of source code.

Function-point and object-point counts can be used in conjunction with lines of code-estimation models. The final code size is calculated from the number of function points. Using historical data analysis, the average number of lines of code, AVC, in a particular language required to implement a function point can be estimated. Values of AVC vary from 200 to 300 LOC/FP in assembly language to 2 to 40 LOC/FP for a database programming language such as SQL. The estimated code size for a new application is then computed as follows:

Code size = AVC × Number of function points

The programming productivity of individuals working in an organisation is affected by a number of factors. Some of the most important of these are summarised in Figure 26.3. However, individual differences in ability are usually more significant than any of these factors. In an early assessment of productivity, Sackman et al. (Sackman, et al., 1968) found that some programmers were more than 10 times

Figure 26.3 Factors affecting software engineering productivity

Factor	Description
Application domain experience	Knowledge of the application domain is essential for effective software development. Engineers who already understand a domain are likely to be the most productive.
Process quality	The development process used can have a significant effect on productivity. This is covered in Chapter 28.
Project size	The larger a project, the more time required for team communications. Less time is available for development so individual productivity is reduced.
Technology support	Good support technology such as CASE tools and configuration management systems can improve productivity.
Working environment	As I discussed in Chapter 25, a quiet working environment with private work areas contributes to improved productivity.

more productive than others. My experience is that this is still true. Large teams are likely to have a mix of abilities and experience and so will have 'average' productivity. In small teams, however, overall productivity is mostly dependent on individual aptitudes and abilities.

Software development productivity varies dramatically across application domains and organisations. For large, complex, embedded systems, productivity has been estimated to be as low as 30 LOC/pm. For straightforward, well-understood application systems, written in a language such as Java, it may be as high as 900 LOC/pm. When measured in terms of object points, Boehm et al. (Boehm, et al., 1995) suggest that productivity varies from 4 object points per month to 50 per month, depending on the type of application, tool support and developer capability.

The problem with measures that rely on the amount produced in a given time period is that they take no account of quality characteristics such as reliability and maintainability. They imply that more always means better. Beck (Beck, 2000), in his discussion of extreme programming, makes an excellent point about estimation. If your approach is based on continuous code simplification and improvement, then counting lines of code doesn't mean much.

These measures also do not take into account the possibility of reusing the software produced, using code generators and other tools that help create the software. What we really want to estimate is the cost of deriving a particular system with given functionality, quality, performance, maintainability, and so on. This is only indirectly related to tangible measures such as the system size.

As a manager, you should not use productivity measurements to make hasty judgements about the abilities of the engineers on your team. If you do, engineers may compromise on quality in order to become more 'productive'. It may be the case that the 'less-productive' programmer produces more reliable code—code that is easier to understand and cheaper to maintain. You should always, therefore, think of productivity measures as providing partial information about programmer productivity. You also need to consider other information about the quality of the programs that are produced.

26.2 Estimation techniques

There is no simple way to make an accurate estimate of the effort required to develop a software system. You may have to make initial estimates on the basis of a high-level user requirements definition. The software may have to run on unfamiliar computers or use new development technology. The people involved in the project and their skills will probably not be known. All of these mean that it is impossible to estimate system development costs accurately at an early stage in a project.

Furthermore, there is a fundamental difficulty in assessing the accuracy of different approaches to cost-estimation techniques. Project cost estimates are often self-fulfilling. The estimate is used to define the project budget, and the product is adjusted so that the budget figure is realised. I do not know of any controlled experiments with project costing where the estimated costs were not used to bias the experiment. A controlled experiment would not reveal the cost estimate to the project manager. The actual costs would then be compared with the estimated project costs. However, such an experiment is probably impossible because of the high costs involved and the number of variables that cannot be controlled.

Nevertheless, organisations need to make software effort and cost estimates. To do so, one or more of the techniques described in Figure 26.4 may be used (Boehm, 1981). All of these techniques rely on experience-based judgements by project managers who use their knowledge of previous projects to arrive at an estimate of the resources required for the project. However, there may be important differences between past and future projects. Many new development methods and techniques have been introduced in the last 10 years. Some examples of the changes that may affect estimates based on experience include:

1. Distributed object systems rather than mainframe-based systems

2. Use of web services

3. Use of ERP or database-centred systems

4. Use of off-the-shelf software rather than original system development

5. Development for and with reuse rather than new development of all parts of a system

Figure 26.4 Cost-estimation techniques

Technique	Description
Algorithmic cost modelling	A model is developed using historical cost information that relates some software metric (usually its size) to the project cost. An estimate is made of that metric and the model predicts the effort required.
Expert judgement	Several experts on the proposed software development techniques and the application domain are consulted. They each estimate the project cost. These estimates are compared and discussed. The estimation process iterates until an agreed estimate is reached.
Estimation by analogy	This technique is applicable when other projects in the same application domain have been completed. The cost of a new project is estimated by analogy with these completed projects. Myers (Myers, 1989) gives a very clear description of this approach.
Parkinson's Law	Parkinson's Law states that work expands to fill the time available. The cost is determined by available resources rather than by objective assessment. If the software has to be delivered in 12 months and 5 people are available, the effort required is estimated to be 60 person-months.
Pricing to win	The software cost is estimated to be whatever the customer has available to spend on the project. The estimated effort depends on the customer's budget and not on the software functionality.

6.   Development using scripting languages such as TCL or Perl (Ousterhout, 1998)

7.   The use of CASE tools and program generators rather than unsupported software development.

If project managers have not worked with these techniques, their previous experience may not help them estimate software project costs. This makes it more difficult for them to produce accurate costs and schedule estimates.

You can tackle the approaches to cost estimation shown in Figure 26.4 using either a top-down or a bottom-up approach. A top-down approach starts at the system level. You start by examining the overall functionality of the product and how that functionality is provided by interacting sub-functions. The costs of system-level activities such as integration, configuration management and documentation are taken into account.

The bottom-up approach, by contrast, starts at the component level. The system is decomposed into components, and you estimate the effort required to develop each of these components. You then add these component costs to compute the effort required for the whole system development.

The disadvantages of the top-down approach are the advantages of the bottom-up approach and vice versa. Top-down estimation can underestimate the costs of solving difficult technical problems associated with specific components such as interfaces to nonstandard hardware. There is no detailed justification of the estimate that is produced. By contrast, bottom-up estimation produces such a justification and considers each component. However, this approach is more likely to underestimate the costs of system activities such as integration. Bottom-up estimation is also more expensive. There must be an initial system design to identify the components to be costed.

Each estimation technique has its own strengths and weaknesses. Each uses different information about the project and the development team, so if you use a single model and this information is not accurate, your final estimate will be wrong. For large projects, therefore, you should use several cost estimation techniques and compare their results. If these predict radically different costs, you probably do not have enough information about the product or the development process. You should look for more information about the product, process or team and repeat the costing process until the estimates converge.

These estimation techniques are applicable where a requirements document for the system has been produced. This should define all users and system requirements. You can therefore make a reasonable estimate of the system functionality that is to be developed. In general, large systems engineering projects will have such a requirements document.

However, in many cases, the costs of many projects must be estimated using only incomplete user requirements for the system. This means that the estimators have very little information with which to work. Requirements analysis and specification is expensive, and the managers in a company may need an initial cost estimate for the system before they can have a budget approved to develop more detailed requirements or a system prototype.

Under these circumstances, "pricing to win" is a commonly used strategy. The notion of pricing to win may seem unethical and unbusinesslike. However, it does have some advantages. A project cost is agreed on the basis of an outline proposal. Negotiations then take place between client and customer to establish the detailed project specification. This specification is constrained by the agreed cost. The buyer and seller must agree on what is acceptable system functionality. The fixed factor in many projects is not the project requirements but the cost. The requirements may be changed so that the cost is not exceeded.

For example, say a company is bidding for a contract to develop a new fuel delivery system for an oil company that schedules deliveries of fuel to its service stations. There is no detailed requirements document for this system so the developers estimate that a price of $900,000 is likely to be competitive and within the oil company's budget. After they are granted the contract, they negotiate the detailed requirements of the system so that basic functionality is delivered; then they estimate the additional costs for other requirements. The oil company does not necessarily lose here because it has awarded the contract to a company that it can trust. The additional requirements may be funded from a future budget, so that the oil company's budgeting is not disrupted by a very high initial software cost.

26.3 Algorithmic cost modelling

Algorithmic cost modelling uses a mathematical formula to predict project costs based on estimates of the project size, the number of software engineers, and other process and product factors. An algorithmic cost model can be built by analysing the costs and attributes of completed projects and finding the closest fit formula to actual experience.

Algorithmic cost models are primarily used to make estimates of software development costs, but Boehm (Boehm, et al., 2000) discusses a range of other uses for algorithmic cost estimates, including estimates for investors in software companies, estimates of alternative strategies to help assess risks, and estimates to inform decisions about reuse, redevelopment or outsourcing.

In its most general form, an algorithmic cost estimate for software cost can be expressed as:

$$\text{Effort} = A \times \text{Size}^B \times M$$

A is a constant factor that depends on local organisational practices and the type of software that is developed. Size may be either an assessment of the code size of the software or a functionality estimate expressed in function or object points. The value of exponent B usually lies between 1 and 1.5. M is a multiplier made by combining process, product and development attributes, such as the dependability requirements for the software and the experience of the development team

Most algorithmic estimation models have an exponential component (B in the above equation) that is associated with the size estimate. This reflects the fact that costs do not normally increase linearly with project size. As the size of the software increases, extra costs are incurred because of the communication overhead of larger teams, more complex configuration management, more difficult system integration, and so on. Therefore, the larger the system, the larger the value of this exponent.

Unfortunately, all algorithmic models suffer from the same fundamental difficulties:

1. *It is often difficult to estimate* Size *at an early stage in a project when only a specification is available.* Function-point and object-point estimates are easier to produce than estimates of code size but are often still inaccurate.

2. *The estimates of the factors contributing to* B *and* M *are subjective.* Estimates vary from one person to another, depending on their background and experience with the type of system that is being developed.

The number of lines of source code in the delivered system is the basic metric used in many algorithmic cost models. Size estimation may involve estimation by analogy with other projects, estimation by converting function or object points to code size, estimation by ranking the sizes of system components and using a known reference component to estimate the component size, or it may simply be a question of engineering judgement.

Accurate code size estimation is difficult at an early stage in a project because the code size is affected by design decisions that have not yet been made. For example, an application that requires complex data management may either use a commercial database or implement its own data-management system. If a commercial database is used, the code size will be smaller but additional effort may be needed to overcome the performance limitations of the commercial product.

The programming language used for system development also affects the number of lines of code to be developed. A language such as Java might mean that more lines of code are necessary than if C (say) were used. However, this extra code allows more compile-time checking so validation costs are likely to be reduced. How should this be taken into account? Furthermore, it may be possible to reuse a significant amount of code from previous projects and the size estimate has to be adjusted to take this into account.

If you use an algorithmic cost estimation model, you should develop a range of estimates (worst, expected and best) rather than a single estimate and apply the costing formula to all of them. Estimates are most likely to be accurate when you understand the type of software that is being developed, when you have calibrated the costing model using local data, and when programming language and hardware choices are predefined.

The accuracy of the estimates produced by an algorithmic model depends on the system information that is available. As the software process proceeds, more information becomes available so estimates become more and more accurate. If the initial estimate of effort required is x months of effort, this range may be from $0.25x$ to $4x$ when the system is first proposed. This narrows during the development process, as shown in Figure 26.5. This figure, adapted from Boehm's paper (Boehm, et al., 1995), reflects experience of a large number of software development projects. Of course, just before the system is delivered, a very accurate estimate can be made.

26.3.1 The COCOMO model

A number of algorithmic models have been proposed as the basis for estimating the effort, schedule and costs of a software project. These are conceptually similar but use different parameter values. The model that I discuss here is the COCOMO model. The COCOMO model is an empirical model that was derived by collecting data from a large number of software projects. These data were analysed to discover formulae that were the best fit to the observations. These formulae link the size of the system and product, project and team factors to the effort to develop the system.

I have chosen to use the COCOMO model for several reasons:

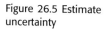

Figure 26.5 Estimate uncertainty

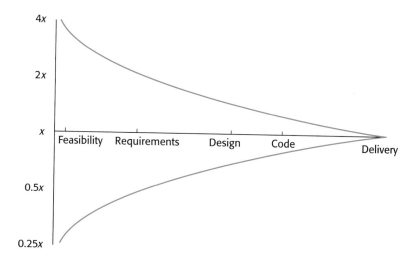

1. It is well documented, available in the public domain and supported by public domain and commercial tools.

2. It has been widely used and evaluated in a range of organisations.

3. It has a long pedigree from its first instantiation in 1981 (Boehm, 1981), through a refinement tailored to Ada software development (Boehm and Royce, 1989), to its most recent version, COCOMO II, published in 2000 (Boehm, et al., 2000).

The COCOMO models are comprehensive, with a large number of parameters that can each take a range of values. They are so complex that I cannot give a complete description here. Rather, I simply discuss their essential characteristics to give you a basic understanding of algorithmic cost models.

The first version of the COCOMO model (COCOMO 81) was a three-level model where the levels corresponded to the detail of the analysis of the cost estimate. The first level (basic) provided an initial rough estimate; the second level modified this using a number of project and process multipliers; and the most detailed level produced estimates for different phases of the project. Figure 26.6 shows the basic COCOMO formula for different types of projects. The multiplier **M** reflects product, project and team characteristics.

COCOMO 81 assumed that the software would be developed according to a waterfall process (see Chapter 4) using standard imperative programming languages such as C or FORTRAN. However, there have been radical changes to software development since this initial version was proposed. Prototyping and incremental development are commonly used process models. Software is now often developed by

Project complexity	Formula	Description
Simple	$PM = 2.4\ (KDSI)^{1.05} \times M$	Well-understood applications developed by small teams
Moderate	$PM = 3.0\ (KDSI)^{1.12} \times M$	More complex projects where team members may have limited experience of related systems
Embedded	$PM = 3.6\ (KDSI)^{1.20} \times M$	Complex projects where the software is part of a strongly coupled complex of hardware, software, regulations and operational procedures

Figure 26.6 The basic COCOMO 81 model

assembling reusable components with off-the-shelf systems and 'gluing' them together with scripting language. Data-intensive systems are developed using a database programming language such as SQL and a commercial database management system. Existing software is re-engineered to create new software. CASE tool support for most software process activities is now available.

To take these changes into account, the COCOMO II model recognises different approaches to software development such as prototyping, development by component composition and use of database programming. COCOMO II supports a spiral model of development (see Chapter 4) and embeds several sub-models that produce increasingly detailed estimates. These can be used in successive rounds of the development spiral. Figure 26.7 shows COCOMO II sub-models and where they are used.

The sub-models that are part of the COCOMO II model are:

1. *An application-composition model* This assumes that systems are created from reusable components, scripting or database programming. It is designed to make estimates of prototype development. Software size estimates are based on application points, and a simple size/productivity formula is used to estimate the effort required. Application points are the same as object points discussed in Section 26.1, but the name was changed to avoid confusion with objects in object-oriented development.

2. *An early design model* This model is used during early stages of the system design after the requirements have been established. Estimates are based on function points, which are then converted to number of lines of source code. The formula follows the standard form discussed above with a simplified set of seven multipliers.

3. *A reuse model* This model is used to compute the effort required to integrate reusable components and/or program code that is automatically generated by design or program translation tools. It is usually used in conjunction with the post-architecture model.

4. *A post-architecture model* Once the system architecture has been designed, a more accurate estimate of the software size can be made. Again this model uses

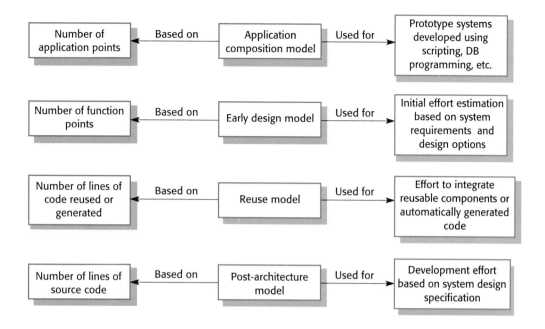

Figure 26.7 The
COCOMO II models

the standard formula for cost estimation discussed above. However, it includes
a more extensive set of 17 multipliers reflecting personnel capability and product and project characteristics.

Of course, in large systems, different parts may be developed using different technologies, and you may not have to estimate all parts of the system to the same level
of accuracy. In such cases, you can use the appropriate sub-model for each part of
the system and combine the results to create a composite estimate.

The application-composition model

The application-composition model was introduced into COCOMO II to support the
estimation of effort required for prototyping projects and for projects where the software is developed by composing existing components. It is based on an estimate
of weighted application points (object points) divided by a standard estimate of
application-point productivity. The estimate is then adjusted according to the difficulty of developing each object point (Boehm, et al., 2000). Programmer productivity also depends on the developer's experience and capability as well as the
capabilities of the CASE tools used to support development. Figure 26.8 shows the
levels of object-point productivity suggested by the model developers (Boehm, et
al., 1995).

Application composition usually involves significant software reuse, and some
of the total number of application points in the system may be implemented with
reusable components. Consequently, you have to adjust the estimate based on the

Figure 26.8 Object-point productivity

Developer's experience and capability	Very low	Low	Nominal	High	Very high
CASE maturity and capability	Very low	Low	Nominal	High	Very high
PROD (NOP/month)	4	7	13	25	50

total number of application points to take into account the percentage of reuse expected. Therefore, the final formula for effort computation for system prototypes is:

$$PM = (NAP \times (1 - \%reuse/100)) / PROD$$

PM is the effort estimate in person-months. **NAP** is the total number of application points in the delivered system. **%reuse** is an estimate of the amount of reused code in the development. **PROD** is the object-point productivity as shown in Figure 26.8. The model simplistically assumes that there is no additional effort involved in reuse.

The early design model

This model is used once user requirements have been agreed and initial stages of the system design process are underway. However, you don't need a detailed architectural design to make these initial estimates. Your goal at this stage should be to make an approximate estimate without undue effort. Consequently, you make various simplifying assumptions, such as that the effort involved in integrating reusable code is zero. Early design estimates are most useful for option exploration where you need to compare different ways of implementing the user requirements.

The estimates produced at this stage are based on the standard formula for algorithmic models, namely:

$$Effort = A \times Size^B \times M$$

Based on his own large data set, Boehm proposes that the coefficient **A** should be 2.94. The size of the system is expressed in KSLOC, which is the number of thousands of lines of source code. You calculate KSLOC by estimating the number of function points in the software. You then use standard tables that relate software size to function points for different programming languages to compute an initial estimate of the system size in KSLOC.

The exponent **B** reflects the increased effort required as the size of the project increases. This is not fixed for different types of systems, as in COCOMO 81, but can vary from 1.1 to 1.24 depending on the novelty of the project, the development flexibility, the risk resolution processes used, the cohesion of the development team and the process maturity level (see Chapter 28) of the organisation. I discuss how the value of this exponent is calculated using these parameters in the description of the COCOMO II post-architecture model.

The multiplier **M** in COCOMO II is based on a simplified set of seven project and process characteristics that influence the estimate. These can increase or decrease the effort required. These characteristics used in the early design model are product reliability and complexity (**RCPX**), reuse required (**RUSE**), platform difficulty (**PDIF**), personnel capability (**PERS**), personnel experience (**PREX**), schedule (**SCED**) and support facilities (**FCIL**). You estimate values for these attributes using a six-point scale where 1 corresponds to very low values for these multipliers and 6 corresponds to very high values.

This results in an effort computation as follows:

$$PM = 2.94 \times Size^B \times M$$

where:

$$M = PERS \times RCPX \times RUSE \times PDIF \times PREX \times FCIL \times SCED$$

The reuse model

As I have discussed in Chapters 18 and 19, software reuse is now common, and most large systems include a significant percentage of code that is reused from previous developments. The reuse model is used to estimate the effort required to integrate reusable or generated code.

COCOMO II considers reused code to be of two types. Black-box code is code that can be reused without understanding the code or making changes to it. The development effort for black-box code is taken to be zero. Code that has to be adapted to integrate it with new code or other reused components is called white-box code. Some development effort is required to reuse this because it has to be understood and modified before it can work correctly in the system.

In addition, many systems include automatically generated code from program translators that generate code from system models. This is a form of reuse where standard templates are embedded in the generator. The system model is analysed, and code based on these standard templates with additional details from the system model is generated. The COCOMO II reuse model includes a separate model to estimate the costs associated with this generated code.

For code that is automatically generated, the model estimates the number of person months required to integrate this code. The formula for effort estimation is:

$$PM_{Auto} = (ASLOC \times AT/100) / ATPROD \qquad \text{// Estimate for generated code}$$

AT is the percentage of adapted code that is automatically generated and **ATPROD** is the productivity of engineers in integrating such code. Boehm et al. (Boehm, et al., 2000) have measured **ATPROD** to be about 2,400 source statements per month. Therefore, if there is a total of 20,000 lines of white-box reused code in a system and 30% of this is automatically generated, then the effort required to integrate this generated code is:

(20,000 × 30/100) / 2400 = 2.5 person months   //Generated code example

The other component of the reuse model is used when a system includes some new code and some reused white-box components that have to be integrated. In this case, the reuse model does not compute the effort directly. Rather, based on the number of lines of code that are reused, it calculates a figure that represents the equivalent number of lines of new code.

Therefore, if 30,000 lines of code are to be reused, the new equivalent size estimate might be 6,000. Essentially, reusing 30,000 lines of code is taken to be equivalent to writing 6,000 lines of new code. This calculated figure is added to the number of lines of new code to be developed in the COCOMO II post-architecture model.

The estimates in this reuse model are:

ASLOC–the number of lines of code in the components that have to be adapted;
ESLOC–the equivalent number of lines of new source code.

The formula used to compute **ESLOC** takes into account the effort required for software understanding, for making changes to the reused code and for making changes to the system to integrate that code. It also takes into account the amount of code that is automatically generated where the development effort is calculated, as explained earlier in this section.

The following formula is used to calculate the number of equivalent lines of source code:

$$\text{ESLOC} = \text{ASLOC} \times (1 - \text{AT}/100) \times \text{AAM}$$

ASLOC is reduced according to the percentage of automatically generated code. **AAM** is the Adaptation Adjustment Multiplier, which takes into account the effort required to reuse code. Simplistically, **AAM** is the sum of three components:

1. An adaptation component (referred to as **AAF**) that represents the costs of making changes to the reused code. This includes components that take into account design, code and integration changes.

2. An understanding component (referred to as **SU**) that represents the costs of understanding the code to be reused and the familiarity of the engineer with the code. **SU** ranges from 50 for complex unstructured code to 10 for well-written, object-oriented code.

3. An assessment factor (referred to as **AA**) that represents the costs of reuse decision-making. That is, some analysis is always required to decide whether code can be reused, and this is included in the cost as **AA**. **AA** varies from 0 to 8 depending on the amount of analysis effort required.

The reuse model is a nonlinear model. Some effort is required if reuse is considered to make an assessment of whether reuse is possible. Furthermore, as more and more reuse is contemplated, the costs per code unit reused drop as the fixed understanding and assessment costs are spread across more lines of code.

The post-architecture level

The post-architecture model is the most detailed of the COCOMO II models. It is used once an initial architectural design for the system is available so the sub-system structure is known.

The estimates produced at the post-architecture level are based on the same basic formula ($PM = A \times Size^B \times M$) used in the early design estimates. However, the size estimate for the software should be more accurate by this stage in the estimation process. In addition, a much more extensive set of product, process and organisational attributes (17 rather than 7) are used to refine the initial effort computation. It is possible to use more attributes at this stage because you have more information about the software to be developed and the development process.

The estimate of the code size in the post-architecture model is computed using three components:

1. An estimate of the total number of lines of new code to be developed

2. An estimate of the equivalent number of source lines of code (ESLOC) calculated using the reuse model

3. An estimate of the number of lines of code that have to be modified because of changes to the requirements.

These three estimates are added to give the total code size in KSLOC that you use in the effort computation formula. The final component in the estimate—the number of lines of modified code—reflects the fact that software requirements always change. The system programs have to reflect these requirements changes so additional code has to be developed. Of course, estimating the number of lines of code that will change is not easy, and there will often be even more uncertainty in this figure than in development estimates.

The exponent term (B) in the effort computation formula had three possible values in COCOMO 1. These were related to the levels of project complexity. As projects become more complex, the effects of increasing system size become more significant. However, good organisational practices and procedures can control this 'diseconomy of scale'. This is recognised in COCOMO II, where the range of values for the exponent B is continuous rather than discrete. The exponent is based on five scale factors, as shown in Figure 26.9. These factors are rated on a six-point scale from Very low to Extra high (5 to 0). You should then add the ratings, divide them by 100 and add the result to 1.01 to get the exponent that should be used.

To illustrate this, imagine that an organisation is taking on a project in a domain where it has little previous experience. The project client has not defined the

Figure 26.9 Scale
factors used in the
COCOMO II
exponent
computation

Scale factor	Explanation
Precedentedness	Reflects the previous experience of the organisation with this type of project. Very low means no previous experience; Extra high means that the organisation is completely familiar with this application domain.
Development flexibility	Reflects the degree of flexibility in the development process. Very low means a prescribed process is used; Extra high means that the client sets only general goals.
Architecture/risk resolution	Reflects the extent of risk analysis carried out. Very low means little analysis; Extra high means a complete and thorough risk analysis.
Team cohesion	Reflects how well the development team know each other and work together. Very low means very difficult interactions; Extra high means an integrated and effective team with no communication problems.
Process maturity	Reflects the process maturity of the organisation. The computation of this value depends on the CMM Maturity Questionnaire, but an estimate can be achieved by subtracting the CMM process maturity level from 5.

process to be used and has not allowed time in the project schedule for significant risk analysis. A new development team must be put together to implement this system. The organisation has recently put a process improvement programme in place and has been rated as a Level 2 organisation according to the CMM model (see Chapter 28). Possible values for the ratings used in exponent calculation are:

- *Precedentedness* This is a new project for the organisation—rated Low (4)
- *Development flexibility* No client involvement—rated Very high (1)
- *Architecture/risk resolution* No risk analysis carried out—rated Very low (5)
- *Team cohesion* New team so no information—rated Nominal (3)
- *Process maturity* Some process control in place—rated Nominal (3)

The sum of these values is 16, so you calculate the exponent by adding 0.16 to 1.01, getting a value of 1.17.

The attributes (Figure 26.10) that are used to adjust the initial estimates and create multiplier M in the post-architecture model fall into four classes:

1. Product attributes are concerned with required characteristics of the software product being developed.

2. Computer attributes are constraints imposed on the software by the hardware platform.

Figure 26.10 Project
cost drivers

Attribute	Type	Description
RELY	Product	Required system reliability
CPLX	Product	Complexity of system modules
DOCU	Product	Extent of documentation required
DATA	Product	Size of database used
RUSE	Product	Required percentage of reusable components
TIME	Computer	Execution time constraint
PVOL	Computer	Volatility of development platform
STOR	Computer	Memory constraints
ACAP	Personnel	Capability of project analysts
PCON	Personnel	Personnel continuity
PCAP	Personnel	Programmer capability
PEXP	Personnel	Programmer experience in project domain
AEXP	Personnel	Analyst experience in project domain
LTEX	Personnel	Language and tool experience
TOOL	Project	Use of software tools
SCED	Project	Development schedule compression
SITE	Project	Extent of multisite working and quality of inter-site communications

3. Personnel attributes are multipliers that take the experience and capabilities of the people working on the project into account.

4. Project attributes are concerned with the particular characteristics of the software development project.

Figure 26.11 shows how these cost drivers influence effort estimates. I have taken a value for the exponent of 1.17 as discussed in the above example and assumed that **RELY, CPLX, STOR, TOOL** and **SCED** are the key cost drivers in the project. All of the other cost drivers have a nominal value of 1, so they do not affect the computation of the effort.

Figure 26.11 The
effect of cost drivers
on effort estimates

Exponent value	1.17
System size (including factors for reuse and requirements volatility)	128,000 DSI
Initial COCOMO estimate without cost drivers	**730 person-months**
Reliability	Very high, multiplier = 1.39
Complexity	Very high, multiplier = 1.3
Memory constraint	High, multiplier = 1.21
Tool use	Low, multiplier = 1.12
Schedule	Accelerated, multiplier = 1.29
Adjusted COCOMO estimate	**2306 person-months**
Reliability	Very low, multiplier = 0.75
Complexity	Very low, multiplier = 0.75
Memory constraint	None, multiplier = 1
Tool use	Very high, multiplier = 0.72
Schedule	Normal, multiplier = 1
Adjusted COCOMO estimate	**295 person-months**

In Figure 26.11, I have assigned maximum and minimum values to the key cost drivers to show how they influence the effort estimate. The values taken are those from the COCOMO II reference manual (Boehm, 1997). You can see that high values for the cost drivers lead an effort estimate that is more than three times the initial estimate, whereas low values reduce the estimate to about one third of the original. This highlights the vast differences between different types of project and the difficulties of transferring experience from one application domain to another.

This formulae proposed by the developers of the COCOMO II model reflects their experience and data, but it is an extremely complex model to understand and use. There are many attributes and considerable scope for uncertainty in estimating their values. In principle, each user of the model should calibrate the model and the attribute values according to its own historical project data, as this will reflect local circumstances that affect the model.

In practice, however, few organisations have collected enough data from past projects in a form that supports model calibration. Practical use of COCOMO II therefore has to start with the published values for the model parameters, and it is impossible for a user to know how closely these relate to their own situation. This means that the practical use of the COCOMO model is limited. Very large organisations may have the resources to employ a cost-modelling expert to adapt and use the COCOMO II models. However, for the majority of companies, the cost of calibrating and learning to use an algorithmic model such as the COCOMO model is so high that they are unlikely to introduce this approach.

26.3.2 Algorithmic cost models in project planning

One of the most valuable uses of algorithmic cost modelling is to compare different ways of investing money to reduce project costs. This is particularly important where you have to make hardware/software cost trade-offs and where you may have to recruit new staff with specific project skills. The algorithmic code model helps you assess the risks of each option. Applying the cost model reveals the financial exposure that is associated with different management decisions.

Consider an embedded system to control an experiment that is to be launched into space. Spaceborne experiments have to be very reliable and are subject to stringent weight limits. The number of chips on a circuit board may have to be minimised. In terms of the COCOMO model, the multipliers based on computer constraints and reliability are greater than 1.

There are three components to be taken into account in costing this project:

1. The cost of the target hardware to execute the system

2. The cost of the platform (computer plus software) to develop the system

3. The cost of the effort required to develop the software.

Figure 26.13 shows some possible options for this project. These include spending more on target hardware to reduce software costs or investing in better development tools.

Additional hardware costs may be acceptable because the system is a specialised system that does not have to be mass-produced. If hardware is embedded in consumer products, however, investing in target hardware to reduce software costs increases the unit cost of the product, irrespective of the number sold, which is usually undesirable.

Figure 26.13 shows the hardware, software and total costs for the options A–F shown in Figure 26.12. Applying the COCOMO II model without cost drivers predicts an effort of 45 person-months to develop an embedded software system for this application. The average cost for one person-month of effort is $15,000.

The relevant multipliers are based on storage and execution time constraints (TIME and STOR), the availability of tool support (cross-compilers, etc.) for the development system (TOOL), and development team's experience platform experience (LTEX). In all options, the reliability multiplier (RELY) is 1.39, indicating that significant extra effort is needed to develop a reliable system.

The software cost (SC) is computed as follows:

SC = Effort estimate × RELY × TIME × STOR × TOOL × EXP × $15,000

Option A represents the cost of building the system with existing support and staff. It represents a baseline for comparison. All other options involve either more hardware expenditure or the recruitment (with associated costs and risks) of new staff. Option B shows that upgrading hardware does not necessarily reduce costs. The staff lack experience with the new hardware so the increase in the experience multiplier negates the reduction in the STOR and TIME multipliers. It is actually more cost-effective to upgrade memory rather than the whole computer configuration.

Figure 26.12
Management options

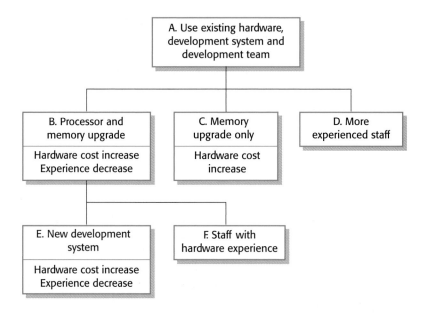

Option	RELY	STOR	TIME	TOOLS	LTEX	Total effort	Software cost	Hardware cost	Total cost
A	1.39	1.06	1.11	0.86	1	63	949393	100000	1049393
B	1.39	1	1	1.12	1.22	88	1313550	120000	1402025
C	1.39	1	1.11	0.86	1	60	895653	105000	1000653
D	1.39	1.06	1.11	0.86	0.84	51	769008	100000	897490
EX	1.39	1	1	0.72	1.22	56	844425	220000	1044159
F	1.39	1	1	1.12	0.84	57	851180	120000	1002706

Figure 26.13 Cost of
Management options

Option D appears to offer the lowest costs for all basic estimates. No additional hardware expenditure is involved but new staff must be recruited onto the project. If these are already available in the company, this is probably the best option to choose. If not, they must be recruited externally, which involves significant costs and risks. These may mean that the cost advantages of this option are much less significant than suggested by Figure 26.13. Option C offers a saving of almost $50,000 with virtually no associated risk. Conservative project managers would probably select this option rather than the riskier Option D.

The comparisons show the importance of staff experience as a multiplier. If good quality people with the right experience are recruited, this can significantly reduce project costs. This is consistent with the discussion of productivity factors in

Section 26.1. It also reveals that investment in new hardware and tools may not be cost-effective. Some engineers may prefer this option because it gives them an opportunity to learn about and work with new systems. However, the loss of experience is a more significant effect on the system cost than the savings that arise from using the new hardware system.

26.4 Project duration and staffing

As well as estimating the effort required to develop a software system and the overall project costs, project managers must also estimate how long the software will take to develop and when staff will be needed to work on the project. The development time for the project is called the project schedule. Increasingly, organisations are demanding shorter development schedules so that their products can be brought to market before their competitor's.

The relationship between the number of staff working on a project, the total effort required and the development time is not linear. As the number of staff increases, more effort may be needed. The reason for this is that people spend more time communicating and defining interfaces between the parts of the system developed by other people. Doubling the number of staff (for example) therefore does not mean that the duration of the project will be halved.

The COCOMO model includes a formula to estimate the calendar time (TDEV) required to complete a project. The time computation formula is the same for all COCOMO levels:

$$TDEV = 3 \times (PM)^{(0.33+0.2*(B-1.01))}$$

PM is the effort computation and B is the exponent computed, as discussed above (B is 1 for the early prototyping model). This computation predicts the nominal schedule for the project.

However, the predicted project schedule and the schedule required by the project plan are not necessarily the same thing. The planned schedule may be shorter or longer than the nominal predicted schedule. However, there is obviously a limit to the extent of schedule changes, and the COCOMO II model predicts this:

$$TDEV = 3 \times (PM)^{(0.33+0.2*(B-1.01))} \times SCEDPercentage/100$$

SCEDPercentage is the percentage increase or decrease in the nominal schedule. If the predicted figure then differs significantly from the planned schedule, it suggests that there is a high risk of problems delivering the software as planned.

To illustrate the COCOMO development schedule computation, assume that 60 months of effort are estimated to develop a software system (Option C in Figure

26.12). Assume that the value of exponent B is 1.17. From the schedule equation, the time required to complete the project is:

TDEV = 3 × (60)$^{0.36}$ = 13 months

In this case, there is no schedule compression or expansion, so the last term in the formula has no effect on the computation.

An interesting implication of the COCOMO model is that the time required to complete the project is a function of the total effort required for the project. It does not depend on the number of software engineers working on the project. This confirms the notion that adding more people to a project that is behind schedule is unlikely to help that schedule to be regained. Myers (Myers, 1989) discusses the problems of schedule acceleration. He suggests that projects are likely to run into significant problems if they try to develop software without allowing sufficient calendar time.

KEY POINTS

■ There is not necessarily a simple relationship between the price charged for a system and its development costs. Organisational factors may mean that the price charged is increased to compensate for increased risk or decreased to gain competitive advantage.

■ Factors that affect software productivity include individual aptitude (the dominant factor), domain experience, the development process, the size of the project, tool support and the working environment.

■ Software is often priced to gain a contract, and the functionality of the system is then adjusted to meet the estimated price.

■ There are various techniques of software cost estimation. In preparing an estimate, several different techniques should be used. If the estimates diverge widely, this means that inadequate estimating information is available.

■ The COCOMO II costing model is a well-developed algorithmic cost model that takes project, product, hardware and personnel attributes into account when formulating a cost estimate. It also includes a means of estimating development schedules.

■ Algorithmic cost models can be used to support quantitative option analysis. They allow the cost of various options to be computed and, even with errors, the options can be compared on an objective basis.

■ The time required to complete a project is not simply proportional to the number of people working on the project. Adding more people to a late project can increase rather than decrease the time required to finish the project.

Dividing the effort required on a project by the development schedule does not give a useful indication of the number of people required for the project team. Generally, only a small number of people are needed at the start of a project to carry out the initial design. The team then builds up to a peak during the development and testing of the system, and finally the team size declines as the system is prepared for deployment. A very rapid buildup of project staff has been shown to correlate with project schedule slippage. Project managers should therefore avoid adding too many staff to a project early in its lifetime.

The effort build-up can be modelled by what is called a Rayleigh curve (Londeix, 1987) and Putnam's estimation model (Putnam, 1978), which incorporates a model of project staffing based around these curves. Putnam's model also includes development time as a key factor. As development time is reduced, the effort required to develop the system grows exponentially.

FURTHER READING

'Ten unmyths of project estimation'. A pragmatic article that discusses the practical difficulties of project estimation and challenges some fundamental assumptions in this area. (P. Armour, *Comm. ACM*, 45(11), November 2002.)

Software Cost Estimation with COCOMO II. This is the definitive book on the COCOMO II model. It provides a complete description of the model with many examples and includes software that implements the model. It's extremely detailed and not light reading. Boehm's paper below is, in my view, an easier introduction to the model. (B. Boehm, et al., 2000, Prentice Hall.)

Software Project Management: Readings and Cases. A selection of papers and case studies on software project management that is particularly strong in its coverage of algorithmic cost modelling. (C. F. Kemerer (ed.), 1997, Irwin.)

'Cost models for future software life cycle processes: COCOMO II'. An introduction to the COCOMO II cost estimation model that includes rationale for the formulae used. Easier to read than the definitive book. (B. Boehm *et al., Annals of Software Engineering*, 1, Balzer Science Publishers, 1995.)

EXERCISES

26.1 Under what circumstance might a company charge a much higher price for a software system than that suggested by the cost estimate plus a normal profit margin?

26.2 Describe two metrics that have been used to measure programmer productivity. Comment briefly on the advantages and disadvantages of each of these metrics.

26.3   In the development of large, embedded real-time systems, suggest five factors that are likely to have a significant effect on the productivity of the software development team.

26.4   Cost estimates are inherently risky irrespective of the estimation technique used. Suggest four ways in which the risk in a cost estimate can be reduced.

26.5   Why should several estimation techniques be used to produce a cost estimate for a large, complex software system?

26.6   A software manager is in charge of the development of a safety-critical software system that is designed to control a radiotherapy machine to treat patients suffering from cancer. This system is embedded in the machine and must run on a special-purpose processor with a fixed amount of memory (8 Mbytes). The machine communicates with a patient database system to obtain the details of the patient and, after treatment, automatically records the radiation dose delivered and other treatment details in the database.

The COCOMO method is used to estimate the effort required to develop this system and an estimate of 26 person-months is computed. All cost driver multipliers were set to 1 when making this estimate.

Explain why this estimate should be adjusted to take project, personnel, product and organisational factors into account. Suggest four factors that might have significant effects on the initial COCOMO estimate and propose possible values for these factors. Justify why you have included each factor.

26.7   Give three reasons why algorithmic cost estimates prepared in different organisations are not directly comparable

26.8   Explain how the algorithmic approach to cost estimation may be used by project managers for option analysis. Suggest a situation where managers may choose an approach that is not based on the lowest project cost.

26.9   Some very large software projects involve writing millions of lines of code. Suggest how useful the cost estimation models are likely to be for such systems. Why might the assumptions on which they are based be invalid for very large software systems?

26.10 Is it ethical for a company to quote a low price for a software contract knowing that the requirements are ambiguous and that they can charge a high price for subsequent changes requested by the customer?

26.11 Should measured productivity be used by managers during the staff appraisal process? What safeguards are necessary to ensure that quality is not affected by this?

27

Quality management

Objectives

The objectives of this chapter are to introduce software quality management and software measurement. When you have read this chapter, you will:

- understand the quality management process and the central process activities of quality assurance, quality planning and quality control;

- understand the importance of standards in the quality management process;

- understand what software metrics are and the differences between predictor metrics and control metrics;

- understand how measurement may be helpful in assessing some software quality attributes;

- be aware of the current limitations of software measurement.

Contents

The quality of software has improved significantly over the past 15 years. One reason for this is that companies have adopted new techniques and technology such as the use of object-oriented development and associated CASE support. In addition, however, there has been a greater awareness of the importance of software quality management and the adoption of quality management techniques from manufacturing in the software industry.

However, software quality is a complex concept that is not directly comparable with quality in manufacturing. In manufacturing, the notion of quality has been that the developed product should meet its specification (Crosby, 1979). In an ideal world this definition should apply to all products but, for software systems, there are problems with this:

1. The specification should be oriented towards the characteristics of the product that the customer wants. However, the development organisation may also have requirements (such as maintainability requirements) that are not included in the specification.

2. We do not know how to specify certain quality characteristics (e.g., maintainability) in an unambiguous way.

3. As I discussed in Part 1, which covered requirements engineering, it is very difficult to write complete software specifications. Therefore, although a software product may conform to its specification, users may not consider it to be a high-quality product because it does not meet their expectations.

You have to recognise the problems with existing software specifications and therefore design quality procedures that do not rely on having a perfect specification. In particular, software attributes such as maintainability, security or efficiency cannot be specified explicitly. However, they have a large effect on the perceived quality of the system. I discuss these attributes in Section 27.3.

Some people think that quality can be achieved by defining standards, and organisational quality procedures that check that these standards are followed by the software development team. Their argument is that standards should encapsulate good practice; following this good practice inevitably leads to high-quality products. In practice, however, I think that there is much more to quality management than standards and the associated bureaucracy to ensure that these have been followed.

Good quality managers aim to develop a 'quality culture' where everyone responsible for product development is committed to achieving a high level of product quality. They encourage teams to take responsibility for the quality of their work and to develop new approaches to quality improvement. While standards and procedures are the basis of quality management, experienced quality managers recognise that there are intangible aspects to software quality (elegance, readability, etc.) that cannot be embodied in standards. They support people who are interested in these intangible aspects of quality and encourage professional behaviour in all team members.

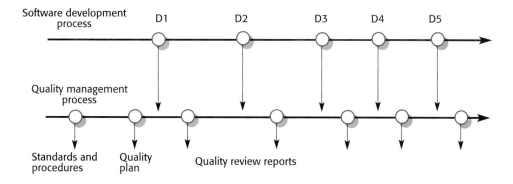

Software development process

D1   D2   D3   D4   D5

Quality management process

Standards and procedures

Quality plan

Quality review reports

Figure 27.1 Quality management and software development

Formalised quality management is particularly important for teams that are developing large and complex systems. The quality documentation is a record of what has been done by each sub-group in the project. It helps people check that important tasks have not been forgotten or that one part of the team has not made incorrect assumptions about what other teams have done. The quality documentation is also a means of communication over the lifetime of a system. It allows the groups responsible for system evolution to trace what the development team have done.

For smaller systems, quality management is still important but a more informal approach can be adopted. Not as much paperwork is needed because a small development team can communicate informally. The key quality issue for small systems development is establishing a quality culture and ensuring that all team members have a positive approach to software quality.

Software quality management for large systems can be structured into three main activities:

1. *Quality assurance* The establishment of a framework of organisational procedures and standards that lead to high-quality software

2. *Quality planning* The selection of appropriate procedures and standards from this framework, adapted for a specific software project

3. *Quality control* The definition and enactment of processes that ensure the software development team have followed project quality procedures and standards

Quality management provides an independent check on the software development process. The quality management process checks the project deliverables to ensure that they are consistent with organisational standards and goals (Figure 27.1). The quality assurance team should be independent from the development team so that they can take an objective view of the software. They report problems and difficulties to senior management in the organisation.

An independent team should be responsible for quality management and should report to management above the project manager level. The quality management team should not be associated with any particular development group but should take organisation-

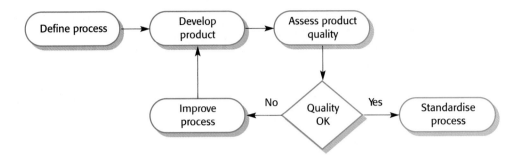

Figure 27.2 Process-based quality

wide responsibility for quality management. The reason for this is that project managers have to maintain the project budget and schedule. If problems arise, they may be tempted to compromise on product quality so that they meet their schedule. An independent quality management team ensures that the organisational goals of quality are not compromised by short-term budget and schedule considerations.

27.1 Process and product quality

A fundamental assumption of quality management is that the quality of the development process directly affects the quality of delivered products. This assumption comes from manufacturing systems where product quality is intimately related to the production process. In an automated manufacturing system, the process involves configuring, setting up and operating the machines involved in the process. Once the machines are operating correctly, product quality naturally follows. You measure the quality of the product and change the process until you achieve the quality level that you need. Figure 27.2 illustrates this process-based approach to achieving product quality.

There is a clear link between process and product quality in manufacturing because the process is relatively easy to standardise and monitor. Once manufacturing systems are calibrated, they can be run again and again to output high-quality products. However, software is not manufactured but is designed. Software development is a creative rather than a mechanical process, so the influence of individual skills and experience is significant. External factors, such as the novelty of an application or commercial pressure for an early product release, also affect product quality irrespective of the process used.

In software development, therefore, the relationship between process quality and product quality is more complex. It is difficult to measure software quality attributes, such as maintainability, even after using the software for a long period. Consequently, it is hard to tell how process characteristics influence these attributes. Furthermore, because of the role of design and creativity in the software process, you can't predict how process changes will influence the quality of the product.

However, experience has shown that process quality has a significant influence on the quality of the software. Process quality management and improvement can certainly lead to fewer defects in delivered software.

Process quality management involves:

1. Defining process standards such as how and when reviews should be conducted

2. Monitoring the development process to ensure that the standards are being followed

3. Reporting the software process to project management and to the buyer of the software

One problem with process-based quality assurance is that the quality assurance (QA) team may insist that standard processes should be used irrespective of the type of software that is being developed. For example, process quality standards for critical systems may specify that specification must be complete and approved before implementation can begin. However, some critical systems may require prototyping where programs are implemented without a complete specification. I have experienced situations where the quality management team suggests that this prototyping should not be carried out because the prototype quality cannot be monitored. In such situations, senior management have to intervene to ensure that the quality process supports rather than hinders product development.

27.2 Quality assurance and standards

Quality assurance is the process of defining how software quality can be achieved and how the development organisation knows that the software has the required level of quality. As I have suggested, the QA process is primarily concerned with defining or selecting standards that should be applied to the software development process or software product. As part of the QA process, you may select and procure tools and methods to support these standards.

The two types of standards that may be established as part of the quality assurance process are:

1. *Product standards* These standards apply to the software product being developed. They include document standards, such as the structure of requirements documents; documentation standards, such as a standard comment header for an object class definition; and coding standards that define how a programming language should be used.

2. *Process standards* These standards define the processes that should be followed during software development. They may include definitions of specification,

design and validation processes and a description of the documents that should be written in the course of these processes.

As I suggested in Section 27.1, there is a close link between product and process standards. Product standards apply to the output of the software process and, in many cases, process standards include specific process activities that ensure that product standards are followed.

Software standards are important for several reasons:

1. They are based on knowledge about the best or most appropriate practice for the company. This knowledge is often only acquired after a great deal of trial and error. Building it into a standard helps the company avoid repeating past mistakes. Standards capture wisdom that is of value to the organisation.

2. They provide a framework for implementing the quality assurance process. Given that standards encapsulate best practice, quality assurance involves ensuring that standards have been properly followed.

3. They assist in continuity where work carried out by one person is taken up and continued by another. Standards ensure that all engineers within an organisation adopt the same practices. Consequently, learning effort when starting new work is reduced.

The development of software engineering project standards is a difficult and time-consuming process. National and international bodies such as the US DoD, ANSI, BSI, NATO and the IEEE have been active in the production of standards. These are general standards that can be applied across a range of projects. Bodies such as NATO and other defence organisations may require that their own standards are followed in software contracts.

National and international standards have been developed covering software engineering terminology, programming languages such as Java and C++, notations such as charting symbols, procedures for deriving and writing software requirements, quality assurance procedures, and software verification and validation processes (IEEE, 2003).

Quality assurance teams that are developing standards for a company should normally base their organisational standards on national and international standards. Using these standards as a starting point, the quality assurance team should draw up a standards 'handbook'. This should define the standards that are needed by their organisation. Examples of standards that might be included in such a handbook are shown in Figure 27.3.

Software engineers sometimes consider standards to be bureaucratic and irrelevant to the technical activity of software development. This is particularly likely when the standards require tedious form filling and work recording. Although they usually agree about the general need for standards, engineers often find good reasons why standards are not necessarily appropriate to their particular project.

Figure 27.3 Product
and process
standards

Product standards	Process standards
Design review form	Design review conduct
Requirements document structure	Submission of documents to CM
Method header format	Version release process
Java programming style	Project plan approval process
Project plan format	Change control process
Change request form	Test recording process

To avoid these problems, quality managers who set the standards need to be adequately resourced and should take the following steps:

1. Involve software engineers in the selection of product standards. They should understand why standards have been designed and so are more likely to be committed to these standards. The standards document should not simply state a standard to be followed but should include a rationale of why particular standardisation decisions have been made.

2. Review and modify standards regularly to reflect changing technologies. Once standards are developed, they tend to be enshrined in a company standards handbook, and management is often reluctant to change them. A standards handbook is essential but it should evolve to reflect changing circumstances and technology.

3. Provide software tools to support standards wherever possible. Clerical standards are the cause of many complaints because of the tedious work involved in implementing them. If tool support is available, you don't need much extra effort to follow the software development standards.

Process standards may cause difficulties if an impractical process is imposed on the development team. Different types of software need different development processes. There is no point in prescribing a particular way of working if it is inappropriate for a project or project team. Each project manager should therefore have the authority to modify process standards according to individual circumstances. However, standards that relate to product quality and the post-delivery process should be changed only after careful consideration.

The project manager and the quality manager can avoid the problems of inappropriate standards by careful quality planning early in the project. They should decide which of the standards in the handbook should be used without change, which should be modified and which should be ignored. New standards may have to be created

Figure 27.4 Areas covered by the ISO 9001 model for quality assurance

Management responsibility	Quality system
Control of nonconforming products	Design control
Handling, storage, packaging and delivery	Purchasing
Purchaser-supplied products	Product identification and traceability
Process control	Inspection and testing
Inspection and test equipment	Inspection and test status
Contract review	Corrective action
Document control	Quality records
Internal quality audits	Training
Servicing	Statistical techniques

in response to a particular project requirement. For example, standards for formal specifications may be required if these have not been used in previous projects. As the team gains experience with them, you should plan to modify and extend these new standards.

27.2.1 ISO 9000

An international set of standards that can be used in the development of a quality management system in all industries is called ISO 9000. ISO 9000 standards can be applied to a range of organisations from manufacturing to service industries. ISO 9001 is the most general of these standards and applies to organisations concerned with the quality process in organisations that design, develop and maintain products. A supporting document (ISO 9000-3) interprets ISO 9001 for software development. Several books describing the ISO 9001 standard are available (Johnson, 1993; Oskarsson and Glass, 1995; Peach, 1996; Bamford and Deibler, 2003).

The ISO 9001 standard isn't specifically aimed at software development but sets out general principles that can be applied to software. The ISO 9001 standard describes various aspects of the quality process and lays out the organisational standards and procedures that a company should define. These should be documented in an organisational quality manual. The process definition should include descriptions of the documentation required to demonstrate that the defined processes have been followed during product development.

The ISO 9001 standard does not define the quality processes that should be used. In fact, it does not constrain the processes used in any organisation in any way. This allows flexibility across industrial sectors and means that small companies can

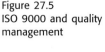

Figure 27.5
ISO 9000 and quality
management

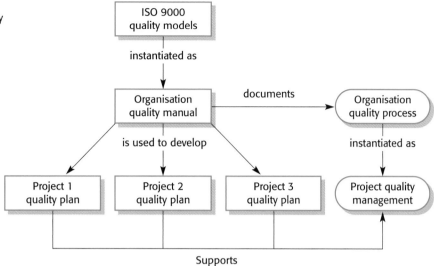

have fairly unbureaucratic processes and still be ISO 9000 compliant. However, this flexibility means that you cannot make any assumptions about the similarity or differences between the processes in ISO 9000 compliant companies.

Figure 27.4 shows the areas covered in ISO 9001. I do not have space here to discuss this standard in any depth. Ince (Ince, 1994) and Oskarrson and Glass (Oskarsson and Glass, 1995) give more detailed accounts of how the standard can be used to develop software quality management processes. The relationships between ISO 9000, the quality manual and individual project quality plans are shown in Figure 27.5. I have derived this figure from a model given in Ince's book (Ince, 1994).

The quality assurance procedures in an organisation are documented in a quality manual that defines the quality process. In some countries, accreditation authorities certify that the quality process as expressed in the quality manual conforms to the ISO 9001 standard. Increasingly, customers look for ISO 9000 certification in a supplier as an indicator of how seriously that supplier takes quality.

Some people think that ISO 9000 certification means that the quality of the software produced by certified companies will be better than that from uncertified companies. This is certainly not the case. The ISO 9000 standard is simply concerned with the definition of processes to be used in a company and associated documentation as control processes that can explicitly show that these processes have been followed. It is not concerned with ensuring that these processes reflect best practice, or with product quality.

Therefore, a company could define product-testing procedures (say) that led to incomplete software testing. So long as these procedures were followed and documented, the company would be following the ISO 9001 standard. While this situation is unlikely, there is no doubt that some company standards are fairly weak and make little contribution to real software quality.

27.2.2   Documentation standards

Documentation standards in a software project are important because documents are the only tangible way of representing the software and the software process. Standardised documents have a consistent appearance, structure and quality, and should therefore be easier to read and understand.

There are three types of documentation standards:

1. *Documentation process standards* These standards define the process that should be followed for document production.

2. *Document standards* These standards govern the structure and presentation of documents.

3. *Document interchange standards* These standards ensure that all electronic copies of documents are compatible.

Documentation process standards define the process used to produce documents. This means that you set out the procedures involved in document development and the software tools used for document production. You should also define checking and refinement procedures to ensure that high-quality documents are produced.

Document process quality standards must be flexible and able to cope with all types of documents. For working papers or electronic memos, there is no need for explicit quality checking. However, for formal documents—that is, those that will be used for further development or released to customers—you should use a formal quality process. Figure 27.6 is a model of one possible documentation process.

Drafting, checking, revising and redrafting is an iterative process. It should continue until a document of acceptable quality is produced. The acceptable quality level depends on the document type and the potential readers of the document.

Document standards should apply to all documents produced during a software development project. Documents should have a consistent style and appearance, and documents of the same type should have a consistent structure. Although document standards should be adapted to the needs of a specific project, it is good practice for the same 'house style' to be used in all of the documents produced by an organisation.

Examples of document standards that may be developed are:

1. *Document identification standards* As large system development projects may produce thousands of documents, each document should be uniquely identified. For formal documents, this identifier may be the formal identifier defined by the configuration manager. For informal documents, the project manager may define the form of the document.

2. *Document structure standards* Each class of document produced during a software project should follow some standard structure. Structure standards should define the sections to be included and should specify the conventions used for

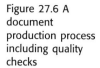

Figure 27.6 A document production process including quality checks

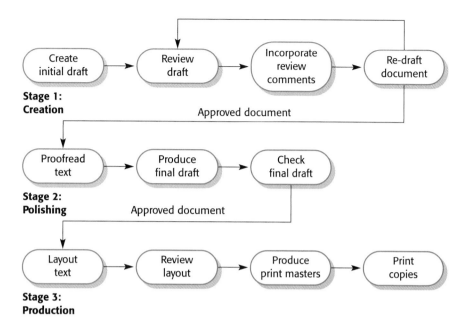

page numbering, page header and footer information, and section and sub-section numbering.

3. *Document presentation standards* Document presentation standards define a 'house style' for documents and contribute significantly to document consistency. They include the definition of fonts and styles used in the document, the use of logos and company names, the use of colour to highlight document structure, and so on.

4. *Document update standards* As a document evolves to reflect changes in the system, a consistent way of indicating document changes should be used. You can use cover colour to indicate document version and change bars in the margin to indicate modified or added paragraphs. However, I advise against the use of change tracking as supported in some commonly used word processors. If there are more than two authors, I find change tracking becomes confusing rather than helpful.

Document interchange standards are important as electronic copies of documents are interchanged. The use of interchange standards allows documents to be transferred electronically and re-created in their original form.

Assuming that the use of standard tools is mandated in the process standards, interchange standards define the conventions for using these tools. Examples of interchange standards include the use of a standard style sheet if a word processor is used or limitations on the use of document macros to avoid possible virus infection. Interchange standards may also limit the fonts and text styles used because of differing printer and display capabilities.

27.3 Quality planning

Quality planning is the process of developing a quality plan for a project. The quality plan should set out the desired software qualities and describe how these are to be assessed. It therefore defines what 'high quality' software actually means. Without this definition, engineers may make different and sometimes conflicting assumptions about which product attributes should be optimised.

The quality plan should select those organisational standards that are appropriate to a particular product and development process. New standards may have to be defined if the project uses new methods and tools. Humphrey (Humphrey, 1989), in his classic book on software management, suggests an outline structure for a quality plan. This includes:

1. *Product introduction* A description of the product, its intended market and the quality expectations for the product.

2. *Product plans* The critical release dates and responsibilities for the product along with plans for distribution and product servicing.

3. *Process descriptions* The development and service processes that should be used for product development and management.

4. *Quality goals* The quality goals and plans for the product including an identification and justification of critical product quality attributes.

5. *Risks and risk management* The key risks that might affect product quality and the actions to address these risks.

Quality plans obviously differ in detail depending on the size and the type of system that is being developed. However, when writing quality plans, you should try to keep them as short as possible. If the document is too long, people will not read it, which will defeat the purpose of producing the quality plan.

There is a wide range of potential software quality attributes (Figure 27.7) that you should consider during the quality-planning process. In general, it is not possible for any system to be optimised for all of these attributes. In the quality plan, you should therefore define the most important quality attributes for the software that is being developed. It may be that efficiency is critical and other factors have to be sacrificed to achieve this. If you have stated this in the quality plan, the engineers working on the development can cooperate to achieve this. The plan should also include a definition of the quality assessment process. This should be a standard way of assessing whether some quality, such as maintainability or robustness, is present in the product.

Figure 27.7 Software
quality attributes

Safety	Understandability	Portability
Security	Testability	Usability
Reliability	Adaptability	Reusability
Resilience	Modularity	Efficiency
Robustness	Complexity	Learnability

Figure 27.7 Software quality attributes

27.4 Quality control

Quality control involves monitoring the software development process to ensure that quality assurance procedures and standards are being followed. As I discussed earlier in the chapter (see Figure 27.1), the deliverables from the software process are checked against the defined project standards in the quality control process.

There are two complementary approaches that may be used to check the quality of project deliverables:

1. Quality reviews where the software, its documentation and the processes used to produce that software are reviewed by a group of people. The review is responsible for checking that the project standards have been followed and that software and documents conform to these standards. Deviations from the standards are noted and the project manager is alerted to them.

2. Automated software assessment where the software and the documents that are produced are processed by some program and compared to the standards that apply to that particular development project. This automated assessment may involve measuring some software attributes and comparing these measurements with some desirable level. I discuss software measurement and metrics in Section 27.5.

27.4.1 Quality reviews

Reviews are the most widely used method of validating the quality of a process or product. They involve a group of people examining part or all of a software process, system, or its associated documentation to discover potential problems. The conclusions of the review are formally recorded and passed to the author or whoever is responsible for correcting the discovered problems.

Figure 27.8 briefly describes several types of review, including reviews for quality management. Program inspections have already been covered in Chapter 22.

Figure 27.8 Types of
review

Review type	Principal purpose
Design or program inspections	To detect detailed errors in the requirements, design or code. A checklist of possible errors should drive the review.
Progress reviews	To provide information for management about the overall progress of the project. This is both a process and a product review and is concerned with costs, plans and schedules.
Quality reviews	To carry out a technical analysis of product components or documentation to find mismatches between the specification and the component design, code or documentation and to ensure that defined quality standards have been followed.

Figure 27.8 Types of review

Progress reviews are part of the management process as discussed in Chapter 5. The review processes have a lot in common; I already described the process of setting up a review in Chapter 22.

The remit of the review team is to detect errors and inconsistencies and point them out to the designer or document author. Reviews are document-based but are not limited to specifications, designs or code. Documents such as process models, test plans, configuration management procedures, process standards and user manuals may all be reviewed.

The review team should have a core of three to four people who are selected as principal reviewers. One member should be a senior designer who can take the responsibility for making significant technical decisions. The principal reviewers may invite other project members, such as the designers of related sub-systems, to contribute to the review. They may not be involved in reviewing the whole document. Rather, they concentrate on those parts that affect their work. Alternatively, the review team may circulate the document being reviewed and ask for written comments from a broad spectrum of project members.

Documents to be reviewed must be distributed well in advance of the review to allow reviewers time to read and understand them. Although this delay can disrupt the development process, reviewing is ineffective if the review team have not properly understood the documents before the review takes place.

The review itself should be relatively short (two hours at most). The author of the document being reviewed should 'walk through' the document with the review team. One team member should chair the review and another should formally record all review decisions and actions to be taken. During the review, the chair is responsible for ensuring that all written comments are considered. The review chair should sign a record of comments and actions agreed upon during the review. This record is then filed as part of the formal project documentation. If only minor problems are discovered, a further review may be unnecessary. The chairman is responsible for ensuring that the required changes are made. If major changes are necessary, a follow-on review may be arranged.

27.5 Software measurement and metrics

Quality reviews are expensive and time-consuming and inevitably delay the completion of a software system. Ideally, it would be possible to accelerate the review process by using tools to process the software design or program and make some automated assessments of the software quality. These assessments could check that the software had reached the required quality threshold and, where this has not been achieved, highlight areas of the software where the review should focus.

Software measurement is concerned with deriving a numeric value for some attribute of a software product or a software process. By comparing these values to each other and to standards that apply across an organisation, you may be able to draw conclusions about the quality of software or software processes. For example, say an organisation plans to introduce a new software-testing tool. Before introducing the tool, you record the number of software defects discovered in a given time; after introducing the tool, you repeat this process. If more defects have been found in the same amount of time after introducing the tool, then you may decide that it provides useful support for the software validation process.

There are two ways in which software product measurements may be used:

1. *To make general predictions about a system.* By measuring the characteristics of system components and then aggregating these measurements, you can derive a general estimate of some system attribute such as the number of faults in the system.

2. *To identify anomalous components.* Measurements can identify individual components whose characteristics deviate from some norm. For example, you can measure components to discover those with the highest complexity and, assuming these are likely to have more errors, concentrate on these components during the review process.

A software metric is any type of measurement that relates to a software system, process or related documentation. Examples are measures of the size of a product in lines of code; the Fog index (Gunning, 1962), which is a measure of the readability of a passage of written text; the number of reported faults in a delivered software product; and the number of person-days required to develop a system component.

A number of large companies such as Hewlett-Packard (Grady, 1993), AT&T (Barnard and Price, 1994) and Nokia (Kilpi, 2001) have introduced metrics programmes and are using collected metrics in their quality management processes. Most of the focus has been on collecting metrics on program defects and the verification and validation

Figure 27.9 Predictor and control measurements

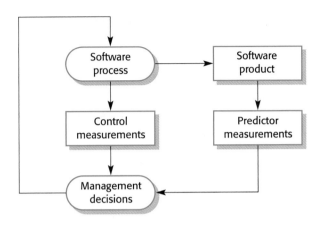

processes. Offen and Jeffrey (Offen and Jeffrey, 1997) and Hall and Fenton (Hall and Fenton, 1997) discuss the introduction of metrics programmes in industry. The ami (application of metrics in industry) handbook (Pulford, et al., 1996) gives detailed advice on measurement and using measurement for process improvement.

However, most companies still do not use systematic software measurement to assess software quality. One reason is that, in many companies, the software processes are poorly defined and controlled, and are not sufficiently mature to make use of measurements. Another reason is that there are no standards for metrics and hence there is limited tool support for data collection and analysis. Most companies will not be prepared to introduce measurement until these standards and tools are available.

Software metrics may be either control metrics or predictor metrics. Both control and predictor metrics may influence management decision making as shown in Figure 27.9. Control metrics are usually associated with software processes; predictor metrics are associated with software products. Examples of control or process metrics are the average effort and time required to repair reported defects. Examples of predictor metrics are the complexity of a module, the average length of identifiers in a program, and the number of attributes and operations associated with objects in a design. In this chapter, because I concentrate on measurement to predict software product quality, I focus on predictor metrics. I discuss control metrics in the Chapter 28.

It is often impossible to measure software quality attributes directly. Quality attributes such as maintainability, understandability and usability are external attributes that relate to how developers and users see the software. They are affected by many factors and there is no simple way to measure them. Rather, you have to measure some internal attribute of the software (such as its size) and assume that a relationship exists between what you can measure and what you really want to know. Ideally, there should be a clear and validated relationship between the internal and the external software attributes.

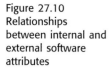

Figure 27.10
Relationships
between internal and
external software
attributes

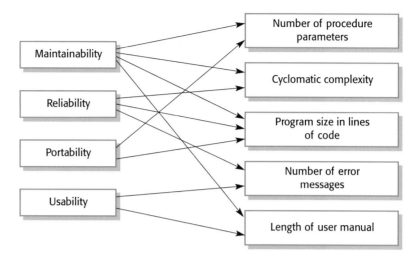

Figure 27.10 shows some external quality attributes that might be of interest and internal attributes that might be related to them. The diagram suggests that there may be relationships between external and internal attributes, but it does not say what that relationship is. If the measure of the internal attribute is to be a useful predictor of the external software characteristic, three conditions must hold (Kitchenham, 1990):

1. The internal attribute must be measured accurately.

2. A relationship must exist between what we can measure and the external behavioural attribute in which we are interested.

3. This relationship is understood, has been validated and can be expressed in terms of a formula or model.

Model formulation involves identifying the functional form of the model (linear, exponential, etc.) by analysis of collected data, identifying the parameters that are to be included in the model and calibrating these using existing data. Such model development, if it is to be trusted, requires significant experience in statistical techniques and, ideally, someone with statistical knowledge and experience should define the model to be used.

27.5.1 The measurement process

A software measurement process that may be part of a quality control process is shown in Figure 27.11. Each of the components of the system is analysed separately, and the values of the metric compared both with each other and, perhaps, with historical measurement data collected on previous projects. Anomalous

Figure 27.11 The
process of product
measurement

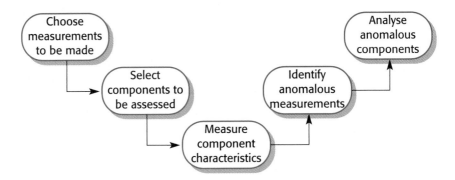

measurements should be used to focus the quality assurance effort on components
that may have quality problems.

The key stages in this process are:

1. *Choose measurements to be made* The questions that the measurement is
    intended to answer should be formulated and the measurements required to answer
    these questions defined. Measurements that are not directly relevant to these
    questions need not be collected. Basili's GQM (Goal-Question-Metric)
    paradigm (Basili and Rombach, 1988), discussed in the next chapter, is a good
    approach to use when deciding what data is to be collected.

2. *Select components to be assessed* It may not be necessary or desirable to assess
    metric values for all of the components in a software system. In some cases,
    you can select a representative selection of components for measurement. In
    others, components that are particularly critical, such as core components that
    are in almost constant use, should be assessed.

3. *Measure component characteristics* The selected components are measured and
    the associated metric values computed. This normally involves processing the
    component representation (design, code, etc.) using an automated data collec-
    tion tool. This tool may be specially written or may already be incorporated in
    CASE tools that are used in an organisation.

4. *Identify anomalous measurements* Once the component measurements have been
    made, you should compare them to each other and to previous measurements
    that have been recorded in a measurement database. You should look for unusu-
    ally high or low values for each metric, as these suggest that there could be
    problems with the component exhibiting these values.

5. *Analyse anomalous components* Once components that have anomalous values
    for particular metrics have been identified, you should examine these compo-
    nents to decide whether the anomalous metric values mean that the quality of
    the component is compromised. An anomalous metric value for complexity (say)
    does not necessarily mean a poor quality component. There may be some other

reason for the high value and it may not mean that there are component quality problems.

You should always maintain collected data as an organisational resource and keep historical records of all projects even when data has not been used during a particular project. Once a sufficiently large measurement database has been established, you can then make comparisons across projects and refine specific metrics to help gather the information that the company needs for quality improvement.

27.5.2 Product metrics

Product metrics are concerned with characteristics of the software itself. Unfortunately, the software characteristics that can be easily measured, such as size and cyclomatic complexity, do not have a clear and consistent relationship with quality attributes such as understandability and maintainability. The relationships vary depending on the development processes and technology and the type of system that is being developed. To discover and validate the relationships between external and internal attributes, you need to collect a large amount of data from existing systems. You can then use this to discover how the software product attributes are related to the external qualities in which you are interested.

Product metrics fall into two classes:

1. *Dynamic metrics* that are collected by measurements made of a program in execution

2. *Static metrics* that are collected by measurements made of representations of the system such as the design, program or documentation

These types of metrics are related to different quality attributes. Dynamic metrics help to assess the efficiency and the reliability of a program. Static metrics help to assess the complexity, understandability and maintainability of a software system.

Dynamic metrics are usually fairly closely related to software quality attributes. It is fairly easy to measure the execution time required for particular functions and to assess the time required to start up a system. These relate directly to the system's efficiency. Similarly, the number of system failures and the type of failure can be logged and related directly to the reliability of the software as discussed in Chapter 24.

Static metrics, on the other hand, have an indirect relationship with quality attributes. A large number of these metrics have been proposed, and many experiments have tried to derive and validate the relationships between these metrics and system complexity, understandability and maintainability. Figure 27.12 describes several static product metrics that have been used for quality assessment. Of these, program or component length and control complexity seem to be the most reliable predictors of understandability, system complexity and maintainability.

Figure 27.12 Static
software product
metrics

Software metric	Description
Fan-in/Fan-out	*Fan-in* is a measure of the number of functions or methods that call some other function or method (say X). *Fan-out* is the number of functions that are called by function X. A high value for fan-in means that X is tightly coupled to the rest of the design and changes to X will have extensive knock-on effects. A high value for fan-out suggests that the overall complexity of X may be high because of the complexity of the control logic needed to coordinate the called components.
Length of code	This is a measure of the size of a program. Generally, the larger the size of the code of a component, the more complex and error-prone that component is likely to be. Length of code has been shown to be one of the most reliable metrics for predicting error-proneness in components.
Cyclomatic complexity	This is a measure of the control complexity of a program. This control complexity may be related to program understandability. I discuss how to compute cyclomatic complexity in Chapter 22.
Length of identifiers	This is a measure of the average length of distinct identifiers in a program. The longer the identifiers, the more likely they are to be meaningful and hence the more understandable the program.
Depth of conditional nesting	This is a measure of the depth of nesting of if-statements in a program. Deeply nested if statements are hard to understand and are potentially error-prone.
Fog index	This is a measure of the average length of words and sentences in documents. The higher the value for the Fog index, the more difficult the document is to understand.

Figure 27.12 Static software product metrics

The metrics in Figure 27.12 are generic but more specific object-oriented metrics have also been proposed (Figure 27.13). The best-known object-oriented metrics were proposed by Chidamber and Kemerer (Chidamber and Kemerer, 1994) and there are some tools available to collect these metrics. Some of these metrics have been derived from the older metrics shown in Figure 27.12 but others are unique to object-oriented systems. El-Amam (El-Amam, 2001), in an excellent review of object-oriented metrics, discusses some of these studies and concludes that we do not yet have sufficient evidence to understand how object-oriented metrics relate to external software qualities.

The specific metrics that are relevant depend on the project, the goals of the quality management team and the type of software that is being developed. All of the metrics shown in Figures 27.12 and 27.13 may be useful in some situations. Equally, however, there will be other situations where they are inappropriate. When

Figure 27.13 Object-oriented metrics

Object-oriented metric	Description
Depth of inheritance tree	This represents the number of discrete levels in the inheritance tree where sub-classes inherit attributes and operations (methods) from super-classes. The deeper the inheritance tree, the more complex the design. Many object classes may have to be understood to understand the object classes at the leaves of the tree.
Method fan-in/fan-out	This is directly related to fan-in and fan-out, as described in Figure 27.12, and means essentially the same thing. However, it may be appropriate to make a distinction between calls from other methods within the object and calls from external methods.
Weighted methods per class	This is the number of methods included in a class, weighted by the complexity of each method. Therefore, a simple method may have a complexity of 1 and a large and complex method may have a much higher value. The larger the value for this metric, the more complex the object class. Complex objects are more likely to be more difficult to understand. They may not be logically cohesive so cannot be reused effectively as super-classes in an inheritance tree.
Number of overriding operations	This is the number of operations in a super-class that are overridden in a sub-class. A high value for this metric indicates that the super-class used may not be an appropriate parent for the sub-class.

introducing software measurement as part of the quality management process, organisations have to experiment to discover the most appropriate metrics for their needs.

27.5.3 Analysis of measurements

One of the problems with collecting quantitative data about software and software projects is understanding what that data really means. It is easy to misinterpret data and make inferences that are incorrect. Measurements must be carefully analysed to understand what they really mean.

To illustrate how collected data can be interpreted in different ways, consider the following scenario. To make this easier to understand, I have used a process rather than a product metric, but the essential message is the same; the reasons for change may often be difficult to understand.

A manager decides to monitor the number of change requests submitted by customers based on an assumption that there is a relationship between these change requests and product usability and suitability. The higher the number of change requests, the less the software meets the needs of the customer.

Processing change requests and changing the software is expensive. The organisation therefore decides to modify its process to increase customer satisfaction and, at the same time, reduce the costs of change. The intent is that the process changes will result in better products and fewer change requests.

Process changes are initiated to increase customer involvement in the software design process. Beta testing of all products is introduced and customer-requested modifications are incorporated in the delivered product. New versions of products, developed with this modified process, are delivered. In some cases, the number of change requests is reduced; in others, it is increased. The manager is baffled and cannot assess the effects of the process changes on the product quality.

To understand why this kind of thing can happen, you have to understand why change requests are made. One reason is that the delivered software does not do what customers want it to do. Another possibility is that the software is very good and is widely and heavily used, sometimes for purposes for which it was not originally designed. Because there are so many people using it, it is natural that more change requests are generated.

A third possibility is that the company producing the software is responsive to customers' change requests. Customers are therefore satisfied with the service they receive. They generate a lot of change requests because they know that these requests will be taken seriously. Their suggestions will probably be incorporated in later versions of the software.

The number of change requests might decrease because the process changes have been effective and have made the software more usable and suitable. Alternatively, the number might decrease because the product has lost market share to a rival product. There are consequently fewer product users. The number of change requests might increase because there are more users, because the beta-testing process has convinced users that the company is willing to make changes, or because the beta-test sites were not typical of most usage of the program.

To analyse the change request data, you do not simply need to know the number of change requests. You need to know who made the request, how they use the software and why the request was made. You need to know whether there are external factors such as modifications to the change request procedure or market changes that might have an effect. With this information, it is then possible to find out whether the process changes have been effective in increasing product quality.

This illustrates that interpreting quantitative data about a product or a process is subjective. Processes and products that are being measured are not insulated from their environment, and changes to that environment may make comparisons of data invalid. Quantitative data about human activities cannot always be taken at face value. Underlying reasons that might account for the measured value have to be investigated.

KEY POINTS

■ Software quality management is concerned with ensuring that software has a low number of defects and that it reaches the required standards of maintainability, reliability, portability and so on. Quality management activities include quality assurance that sets the standards for software development, quality planning, and quality control that checks the software against the defined standards.

■ You should document a set of quality assurance procedures in an organisational quality manual. This may be based on the generic model for a quality manual suggested in the ISO 9000 standards.

■ Software standards are important to quality assurance as they represent an identification of 'best practice'. The quality control process is concerned with checking that the software process and the software being developed conform to these standards.

■ Reviews of the software process deliverables involve a team of people who check that quality standards are being followed. Reviews are the most widely used technique for assessing quality.

■ Software measurement can be used to gather quantitative data about software and the software process. You may be able to use the values of the software metrics that are collected to make inferences about product and process quality.

■ Product quality metrics are particularly valuable for highlighting anomalous components that may have quality problems. These components should then be analysed in more detail.

■ There are no standardised and universally applicable software metrics. Organisations must select metrics and analyse measurements based on local knowledge and circumstances.

FURTHER READING

Software Quality Assurance: From Theory to Implementation. An excellent, up-to-date look at the principles and practice of software quality assurance. It includes a discussion of standards such as ISO 9001. (D. Galin, 2004, Addison-Wesley.)

Metrics and Models for Software Quality Engineering, 2nd ed. This is a very comprehensive discussion of software metrics covering process, product and object-oriented metrics. It also includes some background on the mathematics required to develop and understand models based on software measurement. (S. H. Kan, 2003, Addison-Wesley.)

'Making sense of measurement for small organisations'. This is an interesting article about the practical application of metrics. It makes the point that all uses of metrics have to take their context into account. (K. Kautz, *IEEE Software,* March/April 1999.)

A Quantitative Approach to Software Management: The ami Handbook. This is an excellent how-to guide introducing a measurement programme and using the results for process improvement. Unfortunately, it is now out of print, but it should be available in good libraries. (K. Pulford, et al., 1996, Addison-Wesley.)

EXERCISES

27.1 Explain why a high-quality software process should lead to high-quality software products. Discuss possible problems with this system of quality management.

27.2 Explain how standards may be used to capture organisational wisdom about effective methods of software development. Suggest four types of knowledge that might be captured in organisational standards.

27.3 Discuss the assessment of software quality according to the quality attributes shown in Figure 27.7. You should consider each attribute in turn and explain how it might be assessed

27.4 Design an electronic form that may be used to record review comments and that could be used to electronically mail comments to reviewers.

27.5 Briefly describe possible standards that might be used for:

■ The use of control constructs in C, C++ or Java

■ Reports which might be submitted for a term project in a university

■ The process of making and approving changes to a program (see Chapter 29)

■ The process of purchasing and installing a new computer.

27.6 Assume you work for an organisation that develops database products for microcomputer systems. This organisation is interested in quantifying its software development. Write a report suggesting appropriate metrics and suggest how these can be collected.

27.7 Explain why design metrics are, by themselves, an inadequate method of predicting design quality.

27.8 Consult the literature and find other design quality metrics that have been suggested apart from those discussed here. Consider these metrics in detail and assess whether they are likely to be of real value.

27.9 Explain why it is difficult to validate the relationships between internal product attributes such as cyclomatic complexity and external attributes such as maintainability.

27.10 Suggest how automated software measurement could be used to support extreme programming (discussed in Chapter 17).

27.11 Do software standards stifle technological innovation?

27.12 A colleague who is a very good programmer produces software with a low number of defects but she consistently ignores organisational quality standards. How should the managers in the organisation react to this behaviour?

28

Process improvement

Objectives

The objective of this chapter is to explain how software processes can be improved to produce better software. When you have read this chapter, you will:

■ understand the principles of software process improvement and why process improvement is worthwhile;

■ understand how software process factors influence software quality and the productivity of software developers;

■ be able to develop simple models of software processes;

■ understand the notions of process capability and process maturity and the general form of the CMMI model for process improvement.

Contents

As I discussed in Chapter 27, there is a close link between the quality of a development process and the quality of the products developed using that process. Consequently, many software engineering companies have turned to software process improvement as a way of enhancing the quality of their software. *Process improvement* means understanding existing processes and changing these processes to increase product quality and/or reduce costs and development time. Most of the literature on process improvement has focused on perfecting processes to improve product quality and, in particular, to reduce the number of defects in delivered software. Once this has been achieved, the principal goals might be cost or schedule reductions.

Software processes are inherently complex and involve a very large number of activities. Like products, processes also have attributes or characteristics as shown in Figure 28.1. It is not possible to make process improvements that optimise all process attributes simultaneously. For example, if your aim is to have a rapid development process, then you may have to reduce the process visibility. Making a process visible means producing documents at regular intervals. This, inevitably, slows down the process.

Process improvement does not simply mean adopting particular methods or tools or using some model of a process that has been used elsewhere. Although organisations that develop the same type of software clearly have much in common, there are always local organisational factors, procedures and standards that influence the process. You will rarely be successful in introducing process improvements if you simply attempt to change the process to one that is used somewhere else. You should always look on process improvement as specific to an organisation or a part of a larger organisation.

Process improvement is a cyclical activity, as shown in Figure 28.2. It involves three principal stages:

1. *Process measurement* Attributes of the current project or the product are measured. The aim is to improve the measures according to the goals of the organisation involved in process improvement.

2. *Process analysis* The current process is assessed, and process weaknesses and bottlenecks are identified. Process models that describe the process are usually developed during this stage.

3. *Process change* Changes to the process that have been identified during analysis are introduced.

I cover each of these activities in separate sections later in this chapter. Each stage of the process may last several months; process improvement is a long-term activity. It is also a continuous activity as, whatever new processes are introduced, the business environment will change and these processes will themselves have to evolve to take these changes into account.

Figure 28.1 Process
characteristics

Process characteristic	Description
Understandability	To what extent is the process explicitly defined and how easy is it to understand the process definition?
Visibility	Do the process activities culminate in clear results so that the progress of the process is externally visible?
Supportability	To what extent can CASE tools be used to support the process activities?
Acceptability	Is the defined process acceptable to and usable by the engineers responsible for producing the software product?
Reliability	Is the process designed in such a way that process errors are avoided or trapped before they result in product errors?
Robustness	Can the process continue in spite of unexpected problems?
Maintainability	Can the process evolve to reflect changing organisational requirements or identified process improvements?
Rapidity	How fast can the process of delivering a system from a given specification be completed?

Figure 28.2 The
process improvement
cycle

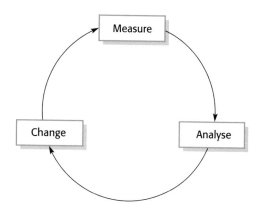

28.1 Process and product quality

Process improvement is based on the assumption that the quality of the product development process is critical to product quality. The notion of process improvement is the brainchild of American engineer W. E. Deming, who worked with Japanese industry after World War II to improve quality. Japanese industry has been committed to continuous process improvement for many years, which has led to the acknowledged high quality of Japanese manufactured goods.

Deming (and others) introduced the idea of statistical quality control. This is based on measuring the number of product defects and relating these defects to the process. The aim is to reduce the number of product defects by improving the process until it is repeatable. That is, the results of the process are predictable and the number of defects reduced. The process is then standardised and a further improvement cycle begins.

Humphrey, in his seminal book on process management (Humphrey, 1988) argues that the same techniques can be applied to software engineering. He states:

> *W. E. Deming, in his work with the Japanese industry after World War II, applied the concepts of statistical process control to industry. While there are important differences, these concepts are just as applicable to software as they are to automobiles, cameras, wristwatches and steel.*

While there are clearly similarities, I do not agree with Humphrey that results from manufacturing engineering can be transferred directly to software engineering. Where manufacturing is involved, the process/product relationship is very obvious. Improving a process so that defects are avoided will lead to better products. This link is less obvious when the product is intangible and dependent, to some extent, on intellectual processes that cannot be automated. Software quality is not dependent on a manufacturing process but on a design process where individual human capabilities are significant. In some classes of product, the process used is the most significant determinant of product quality. However, for innovative applications in particular, the people involved in the process may be more important than the process used.

For software products, or any other intellectual products such as books or films where the quality of the product depends on its design, four main factors affect product quality. These are shown in Figure 28.3.

The influence of each of these factors depends on the size and type of the project. For very large systems that include separate sub-systems, developed by teams who may be working in different locations, the principal factor that affects product quality is the software process. The major problems with large projects are integration, project management and communications. There is usually a mix of abilities and experience in the team members and, because the development process usually takes place over a number of years, the development team is volatile. It may change completely over the lifetime of the project. Therefore, particularly skilled or talented individuals don't usually have a dominant effect over the lifetime of the project.

For small projects, however, where there are only a few team members, the quality of the development team is more important than the development process used. If the team has a high level of ability and experience, the quality of the product is likely to be high. If the team is inexperienced and unskilled, a good process may limit the damage but will not, in itself, lead to high-quality software.

Figure 28.3 Principal
software product
quality factors

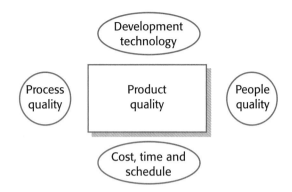

Where teams are small, good development technology is particularly important. The small team cannot devote a lot of time to tedious administrative procedures. The team members spend much of their time designing and programming the system, so good tools can significantly affect their productivity. For large projects, a basic level of development technology is essential for information management. Paradoxically, sophisticated CASE tools are often less important in large projects. Team members spend a smaller proportion of their time in development activities and more time communicating and understanding other parts of the system. This is the dominant factor affecting their productivity. Development tools make no difference to this.

The base of the rectangle in Figure 28.3 is absolutely critical. If a project, irrespective of size, is under-budgeted or planned with an unrealistic delivery schedule, the product quality will be affected. A good process requires resources for its effective implementation. If these resources are insufficient, the process cannot work effectively. If resources are inadequate, only excellent people can save a project. Even then, if the deficit is too great, the product quality will be degraded.

All too often, the real cause of software quality problems is not poor management, inadequate processes or poor quality training. Rather, it is the fact that organisations must compete to survive. To gain a contract, a company may underestimate the effort required or promise rapid delivery of a system. In an attempt to meet these commitments, the company may have to sacrifice software quality.

28.2 Process classification

Software processes can be observed in all organisations, from one-person companies to large multinationals. These processes are of different types depending on the degree of formality of the process, the types of products developed, the size of the organisation, and so on. There are four classes of software processes:

Figure 28.4 Process
applicability

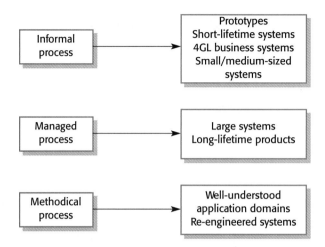

1. *Informal processes* When there is no strictly defined process model, the development team chooses the process that they will use. Informal processes may use formal procedures such as configuration management, but the procedures and the relationships between procedures are defined as required by the development team.

2. *Managed processes* A defined process model is used to drive the development process. The process model defines the procedures, their scheduling and the relationships between the procedures.

3. *Methodical processes* When some defined development method or methods (such as systematic methods for object-oriented design) are used, these processes benefit from CASE tool support for design and analysis processes.

4. *Improving processes* Processes that have inherent improvement objectives have a specific budget for improvements and procedures for introducing such improvements. As part of this, quantitative process measurement may be introduced.

These classifications obviously overlap, and a process may fall into several classes. For example, the process may be informal in that it is chosen by the development team. The team may choose to use a particular design method. They may also have a process-improvement capability. In this case, the process would be classified as *informal, methodical* and *improving*.

These classifications are useful because they serve as a basis for multidimensional process improvement. They help organisations choose an appropriate process for their unique product development requirements. Figure 28.4 shows different types of product and the type of process that might be used for their development. Improving processes are not shown on this diagram because any type of process can be an improving process.

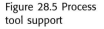

Figure 28.5 Process tool support

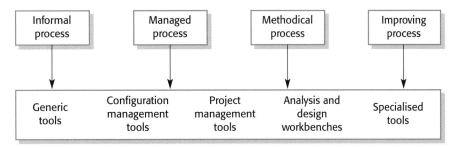

The classes of system shown on the right in Figure 28.4 may overlap. Therefore, small systems that are re-engineered may be developed using a methodical process. Large systems always need a managed process. However, design methods are not suited to all types of applications, and large systems in particular may include sub-systems of different types. Rather than force a single method on the designers, these systems may be developed using a managed process that is not based on any particular method.

Process classification provides a basis for choosing the right process for the product that is being developed. For example, a program that will support a transition from one type of computer system to another has a relatively short lifetime. Its development does not require the standards and management procedures that are appropriate for software that will be used for many years.

Process classification recognises that the process affects product quality. It does not assume, however, that the process is always the dominant factor. It provides a basis for improving many types of processes. Different types of process improvement may be applied to the different types of process. For example, the improvements to methodical processes might be based on better method training, better integration of requirements and design, improved CASE tools and so on.

Most software processes now have some CASE tool support, so they are *supported processes*. Analysis and design workbenches are used to support methodical processes. However, processes may have other kinds of tool support (for example, prototyping tools, testing tools) irrespective of whether a structured design method is used.

The tool support that can be effective in supporting processes depends on the process classification. For example, generic tools such as prototyping languages, compilers, debuggers and word processors can be used in informal processes. However, informal processes rarely use more specialised tools in a consistent way. Figure 28.5 shows that a spectrum of tools can be used in software development. The effectiveness of particular tools depends on the type of process used.

Analysis and design CASE tools are only likely to be cost effective with a methodical process. Specialised tools provide specific support for individual process activities. For example, a team involved in multisite development may create a display tool that shows the work going on at each site. Sometimes, these specialised tools may be developed specially to improve the process.

28.3 Process measurement

Process measurements are quantitative data about the software process. Humphrey (Humphrey, 1989), in his book on process improvement, argues that the measurement of process and product attributes is essential for process improvement. He also suggests that measurement has an important role to play in small-scale, personal process improvement (Humphrey, 1995). Process measurements can be used to assess whether the efficiency of a process has been improved. For example, the effort and time devoted to testing can be monitored. Effective improvements to the testing process should reduce the effort, testing time or both. However, process measurements on their own cannot be used to determine whether product quality has improved. Product quality data (see Chapter 27) should also be collected and related to the process activities.

Three classes of process metric can be collected:

1. *The time taken for a particular process to be completed* This can be the total time devoted to the process, calendar time, the time spent on the process by particular engineers and so on.

2. *The resources required for a particular process* The resources might include total effort in person-days, travel costs and computer resources.

3. *The number of occurrences of a particular event* Examples of events that might be monitored include the number of defects discovered during code inspection, the number of requirements changes requested and the average number of lines of code modified in response to a requirements change.

The first two types of measurement can be used to discover whether process changes have improved the efficiency of a process. Say there are fixed points in a software development process such as the acceptance of requirements, the completion of architectural design or the completion of test data generation. You may be able to measure the time and effort required to move from one of these fixed points to another. After changes have been introduced, measurements of system attributes can show whether the process changes have actually been beneficial in reducing the time or effort required.

Measurements of the number of events that occur can have a more direct bearing on software quality. For example, increasing the number of defects discovered by changing the program inspection process will probably be reflected in improved product quality. However, this has to be confirmed by subsequent product measurements.

The fundamental difficulty in process measurement is knowing what to measure. Basili and Rombach (Basili and Rombach, 1988) have proposed what they call the GQM (Goal-Question-Metric) paradigm. This is used to help decide what measurements should be taken and how they should be used. This approach relies on the identification of:

1. *Goals* What the organisation is trying to achieve. Examples of goals might be improved programmer productivity, shorter product development time and increased product reliability.

2. *Questions* These are refinements of goals where specific areas of uncertainty related to the goals are identified. Normally, a goal will have a number of associated questions that need to be answered. Examples of questions related to the above goals are:

    *   How can the number of debugged lines of code be increased?
    *   How can the time required to finalise product requirements be reduced?
    *   How can more effective reliability assessments be made?

3. *Metrics* These are the measurements that need to be collected to help answer the questions and to confirm whether process improvements have achieved the desired goal. In the above examples, measurements that might be made include the productivity of individual programmers in lines of code and their level of experience, the number of formal communications between client and contractor for each requirements change and the number of tests required to cause product failure.

The advantage of this approach applied to process improvement is that it separates organisational concerns (the goals) from specific process concerns (the questions). It focuses data collection and suggests that collected data should be analysed in different ways depending on the question it is intended to answer. Basili and Green (Basili and Green, 1993) describe how this approach has been used in a long-term, measurement-based process improvement programme.

The GQM approach has been developed and combined with the SEI's capability maturity model (Paulk, et al., 1995) in the ami method (Pulford, et al., 1996) of software process improvement. The developers of the ami method propose a staged approach to process improvement where measurement is introduced when an organisation has introduced some discipline into its processes. It provides guidelines and practical advice on implementing measurement-based process improvement.

28.4 Process analysis and modelling

Process analysis and modelling involve studying existing processes and developing an abstract model of these processes that captures their key characteristics. These models help you understand the process and communicate that understanding to others. Throughout the book, I have used process model fragments to discuss specific activities such as requirements engineering and software design. I have suggested, in Figure 28.2, that process analysis follows process measurement. This is a simplification because, in reality, these activities are intertwined. You need to carry out some analysis to know what to measure, and, when making measurements, you inevitably develop a deeper understanding of the process being measured.

Process analysis is concerned with studying existing processes in order to understand the relationships between the parts of the process. The initial stages of process analysis are qualitative: The analyst is simply trying to discover the key features of the model. Later stages may be quantitative and make use of collected process measurements. After the analysis is complete, you should describe and document the process using a software process model (Huff, 1996).

The starting point for process analysis should be whatever 'formal' process model is used. Many organisations have such a formal model, which may be imposed on them by the software customer. This standard defines the critical activities and life-cycle deliverables that must be produced.

Formal models can serve as a useful starting point for process analysis. However, they rarely include enough detail or reflect the real activities of software development. Formal process models are fairly abstract and define only the principal process activities and deliverables. It is usually necessary to 'look inside' the model to find the real process. Furthermore, the actual process often differs significantly from the formal model, although the specified deliverables will usually be produced.

Techniques of process analysis include:

1. *Questionnaires and interviews* The engineers working on a project are questioned about what actually goes on. The answers to a formal questionnaire are refined during personal interviews with those involved in the process. The discussion can be structured around a version of the process model that is refined as new information becomes available.

2. *Ethnographic studies* As discussed in Chapter 7, ethnographic studies may be used to understand the nature of software development as a human activity. Such analysis reveals subtleties and complexities that may not be discovered using other techniques.

Each of these approaches has advantages and disadvantages. Questionnaire-based analysis can be carried out fairly quickly once the right questions have been identified. However, if the questions are badly worded or inappropriate, you will end up with an incomplete or inaccurate model of the process. Furthermore, questionnaire-based analysis may appear to be like assessment. The engineers being questioned may give the answers that they think you want to hear rather than the truth about the process used.

Interviews with the people involved in the process are more open ended than questionnaires. You start with a prepared script of questions but adapt these according to the responses that you get from different people. If you give participants an opportunity to discuss issues more widely, you may find that the process participants talk about process problems, the ways that the process is changed in practice, etc.

Ethnographic analysis is more likely to discover the true process used. However, it is a prolonged activity that can last several months. It relies on external observation of the process as it is being enacted. To do a complete analysis, you have to be involved from the initial stages of a project through to product delivery and maintenance. For large projects, this could take several years, so it is clearly impractical in those situations. Ethnographic analysis, therefore, is most useful when an in-depth understanding of process fragments is required. You carry out a smaller-scale study focusing on process details.

Process models are simplified views of software processes that show the activities and outputs of the process. The process models used in this book present a high-level view of the processes concerned. At this abstract level, these processes are the same in many organisations. However, these generic models have different instantiations in different companies depending on the type of software being developed and the organisational environment. Detailed process models are not usually the same across organisations.

Abstract or generic process models are a useful basis for discussing processes. However, they do not include enough information for process analysis and improvement. Process improvement needs information about activities, deliverables, people, communications, schedules and other organisational processes that affect the software development process. Figure 28.6 explains what might be included in a detailed process model.

You should record the timing of and the dependencies between activities, deliverables and communications in the process model. Sometimes activities can be carried out in parallel and other times they must occur in sequence. They may be interleaved so that the same person is involved in several activities. Deliverables may be dependent on other deliverables or on communications between engineers working on the process.

In the examples of process models in this book, I show the approximate sequence of activities from left to right. Activities that may be carried out in parallel are, as far as possible, aligned vertically.

Detailed process models are extremely complex. For example, consider the process fragments shown in Figures 28.7 and 28.8. These describe the process of testing a single module in a large system that uses a strictly controlled configuration management process (see Chapter 29). The software being tested and the test data are under configuration control. Figure 28.7 shows the role responsible for the testing process, process inputs and outputs, and pre- and post-conditions.

Figure 28.8 shows the decomposed process 'test module' as a number of separate activities. This fragment shows only the activities in the relatively simple activity of module testing. Four streams of activities are concerned with preparing test data, writing a test harness for the module, running the tests and reporting on the

Figure 28.6 Elements
of a process model

Process model element	Description
Activity (shown as a round-edged rectangle with no drop shadow)	An activity has a clearly defined objective, entry and exit conditions. Examples of activities are preparing a set of test data to test a module, coding a function or a module and proofreading a document. Generally, an activity is atomic; that is, it is the responsibility of one person or group. It is not decomposed into sub-activities.
Process (shown as a round-edged rectangle with drop shadow)	A process is a coherent set of activities whose objective is generally agreed within an organisation. Examples of processes are requirements analysis, architectural design and test planning.
Deliverable (shown as a rectangle with drop shadow)	A deliverable is a tangible output of an activity that is predicted in a project plan.
Condition (shown as a parallelogram)	A condition is either a pre-condition that must hold before a process or activity can start or a post-condition that holds after a process or activity has finished.
Role (shown as a circle with drop shadow)	A role is a bounded area of responsibility. Examples of roles might be configuration manager, test engineer and software designer. One person may have several roles and a single role may be associated with several different people.
Exception (not shown in examples here but may be represented as a double-edged box)	An exception is a description of how to modify the process if some anticipated or unanticipated event occurs. Exceptions are often undefined, and it is left to the ingenuity of the project managers and engineers to handle the exception.
Communication (shown as an arrow)	Communication is an interchange of information between people or between people and supporting computer systems. Communications may be informal or formal. Formal communications might be the approval of a deliverable by a project manager; informal communications might be the interchange of e-mail to resolve ambiguities in a document.

tests. The activities in the preparation streams would normally be interleaved. Obviously, the preparation activities precede the execution and reporting activities.

I have left out information on process pre- and post-conditions and process inputs and outputs in this diagram because this information would make the model more complex and difficult to understand. Rather than trying to get all information into

Figure 28.7 The module testing process

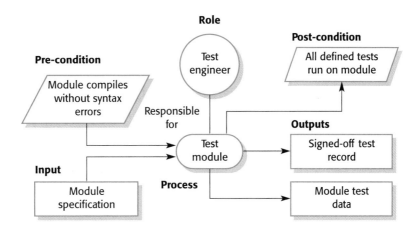

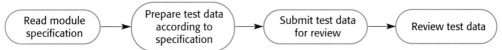

TEST DATA PREPARATION

MODULE TEST HARNESS PREPARATION

TEST EXECUTION

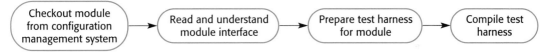

TEST REPORTING

Write report on module testing including details of discovered problems → Submit report for approval → Submit test results to CM

Figure 28.8 The activities involved in module testing

a single model, you may need to make several models at different levels of abstraction. These should be related using common elements such as activities or deliverables. Some models should be primarily concerned with process activities, others with control information that drives the process execution.

28.4.1 Process exceptions

Software processes are very complex entities. While there may be a defined process model in an organisation, this can only ever represent the ideal situation where the development team is not faced with any unanticipated problems. In reality, unanticipated problems are a fact of everyday life for project managers. The 'ideal' process model must be modified dynamically as solutions to these problems are found. Examples of the kinds of exceptions that a project manager may have to deal with include:

1. Several key people becoming ill at the same time just before a critical project review

2. A serious breach in computer security that means all external communications are out of action for several hours

3. An organisational reorganisation that means that managers have to spend much of their time working on organisational matters rather than on project management

4. An unanticipated request to write proposals for new projects that means effort must be transferred from the project to a proposal.

In general, the effect of an exception is that, somehow, the resources, budgets or schedules of a project are changed. It is difficult to predict all exceptions in advance and to incorporate them into a formal process model. You therefore often have to work out how to handle exceptions and then dynamically change the 'standard' process to cope with these unexpected circumstances. Process models therefore are inevitably incomplete, and the process manager is responsible for dealing with exceptions and adapting the process as required.

28.5 Process change

Process change involves making modifications to the existing process. You may do this by introducing new practices, methods or tools, by changing the ordering of process activities, by introducing or removing deliverables from the process, or by introducing new roles and responsibilities. You should set goals for process improvement such as 'reduce the number of defects discovered during integration testing by 25%'. These goals should drive the process changes and, after the changes have been implemented, be used to measure progress.

There are five key stages in the process change process (Figure 28.9):

1. *Improvement identification* This stage is concerned with using the results of the process analysis to identify quality, schedule or cost bottlenecks where process factors might adversely influence the product quality. Process improvement

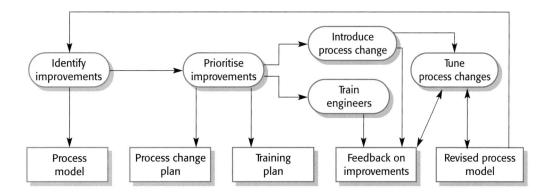

Figure 28.9 The process change process

should focus on loosening these bottlenecks by proposing new procedures, methods and tools to address the problems.

2. *Improvement prioritisation* This stage is concerned with assessing the possible changes and prioritising them for implementation. When many possible changes have been identified, it is usually impossible to introduce them all at once; you have to decide which are most important. You may make these decisions based on the need to improve specific process areas, the costs of introducing the change, the impact of the change on the organisation and other factors.

3. *Process change introduction* Process change introduction means putting new procedures, methods and tools into place, and integrating them with other process activities. You must allow enough time to introduce changes and to ensure that these changes are compatible with other process activities and with organisational procedures and standards.

4. *Process change training* Without training, it is not possible to gain the full benefits from process changes. Process managers and software engineers may simply refuse to accept the new process. All too often, process changes have been imposed without adequate training, and the effects of these changes have been to degrade rather than improve product quality.

5. *Change tuning* Proposed process changes will never be completely effective as soon as they are introduced. You need a tuning phase where minor problems are discovered, and modifications to the process are proposed and are introduced. This tuning phase should last for several months until the development engineers are happy with the new process.

Once a change has been introduced, the improvement process can iterate with further analysis used to identify process problems, propose improvements, and so on. It is impractical to introduce too many changes at the same time. Apart from the problems of training that this causes, introducing too many changes makes it impossible to assess the effect of each change on the process.

As a manager, you have to be sensitive to the feelings of the people in your team when introducing process change. Business process re-engineering (Hammer, 1990; Ould, 1995), a fashion of the 1990s that involved making radical process changes, was largely unsuccessful because it failed to take the legitimate concerns of the people involved into account. People felt that their expertise was being ignored and their jobs changed without consultation. They actively resisted the changes and ensured that the changes would not work.

There is no question that some people feel threatened by change and concerned that they may lose their job or be unable to cope with new ways of working. You have to involve the team all the way through the change process, understand their doubts and involve them in planning the new process. By making them stakeholders in the process change, it is much more likely that they will wish to make it work.

28.6 The CMMI process improvement framework

The Software Engineering Institute (SEI) was established to improve the capabilities of the US software industry. In the mid-1980s, the SEI initiated a study of ways of assessing the capabilities of software contractors. The outcome of this capability assessment was the SEI Software Capability Maturity Model (CMM) (Paulk, et al., 1993) (Paulk, et al., 1995). This has been tremendously influential in convincing the software engineering community to take process improvement seriously. The Software CMM was followed by a range of other capability maturity models, including the People Capability Maturity Model (P-CMM) (Curtis, et al., 2001), discussed in Chapter 25.

Other organisations have developed comparable process maturity models. The SPICE approach to capability assessment and process improvement (Paulk and Konrad 1994) is more flexible than the SEI model. It includes maturity levels comparable with the SEI levels but also identifies processes, such as customer-supplier processes, that cut across these levels. As the level of maturity increases, the performance of these key processes must improve.

The Bootstrap project had the goal of extending and adapting the SEI maturity model to make it applicable across a wider range of companies. The Bootstrap model (Haase, et al., 1994; Kuvaja, et al., 1994) uses the SEI's maturity levels but also proposes:

1. Guidelines for a company-wide quality system to support process improvement

2. An important distinction between organisation, methodology and technology

3. A base process model (based on the model used in the European Space Agency) that may be adopted.

In an attempt to integrate the plethora of models that have been developed (including its own models), the SEI embarked on a new programme to develop an integrated capability model (CMMI). This supersedes the Software and Systems Engineering CMMs and integrates other engineering models. It has two instantiations, staged and continuous, and addresses some of the reported weaknesses in the Software CMM.

The CMMI model (Ahern, et al., 2001) is intended to be a framework for process improvement that has broad applicability across a range of companies. Its staged version is compatible with the Software CMM and allows an organisation's system development and management processes to be assessed and assigned a maturity level from 1 to 5. Its continuous version allows for a finer-grain classification and rates 24 process areas (see Figure 28.10) on a scale from 1 to 6.

The model is very complex (more than 1,000 pages of description), so I have radically simplified it for discussion here:

1. *Process areas* The CMMI identifies 24 process areas that are relevant to software process capability and improvement. These are organised into four groups in the continuous CMMI model. These groups and related process areas are listed in Figure 28.10.

2. *Goals* Goals are abstract descriptions of a desirable state that should be attained by an organisation. The CMMI has specific goals that are associated with each process area and that define the desirable state for that area. It also defines generic goals that are associated with the institutionalisation of good practice. Figure 28.11 shows some specific and generic goals in the CMMI.

3. *Practices* Practices in the CMMI are descriptions of ways to achieving a goal. Up to seven specific and generic practices may be associated with each goal within each process area. Examples of recommended practices are shown in Figure 28.12. However, the CMMI recognises that it is the goal rather than the way that goal is reached that is important. Organisations may use any appropriate practices to achieve any of the CMMI goals—they do not have to take the CMMI recommendations.

Generic goals and practices are not technical but are associated with the institutionalisation of good practice. What this means depends on the maturity of the organisation. Therefore, for a young organisation at an early stage of maturity development, institutionalisation may mean following established plans and processes. However, for an organisation with more mature, advanced processes, institutionalisation may mean controlling the process using statistical and other quantitative techniques.

A CMMI assessment involves examining the processes in an organisation and rating these on a six-point scale that relates to the level of maturity in each process area. The six-point scale assigns a level to a process as follows:

Figure 28.10 Process
areas in the CMMI

Category	Process area
Process management	Organisational process definition Organisational process focus Organisational training Organisational process performance Organisational innovation and deployment
Project management	Project planning Project monitoring and control Supplier agreement management Integrated project management Risk management Integrated teaming Quantitative project management
Engineering	Requirements management Requirements development Technical solution Product integration Verification Validation
Support	Configuration management Process and product quality management Measurement and analysis Decision analysis and resolution Organisational environment for integration Causal analysis and resolution

Figure 28.11
Examples of goals in
the CMMI

Goal	Process area
Corrective actions are managed to closure when the project's performance or results deviate significantly from the plan.	Specific goal in project monitoring and control
Actual performance and progress of the project is monitored against the project plan.	Specific goal in project monitoring and control
The requirements are analysed and validated, and a definition of the required functionality is developed.	Specific goal in requirements development
Root causes of defects and other problems are systematically determined.	Specific goal in causal analysis and resolution
The process is institutionalised as a defined process.	Generic goal

Figure 28.12
Practices and
associated goals in
the CMMI

Practice	Associated goal
Analyse derived requirements to ensure that they are necessary and sufficient.	The requirements are analysed and validated, and a definition of the required functionality is developed.
Validate requirements to ensure that the resulting product will perform as intended in the user's environment using multiple techniques as appropriate.	
Select the defects and other problems for analysis.	Root causes of defects and other problems are systematically determined.
Perform causal analysis of selected defects and other problems and propose actions to address them.	
Establish and maintain an organisational policy for planning and performing the requirements development process.	The process is institutionalised as a defined process.
Assign responsibility and authority for performing the process, developing the work products and providing the services of the requirements development process.	

1. *Not performed* One or more of the specific goals associated with the process area is not satisfied.

2. *Performed* The goals associated with the process area are satisfied, and for all processes the scope of the work to be performed is explicitly set out and communicated to the team members.

3. *Managed* At this level, the goals associated with the process area are met and organisational policies are in place that define when each process should be used. There must be documented plans, and resource management and process monitoring procedures must be in place across the institution.

4. *Defined* This level focuses on organisational standardisation and deployment of processes. Each project in an organisation has a managed process that is tailored from a defined set of organisational processes. Process assets and process measurements must be collected and used for future process improvements.

5. *Quantitatively managed* At this level, there is an organisational responsibility to use statistical and other quantitative methods to control sub-processes. That is, collected process and product measurements must be used in process management.

6.   *Optimizing* At this highest level, the organisation must use the process and product measurements to drive process improvement. Trends must be analysed and the processes adapted to changing business needs.

Of course, this description of the capability levels is simplified, but you can generally think of the levels as progressive, with explicit process descriptions at the lowest levels, through process standardisation to process change and improvement driven by measurements of the process and the software.

28.6.1   The staged CMMI model

The staged CMMI model is comparable with the Software CMM in that it provides a means to assess an organisation's process capability at one of five levels. It prescribes the goals that should be achieved at each of these levels. Process improvement is achieved by implementing practices at each level, moving from the lower to the higher levels in the model. The five levels in the staged CMMI model are shown in Figure 28.13.

Each maturity level has an associated set of process areas and generic goals. For example, the process areas as defined in the model associated with the second level (the managed level) are:

1.   *Requirements management* Manage the requirements of the project's products and product components, and identify inconsistencies between those requirements and the project's plans and work products.

2.   *Project planning* Establish and maintain plans that define project activities.

3.   *Project monitoring and control* Provide understanding into the project's progress so that appropriate corrective actions can be taken when the project's performance deviates significantly from the plan.

4.   *Supplier agreement management* Manage the acquisition of products and services from suppliers external to the project for which a formal agreement exists.

5.   *Measurement and analysis* Develop and sustain a measurement capability that is used to support management information needs.

6.   *Process and product quality assurance* Provide staff and management with objective insight into the processes and associated work products.

7.   *Configuration management* Establish and maintain the integrity of work products using configuration identification, configuration control, configuration status accounting and configuration audits.

As well as these specific practices, organisations operating at the second level in the CMMI model should have achieved the generic goal of institutionalising each of the processes as a managed process. Examples of institutional practices

Figure 28.13 The
CMMI staged model

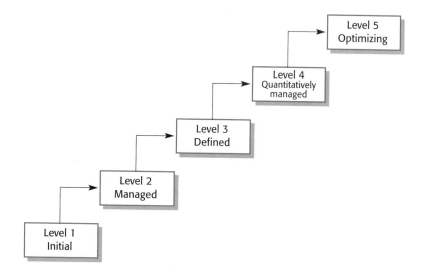

associated with project planning that lead to the project-planning process being a managed process are:

* Establish and maintain an organisational policy for planning and performing the project planning process.
* Provide adequate resources for performing the project management process, developing the work products and providing the services of the process.
* Monitor and control the project-planning process against the plan and take appropriate corrective action.
* Review the activities, status and results of the project-planning process with high-level management and resolve issues.

The advantage of the staged CMMI, apart from its compatibility with the Software CMM, is that it defines a clear improvement pathway for organisations. They move from the second to the third level, and so on. Its disadvantage is that it may be more appropriate to introduce goals and practices at higher levels before lower-level practices. When an organisation does this, a maturity assessment will give a misleading picture of its capability.

28.6.2 The continuous CMMI model

Continuous maturity models do not classify an organisation according to discrete levels. Rather, they are finer-grained models that consider individual or groups of practices and assess the use of each practice. The maturity assessment is not, there-

Figure 28.14 A
process capability
profile

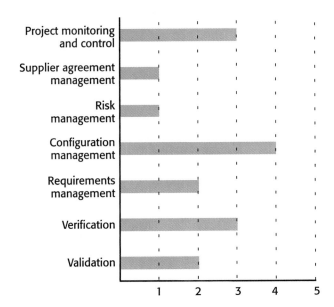

Figure 28.14 A
process capability
profile

fore, a single value but a set of values showing the organisation's maturity for each process or process group.

The continuous CMMI rates each process area as shown in Figure 28.10 and assigns a capability assessment level from 1 to 6 (as just described) to each process area.

Normally, organisations operate at different maturity levels for different process areas. Consequently, the result of a continuous CMMI assessment is a capability profile showing each process area and its associated capability assessment. A fragment of a capability profile that shows processes at different capability levels is shown in Figure 28.14. Organisations may develop actual and target capability profiles where the target profile reflects the capability level for that process area that they would like to reach.

The principal advantage of the continuous model is that organisations can pick and chose processes to improve according to their own needs and requirements. In my experience, different types of organisations have different requirements for process improvement. For example, a company that develops software for the aerospace industry may focus on improvements in system specification, configuration management and validation, whereas a web development company may be more concerned with customer-facing processes. The staged model requires companies to focus on the different stages in turn. By contrast, the continuous CMMI allows more discretion and flexibility while retaining the CMMI support.

KEY POINTS

■ Process improvement involves process analysis, standardisation, measurement and change. Training is essential if process improvement is to be effective.

■ Processes can be classified as informal, managed, methodical and improving. This classification can be used to identify process tool support.

■ The process improvement cycle involves process measurement, process analysis, and modelling and process change.

■ Measurement should be used to answer specific questions about the software process used. These questions should be based on organisational improvement goals.

■ Three types of process metrics used in the measurement process are time metrics, resource utilisation metrics and event metrics.

■ Process models include descriptions of activities, sub-processes, roles, exceptions, communications, deliverables and other processes.

■ The CMMI process maturity model is an integrated process improvement model that supports both staged and continuous process improvement.

■ Process improvement in the CMMI model is based on reaching a set of goals related to good software engineering practice and describing, standardising and controlling the practices used to achieve these goals. The CMMI model includes recommended practices that may be used, but these are not obligatory.

FURTHER READING

CMMI Distilled. The only concise summary of the CMMI approach at the time of this writing. It is easier to read if you already understand the Software CMM, as it lacks general introductory material on process improvement. (D. M. Ahern, et al., 2001, Addison-Wesley.)

'Can you trust software capability evaluations'. This article takes a sceptical look at the subject of capability evaluation and discusses why these evaluations may not give a true picture of an organisation's maturity. (E. O'Connell and H. Saiedian, *IEEE Computer*, 33(2), February 2000.)

Trends in Software: Software Process Modelling and Technology. This book includes a good selection of overview papers that cover aspects of software processes, including process modelling, process support and the use of the CMM. (A. Fuggetta and A. Wolf (eds.), 1996, John Wiley & Sons.)

Managing the Software Process. A classic text on software process improvement that first publicised the notion of a structured approach to process improvement. Although this book is more than 15 years old, the advice in this book is still very relevant, especially for very large software projects. (W. S. Humphrey, 1988, Addison-Wesley.)

EXERCISES

28.1 Suggest process models for the following processes:

■ Lighting a wood fire

■ Cooking a three-course meal (you chose the menu)

■ Writing a small (50-line) program.

28.2 Under what circumstances is product quality likely to be determined by the quality of the development team? Give examples of the types of software product that are particularly dependent on individual talent and ability.

28.3 Explain why a methodical process is not necessarily a managed process as defined in Section 28.2.

28.4 Suggest three specialised software tools that might be developed to support a process improvement programme in an organisation.

28.5 Assume that the goal of process improvement in an organisation is to increase the number of reusable components that are produced during development. Suggest three questions in the GQM paradigm that this might lead to.

28.6 Describe three types of software process metric that may be collected as part of a process improvement process. Give one example of each type of metric.

28.7 Design a process for assessing and prioritising process change proposals. Document this process as a process model showing the roles involved in this process.

28.8 Give two advantages and two disadvantages of the approach to process assessment and improvement that is embodied in the process improvement frameworks such as the CMMI.

28.9 Under what circumstances would you recommend the use of the staged representation of the CMMI?

28.10 What is the difference between generic and specific goals in the CMMI?

28.11 What are the advantages and disadvantages of using a goal-based rather than a practice-based maturity model?

28.12 Are process improvement programmes, which involve measuring the work of people in the process and changing the process, inherently dehumanising? What resistance to a process improvement programme might arise?

29

Configuration management

Objectives

The objective of this chapter is to introduce the process of managing the code and documentation of an evolving software system. When you have read this chapter, you will:

- understand why software configuration management is required for complex software systems;

- have been introduced to four fundamental configuration management activities—configuration management planning, change management, version and release management, and system building;

- understand how CASE tools for configuration management are used to support configuration management processes.

Contents

Configuration management (CM) is the development and use of standards and procedures for managing an evolving software system. As I discussed in Chapter 7, system requirements always change during development and use, and you have to incorporate these requirements into new versions of the system. You need to manage evolving systems because it is easy to lose track of what changes have been incorporated into what system version. Versions incorporate proposals for change, corrections of faults and adaptations for different hardware and operating systems. There may be several versions under development and in use at the same time. If you don't have effective configuration management procedures in place, you may waste effort modifying the wrong version of a system, deliver the wrong version of a system to customers or lose track of where the software source code is stored.

Configuration management procedures define how to record and process proposed system changes, how to relate these to system components and the methods used to identify different versions of the system. Configuration management tools are used to store versions of system components, build systems from these components and track the releases of system versions to customers.

Configuration management is sometimes considered to be part of software quality management (covered in Chapter 27), with the same manager sharing quality management and configuration management responsibilities. The software is initially released by the development team for quality assurance. The QA team checks that the system is of acceptable quality. It then becomes a controlled system, which means that changes to the system have to be agreed on and recorded before they are implemented. Controlled systems are sometimes called *baselines* because they are a starting point for further, controlled evolution.

There are many reasons why systems exist in different configurations. Configurations may be produced for different computers, for different operating systems, incorporating client-specific functions and so on (Figure 29.1). Configuration managers are responsible for keeping track of the differences between software versions, for ensuring that new versions are derived in a controlled way and for releasing new versions to the right customers at the right time.

The definition and use of configuration management standards is essential for quality certification in both the ISO 9000 and the CMM and CMMI standards (Paulk, et al., 1995; Ahern, et al., 2001; Peach, 1996). An example of such a standard is IEEE 828-1998, which is a standard for configuration management plans. Within a company, these standards should be incorporated into the quality handbook or configuration management guide. Of course, the generic external standards may be used as a basis for more detailed organisational standards that are tailored to a specific environment.

In a traditional software development process based on the 'waterfall' model (see Chapter 4), software is delivered to the configuration management team after development is complete and the individual software components have been tested. This team then takes over the responsibility for building the complete system and for managing system testing. Faults that are discovered during system testing are passed back to the development team for repair. After the faults have been repaired, the development team delivers a new version of the repaired component to the quality

Figure 29.1 System
families

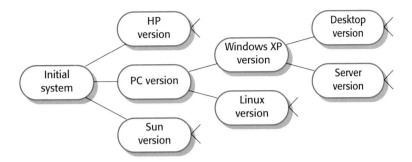

assurance team. If the quality is acceptable, this then may become the new baseline for further system development.

This model, where the CM team controls the system integration and testing processes, has influenced the development of configuration management standards. Most
CM standards have an embedded assumption that a waterfall model will be used
for system development (Bersoff and Davis, 1991). This means that the standards
have to be adapted to modern software development approaches based on incremental specification and development. Hass (Hass, 2003) discusses some of these
adaptations for software development processes such as agile development.

To cater for incremental development, some organisations have developed a modified approach to configuration management that supports concurrent development
and system testing. This approach relies on a very frequent (at least daily) build of
the whole system from its components:

1.   The development organisation sets a delivery time (say 2 p.m.) for system com-
     ponents. If developers have new versions of the components that they are writ-
     ing, they must deliver them by that time. Components may be incomplete but
     should provide some basic functionality that can be tested.

2.   A new version of the system is built from these components by compiling and
     linking them to form a complete system.

3.   This system is then delivered to the testing team, which carries out a set of pre-
     defined system tests. At the same time, the developers are still working on their
     components, adding to the functionality and repairing faults discovered in pre-
     vious tests.

4.   Faults that are discovered during system testing are documented and returned
     to the system developers. They repair these faults in a subsequent version of
     the component.

The advantages of using daily builds of software are that the chances of finding
problems stemming from component interactions early in the process are increased.
Furthermore, daily building encourages thorough unit testing of components.

Psychologically, developers are put under pressure not to 'break the build', that is, deliver versions of components that cause the whole system to fail. They are therefore reluctant to deliver new component versions that have not been properly tested. Less system testing time is spent discovering and coping with software faults that should have been found during unit testing.

The successful use of daily builds requires a very stringent change management process to keep track of the problems that have been discovered and repaired. It also leads to a very large number of system and component versions that must be managed. Good configuration management is therefore essential for this approach to be successful.

Configuration management in agile and rapid development approaches cannot be based around rigid procedures and paperwork. While these may be necessary for large, complex projects, they slow down the development process. Careful record-keeping is essential for large, complex systems developed across several sites, but it is unnecessary for small projects. In these projects, all team members work together in the same room, and the overhead involved in record keeping slows down the development process. However, this does not mean that CM should be completely abandoned when rapid development is required. Rather, agile processes use simple CM tools, such as version management and system-building tools, that enforce some control. All team members have to learn to use these tools and conform to the disciplines that they impose.

29.1 Configuration management planning

A configuration management plan describes the standards and procedures that should be used for configuration management. The starting point for developing the plan should be a set of configuration management standards, and these should be adapted to fit the requirements and constraints of each specific project. The CM plan should be organised into a number of sections that:

1. Define what is to be managed (the configuration items) and the scheme that you should use to identify these entities.

2. Set out who is responsible for the configuration management procedures and for submitting controlled entities to the configuration management team.

3. Define the configuration management policies that all team members must use for change control and version management.

4. Specify the tools that you should use for configuration management and the processes for using these tools.

5. Describe the structure of the configuration database that is used to record configuration information and the information that should be maintained in that database (the configuration records).

You may also include other information in the CM plan such as the management of software from external suppliers and the auditing procedures for the CM process in the CM plan.

An important part of the CM plan is the definition of responsibilities. The plan should define who is responsible for the delivery of each document or software component to quality assurance and configuration management. It may also define the reviewers of each document. The person responsible for document delivery need not be the same as the person responsible for producing the document. To simplify interfaces, project managers or team leaders are often responsible for all of the documents produced by their team.

29.1.1 Configuration item identification

In a large software system, there may be thousands of source code modules, test scripts, design documents and so on. These are produced by different people and, when created, may be assigned similar or identical names. To keep track of all this information so that the right file can be found when it is needed, you need a consistent identification scheme for all items in the configuration management system.

During the configuration management planning process, you decide exactly which items (or classes of items) are to be controlled. Documents or groups of related documents under configuration control are formal documents or configuration items. Project plans, specifications, designs, programs and test data suites are normally maintained as configuration items. All documents that may be useful for future system evolution should be controlled by the configuration management system.

However, this does not mean that every document or file produced must be placed under configuration control. Documents such as technical working documents that present a snapshot of ideas for further development, minutes of group meetings, outline plans and proposals, and so on may not have long-term relevance and are not needed for future maintenance of the system.

The configuration item identification scheme must assign a unique name to all documents under configuration control. This name may reflect the type of item, the part of the system that it applies to, the creator of the item and so on. In your naming scheme, you may wish to reflect relationships between items by ensuring that related documents have a common root to their name. Therefore, you might define a hierarchical naming scheme with names such as:

PCL-TOOLS/EDIT/FORMS/DISPLAY/AST-INTERFACE/CODE
PCL-TOOLS/EDIT/HELP/QUERY/HELPFRAMES/FR-1

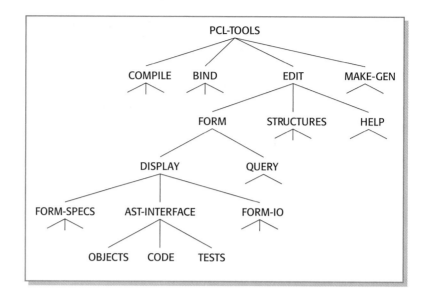

Figure 29.2 A
configuration
hierarchy used to
assign item
identifiers

The initial part of the name is the project name, PCL-TOOLS. In this project, there are a number of separate tools being developed, so the tool name (EDIT) is used as the next part of the name. Each tool includes differently named modules whose name makes up the next component of the item identifier (FORMS, HELP). This decomposition process continues until the base-level formal documents are referenced (Figure 29.2). The leaves of the documentation hierarchy are the formal configuration items. Figure 29.2 shows that three formal items are required for each code component: an object description (OBJECTS), the source code of the component (CODE) and a set of tests for that component (TESTS). Items such as help frames are also managed and have different names (FR-1, in the preceding example).

Hierarchical naming schemes are simple and easily understood, and sometimes they can map to the directory structures used to store project files. However, they reflect the structure of the project where the software was developed. The configuration item names associate components with a particular project and so may reduce the opportunities for reuse. It can be very hard to find related components (e.g., all components developed by the same programmer) where the relationship is not reflected in the item-naming scheme.

29.1.2 The configuration database

The configuration database is used to record all relevant information about system configurations and configuration items. You use the CM database to help assess the impact of system changes and to generate reports for management about the CM process. As part of the CM planning process, you should define the CM database schema, the forms to collect information to be recorded in the database and procedures for recording and retrieving project information.

A configuration database does not just include information about configuration items. It may also record information about users of components, system customers, execution platforms, proposed changes and so forth. It should be able to provide answers to a variety of queries about system configurations. Typical queries might be:

1. Which customers have taken delivery of a particular version of the system?

2. What hardware and operating system configuration is required to run a given system version?

3. How many versions of a system have been created and what were their creation dates?

4. What versions of a system might be affected if a particular component is changed?

5. How many change requests are outstanding on a particular version?

6. How many reported faults exist in a particular version?

Ideally, the configuration database should be integrated with the version management system that is used to store and manage the formal project documents. This approach, supported by some integrated CASE tools, makes it possible to link changes directly with the documents and components affected by the change. Links between documents (such as design documents) and program code may be maintained so that you can find everything that you have to modify when a change is proposed.

However, integrated CASE tools for configuration management are expensive. Many companies do not use them but maintain their configuration database separate from their version control systems. They store configuration items as files in a directory structure or in a version management system such as CVS (Berliner, 1990), discussed later in this chapter.

The configuration database stores information about the configuration items and references their names in the version management system or filestore. While this is a relatively cheap and flexible approach, the problem with it is that configuration items may be changed without going through the configuration database. Therefore, you can't be completely sure that the configuration database is an up-to-date description of the state of the system.

29.2 Change management

Change is a fact of life for large software systems. As I have discussed in earlier chapters, organisational needs and requirements change during the lifetime of a system.

Figure 29.3 The
change management
process

Request change by completing a change request form
Analyze change request
if change is valid **then**
    Assess how change might be implemented
    Assess change cost
    Record change request in database
    Submit request to change control board
    if change is accepted **then**
        repeat
            make changes to software
            record changes and link to associated change request
            submit changed software for quality approval
        until software quality is adequate
        create new system version
    else
        reject change request
else
    reject change request

This means that you have to make corresponding changes to the software system. To ensure that the changes are applied to the system in a controlled way, you need a set of tool-supported, change management procedures.

Change management procedures are concerned with analysing the costs and benefits of proposed changes, approving those changes that are worthwhile and tracking which components of the system have been changed. The change management process (Figure 29.3) should come into effect when the software or associated documentation is baselined by the configuration management team.

The first stage in the change management process is to complete a change request form (CRF) describing the change required to the system. As well as recording the change required, the CRF records the recommendations regarding the change, the estimated costs of the change and the dates when the change was requested, approved, implemented and validated. The CRF may also include a section where an analyst outlines how the change is to be implemented.

An example of a partially completed change request form is shown in Figure 29.4. The change request form is usually defined during the CM planning process. This is an example of a CRF that might be used in a large complex systems engineering project. For smaller projects, I recommend that change requests should be formally recorded, but the CRF should focus on describing the change required with less focus on implementation issues. The engineer making the change decides how to implement that change in these situations.

Once a change request form has been submitted, it should be registered in the configuration database. The change request is then analysed to check that the change requested is necessary. Some change requests may be due to misunderstandings

Figure 29.4 A
partially completed
change request form

Change Request Form

Project: Proteus/PCL-Tools   **Number:** 23/02
Change requester: I. Sommerville   **Date:** 1/12/02
Requested change: When a component is selected from the structure, display the
name of the file where it is stored.

Change analyser: G. Dean   **Analysis date:** 10/12/02
Components affected: Display-Icon.Select, Display-Icon.Display

Associated components: FileTable

Change assessment: Relatively simple to implement as a file name table is
available. Requires the design and implementation of a display field. No changes to
associated components are required.

Change priority: Low
Change implementation:
Estimated effort: 0.5 days
Date to CCB: 15/12/02   **CCB decision date:** 1/2/03
CCB decision: Accept change. Change to be implemented in Release 2.1.
Change implementor: **Date of change:**
Date submitted to QA: **QA decision:**
Date submitted to CM:
Comments

---

rather than system faults and no system change is necessary. Others may refer to
already known faults. If the analysis discovers that a change request is invalid, duplicated or has already been considered, the change is rejected. You should tell the
person who submitted the change request why it has been rejected.

For valid changes, the next stage of the process is change assessment and costing. The impact of the change on the rest of the system must be checked. This involves
identifying all of the components affected by the change using information from
the configuration database and the source code of the software. If making the change
means that further changes elsewhere in the system are needed, this clearly
increases the cost of change implementation. Next, the required changes to the system modules are assessed. Finally, the cost of making the change is estimated, taking into account the costs of changing related components.

A change control board (CCB) should review and approve all change requests unless
the changes simply involve correcting minor errors on screen displays, web pages or
in documents. The CCB considers the impact of the change from a strategic and organisational rather than a technical point of view. The board should decide whether the
change is economically justified and should prioritise the changes that have been accepted.

The term *change control board* implies a rather grand group that makes change
decisions. Such formally structured CCBs, including senior client and contractor staff,
are a requirement of military projects. However, for small or medium-sized projects,
the CCB may simply consist of a project manager plus one or two engineers who are

not directly involved in the software development. In some cases, the CCB may be a single change reviewer who gives advice on whether changes are justifiable.

Change management for generic, shrink-wrapped software products rather than systems that are tailored for a specific customer has to be handled in a slightly different way. In these systems, the customer is not directly involved so the relevance of the change to the customer's business is not an issue. Change requests in these products are usually associated with bugs in the system that have been discovered during system testing or by customers after the software has been released. Customers may use a web page or e-mail to report bugs. A bug management team then checks that the bug reports are valid and translates them into formal system change requests. As with other types of systems, changes have to be prioritised for implementation and bugs may not be repaired if the repair costs are too high.

During development, when new versions of the system are created through daily (or more frequent) system builds, a simpler change management process is used. Problems and changes must still be recorded, but changes that affect only individual components and modules need not be independently assessed. They are passed directly to the system developer. The system developer either accepts them or makes a case why they are not required. Changes that affect system modules produced by different development teams, however, should be assessed by a change control authority who prioritises them for implementation.

In some agile methods, such as extreme programming, customers are directly involved in deciding whether a change should be implemented. When they propose a change to the system requirements, they work with the team to assess the impact of that change and then decide whether the change should take priority over the features planned for the next increment of the system. However, changes that involve software improvement are left to the discretion of the programmers working on the system. Refactoring, where the software is continually improved, is not seen as an overhead but rather as a necessary part of the development process.

As software components are changed, a record of the changes made to each component should be maintained. This is sometimes called the *derivation history* of a component. A good way to keep the derivation history is in a standardised comment at the beginning of the component source code (see Figure 29.5). This comment should reference the change request that triggered the software change. You can then write simple scripts that scan all components and process the derivation histories to produce component change reports. A similar approach can be used for web pages. For published documents, records of changes incorporated in each version are usually maintained in a separate page at the front of the document.

29.3 Version and release management

The processes involved in version and release management are concerned with identifying and keeping track of the versions of a system. Version managers devise

Figure 29.5
Component header
information

```
// BANKSEC project (IST 6087)
//
// BANKSEC-TOOLS/AUTH/RBAC/USER_ROLE
//
// Object: currentRole
// Author: N. Perwaiz
// Creation date: 10th November 2002
//
// (c) Lancaster University 2002
//
// Modification history
// Version    Modifier      Date          Change        Reason
// 1.0        J. Jones      1/12/2002     Add header     Submitted to CM
// 1.1        N. Perwaiz    9/4/2003      New field      Change req. R07/02
```

procedures to ensure that versions of a system may be retrieved when required and are not accidentally changed by the development team. For products, version managers work with marketing staff and, for custom systems with customers, to plan when new releases of a system should be created and distributed for deployment.

A system version is an instance of a system that differs, in some way, from other instances. Versions of the system may have different functionality, enhanced performance or repaired software faults. Some versions may be functionally equivalent but designed for different hardware or software configurations. Versions with only small differences are sometimes called *variants*.

A system release is a version that is distributed to customers. Each system release should either include new functionality or should be intended for a different hardware platform. There are normally many more versions of a system than releases. Versions are created within an organisation for internal development or testing and are not intended for release to customers

As I discuss in Section 29.5, CASE tools are now always used to support version management. These tools manage the storage of each version of the software and control access to system components. Components must be checked out from the system for editing. Re-entering (checking in) the component creates a new version, and an identifier is assigned by the version management system. While tools obviously differ significantly in the features offered and their user interfaces, the general principles of version management covered here are the basis for all support tools.

29.3.1 Version identification

To create a particular version of a system, you have to specify the versions of the system components that should be included in it. In a large software system, there are hundreds of software components, each of which may exist in several different versions. There must therefore be an unambiguous way to identify each component version to ensure that the right components are included in the system. However, you cannot use the configuration item name for version identification because there may be several versions of each identified configuration item.

Instead, three basic techniques are used for component version identification:

1. *Version numbering* The component is given an explicit, unique version number. This is the most commonly used identification scheme.

2. *Attribute-based identification* Each component has a name (such as the configuration item name, which is not unique across versions) and an associated set of attributes for each version (Estublier and Casallas, 1994). Components are therefore identified by specifying their name and attribute values.

3. *Change-oriented identification* Each component is named as in attribute-based identification but is also associated with one or more change requests (Munch, et al., 1993). That is, it is assumed than each version of the component has been created in response to one or more change requests. The component version is identified by the set of change requests that apply to the component.

Version numbering

In a simple version-numbering scheme, a version number is added to the component or system name. Therefore, you might refer to Solaris 4.3 (version 4.3 of the Solaris system) and version 1.4 of component **getToken**. If the first version is called 1.0, subsequent versions are 1.1, 1.2, and so on. At some stage, a new release is created (release 2.0) and the process starts again at version 2.1. The scheme is linear, based on the assumption that system versions are created in sequence. Most version management tools (see Section 29.5) such as RCS (Tichy, 1985) and CVS (Berliner, 1990) support this approach to version identification.

I illustrate this approach and the derivation of a number of different system versions in Figure 29.6. The arrows in this diagram point from the source version to the new version created from that source. Notice that the derivation of versions is not necessarily linear and versions with consecutive version numbers may be produced from different baselines. For example, in Figure 29.6, version 2.2 is created from version 1.2 rather than from version 2.1. In principle, any existing version may be used as the starting point for a new version of the system.

This scheme is simple, but you need to maintain a lot of extra information to keep track of the differences between versions and the relationships between system change proposals and versions. For example, versions 1.1 and 1.2 of a system might differ because version 1.2 has been produced using a different graphics library. The name tells you nothing about the version or why it was created. Consequently, you need to keep records in the configuration database that describe each version and why it was produced. You may also need to explicitly link change requests to the different versions of each component.

Figure 29.6 Version
derivation structure

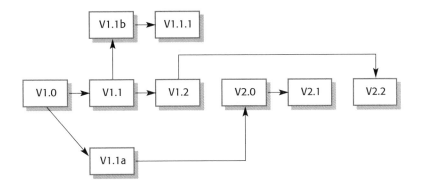

Attribute-based identification

A fundamental problem with explicit version naming schemes is that they do not
reflect the many attributes that may be used to identify versions. Examples of these
identifying attributes are:

- Customer
- Development language
- Development status
- Hardware platform
- Creation date

   If each version is identified by a unique set of attributes, it is easy to add new versions that are derived from any of the existing versions. These are identified using a
unique set of attribute values. They share most of these values with their parent version so relationships between versions are maintained. You can retrieve specific versions by specifying the attribute values required. Functions on attributes support queries
such as 'the most recently created version' or 'the version created between given dates'.
   For example, the version of the software system AC3D developed in Java for
Windows XP in January 2003 would be identified:

AC3D (language = Java, platform = XP, date = Jan2003)

Using a general specification of the components in AC3D, the version management tool selects the versions of components that have the attributes 'Java', 'XP'
and 'Jan2003'.
   Attribute-based identification may be implemented directly by the version management system, with component attributes maintained in a system database.
Alternatively, the attribute identification system may be built as a layer on top of
a hidden version-numbering scheme. The configuration database then maintains the
links between identifying attributes and underlying system and component versions.

Change-oriented identification

Attribute-based identification of system versions removes some of the version retrieval problems of simple version numbering schemes. However, to retrieve a version, you still have to know its associated attributes. Furthermore, you still need to use a separate change management system to discover the relationships between versions and changes.

Change-oriented identification is used to identify system versions rather than components. The version identifiers of individual components are hidden from users of the CM system. Each system change that has been implemented has an associated change set that describes the requested changes made to the different system components. Change sets may be applied in sequence so that, in principle at least, the version may incorporate an arbitrary set of changes. For example, the set of changes to a system that were made to adapt it for Linux rather than Solaris could be applied, followed by the changes required to incorporate a new system database. Equally, the Linux/Solaris changes could be followed by changes that converted the user interface language from English to Italian.

In practice, of course, it isn't possible to apply arbitrary sets of changes to a system. The change sets may be incompatible so that applying change set A followed by change set D may create an invalid system. Furthermore, change sets may conflict in that different changes affect the same code of the system. If the code has been changed by change set A, then change set D may no longer work. To address these difficulties, version management tools that support change-oriented identification allow system consistency rules to be specified. These limit the ways in which change sets may be combined.

29.3.2 Release management

A system release is a version of the system that is distributed to customers. System release managers are responsible for deciding when the system can be released to customers, managing the process of creating the release and the distribution media, and documenting the release to ensure that it may be re-created exactly as distributed if this is necessary.

A system release is not just the executable code of the system. The release may also include:

1. *Configuration files* defining how the release should be configured for particular installations

2. *Data files* that are needed for successful system operation

3. *An installation program* that is used to help install the system on target hardware

4. *Electronic and paper documentation* describing the system

5. *packaging and associated publicity* that have been designed for that release.

Release managers cannot assume that customers will always install new system releases. Some system users may be happy with an existing system. They may consider it not worth the cost of changing to a new release. New releases of the system cannot, therefore, rely on the installation of previous releases. To illustrate this problem, consider the following scenario:

1. Release 1 of a system is distributed and put into use.

2. Release 2 requires the installation of new data files, but some customers do not need the facilities of release 2 so remain with release 1.

3. Release 3 requires the data files installed in release 2 and has no new data files of its own.

The software distributor cannot assume that the files required for release 3 have already been installed in all sites. Some sites may go directly from release 1 to release 3, skipping release 2. Some sites may have modified the data files associated with release 2 to reflect local circumstances. Therefore, the data files must be distributed and installed with release 3 of the system.

Release decision making

Preparing and distributing a system release is an expensive process, particularly for mass-market software products. If releases are too frequent, customers may not upgrade to the new release, especially if it is not free. If system releases are infrequent, market share may be lost as customers move to alternative systems. This, of course, does not apply to custom software developed specially for an organisation. For custom software, infrequent releases may mean increasing divergence between the software and the business processes that it is designed to support.

The various technical and organisational factors that you should take into account when deciding to create a new system release are shown in Figure 29.7.

Release creation

Release creation is the process of creating a collection of files and documentation that includes all of the components of the system release. The executable code of the programs and all associated data files must be collected and identified. Configuration descriptions may have to be written for different hardware and operating systems and instructions prepared for customers who need to configure their own systems. If machine-readable manuals are distributed, electronic copies must be stored with the software. Scripts for the installation program may have to be written. Finally, when all information is available, the release directory is handed over for distribution.

Figure 29.7 Factors
influencing system
release strategy

Factor	Description
Technical quality of the system	If serious system faults are reported which affect the way in which many customers use the system, it may be necessary to issue a fault repair release. However, minor system faults may be repaired by issuing patches (often distributed over the Internet) that can be applied to the current release of the system.
Platform changes	You may have to create a new release of a software application when a new version of the operating system platform is released.
Lehman's fifth law (see Chapter 21)	This suggests that the increment of functionality that is included in each release is approximately constant. Therefore, a system release with significant new functionality may have to be followed by a repair release.
Competition	A new system release may be necessary because a competing product is available.
Marketing requirements	The marketing department of an organisation may have made a commitment for releases to be available at a particular date.
Customer change proposals	For customised systems, customers may have made and paid for a specific set of system change proposals, and they expect a system release as soon as these have been implemented.

The normal distribution medium for system releases is now optical disks (CD-ROM or DVD) that can store from 600 Mbytes to 4 Gbytes of data. In addition, software may be released online, allowing customers to download it from the Internet, although many people find it takes too long to download large files and prefer CD-ROM distribution.

There are very high marketing and packaging costs associated with distributing new releases of software products, so product vendors usually create new releases only for new platforms or to add significant new functionality. They then charge users for this new software. When problems are discovered in an existing release, the vendors usually make patches to repair the existing software available on a web site for downloading by customers.

Apart from the costs of finding and downloading the new release, the problem is that many customers may never discover the existence of these repairs or may not have the technical knowledge to install them. They may instead continue using their existing, faulty system with the consequent risks to their business. In some situations, where the patch is designed to repair security loopholes, the risks of failing to install the patch can mean that the business is susceptible to external attacks.

Release documentation

When a system release is produced, it must be documented to ensure that it can be re-created exactly in the future. This is particularly important for customised, long-lifetime embedded systems such as those controlling complex machines. Customers may use a single release of these systems for many years and may require specific changes to a particular software release long after its original release date.

To document a release, you have to record the specific versions of the source code components that were used to create the executable code. You must keep copies of the source and executable code and all data and configuration files. You should also record the versions of the operating system, libraries, compilers and other tools used to build the software. These may be required to build exactly the same system at some later date. This may mean that you have to store copies of the platform software and the tools used to create the system in the version management system along with the source code of the target system.

29.4 System building

System building is the process of compiling and linking software components into a program that executes on a particular target configuration. When you are building a system from its components, you have to think about the following questions:

1. Have all the components that make up a system been included in the build instructions?

2. Has the appropriate version of each required component been included in the build instructions?

3. Are all required data files available?

4. If data files are referenced within a component, is the name used the same as the name of the data file on the target machine?

5. Is the appropriate version of the compiler and other required tools available? Current versions of software tools may be incompatible with the older versions used to develop the system.

Nowadays, software configuration management tools or, sometimes, the programming environment are used to automate the system-building process. The CM team writes a build script that defines the dependencies between the system components. This script also defines the tools used to compile and link the system components. The system-building tool interprets the build script and calls other programs as required to build the executable system from its components. This is illustrated in

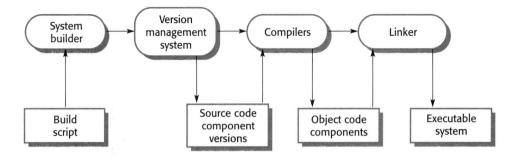

Figure 29.8 System building

Figure 29.8. In some programming environments (such as Java development environments), the build script is created automatically by parsing the source code and discovering which components are called. Of course, in this situation, the name of the stored component has to be the same as the name of the program component.

Dependencies between components are specified in the build script. This provides information so that the system-building tool can decide when the source code of components must be recompiled and when existing object code can be reused. In many tools, these build-script dependencies are often specified as dependencies between the physical files in which the source code and object code of components are stored. However, when there are multiple source code files representing multiple versions of components, it may be difficult to tell which source files were used to derive object-code components. This confusion is particularly likely when the correspondence between source and object code files relies on them having the same name but a different suffix (e.g., .c and .o). This problem can only be solved when the version management and system-building tools are integrated.

29.5 CASE tools for configuration management

Configuration management processes are usually standardised and involve the application of predefined procedures. They require careful management of very large amounts of data, and attention to detail is essential. When a system is being built from component versions, a single configuration management mistake can mean that the software will not work properly. Consequently, CASE tool support is essential for configuration management, and, since the 1970s, many software tools covering different areas of configuration management have been produced.

These tools can be combined to create a configuration management workbench to support all CM activities. There are two types of CM workbench:

1. *Open workbenches* Tools for each stage in the CM process are integrated through standard organisational procedures for using these tools. There are many commercial

and open-source CM tools available for specific purposes. Change management can be supported by bug-tracking tools such as Bugzilla, version management by using tools such as RCS (Tichy, 1985) or CVS (Berliner, 1990), and system building by using tools such as make (Feldman, 1979; Oram and Talbott, 1991) or imake (DuBois, 1996). These are all open-source tools that are freely available.

2. *Integrated workbenches* These workbenches provide integrated facilities for version management, system building and change tracking. For example, Rational's Unified Change Management process relies on an integrated CM workbench incorporating ClearCase (White, 2000) for system building and version management and ClearQuest for change tracking. The advantages of integrated CM workbenches are that data exchange is simplified, and the workbench includes an integrated CM database. Integrated SCM workbenches have been derived from earlier systems such as Lifespan (Whitgift, 1991) for change management and DSEE (Leblang and Chase, 1987) for version management and system building. However, integrated CM workbenches are complex and expensive, and many organisations prefer to use cheaper and simpler individual tool support.

Many large systems are developed at different sites, and these need SCM tools that support multisite working with multiple data stores for configuration items. While most SCM tools are designed for single site working, some tools, such as CVS, have facilities for multisite support (Vesperman, 2003).

29.5.1 Support for change management

Each person involved in the change management process is responsible for some activity. They complete this activity, then pass on the forms and associated configuration items to someone else. The procedural nature of this process means that a change process model can be designed and integrated with a version management system. This model may then be interpreted so that the right documents are passed to the right people at the right time.

There are several change management tools available, from relatively simple, open-source tools such as Bugzilla to comprehensive integrated systems such as Rational ClearQuest. These tools provide some or all of the following facilities to support the process:

1. *A form editor* that allows change proposal forms to be created and completed by people making change requests.

2. *A workflow system* that allows the CM team to define who must process the change request form and the order of processing. This system will also automatically pass forms to the right people at the right time and inform the relevant team members of the progress of the change. E-mail is used to provide progress updates for those involved in the process.

3. *A change database* that is used to manage all change proposals and that may be linked to a version management system. Database query facilities allow the CM team to find specific change proposals.

4. *A change-reporting system* that generates management reports on the status of change requests that have been submitted.

29.5.2 Support for version management

Version management involves managing large amounts of information and ensuring that system changes are recorded and controlled. Version management tools control a repository of configuration items where the contents of that repository are immutable (i.e., cannot be changed). To work on a configuration item, you must check it out of the repository into a working directory. After you have made the changes to the software, you check it back into the repository and a new version is automatically created.

All version management systems provide a comparable basic set of capabilities although some have more sophisticated facilities than others. Examples of these capabilities are:

1. *Version and release identification* Managed versions are assigned identifiers when they are submitted to the system. Different systems support the different types of version identification discussed in Section 29.3.1.

2. *Storage management* To reduce the storage space required by multiple versions that are largely the same, version management systems provide storage management facilities so that versions are described by their differences from some master version. Differences between versions are represented as a *delta*, which encapsulates the instructions required to recreate the associated system version. This is illustrated in Figure 29.9, which shows how backward deltas may be applied to the latest version of a system to re-create earlier system versions. The latest version is version 1.3. To create version 1.2, you apply the change delta that re-creates that version.

3. *Change history recording* All of the changes made to the code of a system or component are recorded and listed. In some systems, these changes may be used to select a particular system version.

4. *Independent development* Multiple versions of a system can be developed in parallel and each version may be changed independently. For example, release 1 can be modified after development of release 2 is in progress by adding new level-1 deltas. The version management system keeps track of components that have been checked out for editing and ensures that changes made to the same component by different developers do not interfere. Some systems allow only one instance of a component to be checked out for editing; others resolve potential clashes when the edited components are checked back into the system.

Figure 29.9 Delta-based versioning

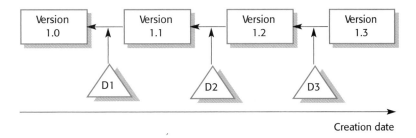

5. *Project support* The system can support multiple projects as well as multiple files. In project support systems, such as CVS, it is possible to check in and check out all of the files associated with a project rather than having to work with one file at a time.

29.5.3 Support for system building

System building is a computationally intensive process. Compiling and linking all of the components of a large system can take several hours. There may be hundreds of files involved, with the consequent possibility of human error if these are compiled and linked manually. System-building tools automate the build process to reduce the potential for human error and, where possible, minimise the time required for system building.

System-building tools may be standalone, such as derivatives of the Unix make utility (Oram and Talbott, 1991), or may be integrated with version management tools. Facilities provided by system-building CASE tools may include:

1. *A dependency specification language and associated interpreter* Component dependencies may be described and recompilation minimised. I explain this in more detail later in this section.

2. *Tool selection and instantiation support* The compilers and other processing tools that are used to process the source code files may be specified and instantiated as required.

3. *Distributed compilation* Some system builders, especially those that are part of integrated CM systems, support distributed network compilation. Rather than all compilations being carried out on a single machine, the system builder looks for idle processors on the network and sets off a number of parallel compilations. This significantly reduces the time required to build a system.

4. *Derived object management* Derived objects are objects created from other source objects. Derived object management links the source code and the derived objects and rederives only an object when this is required by source code changes.

Figure 29.10
Component
dependencies

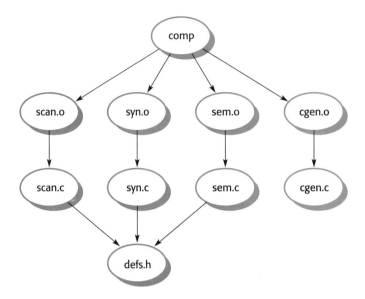

Managing derived objects and minimising recompilation is best explained using a simple example. Consider a situation where a compiler program called **comp** is created out of four object modules named **scan.o**, **syn.o**, **sem.o** and **cgen.o**. Each object module is created from a source code module with corresponding names (**scan.c**, **syn.c**, **sem.c** and **cgen.c**). A file of variable and constant declarations called **defs.h** is shared by **scan.c**, **syn.c** and **sem.c** (Figure 29.10). In Figure 29.10, the arrows mean 'depends on'—the entity at the base of the arrow depends on the entity at its head. Therefore, **comp** depends on **scan.o**, **syn.o**, **sem.o** and **cgen.o**, **scan.o** depends on **scan.c**, and so on.

If **scan.c** is changed, the system-building tool can detect that the derived object **scan.o** must be re-created. It does this by comparing the modification times of **scan.o** and **scan.c** and detects that **scan.c** has been modified after **scan.o**. It then calls the C compiler to compile **scan.c** to create a new derived object, **scan.o**.

The build tool then uses the dependency link between **comp** and **scan.o** to detect that **comp** must be recreated by linking **scan.o**, **syn.o**, **sem.o** and **cgen.o**. The system can detect that the other object code components are unchanged, so recompilation of their source code is not required.

Most system-building tools use the file modification date as the key attribute in deciding whether recompilation is required. If a source code file is modified after its corresponding object code file, then the object code file is re-created. Essentially, there can only ever be one version of the object code corresponding to the most recently changed source code component. When a new version of a source code component is re-created, the object code for the previous version is lost.

However, some tools use a more sophisticated approach to derived object management. They tag derived objects with the version identifier of the source code used to generate these objects. Within the limits of storage capacity, they maintain all derived objects. Therefore, it is usually possible to recover the object code of all versions of source code components without recompilation.

KEY POINTS

▨ Configuration management is the management of system change. When a system is maintained, the role of the CM team is to ensure that changes are incorporated in a controlled way.

▨ In a large project, a formal document-naming scheme should be established and used as a basis for keeping track of the versions of all project documents.

▨ The CM team should be supported by a configuration database that records information about system changes and change requests that are outstanding. Projects should have some formal means of requesting system changes.

▨ When setting up a configuration management scheme, a consistent scheme of version identification should be established. Versions may be identified by version number, by an associated set of attributes or by the proposed system changes that they implement.

▨ System releases include executable code, data files, configuration files and documentation. Release management involves making decisions on system release dates, preparing all information for distribution and documenting each system release.

▨ System building is the process of assembling system components into an executable program to run on some target computer system.

▨ CASE tools are available to support all configuration management activities. These include tools such as CVS to manage system versions, tools to support change management and system-building tools.

▨ CASE tools for CM may be standalone tools supporting change management, version management and system building, or may be integrated workbenches that provide a single interface to all CM support.

FURTHER READING

Configuration Management Principles and Practice. This very comprehensive book covers standards and traditional approaches to CM as well as CM approaches that are more appropriate to modern processes such as agile software development. (A.M.J. Hass, 2002, Addison-Wesley.)

'A layered architecture for uniform version management'. This paper discusses the different approaches to software version management and proposes a basic model that can accommodate all of them. It includes a particularly good survey of background work in this area. (B. Westfechel, et al., *IEEE Transactions on Software Engineering*, 27 (12), December 2001.)

'Software configuration management: A roadmap'. This overview paper discusses the evolution of

SCM and identifies research challenges that remain in this area. (J. Estublier, *Proc. Int. Conf. on Software Engineering*, 2000. IEEE Press.)

Trends in Software: Configuration Management. This is a collection of papers on aspects of configuration management, by authors who are active researchers and practitioners in this field. It's a good introduction for students and practitioners who are interested in advanced CM topics. Most of these problems have not yet been solved. (W. Tichy (ed.), 1995, John Wiley & Sons.)

EXERCISES

29.1 Explain why you should not use the title of a document to identify the document in a configuration management system. Suggest a standard for a document identification scheme that may be used for all projects in an organisation.

29.2 Using an object-oriented approach (see Chapter 8), design a model of a configuration database that records information about system components, versions, releases and changes. Some requirements for the data model are as follows:

- It should be possible to retrieve all versions or a single identified version of a component.

- It should be possible to retrieve the 'latest' version of a component.

- It should be possible to find out which change requests have been implemented by a particular version of a system.

- It should be possible to discover which versions of components are included in a specified version of a system.

- It should be possible to retrieve a particular release of a system according to either the release date or the customers to whom the release was delivered.

29.3 Using a data-flow diagram, describe a change management procedure that might be used in a large organisation concerned with developing software for external clients. Changes may be suggested either from external or internal sources.

29.4 How does the use of a project-based configuration management system such as CVS simplify the version management process?

29.5 Explain why an attribute-based version identification system makes it easier to discover all of the components making up a specific version of a system.

29.6 Describe the difficulties that may arise when building a system from its components. What particular problems might occur when a system is built on a host computer for some target machine?

29.7 With reference to system building, explain why you may sometimes have to maintain obsolete computers on which large software systems were developed.

29.8   A common problem with system building occurs when physical file names are incorporated in system code and the file structure implied in these names differs from that of the target machine. Write a set of programmer's guidelines that help avoid this and other system-building problems that you can think of.

29.9   Describe five factors that should be taken into account by engineers during the process of building a release of a large software system.

29.10   Describe two ways in which system-building tools can optimise the process of building a version of a system from its components.

Glossary

abstract data type

A type whose representation is concealed and that is defined by its operations.

activity (PERT) chart

A chart used by project managers to show the dependencies between tasks that have to be completed. The chart shows the tasks, the time expected to complete these tasks and the task dependencies. The critical path is the longest path (in terms of the time required to complete the tasks) through the activity chart. The critical path defines the minimum time required to complete the project.

Ada

A programming language that was developed for the US Department of Defense as a standard language for developing military software. It is based on programming language research from the 1970s and includes constructs such as abstract data types and support for concurrency. It is still used for large, complex military and aerospace systems.

agile methods

Methods of software development that are geared to rapid software delivery. The software is developed and delivered in increments, and process documentation and bureaucracy are minimised.

algorithmic cost modelling

An approach to software cost estimation where a formula is used to estimate the project cost. The parameters in the formula are attributes of the project and the software itself.

application family

A set of software application programs that have a common architecture and generic functionality. These can be tailored to the needs of specific customers by modifying components and program parameters.

application framework

A generic structure in some specific domain that can form the basis of a family of applications. Application frameworks are generally implemented as a set of concrete and abstract classes that are specialised and instantiated to create an application.

Application Program Interface (API)

An interface, generally specified as a set of operations, which is defined by an application program that allows access to the program's functionality. This means that this functionality can be called on directly by other programs and not just accessed through the user interface.

aspect-oriented software development

An approach to software development that combined generative and component-based development. Cross-cutting concerns are identified in a program and the implementation of these concerns is defined as aspects. A program weaver then weaves the aspects into the appropriate places in the program.

availability

The readiness of a system to deliver services when requested. Availability is usually expressed as a decimal number, so an availability of 0.999 means that the system can deliver services for 999 out of 1000 time units.

bar (Gantt) chart

A chart used by project managers to show the project tasks, the schedule associated with these tasks and the people who will work on them. It shows the tasks start and end dates and the staff allocations against a timeline.

C

A programming language that was originally developed to help implement the Unix system. C is a relatively low-level system implementation language that allows access to the system hardware and that can be compiled to efficient code. It is still widely used for low-level systems programming.

C++

An object-oriented programming language that is a superset of C.

Computer-Aided Software Engineering (CASE)

The process of developing software using automated support.

CASE tool

A software tool, such as a design editor or a program debugger, used to support an activity in the software development process.

CASE workbench

An integrated set of CASE tools that work together to support a major process activity such as software design or configuration management.

client–server architecture

An architectural model for distributed systems where the system functionality is offered as a set of services provided by a server. These are accessed by client computers that make use of the services. Variants of this approach, such as three-tier client–server architectures, use multiple servers.

Cleanroom software engineering

An approach to software development where the aim is to avoid introducing faults into the software (by analogy with a cleanroom used in semiconductor fabrication). The process involves formal software specification, structured transformation of a specification to a program, the development of correctness arguments and statistical program testing.

CMMI

An integrated approach to process capability maturity modelling. It supports discrete and continuous maturity modelling and integrates systems and software engineering process maturity models.

code of ethics and professional practice

A set of guidelines that set out expected ethical and professional behaviour for software engineers. This was defined by the major US professional societies (the ACM and the IEEE) and defines ethical behaviour under eight headings: public, client and employer, product, judgement, management, colleagues, profession and self.

COM+

A component model designed for use on Microsoft platforms.

Common Request Broker Architecture (CORBA)

A set of standards proposed by the OMG that define a distributed object model and object communications.

component

A deployable, independent unit of software that is completely defined and accessed through a set of interfaces.

component model

A set of standards for component implementation, documentation and deployment. These cover the specific interfaces that may be provided by a component, component naming, component interoperation and component composition. Component models provide the basis for middleware to support executing components.

component-based software engineering (CBSE)

The development of software by composing independent, deployable components.

configuration item

A machine-readable unit, such as a document or a source code file, that is subject to change and where the change has to be controlled by a configuration management system.

configuration management

The process of managing the changes to an evolving software product. Configuration management involves configuration planning, version management, system building and change management.

Constructive Cost Modelling (COCOMO)

Perhaps the best-known algorithmic cost estimation model.

CORBA component model

A component model designed for use for the CORBA platform.

critical system

A computer system whose failure can result in significant economic, human or environmental losses.

data processing system

A system whose aim is to process large amounts of structured data. These systems usually process the data in batches and follow an input-process-output model. Examples of data processing systems are billing and invoicing systems, and payment systems.

dependability

The dependability of a system is an aggregate property that takes into account the system's safety, reliability, availability, security and other attributes. The dependability of a system reflects the extent to which it can be trusted by its users.

dependability requirement

A system requirement that is included to help achieve the required dependability for a system. Non-functional dependability requirements specify dependability attribute values; functional dependability requirements are functional requirements to avoid, detect, tolerate or recover from system faults and failures.

dependability case

A structured document that is used to back up claims made by a system developer about the dependability of a system.

design pattern

A well-tried solution to a common problem that captures experience and good practice in a form that can be reused. It is an abstract representation than can be instantiated in a number of ways.

distributed system

A software system where the software sub-systems or components execute on different processors.

distributed object system

A distributed system where the executing components are objects.

domain

A specific problem or business area where software systems are used. Examples of domains are real-time control, business data processing and telecommunications switching.

domain model
A definition of domain abstractions such as policies, procedures, objects, relationships and events. It serves as a base of knowledge about some problem area.

emergent property
A property that only becomes apparent once all of the components of the system have been integrated to create the system.

enterprise Java beans (EJB)
A Java-based component model.

ethnography
An observational technique that may be used in requirements elicitation and analysis. The ethnographer immerses himself or herself in the users' environment and observes their day-to-day work habits. Requirements for software support can be inferred from these observations.

event-based systems
Systems where the control of operation is determined by events that are generated in the system's environment. Most real-time systems are event-based systems.

extreme programming (XP)
An agile method of software development that includes practices such as scenario-based requirements, test-first development and pair programming.

fault avoidance
Developing software in such a way that faults are not introduced into that software.

fault detection
The use of processes and run-time checking to detect and remove faults in a program before these result in a system failure.

fault tolerance
The ability of a system to continue in execution even after faults have occurred.

formal methods
Methods of software development that are based on mathematically rigorous approaches and that model the software using formal mathematical constructs such as predicates and sets.

formal specification, algebraic
A method of mathematical system specification where a system or component is specified by defining relationships between the operations defined in its external interfaces.

formal specification, model-based
A method of mathematical system specification where a system or component is specified by defining pre-conditions, post-conditions and invariants that apply to the system state.

information hiding
Using programming language constructs to conceal the representation of data structures and to control external access to these structures.

incremental development
An approach to software development where the software is delivered and deployed in increments.

interface
A specification of attributes and operations associated with a software component. The interface is used as the means of accessing the component's functionality.

ISO 9000
A standard for quality management processes that is defined by the International Standards Organisation (ISO).

iterative development
An approach to software development where the processes of specification, design, programming and testing are interleaved.

Java
An object-oriented programming language that was designed by Sun with the aim of platform independence.

language processing system
A system that translates one language to another. For example, a compiler is a language processing system that translates program source code to object code.

legacy system
A socio-technical system that is useful or essential to an organisation but which has been developed using obsolete technology or methods. Because legacy systems often perform critical business functions, they have to be maintained.

maintenance
The process of making changes to a system after it has been put into operation.

middleware
The infrastructure software in a distributed system. It helps manage interactions between the distributed entities in the system and the system databases. Examples of middleware are an object request broker and a transaction management system.

object class
An object class defines the attributes and operations of objects. Objects are created at run-time by instantiating the class definition. The object class name can be used as a type name in some object-oriented languages.

object model
A model of a software system that is structured and organised as a set of object classes and the relationships between these classes. Various different perspectives on the model may exist such as a state perspective and a sequence perspective.

object-oriented (OO) development

An approach to software development where the fundamental abstractions in the system are independent objects. The same type of abstraction is used during specification, design and development.

object constraint language (OCL)

A language that is part of the UML, used to define predicates that apply to object classes and interactions in a UML model.

Object Management Group (OMG)

A group of companies formed to develop standards for object-oriented development. Examples of standards promoted by the OMG are CORBA, UML and MDA.

peer-to-peer system

A distributed system where there is no distinction between clients and servers. Computers in the system can act as both clients and servers. Peer-to-peer applications include file sharing, instant messaging and cooperation support systems.

People Capability Maturity Model (P-CMM)

A process maturity model that reflects how effective an organisation is at managing the skills, training and experience of the people in that organisation.

process improvement

The process of making changes to a process with the aim of making that process more predictable or to improve the quality of its outputs. For example, if your aim is to reduce the number of defects in the delivered software, you might improve the process by adding new validation activities.

process model

An abstract representation of a process. Process models may be developed from various perspectives and may show the activities involved in a process, the artefacts used in the process, constraints that apply to the process and the roles of the people enacting the process.

process maturity model

A model of the extent to which a process includes good practice and reflective and measurement capabilities that are geared to process improvement.

program evolution dynamics

The study of the ways in which an evolving software system changes.

program generator

A program that generates another program from a high-level, abstract specification. The generator embeds knowledge that is reused in each generation activity.

program inspection

A verification process where a group of inspectors examine a program, line by line, with the aim of detecting program errors.

quality assurance (QA)

The overall process of defining how software quality can be achieved and how the development organisation knows that the software has the required level of quality.

quality control (QC)

The process of ensuring that a software development team is following quality standards.

quality plan

A plan that defines the quality processes and procedures that should be used. This involves selecting and instantiating standards for products and processes and defining the required quality attributes of the system.

rapid application development (RAD)

An approach to software development aimed at rapid delivery of the software. It often involves the use of database programming and development support tools such as screen and report generators.

Rational Unified Process (RUP)

A generic software process model that presents software development as a four-phase iterative activity where the phases are inception, elaboration, construction and transition. Inception establishes a business case for the system, elaboration defines the architecture, construction implements the system and transition deploys the system in the customer's environment.

real-time system

A system that has to respond to and process external events in 'real-time'. The correctness of the system does not just depend on what it does but also on how quickly it does it. Real-time systems are usually organised as a set of cooperating sequential processes.

re-engineering

Modifying a software system to make it easier to understand and change. Re-engineering often involves software and data restructuring and organisation, program simplification and redocumentation.

re-engineering, business process

Changing a business process to meet some new organisational objectives such as reduced cost and faster execution.

reference architecture

A generic system architecture that is an idealised architecture that includes all the features that systems might incorporate. This is a way of informing designers about the general structure of that class of system.

release

A version of a software system that is made available to system customers.

reliability

The ability of a system to deliver services as specified. Reliability can be specified quantitatively as a probability of failure on demand or as the rate of occurrence of failure.

reliability growth modelling
The development of a model of how the reliability of a system changes (hopefully improves) as it is tested and program defects are removed.

requirement, functional
A statement of some function or feature that should be implemented in a system.

requirement, non-functional
A statement of a constraint or expected behaviour that applies to a system. This constraint may refer to the emergent properties of the software that is being developed or to the development process.

requirements management
The process of managing changes to requirements to ensure that the changes made are properly analysed and tracked through the system.

risk
An undesirable outcome that poses a threat to the achievement of some objective. A process risk threatens the schedule or cost of a process; a product risk is a risk that may mean that some of the system requirements may not be achieved.

risk management
The process of identifying risks, assessing their severity, planning measures to put in place if the risks arise and monitoring the software and the software process for risks.

safety
The ability of a system to operate without catastrophic failure.

safety case
A structured argument that a system is safe. Usually required by regulators such as nuclear safety regulators.

scenario
A description of one typical way in which a system is used or a user carried out some activity.

security
The ability of a system to protect itself against accidental or deliberate intrusion.

sequence diagram
A diagram that shows the sequence of interactions required to complete some operation. In the UML, sequence diagrams may be associated with use-cases.

server
A program that provides some service to other (client) programs.

software architecture
A model of the fundamental structure and organisation of a software system.

software metric
An attribute of a software system or process that can be expressed numerically and measured. Process metrics are attributes of the process such as the time taken to complete a task; product metrics are attributes of the software itself such as size or complexity.

software product line
See application family.

socio-technical system
A system, including hardware and software components, that has defined operational processes followed by human operators and that operates within an organisation. It is therefore influenced by organisational policies, procedures and structures.

software process
The related set of activities and processes that are involved in developing and evolving a software system.

software life cycle
Often used as another name for the software process. Originally coined to refer to the waterfall model of the software process.

spiral model
A model of a development process where the process is represented as a spiral with each round of the spiral incorporating the different stages in the process. As you move from one round of the spiral to another, you repeat all of the stages of the process.

static analysis
Tool-based analysis of a program's source code to discover errors and anomalies. Anomalies such as successive assignments to a variable with no intermediate use may be programming errors.

structured method
A method of software design that defines the system models that should be developed, the rules and guidelines that should apply to these models and a process to be followed in developing the design.

Structured Query Language (SQL)
A standard language used for relational database programming.

system building
The process of compiling the components or units that make up a system and linking these with other components to create an executable program. System building is normally automated so that recompilation is minimised. This automation may be built in to the language processing system (as in Java) or may involve CASE tools to support system building.

systems engineering
A process that is concerned with specifying a system, integrating its components and testing that the system meets its requirements. System engineering is concerned with the whole socio-technical system—software, hardware and operational processes—not just the system software.

transaction
A unit of interaction with a computer system. Transactions are independent and atomic (they are not broken down into smaller units) and are a fundamental unit of recovery, consistency and concurrency.

transaction processing system

A system that ensures that transactions are processed in such a way so that they do not interfere with each other and so that individual transaction failure does not affect other transactions or the system's data.

Unified Modeling Language (UML)

A graphical language that is used in object-oriented development that includes a several types of system model that provide different views of a system. The UML has become a de facto standard for object-oriented modelling.

use-case

A specification of one type of interaction with a system.

user interface design

The process of designing the way in which system users access the system functionality and information produced by the system is displayed.

user interface design principles

A set of principles that embody good practice for user interface design.

validation

The process of checking that a system meets the needs and expectations of the customer.

verification

The process of checking that a system meets its specification.

waterfall model

A software process model where there are discrete development stages: specification, design, implementation, testing and maintenance. In principle, one stage must be complete before progress to the next stage is possible. In practice, there is iteration between stages.

web service

An independent software component that can be accessed through the Internet using standard protocols. SOAP (Standard Object Access Protocol) is used for web service information exchange. WSDL (Web Service Definition Language) is used to define the web service interfaces.

Wizard-of-Oz prototyping

An approach to user interface prototyping where commands input by a user are interpreted by a person who responds as if he or she were the computer.

XML

Extended Markup Language. XML is a text markup language that supports the interchange of structured data. Each data field is delimited by tags that give information about that field. XML is now very widely used and has become the basis of protocols for web services.

Z

A model-based, formal specification language developed at the University of Oxford in England.

Definitions of many other terms are available in the on-line glossary accessible through the book's web site.

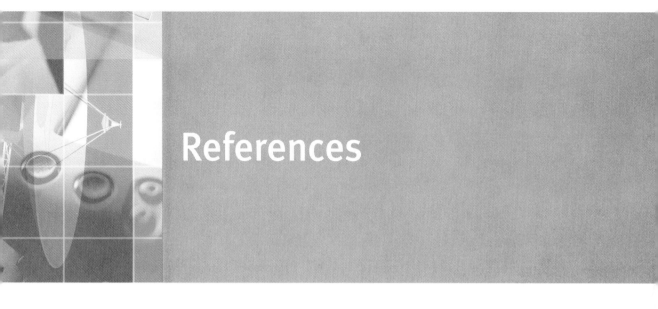

References

Abbott, R. (1983). Program design by informal English descriptions. *Comm. ACM,* 26(11), 882–94. (Ch. 14)

Abdel-Ghaly, A. A., Chan, P. Y., *et al.* (1986). Evaluation of competing software reliability predictions. *IEEE Trans. on Software Engineering,* **SE-12**(9), 950–67. (Ch. 24)

Ackroyd, S., Harper, R., *et al.* (1992). *Information Technology and Practical Police Work.* Milton Keynes: Open University Press. (Ch. 2)

Adams, E. N. (1984). Optimizing preventative service of software products. *IBM J. Res. & Dev.,* **28**(1), 2–14. (Ch. 3)

Ahern, D. M., Clouse, A., *et al.* (2001). *CMMI Distilled.* Reading, MA: Addison-Wesley. (Chs. 28, 29)

Albrecht, A. J. (1979). Measuring application development productivity. *Proc. SHARE/GUIDE IBM Application Development Symposium.* (Ch. 26)

Albrecht, A. J. and Gaffney, J. E. (1983). Software function, lines of code and development effort prediction: a software science validation. *IEEE Trans. on Software Engineering,* **SE-9**(6), 639–47. (Ch. 26)

Alexander, C., Ishikawa, S., *et al.* (1977). *A Pattern Language.* Oxford: Oxford University Press. (Ch. 18)

Ambler, S. W. and Jeffries, R. (2002). *Agile Modeling.* New York: John Wiley & Sons. (Ch. 17)

Anderson, R. (2001). *Security Engineering: A Guide to Building Dependable Distributed Systems.* Chichester: John Wiley & Sons. (Ch. 24)

Appelrath, H.-J. and Ritter, J. (2000). *SAP R/3 Implementation: Methods and Tools (SAP Excellence).* Berlin: Springer-Verlag. (Ch. 13)

Armour, P. (2002). Ten unmyths of project estimation. *Comm. ACM,* **45**(11), 15–18. (Ch. 26)

Aron, J. D. (1974). *The Program Development Process.* Reading, MA: Addison-Wesley. (Ch. 25)

Arthur, L. J. (1988). *Software Evolution.* New York: John Wiley & Sons. (Ch. 21)

Avizienis, A. (1985). The N-version approach to fault-tolerant software. *IEEE Trans. on Software Engineering,* **SE-11**(12), 1491–501. (Ch. 20)

Avizienis, A. A. (1995). A methodology of N-version programming. In *Software Fault Tolerance* (M. R. Lyu, ed.). New York: John Wiley & Sons, 23–46. (Ch. 20)

Bagert, D. J. (2002). Texas licensing of software engineers: all's quiet for now. *Comm. ACM,* **45**(11), 92–4. (Ch. 24)

Baker, F. T. (1972). Chief programmer team management of production programming. *IBM Systems J.,* **11**(1), 56–73. (Ch. 25)

Baker, T. (2002). Lessons learned integrating COTS into systems. *Proc. ICCBSS 2002 (1st Int. Conf on COTS-based Software Systems),* Orlando, FL: Springer-Verlag. (Ch. 18)

Balk, L. D. and Kedia, A. (2000). PPT: a COTS integration case study. *Proc. Int. Conf. on Software Engineering,* Limerick, Ireland: ACM Press. (Ch. 18)

Bamford, R. and Deibler, W. J., eds. (2003). ISO 9001: 2000 for Software and Systems Providers: An Engineering Approach. CRC Press. (Ch. 27)

Banker, R. D., Datar, S. M., *et al.* (1993). Software complexity and maintenance costs. *Comm. ACM,* **36**(11), 81–94. (Chs. 21, 26)

Banker, R., Kauffman, R., *et al.* (1994). An empirical test of object-based output measurement metrics in a computer-aided software engineering (CASE) environment. *J. of Management Info. Sys.,* **8**(3), 127–50. (Ch. 26)

Bansler, J. P. and Bødker, K. (1993). A reappraisal of structured analysis: design in an organizational context. *ACM Trans. on Information Systems,* **11**(2), 165–93. (Ch. 4)

Barker, R. (1989). *CASE* Method: Entity Relationship Modelling.* Wokingham: Addison-Wesley. (Ch. 8)

Barnard, J. and Price, A. (1994). Managing code inspection information. *IEEE Software,* **11**(2), 59–69. (Chs. 22, 27)

Basili, V. and Green, S. (1993). Software process improvement at the SEL. *IEEE Software,* **11**(4), 58–66. (Ch. 28)

Basili, V. R. and Rombach, H. D. (1988). The TAME project: towards improvement-oriented software environments. *IEEE Trans. on Software Engineering,* **14**(6), 758–73. (Chs. 27, 28)

Bass, B. M. and Dunteman, G. (1963). Behaviour in groups as a function of self, interaction and task orientation. *J. Abnorm. Soc. Psychology,* **66**(4), 19–28. (Ch. 25)

Bass, L., Clements, P., *et al.* (2003). *Software Architecture in Practice, 2nd edn.* Boston: Addison-Wesley. (Ch. 11)

Baumer, D., Gryczan, G., *et al.* (1997). Framework development for large systems. *Comm. ACM,* **40**(10), 52–9. (Ch. 18)

Beck, K. (1999). Embracing change with extreme programming. *IEEE Computer,* **32**(10), 70–8. (Chs. 6, 17)

Beck, K. (2000). *Extreme Programming Explained.* Boston: Addison-Wesley. (Chs. 4, 17, 25, 26)

Beck, K. and Cunningham, W. (1989). A laboratory for teaching object-oriented thinking. *Proc. OOPSLA'89,* New Orleans: ACM Press. (Ch. 14)

Bentley, R., Rodden, T., *et al.* (1992). Ethnographically informed systems design for air traffic control. *Proc. CSCW'92,* Toronto: ACM Press. (Ch. 16)

Berczuk, S. P. and Appleton, B. (2002). *Software Configuration Management Patterns: Effective Teamwork, Practical Integration.* Boston: Addison-Wesley. (Ch. 18)

Berghel, H. (2001). The code red worm. *Comm. ACM,* **44**(12), 15–19. (Ch. 3)

Berliner, B. (1990). CVS II: parallelizing software development. *Proc. 1990 Winter USENIX Conference,* Washington, DC: USENIX Assoc. (Ch. 29)

Bernstein, P. A. (1996). Middleware: a model for distributed system services. *Comm. ACM,* **39**(2), 86–97. (Ch. 12)

Bersoff, E. H. and Davis, A. M. (1991). Impact of life cycle models on software configuration management. *Comm. ACM,* **34**(8), 104–18. (Ch. 29)

Bezier, B. (1990). *Software Testing Techniques, 2nd edn.* New York: Van Nostrand Rheinhold. (Ch. 23)

Biggerstaff, T. (1998). A perspective of generative reuse. *Annals of Software Engineering,* **5**, 169–226. (Ch. 18)

Bishop, P. and Bloomfield, R. E. (1995). The SHIP safety case approach. *Proc. Safecomp'95,* Belgirate, Italy: Springer-Verlag. (Ch. 24)

Bishop, P. and Bloomfield, R. E. (1998). A methodology for safety case development. *Proc. Safety-critical Systems Symposium,* Birmingham, UK: Springer-Verlag. (Ch. 24)

Blevins, D. (2001). Overview of the Enterprise Java Beans component model. In *Component-Based Software Engineering* (G. T. Heineman and W. T. Councill, eds.). Boston: Addison-Wesley, 589–606 (Ch. 19)

Boehm, B. (1997). *COCOMO II Model Definition Manual.* Center for Software Engineering, Univ. of Southern California (http://sunset.usc.edu/research/COCOMOII). (Ch. 26)

Boehm, B. and Abts, C. (1999). COTS integration: plug and pray? *IEEE Computer,* **32**(1), 135–8. (Ch. 18)

Boehm, B. and Royce, W. (1989). Ada COCOMO and the Ada process model. *Proc. 5th COCOMO Users' Group Meeting,* Pittsburgh: Software Engineering Institute. (Ch. 26)

Boehm, B. W. (1979). Software engineering; R & D trends and defense needs. In *Research Directions in Software Technology* (P. Wegner, ed.). Cambridge, MA: MIT Press, 1–9. (Ch. 22)

Boehm, B. W. (1981). *Software Engineering Economics.* Englewood Cliffs, NJ: Prentice Hall. (Ch. 26)

Boehm, B. W. (1988). A spiral model of software development and enhancement. *IEEE Computer,* **21**(5), 61–72. (Chs. 4, 5)

Boehm, B. W., Abts, C., *et al.* (2000). *Software Cost Estimation with COCOMO II.* Upper Saddle River, NJ: Prentice Hall. (Chs. 19, 22, 26)

Boehm, B. W., McClean, R. L., *et al.* (1975). Some experience with automated aids to the design of large-scale reliable software. *IEEE Trans. on Software Engineering,* **SE-1**(1), 125–33. (Ch. 3)

Boehm, B., Clark, B., *et al.* (1995). Cost models for future life cycle processes: COCOMO 2. *Annals of Software Engineering,* **1**, 57–94. (Ch. 26)

Bolognesi, T. and Brinksma, E. (1987). Introduction to the ISO specification language LOTOS. *Computer Networks,* **14**(1), 25–59. (Ch. 10)

Booch, G. (1987). *Software Components with Ada: Structures, Tools, and Subsystems.* Menlo Park, CA: Benjamin-Cummings. (Ch. 18)

Booch, G. (1994). *Object-Oriented Analysis and Design with Applications.* Redwood City, CA: Benjamin-Cummings. (Chs. 1, 4, 8, 14)

Booch, G., Rumbaugh, J., *et al.* (1999). *The Unified Modeling Language User Guide.* Reading, MA: Addison-Wesley. (Ch. 1, 4, 8)

Borchers, J. (2001). *A Pattern Approach to Interaction Design.* New York: John Wiley & Sons. (Ch. 18)

Bosch, J. (2000). *Design and Use of Software Architectures.* Harlow: Addison-Wesley. (Ch. 11)

Bourne, S. R. (1978). The Unix shell. *Bell Sys. Tech. J.,* **57**(6), 1971–90. (Ch. 17)

Bracket, M. H. (1994). *Data Sharing Using a Common Data Architecture.* New York: John Wiley & Sons. (Ch. 13)

Brazendale, J. and Bell, R. (1994). Safety-related control and protection systems: standards update. *IEEE Computing and Control Engineering J.,* **5**(1), 6–12. (Ch. 9)

Brilliant, S. S., Knight, J. C., *et al.* (1990). Analysis of faults in an N-version software experiment. *IEEE Trans. on Software Engineering,* **16**(2), 238–47. (Ch. 20)

Brinch-Hansen, P. (1973). *Operating System Principles.* Englewood Cliffs, NJ: Prentice Hall. (Ch. 15)

Brooks F. P. (1975). *The Mythical Man Month.* Reading, MA: Addison-Wesley. (Ch. 25)

Brown, A. W., Earl, A. N., *et al.* (1992). *Software Engineering Environments.* London: McGraw-Hill. (Ch. 11)

Budgen, D. (2003). *Software Design, 2nd edn.* Harlow: Addison-Wesley. (Ch. 8)

Burns, A. and Wellings, A. (2001). *Real-Time Systems and Programming Languages.* Harlow: Addison-Wesley. (Ch. 15)

Butler, H. (1994). Virtual remote: the centralized expert. *HP Journal,* **45**(5), http://www.hpl.hp.com/hpjournal/94oct/oct94a13.htm. (Ch. 18)

Buxton, J. (1980). *Requirements for Ada Programming Support Environments: Stoneman.* Washington, DC: US Department of Defense. (Ch. 11)

Checkland, P. (1981). *Systems Thinking, Systems Practice.* Chichester: John Wiley & Sons. (Ch. 2)

Checkland, P. and Scholes, J. (1990). *Soft Systems Methodology in Action.* Chichester: John Wiley & Sons. (Ch. 2)

Chen, P. (1976). The entity relationship model—towards a unified view of data. *ACM Trans. on Database Systems,* **1**(1), 9–36. (Ch. 8)

Chidamber, S. and Kemerer, C. (1994). A metrics suite for object-oriented design. *IEEE Trans. on Software Engineering,* **20**(6), 476–93. (Ch. 27)

Chikofsky, E. J. and Cross, J. H. (1990). Reverse engineering and design recovery: a taxonomy. *IEEE Software,* **7**(1), 13–17. (Ch. 21)

Clements, P., Bachmann, F., *et al.* (2002). *Documenting Software Architectures: Views and Beyond.* Boston: Addison-Wesley. (Ch. 11)

Coad, P. and Yourdon, E. (1990). *Object-Oriented Analysis.* Englewood Cliffs, NJ: Prentice Hall. (Chs. 8, 14)

Cobb, R. H. and Mills, H. D. (1990). Engineering software under statistical quality control. *IEEE Software,* **7**(6), 44–54. (Ch. 22)

Cockburn, A. (2001). *Agile Software Development.* Reading, MA: Addison-Wesley. (Ch. 17)

Codd, E. F. (1979). Extending the database relational model to capture more meaning. *ACM Trans. on Database Systems,* **4**(4), 397–434. (Ch. 8)

Cohen, B., Harwood, W. T., *et al.* (1986). *The Specification of Complex Systems.* Wokingham: Addison-Wesley. (Ch. 10)

Constantine, L. L. and Yourdon, E. (1979). *Structured Design.* Englewood Cliffs, NJ: Prentice Hall. (Chs. 4, 8)

Cooling, J. (2003). *Software Engineering for Real-Time Systems.* Harlow: Addison-Wesley. (Ch. 15)

Coulouris, G., Dollimore, J., *et al.* (2001). *Distributed Systems: Concepts and Design.* Harlow: Addison-Wesley. (Ch. 12)

Councill, W. T. and Heineman, G. T. (2001). Definition of a software component and its elements. In *Component-Based Software Engineering* (G. T. Heineman and W. T. Councill, eds.). Boston: Addison-Wesley, 5–20. (Ch. 19)

Crabtree, A. (2003). *Designing Collaborative Systems: A Practical Guide to Ethnography.* London: Springer. (Ch. 16)

Crosby, P. (1979). *Quality Is Free.* New York: McGraw-Hill. (Ch. 27)

Curtis, B., Hefley, W. E., *et al.* (2001). *The People Capability Model: Guidelines for Improving the Workforce.* Boston: Addison-Wesley. (Chs. 25, 28)

Cusamano, M. (1989). The software factory: a historical interpretation. *IEEE Software,* **6**(2), 23–30. (Ch. 18)

Czarnecki, K. and Eisenecher, U. (2000). *Generative Programming: Methods, Tools, and Applications.* Boston: Addison-Wesley. (Ch. 18)

Davis, A. M. (1993). *Software Requirements: Objects, Functions, & States.* Englewood Cliffs, NJ: Prentice Hall. (Ch. 6)

Dehbonei, B. and Mejia, F. (1995). Formal development of safety-critical software systems in railway signalling. In *Applications of Formal Methods* (M. Hinchey and J. P. Bowen, eds.). London: Prentice Hall, 227–52. (Ch. 10)

DeMarco, T. (1978). *Structured Analysis and System Specification.* New York: Yourdon Press. (Ch. 8)

DeMarco, T. and Boehm, B. (2002). The agile methods fray. *IEEE Computer,* **35**(6), 90–2. (Ch. 17)

DeMarco, T. and Lister, T. (1985). Programmer performance and the effects of the workplace. *Proc. 8th Int. Conf. on Software Engineering,* London: IEEE Press. (Ch. 25)

DeMarco, T. and Lister, T. (1999). *Peopleware: Productive Projects and Teams.* New York: Dorset House. (Ch. 25)

DeMarco, T. (1978). *Structured Analysis and System Specification.* New York: Yourdon Press. (Ch. 1)

Diaper, D. (1989). *Task Analysis for Human-Computer Interaction.* Chichester: Ellis Horwood. (Ch. 16)

Dijkstra, E. W. (1968). Cooperating sequential processes. In *Programming Languages* (F. Genuys, ed.). London: Academic Press, 43–112. (Ch. 15)

Dijkstra, E. W. (1968). Goto statement considered harmful. *Comm. ACM,* **11**(3), 147–8. (Ch. 20)

Dijkstra ,E. W., Dahl, O. J., *et al.* (1972). *Structured Programming.* London: Academic Press. (Ch. 23)

Dix, A., Finlay, J., *et al.* (2004). *Human Computer Interaction, 3rd edn.* Harlow: Addison-Wesley. (Ch. 16)

Douglass, B. P. (1999). *Real-Time UML: Developing Efficient Objects for Embedded Systems, 2nd edn.* Boston: Addison-Wesley. (Ch. 15)

DuBois, P. (1996). *Software Portability with imake, 2nd edn.* Sebastopol, CA: O'Reilly & Associates. (Ch. 29)

Easterbrook, S., Lutz, R., *et al.* (1998). Experiences using lightweight formal methods for requirements modeling. *IEEE Trans. on Software Engineering,* **24**(1), 4–14. (Ch. 10)

ECMA. (1991). A reference model for frameworks of computer-assisted software engineering environments. In *Reprints of the Seventh International Software Process Workshop,* Yountville, CA: ACM Press. (Ch. 11)

Ehrlich, W., Prasanna, B., *et al.* (1993). Determining the cost of a stop-test decision. *IEEE Software,* **9**(4), 33–42. (Ch. 24)

El-Amam, K. (2001). *Object-Oriented Metrics: A Review of Theory and Practice.* (Ch. 27)

Elliott, J., Eckstein, R., *et al.* (2002). *Java Swing, 2nd edn.* Sebastopol, CA: O'Reilly & Associates Inc. (Ch. 16)

Ellison, R. J., Fisher, D. A., *et al.* (1999). Survivability: protecting your critical systems. *IEEE Internet Computing,* **3**(6), 55–63. (Ch. 3)

Ellison, R. J., Linger, R. C., *et al.* (1999). Survivable network system analysis: a case study. *IEEE Software,* **16**(4), 70–7. (Ch. 3)

Ellison, R., Linger, R., *et al.* (2002). Foundations of survivable systems engineering. *Crosstalk: The Journal of Defense Software Engineering,* **12**, 10–15. (Ch. 3)

Elrad, T., Askit, M., *et al.* (2001). Discussing aspects of AOP. *Comm. ACM,* **44**(10), 33–8. (Ch. 18)

Endres, A. (1975). An analysis of errors and their causes in system programs. *IEEE Trans. on Software Engineering,* **SE-1**(2), 140–9. (Ch. 3)

Erlikh, L. (2000). Leveraging legacy system dollars for e-business. *IT Pro,* **May/June 2000,** 17–23. (Ch. 21)

Estublier, J. and Casallas, R. (1994). The Adele configuration manager. In *Configuration Management* (W. Tichy, ed.). Chichester: John Wiley & Sons, 99–134. (Ch. 29)

Evans, D. and Larochelle, D. (2002). Improving security using extensible lightweight static analysis. *IEEE Software,* **19**(1), 42–51. (Ch. 22)

Ewald, T. (2001). Overview of COM+. In *Component-Based Software Engineering* (G. T. Heineman and W. T. Councill, eds.). Boston: Addison-Wesley, 573–88. (Ch. 19)

Fagan, M. E. (1976). Design and code inspections to reduce errors in program development. *IBM Systems J.,* **15**(3), 182–211. (Ch. 22)

Fagan, M. E. (1986). Advances in software inspections. *IEEE Trans. on Software Engineering,* **SE-12**(7), 744–51. (Ch. 22)

Fayad, M. E. and Schmidt, D. C. (1997). Object-oriented application frameworks. *Comm. ACM,* **40**(10), 32–8. (Ch. 18)

Feldman, S. I. (1979). MAKE—a program for maintaining computer programs. *Software-Practice and Experience,* **9**(4), 255–65. (Ch. 29)

Firesmith, D. G. (2003). Analysing and specifying reusable security requirements. *Journal of Object Technology,* **2**(1), 53–68. (Ch. 9)

Foster, I., Kesselman, C., *et al.* (2002). Grid services for distributed system integration. *IEEE Computer,* **35**(6), 37–46. (Ch. 12)

Frewin, G. D. and Hatton, B. J. (1986). Quality management—procedures and practises. *IEE/BCS Software Engineering J.,* **1**(1), 29–38. (Ch. 22)

Fromme, B. and Walker, J. (1993). An open architecture for tool and process integration. *Proc. 6th Conf. on Software Engineering Environments,* Reading, UK: IEEE Press. (Ch. 11)

Fuggetta, A. (1993). A classification of CASE technology. *IEEE Computer,* **26**(12), 25–38. (Ch. 4)

Fujiwara, E. and Pradhan, D. K. (1990). Error-control coding in computers. *IEEE Computer,* **23**(7), 63–72. (Ch. 20)

Furey, S. and Kitchenham, B. (1997). Point/counterpoint: function points. *IEEE Software,* **14**(2), 28–31. (Ch. 26)

Futatsugi, K., Goguen, J. A., *et al.* (1985). Principles of OBJ2. *Proc. 12th ACM Symp. on Principles of Programming Languages,* New Orleans: ACM Press. (Ch. 10)

Gamma, E., Helm, R., *et al.* (1995). *Design Patterns: Elements of Reusable Object-Oriented Software.* Reading, MA: Addison-Wesley. (Ch. 18)

Gane, C. and Sarson, T. (1979). *Structured Systems Analysis.* Englewood Cliffs, NJ: Prentice Hall. (Chs. 4, 8)

Garlan, D. and Shaw, M. (1993). An introduction to software architecture. *Advances in Software Engineering and Knowledge Engineering,* **1**, 1–39. (Chs. 11, 13)

Garlan, D., Allen, R., *et al.* (1995). Architectural mismatch: why reuse is so hard. *IEEE Software,* **12**(6), 17–26. (Ch. 18)

Garlan, D., Kaiser, G. E., *et al.* (1992). Using tool abstraction to compose systems. *IEEE Computer,* **25**(6), 30–8. (Ch. 11)

Garmus, D. and Herron, D. (2000). *Function Point Analysis: Measurement Practices for Successful Software Projects.* Boston: Addison-Wesley. (Ch. 26)

Gilb, T. and Graham, D. (1993). *Software Inspection.* Wokingham: Addison-Wesley. (Ch. 22)

Goldberg, A. and Robson, D. (1983). *Smalltalk-80. The Language and Its Implementation.* Reading, MA: Addison-Wesley. (Ch. 16)

Gollmann, D. (1999). *Computer Security.* Chichester: John Wiley & Sons. (Ch. 24)

Gomaa, H. (1993). *Software Design Methods for Concurrent and Real-Time Systems.* Reading, MA: Addison-Wesley. (Ch. 15)

Gordon, V. S. and Bieman, J. M. (1995). Rapid prototyping: lessons learned. *IEEE Software,* **12**(1), 85–95. (Ch. 17)

Gotterbarn, D., Miller, K., et al. (1999). Software engineering code of ethics is approved. *Comm. ACM,* **42**(10), 102–7. (Ch. 1)

Grady, R. B. (1993). Practical results from measuring software quality. *Comm. ACM,* **36**(11), 62–8. (Ch. 27)

Grady, R. B. and Van Slack, T. (1994). Key lessons in achieving widespread inspection use. *IEEE Software,* **11**(4), 46–57. (Ch. 22)

Graham, I. (1994). *Object-Oriented Methods, 2nd edn.* Wokingham: Addison-Wesley. (Ch. 14)

Griss, M. L. and Wosser, M. (1995). Making reuse work at Hewlett-Packard. *IEEE Software,* **12**(1), 105–7. (Ch. 18)

Groff, J. R., Weinberg, P. N., *et al.* (2002). *SQL: The Complete Reference, 2nd edn.* New York: McGraw-Hill Osborne. (Ch. 17)

Grudin, J. (1989). The case against user interface consistency. *Comm. ACM,* **32**(10), 1164–73. (Ch. 16)

Guimaraes, T. (1983). Managing application program maintenance expenditures. *Comm. ACM,* **26**(10), 739–46. (Ch. 21)

Gunning, R. (1962). *Techniques of Clear Writing.* New York: McGraw-Hill. (Ch. 27)

Guttag, J. (1977). Abstract data types and the development of data structures. *Comm. ACM,* **20**(6), 396–405. (Ch. 10)

Guttag, J., Horning, J., *et al.* (1993). *Larch: Languages and Tools for Formal Specification.* Heidelberg: Springer-Verlag. (Ch. 10)

Haase, V., Messnarz, R., *et al.* (1994). Bootstrap: fine tuning process assessment. *IEEE Software,* **11**(4), 25–35. (Ch. 28)

Hall, A. (1990). Seven myths of formal methods. *IEEE Software,* **7**(5), 11–20. (Ch. 10)

Hall, A. (1996). Using formal methods to develop an ATC information system. *IEEE Software,* **13**(2), 66–76. (Chs. 3, 9, 10)

Hall, A. and Chapman, R. (2002). Correctness by construction: developing a commercially secure system. *IEEE Software,* **19**(1), 18–25. (Ch. 3, 9, 10)

Hall, E. (1998). *Managing Risk: Methods for Software Systems Development.* Reading, MA: Addison-Wesley. (Ch. 5)

Hall, T. and Fenton, N. (1997). Implementing effective software metrics programs. *IEEE Software,* **14**(2), 55–64. (Ch. 27)

Halstead, M. H. (1977). *Elements of Software Science.* Amsterdam: North-Holland. (Ch. 21)

Hamlet, D. (1992). Are we testing for true reliability? *IEEE Software,* **9**(4), 21–7. (Ch. 24)

Hammer, M. (1990). Reengineering work: don't automate, obliterate. *Harvard Business Review,* **July-August 1990**, 104–12. (Ch. 28)

Hammer, M. and McLeod, D. (1981). Database descriptions with SDM: A semantic database model. *ACM Trans. on Database Sys.,* **6**(3), 351–86. (Ch. 8)

Hardin, D., Frerking, M., *et al.* (2002). Getting down and dirty: device-level programming using the real-time specification for Java. *Proc. Fifth IEEE International Symp. on Object-Oriented Real-Time Distributed Computing,* Washington, DC: IEEE Computer Society Press. (Ch. 15)

Harel, D. (1987). Statecharts: a visual formalism for complex systems. *Sci. Comput. Programming,* **8**(3), 231–74. (Chs. 8, 14, 15)

Harel, D. (1988). On visual formalisms. *Comm. ACM,* **31**(5), 514–30. (Chs. 8, 15)

Harold, E. R. and Means, W. S. (2002). *XML in a Nutshell.* Sebastopol. CA: O'Reilly & Associates. (Ch. 13)

Hass, A. M. J. (2003). *Configuration Management: Principles and Practice.* Boston: Addison-Wesley. (Ch. 29)

Hayes, I. (1987). *Specification Case Studies.* London: Prentice Hall. (Ch. 10)

Heninger, K. L. (1980). Specifying software requirements for complex systems: new techniques and their applications. *IEEE Trans. on Software Engineering,* **SE-6**(1), 2–13. (Ch. 6)

Highsmith, J. A. (2000). *Adaptive Software Development: A Collaborative Approach to Managing Complex Systems.* New York: Dorset House. (Ch. 17)

Higuera-Toledano, M. T. and Issarny, V. (2000). Java embedded real-time systems: an overview of existing solutions. *Proc. Third IEEE International Symp. on Object-Oriented Real-Time Distributed Computing,* Newport Beach, CA: IEEE Computer Society Press. (Ch. 15)

Hoare, C. A. R. (1974). Monitors: an operating system structuring concept. *Comm. ACM,* **21**(8), 666–77. (Ch. 15)

Hoare, C. A. R. (1985). *Communicating Sequential Processes.* London: Prentice Hall. (Ch. 10)

Hofmeister, C., Nord, R., *et al.* (2000). *Applied Software Architecture.* Boston: Addison-Wesley. (Ch. 11)

Horswill, J. and Miller, S. A. (2000). *Designing and Programming CICS Applications.* Sebastopol, CA: O'Reilly & Associates. (Ch. 13)

Huang, Y. and Kintala, C. M. R. (1993). Software implemented fault tolerance: technologies and experience. *Proc. 23rd Fault-tolerant Computing Symposium (FTCS-23),* Toulouse, France: IEEE Computer Society Press. (Ch. 20)

Huff, C. C. (1992). Elements of a realistic CASE tool adoption budget. *Comm. ACM,* **35**(4), 45–54. (Ch. 4)

Huff, K. E. (1996). Software process modeling. In *Trends in Software: Software Process* (A. Fuggetta and A. Wolf, eds.). Chichester: John Wiley & Sons, 1–24. (Ch. 28)

Huff, C. and Martin, C. D. (1995). Computing consequences: a framework for teaching ethical computing. *Comm. ACM,* **38**(12), 75–84. (Ch. 1)

Hughes, J. A., O'Brien, J., *et al.* (1997). Designing with ethnography: a presentation framework for design. *Proc. DIS'97,* Amsterdam: ACM Press. (Ch. 16)

Hull, R. and King, R. (1987). Semantic database modeling: survey, applications and research issues. *ACM Computing Surveys,* **19**(3), 201–60. (Ch. 8)

Humphrey, W. (1989). *Managing the Software Process.* Reading, MA: Addison-Wesley. (Chs. 22, 27. 28)

Humphrey, W. S. (1988). Characterizing the software process. *IEEE Software,* **5**(2), 73–9. (Ch. 28)

Humphrey, W. S. (1995). *A Discipline for Software Engineering.* Reading, MA: Addison-Wesley. (Ch. 28)

IEC. (1998). *Standard IEC 61508: Functional safety of electrical/electronic/programmable electronic safety-related systems.* (Ch. 9)

IEEE. (1998). IEEE recommended practice for software requirements specifications. In *IEEE Software Engineering Standards Collection.* Los Alamitos, CA: IEEE Computer Society Press. (Ch. 6)

IEEE. (2003). *IEEE Software Engineering Standards Collection on CD-ROM.* Los Alamitos, CA: IEEE Computer Society Press. (Ch. 27)

Ince, D. (1994). *ISO 9001 and Software Quality Assurance.* London: McGraw-Hill. (Ch. 27)

Jackson, M. A. (1983). *System Development.* London: Prentice Hall. (Chs. 1, 8)

Jackson, M. A. (1995). *Requirements and Specifications.* Wokingham: Addison-Wesley. (Ch. 6)

Jacky, J. (1995). Specifying a safety-critical control system. *IEEE Trans. on Software Engineering,* **21**(2), 99–106. (Ch. 10)

Jacky, J. (1997). *The Way of Z: Practical Programming with Formal methods.* Cambridge, UK: Cambridge University Press. (Ch. 10)

Jacky, J., Unger, J., *et al.* (1997). Experience with Z: developing a control program for a radiation therapy machine. *Proc. ZUM'97,* Reading: Springer. (Ch. 10)

Jacobsen, I., Christerson, M., *et al.* (1993). *Object-Oriented Software Engineering.* Wokingham: Addison-Wesley. (Chs. 6, 8, 15)

Jacobsen, I., Griss, M., *et al.* (1997). *Software Reuse.* Reading, MA: Addison-Wesley. (Chs. 18, 19)

Jahanian, F. and Mok, A. K. (1986). Safety analysis of timing properties in real-time systems. *IEEE Trans. on Software Engineering,* **SE-12**(9), 890–904. (Ch. 9)

Janis, I. L. (1972). *Victims of Groupthink. A Psychological Study of Foreign Policy Decisions and Fiascos.* Boston: Houghton Mifflin. (Ch. 25)

Jelinski, Z. and Moranda, P. B. (1972). Software reliability research. In *Statistical Computer Performance Evaluation* (W. Frieberger, ed.). New York: Academic Press, 465–84. (Ch. 24)

Johnson, P. L. (1993). *ISO 9000: Meeting the New International Standards.* New York: McGraw-Hill. (Ch. 27)

Jones, C. B. (1980). *Software Development—A Rigorous Approach.* London: Prentice Hall. (Ch. 10)

Jones, C. B. (1986). *Systematic Software Development Using VDM.* London: Prentice Hall. (Chs. 10, 22)

Kafura, D. and Reddy, G. R. (1987). The use of software complexity metrics in software maintenance. *IEEE Trans. on Software Engineering,* **SE-13**(3), 335–43. (Ch. 21)

Kan, S. H. (2003). *Metrics and Models in Software Quality Engineering.* Boston: Addison-Wesley. (Ch. 24)

Kiczales, G., Hilsdale, E., *et al.* (2001). Getting started with AspectJ. *Comm. ACM,* **44**(10), 59–65. (Ch. 18)

Kilpi, T. (2001). Implementing a software metrics program at Nokia. *IEEE Software,* **18**(6), 72–7. (Ch. 27)

Kit, E. (1995). *Software Testing in the Real World: Improving the Process.* Reading, MA: Addison-Wesley. (Ch. 22)

Kitchenham, B. (1990). Measuring software development. In *Software Reliability Handbook* (P. Rook, ed.). Amsterdam: Elsevier, 303–31. (Ch. 27)

Kleppe, A., Warmer, J., *et al.* (2003). *MDA Explained: The Model-Driven Architecture—Practice and Promise.* Boston: Addison-Wesley. (Ch. 14)

Knight, J. C. and Leveson, N. G. (1986). An experimental evaluation of the assumption of independence in multi-version programming. *IEEE Trans. on Software Engineering,* **SE-12**(1), 96–109. (Ch. 20)

Knight, J. C. and Leveson, N. G. (2002). Should software engineers be licensed? *Comm. ACM,* **45**(11), 87–90. (Ch. 24)

Knuth, D. E. (1971). *The Art of Computer Programming: Fundamental Algorithms.* Reading, MA: Addison-Wesley. (Ch. 18)

Kotonya, G. and Sommerville, I. (1998). *Requirements Engineering: Processes and Techniques.* Chichester: John Wiley & Sons. (Ch. 6)

Kreger, H. (2001). *Web Services Conceptual Architecture (WSCA 1.0).* IBM. www.ibm.com/software/solutions/ webservices/pdf/WSCA.pdf (Ch. 12)

Krutchen, P. (2000). *The Rational Unified Process—An Introduction.* Reading, MA: Addison-Wesley. (Chs. 4, 8)

Kumaran, S. I. (2001). *JINI Technology: An Overview.* Englewood Cliffs, NJ: Prentice Hall. (Ch. 12)

Kuvaja, P., Similä, J., *et al.* (1994). *Software Process Assessment and Improvement: The BOOT-STRAP Approach.* Oxford: Blackwell Publishers. (Ch. 28)

Lamping, J., Rao, R., *et al.* (1995). A focus + context technique based on hyperbolic geometry for visualising large hierarchies. *Proc. CHI'95,* Denver, CO: ACM Press. (Ch. 16)

Laprie, J.-C. (1995). Dependable computing: concepts, limits, challenges. *Proc. 25th IEEE Symposium on Fault-Tolerant Computing,* Pasadena, CA: IEEE Press. (Ch. 3)

Laprie, J.-C., Arlat, J., *et al.* (1995). Architectural issues in software fault tolerance. In *Software Fault Tolerance* (M. R. Lyu, ed.). New York: John Wiley & Sons 47–80. (Ch. 20)

Larman, C. (2002). *Applying UML and Patterns: An Introduction to Object-Oriented Analysis and Design and the Unified Process.* Englewood Cliffs, NJ: Prentice Hall. (Ch. 17)

Laudon, K. (1995). Ethical concepts and information technology. *Comm. ACM,* **38**(12), 33–9. (Ch. 1)

Leblang, D. B. and Chase, R. P. (1987). Parallel software configuration management in a network environment. *IEEE Software,* **4**(6), 28–35. (Ch. 29)

Lehman, M. M. (1996). Laws of software evolution revisited. *Proc. European Workshop on Software Process Technology (EWSPT'96),* Nancy, France: Springer-Verlag. (Ch. 21)

Lehman, M. M. and Belady, L. (1985). *Program Evolution: Processes of Software Change.* London: Academic Press. (Ch. 21)

Lehman, M. M., Perry, D. E., *et al.* (1998). On evidence supporting the FEAST hypothesis and the laws of software evolution. *Proc. Metrics'98,* Bethesda, MD: IEEE Computer Society Press. (Ch. 21)

Lehman, M. M., Ramil, J. F., *et al.* (2001). An approach to modelling long-term growth trends in software systems. *Proc. Int. Conf. on Software Maintenance,* Florence, Italy: IEEE Computer Society Press. (Ch. 21)

Leveson, N. and Stolzy, J. (1987). Safety analysis using Petri nets. *IEEE Transactions on Software Engineering,* **13**(3), 386–97. (Ch. 9)

Leveson, N. G. (1985). Software safety. In *Resilient Computing Systems* (T. Anderson, ed.). London: Collins, 12343. (Chs. 3, 9)

Leveson, N. G. (1995). *Safeware: System Safety and Computers.* Reading, MA: Addison-Wesley. (Chs. 9, 20)

Leveson, N. G. and Harvey, P. R. (1983). Analysing software safety. *IEEE Trans. on Software Engineering,* **SE-9**(5), 569–79. (Ch. 9)

Lewis, P. M., Bernstein, A. J., *et al.* (2003). *Databases and Transaction Processing: An Application-Oriented Approach.* Boston: Addison-Wesley. (Ch. 13)

Lientz, B. P. and Swanson, E. B. (1980). *Software Maintenance Management.* Reading, MA: Addison-Wesley. (Ch. 21)

Linger, R. C. (1994). Cleanroom process model. *IEEE Software,* **11**(2), 50–8. (Chs. 4, 22)

Liskov, B. and Guttag, J. (1986). *Abstraction and Specification in Program Development.* Cambridge, MA: MIT Press. (Ch. 10)

Littlewood, B. (1990). Software reliability growth models. In *Software Reliability Handbook* (P. Rook, ed.). Amsterdam: Elsevier, 401–12. (Chs. 3, 24)

Littlewood, B. and Verrall, J. L. (1973). A Bayesian reliability growth model for computer software. *Applied Statistics,* **22**, 332–46. (Ch. 24)

Londeix, B. (1987). *Cost Estimation for Software Development.* Wokingham: Addison-Wesley. (Ch. 26)

Lovelock, C., Vandermerwe, S., *et al.* (1996). *Services Marketing.* Englewood Cliffs, NJ: Prentice Hall. (Ch. 12)

Lutz, M. (1996). *Programming Python.* Sebastopol, CA: O'Reilly & Associates. (Ch. 17)

Lutz, R. R. (1993). Analysing software requirements errors in safety-critical embedded systems. *Proc. RE'93,* San Diego CA: IEEE Computer Society Press. (Chs. 3, 22, 23)

MacDonell, S. G. (1994). Comparative review of functional complexity assessment methods for effort estimation. *BCS/IEE Software Engineering J.,* **9**(3), 107–17. (Ch. 26)

Marshall, J. E. and Heslin, R. (1975). Boys and girls together: sexual composition and the effect of density on group size and cohesiveness. *J. of Personality and Social Psychology,* **35**(5), 952–61. (Ch. 25)

Martin, D., Rodden, T., *et al.* (2001). Finding patterns in the fieldwork. *Proc. ECSCW'01,* Bonn: Kluwer. (Ch. 18)

Martin, D., Rouncefield, M., *et al.* (2002). Applying patterns of interaction to work (re)design: e-government and planning. *Proc CHI'2002,* ACM Press. (Ch. 18)

Maslow, A. A. (1954). *Motivation and Personality.* New York: Harper and Row. (Ch. 25)

Massol, V. and Husted, T. (2003). *JUnit in Action.* Greenwich, CT: Manning. (Ch. 23)

Matsumoto, Y. (1984). Some experience in promoting reusable software: presentation in higher abstract levels. *IEEE Trans. on Software Engineering,* **SE-10**(5), 502–12. (Ch. 18)

McCabe, T. J. (1976). A complexity measure. *IEEE Trans. on Software Engineering,* **SE-2**(4), 308–20. (Ch. 21)

McCue, G. M. (1978). IBM's Santa Teresa laboratory: architectural design for program development. *IBM Systems J.,* **17**(1), 4–25. (Ch. 25)

McDougall, P. (2000). The power of peer-to-peer. *Information Week,* August 28, http://www.informationweek.com. (Ch. 12)

McGuffin, R. W., Elliston, A. E., *et al.* (1979). CADES—software engineering in practice. *Proc. 4th Int. Conf. on Software Engineering,* Munich: IEEE Computer Society Press. (Ch. 11)

McIlroy, M. D. (1968). Mass-produced software components. *Proc. NATO Conf. on Software Engineering,* Garmisch, Germany: Springer-Verlag. (Ch. 18)

Meyer, B. (1992). Design by contract. *IEEE Computer,* **25**(10), 40–51. (Ch. 19)

Meyer, B. (2003). The grand challenge of trusted components. *Proc. ICSE 25: Int. Conf. on Software Engineering,* Portland, OR: IEEE Press. (Ch. 19)

Mili, H., Mili, A., *et al.* (2002). *Reuse-Based Software Engineering.* New York: John Wiley & Sons. (Ch. 19)

Miller, G. A. (1957). The magical number 7 plus or minus two: Some limits on our capacity for processing information. *Psychological Review,* **63**, 81–97. (Ch. 16)

Mills, H. D., Dyer, M., *et al.* (1987). Cleanroom software engineering. *IEEE Software,* **4**(5), 19–25. (Chs. 3, 4, 22)

Mitschele-Thiel, A. (2001). *Systems Engineering with SDL: Developing Performance-Critical Communication Systems.* Chichester: John Wiley & Sons. (Ch. 22)

MOD, (1995). *The Procurement of Safety Critical Software (Revised edn).* UK Ministry of Defence, Interim Standard, 00–55. (Ch. 22)

Mosley, D. J. and Posey, B. A. (2002). *Just Enough Test Automation.* Englewood Cliffs, NJ: Prentice Hall. (Ch. 23)

Mumford, E. (1989). User participation in a changing environment—why we need it. In *Participation in Systems Development* (K. Knight, ed.). London: Kegan Paul. (Ch. 2)

Munch, B. P., Larsen, J-O., *et al.* (1993). Uniform versioning: the change-oriented model. *Proc. 4th Workshop on Software Configuration Management,* Baltimore, MD: ACM Press. (Ch. 29)

Musa, J. D. (1993). Operational profiles in software reliability engineering. *IEEE Software,* **10**(2), 14–32. (Ch. 24)

Musa, J. D. (1998). *Software Reliability Engineering: More Reliable Software, Faster Development and Testing.* New York: McGraw-Hill. (Ch. 24)

Musciano, C. and Kennedy, B. (2002). *HTML & XHTML: The Definitive Guide.* Sebastopol, CA: O'Reilly & Associates. (Ch. 16)

Myers, W. (1989). Allow plenty of time for large-scale software. *IEEE Software,* **6** (4), 92–9. (Ch. 26)

Nakajo, T. and Kume, H. (1991). A case history analysis of software error-cause relationships. *IEEE Trans. on Software Engineering,* **18**(8), 830–8. (Ch. 3)

Neil, M., Ostrolenk, G., *et al.* (1998). Lessons from using Z to specify a software tool. *IEEE Trans. on Software Engineering,* **24**(1), 15–23. (Ch. 10)

Neilsen ,J. (1993). *Usability Engineering.* New York: Academic Press. (Ch. 16)

Nii, H. P. (1986). Blackboard systems, parts 1 and 2. *AI Magazine,* **7**(3 and 4), 38–53 and 62–9. (Ch. 11)

Nilsen, K. (1998). Adding real-time capabilities to Java. *Comm. ACM,* **41**(6), 49–56. (Ch. 15)

Norman, D. A. and Draper, S. W. (1986). *User-Centered System Design.* Hillsdale, NJ: Lawrence Erlbaum. (Ch. 16)

Nosek, J. T. and Palvia, P. (1990). Software maintenance management: changes in the last decade. *Software Maintenance: Research and Practice,* **2**(3), 157–74. (Ch. 21)

Nuseibeh, B. (1997). Ariane 5: who dunnit? *IEEE Software,* **14**(3), 15–16. (Ch. 18)

O'Connor, J., Mansour, C., *et al.* (1994). Reuse in command and control systems. *IEEE Software,* **11**(4), 70–9. (Ch. 18)

Offen, R. J. and Jeffrey, R. (1997). Establishing software measurement programs. *IEEE Software,* **14**(2), 45–54. (Ch. 27)

O'Leary, D. E. (2000). *Enterprise Resource Planning Systems: Systems, Life Cycle, Electronic Commerce and Risk.* Cambridge, UK: Cambridge University Press. (Ch. 18)

Oram, A. (2001). *Peer-to-Peer: Harnessing the Power of Disruptive Technologies.* Sebastopol, CA: O'Reilly & Associates. (Ch. 12)

Oram, A. and Talbott, S. (1991). *Managing Projects with make, 2nd edn.* Sebastopol, CA: O'Reilly & Associates. (Ch. 29)

Orcero, D. S. (2000). The code analyser LCLint. *Linux Journal,* 73, http://www.linuxjournal.com/article.php?sid=3599. (Ch. 22)

Orfali, R. and Harkey, D. (1998). *Client/Server Programming with Java and CORBA.* New York: John Wiley & Sons. (Ch. 12)

Oskarsson, O. and Glass, R. L. (1995). *An ISO 9000 Approach to Building Quality Software.* Englewood Cliffs, NJ: Prentice Hall. (Ch. 27)

Ould, M. A. (1999). *Managing Software Quality and Business Risk.* Chichester: John Wiley & Sons. (Ch. 5)

Ould, M. A. (1995). *Business Processes: Modelling and Analysis for Re-engineering and Improvement.* Chichester: John Wiley & Sons. (Ch. 28)

Ousterhout, J. (1994). *TCL and the TK toolkit.* Reading, MA: Addison-Wesley. (Ch. 17)

Ousterhout, J. K. (1998). Scripting: higher-level programming for the 21st century. *IEEE Computer,* **31**(3), 23–30. (Chs. 17, 26)

Palmer, S. R. and Felsing, J. M. (2002). *A Practical Guide to Feature-Driven Development.* Englewood Cliffs, NJ: Prentice Hall. (Ch. 17)

Parnas, D. L., van Schouwen, J., *et al.* (1990). Evaluation of safety-critical software. *Comm. ACM,* **33** (6), 636–51. (Chs. 20, 24)

Paulk, M. C. and Konrad, M. (1994). An overview of ISO's SPICE project. *IEEE Computer,* **27**(4), 68–70. (Ch. 28)

Paulk, M. C., Curtis, B., *et al.* (1993). Capability maturity model, version 1.1. *IEEE Software,* **10**(4), 18–27. (Ch. 28)

Paulk, M. C., Weber, C. V., *et al.* (1995). *The Capability Maturity Model: Guidelines for Improving the Software Process.* Reading, MA: Addison-Wesley. (Chs. 28, 29)

Peach, R. W. (1996). *The ISO 9000 Handbook, 3rd edn.* New York: Irwin Professional. (Chs. 27, 29)

Perrow, C. (1984). *Normal Accidents: Living with High-Risk Technology.* New York: Basic Books. (Ch. 3)

Peterson, J. L. (1981). *Petri Net Theory and the Modeling of Systems.* New York: McGraw-Hill. (Chs. 9, 10)

Pfaff, G. and ten Hagen, P. J. W. (1985). *Seeheim Workshop on User Interface Management Systems.* Heidelberg: Springer-Verlag. (Ch. 16)

Pfarr, T. and Reis, J. E. (2002). The integration of COTS/GOTS within NASA's HST command and control system. *Proc. ICCBSS 2002 (1st Int. Conf on COTS-based Software Systems),* Orlando, FL: Springer-Verlag. (Ch. 18)

Pfleeger, C. P. (1997). *Security in Computing, 2nd edn.* Englewood Cliffs, NJ: Prentice Hall. (Ch. 3)

Pope, A. (1998). *CORBA.* Harlow: Addison-Wesley. (Ch. 19)

Potter, B., Sinclair, J., *et al.* (1996). *An Introduction to Formal Specification and Z.* London: Prentice Hall. (Ch. 10)

Preiser, W. and Ostoff, E. (2001). *The Universal Design Handbook.* New York: McGraw-Hill. (Ch. 16)

Pritchard, J. (1999). *COM and CORBA Side by Side: Architectures, Strategies, and Implementations.* Boston: Addison-Wesley. (Ch. 12)

Prowell, S. J., Trammell, C. J., *et al.* (1999). *Cleanroom Software Engineering: Technology and Process.* Reading, MA: Addison-Wesley. (Chs. 4, 10, 22, 24)

Pulford, K., Kuntzmann-Combelles, A., *et al.* (1996). *A Quantitative Approach to Software Management.* Wokingham: Addison-Wesley. (Chs. 27, 28)

Pullum, L. L. (2001). *Software Fault Tolerance Techniques and Implementation.* Norwood, MA: Artech House. (Ch. 20)

Putnam, L. H. (1978). A general empirical solution to the macro software sizing and estimating problem. *IEEE Trans. on Software Engineering,* **SE-4**(3), 345–61. (Ch. 26)

Randell, B. (1975). System structure for software fault tolerance. *IEEE Trans. on Software Engineering,* **SE-1**(2), 220–32. (Ch. 20)

Randell, B. and Xu, J. (1995). The evolution of the recovery block concept. In *Software Fault Tolerance* (M. R. Lyu, ed.). New York: John Wiley & Sons, 1–22. (Ch. 20)

Rankin, C. (2002). The software testing automation framework. *IBM Systems J.,* **41**(1), 126–40. (Ch. 23)

Redmill, F. (1998). IEC 61508: principles and use in the management of safety. *IEEE Computing and Control Engineering J.,* **9**(10), 205–13. (Ch. 9)

Reiss, S., P. (1990). Connecting tools using message passing in the field environment. *IEEE Software,* **7**(4), 57–66. (Ch. 11)

Rettig, M. (1994). Practical programmer: prototyping for tiny fingers. *Comm. ACM,* **37**(4), 21–7. (Ch. 17)

Rittel, H. and Webber, M. (1973). Dilemmas in a general theory of planning. *Policy Sciences*, 4, 155–69. (Ch. 2)

Robertson, S. and Robertson, J. (1999). *Mastering the Requirements Process.* Harlow: Addison-Wesley. (Ch. 6)

Robinson, P. J. (1992). *Hierarchical Object-Oriented Design.* Englewood Cliffs, NJ: Prentice Hall. (Chs. 4, 8, 14)

Ross, D. T. (1977). Structured analysis (SA): a language for communicating ideas. *IEEE Trans. on Software Engineering,* **SE-3**(1), 16–34. (Ch. 6)

Royce, W. W. (1970). Managing the development of large software systems: concepts and techniques. *Proc. IEEE WESTCON,* Los Angeles CA: IEEE Computer Society Press. (Ch. 4)

Rubin, K. and Goldberg, A. (1992). Object behaviour analysis. *Comm. ACM,* **35**(9), 48–62. (Ch. 14)

Rumbaugh, J., Blaha, M., *et al.* (1991). *Object-Oriented Modeling and Design.* Englewood Cliffs, NJ: Prentice Hall. (Chs. 1, 4, 8)

Rumbaugh, J., Jacobson, I., *et al.* (1999). *The Unified Modeling Language Reference Manual.* Reading, MA: Addison-Wesley. (Chs. 1, 4, 8, 14)

Rumbaugh, J., Jacobson, I., *et al.* (1999). *The Unified Software Development Process.* Reading, MA: Addison-Wesley. (Chs. 1, 4, 8)

Sackman, H., Erikson, W. J., *et al.* (1968). Exploratory experimentation studies comparing on-line and off-line programming performance. *Comm. ACM,* **11**(1), 3–11. (Ch. 26)

Schmidt, D. C. (1997). Applying design patterns and frameworks to develop object-oriented communications software. In *Handbook of Programming Languages, Vol. 1* (P. Salus, ed.). London: Macmillan Computer Publishing. (Ch. 18)

Schneidewind, N. F. and Keller, T. W. (1992). Applying reliability models to the space shuttle. *IEEE Software,* **9**(4), 28–33. (Ch. 24)

Schoman, K. and Ross, D. T. (1977). Structured analysis for requirements definition. *IEEE Trans. on Software Engineering,* **SE-3**(1), 6–15. (Ch. 6)

Schwaber, K. and Beedle, M. (2001). *Agile Software Development with Scrum.* Englewood Cliffs, NJ: Prentice Hall. (Ch. 17)

Scott, J. E. (1999). The FoxMeyer Drug's bankruptcy: was it a failure of ERP? *Proc. Association for Information Systems 5th Americas Conf. on Information Systems,* Milwaukee, WI. (Ch. 18)

Selby, R. W., Basili, V. R., *et al.* (1987). Cleanroom software development: an empirical evaluation. *IEEE Trans. on Software Engineering,* **SE-13**(9), 1027–37. (Chs. 4, 22)

Sheldon, F. T., Kavi, K. M., *et al.* (1992). Reliability measurement: from theory to practice. *IEEE Software,* **9**(4), 13–20. (Ch. 24)

Shlaer, S. and Mellor, S. (1988). *Object-Oriented Systems Analysis: Modeling the World in Data.* Englewood Cliffs, NJ: Yourdon Press. (Ch. 14)

Shneiderman, B. (1998). *Designing the User Interface, 3rd edn.* Reading, MA: Addison-Wesley. (Ch. 16)

Siegal, J. (1998). OMG overview: CORBA and the OMA in enterprise computing. *Comm. ACM,* **41**(10), 37–43. (Ch. 12)

Silberschatz, A., Galvin, P. B., *et al.* (2002). *Operating System Concepts, 6th edn.* New York: John Wiley & Sons. (Ch. 15)

Skonnard, A. and Gudgin, M. (2002). *Essential XML Quick Reference: A Programmer's Reference to XML, XPath, XSLT, XML Schema, SOAP, and More.* Boston: Addison-Wesley. (Ch. 12)

Snyder, C. (2003). *Paper Prototyping: The Fast and Easy Way to Design and Refine User Interfaces.* San Francisco: Morgan Kaufmann. (Ch. 16)

Spafford, E. (1989). The Internet worm: crisis and aftermath. *Comm. ACM,* **32**(6), 678–87. (Ch. 3)

Spivey, J. M. (1990). Specifying a real-time kernel. *IEEE Software,* **7**(5), 21–8. (Ch. 10)

Spivey, J. M. (1992). *The Z Notation: A Reference Manual, 2nd edn.* London: Prentice Hall. (Chs. 10, 22)

Stal, M. (2002). Web services: beyond component-based computing. *Comm. ACM,* **45**(10), 71–6. (Ch. 12)

Stapleton, J. (1997). *DSDM Dynamic Systems Development Method.* Harlow: Addison-Wesley. (Ch. 17)

Stephens, M. and Rosenberg, D. (2003). *Extreme Programming Refactored.* Berkley, CA: Apress. (Ch. 17)

Stevens, P. and Pooley, R. (1999). *Software Engineering with Objects and Components.* Harlow: Addison-Wesley. (Ch. 6)

Storey, N. (1996). *Safety-Critical Computer Systems.* Harlow: Addison-Wesley. (Chs. 9, 20)

Suchman, L. (1983). Office procedures as practical action. *ACM Trans. on Office Information Systems,* **1**(3), 320–28. (Ch. 16)

Swartz, A. J. (1996). Airport 95: automated baggage system? *ACM Software Engineering Notes,* **21**(2), 79–83. (Ch. 2)

Symons, C. R. (1988). Function-point analysis: difficulties and improvements. *IEEE Trans. on Software Engineering,* **14**(1), 2–11. (Ch. 26)

Szyperski, C. (2002). *Component Software: Beyond Object-Oriented Programming, 2nd edn.* Harlow: Addison-Wesley. (Chs. 12, 19)

Tanenbaum, A. S. (2001). *Modern Operating Systems, 2nd edn.* Englewood Cliffs, NJ: Prentice Hall. (Ch. 15)

Thayer, R. H. (1997). Software system engineering: an engineering process. In *Software Requirements Engineering* (R. H. Thayer and M. Dorfmann, eds.). Los Alamitos: IEEE Computer Society Press, 84106. (Ch. 2)

Thayer, R. H. (2002). Software system engineering: a tutorial. *IEEE Computer,* **35**(4), 6873. (Ch. 2)

Tichy, W. (1985). RCS—a system for version control. *Software Practice and Experience,* **15**(7), 637–54. (Ch. 29)

Tracz, W. (2001). COTS myths and other lessons learned in component-based software development. In *Component-Based Software Engineering* (G. T. Heineman and W. T. Councill, eds.). Boston: Addison-Wesley, 99–112. (Ch. 18)

Turner, M., Budgen, D., *et al.* (2003). Turning software into a service. *IEEE Computer,* **36**(10), 38–45. (Ch. 12)

Ulrich, W. M. (1990). The evolutionary growth of software reengineering and the decade ahead. *American Programmer,* **3**(10), 14–20. (Ch. 21)

Vesperman, J. (2003). *Essential CVS.* Sebastopol, CA: O'Reilly & Associates. (Ch. 29)

Wall, L., Christiansen, T., *et al.* (1996). *Programming Perl.* Sebastopol, CA: O'Reilly & Associates. (Ch. 17)

Wang, N., Schmidt, D. C., *et al.* (2001). Overview of the CORBA component model. In *Component-Based Software Engineering* (G. T. Heineman and W. T. Councill, eds.). Boston: Addison-Wesley, 557–72. (Ch. 19)

Ward, P. and Mellor, S. (1985). *Structured Development for Real-Time Systems.* Englewood Cliffs, NJ: Prentice Hall. (Ch. 8)

Warmer, J. and Kleppe, A. (1998). *The Object Constraint Language: Precise Modeling with UML.* Boston: Addison-Wesley. (Ch. 19)

Warren, I. (1998). *The Renaissance of Legacy Systems.* London: Springer. (Ch. 21)

Weinberg, G. (1971). *The Psychology of Computer Programming.* New York: Van Nostrand. (Chs. 17, 25)

Weinreich, R. and Sametinger, J. (2001). Component models and component services: concepts and principles. In *Component-Based Software Engineering* (G. T. Heineman and W. T. Councill, eds.). Boston: Addison-Wesley, 33–48. (Ch. 19)

Weiss, S. (2002). *Handheld Usability.* New York: John Wiley & Sons. (Ch. 16)

White, B. A. (2000). *Software Configuration Management Strategies and Rational ClearCase.* Reading, MA: Addison-Wesley. (Ch. 29)

White, S., Alford, M., *et al.* (1993). Systems engineering of computer-based systems. *IEEE Computer,* **26**(11), 54–65. (Ch. 2)

Whitgift, D. (1991). *Software Configuration Management: Methods and Tools.* Chichester: John Wiley & Sons. (Ch. 29)

Whittaker, J. W. (2002). *How to Break Software: A Practical Guide to Testing.* Boston: Addison-Wesley. (Ch. 23)

Williams, L., Kessler, R. R., *et al.* (2000). Strengthening the case for pair programming. *IEEE Software,* **17**(4), 19–25. (Ch. 17)

Wirfs-Brock, R. J. and Johnson, R. E. (1990). Surveying current research in object-oriented design. *Comm. ACM,* **33**(9), 104–24. (Ch. 18)

Wirfs-Brock, R., Wilkerson, B., *et al.* (1990). *Designing Object-Oriented Software.* Englewood Cliffs, NJ: Prentice Hall. (Ch. 14)

Wordsworth, J. (1996). *Software Engineering with B.* Wokingham: Addison-Wesley. (Chs. 4, 9, 10, 22)

Wordsworth, J. B. (1991). The CICS application programming interface definition. *Proc. Z User Workshop,* Oxford, Berlin: Springer-Verlag. (Ch. 10)

Zimmermann, H. (1980). OSI reference model—the ISO model of architecture for open systems interconnection. *IEEE Transactions on Communications,* **COM-28**(4), 425–32. (Ch. 11)

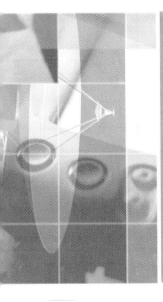

Index

A

N

O

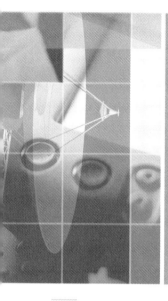

Author Index

H

Hailpern, 536
Hall, 45, 194, 219, 221, 236
Halstead, 497
Hammer, 178
Hardin, 342
Harel, 176, 332, 345
Harker, 162
Harkey, 270
Harold, 294
Harvey, 201
Hatton, 520
Hayes, 230
Heath, 157
Heineman, 442, 460
Helm, 438
Heninger, 131, 138
Highsmith, 396
Higuera-Toledano, 342
Hnich, 461
Hoare, 344
Hofmeister, 242
Horswill, 299
Huang, 482
Huff, 17, 86
Hughes, 157, 380
Hull, 178
Humphrey, 520, 525

I

Issarny, 342

J

Jackson, 11, 41, 130, 188
Jacky, 219, 230
Jacobsen, 154, 182, 188, 315, 337, 451
Jahanian, 199
Jeffries, 396
Johnson, 427, 438
Jones, 230, 532

Jonsson, 461

K

Kafura, 497
Kazman, 256, 264
Kedia, 429
Kennedy, 363
Kiczales, 426
Kifer, 310
Kindberg, 290
King, 178
Kintala, 482
Kit, 520
Kiziltan, 461
Kleppe, 314, 457
Knight, 485
Knuth, 421
Kotonya, 121, 136, 140, 149, 167
Kreger, 286
Krutchen, 83, 90, 188
Kumaran, 286
Kume, 56

L

Lamping, 373
Laprie, 44, 485
Larman, 144, 337, 396
Larochelle, 529
Laudon, 17
Lehman, 490, 492
Leveson, 56, 196, 199, 201, 485
Lewis, 310, 510
Lientz, 493
Linger, 49, 66, 532, 534, 536
Liskov, 223
Lister, 112
Littlewood, 53
Lovelock, 285
Luff, 157
Luqi, 236
Lutz, 56, 407, 531
Lyu, 487